LANGUAGE ISSUES

▼

READINGS FOR TEACHERS

DIANE BENNETT DURKIN
University of California, Los Angeles

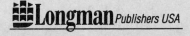 **Longman** *Publishers USA*

Language Issues: Readings for Teachers

Longman, 10 Bank Street, White Plains, N.Y. 10606

Associated companies:
Longman Group Ltd., London
Longman Cheshire Pty., Melbourne
Longman Paul Pty., Auckland
Copp Clark Longman Ltd., Toronto

Senior acquisitions editor: Laura McKenna
Production editor: Linda Moser/Professional Book Center
Cover design: Joseph DePinho
Production supervisor: Richard Bretan

For Michael and Celia
Without whom not

Library of Congress Cataloging-in-Publication Data
Language issues : readings for teachers / Diane Bennett Durkin
   [editor].
        p.   cm.
    Includes bibliographical references and index.
    ISBN 0-8013-0951-4
    1. Language and languages—Study and teaching.   I. Durkin, Diane
Bennett.
    P51.L346   1995
    418—dc20

94-7046
CIP

2 3 4 5 6 7 8 9 10 - CRS - 98 97 96 95

Contents

CHAPTER 3   ACQUIRING A SECOND LANGUAGE: A SOCIOLINGUISTIC APPROACH   176

CHAPTER 4   UNDERSTANDING LANGUAGE DIVERSITY AND LANGUAGE CHANGE   259

CHAPTER 5   ACHIEVING GRAMMATICAL COMPETENCE   331

CHAPTER 6   **DEVELOPING LITERACY**   404

Preface

This book presents complex and often technical linguistic knowledge in ways directly applicable to teachers' needs. Because introductory courses and textbooks in linguistics usually attempt to build a knowledge base, reserving applications for more advanced study, they do not often present materials directly addressing teaching issues. In contrast, this book begins with teachers' concerns—the language issues they daily face. It then brings together readings in linguistics that bear on the kinds of language questions, controversies, and choices that teachers confront. It does not ask readers to master extensive technical knowledge and then leave them to determine how such knowledge applies.

The readings are organized around those language experiences that provoke teachers' questions. The chapter titles identify these experiences: "Acquiring a First Language"; "Acquiring a Second Language—A Psycholinguistic Approach"; "Acquiring a Second Language—A Sociolinguistic Approach"; "Understanding Language Diversity and Language Change"; "Achieving Grammatical Competence"; and "Developing Literacy." What teachers need to understand about language—and it is broad and sometimes technical—should be directly relevant to fostering these language competencies. Most textbooks do not offer or organize studies that directly address classroom concerns.

Significantly, controversies surround each of these areas of language growth, especially second language acquisition and the teaching of standard English to nonstandard dialect speakers. The readings attempt to present these controversies, in both theory and practice, and encourage the examination of underlying assumptions. Furthermore, along with the introductions and discussion and writing questions, the readings underscore the implications of practical choices—their effect on the education of increasingly language-diverse students.

As these controversies unfold, two central perspectives emerge, helping to shape and unify the text. Throughout the book, the readings fall loosely into cognitive or social perspectives. In chapter 1, "Acquiring a First Language," the first two readings offer a cognitive approach and the second two present a social perspective. In the next two chapters, "Acquiring a Second Language—A Psycholinguistic Approach," and "Acquiring a Second Language—A Sociolinguistic Approach," these perspectives generate separate chapters. In the last three chapters, the readings typically combine these two orientations in ways that invite interesting analyses. Significantly, both these perspectives—cognitive and social—suggest themes that recur throughout the text: the need to see error as a sign of learning, the importance of social purposes and context in developing language, and the need for skepticism concerning drill, isolated skills, and a "back to basics movement" generally.

These themes evolve and deepen because the six chapters, and the readings within them, build on each other, reflecting forward and backward. The first chapter, "Acquiring a First Language," presents underlying principles of all language acquisition from cognitive and social perspectives. These principles are referred to in subsequent chapters, most explicitly in chapters 2 and 3 on second language acquisition. The first chapter also anticipates the principles of integrating grammar instruction into writing processes, discussed in chapter 5, "Achieving Grammatical Competence." The last chapter, "Developing Literacy," unites insights from previous chapters, revealing how principles of language acquisition, grammar instruction, and linguistic diversity have been successfully applied to the teaching of reading and writing.

The apparatus of this book provides an additional unifying feature. Just as the readings attempt to weld theory to practice, so does the apparatus, in ways that other linguistics books do not. Chapter introductions include not only sections on issues and principles but also a section on professional applications. In addition, the introductions connect chapter readings to each other and to readings in other chapters. Introductions to individual readings extend such connections, identifying underlying themes and principles. The "Theory and Implications" questions ask students to develop their own connections and to evaluate methods implied by such connections. Finally, the "Professional Concerns" questions ask students to connect theory and practice by having them assume specific pedagogical roles and situations; students are asked to write about language issues from the perspective of these roles.

Some of the criteria for selecting these readings may now be clear: They had to be comprehensive and consolidating; they had to present theory in nontechnical but incisive terms; they had to offer or suggest immediate practical implications to language issues; and they had to address the developing perspectives and themes of the text. But another criterion, not immediately evident, was equally important. The selections also had to be forceful, cogent presentations offering examples that reflect the experiences of teachers. This cogency is achieved in different ways by different articles: Some bring alive language controversies through portraits of individual students, their language, or their writing; others bring such controversies home through the clarity and simplicity of the language, the gift of making the complex simple. As a result, some of the selections are older, classic essays in linguistics often cited in the literature. These are balanced by recent articles, also chosen for clarity and impact, that suggest where concerns in the field now lie.

Introduction

Language Issues: Readings for Teachers is a linguistics reader for undergraduate and graduate prospective teachers, K-12 and in-service professionals. It offers readings in first and second language acquisition, dialects, grammar, and the development of literacy. Although each of these areas could comprise a text, *Language Issues* frames the essential controversies of these fields, highlighting teachers' practical concerns about error. The essays included here consolidate research, present it in a nontechnical manner, and demonstrate its practical applications. Furthermore, the readings are interrelated, each informing the other: Principles of first language acquisition form the groundwork for questions and controversies in second language acquisition, especially concerning the role of error in learning. Dialect issues, which also involve attitudes toward error, build on first and second language acquisition principles. Grammatical and historical descriptions of the language further support pedagogies deriving from general language acquisition studies. Finally, wholistic reading and writing theories, which welcome error in initial literacy, evolve out of principles for many of these areas. Thus the book offers a grounding for the practical concerns teachers face in developing their students' oral and written language skills.

This is a book about language *issues,* with particular emphasis on interpreting the nature, source, and role of error. For instance, it offers readings that raise such specific questions as: how to view and respond to error in the multilingual classroom; how to respond to the current "back to basics" movement; whether or not grammar instruction improves language use; how grammar can be used to produce thought, not simply correct language use; how to respond to dialect differences; and how the acquisition of reading and writing skills reflects language acquisition generally. Teachers' approaches to these issues determine the success or failure of their students. In particular, error-centered instruction inhibits learning for all students by undermining the unmonitored, natural processes of language acquisition, placing concern for isolated skills and superficial form above attention to global meaning. And as language issues have a disproportionate effect on minority students, these groups are especially handicapped by uninformed teaching methods.

This book arose out of a frustration with so many language texts that seem fragmented or overgeneralized, with phonemics leading in one direction, brain physiology in another. Rather than take an information or topic approach to so broad a subject as language, this book takes a problem approach. Instead of assuming a limited audience of readers on the way to becoming linguists, it assumes a wide audience of teachers who face particular, practical language issues. Furthermore, whereas most texts on language avoid a central philosophy, underlying themes, and a concern for practice, this text offers such a philosophy and joins theory and practice.

The theme of the role that errors play in learning helps to unify theory and practice. Our knowledge of how children acquire a first and a second language, become bidialectal, implement a grammar, and first learn to read and write depends on our knowledge of error. We need demonstrations of the idea that errors can be signs of acquisition, of progress, of cultural difference, and of learning strategies. We need proof that errors are not simply signs of deficits. Teachers need to learn to "read" error, not just mark it.

Reading error requires linguistic knowledge. For instance, linguists have shown that syntax errors in first language acquisition often reflect normal hypothesizing of general rules, with refinements postponed to a later learning stage—an efficient acquisition strategy. Second language acquisition errors can reflect a similar concern for efficiency, with acquirers seeking the most generally applicable rules first. In addition, dialect "errors" can indicate interference from different "native" grammatical structures and logic, as well as a different phonemic system. Furthermore, some errors in early reading can reveal active, logical guessing from context and a positive concentration on meaning over form; errors in initial writing, such as those deriving from invented spelling, similarly reveal logical guesses based on phonetics. This book thus offers interactive readings in linguistics that apply to the practical concerns of teachers. With the aid of follow-up questions, it will help teachers question, if not abolish, the debilitating ideas and attitudes about error that have dominated language instruction.

The goals of this book are to address issues that all teachers face and to encourage informed language instruction across disciplines. It accomplishes these goals by providing teachers with readings that suggest priorities and practical guidelines. These readings are meant to be broad, consolidating, illustrative selections sufficiently detailed to avoid the homogenizing tendency of textbooks that try to present panoramas of findings. Rather than offer one voice to summarize divergent fields, the readings offer the voices of the researchers themselves where they are most immediate, most comprehensive, and most interactive. These voices often indirectly support or qualify one another, as if in an ongoing conversation. Despite divergent interests, together they illustrate an emerging consensus on key concerns, language principles, and practical implications. The variety of voices themselves makes this a unique book, one that reveals the commitment underlying the multidimensional arena of language study.

ACKNOWLEDGMENTS

The author would like to thank the following reviewers for their suggestions:

Maria Brisk, Boston University
Barbara Decker, Louisiana State University, Shreveport
Diana Dreyer, Slippery Rock University
Gisela Ernst, Washington State University
Nidia Gonzales-Edfelt, San Francisco State University
Joan Hall, University of Georgia
Stevie Hoffman, University of Missouri, Columbia
Elaine Horwitz, University of Texas, Austin
Pam McCollum, University of Colorado, Boulder
Mary McGroarty, Northern Arizona University
Teresa Pica, University of Pennsylvania
Milagros Seda, University of Texas, El Paso
Merritt Stark, Henderson State University
Leo Vanlier, Monterey Institute of International Study
Karen Webb, University of Kentucky, Lexington

chapter 1

Acquiring a First Language

THE ISSUES

Because our memories of our first words are short and our recollections of school-based grammar instruction are long, confusion abounds as to the nature of first language acquisition. We often think we "learned" the complexities of speech through the practice and correction methods we experienced in school. However, recent research based on increasingly accurate recordings and analyses demonstrates the innate, perhaps even preprogrammed processes involved. Indeed it appears that we learn to speak fluently even without benefit of correction, and that we acquire a sophisticated grammar long before we enter school. We have the impressive ability to derive rules, apply them to new situations to produce sentences never heard before, and make mistakes that are both predictable and necessary.

The research emphasizing innate aptitudes draws on the generative-transformational grammar of Noam Chomsky and stresses the innately creative, non-behaviorist model of early language acquisition. In sum, children need no drills, nor do they "copy" or imitate what they hear based on external rewards or punishments; they do not piece together isolated language behaviors to produce language. Rather they have the innate, cognitive capacity to derive underlying rules to generate new sentences. Although crucial in the advances it brought—particularly in dispelling mechanistic behaviorist assumptions—this cognitive research is now triggering new contrary concerns for social or environmental factors. A number of debates are now under way.

The research in first language (L1) acquisition raises central issues about the nature of language and learning. It catapults us into ongoing controversies

1

between nature and nurture, between behaviorist and creative constructionist learning models, and between isolated skill and whole language approaches to instruction. The principles derived from this research clearly have implications for instruction—for first and second language instruction to be sure, but for broader language learning, including reading and writing instruction, as well.

The controversies raised by this research are central to teachers. Is language learning innate, or do children need special linguistic instruction to acquire language fully? Do children learn language through passive imitation, correction, and explicit teaching, or do they actively formulate rules, depending little on specific input and correction? Do children learn language in small pieces, such as individual words and then phrases, or do they learn it as a grammatical system?

Teachers are particularly interested in such questions because these issues bear on instruction. The nature position suggests important lines of inquiry. If children before the age of five naturally acquire most of their syntax without formal instruction, what are the implications for language teaching, especially formal grammar instruction? Indeed if children are "prewired" for language acquisition, what purpose does any explicit instruction serve, especially the creation of a sequenced language syllabus? If children learn by naturally generating rules and not by imitating adult models or other forms of nurture, does it matter that students go uncorrected or that they are exposed to incorrect models? And if children are prewired, how can such wiring be used to best advantage in reading and writing instruction?

The nurture position challenges the view that language acquisition excludes environmental factors. It raises a problematic question: If children are impervious to correction and modeling—if they automatically hypothesize rules in a preset sequence, depending neither on a particular kind of input nor on imitation— why do parents intuitively modify their own speech when talking to children? Although Chomsky has demonstrated that most adult speech with its false starts and convoluted syntax provides poor models for children, other research shows that the language directed at children is often highly regularized, carefully structured to teach obvious contrasts, and intuitively adjusted to the level of the child's developing grammar. This research shows that across many cultures and particularly within the middle class, caregivers simplify the phonology, syntax, and vocabulary of their speech. They exaggerate intonation and use a higher pitch than normal. In general, they heighten language regularities, limit content to the here and now, and underscore key language contrasts. Furthermore, caregivers across many cultures expand children's sentences to complete the grammar, with the result that children imitate modeled sentences, especially when there is only a moderate discrepancy between the adult grammar and the grammar the child is currently developing. Indeed, caregivers intuitively use a grammar that is about six months in advance of the child's own. Such research raises important questions affecting pedagogy: What specific effect do these modifications have on children's language acquisition? What are the intuitive language teaching methods that caregivers use and that teachers can incorporate? Is language acquisition then as much nurture as it is nature?

PRINCIPLES OF FIRST LANGUAGE ACQUISITION

Recent research suggests some answers to these questions, though they are equivocal ones. Studies suggest that first language learning is principally innate, but that it is also influenced by caregivers' responses. Such studies support a creative constructionist approach to language learning over a behaviorist approach, but they also show that caregivers and teachers modify behavior by deliberate language shaping. In addition, research indicates that children isolate grammatical rules in a preset order, but it also demonstrates that children use imitation and require some modeling to further language development. Moreover, research indicates that children, even at the one-word stage, approach language as a system, not as isolated units, but that children do practice specific phrases and routines, which helps them to carry on conversations. Thus recent studies sketch out broad answers but make problematic any commitment to one set of assumptions over another.

Despite these equivocations, the greatest impact of this research lies in its demonstration that children who have been exposed to complex language patterns from birth have the innate capacity to extract regularities of the language and begin formulating rules. Children approach language as a whole, as a communicative tool, not as a series of isolated words or references. Even as early as six weeks, children have identified different intonation patterns and have begun to duplicate them. At 18 months, by which time they have begun to use individual words, children babble groups of nonsense words as if carrying on full conversations. And the single words they first use fall into grammatical patterns, the rudimentary forms implying a full syntax. Children are not just imitating words to identify single objects; they are offering full propositions.

Because children approach language as a system used to communicate ideas, they isolate those features that best accomplish that purpose. For example, they learn content words (nouns and verbs) before function words (prepositions, determiners, etc.). And when they begin to isolate syntactic rules, they choose first those rules that are most regular and that have the broadest communicative power, leaving until a later stage those rules that govern fewer forms. For instance, they learn that *ed* added to the verb stem indicates the past, and such a rule provides them with immense communicative power; only later do they learn the irregular forms of the past tense—with much less communicative benefit. Thus, cognitive complexity and syntactic complexity, along with innate developmental stages, become the key factors of acquisition. These factors contrast sharply with earlier concerns for teacher and parent behaviors. They call into question such isolated practices as flash cards, pronunciation and word drills, repetitions, correction for minute errors, and modeling.

Interestingly, the emphasis on universal cognitive processes over imitation and modeling has led to new research on social factors that influence acquisition. The new research emphasizes that context and motivation—for instance, the roles children enact, the rules they have for conversation and play, and the strategies available to them as children—are central to understanding early language acquisition. Like the cognitivists, the social interaction theorists believe that children seek to convey meaning and that this effort explains children's early language; they too condemn behaviorist, drill-based approaches to acquisition that seem to ignore meaning. But unlike the cognitivists, they see children's meanings as complex, not as simple one-to-one relationships between word and external reality. They believe children's meanings are shaped by unequal parent-child roles and by unequal communicative abilities. For instance, by understanding children's desire to enter conversations and confirm comprehension, social interaction theorists can interpret the social function of children's and parents' repetitions. Making meaning even more complex, some social interactionists posit a complex, reciprocal relationship between words and referenced "reality" whereby children create their own social reality. For instance, a child assumes the role of mother and reconstructs another child's understanding of "owning" and "sharing" a toy; the children then create meanings that emerge from that newly established reality.

PROFESSIONAL APPLICATIONS

The significance of the cognitive and social dichotomies extends beyond the arena of grammar into reading and writing theory and language arts generally. Some of the principles established by this research will be recalled in later sections on acquiring a second language, experiencing language varieties and language change, and teaching reading and writing. The principles established here are thus the basis for subsequent chapters of this book and it is hoped they will help teachers to assess language theories encountered throughout their teaching careers.

Immediate practical applications of the research abound as well. Most importantly, studies suggest that teachers should offer a rich, interactive language environment, one that allows children to develop innate language skills. The environment should be student-centered, with children talking to each other as much as to the teacher. Such an environment might include learning centers, collaborative projects, peer editing groups, and student-led discussions. Teachers might try to engineer social roles and contexts that approximate the social roles children assume outside of class, roles that heighten verbal interaction, such as customers ordering meals at a restaurant, patrons conducting business at banks or markets, and friends negotiating rules for a game. Furthermore teachers should avoid assessing children's speech as if it reflected only what the teacher had taught. Finally, teachers should see grammatical errors as developmental—as signs of a transitional grammar. They should concentrate on content, helping children extend the functions of their language.

OVERVIEW OF THE READINGS

The readings in this chapter survey and juxtapose the essential principles of language acquisition. They begin with a consolidating essay that draws on central areas of language acquisition: phonology, or how we put sounds together to form words; morphology, or how the smallest units of meaning combine to form words; syntax, or how words come together to form sentences; semantics, or how to interpret the meaning or words and sentences; and pragmatics, or how to participate in conversation.

Breyne Arlene Moskowitz's "The Acquisition of Language" defines basic terms and explains central issues, allowing readers to view the field as a whole before confronting articles with more specific concerns. In this piece, the reader is first introduced to ideas with important implications for language instruction: that learning is achieved through active rule hypothesizing, not through memorization or drill; that errors are signs of a developing grammar, not mistakes; and that the preset order of acquisition depends on such criteria as regularity and grammatical difficulty, not on exposure, drill, or the teacher's syllabus.

Derek Bickerton's "Creole Languages" throws additional light on universal language acquisition principles through the study of how creoles develop out of pidgins. Immigrant laborers, with different complete first language systems, develop rudimentary "pidgins" with simplified grammars and limited vocabularies to communicate with each other and with overseers. Their children, exposed to only rudimentary language forms, on their own develop full language systems called *creoles*—systems as complex as any of the world's existing languages. These children are not born speaking a pidgin on their way to creole; they speak creole, an autonomously developed complex language system. Thus contact, and with it imitation and explicit instruction, seems less a key factor than children's innate abilities to develop full language structures. And the similarities among different creoles in different regions of the world further underscore innate processes.

Elinor Ochs Keenan's "Making It Last: Repetition in Children's Discourse" critiques the emphasis on inner processes, offering a perspective on language acquisition from the field of study called *pragmatics,* the study of how different social goals, conventions, and contexts influence language. Keenan views child language as a social act. Thus she does not focus on the grammar of isolated sentences and its growth toward static adult models, but rather on exchanges and the communicative (pragmatic) functions of those exchanges. Her essay specifically addresses repetition. Children's repetitions are significant because they so obviously play a role in language acquisition, yet this role has been down-played. According to Moskowitz, from the standpoint of grammar and innate abilities, repetition can only be viewed as simple imitation or mimicry and thus seems irrelevant to language acquisition. Viewed as a social act, however, repetition functions as a way of answering questions, verifying messages, requesting attention, and establishing the topic of subsequent discussion. This pragmatic view of children's language abilities is important because it investigates children's full communicative competence. It thus corresponds to similar investigations in second language acquisition, as we shall see in the next chapter.

The final selection, Peter French and Bencie Woll's "Context, Meaning and Strategy in Parent-Child Conversation," adds new insight into the nature versus nurture debate. Like Keenan, these researchers argue that formal and cognitive complexity alone cannot explain language acquisition; social factors are also important considerations. However, French and Woll introduce the idea that the context or social environment is not a stable reference point, easily identified and then referred to as a static entity. They argue that the social context is itself established or created through language, and that it has a reciprocal effect upon the meaning of what is said. The notion of reciprocal effect introduces the idea that meaning is created through interaction, as in a play situation in which children define each other's roles and the surrounding reality. For instance, children may become fairy children, designate an ordinary tunnel as a "wishing tunnel," and hold their breath and make wishes while passing through. Thus French and Woll caution us against overly simplistic ideas of a static context and ask us to observe the contexts that children bring into being. Their view of context posits children as active creators, learners, and language users. They favor a social over a cognitive view, but more importantly emphasize a creative constructionist view of language over a representational one. This perspective is highly antithetical to a behaviorist, teacher-directed, drill-based view of acquisition, as are all the essays in this chapter.

The Acquisition of Language*

BREYNE ARLENE MOSKOWITZ

"The Acquisition of Language," first published in Scientific American, *offers a comprehensive overview of first language acquisition research. It is one of those introductory essays that are rare in linguistics—broad without being simplistic, technical without requiring technical knowledge, consolidating without losing rich detail. Drawing on phonetics, morphology, and syntax, Moskowitz offers the essential principles of first language acquisition, a review of major research areas, and a brief summary of research bearing on this issue.*

Some of the essential principles she presents underlie other language arenas and are referred to in later chapters. For this reason, they are listed here.

1. *The distinction between unconscious, tacit learning and school-based, conscious learning. Moskowitz vivifies this distinction, which becomes so important in second language (L2) learning.*
2. *The Chomskyan distinction between internal grammar, developed by (unconscious) rule formation and capable of producing sentences never heard before, and a behaviorist grammar based on imitation and drill and limited to sentences already heard.*
3. *The Chomskyan distinction between the child as active learner—who analyzes language in predictable ways—and the passive learner—who can only repeat what is heard and learns only through repetitive practice.*
4. *The apparent preset order of acquisition, based on the breadth and regularity of the rule acquired (exceptions are learned last) and the imperviousness of children to correction. This emphasis on stages, order, and imperviousness to correction corresponds to Piagetian views of developmental stages.*

* Moskowitz, B. A., "The Acquisition of Language" reprinted by permission of the publishers from *Language Acquisition* by Jill G. deVilliers and Peter A. deVilliers. Cambridge, Mass.: Harvard University Press. Copyright © 1978 by the President and Fellows of Harvard College.

5. *The superiority of engaging children in natural conversations rather than expanding their sentences (repeating them with fuller syntax).*
6. *The importance of viewing language not simply as a logical system but as a communicative tool that depends on interaction.*
7. *The importance of "caretaker speech," a distinct register (vocabulary adopted to particular situations) that seems ideally suited to underscore language regularities.*
8. *The caretaker's intuitive use of a syntax six months in advance of the child's own.*

Although Moskowitz does not explore the potential conflicts between the first five principles and the last three listed above, she consolidates well the main insights from the two key fields represented: psycholinguistics and sociolinguistics. The main thrust of her essay is on universal cognitive principles, the necessary developmental stages that children undergo irrespective of age, intelligence, exposure, or language community. Later readings in this chapter, particularly Keenan's piece on repetition, will point up some of the conflicting assumptions and challenge the Piagetian and Chomskyan views shaping this research.

An adult who finds herself in a group of people speaking an unfamiliar foreign language may feel quite uncomfortable. The strange language sounds like gibberish: mysterious strings of sound, rising and falling in unpredictable patterns. Each person speaking the language knows how to interpret other people's strings, but the individual who does not know anything about the language cannot pick out separate words or sounds, let alone discern meanings. She may feel overwhelmed, ignorant and even childlike. It is possible that she is returning to a vague memory from her very early childhood, because the experience of an adult listening to a foreign language comes close to duplicating the experience of an infant listening to the "foreign" language spoken by everyone around her. Like the adult, the child is confronted with the task of learning a language about which she knows nothing.

The task of acquiring language is one for which the adult has lost most of her aptitude but one the child will perform with remarkable skill. Within a short span of time and with almost no direct instruction the child will analyze the language completely. In fact, although many subtle refinements are added between the ages of five and ten, most children have completed the greater part of the basic language-acquisition process by the age of five. By that time a child will have dissected the language into its minimal separable units of sound and meaning; she will have discovered the rules for recombining sounds into words, the meanings of individual words and the rules for recombining words into meaningful sentences, and she will have internalized the intricate patterns of taking turns in dialogue. All in all she will have established herself linguistically as a full-fledged member of a social community, informed about the most subtle details of her native language as it is spoken in a wide variety of situations.

The speed with which children accomplish the complex process of language acquisition is particularly impressive. Ten linguists working full time for ten years to analyze the structure of the English language could not program a computer with the ability for language acquired by an average child in the first ten or even five years of life. In spite of the scale of the task and even in spite of adverse conditions—emotional instability, physical disability and so on—children learn to speak. How do they go about it? By what process does a child learn language?

WHAT IS LANGUAGE?

In order to understand how language is learned it is necessary to understand what language is. The issue is confused by two factors. First, language is learned in early childhood, and adults have few memories of the intense effort that went into the learning process, just as they do not remember the process of learning to walk. Second, adults do have conscious memories of being taught the few grammatical rules that are prescribed as "correct" usage, or the norms of "standard" language. It is difficult for adults to dissociate their memories of school lessons from those of true language learning, but the rules learned in school are only the conventions of an educated society. They are arbitrary finishing touches of embroidery on a thick fabric of language that each child weaves for herself before arriving in the English teacher's classroom. The fabric is grammar: the set of rules that describe how to structure language.

The grammar of language includes rules of phonology, which describe how to put sounds together to form words; rules of syntax, which describe how to put words together to form sentences; rules of semantics, which describe how to interpret the meaning of words and sentences; and rules of pragmatics, which describe how to participate in a conversation, how to sequence sentences and how to anticipate the information needed by an interlocutor. The internal grammar each adult has constructed is identical with that of every other adult in all but a few superficial details. Therefore each adult can create or understand an infinite number of sentences she has never heard before. She knows what is acceptable as a word or a sentence and what is not acceptable, and her judgments on these issues concur with those of other adults. For example, speakers of English generally agree that the sentence "Ideas green sleep colorless furiously" is ungrammatical and that the sentence "Colorless green ideas sleep furiously" is grammatical but makes no sense semantically. There is similar agreement on the grammatical relations represented by word order. For example, it is clear that the sentences "John hit Mary" and "Mary hit John" have different meanings although they consist of the same words, and that the sentence "Flying planes can be dangerous" has two possible meanings. At the level of individual words all adult speakers can agree that "brick" is an English word, that "blick" is not an English word but could be one (that is, there is an accidental gap in the adult lexicon, or internal vocabulary) and that "bnick" is not an English word and could not be one.

How children go about learning the grammar that makes communication possible has always fascinated adults, particularly parents, psychologists, and investigators of language. Until recently diary keeping was the primary method of study in this area. For example, in 1877 Charles Darwin published an account of his son's development that includes notes on language learning. Unfortunately most of the diarists used inconsistent or incomplete notations to record what they heard (or what they thought they heard), and most of the diaries were only partial listings of emerging types of sentences with inadequate information on developing word meanings. Although the very best of them, such as W. F. Leopold's classic *Speech Development of a Bilingual Child,* continue to be a rich resource of contemporary investigators, advances in audio and video recording equipment have made modern diaries generally much more valuable. In the 1960s, however, new discoveries inspired linguists and psychologists to approach the study of language acquisition in a new, systematic way, oriented less toward long-term diary keeping and more toward a search for the patterns in a child's speech at any given time.

An event that revolutionized linguistics was the publication in 1957 of Noam Chomsky's *Syntactic Structures.* Chomsky's investigation of the structure of grammars revealed that language systems were far deeper and more complex than had been suspected. And of course if linguistics was more complicated, then language learning had to be more complicated. In the . . . years since the publication of *Syntactic Structures* the disciplines of linguistics and child language have come of age. The study of the acquisition of language has benefited not only from the increasingly sophisticated understanding of linguistics but also from the improved understanding of cognitive development as it is related to language. The improvements in recording technology have made experimentation in this area more reliable and more detailed, so that investigators framing new and deeper questions are able to accurately capture both rare occurrences and developing structures.

The picture that is emerging from the more sophisticated investigations reveals the child as an active language learner, continually analyzing what she hears and proceeding in a methodical, predictable way to put together the jigsaw puzzle of language. Different children learn language in similar ways. It is not known how many processes are involved in language learning, but the few that have been observed appear repeatedly, from child to child and from language to language. All the examples I shall discuss here concern children who are learning English, but identical processes have been observed in children learning French, Russian, Finnish, Chinese, Zulu and many other languages.

Children learn the systems of grammar—phonology, syntax, semantics, lexicon and pragmatics—by breaking each system down into its smallest combinable parts and then developing rules for combining the parts. In the first two years of life a child spends much time working on one part of the task, disassembling the language to find the separate sounds that can be put together to form words and the separate words that can be put together to form sentences. After the age of two the basic process continues to be refined, and many more sounds and words are produced. The other part of language acquisition—developing rules for combining the basic elements of language—is carried out in a very methodical way: the most general rules are hypothesized first, and as time passes they are successively narrowed down by the addition of more precise rules applying to a more restricted set of sentences. The procedure is the same in any area of language learning, whether the child is acquiring syntax or phonology or semantics. For example, at the earliest stage of acquiring negatives a child does not have at her command the same range of negative structures that an adult does. She has constructed only a single very general rule: Attach "no"

(1)	(2)	(3)	(4)	(5)	(6)
boy		boys	boysəz	boys	boys
cat		cats	catsəz	cats	cats
			catəz		
man	men	mans	mansəz	mans	men
			menəz		
house		house	housəz	houses	houses
foot		foots	footsəz	feets	feet
feet		feets	feetsəz		

Sorting out of competing pronunciations that result in the correct plural forms of nouns takes place in the six stages shown in this illustration. Children usually learn the singular forms of nouns first (1), although in some cases an irregular plural form such as "feet" may be learned as a singular or as a free variant of a singular. Other irregular plurals may appear for a brief period (2), but soon they are replaced by plurals made according to the most general rule possible: To make a noun plural add the sound "s" or "z" to it (3). Words such as "house" or "rose," which already end in an "s"- or "z"-like sound, are usually left in their singular forms at this stage. When words of this type do not have irregular plural forms, adults make them plural by adding an "əz" sound. (The vowel "ə" is pronounced like the unstressed word "a.") Some children demonstrate their mastery of this usage by tacking "əz" endings indiscriminately onto nouns (4). That stage is brief and use of the ending is quickly narrowed down (5). At this point only irregular plurals remain to be learned, and since no new rule-making is needed, children may go on to harder problems and leave final stage (6) for later.

to the beginning of any sentence constructed by the other rules of grammar. At this stage all negative sentences will be formed according to that rule.

Throughout the acquisition process a child continually revises and refines the rules of her internal grammar, learning increasingly detailed subrules until she achieves a set of rules that enables her to create the full array of complex, adult sentences. The process of refinement continues at least until the age of ten and probably considerably longer for most children. By the time a child is six or seven, however, the changes in her grammar may be so subtle and sophisticated that they go unnoticed. In general children approach language learning economically, devoting their energy to broad issues before dealing with specific ones. They cope with clear-cut questions first and sort out the details later, and they may adopt any one of a variety of methods for circumventing details of a language system they have not yet dealt with.

PREREQUISITES FOR LANGUAGE

Although some children verbalize much more than others and some increase the length of their utterances much faster than others, all children overgeneralize a single rule before learning to apply it more narrowly and before constructing other less widely applicable rules and all children speak in one-word sentences before they speak in two-word sentences. The similarities in language learning for different children and different languages are so great that many linguists have believed at one time or another that the human brain is preprogrammed for language learning. Some linguists continue to believe language is innate and only the surface details of the particular language spoken in a child's environment need to be learned. The speed with which children learn language gives this view much appeal. As more parallels between language and other areas of cognition are revealed, however, there is greater reason to believe any language specialization that exists in the child is only one aspect of more general cognitive abilities of the brain.

Whatever the built-in properties the brain brings to the task of language learning may be, it is now known that a child who hears no language learns no language, and that a child learns only the language spoken in her environment. Most infants coo and babble during the first six months of life, but congenitally deaf children have been observed to cease babbling after six months, whereas normal infants continue to babble. A child does not learn language, however, simply by hearing it spoken. A boy with normal hearing but with deaf parents who communicated by the American Sign Language was exposed to television every day so that he would learn English. Because the child was asthmatic and was confined to his home he interacted only with people at home, where his family and all their visitors communicated in sign language. By the age of three he was fluent in sign language but neither understood nor spoke English. It appears that in order to learn a language a child must also be able to interact with real people in that language. A television set does not suffice as the sole medium for language learning because, even though it can ask questions, it cannot respond to a child's answers. A child, then, can develop language only if there is language in her environment and if she can employ that language to communicate with other people in her immediate environment.

CARETAKER SPEECH

In constructing a grammar children have only a limited amount of information available to them, namely the language they hear spoken around them. (Until about the age of three a child models her language on that of her parents; afterward the language of her peer group tends to become more important.) There is no question, however, that the language environments children inhabit are restructured, usually unintentionally, by the adults who take care of them. Recent studies show that there are several ways caretakers systematically modify the child's environment, making the task of language acquisition simpler.

Caretaker speech is a distinct speech register that differs from others in its simplified vocabulary, the systematic phonological simplification of some words, higher pitch, exaggerated intonation, short, simple sentences and a high proportion of questions (among mothers) or imperatives (among fathers). Speech with the first two characteristics is formally designated Baby Talk. Baby Talk is a subsystem of caretaker speech that has been studied over a wide range of languages and cultures. Its characteristics appear to be universal: in languages as diverse as English, Arabic, Comanche, and Gilyak (a Paleo-Siberian language) there are simplified vocabulary items for terms relating to food, toys, animals and body functions. Some words are phonologically simplified, frequently by the duplication of syllables, as in "wawa" for "water" and "choo-choo" for "train," or by the reduction of consonant clusters, as in "tummy" for "stomach" and "scambled eggs" for "scrambled eggs." (Many types of phonological simplification seem to mimic the phonological structure of an infant's own early vocabulary.)

Perhaps the most pervasive characteristic of caretaker speech is its syntactic simplification. While a child is still babbling, adults may address long, complex sentences to her, but as soon as she begins to utter meaningful, identifiable words they almost invariably speak to her in very simple sentences. Over the next few years of the child's language development the speech addressed to her by her caretakers may well be describable by a grammar only six months in advance of her own.

The functions of the various language modifications in caretaker speech are not equally apparent. It is possible that higher pitch and exaggerated intonation serve to alert a child to pay attention to what she is hearing. As for Baby Talk, there is no reason to believe the use of phonologically simplified words in any way affects a child's learning of pronunciation. Baby Talk may have only a psychological function, marking speech as being affectionate. On the other hand, syntactic simplification has a clear function. Consider the speech adults address to other adults; it is full of false starts and long, rambling, highly complex sentences. It is not surprising that elaborate theories of innate language ability arose during the years when linguists examined the speech adults addressed to adults and assumed that the speech addressed to children was similar. Indeed, it is hard to imagine how a child could derive the rules of language from such input. The wide study of caretaker speech conducted over the past eight years has shown that children do not face this problem. Rather it appears they construct their initial grammars on the basis of the short, simple, grammatical sentences that are addressed to them in the first year or two they speak.

CORRECTING LANGUAGE

Caretakers simplify children's language-analysis task in other ways. For example, adults talk with other adults about complex ideas, but they talk with children about the here and now, minimizing discussion of feelings, displaced events and so on. Adults accept children's syntactic and phonological "errors," which are a normal part of the acquisition process. It is important to understand that when children make such errors, they are not producing flawed or incomplete replicas of adult sentences; they are producing sentences that are correct and grammatical with respect to their own current internalized grammar. Indeed, children's errors are essential data for students of child language because it is the consistent departures from the adult model that indicate the nature of a child's current hypotheses about the grammar of language. There are a number of memorized, unanalyzed sentences in any child's output of language. If a child says, "Nobody likes me," there is no way of knowing whether she has memorized the sentence

(1)	(2)	(3)	(4)	(5)	(6)
walk		walked	walkedəd	walked	walked
play		played	playedəd	played	played
need		need	needəd	needed	needed
			camedəd		
come	came	comed	comedəd	comed	came
			goed		
go	went	goed	wentəd	goed	went

Development of past-tense forms of verbs also takes place in six stages. After the present-tense forms are learned (1) irregular past-tense forms may appear briefly (2). The first and most general rule that is postulated is: To put a verb into the past tense, add a "t" or "d" sound (3). In adult speech, verbs such as "want" or "need," which already end in a "t" or "d" sound, are put into the past tense by adding "əd" sound. Many children go through a brief stage in which they add "əd" endings to any existing verb forms (4). Once the use of "əd" ending has been narrowed down (5), only irregular past-tense forms remain to be learned (6).

intact or has figured out the rules for constructing the sentence. On the other hand, a sentence such as "Nobody don't like me" is clearly not a memorized form but one that reflects an intermediate stage of a developing grammar.

Since each child's utterances at a particular stage are from her own point of view grammatically correct, it is not surprising that children are fairly impervious to the correction of their language by adults, indeed to any attempts to teach them language. Consider the boy who lamented to his mother, "Nobody don't like me." His mother seized the opportunity to correct him, replying, "Nobody likes me." The child repeated his original version and the mother her modified one a total of eight times until in desperation the mother said, "Now listen carefully! Nobody likes me." Finally her son got the idea and dutifully replied, "Oh! Nobody don't likes me." As the example demonstrates, children do not always understand exactly what it is the adult is correcting. The information the adult is trying to impart may be at odds with the information in the child's head, namely the rules the child is postulating for producing language. The surface correction of a sentence does not give the child a clue about how to revise the rule that produced the sentence.

It seems to be virtually impossible to speed up the language-learning process. Experiments conducted by Russian investigators show that it is extremely difficult to teach children a detail of language more than a few days before they would learn it themselves. Adults sometimes do, of course, attempt to teach children rules of language, expecting them to learn by imitation, but Courtney B. Cazden of Harvard University found that children benefit less from frequent adult correction of their errors than from true conversational interaction. Indeed, correcting errors can interrupt that interaction, which is, after all, the function of language. (One way children may try to secure such interaction is by asking "Why?" Children go through a stage of asking a question repeatedly. It serves to keep the conversation going, which may be the child's real aim. For example, a two-and-a-half-year-old named Stanford asked "Why?" and was given the nonsense answer: "Because the moon is made of green cheese." Although the response was not at all germane to the conversation, Stanford was happy with it and again asked "Why?" Many silly answers later the adult had tired of the conversation but Stanford had not. He was clearly not seeking information. What he needed was to practice the form of social conversation before dealing with its function. Asking "Why?" served that purpose well.)

In point of fact adults rarely correct children's ungrammatical sentences. For example, one mother, on hearing "Tommy fall my truck down," turned to Tommy with "Did you fall Stevie's truck down?" Since imitation seems to have little role in the language-acquisition process, however, it is probably just as well that most adults are either too charmed by children's errors or too busy to correct them.

Practice does appear to have an important function in the child's language learning process. Many children have been observed purposefully practicing language when they are alone, for example in a crib or a playpen. Ruth H. Weir of Stanford University hid a tape recorder in her son's bedroom and recorded his talk after he was put to bed. She found that he played with words and phrases, stringing together sequences of similar sounds and of variations on a phrase or on the use of a word: "What color . . . what color blanket . . . what color mop . . . what color glass . . . what color TV . . . red ant . . . fire . . . like lipstick . . . blanket . . . now the blue blanket . . . what color TV . . . what color horse . . . then what color table . . . then what color fire . . . here yellow spoon." Children who do not have much opportunity to be alone may use dialogue in a similar fashion. When Weir tried to record the bedtime monologues of her second child, whose room adjoined that of the first, she obtained through-the-wall conversations instead.

THE ONE-WORD STAGE

The first stage of child language is one in which the maximum sentence length is one word; it is followed by a stage in which the maximum sentence length is two words. Early in the one-word stage there are only a few words in a child's vocabulary, but as months go by her lexicon expands with increasing rapidity. The early words are primarily concrete nouns and verbs; more abstract words such as adjectives are acquired later. By the time the child is uttering two-word sentences with some regularity, her lexicon may include hundreds of words.

When a child can say only one word at a time and knows only five words in all, choosing which one to say may not be a complex task. But how does she decide which word to say when she knows 100 words or more? Patricia M. Greenfield of the University of California at Los Angeles and Joshua H. Smith of Stanford have suggested that an important criterion is informativeness, that is, the child selects a word reflecting what is new in a particular situation. Greenfield and Smith also found that a newly acquired word is first used for naming and only later for asking for something.

Superficially the one-word stage seems easy to understand: a child says one word at a time, and so each word is a complete sentence with its own sentence intonation. Ten years ago a child in the one-word stage was thought to be learning word meanings but not syntax. Recently, however, students of child language have seen less of a distinction between the one-word stage as a period of word learning and the subsequent period, beginning with the two-word stage, as one of syntax acquisition. It now seems clear that the infant is engaged in an enormous amount of syntactic analysis in the one-word stage, and indeed that her syntactic abilities are reflected in her utterances and in her accurate perception of multiword sentences addressed to her.

Ronald Scollon of the University of Hawaii and Lois Bloom of Columbia University have pointed out independently that important patterns in word choice in the one-word stage can be found by examining larger segments of children's speech. Scollon observed that a nineteen-month-old named Brenda was able to use a vertical construction (a series of one-word sentences) to express what an adult might say with a horizontal construction (a multiword sentence). Brenda's pronunciation, which is represented phonetically below, was imperfect and Scollon did not understand her words at the time. Later, when he transcribed the tape of their conversation, he heard the sound of a passing car immediately preceding the conversation and was able to identify Brenda's words as follows:

BRENDA: "Car [*pronounced 'ka'*]. Car. Car. Car."
SCOLLON: "What?"
BRENDA: "Go. Go."
SCOLLON: [*Undecipherable.*]
BRENDA: "Bus [*pronounced 'baish'*] Bus. Bus. Bus. Bus. Bus. Bus. Bus. Bus."
SCOLLON: "What? Oh, bicycle? Is that what you said?"
BRENDA: "Not ['*na'*]."
SCOLLON: "No?"
BRENDA: "Not."
SCOLLON: "No. I got it wrong."

Brenda was not yet able to combine two words syntactically to express "Hearing that car reminds me that we went on the bus yesterday. No, not on a bicycle." She could express that concept, however, by combining words sequentially. Thus the one-word stage is not just a time for learning the meaning of words. In that period a child is developing hypotheses about putting words together in meaningful groups. The next step will be to put two words together to form a single sentence.

THE TWO-WORD STAGE

The two-word stage is a time for experimenting with many binary semantic-syntactic relations such as possessor-possessed ("Mommy sock"), actor-action ("Cat sleeping") and action-object ("Drink soup"). When two-word sentences first began to appear in Brenda's speech, they were primarily of the following forms: subject noun and verb (as in "Monster go"), verb and object (as in "Read it") and verb or noun and location (as in "Bring home" and "Tree down"). She also continued to use vertical constructions in the two-word stage, providing herself with a means of expressing ideas that were still too advanced for her syntax. Therefore once again a description of Brenda's isolated sentences does not show her full abilities at this point in her linguistic development. Consider a later conversation Scollon had with Brenda:

BRENDA: "Tape corder. Use it. Use it."

SCOLLON: "Use it for what?"

BRENDA: "Talk. Corder talk. Brenda talk."

Brenda's use of vertical constructions to express concepts she is still unable to encode syntactically is just one example of a strategy employed by children in all areas of cognitive development. As Jean Piaget of the University of Geneva and Dan I. Slobin of the University of California at Berkeley put it, new forms are used for old functions and new functions are expressed by old forms. Long before Brenda acquired the complex syntactic form "Use the tape recorder to record me talking" she was able to use her old forms—two-word sentences and vertical construction—to express the new function. Later, when that function was old, she would develop new forms to express it. The controlled dovetailing of form and function can be observed in all areas of language acquisition. For example, before children acquire the past tense they may employ adverbs of time such as "yesterday" with present-tense verbs to express past time, saying "I do it yesterday" before "I dood it."

Bloom has provided a rare view of an intermediate stage between the one-word and the two-word stages in which the two-word construction—a new form—served only an old function. For several weeks Bloom's daughter Alison uttered two-word sentences all of which included the word "wida." Bloom tried hard to find the meaning of "wida" before realizing that it had no meaning. It was, she concluded, simply a placeholder. This case is the clearest ever reported of a new form preceding new functions. The two-word stage is an important time for practicing functions that will later have expanded forms and practicing forms that will later expand their functions.

TELEGRAPHIC SPEECH

There is no three-word stage in child language. For a few years after the end of the two-word stage children do produce rather short sentences, but the almost inviolable length constraints that characterized the first two stages have disappeared. The absence of a three-word stage has not been satisfactorily explained as yet; the answer may have to do with the fact that many basic semantic relations are binary and few are ternary. In any case a great deal is known about the sequential development in the language of the period following the two-word stage. Roger Brown of Harvard has named that language telegraphic speech. (It should be noted that there is no specific age at which a child enters any of these

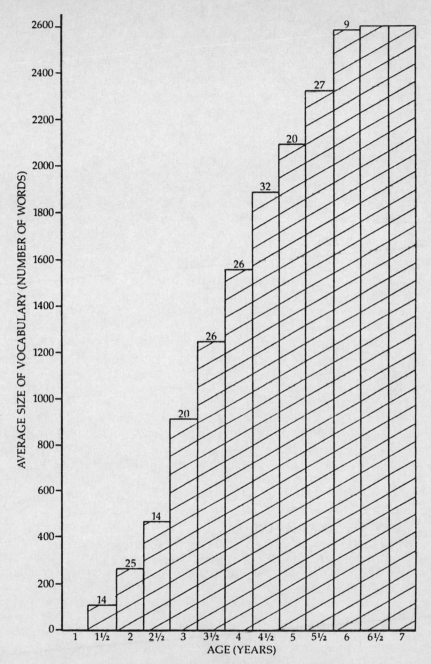

Children's average vocabulary size increases rapidly between the ages of one-and-a-half and six-and-a-half. The numbers over the first ten columns indicate the number of children tested in each sample age group.

Data are based on work done by Madorah E. Smith of the University of Hawaii.

stages of language acquisition and further that there is no particular correlation between intelligence and speed of acquisition.)

Early telegraphic speech is characterized by short, simple sentences made up primarily of content words: words that are rich in semantic content, usually nouns and verbs. The speech is called telegraphic because the sentences lack function "words": tense endings on verbs and plural endings on nouns, prepositions, conjunctions, articles and so on. As the telegraphic-speech stage progresses, function words are gradually added to sentences. This process has possibly been studied more thoroughly than any other in language acquisition, and a fairly predictable order in the addition of function words has been observed. The same principles that govern the order of acquisition of function words in English have been shown to operate in many other languages, including some, such as Finnish and Russian, that express the same grammatical relations with particularly rich systems of noun and verb suffixes.

In English many grammatical relations are represented by a fixed word order. For example, in the sentence "The dog followed Jamie to school" it is clear it is the dog that did the following. Normal word order in English requires that the subject come before the verb, and so people who speak English recognize "the dog" as the subject of the sentence. In other languages a noun may be marked as a subject not by its position with respect to the other words in the sentence but by a noun suffix, so that in adult sentences word order may be quite flexible. Until children begin to acquire suffixes and other function words, however, they employ fixed word order to express grammatical relations no matter how flexible adult word order may be. In English the strong propensity to follow word order rigidly shows up in children's interpretations of passive sentences as "Jamie was followed by the dog." At an early age children may interpret some passive sentences correctly, but by age three they begin to ignore the function words such as "was" and "by" in passive sentences and adopt the fixed word-order interpretation. In other words, since "Jamie" appears before the verb, Jamie is assumed to be the actor, or the noun doing the following.

FUNCTION WORDS

In spite of its grammatical dependence on word order, the English language makes use of enough function words to illustrate the basic principles that determine the order in which such words are acquired. The progressive tense ending "-ing," as in "He going," is acquired first, long before the present-tense third-person singular ending "-s," as in "He goes." The "-s" itself is acquired long before the past tense endings, as in "He goed." Once again the child proves to be a sensible linguist, learning first the tense that exhibits the least variation in form. The "-ing" ending is pronounced only one way, regardless of the pronunciation of the verb to which it is attached. The verb endings "-s" and "-ed," however, vary in their pronunciation: compare "cuts (s)," "cuddles (z)," "crushes (əz)," "walked (t)," "played (d)" and "halted (əd)." (The vowel "ə," called "schwa," is pronounced like the unstressed word "a.") Furthermore, present progressive ("-ing") forms are used with greater frequency than any other tense in the speech children hear. Finally, no verb has an irregular "-ing" form, but some verbs do have irregular third-person present-tense singular forms and many have irregular past-tense forms. (The same pattern of learning earliest those forms that exhibit the least variation shows up much more dramatically in languages such as Finnish and Russian, where the paradigms of inflection are much higher.)

The past tense is acquired after the progressive and present tenses, because the relative time it represents is conceptually more difficult. The future tense ("will" and a verb) is formed regularly in English and is as predictable as the progressive tense, but it is a much more abstract concept than the past tense. Therefore it is acquired much later. In the same way the prepositions "in" and "on" appear earlier than any others, at about the same time as "-ing," but prepositions such as "behind" and "in front of," whose correct usage depends on the speaker's frame of reference, are acquired much later.

It is particularly interesting to note that there are three English morphemes that are pronounced identically but are acquired at different times. They are the plural "-s," the possessive "-s" and the third-person singular tense ending "-s," and they are acquired in the order of listing. Roman Jakobson of Harvard has suggested that the explanation of this phenomenon has to do with the complexity of the different relations the morphemes signal: the singular-plural distinction is at the word level, the possessive relates two nouns at the phrase level and the tense ending relates a noun and a verb at the clause level.

The forms of the verb "to be" — "is," "are" and so on—are among the last of the function words to be acquired, particularly in their present-tense forms. Past- and future-tense forms of "to be" carry tense information, of course, but present-tense forms are essentially meaningless, and omitting them is a very sensible strategy for a child who must maximize the information content of a sentence and place priorities on linguistic structures still to be tackled.

---

(1) Laura (2:2)	(4) Andrew (2:0)
Her want some more.	Put that on.
Her want some more candy.	Andrew put that on.
(2) Laura (2:2)	(5) Andrew (2:1)
Where my tiger?	All wet.
Where my tiger book?	This shoe all wet.
(3) Laura (2:2)	(6) Benjy (2:3)
Let's dooz this.	Broke it.
Let's do this.	Broke it.
Let's do this puzzle.	Broke it I did.

Children correct their speech in ways that reflect the improvements they are currently making on their internal grammar. For example, Laura (1–3) is increasing the length of her sentences, encoding more information by embellishing a noun phrase. Andrew (4, 5) and Benjy (6) appear to be adding subjects to familiar verb-phrase sentences.

(7) Jamie (6:0)

Jamie: Why are you doing that?

Mother: What?

Jamie: Why are you writing what I say down?

Mother: What?

Jamie: Why are you writing down what I say?

(8) Jamie (6:3)

Jamie: Who do you think is the importantest kid in the world except me?

Mother: What did you say, Jamie?

Jamie: Who do you think is the specialest kid in the world not counting me?

(9) Jamie (6:6)

Jamie: Who are you versing?

Mother: What?

Jamie: I wanted to know who he was playing against.

(10) Jamie (6:10)

Jamie: I figured something you might like out.

Mother: What did you say?

Jamie: I figured out something you might like.

Jamie (7–10) seems to be working on much more subtle refinements such as the placement of verb participles, for example the "down" of "writing down." (Each child's age at time of correction is given in years and months.)

Corrections shown here were recorded by Judy S. Reilly of University of California at Los Angeles.

PLURALS

When there are competing pronunciations available, as in the case of the plural and past tenses, the process of sorting them out also follows a predictable pattern. Consider the acquisition of the English plural, in which six distinct stages can be observed. In English, as in many other (but not all) languages, nouns have both singular and plural forms. Children usually use the singular forms first, both in situations where the singular form would be appropriate and in situations where the plural form would be appropriate. In instances where the plural form is irregular in the adult model, however, a child may not recognize it as such and may use it in place of the singular or as a free variant of the singular. Thus in the first stage of acquisition, before either the concept of a plural or the linguistic devices for expressing a plural are acquired, a child may say "two cat" or point to "one feet."

When plurals begin to appear regularly, the child forms them according to the most general rule of English plural formation. At this point it is the child's overgeneralization of the rule, resulting in words such as "mans," "foots" or "feets," that shows she has hypothesized the rule: Add the sound /s/ or /z/ to the end of a word to make it plural. (The slashes indicate pronounced sounds, which are not to be confused with the letters used in spelling.)

For many children the overgeneralized forms of the irregular nouns are actually the earliest /s/ and /z/ plurals to appear, preceding "boys," "cats" and other regular forms by hours or days. The period of overgeneralization is considered to be the third stage in the acquisition of plurals because for many children there is an intermediate second stage in which irregular plurals such as "men" actually do appear. Concerned parents may regard the change from the second-stage "men" to the third-stage "mans" as a regression, but in reality it demonstrates progress from an individual memorized item to the application of a general rule.

In the third stage the small number of words that already end in a sound resembling /s/ or /z/, such as "house," "rose" and "bush," are used without any plural ending. Adults normally make such words plural by adding the suffix /əz/. Children usually relegate this detail to the remainder pile, to be dealt with at a later time. When they return to the problem, there is often a short fourth stage of perhaps a day, in which the child delightedly demonstrates her solution by tacking /əz/ endings indiscriminately onto nouns no matter what sound they end in and no matter how many other plural markings they may already have. A child may wake up one morning and throw herself into this stage with all the zeal of a kitten playing with its first ball of string.

Within a few days the novelty wears off and the child enters a less flamboyant fifth stage, in which only irregular plurals still deviate from the model forms. The rapid progression through the fourth stage does not mean that she suddenly focused her attention on the problem of /əz/ plurals. It is more likely that she had the problem at the back of her mind throughout the third stage. She was probably silently formulating hypotheses about the occurrence of /əz/ and testing them against the plurals she was hearing. Finding the right rule required discovering the phonological specification of the class of nouns that take /əz/ plurals.

Arriving at the sixth and final stage in the acquisition of plurals does not require the formulation of any new rules. All that is needed is the simple memorizing of irregular forms. Being rational, the child relegates such minor details to the lowest-priority remainder pile and turns her attention to more interesting linguistic questions. Hence a five-year-old may still not have entered the last stage. In fact, a child in the penultimate stage may not be at all receptive to being taught irregular plurals. For example, a child named Erica pointed to a picture of some "mouses," and her mother corrected her by saying "mice." Erica and her mother each repeated their own version two more times, and then Erica resolved the standoff by turning to a picture of "ducks." She avoided the picture of the mice for several days. Two years later, of course, Erica was perfectly able to say "mice."

NEGATIVE SENTENCES

One of the pioneering language-acquisition studies of the 1960s was undertaken at Harvard by a research group headed by Brown. The group studied the development in the language of three children over a period of several years. Two members of the group, Ursula Bellugi and Edward S. Klima, looked specifically at the changes in the children's negative sentences over the course of the project. They found that negative structures, like other subsystems of the syntactic component of grammar, are acquired in an orderly, rule-governed way.

When the project began, the forms of negative sentences the children employed were quite simple. It appeared that they had incorporated the following rule into their grammar: To make a sentence negative attach "no" or "not" to the beginning of it. On rare occasions, possibly when a child had forgotten to anticipate the negative, "no" could be attached to the end of a sentence, but negative words could not appear inside a sentence.

In the next stage the children continued to follow this rule, but they had also hypothesized and incorporated into their grammars more complex rules that allowed them to generate sentences in which the negatives "no," "not," "can't" and "don't" appeared after the subject and before the verb. These rules constituted quite an advance over attaching a negative word externally to a sentence. Furthermore, some of the primitive imperative sentences constructed at this stage began with "don't" rather than "no." On the other hand, "can't" never appeared at the beginning of a sentence, and neither "can" nor "do" appeared as an auxiliary, as they do in adult speech: "I can do it." These facts suggest that at this point "can't" and "don't" were unanalyzed negative forms rather than contractions of "cannot" and "do not," but that although "can't" and "don't" each seemed to be interchangeable with "no," they were no longer interchangeable with each other.

In the third stage of acquiring negatives many more details of the negative system had appeared in the children's speech. The main feature of the system that still remained to be worked out was the use of pronouns in negative sentences. At this stage the children said "I didn't see something" and "I don't want somebody to wake me up." The pronouns "somebody" and "something" were later replaced with "nobody" and "nothing" and ultimately with the properly concorded forms "anybody" and "anything."

Many features of telegraphic speech were still evident in the third stage. The form "is" of the verb "to be" was frequently omitted, as in "This no good." In adult speech the auxiliary "do" often functions as a dummy verb to carry tense and other markings; for example, in "I didn't see it," "do" carries the tense and the negative. In the children's speech at this stage "do" appeared occasionally, but the children had not yet figured out its entire function. Therefore in some sentences the auxiliary "do" was omitted and the negative "not" appeared alone, as in "I not hurt him." In other sentences, such as "I didn't did it," the negative auxiliary form of "do" appears to be correct but is actually an unanalyzed, memorized item; at this stage the tense is regularly marked on the main verb, which in this example happens also to be "do."

Many children acquire negatives in the same way that the children in the Harvard study did, but subsequent investigations have shown that there is more than one way to learn a language. Carol B. Lord of U.C.L.A. identified a quite different strategy employed by a two-year-old named Jennifer. From twenty-four to twenty-eight months Jennifer used "no" only as a single-word utterance. In order to produce a negative sentence she simply spoke an ordinary sentence with a higher pitch. For example, "I want put it on" spoken with a high pitch meant "I don't want to put it on." Lord noticed that many of the negative sentences adults addressed to Jennifer were spoken with an elevated pitch. Children tend to pay more attention to the beginning and ending of sentences, and in adult speech negative words usually appear in the middle of sentences. With good reason, then, Jennifer seemed to have hypothesized that one makes a sentence negative by uttering it with a higher pitch. Other children have been found to follow the same strategy. There are clearly variations in the hypotheses children make in the process of constructing grammar.

Stage 1	Stage 2	Stage 3
No . . . wipe finger.	I can't catch you.	We can't make another broom.
No a boy bed.	I can't see you.	I don't want cover on it.
No singing song.	We can't talk.	I gave him some so he won't cry.
No the sun shining.	You can't dance.	No, I don't have a book.
No money.	I don't want it.	I am not a doctor.
No sit there.	I don't like him.	It's not cold.
No play that.	I don't know his name.	Don't put the two wings on.
No fall!	No pinch me.	
Not . . . fit.	Book say no.	A
Not a teddy bear.	Touch the snow no.	I didn't did it.
More . . . no,	This a radiator no.	You didn't caught me.
Wear mitten no.	No square . . . is clown.	I not hurt him.
	Don't bite me yet.	Ask me if I not made mistake.
	Don't leave me.	
	Don't wake me up . . . again.	B
	He not little, he big.	Because I don't want somebody
	That no fish school.	to wake me up.
	That no Mommy.	I didn't see something.
	There no squirrels.	
	He no bite you.	C
	I no want envelope.	I isn't . . . I not sad.
	I no taste them.	This not ice cream.
		This no good.
		I not crying.
		That not turning.
		He not taking the walls down.

Three stages in the acquisition of negative sentences were studied by Ursula Bellugi of the Salk Institute for Biological Studies and Edward S. Klima of the University of California at San Diego. They observed that in the first stage almost all negative sentences appear to be formulated according to the rule: Attach *"no"* or *"not"* to the beginning of a sentence to make it negative. In the second stage additional rules are postulated that allow the formation of sentences in which *"no,"* *"not,"* *"can't"* and *"don't"* appear after the subject and before the verb. In the third stage several issues remain to be worked out, in particular the agreement of pronouns in negative sentences (B), the inclusion of the forms of the verb *"to be"* (C), and the correct use of the auxiliary *"do"* (A). In adult speech the auxiliary *"do"* often carries tense and other functional markings such as the negative; children in the third stage may replace it by *"not"* or use it redundantly to mark tense that is already marked on the main verb.

SEMANTICS

Up to this point I have mainly discussed the acquisition of syntactic rules, in part because in the years following the publication of Chomsky's *Syntactic Structures* child-language research in this area flourished. Syntactic rules, which govern the ordering of words in a sentence, are not all a child needs to know about language, however, and after the first flush of excitement over Chomsky's work investigators began to ask questions about other areas of language acquisition. Consider the development of the rules of semantics, which govern the way words are interpreted. Eve V. Clark of Stanford reexamined old diary studies and noticed that the development in the meaning of words during the first several months of the one-word stage seemed to follow a basic pattern.

The first time children in the studies used a word, Clark noted, it seemed to be as a proper noun, as the name of a specific object. Almost immediately, however, the children generalized the word based on some feature of the original object and used it to refer to many other objects. For example, a child named Hildegard first used "tick-tock" as the name for her father's watch, but she quickly broadened the meaning of the word, first to include all clocks, then all watches, then a gas meter, then a firehose wound on a spool and then a bathroom scale with a round dial. Her generalizations appear to be based on her observation of common features of shape: roundness, dials and so on. In general the children in the diary studies overextended meaning based on similarities of movement, texture, size and, most frequently, shape.

As the children progressed, the meanings of words were narrowed down until eventually they more or less coincided with the meanings accepted by adult speakers of the language. The narrowing-down process has not been studied intensively, but it seems likely that the process has no fixed end point. Rather it appears that the meanings of words continue to expand and contract through adulthood, long after other types of language acquisition have ceased.

One of the problems encountered in trying to understand the acquisition of semantics is that it is often difficult to determine the precise meaning a child has constructed for a word. Some interesting observations have been made, however, concerning the development of the meanings of the pairs of words that function as opposites in adult language. Margaret Donaldson and George Balfour of the University of Edinburgh asked children from three to five years old which one of two cardboard trees had "more" apples on it. They asked other children of the same age which tree had "less" apples. (Each child was interviewed individually.) Almost all the children in both groups responded by pointing to the tree with more apples on it. Moreover, the children who had been asked to point to the tree with "less" apples showed no hesitation in choosing the tree with more apples. They did not act as though they did not know the meaning of "less"; rather they acted as if they did know the meaning and "less" meant "more."

Subsequent studies have revealed similar systematic error making in the acquisition of other pairs of opposites such as "same" and "different," "big" and "little," "wide" and "narrow" and "tall" and "short." In every case the pattern of learning is the same: one word of the pair is learned first and its meaning is overextended to apply to the other word in the pair. The first word learned is always the unmarked word of the pair, that is, the word adults use when they do not want to indicate either one of the opposites. (For example, in the case of "wide" and "narrow," "wide" is the unmarked word: asking "How wide is the road?" does not suggest that the road is wide, but asking "How narrow is the road?" does suggest that the road is narrow.).

Clark observed a more intricate pattern of error production in the acquisition of the words "before" and "after." Consider the four different types of sentence represented by (1) "He jumped the gate before he patted the dog," (2) "Before he patted the dog he jumped the gate," (3) "He patted the dog after he jumped the gate" and (4) "After he jumped the gate he patted the dog." Clark found that the way the children she observed interpreted sentences such as these could be divided into four stages.

In the first stage the children disregarded the words "before" and "after" in all four of these sentence types and assumed that the event of the first clause took place before the event of the second clause. With this order-of-mention strategy the first and fourth sentence types were interpreted correctly but the second and third sentence types were not. In the second stage sentences using "before" were interpreted correctly but an order-of-mention strategy was still adopted for sentences that used "after." Hence sentences of the fourth type were interpreted correctly but sentences of the third type were not. In the next stage both the third and the fourth sentence types were interpreted incorrectly, suggesting that the children had adopted the strategy that "after" actually meant "before." Finally, in the fourth stage both "before" and "after" were interpreted appropriately.

It appears, then, that in learning the meaning of a pair of words such as "more" and "less" or "before" and "after" children acquire first the part of the meaning that is common to both words and only later the part of the meaning that distinguishes the two. Linguists have not yet developed satisfactory ways of separating the components of meaning that make up a single word, but it seems clear that when such components can be identified, it will be established that, for example, "more" and "less" have a large number of components in common and differ only in a single component specifying the pole of the dimension. Beyond the studies of opposites there has been little investigation of the period of semantic acquisition that follows the early period of rampant overgeneralization. How children past the early stage learn the meanings of other kinds of words is still not well understood.

PHONOLOGY

Just as children overgeneralize word meanings and sentence structures, so do they overgeneralize sounds, using sounds they have learned in place of sounds they have not yet acquired. Just as a child may use the word "not" correctly in one sentence but instead of another negative word in a second sentence, so may she correctly contrast /p/ and /b/ at the beginnings of words but employ /p/ at the ends of words, regardless of whether the adult models end with /p/ or /b/. Children also acquire the details of the phonological system in very regular ways.

Child's Lexical Item	First Referents	Other Referents in Order of Occurrence	General Area of Semantic Extension
mooi	moon	cake round marks on windows writing on windows and in books round shapes in books tooling on leather book covers round postmarks letter "o"	shape
bow-wow	dog	fur piece with glass eyes father's cufflinks pearl buttons on dress bath thermometer	shape
kotibaiz	bars of cot	large toy abacus toast rack with parallel bars picture of building with columns	shape
bébé	reflection of child (self) in mirror	photograph of self all photographs all pictures all books with pictures all books	shape
vov-vov	dog	kittens hens all animals at a zoo picture of pigs dancing	shape

(*continued*)

Children overgeneralize word meanings, using words they acquire early in place of words they have not yet acquired. Eve V. Clark of Stanford University has observed that when a word first appears in a child's lexicon, it refers to a specific object but the child quickly extends semantic domain of word, using it to refer to many other

The ways in which they acquire individual sounds, however, are highly idiosyncratic, and so for many years the patterns eluded diarists, who tended to look only at the order in which sounds were acquired. Jakobson made a major advance in this area by suggesting that it was not individual sounds children acquire in an orderly way but the distinctive features of sound, that is, the minimal differences, or contrasts, between sounds. In other words, when a child begins to contrast /p/ and /b/, she also begins to contrast all the other pairs of sounds that, like /p/ and /b/, differ only in the absence or presence of vocal-cord vibration. In English these pairs include /t/ and /d/, and /k/ and the hard /g/. It is the acquisition of this contrast and not of the six individual sounds that is predictable. Jakobson's extensive examination of the diary data for a wide variety of languages supported his theory. Almost all current work in phonological theory rests on the theory of distinctive features that grew out of his work.

Child's Lexical Item	First Referents	Other Referents in Order of Occurrence	General Area of Semantic Extension
ass	goat with rough hide on wheels	things that move: animals, sister, wagon . . . all moving things all things with a rough surface	movement texture
tutu	train	engine moving train journey	movement
fly	fly	specks of dirt dust all small insects child's own toes crumbs of bread a toad	size
quack	ducks on water	all birds and insects all coins (after seeing an eagle on the face of a coin)	size
koko	cockerel's crowing	tunes played on a violin tunes played on a piano tunes played on an accordion tunes played on a phonograph all music merry-go-round	sound
dany	sound of a bell	clock telephone doorbells	sound

things. Eventually meaning of the word is narrowed down until it coincides with adult usage. Clark found that children most frequently base the semantic extension of a word on shape of its first referent.

My own recent work suggests that phonological units even more basic than the distinctive features play an important part in the early acquisition process. At an early stage, when there are relatively few words in a child's repertory, unanalyzed syllables appear to be the basic unit of the sound system. By designating these syllables as unanalyzed I mean that the child is not able to separate them into their component consonants and vowels. Only later in the acquisition process does such division into smaller units become possible. The gradual discovery of successively smaller units that can form the basis of the phonological system is an important part of the process.

At an even earlier stage, before a child has uttered any words, she is accomplishing a great deal of linguistic learning, working with a unit of phonological organization even more primitive than the syllable. That unit can be defined in terms of pitch contours. By the late babbling period children already control the intonation, or pitch modulation, contours of the language they are learning. At that stage the child sounds as if she is uttering reasonably long sentences, and adult listeners may have the impression they are not quite catching the child's words. There are no words to catch, only random strings of babbled sounds with recognizable, correctly produced question or statement intonation contours. The sounds may accidentally be similar to some of those found in adult English. These sentence-length utterances are called sentence units, and in the phonological system of the child at this stage they are comparable to the consonant-and-vowel segments, syllables and distinctive features that appear in the phonological systems of later stages. The syllables and segments that appear when the period of word learning begins are in no way related to the vast repertory of babbling sounds. Only the intonation contours are carried over from the babbling stage into the later period.

No matter what language environment a child grows up in, the intonation contours characteristic of adult speech in that environment are the linguistic information learned earliest. Some recent studies suggest that it is possible to identify the language environment of a child from her babbling intonation during the second year of life. Other studies suggest that children can be distinguished at an even earlier age on the basis of whether or not their language environment is a tone language, that is, a language in which words spoken with different pitches are identifiable as different words, even though they may have the same sequence of consonants and vowels. To put it another way, "ma" spoken with a high pitch and "ma" spoken with a low pitch can be as different to someone speaking a tone language as "ma" and "pa" are to someone speaking English. (Many African and Asian languages are tone languages.) Tones are learned very early, and entire tone systems are mastered long before other areas of phonology. The extremely early acquisition of pitch patterns may help to explain the difficulty adults have in learning the intonation of a second language.

PHONETICS

There is one significant way in which the acquisition of phonology differs from the acquisition of other language systems. As a child is acquiring the phonological system she must also learn the phonetic realization of the system: the actual details of physiological and acoustic phonetics, which call for the coordination of a complex set of muscle movements. Some children complete the process of learning how to pronounce things earlier than others, but differences of this kind are usually not related to the learning of the phonological system. Brown had what has become a classic conversation with a child who referred to a "fis." Brown repeated "fis," and the child indignantly corrected him, saying "fis." After several such exchanges Brown tried "fish," and the child, finally satisfied, replied, "Yes, fis." It is clear that although the child was still not able to pronounce the distinction between the sounds "s" and "sh," he knew such a systematic phonological distinction existed. Such phonetic muddying of the phonological waters complicates the study of this area of acquisition. Since the child's knowledge of the phonological system may not show up in her speech, it is not easy to determine what a child knows about the system without engaging in complex experimentation and creative hypothesizing.

Children whose phonological system produces only simple words such as "mama" and "papa" actually have a greater phonetic repertory than their utterances suggest. Evidence of that repertory is found in the late babbling stage when children are working with sentence units and are making a large array of sounds. They do not lose their phonetic ability overnight, but they must constrain it systematically. Going on to the next-higher stage of language learning, the phonological system, is more important to the child than the details of facile pronunciation. Much later, after the phonological system has been acquired, the details of pronunciation receive more attention.

In the period following the babbling period the persisting phonetic facility gets less and less exercise. The vast majority of a child's utterances fail to reflect her real ability to pronounce things accurately; they do, however, reflect her growing ability to pronounce things systematically. (For a child who grows up learning only one language the movements of the muscles of the vocal tract ultimately become so overpracticed that it is difficult to learn new pronunciations during adulthood. On the other hand, people who learn at least two languages in early childhood appear to retain a greater flexibility of the vocal musculature and are more likely to learn to speak an additional language in their adult years without the "accent" of their native language.)

In learning to pronounce, then, a child must acquire a sound system that includes the divergent systems of phonology and phonetics. The acquisition of phonology differs from that of phonetics in requiring the creation of a representation of language in the mind of the child. This representation is necessary because of the abstract nature of the units of phonological structure. From only the acoustic signal of adult language the child must derive successively more abstract phonological units: first intonations, then syllables, then distinctive features and finally consonant-and-vowel segments. There are, for example, few clear segment boundaries in the acoustic signal the child receives, and so the consonant-and-vowel units could hardly be derived if the child had no internal representation of language.

At the same time that a child is building a phonological representation of language she is learning to manipulate all the phonetic variations of language, learning to produce each one precisely and automatically. The dual process of phonetics and phonology acquisition is one of the most difficult in all of language learning. Indeed, although a great deal of syntactic and semantic acquisition has yet to take place, it is usually at the completion of the process of learning to pronounce that adults consider a child to be a full-fledged language speaker and stop using any form of caretaker speech.

ABNORMAL LANGUAGE DEVELOPMENT

There seems to be little question that the human brain is best suited to language learning before puberty. Foreign languages are certainly learned most easily at that time. Furthermore, it has been observed that people who learn more than one language in childhood have an easier time learning additional languages in later years. It seems to be extremely important for a child to exercise the language-learning faculty. Children who are not exposed to any learnable language during the crucial years, for example children who are deaf before they can speak, generally grow up with the handicap of having little or no language. The handicap is unnecessary: deaf children of deaf parents who communicate by means of the American Sign Language do not grow up without language. They live in an environment where they can make full use of their language-learning abilities, and they are reasonably fluent in sign language by age three, right on the developmental schedule. Deaf children who grow up communicating by means of sign language have a much easier time learning English as a second language than deaf children in oral-speech programs learning English as a first language.

The study of child language acquisition has made important contributions to the study of abnormal speech development. Some investigators of child language have looked at children whose language development is abnormal in the hope of finding the conditions that are necessary and sufficient for normal development; others have looked at the development of language in normal children in the hope of helping children whose language development is abnormal. It now appears that many of the severe language abnormalities found in children can in some way be traced to interruptions of the normal acquisition process. The improved understanding of the normal process is being exploited to create treatment programs for children with such problems. In the past therapeutic methods for children with language problems have emphasized the memorizing of language routines, but methods now being developed would allow a child to work with her own language-learning abilities. For example, the American Sign Language has been taught successfully to several autistic children. Many of these nonverbal and antisocial children have learned in this way to communicate with therapists, in some cases becoming more socially responsive. (Why sign language should be so successful with some autistic children is unclear; it may have to do with the fact that a sign lasts longer than an auditory signal.)

There are still may questions to be answered in the various areas I have discussed, but in general a great deal of progress has been made in understanding child language over the past 20 years. The study of the acquisition of language has come of age. It is now a genuinely interdisciplinary field where psychologists, neurosurgeons and linguists work together to penetrate the mechanisms of perception and cognition as well as the mechanisms of language.

BIBLIOGRAPHY

Bloom, Lois. *One Word at a Time.* The Hague: Mouton, 1975.

Brown, Roger. *A First Language: The Early Stages.* Cambridge, Mass.: Harvard University Press, 1973.

Dil, Anwar S., ed. *Language Structure and Language Use: Essays by Charles A. Ferguson.* Stanford, Calif.: Stanford University Press, 1971.

McNeill, David. *The Acquisition of Language: The Study of Developmental Psycholinguistics.* New York: Harper & Row, 1970.

THEORY AND IMPLICATIONS

1. What key implications for teaching are there in the fact that by the age of five, children have acquired most of the syntax of their language?

2. What is significant, for teaching methods, about the fact that the child of deaf parents who watched television did not learn English?

3. Moskowitz demonstrates that children hypothesize the most general rules first, then successively narrow down these rules by hypothesizing more precise rules that apply to a more restricted set of sentences. Moskowitz shows how this process applies to any area of language learning—syntax, phonology, and semantics. Do you think the process differs in key ways for these three language areas? Explain.

4. Moskowitz portrays language learning as unconscious, tacit learning. Yet the language she uses implies conscious analysis. For instance, she says that children learn by "breaking each system down into its smallest combinable parts and then developing rules for combining the parts." How are we meant to understand this apparent contradiction?

5. If corrections rarely affect children's performance, and if parents rarely correct, why do you think that correction remains crucial to most language curricula?

6. Vertical constructions are seen as one or two word groups spoken in sequence that can express concepts a child is unable to encode syntactically. Why is it, however, that linguists view vertical constructions as indicators of a one-word or two-word stage? Why do they assume a stop at the end of one (or two) words when the child clearly continues to add words? On what basis does the linguist assign a stop after the child's use of two words?

7. What potential conflict do you see between cognitive (innate, universal) factors and social factors as they are incorporated in this article (for example, among the eight principles outlined in the introduction to this article)?

8. What examples of rule hypothesizing have you noticed in young children? What rules are the children using? How are the errors signs of learning?

9. How have certain teaching methods that you have seen or experienced contradicted L1 research? Explain.

10. In determining the order of acquisition of various function words, can meaning (e.g., abstractness, conceptual difficulty, informativeness) sometimes compete with form (e.g., least variation or complexity of syntactical relations)? What other principles than those offered might account for the order of acquisition of various function words?

[handwritten margin notes: Unconscious on the part of the teacher or model. The child is very consciously an alysing lang from the very beginning — innate need to communicate (social beings) also to express himself + get needs met.]

PROFESSIONAL CONCERNS

1. Moskowitz consolidates extensive research on first language acquisition without necessarily explaining how all the studies fit together. What questions does she leave unanswered and what kind of research would be needed to answer them? Could you research such questions in the classroom?

2. Compose a handbook for parents, based on the principles here, for enhancing the language abilities of preschool children. Suggest as many practical activities as you can think of and explain their importance in terms of L1 theory.

3. Research any area of abnormal language development. What principles of L1 acquisition theory underlie this research? Is it primarily cognitive or social? What implications do you see in L1 acquisition theory for the classroom?

Creole Languages*

DEREK BICKERTON

The study of creole languages has added a broad, cross-cultural reinforcement of the theory of innate language processes. This essay, which consolidates and perhaps simplifies more technical studies, underscores the central idea from cognitive studies that language acquisition does not depend on modeling and imitation. Indeed Bickerton seems to imply that language acquisition depends on no specific input or set of external conditions. He postulates the existence of an innate grammar, which children who are deprived of adult models learn independently and consistently.

Bickerton derives such implications from the surprising fact that, across cultures, children of parents of diverse first language backgrounds autonomously develop a creole language as their first language. In each geographical location, the parents, who have a fully developed L1, use only a rudimentary contact pidgin, making it impossible that the children are merely borrowing or imitating. Because of this lack of models, these children are thought to be using some innate language ability to expand the rudimentary pidgin into the fully developed creole. And across cultures and in isolated geographical locations, the creoles they develop are surprisingly similar, which contradicts the notion of cultural contact and borrowing and instead suggests a "universal grammar."

Despite the provocative nature of such research, many questions remain unanswered. In particular, one must question the criteria on which the research postulates a universal grammar underlying the various creoles. Furthermore one might find problematic the equation of creoles with an easier and thus more innate syntax that children of other languages first try to use until they are forced to use another grammar. However, the evidence provides fascinating material for speculation about regularities across cultures.

The ancient Greek historian Herodotus records the story of Psamtik I, pharaoh of Egypt in the seventh century B.C., who set out to discover the original language of humanity. On royal decree two infants were taken away from their parents and put in the care of a mute shepherd, who was instructed to raise the children in isolation from other people. The shepherd was to take note of the first word uttered by the children; "uncorrupted" by the language of their forefathers, Psamtik reasoned, they would begin to speak in the pure tongue from which all other languages were derived. The first intelligible sound the children made was "bekos," which meant bread in the ancient language Phrygian. Therefore, Psamtik maintained, the original language of humanity is Phrygian.

The story has amused generations of linguistics students. Most linguists, who have taken it for granted that no such experiment should ever be carried out, have dismissed the Psamtik experiment as being defective in design and unlikely to yield any useful result. Indeed, the assumption that an "original" vocabulary can be recovered is overoptimistic, and linguistic isolation of the individual, which has been documented in a few cases of severe child abuse, usually results in the absence of language. Nevertheless, a modified form of the experiment has been repeated many times over the past 500 years among the children of slaves and laborers who were pressed into service by the European colonial powers.

These laborers, who were shipped from many parts of the world to tend and harvest crops in Africa, the Indian Ocean region, the Orient, the Caribbean, and Hawaii, were obliged to communicate within their polyglot community by means of the rudimentary speech system called pidgin. Pidgin speech is extremely impoverished in syntax and vocabulary, but for the children born into the colonial community it was the only common language available. From these modest beginnings new native languages evolved among the children, which are generically called creole languages. It can be shown that they exhibit the complexity, nuance, and expressive power universally found in the more established languages of the world.

Taken at face value, the development of many different creole languages suggests that the search for a single, original language is misguided. For many years, however, scholars have noted a remarkable similarity of structure among all the creole languages. It can now be demonstrated, by considering the origin of creole language in Hawaii, that similarities among creoles cannot be accounted for by contact with other languages, either indigenous or imported. The finding suggests that what is common to creole languages may indeed form the basis of the acquisition of language by children everywhere. There is now an impressive body of evidence to support this hypothesis: between the ages of two and four the child born into a community of linguistically competent adults speaks a variety of language whose structure bears a deep resemblance to the structure of creole languages. Hence, by an ironic stroke of justice, the surviving linguistic remnants of colonialism may offer indispensable keys to the study of our own linguistic heritage.

The historical conditions that favored the development of creole languages are well known. Between 1500 and 1900 England, France, the Netherlands, Portugal, and Spain established numerous labor-intensive, agricultural economies on isolated littorals and underpopulated tropical islands throughout the world. The colonies were engaged primarily in monoculture, usually sugar, and their economic viability depended on an abundance of cheap labor imported from distant regions under conditions of chattel slavery. Workers were drawn first from West Africa and later from East Africa, India, and the Orient, and they spoke a variety of mutually incomprehensible languages.

Under more salutary conditions of immigration the workers or their children would eventually have learned the language of the local colonial power, but two factors combined to keep them from doing so. First, the number of speakers of the colonial languages rarely exceeded 20 percent of the total population, and it was often less than 10 percent. In other words, there were relatively few people from whom the dominant language could have been learned. Second, the colonial societies were small, autocratic, and rigidly stratified. There were few chances for prolonged linguistic contact between field laborers and speakers of the dominant language.

Except in Hawaii, there is little reliable documentary evidence concerning the early linguistic history of the colonial societies. It has generally been assumed that pidgin developed as a contact language solely to allow communication between master and workers and among workers from various immigrant groups. Creole languages then arose among the children of the workers through the "expansion" of pidgin; there was little occasion for the children to use the ancestral languages of their parents, and they still lacked access to the language of the dominant culture. What is meant by the term "expansion" has remained obscure until my colleagues and I began our studies in Hawaii.

The unique advantage for the study of creole language in Hawaii is that the details of its formation can be reconstructed at least in part from the speech of people still living. Although Hawaiian contact with Europeans goes back to 1778, it was not until 1876 that a revision in the U.S. tariff laws, allowing the free importation of Hawaiian sugar, enabled Hawaiian sugar plantations to increase their output by several hundred percent. A polyglot force of indentured laborers, made up of Chinese, Filipinos, Japanese, Koreans, Portuguese, Puerto Ricans, and others, began to be assembled, and by 1900 it outnumbered the other groups in Hawaii, both native and European, by a ratio of two to one.

A pidgin based on the Polynesian language Hawaiian initially served as a means of communication between immigrants and the locally born, but the annexation of Hawaii by the U.S. in 1898 eventually led to the replacement of Hawaiian by English. After 1900 the Hawaiian language declined, and pidgin Hawaiian was replaced as a lingua franca by a pidgin based on English. By the time we began our intensive study of language variation in Hawaii in the early 1970's there were still many survivors, both immigrant and locally born, from the years 1900 until 1920.

Our recordings of locally born people make it clear that the process of creolization was under way by 1900 and was certainly complete by 1920. Most of the linguistic features that characterize Hawaiian Creole English are present in the speech of working-class people born in Hawaii since 1905; before that date the proportion of Creole speakers to the rest of the population falls off rapidly. On the other hand, the speech of immigrants is always some form of pidgin, although just what form it takes depends on the date of the immigrant's arrival in Hawaii as well as the immigrant's language background. The pidgin spoken by the earliest immigrants among our subjects is much more rudimentary than that spoken by the later ones, probably because the latter were exposed to Creole as well as pidgin. Nevertheless, the distinction between pidgin and Creole remains fundamental: anyone familiar with Hawaii can quickly identify the ethnic origins of any immigrant on the basis of speech patterns alone. Without a conversational topic or a person's physical appearance as a guide, however, no one can reliably identify the ethnic origins of any locally born speaker solely on the basis of the speaker's pronunciation or the grammatical structure of the utterances.

One of the main characteristics of pidgin, therefore, is its variability from speaker to speaker. Each immigrant seems to have gone about the task of inventing a makeshift language in some individual way. For example, pidgin speakers of Japanese ancestry generally place the verb at the end of a sentence, as in "The poor people all potato eat" ("All that the poor people ate were potatoes"). Filipino pidgin, however, places the verb before the subject: "Work hard these people" ("These people work hard"). More often word order follows no fixed principle except the pragmatic one that old, shared information is stated near the beginning of a sentence and new information near the end.

It is probably the case that anything expressible in Creole, or in English for that matter, can also be expressed in pidgin. Nevertheless, the pidgin speaker is at a great disadvantage, because pidgin lacks many of the building blocks possessed by all native languages. Such everyday necessities of language as articles, prepositions, and auxiliary verbs are either absent or appear sporadically in a quite unpredictable fashion. Pidgin sentences have no subordinate clauses, and single-clause utterances frequently lack verbs.

The first of the following examples was recorded from a pidgin-speaking Korean; omitted words are bracketed in the translation: "And a too much children, small children, house money pay" ("And [I had] too many children, small children, [I had] to pay the rent"). The second example was recorded from a Japanese speaker: "Before mill no more Filipino no nothing" ("Before the mill [was built, there were] no Filipinos here at all"). The third example, recorded from the speech of a retired bus driver, illustrate the heroic measures needed to say anything out of the ordinary in pidgin: "Sometime good road get, sometime, all same bend get, enguru [angle] get, no? Any kind same. All same human life, all same" ("Sometimes there's a good road, sometimes there's like, bends, corners, right? Everything's like that. Human life's just like that").

The language-learning task confronted by the child born into a community of such speakers is far different from the task imposed on the child who is surrounded by linguistically competent adults. The children of English or Chinese parents, for example, are presented with accurate models to follow. Although their mistakes are seldom overtly corrected, they can almost constantly check their own utterances against those of older speakers and adapt them where necessary. When they have mastered the simpler structures of their language, more complex structures are readily available.

For the Hawaiian-born child of immigrant parents, however, there was no consistent linguistic model for the basic word order of simple sentences and often no model at all for the more complicated structures of language. Many such children were born of interethnic or interracial marriages, and so even at home there was little occasion to speak the native language of either parent. Moreover, even among the children not born of linguistically mixed parents there was considerable incentive to abandon the parents' native language and adopt some version of pidgin in the company of peers and neighboring adults. Like first-generation immigrant children elsewhere, the children of Hawaiian immigrants often became bilingual or even trilingual, and they adopted the common language of their peers as a native language in spite of considerable effort by their parents to maintain the ancestral tongue.

The historical evidence is consistent with the view that the structure of Creole arose without significant borrowing from other languages. Bilingual or trilingual children of school age need not (and usually do not) mix up the structural features of the languages they speak, and there is no reason to suppose such crossovers were common in Hawaii. The most compelling argument for the autonomous emergence of Creole, however, is its observed uniformity. How, within a single generation, did such a consistent and uniform language develop out of the linguistic free-for-all that was pidgin in Hawaii? Even if all the children of various immigrant groups had begun by learning the languages of their parents, and even if the differences among the various pidgins had been smoothed by interaction and contact among the children, the homogeneity of the language that developed remains in need of explanation. Fifty years of contact among pidgin-speaking adults were not enough to erase the differences among the national language groups; the homogeneity must have resulted from the differences between children and adults.

One might still suppose the structural uniformity of Creole is derived from certain structures of one of the ancestral languages or perhaps from certain structures of English, the language of the plantation owners. There are numerous differences, however, between the structure of Creole and the structure of any of the languages with which Creole speakers have been in contact. In English, for example, it is possible to refer to an object or a group of objects in a nonspecific way, but English grammar forces the speaker to state in advance whether the number of unspecified objects is one or many, singular or plural. One must say either "I am going to the store to buy a shirt" or "I am going to the store to buy shirts," even though one may not want to commit oneself in advance to buying any particular number of shirts.

In Creole a grammatically neutral marker for number can be employed on the noun "shirt" in order to avoid specifying number: "I stay go da store for buy shirt" ("I am going to the store to buy shirt"). Moreover, in Creole the addition of a definite or an indefinite article to "shirt" changes the meaning of the sentence. In saying "I stay go da store for buy one shirt" the Creole speaker asserts the shirt is a specific one; in the sentence "I stay go da store for buy da shirt" the speaker further presupposes that the listener is already familiar with the shirt the speaker is going to buy.

There are many other features of Creole that distinguish it from English. Whereas in English there is a past tense, which is usually marked with the suffix "-ed," in Creole there is a tense called the anterior tense, which is marked with "bin" for older speakers and with "wen" for younger speakers. The anterior tense is somewhat like the English past perfect: "had walked" in English is "bin walk" in Creole, and "walked" in English is simply "walk" in Creole. In order to distinguish irreal, or possible, actions or processes from actual ones, English employs the conditional or the future tense. In Creole all such irreal circumstances are expressed by the particle "go," which is placed before the main verb and marks what linguists call modality. For example, the sentence "If I had a car, I would drive home" is rendered in Creole as "If I bin get car, I go drive home."

There is also a Creole auxiliary verb that marks what linguists call aspect; it too is placed before the main verb and indicates that the action expressed by

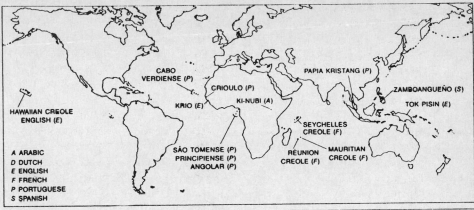

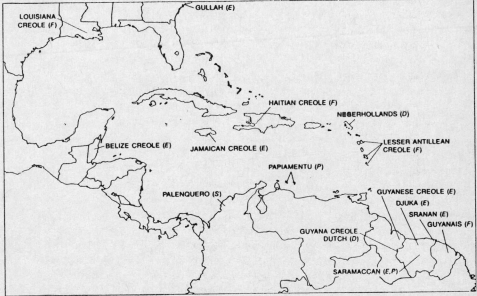

Worldwide distribution of creole languages reflects the historical circumstances of their development. Almost all creoles arose on isolated tropical littorals or islands, where colonial powers had established agricultural economies based on cheap immigrant labor. The geographic dispersion of the colonies suggests that creole languages developed independently of one another. The letters in parentheses after the name of each language indicate the colonial language from which most of the vocabulary of the creole is borrowed.

the verb in nonpunctual, or in other words repeated, habitual, continuing, or incomplete. In order to say "I run in Kapiolani Park every evening" in Creole one must say "I stay run in Kapiolani Park every evening." If the particle "stay" is omitted by the Creole speaker, the action is understood to be completed or nonrepetitive.

In English there is no straightforward way to distinguish purposes that have been accomplished from those that have not. The sentence "John went to Honolulu to see Mary" does not specify whether or not John actually saw Mary. In Creole grammar the ambiguity must be resolved. If John saw Mary and the Creole speaker knows that John saw Mary, the speaker must say, "John bin go Honolulu go see Mary." If John did not see Mary or if the speaker does not know whether or not John saw Mary, the speaker must say, "John bin go Honolulu for see Mary."

Similar distinctions could be drawn between the grammatical structure of Creole and the structure of other contact languages, such as Hawaiian, Ilocano (the language spoken in the north of the Philippine island of Luzon), and Japanese. There are also resemblances, but most of them are confined to idiomatic expressions. For example, the Creole expression "O the pretty," which means "How pretty he [she/it] is," is a literal translation of the Hawaiian-language idiom "O ka nani." In the main, however, our investigations strongly suggest that the basic structures of Creole differ from those of other languages. Although it might seem that some children of immigrants could transfer the structures of their

Pidgin	Hawaiian Creole English
Building—high place—wall part—time—nowtime—and then—now temperature every time give you.	Get one [There is an] electric sign high up on da wall of da building show you what time an' temperature get [it is] right now.
Now days, ah, house, ah, inside, washi clothes machine get, no? Before time, ah, no more, see? And then pipe no more, water pipe no more.	Those days bin get [there were] no more washing machine, no more pipe water like get [there is] inside house nowadays, ah?
No, the men, ah—pau [finished] work—they go, make garden. Plant this, ah, cabbage, like that. Plant potato, like that. And then—all that one—all right, sit down. Make lilly bit story.	When work pau [is finished] da guys they stay go make [are going to make] garden for plant potato an' cabbage an' after little while they go sit down talk story ["shoot the breeze"].
Good, this one. Kaukau [food] any kind this one. Pilipin island no good. No more money.	Hawaii more better than Philippines, over here get [there is] plenty kaukau [food], over there no can, bra [brother], you no more money for buy kaukau [food], 'a'swhy [that's why].

Pidgin and Creole versions of identical sentences illustrate the structural differences between pidgin and Creole in Hawaii. Pidgin, which is spoken only by immigrants, varies widely from speaker to speaker. Although one can probably say anything in pidgin that can be said in English or Creole, the structure of pidgin is extremely rudimentary. Pidgin sentences are little more than strings of nouns, verbs, and adjectives, often arranged to place old, shared information first and new information later in the sentence. Creole arose in Hawaii only among the children of immigrants, and it is much richer in grammatical structure than pidgin. Moreover, the rules of Creole grammar are uniform from speaker to speaker, and they resemble the structural rules of other creoles. English versions of words and phrases are given in brackets.

parents' native languages onto the evolving Creole language, they did not do so. The structural linguistic input that was available to the children was apparently not used in the development of Creole.

Even if it could be demonstrated that all the grammatical structures of Creole were borrowed, cafeteria-style, from one contact language or another, the uniformity of Creole would present a difficult question: How did the speakers who invented Creole come to agree on which structure to borrow from which language? Without such agreement Creole could not be as uniform as it is. Yet it seems highly implausible that the agreement could have been reached so quickly. If there had been massive borrowing from ancestral languages, differences in the version of Creole spoken by various groups would have persisted at least one generation beyond the first generation of speakers.

There is another dimension to the problem of the uniformity of Hawaiian Creole. It turns out that creole languages throughout the world exhibit the same uniformity and even the same grammatical structures that are observed in Hawaii. The finding is all the more remarkable when it is compared with the rather poor

English	Hawaiian Creole English
The two of us had a hard time raising dogs.	Us two bin get hard time raising dog.
John and his friends are stealing the food.	John-them stay cockroach the kaukau.
He doesn't want to play because he's lazy.	He lazy, 'a'swhy he no like play.
How do you expect to finish your house?	How you expect for make pau you house?
It would have been better if I'd gone to Honolulu to buy it.	More better I bin go Honolulu for buy om.
The one who falls first is the loser.	Who go down first is loser.
The man who was going to lay the vinyl had quoted me a price.	The guy gon' lay the vinyl bin quote me price.
There was a woman who had three daughters.	Bin get one wahine she get three daughter.
She can't go because she hasn't any money.	She no can go, she no more money, 'a'swhy.

Structural differences between sentences in Hawaiian Creole and their English equivalents show that the grammar of Creole did not originate as a grammar borrowed from English. For example, the past perfect tense of a verb in Creole is expressed by the particles "bin" or "wen," which precede the main verb, instead of by the suffix "-ed." Nonpunctual, or progressive, aspect is expressed by the word "stay" instead of by the suffix "-ing." In the English sentence "The two of us had a hard time raising dogs" the rules of grammar oblige the speaker to indicate that the noun "dog" is either singular or plural. In the Creole version of the sentence, however, neither singular nor plural is implied. There are also relatively insignificant lexical differences between the two languages: "cockroach" is picturesquely employed as a verb, and "kaukau," which may be derived from the Chinese pidgin term "chow-chow," is a common word for "food." Equally striking structural differences are found between Hawaiian Creole and other languages, such as Chinese, Hawaiian, Japanese, Korean, Portuguese, Spanish, or the Philippine languages, with which speakers of Hawaiian Creole might have been in contact.

correspondence in structure I have noted between Hawaiian Creole and other contact languages in Hawaii. For example, the distinction made in Hawaiian Creole between singular, plural, and neutral number is also made in all other creole languages. Similarly, in all other creole languages there are three invariant particles that act as auxiliary verbs and play the roles that "bin," "go," and "stay" play in Hawaiian Creole.

In Haitian Creole, for example, the word "té" marks the anterior tense of the verb, the word "av(a)" marks irreal modality, and the word "ap" marks the aspect of the verb as nonpunctual. Thus in Haitian Creole the phrase "I have been walking" is rendered "m [I] t'ap [té + ap] maché." Similarly, in Sranan, an English-based creole found in Surinam (formerly Netherlands Guiana), the anterior tense marker is "ben," the irreal modality marker is "sa" and the nonpunctual aspect marker is "e." The phrase "He would have been walking" is rendered "A[he] ben sa e waka." Most important, there is a strict order that must be followed in all creole languages when more than one of these markers is present in a sentence. The particle for tense precedes the particle for modality, and the particle for modality precedes the particle for aspect.

Finally, consider the grammatical distinction I have noted between purposes accomplished and unaccomplished. The same distinction, absent in English, is found in all creoles. In Mauritian Creole, a creole based on the French vocabulary that is used on the island of Mauritius, a sentence such as "He decided to eat meat" can be expressed in two ways. If the subject of the sentence carried out his decision, the sentence is rendered "Li ti desid al mâz lavian," which literally means "He decided go eat meat." If the decision was not carried out, the sentence is rendered as "Li ti desid pu mâz lavian," or literally "He decided for eat meat." In Jamaican Creole the sentence "He went to wash" must be rendered either as "Im gaan fi bied ("He went with the intention of washing") or as "Im gaan go bied ("He went to wash and completed the task").

These examples only suggest the extent of the structural similarities among creole languages. The similarities seem unaffected by the wide geographic dispersion of the creoles and the variation among the languages such as Dutch, English, and French from which they draw the greatest part of their vocabulary. . . .

The linguist's first reaction to such a finding is to look for a common ancestor of the similar languages. For example, it has been conjectured that the linguistic ancestor was a contact language that grew out of Portuguese and certain West African languages in the course of the first Portuguese explorations of Africa in the 15th and 16th centuries. According to the hypothesis, this contact language was subsequently spread around the world by Portuguese sailors, changing its vocabulary but not its syntax or semantics as it entered the sphere of influence of another colonial power. Superficially such an explanation might seem to be consistent with the development of Creole in Hawaii, because Portuguese laborers were brought to the islands in large numbers during the late 19th and early 20th centuries.

There are several serious flaws in the account. First, Hawaiian Creole bears scant resemblance to any of the contact languages, including Portuguese. Second, the claims on linguistic similarity between creoles and Portuguese or between creoles and East African languages are grossly exaggerated. Most important, our study of hundreds of Hawaiian speakers has made it clear that Hawaiian Creole almost certainly originated in Hawaii. We found no surviving immigrant who speaks anything approximating a creole language; instead every immigrant we surveyed speaks some variety of pidgin. If Hawaiian Creole was primarily an imported language, it would have been carried by immigrants, and presumably it would have been learned by others among the immigrant population. One must therefore conclude that Hawaiian Creole arose among the children of immigrants, where it is now found. Moreover, if a creole language could develop in Hawaii without ancestry, it can arise anywhere else in a similar way.

The implications of these findings are far-reaching. Because the grammatical structures of creole languages are more similar to one another than they are to the structures of any other language, it is reasonable to suppose most if not all creoles were invented by the children of pidgin-speaking immigrants. Moreover, since creoles must have been invented in isolation, it is likely that some general ability, common to all people, is responsible for the linguistic similarities.

The suggestion that people are biologically predisposed to use language is not a new one: for more than two decades Noam Chomsky of the Massachusetts Institute of Technology has argued that there is an innate universal grammar underlying all human languages. The universal grammar is postulated largely on the grounds that only by its means could children acquire a system as enormously complex as a human language in the short time they do. Studies by the late Eric H. Lenneberg tend to confirm Chomsky's hypothesis. The acquisition of language resembles the acquisition of other complex and flexible aspects of the child's behavior, such as walking, which are undoubtedly controlled to some degree by neurophysiological development. The universal grammar conjectured by Chomsky is a computing device, somehow realized neurologically, that makes a wide range of grammatical models available to the child. According to Chomsky, the child must then "select" which of the available grammatical models matches the grammar of the language into which the child is born.

The evidence from creole languages suggests that first-language acquisition is mediated by an innate device of a rather different kind. Instead of making a range of grammatical models available, the device provides the child with a single and fairly specific grammatical model. It was only in pidgin-speaking communities, where there was no grammatical model that could compete with the child's innate grammar, that the innate grammatical model was not eventually suppressed. The innate grammar was then clothed in whatever vocabulary was locally available and gave rise to the creole languages heard today.

The implications of this hypothesis call into question an idea that most linguists, including Chomsky, have tacitly accepted for many years, namely that no one of the world's languages is easier or harder for the child to acquire than any other. If there is a creole grammar somehow imprinted in the mind, creole languages should be easier to acquire than other languages. How is it, then, that not all children grow up speaking a creole language? The answer is they do their best to do just that. People around them, however, persist in speaking English or French or some other language, and so the child must modify the grammar of the native creole until it conforms to that of the local language.

	Nonstative Verbs			Stative Verbs		
Verb Form	Hawaiian Creole	Haitian Creole	Sranan	Hawaiian Creole	Haitian Creole	Sranan
Phrase form "He walked"; "He loves"	He walk	Li maché	A waka	He love	Li rêmê	A lobi
Anterior "He had walked"; "He loved"	He bin walk	Li té maché	A ben waka	He bin love	Li té rêmê	A ben lobi
Irreal "He will/would walk"; "He will/would love"	He go walk	L'av(a) maché	A sa waka	He go love	L'av(a) rêmê	A sa lobi
Nonpunctual "He is/was walking"	He stay walk	L'ap maché	A e waka	—	—	—
Anterior + irreal "He would have walked"; He would have loved"	He bin go walk	Li t'av(a) maché	A ben sa waka	He bin go love	Li t'av(a) rêmê	A ben sa lobi

Anterior + nonpunctual "He was/had been walking"	—	He bin stay walk	Li t'ap maché	A ben e waka	—
Irreal + nonpunctual "He will/would be walking"	—	He go stay walk	L'av ap maché	A sa e waka	—
Anterior + irreal + nonpunctual "He would have been walking"	—	He bin go stay walk	Li t'av ap maché	A ben sa e waka	—

Conjugation of the verb is similar in all creole languages, in spite of superficial lexical differences. Moreover, the creole system is quite distinct from the one encountered in English and in most other languages. The table gives conjugations in Hawaiian Creole, Haitian Creole, and Sranan (an English-based creole spoken in Surinam, the former Netherlands Guiana) for stative and nonstative verbs. Stative verbs are verbs such as "like," "want," and "love," which cannot form the nonpunctual aspect; in English, for example, one cannot add "-ing" to a finite stative verb. The base form of the verb refers to the present for stative verbs and to the past for nonstative verbs. The anterior tense is roughly equivalent to the English past tense for stative verbs and to the English past perfect tense for nonstative verbs. The irreal mode includes the English future, conditional, and subjunctive. In all the creole languages the anterior particle precedes the irreal particle, and the irreal particle precedes the nonpunctual particle. In Hawaiian Creole, however, "He gin go walk," "He go go walk" has come to mean "He walked" instead of "He would have walked," and the forms "He bin stay walk," "He go stay walk," and "He bin go stay walk," although they were widespread before World War II, are now almost extinct because of the growing influence of English in Hawaii. The bracketed English translations are provided only as a rough guide to the meaning.

Two kinds of linguistic evidence are relevant for testing the hypothesis. First, if some grammatical structure of creole is at variance with the corresponding grammatical structure of the local language, one should find that children make systematic errors with respect to the structure of the local language. On the other hand, if the two grammatical structures tend to agree, one should find extremely early, rapid, and errorless acquisition of the local-language structure.

Consider the systematic error observed by David McNeill of the University of Michigan in the speech of a four-year-old boy. In one of McNeill's observing sessions the boy complained, "Nobody don't like me," and the boy's mother responded by correcting the sentence: "Nobody likes me." The boy then repeated his sentence and the mother repeated her correction no fewer than eight times. Finally, the child altered his sentence and shouted in exasperation, "Nobody don't likes me."

The error is found in many English-speaking children between three-and-a-half and four years old, including children who are not exposed to dialects of English that employ double negatives. There are many languages, such as French and Spanish, that also employ double negatives, but the only languages that allow negative subjects with negative verbs are creoles. For example, in Papia Kristang, the Portuguese-based creole language of the Malay Peninsula, one can say, "Angkosa nte mersimentu," or literally, "Nothing not-have value." In Guyanese Creole, which is based on English and found in Guyana (formerly British Guiana), one can say, "Non dag na bait non kyat," or literally, "No dog did not bite no cat."

A second instance of systematic error is found in the formation of children's questions. Children learning English often indicate questions only by their

Child Language	English Creole
Where I can put it?	Where I can put om? (Hawaii)
Daddy throw the nother rock.	Daddy t'row one neda rock'tone. (Jamaica)
I go full Angela bucket.	I go full Angela bucket. (Guyana)
Lookit a boy play ball.	Luku one boy a play ball. (Jamaica)
Nobody don't like me.	Nobody no like me. (Guyana)
I no like do that.	I no like do that. (Hawaii)
Johnny big more than me.	Johnny big more than me. (Jamaica)
Let Daddy get pen write it.	Make Daddy get pen write am. (Guyana)
I more better than Johnny.	I more better than Johnny. (Hawaii)

Sentences spoken by children between two and four years old, all born of English-speaking parents, are strikingly similar to sentences in English-based creole languages. The similarities among creole languages and the likelihood that the languages arose independently of one another suggest that creoles develop among children whenever there is no adequate native language to serve as a model. The author conjectures that if children were removed from their native English-language community at the age of about two, they would grow up speaking a language whose vocabulary would be primarily English but whose grammar would be creole.

intonation; the subject and the auxiliary verb are almost never reversed. For example, children repeatedly say things such as "You can fix this?" even though they have heard countless questions such as "Can you fix this?" Similarly, no creole language distinguishes questions and statements on the basis of word order; the difference is marked by intonation alone.

Consider the sentence "A gon' full Angela bucket." Although such a sentence is unacceptable in English, it is perfectly acceptable in Hawaiian Creole, Guyanese Creole, or any of several other creoles related to English. It is synonymous with the sentence "I'm going to fill Angela's bucket," but it differs from the structure of the English sentence in the following ways. First, the first-person pronoun "I" is reduced to "A"; second, the auxiliary verb "am" is omitted; third, the forms "go" or "gon" are used to mark the future tense; fourth, the word "to" in the infinitive is omitted; fifth, the adjective "full" is employed as if it were a transitive verb, and sixth, the possessive marker "-'s" is omitted. All these features are characteristics of creoles, but this sentence was not uttered by a creole speaker. It was spoken by the three-year-old daughter of an English-speaking linguist.

When a feature of the local language matches the structure of creole, children avoid making errors that would otherwise seems quite natural. For example, children learning English acquire the suffix "-ing," which expresses duration, at a very early age. Even before the age of two many children say things such as "I sitting high chair," where the verb expresses a continuing action. One would expect that as soon as the suffix was acquired it would be applied to every possible verb, just as the suffix "-s" that marks the English plural is frequently overgeneralized to nouns such as "foot" and "sheep."

One would therefore expect children to utter ungrammatical sentences such as "I liking Mommy" and "I wanting candy." Remarkably, such errors are almost never heard. Children seem to know implicitly that English verbs such as "like" and "want," which are called stative verbs, cannot be marked by the suffix "-ing" to indicate duration. The distinction between stative and nonstative verbs is fundamental to creole languages, however, and no marker of continuing action can be employed with a stative verb in creoles either.

The distinction between specific and nonspecific reference, which I have already discussed, is an important feature of creole languages. In English the distinction can be subtle, but young children nonetheless acquire it with ease. Michael P. Maratsos of the University of Minnesota constructed a series of sentences for children to complete, for which the completions depended on the distinction between specific and nonspecific reference. For example, the sentence "John has never read a book," which makes nonspecific reference to the noun "book," can be completed by the phrase "and he never will read a book"; it cannot be completed by the phrase "and he never will read the book." Similarly, the sentence "John read a book yesterday," in which a specific book is presupposed, can be completed by the phrase "and he enjoyed the book"; it cannot be completed by the phrase "and he enjoyed a book." Children as young as three years were able to make such distinctions correctly about 90 percent of the time.

Many more studies of language acquisition will have to be carried out before the structure of creole languages can be firmly accepted as the basis of first-language acquisition. Daniel Isaac Slobin of the University of California at Berkeley has suggested that there is a set of processes children apply to any language they hear, which he calls basic child grammar. [Slobin] cites evidence from several languages for the hypothesis, and it now appears that basic child grammar and creole languages may have much in common.

If creole languages represent the manifestation of a neurologically determined program of child development, then Psamtik was by no means the fool he has been taken for. It may be possible to discover, at least in general outline, the structure of human language in the early stages of its development. Moreover, in attempting to reconstruct such a language linguists may be able to answer questions the pharaoh did not even ask: How did human language originate? What are the minimum prerequisites for such a thing as language to arise in a species? If such questions can be answered or even formulated in a precise and coherent way, we shall be much closer to understanding what makes the human species different from others.

BIBLIOGRAPHY

Baker, Philip, and Chris Corne. *Isle de France Creole.* Ann Arbor, MI: Karoma Publishers, 1982.
Bickerton, Derek. *Roots of Language.* Ann Arbor, MI: Karoma Publishers, 1981.
Chomsky, Noam. *Rules and Representations.* New York: Columbia University Press, 1980.
Lenneberg, Eric H. *Biological Foundations of Language.* New York: John Wiley & Sons, 1967.

THEORY AND IMPLICATIONS

1. How do you think that individual children from pidgin-speaking parents come up with forms of creole syntax? Does the article adequately explain this problem? Why or why not? What kind of study might help us learn more about this process?

2. Does this research seem to eliminate all roles for interaction in language acquisition? If so, do you agree with this view? If it does not, where does the research allow room for environmental factors?

3. Look carefully at the evidence for the similarities among creoles. What do you think is the significance of these similarities? Do you agree that they are so striking as to indicate a universal grammar? Explain.

4. What other reasons might there be for children of immigrants to speak a different grammar from their parents? Are innate processes alone responsible?

5. The research implies a correspondence between creole and children's early speech in all cultures. Are there differences as well as similarities? Is the correspondence as strong as the research indicates?

6. What is particularly revealing about the example that children learn the stative and do not overapply the rule?

7. Given that innate processes seem to be at work, what implications does this research have for teaching children from other cultures?

PROFESSIONAL CONCERNS

1. Write a summary of this research for a principal or other educator, indicating what applications the research has for the school's approach to grammar.
2. The idea that learning is suppression is an important one here, perhaps too easily dismissed. What does this mean? In what other ways does learning a language involve suppression? Write a brief summary, for other teachers, of the classroom implications of suppression.
3. The notion of a universal grammar bolsters the idea that children learning a particular language must "suppress" those rules from such a grammar in favor of that particular language. Such a view has major implications for responding to error. What do you think they might be?
4. Do further research on creoles or on pidginization theory. What additional insights, questions, or refutations does this research provide? What implications do they have for language instruction?

Making It Last: Repetition in Children's Discourse*

ELINOR OCHS KEENAN

This essay offers a view of language acquisition in the social context. It moves away from issues of strict grammaticality and linguistic competence to the broader issue of communicative competence, or socially appropriate speech. Addressing repetitions because they are typically misunderstood—thought to have no function in acquisition—Keenan pinpoints the various social uses: Repetitions serve to check meanings, fill up a turn, and sustain dialogue by acknowledging a new topic. One of the specific functions they may have is to make new information into old information, establishing a new basis for discussion.

From the grammatical perspective, however, children repeating adults' speech appear to be simply practicing, often with imperfect ability, adult speech patterns. This view overlooks children's social intent, their attempts at maintaining dialogue, and their awareness of and compensation for their limited resources in conveying meaning. The grammatical view also reduces the function of repetition (and by implication other speech acts) to emulation of the adult model, ignoring any potential communicative purpose. Grammatical competence is presumed to be the child's key goal. As a result, this view assumes that any discrepancy between the child's version and the adult's version is necessarily an error and therefore leads researchers to underestimate children's language abilities and to concentrate on error, not on ability or use.

The importance of Keenan's study lies in its demonstration of the remark-able variety of functions a particular structure might have in the language repertoire of a two-year-old. Her view sharply contrasts not only with the cognitive and grammatical viewpoints, but also with Piaget's views of early childhood egocentrism—of children who speak as if only to themselves, who make no adjustments for listeners, who cannot engage in negotiated meaning, and for whom appropriateness of speech is inconsequential.

> *"The counterfeit is poorly imitated after you"*
> *(Shakespeare)* Sonnets *iii*

INTRODUCTION

One of the most commonplace observations in the psycholinguistic literature is that many young children repeat utterances addressed to them. Just as common-place are generalizations concerning the importance of this behavior to the development of language in the child. We have, on the one extreme, those who consider all linguistic knowledge to be obtained through this vehicle, and on the other extreme, we have those who place no importance whatsoever to the repetitions of young children.

Throughout the 1960s and into the 1970s the literature is dominated by studies which purport to show that language does not develop through repetition. Typically, the class of repeated utterances of the child is compared to the class of spontaneous or free utterances. Over and over these studies show that, with the exception of the child's repetition of adult expansions (Slobin 1968, Brown and Bellugi 1964), repeated utterances are not longer nor transformationally more complex than spontaneous utterances (Ervin 1964, Menyuk 1963, Bloom 1970).

If repetition is irrelevant to language development, we are left with the question: Why do young children repeat the utterances of others with such frequency? This question has not been seriously addressed. At this point in time, we still do not understand what children are doing when they repeat a given utterance. This state of affairs exists because, until quite recently, psycholinguists have been insensitive to the status of utterances as social acts. With some exception (Bloom 1970, Weir 1962, Scollon 1973, Slobin 1968), they have focused on the form of repeated utterances to the exclusion of their function in real communicative situations. An expressed intention of this chapter is to remedy this state of affairs. I present here an analysis of repetition in child language from a pragmatic perspective. By pragmatic perspective, I mean simply one that relates an utterance to its context of use. Context, of course, is an infinitely extendable notion, but can include such things as the speaker's communicative intention, the speaker-hearer relationship, the extralinguistic setting of the utterance, the linguistic setting of the utterance (e.g., prior discourse, topic at hand, etc.), and other areas of background knowledge, such as knowledge of conversational norms and conventions.

Data used to substantiate this presentation are drawn from a number of existing sources. However, I will rely primarily on observations carried out by myself on the spontaneous conversations of twin boys (2:9 at the outset). Their conversations were recorded (video and audio) on a monthly basis over a period of a year.

CHILDREN AS COMMUNICATORS

It is no accident that the positive function of repetition in children's speech has not been investigated. For one thing, perspectives adopted in developmental psycholinguistics are heavily influenced by current paradigms in linguistics. It is only in the past 5 years that pragmatics have been seriously considered within the field. Secondly, within developmental psycholinguistics, there has persisted a stereotype of the child as a noncommunicator. Over and over, we find attempts to set children apart from adults in their verbal activity. We are told that children are egocentric in their speech; that is, they are not interested in directing their talk to an addressee. Copresent individuals are merely used as sounding boards for the child, as the child has no interest in obtaining a response to his utterance. Furthermore, when others talk, the child experiences difficulty in attending and evaluating their communicative intentions. In short, we are told that, unlike adults, children typically do not engage in dialogue. More characteristic of their speech are collective monologues (Piaget 1955).

With this prejudice in hand, the psycholinguist quite naturally believed that the primary motive of the child in interacting with adults was mastery of the adult code. In line with this, it was quite natural for researchers to associate repetition with this goal. Why did children repeat? Behaviorists claimed that young children repeated utterances as an attempt to produce the same utterance themselves. That is, they repeated because they wished to imitate the adult form of an utterance. Repetition in the speech of young children became strongly associated with imitation. In fact, throughout the rationalist counterargument, the association of repetition with imitation was never challenged. It was tacitly accepted that children repeated as an attempt to copy a prior utterance; what was denied was that the attempt was successful, or a means by which mastery was obtained.

Notice here that contextual grounds have subtly entered into the psycholinguist's categorization of repetitions as imitation. The psycholinguist perceives these repetitions as imitations because the repeater is a young child and the initial speaker is an adult. Constrained by the current paradigm, the relationship is translated into that between master of the code and learner of the code. This is important to note as most psycholinguists try to define imitation in terms of repetition alone. That is, they try to treat imitation as a formal relation between two utterances and not as a social act.

I have argued in an earlier paper (Keenan 1974[a]) that attempts to define imitation on formal grounds alone have been unsuccessful and inconsistent. The constraints on what counts as a repetition vary enormously from investigator to investigator. Rodd and Braine (1971), Freedle et al. (1970), and Ervin (1964), for example, consider only immediate responses to an utterance as possible imitations. Bloom et al. (1974), on the other hand, is willing to look to the next five to ten utterances for a candidate imitation. Then there is the problem of cross-utterance similarity. Just how much of the initial utterance must be repeated in order for it to count as an imitation? For many investigators, the repeated utterance could omit but not substitute items of the initial utterance. Further, the repeated utterance had to be a more or less telegraphic version of the adult string, omitting the function words but retaining some or all of the content words. For other investigators (Rodd and Braine 1971), it was sufficient that the child repeat a particular construction under investigation for the utterance to count as an imitation.

On top of these practical difficulties is the fact that repetition alone is neither necessary nor sufficient to characterize imitation. It is not a necessary criterion in that attempts to copy may not, in fact, repeat the prior utterance. Hence there may be innumerable unsuccessful imitations—e.g., inarticulate mutterings, wild stabs, false starts, and the like—which are not repetitions in any accepted sense of the word. Note here, then that when psycholinguists address themselves to the role of imitation in language development, they are considering only successful imitations in their data base. We have no idea whatsoever of the character of these unsuccessful imitations. We don't know what type of adult utterance is responded to in such a way, and we do not know the nature of the distortion. It is evident that even on its own terms, the imitation literature stands on shaky ground.

Repetition is not a sufficient criterion for imitation in that it is possible to find repeated utterances that are not attempts to copy. Slobin illustrated this beautifully in his 1968 article on imitation. He provides the following dialogue between Adam (2:6) and his mother:

MOTHER: It fits in the puzzle someplace.
ADAM: Puzzle? Puzzle someplace?
MOTHER: Turn it around.
ADAM: Turn it around?
MOTHER: No, the other way.
ADAM: Other way?
MOTHER: I guess you have to turn it around.
ADAM: Guess turn it round. Turn round.

In this dialogue, Adam appear first to be using repetition as a vehicle for querying a prior utterance, and then as a vehicle for informing himself and/or agreeing with the mother's comment.

It is clear that all repetitions are not imitations and all imitations are not repetitions. In order to establish a given utterance as an imitation, contextual criteria must be provided as well. Further, it is not sufficient to define the context as simply that of a child interacting with an adult. We have seen that this relationship may be held constant through a variety of social uses of repetition (imitation, query, self-informing). In order to establish that an imitation has taken place, the investigator must somehow contend with the communicative intentions of the child. This is not to say that for an imitation to have taken place the child must have the conscious intention to reproduce a prior utterance. There may be degrees to which the child is aware of his own behavior. It is only to say that the presence or absence of the intention to imitate must be reckoned with. In particular, we can not accept that a repetition overtly elicited in an experimental situation can be equated in all cases with a repetition uttered in spontaneous conversation between caretaker and child. The overtly elicited repetition counts as an imitation because the child has been asked to copy the experimenter's utterance. While this sometimes may be the case in spontaneous conversation, we can not assume all repeats to be of this character. Claims made about the nature of repetition in the laboratory situation, then, should not automatically extend to ordinary verbal interactions between caretaker and child.

Once we address ourselves to the communicative intentions of the child, we can begin investigating a variety of interesting questions. For example, we know that children who repeat utterances increase this activity until about 2:6 and then it begins to decline. It would be interesting to follow a repeater through this cycle, indicating the ways in which the repetition was used in discourse. We could begin asking in what order the different communicative uses of repetition emerge. It may be the case that the child first uses repetition to imitate and later comes to use it to perform other communicative tasks. It may be the case that, as Slobin (1973) has suggested for syntax, the child uses an old form for new functions. That is, some children may latch onto repetition quite early as a device for participating in discourse, and use this device to perform novel communicative tasks. Further, it may be the case that repetition is more appropriate or more efficient for some tasks than others. For example, if you want to copy the utterance of another speaker, then repetition is a good device to employ. Similarly, if the child wishes to let his caretaker know that he has understood ("communication check") the caretaker's utterance, then repetition is appropriate. On the other hand, there are only a few types of questions one can ask by repeating all or part of a prior utterance. It may be the case that as the child becomes competent in a greater number of speech acts, he finds repetition a less and less satisfying device.

A second area of inquiry opened up concerns the differences and similarities between children who rely heavily on repetition and those who rarely repeat (Bloom et al. 1974). The distinction has been posed in the literature as those children who are imitators and those children who are nonimitators. Addressing ourselves to the communicative intentions of children, we may discover that this dichotomy misses the mark. It may be the case that "imitators" are not, in fact, imitating, and that all of these children do similar communicative work; they simply differ in the formal devices used to carry out this work.

REPETITION AND PRIOR DISCOURSE

I would like now to examine in some detail the varied uses of repetition in conversational discourse. In investigating these uses, I look for clues in prior discourse and in subsequent discourse. Here I consider the relation of repetition to prior discourse.

One of the characteristics of the literature on imitation is that it generally ignores the illocutionary force of the utterance that the child is responding to. The utterance repeated by the child is not described as a request for information, request for services, an assertion, a greeting, a rhyme, or song. All utterances are lumped together under the cover term "model sentence." The use of this term, of course, reflects the general assumption that all repetitions are imitations. Furthermore, in comparing an utterance with its repetition, the investigator judges only the extent to which the repetition succeeds as an imitation. It is typical of repetitions, in fact, not to succeed completely. Ervin (1964), for example, mentions that only a small percentage of the spontaneous "imitations" in her data were exact repetitions. As imitations, then, the repetitions of young children are inferior reproductions.

If, on the other hand, children are repeating not to imitate but to satisfy some other communicative obligation, then inexact repetition might be the intended, not unintended, desire of the child. The fact that the child, particularly the child from 2–3 years, fails to copy in entirety a previous utterance in conversation, may reflect the child's competence and not his incompetence. Consider, for example, the model sentences used by Rodd and Braine (1971) in their study of imitation. In this study, the investigator directed to a child of 2:1 years the sentence *Is the baby sitting down?* The child's response was *uhhuh, baby down.* Here, it is perfectly appropriate for the child not to repeat the previous utterance. In fact, it would be inappropriate for the child to produce an exact copy. Clearly, the child has grasped the communicative intentions of the investigator. The child's response shows that the child treated the investigator's utterance not as a model to be imitated, but as a question to be answered. The repetition is far more successful as an answer than as an imitation.

Repetition with omissions is appropriate in response to utterances other than information questions as well. For both adult and child alike, it is appropriate to repeat just one or two words from the utterance of a conversational partner to comment attitudinally:

EXAMPLE 1
(Toby and David at 2:9 conversing with their nanny, Jill)
JILL: And we're going to have hot dogs.
TOBY: Hot dogs! (excitedly)
JILL: And soup.
DAVID: Mmm soup!

To agree with:

EXAMPLE 2
(Toby and David at 2:9 with their nanny, Jill)
JILL: And we're gonna build a fire.
DAVID: Mmm.
TOBY: Oh yeah/build fire.

To self-inform:

EXAMPLE 3
(Toby and David at 2:9 with their nanny, Jill)

JILL: And we're going to cook sausages.

TOBY: Cook sausages.

JILL: And bacon.

TOBY **and** DAVID: Bacon.

JILL: And eggs.

TOBY **and** DAVID: Eggs.

To query:

EXAMPLE 4
(Toby and David at 2:10. Toby engaged in sound play)

TOBY: /diɔt/tziju/i/u/bɔ/ɔt/

DAVID: ˇbɔt

EXAMPLE 5
(Toby and David at 2:11)

DAVID: ˋMy hands are cold.

TOBY: ´Cold.

To imitate:

EXAMPLE 6
(Toby and David at 2:9 with their nanny, Jill)

JILL: Aren't I a good cook? Say "Yes, the greatest!"

TOBY: Yes the greatest. (softly)

JILL: That's right.

DAVID: The greatest! (loudly)

Even in the case of explicit imitation, the child repeats selectively. For example, the child does not repeat the performative verb "say" in the previous utterance. The child has shaped the repetition to satisfy his obligations as a conversational partner. In each case the shaping reflects the child's orientation to the expectations of the prior speaker.

We have established, then, that children are sensitive to the illocutionary force of prior utterances in discourse. They repeat as an attempt to respond appropriately to particular types of utterances. I have mentioned some of these types in the previous discussion, but this mention by no means exhausts the list. In addition to its usefulness in answering questions, commenting, affirming, self-informing, querying, and imitating, repetition may be used to make counterclaims of the following sort:

EXAMPLE 7
(Toby and David at 2:9)

DAVID: You`silly/ you`silly/ you`silly/ you`silly/ you`silly/

TOBY: `You/`you silly/`you silly/`you silly/`no you silly/

Further, repetition may be used to match a claim made by a previous speaker (Keenan and Klein 1974). That is, the second speaker may claim what was predicted by the first speaker holds for the second speaker as well:

EXAMPLE 8
(Toby and David at 2:9 with their nanny, Jill)

DAVID: Doggie bib. (I have) doggie bib. (see). I have doggie bib (2x). (?) bib.

JILL: David's got brown flowers in his.

DAVID: Yeah.

TOBY: (I) have doggie bib.

JILL: (You've got a) doggie bib.

EXAMPLE 9

DAVID: I get them off.

TOBY: I get them off.

In counterclaims and matching claims, we see that an utterance that replicates another in form does not replicate it in meaning. The utterances differ in meaning precisely because they differ in context. In each case, the meaning of the deitic item (*I, you*) depends on who the speaker is and who the addressee is. Such examples indicate the difficulty involved in earlier claims that imitations must preserve the meaning of the model utterance. (Ervin 1964). Preservation of meaning must surely be the exception rather than the norm in repeated utterances. Even if the repeated utterance contains no deitic items, the position of the utterance as a response (i.e., second pair part, cf. Schegloff and Sacks [1973]) makes it pragmatically distinct from the initial utterance.

In addition to the above-mentioned uses of repetition, there are examples in the data of repeating to greet back, to reverse the direction of an order, to reverse the direction of an information question, and to request clarification of an utterance:

EXAMPLE 10
(Toby and David at 2:11)

DAVID: (fae:b)

TOBY: (fae:b). You mean that/

In short, there appears to be no end to the ways in which cross utterance repetition is employed in conversational discourse. Repetition is probably one of the most misunderstood phenomena in psycholinguistics. It is associated with the language of children, who, in turn, are underrated as communicators. It is obvious, however, that with some exceptions, the kind of repetition described here is quite characteristic of adult speakers as well. Any of the following exchanges could appear in adult discourse:

EXAMPLE 11: GREETING

A: Hello.
B: Hello.

EXAMPLE 12: SELF-INFORMING AND/OR DISPLAYING KNOWLEDGE

A: That's Halley's comet.
B: Ah, that's Halley's comet.

EXAMPLE 13: AGREEING

A: That's dreadful.
B: Dreadful.

EXAMPLE 14: MATCHING CLAIM

A: I'm fat.
B: I'm fat.

EXAMPLE 15: COUNTERCLAIM

A: You're thinner than I am.
B: You're thinner than I am.

EXAMPLE 16: QUERYING

A: Yes.
B: Yes?

EXAMPLE 17: ANSWERING

A: Yes?
B: Yes.

EXAMPLE 18: REVERSING DIRECTION OF QUESTION

A: Well?
B: Well?

EXAMPLE 19: IMITATING

A: Say 'cheese.'
B: Cheese.

EXAMPLE 20: COMMENTING

A: But my diet.
B: Diet schmiet. Let's eat.

What then is going on when a child repeats the utterances of a copresent speaker? Is the child learning anything about his language? Is there any way in which repetition is developmentally progressive with respect to language? We can say that in repeating, the child is learning to communicate. He is learning not to construct sentences at random, but to construct them to meet specific communicative needs. He is learning to query, comment, confirm, match a claim and counterclaim, answer a question, respond to a demand, and so on. In short, he is learning the human uses of language, what Dell Hymes has called "communicative competence" (1972).

REPETITION AND SUBSEQUENT DISCOURSE

I would like to turn now to the relation between repetition and discourse subsequent to a repetition. It has been often noted in the literature (Slobin 1968, Brown and Bellugi 1964) that when caretakers repeat and expand the utterances of children, they often do so as a kind of "communication check." The caretaker presents his or her interpretation of the child's utterance to the child for verification.

EXAMPLE 21
(Toby and David at 2:9 with their nanny, Jill)

TOBY: Gramma Ochs/

JILL: Gramma Ochs?

TOBY: Yeah/

EXAMPLE 22
(Toby and David at 2:9 with their nanny, Jill)

TOBY: Airplane/

JILL: Oh. She went on an airplane, did she?

TOBY: Yeah/

It is similarly the case that children repeat the utterances of adults to let them know they have understood their utterances at some basic level. (Examples 1–3 illustrate this point.) It is characteristic of some adults that they in fact wait for such repetitions by the child before proceeding with the discourse. These communication checks are not unique to adult-child interaction, however. They are also prevalent in child-child conversational discourse as well:

EXAMPLE 23
(Toby and David at 2:11)

DAVID: (putting head on Toby's bed) . . . Help me/ David's falling/ help me/ David's falling/ help me/ help me/ help me/ Its got me/ help me/ help me/ oooo/.

TOBY: Help me/. you saying help me/. (See also Example 10)

Children often experience enormous difficulty in getting their message across (Ryan 1974), and many of them come to expect verification of their message through repetition. In the case of Toby and David, when verification was not expressed by a co-conversationalist, the child would solicit it (Keenan 1974[b]; Keenan and Klein 1974). The child would repeat his utterance over and over until it was acknowledged:

EXAMPLE 24
(Toby and David at 2:10 with their nanny, Jill,
in the process of making a picture)

TOBY: Put it Toby's room/

JILL: Toby's got a worm?

TOBY: No/ Put it Toby's room/

JILL: Toby's what?

DAVID: Room/   ⎱
TOBY: Toby's room/   ⎰   (simultaneously)

JILL: Toby's room?

TOBY: Yeah/

DAVID: (?)

JILL: Oh. Put it in Toby's room.

TOBY: Yeah/ (See Example 23 for child-child interaction)

The child might accompany his utterance with an explicit request to attend and acknowledge:

EXAMPLE 25
(Toby and David at 3:0)

TOBY: My big tractors coming/

DAVID: No/ (?)

TOBY: Its coming/ look its coming/ its coming/

DAVID: Now its coming/ Its coming/ Its coming/ look its coming/

TOBY: I see/

In short, children observed in this study established a convention, whereby given an utterance by one partner, some evidence of attentiveness or base comprehension from the other was expected to follow. It is certainly the case that adults in our society depend on communication checks (nods of the head, eye contact, mutterings of "umhum," etc.) in talking with one another. However the dependence does not appear to be as extreme or as frequent as is the case for young children. For example, when one adult native speaker converses with another such speaker, he or she usually assumes that the message has been successfully decoded by the addressee. Adult speakers usually take it for granted that conversational partners "know" in some sense (e.g., are aware of the messages previously exchanged in the course of a particular conversation). In the absence of a challenge from the addressee, a speaker can treat these utterances as shared knowledge (Givon 1974), and in subsequent discourse, he or she can consider these utterances to be known, or old information.

Children, on the other hand, cannot make these assumptions. Because of the production difficulties they experience on all levels (phonological, syntactic, semantic), they cannot assume that their utterances have been decoded. Simply uttering a proposition does not assure that it is "shared knowledge" between speaker and addressee. Hence, what communication checks do is to precisely turn an utterance into shared knowledge. That is, when an addressee repeats (expands) an antecedent utterance, he evidences his knowledge of that utterance. Henceforth, both interlocutors can treat the propositions contained in the utterance as given or old information.

It is often the case in adult discourse that known or old information emerges as the topic of a subsequent utterance. The topic is the unchallengeable or presupposed element about which some new prediction ("comment") is made. Similarly, in the discourse of young children, information made known through repetition may serve as future topics in subsequent discourse. It is often the case that an utterance is produced by one speaker, part or all of it is repeated by the addressee, and the repeated information becomes the topic of a next utterance. For example:

EXAMPLE 26
(Toby and David at 2:10, eating lunch)

TOBY: Piece bread then/

DAVID: No piece bread/ piece bread/ Its gone/

EXAMPLE 27
(Toby and David at 2:11 in bedroom. An alarm clock rings.)

DAVID: Bell/

TOBY: Bell/

DAVID: Bell/ its mommy's/

TOBY: (?) It/

DAVID: Was mommy's alarm clock/

TOBY: "Larm clock/yeah/goes ding dong ding dong/

DAVID: No/ no/ goes fip fip/ fip fip/

These two examples bring out a number of points. Example 26 illustrates the way in which the repeated information may become the topic of a subsequent utterance in the form of a pronoun. Pronouns normally refer to an established or already known referent. In this case, it is perfectly appropriate for the speaker to use a pronoun, because repetition has given the referent this status. In Example 27, we see that the initial utterance *bell* is repeated and treated as the topic of the following utterance *Its mommy's*. Again the known information is represented in the form of a pronoun. On the other hand, the repetition of *alarm clock* later in the dialogue is incorporated directly as topic of *goes ding dong ding dong* without the mediation of a pronoun. Further, Example 27 illustrates nicely the recursive nature of topic-comment sequences in conversational discourse. We see that the new information *bell* serves as old information topic for the comment *was mommy's alarm clock.* However, part of this predicate *alarm clock* becomes old information through repetition by the other child. Having achieved this status, it then becomes the topic of the subsequent utterances *goes ding dong ding dong* and *goes fip fip/fip fip/.* Whole stretches of discourse are linked in this way: New information is transformed into old information through repetition, yielding topics for subsequent discourse. One positive role of repetition in discourse is, then, to establish topic candidates (Keenan 1974[b]). The topic candidates can be utilized in the discourse of either conversational partner. In Example 26, the child who repeats the utterance exploits it as a topic. In Example 27, we have a case in which the child who introduces the new information is the one who topicalizes it in later discourse. (David first points out the existence of a *bell* and later makes a claim about it: *its mommy's,* etc.)

Two additional points need to be made with respect to the role of repetition in establishing topic candidates. The first is that such sequences are characteristic of many adult-child interactions as well as child-child interactions. It is often the case that an adult will present new information, the child will repeat some or all of it, and will use it as the topic of utterances:

EXAMPLE 28
(Toby and David at 2:9 with their nanny, Jill)

JILL: Jiji's going camping this afternoon.
TOBY: Oh yeah/
DAVID: Camping/ oh exciting/   } (simultaneously)

Or the child will initiate an assertion, the adult will repeat it and use it subsequently as a topic:

EXAMPLE 29
(Toby and David at 2:9 with their nanny, Jill)

TOBY: Jiji's wonderful/
JILL: Wonderful. I know it/

With respect to the earlier mentioned topic of children who are imitators and those who are not, it may be worth investigating if the so-called nonimitators engage in conversations primarily like Example 29, whereas the so-called imitators engage in conversation primarily like Example 28. That is, it may be characteristic of some caretaker-child interactions that the caretaker takes an utterance of a child and makes it old information through repetition, using it as a topic in further discourse. This kind of discourse would give a "nonimitative" look to the child's utterances. In other caretaker-child interactions, however, the child himself or herself may transform the utterance of another into old information through repetition ("imitating"), providing either the caretaker or the child with a topic candidate.

Second, now that we understand some of the work that is being carried out through discourse, we can understand more clearly the meaning of any single utterance of an interlocutor (child or adult). For example, we can retrace the history of the discourse to isolate the communicative work of an utterance. In many cases (though by no means in all cases), the first mention of a referent by a child or by an adult talking to a child is simultaneously a claim and a request to be ratified as a topic candidate. The second mention of the referent (the repetition) ratifies the information as known, and subsequent mentions take for granted that it is established, old information.

Furthermore, without discourse history, it would be difficult to separate what is new information from what is old information in any single utterance. That is, it would be difficult to isolate what is being asserted from what is already taken for granted or presupposed. The linguist cannot, for example, rely on the range of syntactic cues expressing old information in adult speech. The use of pronouns to express old information is a relatively late development in child language (Bloom et al. 1975). Further, even if pronouns are available for this purpose as in the speech of Toby and David, there still is an absence of definite articles, relative clause nominalizations, and other syntactic means for codifying taken-for-granted information. For many children, taken-for-granted information is marked through discourse and not through syntax. Ratification of a word, phrase, etc., in discourse is sufficient in itself to establish these items as presupposed in subsequent utterances. This is the case in Example 27, where *alarm clock* is the old information, or topic addressed by the next two utterances *goes ding dong ding dong* and *no/no/ goes fip fip/ fip fip/*. We end this chapter with the hypothesis that cross-utterance repetition anticipates the syntactic marking of old information, and the heavy reliance on repetition gives way once syntactic devices for topicalization emerge in the child's speech corpus.

REFERENCES

Bloom, Lois. 1970. *Language development.* Cambridge, Massachusetts: M.I.T.

Bloom, Lois, Lois Hood, and Patsy Lightbrown. 1974. Imitation in language development: If, when and why. *Cognitive Psychology* 6: 380–420.

Bloom, Lois, Patsy Lightbrown, and Lois Hood. 1975. *Structure and variation in child language.* Monograph of the Society for Research in Child Development.

Brown, Roger and Ursula Bellugi. 1964. Three processes in the child's acquisition of syntax. *Harvard Educational Review,* 34: 133–151.

Ervin, Susan M. 1964. Imitation and structural change in children's language. In *New directions in the study of language,* edited by Eric H. Lenneberg. Cambridge, Massachusetts: M.I.T. Press, pp. 163–189.

Freedle, Roy O., Terrence J. Keeney, and Nancy D. Smith. 1970. Effects of mean depth and grammaticality on children's imitation of sentences. *Journal of Verbal Learning and Verbal Behavior.* 9: 149–154.

Givon, Talmy. 1974. "Towards a discourse definition of syntax." Unpublished manuscript.

Hymes, Dell. 1972. On communicative competence. In *Sociolinguistics,* edited by J. B. Pride and Janet Holmes. Harmondsworth: Penguin.

Keenan, Elinor O. 1974[a]. Again and again: The pragmatics of imitation in child language. Paper presented at the Annual Meeting of the American Anthropological Association.

————. 1974[b]. Conversational competence in children. *Journal of Child Language.* 1: 163–183.

Keenan, Elinor O. and Ewan Klein. 1974. Coherency in children's discourse. Paper presented at the Linguistics Society of America Meetings (summer).

Menyuk, Paula. 1963. A preliminary evaluation of grammatical capacity in children. *Journal of Verbal Learning and Verbal Behavior.* 2: 429–439.

Piaget, Jean. 1955. *The language and thought of the child.* Cleveland: Meridian Books.

Rodd, Linda J. and Martin D. S. Braine. 1971. Children's imitations of syntactic constructions as a measure of linguistic competence. *Journal of Verbal Learning and Verbal Behavior.* 10: 430–443.

Ryan, Joanna. 1974. Early language development: Toward a communicational analysis. In *The integration of the child into a social world,* edited by Martin P. M. Richards. London: Cambridge Univ. Press, pp. 185–213.

Schegloff, Emmanuel and Harvey Sacks. 1973. Opening up closings. *Semiotica.* 8:289–327.

Scollon, Ronald. 1973. A real early stage: An unzipped condensation of a dissertation on child language. Department of Linguistics, University of Hawaii, Working Papers in Linguistics. 5:6, 67–81.

Slobin, Dan I. 1968. Imitation and grammatical development in children. In *Contemporary issues in developmental psychology,* edited by N. S. Endler *et al.* New York: Holt, Rinehart and Winston, pp. 437–443.

Slobin, D. 1973. *The Ontogenesis of Grammar.* Working Paper No. 33, Language Behavior Research Laboratory. Berkeley: University of California.

Weir, Ruth H. 1962. *Language in the crib.* The Hague: Mouton.

THEORY AND IMPLICATIONS

1. Imagine a debate between psycholinguists and sociolinguists over the role of repetition in language acquisition. How might the debate go?

2. Why does the author wish to show that repetitions are not equatable with imitations? What significance does the distinction have, then, for teachers' attitudes toward children's repetitions?

3. What uses, other than information checks, might adults have for repetition? Think of other language contexts, including written documents, that employ repetition. What functions does repetition serve?

4. What is the significance, for the sociolinguist, of the utterance prior to the repetition?

5. Keenan develops the argument that children use repetitions for adult communicative purposes. Could children have their own purposes that researchers are not attuned to noticing? What might these be?

6. Keenan's argument focuses on psycholinguists' misinterpretation of repetitions. What other types of utterances that psycholinguists discuss might be similarly misunderstood because interpreters ignore children's intentions? How might these utterances be misinterpreted?

7. What are the problematic implications of viewing children's repetitions solely as imitations of "model" sentences?

8. How might repetition be incorporated into the classroom in ways that promote language learning?

PROFESSIONAL CONCERNS

1. Keenan develops the argument that children use repetitions for adult communicative purposes. Looking carefully at the examples of exchanges between children, identify some of the interpretive difficulties observers have when assigning such purposes to children's repetitions. How do these difficulties reflect problems teachers face in identifying children's purposes in the classroom?

2. Perform an observation of adult uses of repetition. Tape record, if possible, the exchanges and record the situation, gestures, and expressions that contribute to the context. Then try to categorize the various communicative functions of adult repetition, noting also the difficulties in arriving at your conclusions.

3. The social functions of language are often difficult to identify because they can be broad and variable. Design a study in which you try to identify the social function of some language feature. Try to investigate its various uses and point out the implications for language instruction.

Context, Meaning and Strategy in Parent–Child Conversation*

PETER FRENCH AND BENCIE WOLL

This essay complements Keenan's study because it highlights the importance of the social context and emphasizes the child's social purposes and strategies. Indeed both essays show us children's resources, perspectives, and achievements— independent of adult models or goals—and caution against underestimating children's abilities as communicators. Moreover, both insist on investigating not individual words or sounds but whole discourse—conversations and exchanges— and widening that investigation to include the social rules and occasions that generate the discourse.

However, French and Woll differ from Keenan in their more dynamic view of the relationship between language and social context. Whereas Keenan assumes a set reality of children's broad social goals and language strategies—independent variables that affect the child—French and Woll emphasize the dynamic, reciprocal, and creative relationship between children's social goals and the language they use. They note that children don't simply respond to a preexisting reality but also help to "constitute" it. For example, once they have created roles for each other as, say, "mother" and "baby," children may enact a series of exchanges, including handing the other child a bottle or trying to diaper her, that reflect this new "reality." Thus French and Woll see language less as a necessary and mundane instrument of social action than as a creator of the social context.

The view of social context presented here differs from that of many sociolinguists regarding independent social variables—a view often reflecting

* French, P., and B. Woll, "Context, meaning and strategy in parent-child conversation," in Wells, G., et al., *Language at Home and School,* Vol. 1: *Learning through Interaction.* Copyright © 1983 by Cambridge University Press. Reprinted by permission of the publisher.

M. A. Halliday's "field," "tenor," and mode" (where, with whom, and what is being discussed). Halliday's views surface in Donna Johnson's "ESL Children as Teachers: A Social View of Language Use" in chapter 3. In contrast, French and Woll describe "interactions" in which language affects social relations as much as social relations affect language.

In the present chapter we shall be considering the relationship of language to the social context, and the role which context plays in the child's productive mastery of meaning and interactive skills. The view of language which we take here is a constitutive one: not only do participants rely upon context in making sense of one another's utterances but, in quite important ways, that context is brought into being or constituted through the use of language. From this position, social settings and relationships are not seen as independent or external variables which operate upon the child to determine his language development. Rather, they are established and maintained by the concrete interactional behaviors through which the child enacts them in collaboration with those around him. The means by which they are enacted are largely linguistic: it is through the use of language that the child, his parents and his peers constitute and display their social relationships, one with another. In this sense, then, we may look upon social settings and relationships as interactional achievements. As such, their existence is as much dependent upon the participants' use of language as that use of language is dependent upon them. . . .

The relationship of language to context which we are proposing here, then, is one of *reciprocal* constitution: not only does language gain its sense from the context or setting in which it occurs, but settings in turn take on their particular meaning for that occasion *via* the language that occurs.

Although such observations may appear self-evident, they significantly affect our conception of the process of meaning development. For rather than seeing this process as simply one of learning to express an independent reality in terms of pre-established lexical categories, a reciprocally constitutive conception of language leads to a view of the child as an active participant in the social production of that reality. It is through the child's progressive mastery of his native language that he is able to participate in the construction of order and meaning in his environment. The psychological import of this process has been documented both by Wells (1975; 1982) and by Bruner (1964), who suggests that "Once the child has succeeded in internalizing language as a cognitive instrument, it becomes possible for him to represent and *systematically transform* the regularities of experience with far greater flexibility and power than before" (1964: 4; our emphasis). . . .

THE PARENT–CHILD RELATIONSHIP AS CONVERSATION

In the second part of this chapter we shall consider the enactment of the parent–child relationship through conversation in much more detail. That is, we shall be looking at some concrete interactional practices through which children manage their unequal status in relation to adults. However, we should point out that this competence involves much more than simply enacting a set of abstractly specifiable procedures; the parent–child relationship (in common with all other facets of social life) must be *locally* managed: what either participant says, and how he behaves, are subject to the constraints of the particular occasion, including what has happened in the course of the interaction up to that particular point. Further, children are quite resourceful in the management of interactions with their parents: not only do they manage successfully to display a respect for the conversational restrictions which their parents may place upon them, but they can do so while at the same time circumventing those restrictions. The strategies which children use in this respect have important consequences for the view we take of the interactional learning process. For although we pointed out earlier that, over time, the child's modes of expression approximate more and more closely to those of the adult system, it seems clear to us that to conceive of the entire social learning process solely in terms of becoming more "adult-like" is to remain insensitive to features of children's conversational practice. In fact, we would argue that the particular strategies we shall consider here are developed as solutions to the problems children face *as* children.

Specifically, for example, children may quite regularly find themselves having difficulty in engaging their parents as conversational partners. In order to bypass these problems, however, they enter into engagement strategies which are, in some respects, distinctive to them as children (cf. French, 1980). These strategies, we shall maintain, are all related to elements of language structure, and are (a) learned at some early point in children's interactional careers and (b) discarded, or at least used less frequently, at later points, as the child gradually achieves a more equal interactional status with his adult interlocutors. However, our knowledge of children's interactional strategies is, as yet, rudimentary: the ones we discuss here derive specifically from and build upon some fairly recent and, for us, exciting developments in the field of conversational analysis. And it may well be that as our knowledge of adult–child conversation increases, the defects just outlined in the traditional view of socialization will become even more apparent.

CHILDREN TALKING TO ADULTS: PARTICIPANT ASYMMETRIES

If one were asked to provide two general characteristics of the research on conversational interaction, one might mention firstly the focus upon rather "special" types of social relationship or social setting. Even though the aim of much of this work has been to extract generalized, or even universal, interactional processes and structures, researchers have nevertheless been led into considering the distinctive features of relatively unusual interactional contexts. Thus we find in the literature accounts of how, for example, turn-taking in conversation is organized in courtrooms (Atkinson & Drew, 1979), or of the manipulative quality of talk between psychiatrists and their patients (Labov & Fanshel, 1977). As a second characteristic one might point to the fact that a great many settings which have been studied are constituted not by participants of equal interactional standing, but by speakers who "take on," for the purposes of the occasion, unequal conversational rights. So, for instance, in order to get through the business of a court, the judge may, at his discretion, interrupt a line of cross-examination and question its relevance to charges against the defendant. He may sustain an objection raised by one counsel, and thus terminate a series of questions to the defendant already begun by the other. And, of course, he is responsible both for opening the proceedings and for deciding if and when to adjourn. None of these rights pertain to other participants in courtroom inter-action, and because of this we may say that conversational rights are asym-metrically distributed among those present.

This general point is applicable to a great many social occasions when adults convene for "formal" or "official" interactional purposes; it also applies to the much more spontaneous, interactions between children and adults. As Speier (1976) points out:

> The manner in which . . . [children] can participate in conversations with adults is internally controlled by an asymmetrical distribution of speakers' rights, wherein adults claim rights of local control over con-versation with children, and children are obliged to allow them that control. Children's failure to do so can be met with the sanctioning power of adults. (p. 101)

Despite the parallel we have drawn between the asymmetrically distributed conversational rights of adults participating in "official" transactions, and those in operation for adult–child talk, there is an important difference. This concerns the fact that, as adults go about their daily business and "move" from one social setting to another, they may, and in many cases they are expected to, change their social identities accordingly. These changes in identity are displayed to us, for the most part, through their conversational activities. So, for example, to return to our hypothetical judge, though he may well exercise his interactional rights as a judge whilst sitting at the bench in a courtroom, he would soon find that he was required to account for himself if he were, for example, constantly to interrupt the conversation between two of his colleagues during a lunch engagement, or attempt to adjourn a dinner party at the home of a friend. Adults, then, do not have preferential rights or restrictions in conversation that operate across all the situations in which they participate; rather, these change depending upon whom they are interacting with and to what end. On the other hand, children's conversational rights tend to be rather more stable across settings.

Generally speaking, *whenever* they interact with adults, they may be expected to display their identity or position as children by observing the convention that their interlocutors assume conversational rights over and above their own. These rights include at least the following:

(i) to refuse to engage with a child in conversation;
(ii) to veto a child's attempts to introduce some topic into the conversation;
(iii) to "protect" a conversation already in progress with someone else against interruption from a child;

(iv) to enforce silence upon a child or to disengage from conversation with him;

(v) to dismiss or remove a child from the conversational setting;

(vi) to sanction or override a child's protest against the exercise of any of the rights cited in (i)–(v) above.

These restricted conversational rights are not confined to children's interactions with adults; an adult may also "step in on" and curtail a child's interaction with his peers. As Speier (1976) suggests, "Much parental work is of a sort that calls for monitoring of children's activity from a distance, and that work is specially entitled with the right to intervene if deemed necessary" (p. 101). The issue of restricted conversational rights thus affects the child's interactional life in more pervasive ways than it does that of the adult. However, this is not to suggest that the child will necessarily experience this as a *problem*. As we mentioned earlier, it seems clear that they develop and deploy strategies for forestalling or bypassing many difficulties which might arise from their inferior status.

The following discussion is devoted to a consideration of the forms these strategies may take. In order to focus this discussion more clearly, we shall first of all consider the strategies available to children for engaging a reluctant, unwilling, or otherwise engaged adult in conversational exchange. Some passing comments made by Sacks et al. (1974) offer a preliminary illustration. Sacks notes that, around the age of 3 years, many children begin conversations with an adult in a similar way. They use openers like: "You know what, Daddy?" or "You know something, Mummy?" (1974: 229). One interesting feature of such questions is that, unlike most questions, they constrain their recipients to produce an answer which is also a further question—i.e. "What?" They thus carry some guarantee that the floor will be almost immediately returned to the first speaker, who will then be able to proceed with whatever topic or purpose he had in mind when initiating the conversation. As Sacks (Sacks et al. 1974) says, the child

> is thereby provided with the opportunity to say whatever it is he wanted to say in the first place, not now, however, on his own say-so, but as a matter of obligation.
> In that case then . . . we may take it that kids take it that they have restricted rights which consist of a right to begin, to make a first statement and not much more. Thereafter they proceed only if requested to. And, it that is their situation as they see it, they surely have evolved a nice solution to it. (p. 231)

To relate this to the conversational privileges appertaining to parents set out above, we can see from (ii) that a parent may, at her discretion, attempt to prevent a child from introducing a particular topic into a conversation. However, by means of a strategy like "You know what, Mummy?," the child is not only able to introduce his topic, but is able to introduce it in response to the parent's invitation. In this way, then, the child not only "gets his way," but in doing so is also seen to respect the superior interactional right of his parent—i.e., by "displaying his recognition of who's in charge" (Hustler, 1981).

Our own data reveal a rather similar strategy. Given that a parent may, if she sees fit, make it clear to a child that other matters are to take priority over his wish to engage her in conversation (cf. (i) above), one way of overcoming this problem may be to direct some question to her which will require clarification. Should the parent then make an issue of the question's terms of reference through a request for clarification, the child is then in a position to reproduce that question in a more explicit form, and thus set up a constraint for the parent to take part in conversation with him through providing an answer to it. Indeed, this strategy for gaining conversational access may be seen to operate in the following interaction between Tony and his mother:

[*Mother is busy washing the table.
Tony has been asking questions
about what she is doing*]

TONY: It dirty is it?

MOTHER: That's right
'Cos it's dirty

TONY: Mummy (v)
Off these Mummy (v)?

. .37. .

[*T. plays with cutlery*]

TONY: Why Mummy (v)?
Why?

MOTHER: Why what?

TONY: Why throw that in dustbin
lorry (= pedal bin) Mummy
(v)?

MOTHER: It's rubbish

TONY: Oh
More haw haw (= horses)
please Mummy (v)

[*"haw haw" = horses.
Mother has been playing horses
with T. and he wants to play
again*]
MOTHER: * * * * *
(Tony, 2 years, 9 months)

Having successfully engaged his mother in one interchange through the initial question in the sequence, his subsequent attempts to re-engage her ("Mummy Off these Mummy?") fail to elicit a response. However, after quite a lengthy pause, we find Tony again attempting engagement by means of the elliptical questions "Why Mummy? Why?," for which there is no apparent referent. However, in her attempt to clarify what it is that Tony is referring to, his mother simultaneously and unavoidably invites him to re-present his question in a form which is comprehensible to her. In so doing, Tony is able both to fulfill his initial aim of gaining conversational access to his mother ("T: Why throw that in dustbin lorry

Mummy? M: It's rubbish") and to do so at her request, as is the case with the "You know what?" type of question.

A further occurrence of this engagement strategy occurs the same day when Tony and his mother have gone out into the garden. Mother is dozing in the sunshine while Tony plays on the lawn:

TONY: That could go like that Mummy (v)
  . .6. .
  Mm   *[sounds like a car]*
  . .14. .
  Why Mummy (v)?
  Why?
  . .12. .
  Is this for *?
  Mummy (v)?
  Get up Mummy (v)
  * *
  Hello took took (v) (= tortoise)
  Why Mummy (v)?
  (hums a tune)
  . .28. .
  No!
  No   (Tony, 2 years, 9 months)

There is little in the transcript to which we can refer in order to render any of Tony's question comprehensible. Moreover, since Tony's mother is (or has been) dozing, she too might be expected to have problems in locating any nonlinguistic object or event to which his questions might constitutively refer. We could therefore expect that the type of reply elicited by the questions would once again be a request for clarification, and hence an invitation for him to re-pose his questions in a form which will be understandable and which will then constrain her to answer him. Indeed, that it is some form of engagement or attention of a "come what may" kind that Tony has in mind would seem to be borne out by his more direct "Get up Mummy" following the failure of his "Why Mummy? Why?" to secure him conversational access. Again, then, by exploiting the procedure of posing a question which has as its response a further question, Tony may be seen as, at one and the same time, attempting to overcome the problem of his restricted status as an interactant *and* also observing it. (This may explain why some children are perceived by adults to be always asking "Why?" Such children have perhaps discovered that to ask such a question, even when "conversationally inappropriate," is likely to provide them with an opportunity to give an extended response or explanation.)

The two strategies for gaining conversational access that we have considered so far would seem to require a firm grasp of conversational sequencing rules. The first involves having some idea of how questions like "You know what?" solicit more or less open invitations to introduce whatever topic one has a mind to introduce in the turn after next. And the second involves some knowledge (a) of the general formats in which speakers routinely resolve problems arising from unclear utterances, and (b) that the outcomes of bringing such a format into operation may be an invitation to produce an utterance which will constrain one's interlocutor to engage in further talk. In addition, we might say that a successful performance of the second type of strategy depends minimally upon the child's capacity to gauge the (in)ability of his parent to contextualize and render his talk meaningful.

In this sense, then, we are crediting the child with both a fair degree of knowledge about linguistic communication, and the ability to apply that knowledge in the development of strategies for overcoming problems he faces as a child. Of course, when we speak of "knowledge" in this context we do not mean that children know the rules of conversational sequencing in the sense that they could tell you them if asked, but merely that they behave *as if* they know the rules. We would further point out that in seeing these strategies as being typical of (though not peculiar to) children's communicative practices, we are presenting a challenge to most traditional conceptions of social and interactive learning. Rather than viewing the progression from infancy to adulthood as a process of incrementally learning more and more adult-like interactive behaviors, we are suggesting that, because of children's restricted rights to talk with adults, they may first go through a period in which they develop and put to use interactive strategies which are sensitive to their status as children. On this analysis then, communicative development would consist not in treading some straight and steady path to adult competence, but in learning first of all how to cope with being a child.

Indeed, it would seem that children are quite resourceful in this respect: the strategies discussed above are only two from a wider and more varied set which has been identified. Not all of these involve the child in asking questions. If we return for a moment to the case of the "You know what?" utterance, we can note that this type of question shares features with the sorts of utterance which speakers perform prior to imparting news or telling a story. In fact, a well-tried way of introducing a story or news into conversations is by means of utterances which likewise solicit invitations to proceed. On the whole, however, these utterances—usually termed "story-prefaces" (Sacks, 1968)—would not be functionally identified as questions. Utterances of this kind, such as "An amazing thing just happened . . .," signal to their recipient that what the speaker has in mind is worthy of mention and solicit replies such as "Oh, yes" which act as the go-ahead to bring the story into the conversation.

Much of children's talk to their parents concerns matters which, from an adult point of view, are of a taken-for-granted or obvious nature. In other words, we frequently find children wishing to raise topics or comment upon features of the setting which an adult might let pass without mention. However, because they seem intuitively to recognize that talk about self-evident features of the current situation is of interest and importance to their children, many parents are willing, and sometimes even eager, to cooperate with them in discussing otherwise mundane matters. Thus we find Gavin's mother actively encouraging his talk about the passing traffic:

[*Gavin is standing on a table looking out of the window*]

GAVIN: Lorry

MOTHER: Lorry out there?

GAVIN: There
Out there

MOTHER: Lorry?

GAVIN: Another one

MOTHER: Going is he?

GAVIN: [ə]

MOTHER: Mind you don't fall
(Gavin, 1 year, 9 months)

There are, however, as we have mentioned, occasions when parents may wish to give other matters precedence over discussions of this order. They may, for example, wish to continue a conversation among themselves without interruption from children, and hence they may refuse their children's attempts at conversational engagement (see (iii) above). An instance of this occurs in the following transcript, in which Sally attempts to break into a conversation between her parents:[1]

MOTHER: That was all really—oh she
was talkin about—erm
Julie and
(1 second pause)

{SALLY: Mummy (v)
{
{   FATHER: Julie—Julie and who?
{   MOTHER: Chris
{   FATHER: Julie and who?
{   MOTHER: Julie and Chris
{   (1 second pause)
{   and—and
{SALLY: Got to tell you something
                                         FATHER: Julie
                                         MOTHER: Julie SMITH 'n Chris
                                         FATHER: Mm

{SALLY: THIS is funny
                                         MOTHER: 'n Pat 'n
                                               ($\frac{1}{2}$ second pause)
                                               Just a minute Sally (v)
                                               I've told you before

---

[1] We are indebted to David Hustler for permission both to reproduce this example and to represent his analysis of it.

{SALLY: (inhales noisily)
Erm—Mummy have you got
any of that decorated
paper what's under the
Christmas tree?

> (Sally, 4 years, 10 months; quoted
> from Hustler, 1981. Braces denote
> which utterances occur
> simultaneously)

Bringing together our comments on story-prefaces and the fact that children frequently raise in their talk matters which adults might see as being of a non-noteworthy kind, we shall suggest that a further strategy for engaging a reluctant parent may take the form of the child beginning his talk with an utterance which conventionally marks what is to come as worthy of mention or significant. Looking at Sally's attempts to engage in conversation with her mother, we can see "a progression from what might be viewed as less powerful to more powerful starters" until, upon her third attempt at engagement, she produces what would appear to be a story-preface and, as such, "seems to promise more news of the sort that parents might be interested in" than either her previous attempt or her earlier "Mummy" (Hustler, 1981). As we mentioned earlier, as with "You know what?" questions, what characteristically follows a story-preface is an invitation to proceed, and the pause in the conversation which follows her third attempt might well be regarded as such an invitation. Significantly however, it becomes clear when Sally eventually does gain the floor that her concern is not to impart significant news, but to pose to her mother a request.

So far, then, we have considered both the use of questions which solicit further questions in return and the use of story-prefaces as examples of strategies that children employ in order to get reluctant parents to talk with them. Before concluding this topic, let us consider one further example of interaction which illustrates yet another strategy.

> [*Frank and Louise (brother and
> sister) are playing on the floor.
> Mother is cutting out a sewing
> pattern*]

LOUISE: * * * * *

. .7. .

FRANK: * * to put that <u>one truck</u>

> MOTHER: Nan's * * * (dinner)
> So (you) don't get them all
> out everywhere
> Do you?

FRANK: After we're <going> to Nan's

> MOTHER: Nan's coming over I said
> Nobody's going out

[I.e., because of the recording
  equipment in the home]
[Frank is wandering in and out of
  the lounge, Louise playing on the
  floor, TV is on and Mother is
  watching]

LOUISE: (noises)

. .6. .

LOUISE: Er <get> the red <one>
         (= toy)
FRANK: I'm not doing it <with you>
         I'm going out the back

. . . .

         I'm doing something

. . . .

         I'm doing something Ma (v)

                    MOTHER: What you doing?
                            Come in and shut the door

. .

FRANK: I'm going out the back

                    MOTHER: Get in here and <see> that
                            door's shut
                            (Frank, 4 years, 3 months)

In addition to having rights to refuse children conversational cooperation, we may note that adults also have rights to censure certain topics. Indeed, Mother's reply to Frank's initial attempts to raise the issue of "going out" ("Nan's coming over I said Nobody's going out") might well be heard as decisively putting an end to that topic. Later, though, Frank raises the topic again, this time in the course of withdrawing from a game with his sister ("I'm not doing it <with you> I'm going out the back"). Despite the fact that his mother is present at this utterance, however, she does not take it up and, after a silence of four seconds, Frank produces what might be heard as *less specific* reformulations of his intent: "I'm doing something I'm doing something Ma." It is after the second of these productions that his mother requests a more explicit statement on the matter ("What you doing?") and thus invites him to re-introduce the censured topic. In this way, then, the child manages to override a conversational restriction set up by his parent, and does so, once again, in response to her request.

A further aspect of this sequence which is of interest to our discussion concerns the design of Frank's utterances "I'm doing something . . . I'm doing something Ma." As Wells points out, different utterance types set up different degrees of expectation for a response. So, for example, whereas what are usually termed first parts to adjacency pairs (questions, invitations, etc.) place their recipients under an obligation to produce relevant second parts (answers, replies) in return, other utterance types such as statements and answers seem to allow greater latitude, i.e. acknowledgments of statements and answers may be optional (Wells, MacLure & Montgomery, 1979). Looked at in these terms, Frank's first "I'm doing something" perhaps does not place his mother under any particularly strong constraint to reply. However, as recent work by Wootton (1981) suggests, "one technique for transforming an utterance, at its potential completion point, into one which carries a stronger constraint on its recipient to take a turn" is to append to it a term of address. Thus, having failed to engage his mother in conversation upon his first production of the utterance, after a three-second silence, Frank re-presents it, this time with the appended address term "Ma(v)." It is, then, through the use of this technique, in conjunction with a nonspecific formulation, that Frank is able to secure an invitation to resurrect the topic, earlier vetoed, of his wish to "go out."

Again, then, we can see that children are extremely adept at devising strategies for getting round the conversational restrictions their parents set up for them, and that these strategies are designed in ways which give the impression that the asymmetries of the parent–child relationship are being preserved.

We shall now conclude by pulling together the various lines of analysis we have followed in this [article].

CONCLUSION

We began by outlining one view of the relationship between language and social context. This view is a constitutive view. It suggests that rather than language merely relying upon context for its meaning, there is an important sense in which contexts are actually produced by the language of participants. By taking this view, we have, we believe, secured firm theoretical grounds for taking the conversation itself as the context for the child's developing mastery of meaning. One aspect of conversational practice which may be extremely important for this development is the "formulation" of the child's utterances by his adult inter-locutors. Through this practice, parents are able to remodel the child's meanings in the terms of the adult systems of lexis and syntax. Further, it is suggested that, because certain meanings figure saliently in the conversational enactment of the parent–child relationship (e.g. "prohibitions" from parents), the linguistic forms through which these meanings are expressed emerge at an early point in the child's communicative career.

In pointing to these trends, however, we must be careful not to represent the child's relationship with his parents as something which exists independently of him and which determines his interactive practices. For, in our constitutive view, social relationships are brought into being and displayed through the concrete communicative behaviors of participants. It is, then, at least in part through the child's development of language that he is able to enact his relation-ship with his parents. This enactment, however, consists of much more than merely following through some program or set of rules of a "once-learned-never-forgotten" kind. The child must be able to tailor his behavior in accordance with the specific "needs" and opportunities presented in the interaction at any particular point. Further, he may, whilst appearing to respect the requirements and restrictions his parents place upon him, attempt to circumvent those restric-tions. His strategies for so doing display both detailed knowledge of conversational sequencing rules, and an ability to bring that knowledge to bear upon the needs of the occasion. The picture which begins to emerge, then, is one of the child as an active, resourceful, and even occasionally cunning, conversationalist. In this respect, his interactive behavior is an extremely adaptive response to his social situation and should not be considered as an impoverished version of adult behavior. The view of the child's communicative competence we wish to convey here is one in which rules are invoked and manipulated in accordance with unique situational features—a view for which Widdowson (1979) has found an elegant analogy:

> We may claim that we know how to play the game of chess if we know the moves it is permitted to make with different pieces, that is to say if we know the constitutive rules of the game. But when we are actually engaging an opponent, we do not merely move our pieces in accordance with these rules: we *use* these rules to create openings, to develop a plan of campaign, to make a game of it. (p. 63; original emphasis)

Parents' conversational practices which are now recognized as likely to promote communicative competence in general (Wells & Robinson, 1982) may well facilitate this development, but it is also facilitated by practices that are seemingly restrictive. After all, it is only through facing problems that one can ever have the experience of constructing solutions.

REFERENCES

Atkinson, J. M. & Drew, P. (1979) *Order in Court.* London: Macmillan.

Bruner, J. S. (1964) The course of cognitive growth. *American Psychologist* 19: 1-15.

French, P. (1980) Getting round the rules: on children's strategies for circumventing conversational restrictions. Paper delivered to the Annual Conference of the Association for Child Psychiatry, Tavis Lock Clinic, London, June 1982.

Hustler, D. (1981) Clarification requests: a response to Langford. In French, P. & MacLure, M. (eds) *Adult-Child Conversation: studies in structure and process.* London: Croom Helm.

Labov, W. & Fanshel, D. (1977) *Therapeutic Discourse: psychotherapy as conversation.* New York: Academic Press.

Sacks, H. (1968) Lecture Notes, April 17, Mimeo, University of California,

Sacks, H., Schegloff, E. A. & Jefferson, G. (1974) A simplest systematics for the organization of turn-taking for conversation. *Language* 50: 696-735. Reprinted in Schenkein, J. (ed.) *Studies in the Organisation of Conversational Interaction.* New York: Academic Press, 1978.

Speier, M. (1976) The child as conversationalist: some culture-contact features of conversational interactions between adults and children. In Hammersley, M. & Woods, P. (eds) *The Process of Schooling: a sociological perspective.* London: Routledge & Kegan Paul.

Wells, C. G. (1975) Interpersonal communication and the development of language. Paper given at Third International Symposium on First Language Acquisition, London, September 1975.

Wells, C. G. (1981) Language as interaction, 22-72. In Gordon Wells (ed) *Learning through Interaction: The Study of Language Development.* Cambridge University Press.

———. (1982). Apprenticeship in meaning. In Nelson, K. E. (ed.) *Children's Language,* vol. II. New York: Gardner Press.

Wells, C. G. & Robinson, W. P. (1982) The role of adult speech in language development. In Fraser, C. & Scherer, K. (eds) *Advances in the Social Psychology of Language.* Cambridge University Press.

Wells, C. G., MacLure, M. & Montgomery, M. (1979) Some strategies for sustaining conversation. Paper given at Sixth LACUS Forum. To appear in Werth, P. (ed.) *The Development of Conversation and Discourse.* London: Croom Helm, in press.

Widdowson, H. (1979) Rules and procedures in discourse analysis. In Myers, T. (ed.) *The Development of Conversation and Discourse.* Edinburgh University Press.

Wootton, A. (1981) On children's use of address terms. In French, P. and MacLure, M. (eds) *Adult–Child Conversation: Studies in Structure and Process.* London: Croom Helm.

THEORY AND IMPLICATIONS

1. How do French and Woll, as well as Keenan, distinguish their position from that of the psycholinguists in terms of semantics as well as syntax?

2. Why might French and Woll consider Keenan's emphasis on specific pragmatic goals too reductionistic?

3. Give an example, from your own past or recent experience, of how context is created by language. What implications does this example have for how children learn language and how adults should view it?

4. What is the importance of the concept of "immediate feedback" and how does a social interactionist's view of feedback differ from a cognitivist's view?

5. How are reformulations, which are like expansions, viewed differently here than in the psycholinguist literature?

6. French and Woll emphasize constraints in social roles that children face. Why does such an emphasis not reduce children's language strategies? How might teachers use such roles to increase children's repertoire of language strategies?

7. Why do you think that adults have a difficult time thinking of children's language as constituting reality? What effect might this thinking have on teaching strategies?

8. What implications for vocabulary lessons does this view of children's social construction of meanings have? Why? Give examples.

9. Frequency of occurrence, from the cognitivist perspective, is not seen as affecting syntax acquisition: rather, intrinsic (cognitive) complexity serves as the key determiner. Yet French and Woll argue that the possessive case is learned early because the social relations involved are ones with early social importance. Can you reconcile these two views, or must you choose between them? Why?

PROFESSIONAL CONCERNS

1. The distinction between adult and child strategies is important in this study. Also important is the distinction between language that refers to reality and language that constitutes or creates reality. Write an article for an educational journal explaining what implications these distinctions have for language arts instruction.

2. Write a proposal to an administrator for incorporating more role play into the classroom. Refer to the theories presented here to support your proposal. Be as specific as possible about the role play you are suggesting.

Acquiring a Second Language—
A Psycholinguistic Approach

THE ISSUES

Chapters 2 and 3 address second language acquisition theory and practice, chapter 2 from a psycholinguistic perspective, chapter 3 from a sociolinguistic approach. Although most of the issues, principles, and benefits described underlie research from both perspectives, the readings in both chapters reveal different underlying assumptions, variables, and methods comprising this field.

The field of second language (L2) acquisition is rife with political, ethical, and practical problems. Emotionally charged disagreements abound because our native language, or "mother tongue," represents our most intimate contact with the world; it contains the words through which objects, concepts, judgments, and behavior are first presented. Furthermore, as we know from first language (L1) principles, the child does not learn a language passively, as a set of words overlaid on objects. First language learning involves complex hypothesis formation, usually through intimate contact with caregivers, about the syntactic features of the language. Policies that seek to obliterate the significance of that early learning and treat a language as a mere expediency, contradict the learner's most intimate experience. That deep-rooted experience denies separation of language from background, upbringing, and culture. It proclaims the importance of the mother tongue's role in shaping specific behaviors, associations, and meanings learned through it and insists on language's role in fostering ethnic ties.

Although we know that at a practical level ideas translate easily from language to language, we also know that their social, emotional, and ethnic associations do not. This paradox—that a language seems to be an objective and interchangeable tool, yet shapes one's personal identity—accounts for certain arguments over bilingual education in this country. However resolutely some immigrant groups have suppressed their native language, other groups with very different political, historical, and economic experiences have resisted the domination of English. While the Italians and Greeks quickly lost their first language abilities, the Pennsylvania Dutch, American Indians, and Louisiana French insisted on maintaining their native languages. Similarly, whereas many educators in this country insist on English only, emphasizing homogeneity, others demand an education partly in the native language and recognize ethnic differences and the role a native language plays in L2 acquisition and academic learning. Thus the issue of L2 learning is never simply practical or methodological. It extends to issues of national policy toward first language maintenance and to larger issues, really national values, of ethnicity and cultural diversity.

Although national questions of cultural diversity have for generations remained unresolved, legal questions surrounding English as a Second Language (ESL) have pressed for more immediate resolution. There is good cause for this sense of immediacy. The legal issue of equal opportunity arises when language testing and methods exclude particular language groups from rigorous courses, or place these groups in such courses without the language skills necessary for success. For instance, biased tests consistently place ESL students in remedial classes, where they fall behind native speakers in cognitive skills. Paradoxically, being improperly tested into regular classes can also lead to loss of cognitive skills and ultimate failure in school: Schools are pressured to move English learners (once labeled "LEP," or Limited English Proficiency students) into regular classes; unable to understand the material, these students then begin to fail.

Teachers' methods in these regular classes may further contribute to such failure. When teachers encounter comprehension difficulties, they often inadvertently simplify the task as well as the language. They frequently reduce cognitively complex tasks to isolated skills such as underlining subjects and predicates and practicing simple sentence combining, hoping both to simplify learning and to eradicate embarrassing errors. As ESL students fall further behind in cognitive skills and their persistent errors in surface form mark them as uneducable, they find a new path to remedial classes. Therefore English exposure in rigorous classes can result not in the desired social mobility but rather in discrimination, social stratification, and alienation of whole ethnic groups. This discrimination has led to the groundbreaking Bilingual Education Act of 1968, which now mandates the teaching of major subjects in the native language of the speaker.

Legal issues of equality are also raised by teacher attitudes. Negative attitudes can lead teachers to lower their expectations, and students to acquire negative self-concepts. For instance, ESL learners who raise questions falteringly in English often encounter derision for the repeated errors that native English speakers do not make. Teachers untrained in ESL errors repeatedly correct such errors in ways that question the students' intelligence, thereby creating fear and defeat and impeding learning in the second language learner.

Such attitudes have had specific legal consequences. In the case of *Martin Luther King Junior Elementary School children v. Ann Arbor School District Board,* the stigma and disrespect attached to black English dialect were judged to be a barrier to learning (see chapter 4 on dialects). Teachers' lack of knowledge of the dialect fostered lowered expectations, inappropriate teaching methods, and inappropriate placement of students. Similarly, the accents and errors of ESL students can prompt negative attitudes, which then create a similar cycle of lowered expectations and performance.

PRINCIPLES OF SECOND LANGUAGE ACQUISITION— A COGNITIVE PERSPECTIVE

Given the breadth of cultural, methodological, and finally legal issues, teachers need to understand key second language principles if they are to reduce national uncertainties to manageable choices. Some of these choices are relatively clear: Standard English needs to be taught, for in everyday life, language demarcates and stigmatizes. But other, more complex choices remain: How should we teach standard English without denying individuals their rights to equal education and without forcing students to sacrifice their ethnic identity? How can we keep ESL students in the schools and mainstreamed? Can we mainstream them without reducing the richness of language that native speakers receive? In short, what are the sound and applicable language principles upon which we can make our choices through programs, materials, and placement? Significantly, advances in L1 and L2 acquisition research have prompted radical reevaluations of second language methods. Although these advances do not offer quick fixes, they do suggest approaches to problems of equality, assimilation, and maintenance; respect for minority cultures; and concern for high standards in a mixed language classroom. The readings in this chapter offer no instant solutions but do offer essential principles, based on research, that individual teachers can adapt to their school circumstances.

The following essays, in this first of two chapters on second language acquisition, bring primarily psycholinguistic knowledge to the question of how best to teach ESL students. That knowledge can help us become better teachers of all children of all language backgrounds. Recent language studies can remove misinformation, counter false assumptions, and replace personal and emotional views with empirically derived knowledge. The contributions of applied linguistics include notions of an unconscious but set order of acquisition based on difficulty level; an interlanguage (IL) that functions as a separate, rule-governed language approximating the target language; and errors as signs of learning, not deficiency. Many of the advances in knowledge derive from studies that compare L2 with L1 acquisition, helping to refute commonly held assumptions about learning a second language: that students learn by explicit drill and consciously memorized rules; that L2 learners' errors are botched versions of the target language; that L2 learners' mistakes mostly derive from L1 interference; that learning L2 simultaneously with L1 results in a mixed language; that the more exposure to L2 the better, irrespective of comprehensibility; and that errors always show ignorance and deficiency, not learning. These and other false assumptions lead to wrongheaded teaching strategies, teacher and student frustration, and destructive and ultimately biased language attitudes.

PROFESSIONAL APPLICATIONS

Clearly, teachers of language arts can benefit from a fuller understanding of second language principles. Less obvious, perhaps, is how teachers of subjects other than language arts can benefit. Yet it is these instructors, in particular, who need to understand L2 acquisition principles. The mastery of any subject matter demands effective English; it is during subject matter instruction that ESL students are assumed to understand and use English. Instructors without a background in language acquisition can too easily assume comprehension when none exists, or they can assume uncritically that the "sink-or-swim" (submersion) method of simple exposure works best in the end. A lack of knowledge leads to bias, discrimination, and the failure of instruction.

Teachers of mathematics, music, science, and even physical education need a background in language acquisition to be critical of prevailing attitudes and assumptions about language. They need to understand the bias involved in using submersion methods, the lack of content in a back-to-basics approach, and the need to use positive strategies for increasing ESL students' acquisition of language. For instance, the similarities between L1 and L2 acquisition indicate that teachers should enhance ESL students' competencies through supportive conversation, just as caregivers do when they encourage and applaud children's emerging language. ESL students need a rich, interactive language environment. Even simple methods such as collaborative projects will help them to better master their subjects.

For all teachers, these readings convey a different attitude toward error from that which prevails in the schools today. Current political and educational rhetoric exhorts a return to the isolation of quantifiable skills, rigorous drill, and an intolerance of error. And because the public sees teachers as accountable for all student errors, teachers are particularly vulnerable to this rhetoric. It is hoped that these readings will provide the research, understanding, and professional expertise to counter assaults based on ignorance of language acquisition.

OVERVIEW OF THE READINGS

The readings selected here offer primarily psycholinguistic views of second language acquisition and suggest specific methods that teachers might implement. They offer the theories and hypotheses of important psychologists and psycholinguists in the field. Throughout these readings there is a concern for similarities between first and second language acquisition, the underlying mental processes responsible for our approaches to language. The final reading offers a practical application of cognitive theories to the issue of enhancing L2 acquirers' academic proficiency.

S. P. Corder's "The Significance of Learners' Errors" is a seminal essay from the cognitive perspective that attacks the "habit-formation" theory of second language acquisition, the primary tenet of behaviorism. Through an analysis of errors, Corder demonstrates that the long-held belief that L1 "interferes" with L2 through habit formation does not account for the errors students actually make.

Those errors are systematic and rule-based, reflecting a developing competence. The study thus not only supports L1 acquisition principles, but also emphasizes the importance of error to learning, a fundamental theme of this book.

Stephen Krashen's "Bilingual Education and Second Language Acquisition Theory" extends Corder's concern with innate processes by positing a set of hypotheses about L2 acquisition that emphasize unconscious, tacit learning as opposed to direct, formal instruction. His theories have practical applications in that he uses these hypotheses to judge various bilingual education programs.

Joseph Huang and Evelyn Hatch's "A Chinese Child's Acquisition of English" broadens Corder's and Krashen's emphasis on cognitive factors to reveal the interrelation of cognitive and social factors. They trace the child Paul's movement from imitation to rule formation, showing how social context aids that movement. This helps teachers to identify the role of both rule formation and imitation, and to understand how the movement toward rules itself causes error.

Jim Cummins's "Explaining Patterns of Minority Student Underachievement," written principally from a cognitive perspective, focuses less on L2 processes than on the overall context of minority student achievement. Cummins attacks erroneous explanations based on behavioristic models for the underachievement of minority students, which he attributes to social factors. His central theory explains the cognitive benefits of bilingualism as well as children's necessary attainment of a proficiency "threshold" beyond which students can gain those benefits. He thus addresses cognitive concerns within the framework of such social factors as status relations.

Anna Uhl Chamot and J. Michael O'Malley's "The Cognitive Academic Language Learning Approach" reveals how students can use developing second language proficiency to gain cognitive benefits. Building on Cummins's concern for extending proficiency, these authors offer the important concept of "procedures"— whole tasks that students perform to master subject matter. They present a theory that supports whole language approaches (full texts, whole tasks) for L2 learners as well as for L1 writers.

The Significance of Learners' Errors*

S. P. CORDER

This much cited study discusses the underlying similarity of language processing strategies in first and second language acquisition. Corder emphasizes innate, universal, and cognitive processes.

Specifically, Corder focuses on the weakness of using contrastive analysis (comparing features of L1 and L2 to locate interference) to predict and address errors. He claims that contrastive analysis wrongly assumes that language

---

* Corder, S. P., "The Significance of Learners' Errors" reprinted from *IRAL,* Vol. V/4, 1967, published by Julius Groos Verlag, Heidelberg.

"habits" of L1 interfere with language "habits" of L2 and argues that L2 learners develop a systematic, rule-based, intermediary language that is not simply a compilation of L2 errors. The errors, then, represent a developmental stage, part of a logical system. To predict them, then, we should look not at the features of the L1 but rather at the syntactical complexities of the L2. Although later studies demonstrate that L1 interference is a factor and criticize the methods of this early study, Corder's essay remains a classic argument against behaviorism (habit formation) and a very readable summary of what in later studies will become interlanguage theory.

According to Corder, second language learners who have proper exposure will internalize a grammar. They develop "approximate systems" (later called "interlanguage" or IL), not carryover rules from their first language. These systems are not reductions or simplifications of a more complicated code; instead they comprise a learners' "transitional competence." (Pidginization theorists such as Bickerton in chapter 1 would see this language system as revealing an underlying structure close to the "inner form" of all languages.) This basic language later will more closely approximate the target language.

Viewing the rudimentary code of L2 learners as an "approximate system"— a separate rule-governed grammar—may be overly simplistic. Indeed "system" itself sounds too static in that we now know that L2 learners' competence varies as they sift out rules. But the concept has important pedagogical implications. Just as parents do not expect well-formed sentences from their two-year-old, no teacher should expect fully correct utterances from a new second language learner. Both learners are using intermediate systems based on linguistic strategies, not imitation. The system will develop through gradual complication, not through correction. For L2 development, therefore, it is not drill or imitation that teachers should use, but rather the strategies caregivers use: expansion, conversational input, and attention to content over form. These methods allow the learner to hypothesize rules from the language heard.

The knowledge this view offers to teachers has far-reaching consequences: What is "taught" is not what is "learned"; no syllabus can dictate when learners will hypothesize rules; and given exposure, motivation, and no significant obstacles, students will learn the language. These insights reduce the likelihood of a grammatical syllabus, emphasize a conversation-based program, and help teachers to see "error" (as opposed to "mistakes") as systematic, natural, and part of hypothesis formation.

Interlanguage theory, like pidginization theory, relies on beliefs in universal language strategies. Much of this work derives from Noam Chomsky's theories of a transformational grammar (see chapter 5), by which the numbers of transformations from kernel sentences determine difficulty levels of the syntax. Although Chomsky's prediction of difficulty levels from numbers of transformations has not been validated by research, his notions of a universal language acquisition device (LAD) and processes are reflected in Corder's, Krashen's, and other researchers' emphasis on universal cognitive language learning.

When one studies the standard works on the teaching of modern languages it comes as a surprise to find how cursorily the authors deal with the question of learners' errors and their correction. It almost seems as if they are dismissed as a matter of no particular importance, as possible annoying, distracting, but inevitable by-products of the process of learning a language about which the teacher should make as little fuss as possible. It is of course true that the application of linguistic and psychological theory to the study of language learning added a new dimension to the discussion of errors; people now believed they had a principled means for accounting for these errors, namely that they were the result of interference in the learning of a second language from the habits of the first language. The major contribution of the linguist to language teaching was seen as an intensive contrastive study of the systems of the second language and the mother tongue of the learner; out of this would come an inventory of the areas of difficulty which the learner would encounter and the value of this inventory would be to direct the teacher's attention to these areas so that he might devote special care and emphasis in his teaching to the overcoming, or even avoiding, of these predicted difficulties. Teachers have not always been very impressed by this contribution from the linguist for the reason that their practical experience has usually already shown them where these difficulties lie and they have not felt that the contribution of the linguist has provided them with any significantly new information. They noted for example that many or the errors with which they were familiar were not predicted by the linguist anyway. The teacher has been on the whole, therefore, more concerned with *how* to deal with these areas of difficulty than with the simple identification of them, and here has reasonably felt that the linguist has had little to say to him.

In the field of methodology there have been two schools of thought in respect of learners' errors. Firstly the school which maintains that if we were to achieve a perfect teaching method the errors would never be committed in the first place, and therefore the occurrence of errors is merely a sign of the present inadequacy of our teaching techniques. The philosophy of the second school is that we live in an imperfect world and consequently errors will always occur in spite of our best efforts. Our ingenuity should be concentrated on techniques for dealing with errors after they have occurred.

Both these points of view are compatible with the same theoretical standpoint about language and language learning, psychologically behaviourist and linguistically taxonomic. Their application to language teaching is known as the audiolingual or fundamental skills method.

Both linguistics and psychology are in a state at the present time of what Chomsky has called "flux and agitation" (Chomsky, 1966). What seemed to be well established doctrine a few years ago is now the subject of extensive debate. The consequence of this for language teaching is likely to be far reaching and we are perhaps only now beginning to feel its effects. One effect has been perhaps to shift the emphasis away from a preoccupation with *teaching* towards a study of *learning*. In the first instance this has shown itself as a renewed attack upon the problem of the acquisition of the mother tongue. This has inevitably led to a consideration of the question whether there are any parallels between the processes of acquiring the mother tongue and the learning of a second language. The usefulness of the distinction between acquisition and learning has been emphasized by Lambert (1966) and the possibility that the latter may benefit from a study of the former has been suggested by Carroll (1966).

The differences between the two are obvious but not for that reason easy to explain: that the learning of the mother tongue is inevitable, whereas, alas, we all know that there is no such inevitability about the learning of a second language; that the learning of the mother tongue is part of the whole maturational process of the child, whilst learning a second language normally begins only after the maturational process is largely complete; that the infant starts with no overt language behavior, while in the case of the second language learner such behaviour, of course, exists; that the motivation (if we can properly use the term in the context) for learning a first language is quite different from that for learning a second language.

On examination it becomes clear that these obvious differences imply nothing about the *processes* that take place in the learning of first and second language. Indeed the most widespread hypothesis about how languages are learned, which I have called behaviourist, is assumed to apply in both circumstances. These hypotheses are well enough known not to require detailing here, and so are the objections to them. If then these hypotheses about language learning are being questioned and new hypotheses being set up to account for the process of child language acquisition, it would seem reasonable to see how far they might also apply to the learning of a second language.

Within this new context the study of errors takes on a new importance and will I believe contribute to a verification or rejection of the new hypothesis.

This hypothesis states that a human infant is born with an innate predisposition to acquire language; that he must be exposed to language for the acquisition process to start; that he possesses an internal mechanism of unknown nature which enables him from the limited data available to him to construct a grammar of a particular language. How he does this is largely unknown and is the field of intensive study at the present time by linguists and psychologists. Miller (1964) has pointed out that if we wished to create an automaton to replicate a child's performance, the order in which it tested various aspects of the grammar could only be decided after careful analysis of the successive stages of language acquisition by human children. The first steps therefore in such a study are seen to be a longitudinal description of a child's language throughout the course of its development. From such a description it is eventually hoped to develop a picture of the procedures adopted by the child to acquire language (McNeill, 1966).

The application of this hypothesis to second language learning is not new and is essentially that proposed fifty years ago by H. E. Palmer (1917). Palmer maintained that we were all endowed by nature with the capacity for assimilating language and that this capacity remained available to use in a latent state after the acquisition of a primary language. The adult was seen as capable as the child of acquiring a foreign language. Recent work (Lenneberg, 1967) suggests that the child who fails for any reason i.e. deafness, to acquire a primary language before the age of 12 thereafter rapidly loses the capacity to acquire language behavior at all. This finding does not of course carry with it the implication that the language learning capacity of those who have successfully learned a primary language also atrophies in the same way. It still remains to be shown that the process of learning a second language is of a fundamentally different nature from the process of primary acquisition.

If we postulate the same mechanism, then we may also postulate that the procedures or strategies adopted by the learner of the second language are fundamentally the same. The principal feature that then differentiates the two operations is the presence or absence of motivation. If the acquisition of the first language is a fulfillment of the predisposition to develop language behavior, then the learning of the second language involves the replacement of the predisposition of the infant by some other force. What this consists of is in the context of this paper irrelevant.

Let us say therefore that, *given motivation*, it is inevitable that a human being will learn a second language if he is exposed to the language data. Study of language aptitude does in some measure support such a view since motivation and intelligence appear to be the two principal factors which correlate significantly with achievement in a second language.

I propose therefore as a working hypothesis that some at least of the *strategies* adopted by the learner of a second language are substantially the same as those by which a first language is acquired. Such a proposal does not imply that the course or *sequence* of learning is the same in both cases.

We can now return to the consideration of errors made by learners. When a two-year-old child produces an utterance such as "This mummy chair" we do not normally call this deviant, ill-formed, faulty, incorrect or whatever. We do not regard it as an error in any sense at all, but rather as a normal childlike communication which provides evidence of the state of his linguistic development at that moment. Our response to that behavior has certain of the characteristics of what would be called "correction" in a classroom situation. Adults have a very strong tendency to repeat and expand the child's utterance in an adult version; something like "Yes, dear, that's Mummy's chair."

No one expects a child learning his mother-tongue to produce from the earliest stages only forms which in adult terms are correct or non-deviant. We interpret his "incorrect" utterances as being evidence that he is in the process of acquiring language and indeed, for those who attempt to describe his knowledge of the language at any point in its development, it is the "errors" which provide the important evidence. As Brown and Frazer (1964) point out the best evidence that a child possesses construction rules is the occurrence of systematic errors, since, when the child speaks correctly, it is quite possible that he is only repeating something that he has heard. Since we do not know what the total input has been we cannot rule out this possibility. It is by reducing the language to a simpler system than it is that the child reveals his tendency to induce rules.

In the case of the second language learner it might be supposed that we *do* have some knowledge of what the input has been, since this is largely within the control of the teacher. Nevertheless it would be wise to introduce a qualification here about the control of input (which is of course what we call the syllabus). The simple fact of presenting a certain linguistic form to a learner in the classroom does not necessarily qualify it for the status of input, for the reason that input is "what goes in" not what is *available* for going in, and we may reasonably suppose that it is the learner who controls this input, or more properly his intake. This may well be determined by the characteristics of his language acquisition mechanism and not by those of the syllabus. After all, in the mother-tongue learning situation the data available as input is relatively vast, but it is the child who selects what shall be the input.

Ferguson (1966) has recently made the point that our syllabuses have been based at best upon impressionistic judgments and vaguely conceived theoretical principles where they have had any considered foundations at all. The suggestion that we should take more account of the learner's needs in planning our syllabuses is not new, but has not apparently led to any investigations, perhaps because of the methodological difficulties of determining what the learner's needs might actually be. Carroll (1955) made such a proposal when he suggested it might be worth creating a problem-solving situation for the learner in which he must find, by inquiring either of the teacher or a dictionary appropriate verbal responses for solving the problem. He pointed out that such a hypothesis contained certain features of what was believed to occur in the process of language acquisition by the child.

A similar proposal actually leading to an experiment was made by Mager but not in connection with language teaching (Mager, 1961); it is nevertheless worth quoting his own words:

> Whatever sequencing criterion is used it is one which the user calls a "logical" sequence. But although there are several schemes by which sequencing can be accomplished and, although it is generally agreed that an effective sequence is one which is meaningful to the learner, the information sequence to be assimilated by the learner is traditionally dictated entirely by the instructor. We generally fail to consult the learner in the matter except to ask him to maximize the effectiveness of what-ever sequence we have already decided upon.

He points out as the conclusions he draws from his small scale experiment that the next step would be to determine whether the learner-generated sequence, or, as we might call it, his *built-in syllabus,* is in some way more efficient than the instructor-generated sequence. It seems entirely plausible that it would be so. The problem is to determine whether there exists such a built-in syllabus and to describe it. It is in such an investigation that the study of learners' errors would assume the role it already plays in the study of child language acquisition, since, as has been pointed out, the key concept in both cases is that the learner is using a definite system of language at every point in his development, although it is not the adult system in the one case, nor that of the second language in the other. The learner's errors are evidence of this system and are them-selves systematic.

The use of the term systematic in this context implies, of course, that there may be errors which are random, or, more properly, the systematic nature of which cannot be readily discerned. The opposition between systematic and non-systematic errors is important. We are all aware that in normal adult speech in our native language we are continually committing errors of one sort or another. These, as we have been so often reminded recently, are due to memory lapses, physical states, such as tiredness and psychological conditions such as strong emotion. These are adventitious artefacts of linguistic performance and do not reflect a defect in our knowledge of our own language. We are normally immediately aware of them when they occur and can correct them with more or less complete assurance. It would be quite unreasonable to expect the learner of a second language not to exhibit such slips of the tongue (or pen), since he is subject to similar external and internal conditions when performing in his first or second language. We must therefore make a distinction between those errors which are the product of such chance circumstances and those which reveal his underlying knowledge of the language to date, or, as we may call it his *transitional competence.* The errors of performance will characteristically be unsystematic and the errors of competence, systematic. As Miller (1966) puts it, "It would be meaningless to state rules for making mistakes." It will be useful therefore hereafter to refer to errors of performance as *mistakes,* reserving the term *error* to refer to the systematic errors of the learner from which we are able to reconstruct his knowledge of the language to date, i.e. his *transitional competence.*

Mistakes are of no significance to the process of language learning. However the problem of determining what is a learner's mistake and what a learner's error is one of some difficulty and involves a much more sophisticated study and analysis of errors than is usually accorded them.

A learner's errors, then, provide evidence of the system of the language that he is using (i.e. has learned) at a particular point in the course (and it must be repeated that he is using some system, although it is not yet the right system). They are significant in three different ways. First to the teacher, in that they tell him, if he undertakes a systematic analysis, how far towards the goal the learner has progressed and, consequently, what remains for him to learn. Second, they provide to the researcher evidence of how language is learned or acquired, what strategies or procedures the learner is employing in his discovery of the language. Thirdly (and in a sense this is their most important aspect) they are indispensable to the learner himself, because we can regard the making of errors as a device the learner uses in order to learn. It is a way the learner has of testing his hypotheses about the nature of the language he is learning. The making of errors then is a strategy employed both by children acquiring their mother tongue and by those learning a second language.

Although the following dialogue was recorded during the study of child language acquisition, it bears unmistakable similarities to dialogues which are a daily experience in the second language teaching classroom:

MOTHER: Did Billy have his egg cut up for him at breakfast?
CHILD: Yes, I showeds him.
MOTHER: You what?
CHILD: I showed him.
MOTHER: You showed him?

CHILD: I seed him.

MOTHER: Ah, you saw him.

CHILD: Yes, I saw him.

Here the child, within a short exchange, appears to have tested three hypotheses: one relating to the concord of subject and verb in a past tense, another about the meaning of *show* and *see* and a third about the form of the irregular past tense of *see.* It only remains to be pointed out that if the child had answered *I saw him* immediately, we would have no means of knowing whether he had merely repeated a model sentence or had already learned the three rules just mentioned. Only a longitudinal study of the child's development could answer such a question. It is also interesting to observe the techniques used by the mother to "correct" the child. Only in the case of one error did she provide the correct form herself: *You saw him.* In both the other cases, it was sufficient for her to query the child's utterance in such a form as: *You what?* or *You showed him?* Simple provision of the correct form may not always be the only, or indeed the most effective, form of correction since it bars the way to the learner testing alternative hypotheses. Making a learner try to discover the right form could often be more instructive to both learner and teacher. This is the import of Carroll's proposal already referred to.

We may note here that the utterance of a correct form cannot be taken as proof that the learner has learned the systems which would generate that form in a native speaker, since he may be merely repeating a heard utterance, in which case we should class such behavior, not as language, but in Spolsky's term (Spolsky, 1966) "language-like behavior." Nor must we overlook the fact that an utterance which is superficially non-deviant is not evidence of a mastery of the language systems which would generate it in a native speaker since such an utterance must be semantically related to the situational context. The learner who produced "I want to know the English" might have been uttering an unexceptionable sentiment, but it is more likely that he was expressing the wish to know the English language. Only the situational context could show whether his utterance was an error or not.

Although it has been suggested that the strategies of learning a first and second language may be the same, it is nevertheless necessary at this point to posit a distinction between the two. Whilst one may suppose that the first language learner has an unlimited number of hypotheses about the nature of the language he is learning which must be tested (although strong reasons have been put forward for doubting this) we may certainly take it that the task of the second language learner is a simpler one: that the only hypotheses he needs to test are: "Are the systems of the new language the same or different from those of the language I know?" "And if different, what is their nature?" Evidence for this is that a large number, but by no means all, of his errors, are related to the systems of his mother tongue. These are ascribed to interference from the habits of the mother tongue, as it is sometimes expressed. In the light of the new hypotheses they are best not regarded as the persistence of old habits, but rather as signs that the learner is investigating the systems of the new language. Saporta (1966) makes this point clear, "The internal structure of the (language acquisition) device, i.e. the learner, has gone relatively unexplored except to point out that one of its components is the grammar of the learner's native language. It has generally been assumed that the effect of this component has been inhibitory rather than facilitative." It will be evident that the position taken here is that the learner's possession of his native language is facilitative and that errors are not to be regarded as signs of inhibition, but simply as evidence of his strategies of learning.

We have been reminded recently of Von Humboldt's statement that we cannot really teach language, we can only create conditions in which it will develop spontaneously in the mind in its own way. We shall never improve our ability to create such favorable conditions until we learn more about the way a learner learns and what his built-in syllabus is. When we do know this (and the learner's errors will, if systematically studied, tell us something about this) we may begin to be more critical of our cherished notions. We may be able to allow the learner's innate strategies to dictate our practice and determine our syllabus; we may learn to adapt ourselves to *his* needs rather than impose upon him *our* preconceptions of *how* he ought to learn, *what* he ought to learn and *when* he ought to learn it.

REFERENCES

Brown, R. W. and Fraser, C. The Acquisition of Syntax. In Ursula Bellugi and Roger Brown (Eds). The Acquisition of Language Monograph of the Society for Research in Child Development, Vol. 29 No. 1. 1964.

Carroll, J. B. The study of Language. Harvard University Press, Cambridge 1955.

———. Research in Foreign Language Teaching: The Last Five Years. Report of the Northeast Conference 1966.

Chomsky, N. Research on Language Learning and Linguistics. Report of the Northeast Conference 1966.

Ferguson, C. A. Research on Language Learning. Applied Linguistics. Report of the Northeast Conference 1966.

Lambert, W. A. Some observations on First Language Acquisition and Second Language Learning. (Mimeograph) 1966.

Lenneberg, E. H. The Natural History of Language. In Smith and Miller (Eds). The Genesis of Language. M.I.T. Press. 1966.

Mager, R. F. On the Sequencing of Instructional Content. Psychological Reports 1961 (405–412).

McNeill, D. Developmental Psycholinguists. In F. Smith and G. A Miller (Eds). The Genesis of Language. M.I.T. Press. 1966.

Miller, G. A. The Psycholinguists. Encounter 23.1. 1964

———. Language and Psychology. In E. H. Lenneberg (Ed). New Directions in the Study of Language. M.I.T. Press. 1966.

Palmer, H. E. The Principles of Language Study. 1917. Reprinted in Language and Language Learning, O.U.P. London 1964.

Saporta, S. Applied Linguistics and Generative Grammar. In Valdman, A. (Ed). Trends in Modern Language Teaching. McGraw-Hill. 1966.

Spolsky, B. A Psycholinguistic Critique of Programmed Foreign Language Instruction. IRAL 4.2 (119–129) 1966.

THEORY AND IMPLICATIONS

1. According to Corder, in what ways are L1 and L2 alike? How do these similarities reinforce the idea of innate cognitive processes?
2. Can you think of differences between L1 and L2 acquisition that Corder might be overlooking? Are they significant differences? Why?
3. Do you think that researchers looking at L2 from a social perspective will view motivation as a given? Why?
4. Do you think that contrasting language differences beyond the level of syntax might prove useful? For instance, do you think that comparing different cultures' ways of writing a paragraph or developing an essay might be useful? Why?
5. Given Corder's many reasons for not relying on contrastive analysis to predict errors, why do you suppose teachers continue to use it? What might its usefulness be?
6. What do you think it means to "internalize" a grammar? In your own second language learning experiences, how would you characterize the process of learning rules? Why?
7. Find an article that uses or supports contrastive analysis. Determine whether the errors analyzed as interference errors are clearly interference from L1 or whether they can be explained as errors of transitional competence.
8. Corder views habit formation as an extremely limited view of language learning. Why is Corder so strongly against this behaviorist view of learning? Do you find behaviorism underlying and distorting other language theories you have encountered? Explain the possible distortions and how they have affected language instruction.
9. Given Corder's theories and especially his examples of the child reformulating a statement three times in response to a simple query, what concrete classroom practices do you think would most likely work to enhance L2 acquisition? Why?
10. What progression of hypotheses about grammar do the child's reformulations show? What do you think was the basis for this progression?

PROFESSIONAL CONCERNS

1. At a department meeting, argue against the use of contrastive analysis, both as a means of predicting and as a means of addressing errors among ESL students. Address an audience of English teachers as well as ESL teachers. Make it clear that this issue involves all language teachers.
2. Explain to a group of irate parents that you have good reasons for not using drills, explicit explanations of rules, or imitation exercises to improve the grammar of your ESL students. Anticipate that they will not condone your acceptance of error; they will question your methods, calling them irresponsible. Respond to this attack.
3. Given the universal language processing strategies suggested here, how would you explain to a parent how errors are formed and why they are necessary?

Bilingual Education and Second Language Acquisition Theory*

STEPHEN D. KRASHEN[†]

"Bilingual Education and Second Language Acquisition Theory" surveys and assesses the various bilingual programs and other second language alternatives. To make his assessments, Krashen proposes his now well-known hypotheses of second language acquisition, which make "comprehensible input" and unconscious acquisition keys to assessment. Like Corder, Krashen posits principles of innate, universal language processes such as those involved in first language acquisition: hypothesis formation, mastery of general rules first, and imperviousness to formal instruction.

These principles of universal language processes surface in Krashen's important distinction between "acquisition" and "learning"—between unconscious and rule-conscious learning. They also underlie his "natural order hypothesis"— that children acquire grammatical features in a preset sequence not amenable to direct instruction. And they are apparent in his concern for i + 1, for input just one step beyond the learner's immediate grammatical competence.

Although Krashen's ideas are not new—indeed some critics see his notion of input that is just a little in advance of comprehension as springing from Vygotsky's notion of the zone of proximal development—his distinctions are helpful to teachers and are widely used in schools. This reading is particularly useful because his program assessments are based primarily on linguistic criteria as they shape social, psychological, and educational concerns: Krashen stresses the need for a low-anxiety environment: a "silent period" in which children are quietly hypothesizing and systematizing second language rules, and a tolerance for errors. By keeping his focus on linguistic principles, he avoids generalized educational and psychological criteria such as "feasibility" and "psychological impact."

This reading complements Corder's essay because it extends the theory of universal language processes. However, these processes themselves have been questioned. As Huang and Hatch's studies of conversation show (see next reading), the "natural" order of acquisition perhaps can be accounted for by conversational rules and input. Furthermore Krashen's specific hypotheses are under attack; his key distinction between "acquisition" and "learning" may be unprovable. Certainly his view that "learning" is antithetical to "acquisition" (that it necessarily impedes rather than enhances acquisition) has evoked

---

* Krashen, Stephen D., "Bilingual Education and Second Language Acquisition Theory," in *Schooling and Language Minority Students: A Theoretical Framework*. Copyright © 1991 by Charles F. Leyba, Evaluation, Dissemination & Assessment Center, School of Education, California State University at Los Angeles. Reprinted by permission.

† This paper owes a tremendous debt to the research and thinking of James Cummins. I would also like to thank Professors Merrill Swain and John Oller for a very helpful discussion of Professor Cummins' ideas and their relationship to second language acquisition theory, and to Robin Scarcella for her comments.

controversy. Moreover, "comprehensible input" and "low-anxiety" environment may prove to be overly simplistic variables, reducible to a "what goes in, comes out" theory of language acquisition. Despite these criticisms, Krashen's theories accord well with grammar, reading, and composition theories that view learning as unconscious rule formation, prediction, and approximation centered on meaning, not form.

INTRODUCTION

The impression one gets from the popular press is that bilingual education is a mess. We are told that "basic disagreements range across the entire field of bilingual education" (Trombley, 1980a), that the experts disagree on which programs are best, that those who are supposed to benefit from bilingual education often oppose it, that there is little information about how second languages are acquired, and that basic research on all of these issues is either contradictory or lacking.

While we cannot cover the entire field of bilingual education, we will examine some of these disagreements, certain central issues in bilingual education that appear to be unresolved. In the first section, we will briefly describe the issues, the points of contention. Following this, we will review what is known today about the process of second language acquisition. A third section will show how this new information, along with a considerable amount of excellent thinking and research in bilingualism and bilingual education, helps to resolve some of the issues facing parents and educators today. We will see that while bilingual education does have many unresolved problems, the situation is not nearly as bad as it may appear. Basic research and theory already exist that speak to many of the issues in the field today.

THE ISSUES

The aim of this section is merely to present the issues. This is no easy task. There appear to be a bewildering variety of options and programs, each with its supporters and detractors. I will try to present some of these options and some of the points of debate. This will not be a complete survey; it will, however, cover those questions upon which current research and theory can shed some light. The presentation is in the form of definitions, done in the hope that consistent use of terms will alleviate at least some of the confusion that exists in bilingual education today.

Bilingual Education Programs

While we could use bilingual education as a cover term for practically all of the programs described below, it will be useful to limit it here. Bilingual education refers to situations in which students are able to study subject matter in their first language (L1) while their weaker language skills catch up. This is Trombley's view of bilingual education: "Bilingual Education is intended to permit students who speak little or no English to learn reading, writing, arithmetic and other basic subjects in their primary language while they are acquiring proficiency in English" (September 4, 1980b, p. 1). The theory behind bilingual education is that it allows non-English proficient (NEP) children to keep up in subject matter while acquiring English as a second language.

There are, of course, many varieties of bilingual education. Bilingual education programs vary in at least four ways:

1. Language use (manner). It is possible to present subject matter in the first language and leave it up to the English as a Second Language (ESL) component to provide practice in English (bilingual education + ESL). Most programs provide at least some subject matter in both languages, and there are several ways this can be done. Some provide some subjects in English and others in the first language; others use both languages for the same subject. Here again, there are several possibilities. A common method is speaking in first one language and then the other; an explanation is given in both the first language and in English during the same class hour. This is known as *concurrent translation*.

2. Amount of each language used. Not all programs provide exactly 50 percent exposure to each language. Legarreta (1979) informs us, for example, that in one concurrent translation class, Spanish was used 28 percent of the time and English 72 percent, while in a balanced bilingual class (some subjects in Spanish and others in English), the percentage was 50 percent Spanish and 50 percent English.

3. Type of ESL. There are many ways of teaching the second language. Methods include the still popular audiolingual system, which emphasizes repetition and memorization of phrases and sentences, as well as other grammar-oriented approaches, which stress the conscious understanding of rules of grammar, and more conversational methods.

4. Purpose. Bilingual programs vary with respect to whether they are intended to maintain the children's first language indefinitely (maintenance) or are only to help them ultimately adjust to an all-English program (transitional). It is important to note that the announced goals of both transitional and maintenance programs always include acquisition of the second language and subject matter education.

Alternatives to Bilingual Education

1. Submersion or "Sink or Swim." In submersion programs, NEP children are simply placed in the same classroom as native English speakers and the regular curriculum is followed. There is no organized attempt to provide any special instruction or extra help for these children. Although sympathetic teachers often try to do something, all instruction is in English.

Many people feel that "Sink or Swim" is the best solution. Here are the two most commonly heard arguments for "Sink or Swim," as opposed to bilingual education:

a. Clearly, "Sink or Swim" provides more exposure to English, and the more exposure to English received, the better off children are. In recent letters to the *Los Angeles Times,* several writers claimed that bilingual education condemns children to second-class status since it fails to provide a full exposure to English, thus denying immigrant students full economic and social opportunity (September 19, 1980).

b. Many people, it is maintained, succeeded via "Sink or Swim." Since they had to learn English, and were surrounded by it, they learned, or so the argument goes.

We will return to these points of view later, after looking at theory and the empirical research.

2. Submersion + ESL.   This option is often referred to simply as "ESL," which is a misnomer, since ESL in some form is nearly always a part of bilingual education programs. In submersion plus ESL, NEP children are usually given a separate ESL class for some prescribed period of time, usually an hour per day (termed "pull-out"). The rest of the day is spent in classes with native English speakers, and the NEP students attempt to follow the all-English curriculum.

Those who favor "Sink or Swim" usually support this program as well, on the grounds that it provides more English; more time spent exposed to English; the motivation to learn, since subject matter it taught in English; and the advantages of formal instruction. Lopez, in a letter to the *Los Angeles Times,* speaks for those who hold this view:

Bilingual classes segregate these [non-English-speaking] students and thus seriously reduce their contact with [the] English speakers and, even more importantly, weaken their drive to communicate with others in English. If you have ever taught a class of immigrants, you know that only the most highly motivated will consistently respond in English if they know you speak their native language. . . . You cannot learn English well if you do not have the opportunity to interact with English speakers in thousands of varied situations over a period of years. This should take place not only in special classes (English-as-a-second-language classes are the right idea for immigrant students, but only for a limited time) but also in regular classes as well as extra-class situations. (September 19, 1980)

Lopez describes herself as one who had to learn English herself as a young immigrant and as a bilingual teacher. Her view is shared by some legislators and some members of the communities who are supposedly served by bilingual education. According to Trombley:

Many parents think the key to success in the United States is to learn English, and they do not believe the educators who tell them their children will learn to speak English better in bilingual classes. (September 4, 1980b)

Of course, many legislators, immigrants, and members of minority language communities support bilingual education enthusiastically. We will evaluate these arguments in a later section of this paper.

3. Immersion.   "Immersion" is often used as a synonym for "Sink or Swim," but this term has been used in the professional literature to refer to a very different kind of program. Immersion typically refers to programs in which *majority* language children (e.g., English-speaking children in the United States and Canada) are instructed in a second language, that is, programs in which subject matter is taught in a second language such as Spanish or French. This need not always be the case, however; and theoretically immersion programs are possible for minority children as well.

Typically, immersion students receive all instruction in the second language, with the exception of language arts in the first language. Many programs, however, increase the amount of subject matter instruction in the first language as children progress. Immersion students are also "segregated," that is, native speakers of the second language are not usually included in these programs; and immersion students do not usually receive formal instruction in the second language.

In early immersion, the second language is used in kindergarten and for most subjects starting from the first grade. In late immersion, students may receive one or two years of formal instruction in the second language before starting subject matter instruction in the L2. Late immersion programs begin around sixth grade, but here again there is variation. There are also partial immersion programs in which some subjects are taught in the L2 and some in the L1 (Swain, 1978).

Immersion programs in Canada using French as the second language have been in operation for the last decade and have been carefully followed by researchers. More recently, American immersion programs have been developed using Spanish and other languages.

With this definition of immersion, there really can be no conflict between bilingual education and immersion, since they are aimed at different populations. Nevertheless, immersion is a logical possibility for NEP children (i.e., subject matter instruction in English, segregated from native speakers with L1 language arts), a possibility discussed later. We also see that immersion research is a rich source of information about second language acquisition for bilingual education specialists.

Table 1 reviews the differences between submersion programs and majority child immersion programs.

Summary of the Issues

The issues, then, are these:

1. Does bilingual education retard the development of English as a second language?

TABLE 1 Comparison of submersion and immersion programs

Submersion	(Majority Child) Immersion
Children are mixed with native speakers of the L2.	Children are linguistically segregated.
Language of instruction is the majority language.	Language of instruction is a minority language.
Instruction in L1 language arts is not provided.	Instruction in L1 language arts is provided.

2. Are "Sink or Swim" (submersion) and/or ESL methods better than bilingual education?
3. How should ESL be taught?
4. Is there a place for "immersion" for the NEP child?
5. Which bilingual education options are better for language acquisition?

The answers to these questions, contrary to much popular opinion, are not obvious, and not merely a matter of common sense. They should not be resolved by vote but by consideration of empirically based theory and research. In the following section, we will review current second language acquisition theory, an exercise that will be of great use in discussing the issues listed above.

SECOND LANGUAGE ACQUISITION THEORY

Current second language acquisition theory will be discussed in terms of five hypotheses about second language acquisition:

1. The Acquisition-Learning Hypothesis
2. The Natural Order Hypothesis
3. The Monitor Hypothesis
4. The Input Hypothesis
5. The Affective Filter Hypothesis

These hypotheses are presented here without extensive supporting evidence, as this evidence has been published elsewhere [Krashen, 1981, 1982(b); Dulay *et al.*, 1982].

The Acquisition-Learning Hypothesis

According to this hypothesis, second language acquirers have two distinct ways of developing ability in second languages. Language *acquisition* is similar to the way children develop first language competence. Language acquisition is a subconscious process in two senses: people are often not aware that they are acquiring a language while they are doing so. What they are aware of is using the language for some communicative purpose. Also, they are often not aware of what they have acquired; they usually cannot describe or talk about the rules they have acquired but they have a "feel" for the language. Language *learning* is different. It is knowing about language or formal knowledge of a language. Language learning is thought to profit from explicit presentation of rules and from error correction. Error correction, supposedly, helps the learner come to the correct conscious mental representation of a rule. There is good evidence, however, that error correction does not help subconscious acquisition (Brown *et al.*, 1973).

In everyday terms, *acquisition* is picking up a language. Ordinary equivalents for *learning* include grammar and rules.

The Natural Order Hypothesis

The Natural Order Hypothesis states that students acquire (not learn) grammatical structures in a predictable order; that is, certain grammatical structures tend to be acquired early and others, late. For English, a very well-studied language, function words (grammatical morphemes) such as *-ing* (as in: John is going to work now.) and plural /s/ (as in: two boys) are among the earliest acquired. The third person singular ending /s/ (as in: He lives in New Jersey.) and the possessive /s/ (as in: John's hat) are acquired much later (in children's first language acquisition, possessive and third person endings may come as much as one year later). It appears that the order of acquisition for first language acquisition is not identical to the order of acquisition for second language acquisition, but there are some similarities. For grammatical morphemes in English, children's second language order is similar to adult second language order. There is thus a "first language order" and a "second language order" (Krashen, 1981).

Two disclaimers about order of acquisition and the Natural Order Hypothesis are necessary. First, linguists do not have information about the order of acquisition of every structure in every language. In fact, we have information only about a few structures in a few languages. As we shall see below, this does not present a practical problem. Also, the order is not rigidly obeyed by every acquirer; there is some individual variation. There is significant agreement among acquirers, however, and we can definitely speak of an average order of acquisition.

As we shall see later, the existence of the natural order does *not* imply that we should teach second languages along this order, focusing on earlier acquired items first and later acquired items later. Indeed, there is good evidence that language teaching aimed at acquisition should not employ a grammatical syllabus.

The Monitor Hypothesis

The Acquisition-Learning Hypothesis merely stated that two separate processes for the development of ability in the second language exist. The Monitor Hypothesis states the relationship between acquisition and learning. It seems that acquisition is far more important. It is responsible for our fluency in a second

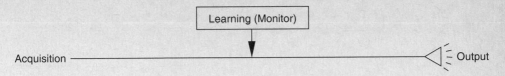

FIGURE 1 Acquisition and learning in second language production

language, our ability to use it easily and comfortable. Conscious learning is not at all responsible for our fluency but has only one function: it can be used as an editor or monitor. This is illustrated in Figure 1.

We use conscious learning to make corrections, to change the output of the acquired system before we speak or write, or sometimes after we speak or write (as in self-correction).

Studies done over the last few years (reviewed in Krashen, 1981) suggest that it is not easy to use the Monitor efficiently. In order to use the Monitor Hypothesis, three *necessary* conditions need to be met. These conditions are *necessary* but not sufficient; that is, even if they are met, second language users may not use the monitor very well.

1. *Time.* In order to use conscious rules, the performer has to have enough time. In normal conversation, there is rarely enough time to consult conscious rules.
2. *Focus on form.* In order to use conscious rules, just having time is not enough. The second language performer must also be focused on form (Dulay and Burt, 1978) or thinking about correctness. Research has indicated that even when performers have time, as when they are writing, they may not fully use the conscious grammar, since they are more concerned with what they are expressing rather than how they are expressing it.
3. *Know the rule.* This is a formidable condition, considering our incomplete knowledge of the structure of language. Linguists concede that they have described only fragments of natural languages, and only a few languages have been worked on to any extent. Teachers and students, of course, have access to only a fraction of the linguists' descriptions.

These three conditions place tremendous limits on the use of conscious grammar—and, again, all three must be met to allow effective grammar use—but even this is no guarantee. Research strongly suggests [Krashen, 1981; 1982(b)] that conscious grammar use is surprisingly light on anything short of a grammar test.

The Input Hypothesis

According to the first three hypotheses, acquisition has the central role in second language performance. If this is so, the crucial question becomes: How do we acquire? Stated in terms of the Natural Order Hypothesis, we can ask how we move from one stage to another, from stage 3, for example, to stage 4 (or more generally from stage i, our current level of competence, to i + 1, the next stage that the acquirer is due to acquire, or ready to acquire).

The Input Hypothesis postulates that we acquire by understanding input containing i + 1; that is, by understanding language that contains input containing structures that are a bit beyond the acquirer's current level. We acquire structure by understanding messages and not focusing on the form of the input or analyzing it. We can do this, we can understand language that contains structures we do not "know" by utilizing context, extra-linguistic information, and our knowledge of the world. In second language classrooms, for example, context is often provided via visual aids (pictures) and discussion of familiar topics.

Our usual approach to second language teaching is very different from the Input Hypothesis. As Hatch (1978) has pointed out, we assume the opposite: We first teach students structures and then try to give them practice in "using" them in communication. According to the Input Hypothesis, on the other hand, we acquire structure not by focusing on structure but by understanding messages containing new structure.

The Input Hypothesis also claims that we do not teach speaking directly. Rather, speaking fluency emerges on its own over time. The best way to "teach" speaking, according to this view, is simply to provide "comprehensible input." Speech will come when the acquirer feels ready. This readiness state arrives at different times for different people, however. Also, early speech is typically not accurate; grammatical accuracy develops over time as the acquirer hears and understands more input.

A third part of the Input Hypothesis is the claim that the "best" input should not be "grammatically sequenced," that is, it should not deliberately aim at i + 1. We are all familiar with language classes that attempt to do this; there is a "structure of the day" (e.g., the aim of today's lesson is to "learn" the past tense), and both teacher and students feel that the aim of the lesson is to learn and practice this structure. Once the day's structure is mastered, we proceed on to the next. The Input Hypothesis claims that such deliberate sequencing is not necessary and may even be harmful! Specifically, it hypothesizes that if there is successful communication, if the acquirer indeed understands the message contained in the input, i + 1 will automatically be provided in just the right quantities. Acquirers will receive comprehensible input containing structures just beyond them if they are in situations involving genuine communication, and these structures will be constantly provided and automatically reviewed.

It may be useful to detail some of the disadvantages of grammatical syllabi, even those that present structures along the natural order. They assume, first of all, that all of our students are at the same level in a given class, that they are all ready for the same i + 1. This is hardly ever true. In most classes, a substantial percentage of students will have already acquired the structure of the day, while another large sub-group is nowhere near ready for it. Thus, a teacher's audience for any given structure is usually a small part of the class. Even if the structure of the day is the appropriate one, how do we know when we have provided enough practice? And what about students who miss the structure due to absence? Under current procedures, they often have to wait until the following year. A third problem is perhaps the most serious: It is practically impossible to discuss any topic of real interest in any depth when the hidden agenda is practice of a structure.

Genuinely interesting and comprehensible input solves these problems. According to the Input Hypothesis, if students can follow the general meaning of a discussion, i + 1 will be provided for all of them, different i + 1 for different students. With natural comprehensible input, students need not worry about missing a class and thereby missing the past tense forever. It will come up again and again, both in class discussion and in reading. Finally, there is no need to worry about contextualizing a different structure every unit. The focus, at all times, is on helping students understand messages and not rules of grammar.

In other words, input for acquisition need not focus only on i + 1, it only needs to contain it. Thus, i + 1 will be supplied, and naturally reviewed, when the acquirer obtains enough "comprehensible input."

Evidence supporting the Input Hypothesis is given in some detail in other publications [Krashen, 1981; 1982(b)] but it is useful to briefly mention two phenomena in second language acquisition that are consistent with this hypothesis. The first is the presence of the *silent period,* a period of time before the acquirer actually starts to speak. The silent period is very noticeable in children's second language acquisition; six- and seven-year-olds, for example, in a new country, may not say anything (except for some memorized sentences and phrases) for several months. According to the Input Hypothesis, this is a time during which they are building up competence via input, by listening. When they are ready, they start to talk.

We generally do not allow adults to have a silent period but insist on production right away. When adults have to talk "too early," before they really have the acquired competence to support production, they have only one choice, and that is to fall back on their first language, an idea first proposed by Newmark (1966). Here is how this works: performers will "think" in their first language, that is, mentally produce the desired sentence in the first language and then fill in the words with second language vocabulary. If time permits, performers will note where the syntax or grammar of the sentence in L1 differs from how this sentence should look in the second language and will use the conscious monitor to make changes. For example, if one wishes to say in French:

(1) The dog ate them.

The learner would mentally produce a sentence similar to (1). Step (2) would be to simply plug in French words, giving:

(2) *Le chien a mangé les.*

Some acquirers may consciously know that sentences like (2) are not correct and, given time, can make the necessary correction, giving:

(3) *Les chien les a mangé.*

According to this view, first language "interference" is not something "getting in the way." It is not interference at all but is the result of falling back on old knowledge. Its cure is more acquisition, or more comprehensible input. It is not restricted to adults but will happen in situations where production demands exceed current competence. It is a fairly common occurrence, and we occasionally see it even in acquisition-rich environments, although the number of first

TABLE 2   The Input Hypothesis

1. We acquire (not learn) language by understanding input that contains structures that are just beyond our current level of competence (i + 1).
2. Speech is not taught directly, but "emerges" on its own. Early speech is typically not grammatically accurate.
3. If input is understood, and there is enough of it, i + 1 is automatically provided. We do not have to deliberately program grammatical structures into the input.

language-influenced errors is generally a small minority of the total number of errors children produce. Sentence (2), in fact, was observed in a child second language acquisition situation in an immersion class in Toronto (Selinker *et al.,* 1975).

Table 2 summarizes the Input Hypothesis.

The Affective Filter Hypothesis

The fifth and final hypothesis deals with the role of "affect," that is, the effect of personality, motivation, and other "affective variables" on the second language acquisition. Briefly, the research literature in second language acquisition tells us that the following affective variables are related to success in second language acquisition:

1. *Anxiety. Low* anxiety relates to second language acquisition. The more the students are "off the defensive" (Stevick, 1976), the better the acquisition.
2. *Motivation.* Higher motivation predicts more second language acquisition. Certain kinds of motivation are more effective in certain situations, moreover. In situations where acquisition of the second language is a practical necessity, "instrumental" motivation relates to second language acquisition; in many other situations, such as those where acquisition of the second language is more of a luxury, "integrative" motivation predicts success in second language acquisition (Gardner and Lambert, 1972).[1]
3. *Self-confidence.* The acquirer with more self-esteem and self-confidence tends to do better in second language acquisition (Krashen, 1981).

I have hypothesized that these affective factors relate more directly to subconscious language acquisition than to conscious learning, because we see stronger relationships between these affective variables when communicative-type tests are used (tests that require the use of the acquired system) and when we test students who have had a chance to *acquire* the language and not just learn it in foreign language classes. Dulay and Burt (1977) have made this relationship more explicit and clear by positing the presence of an "affective filter." According

[1] "Instrumental" motivation is defined as wanting to acquire another language for some practical purpose, e.g., for a profession. "Integrative" motivation occurs when the language is acquired in order to feel a closer sense of identity with another group.

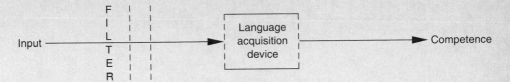

FIGURE 2 The affective filter

When the filter is "up," input may be understood but will not reach the language acquisition device; it will not strike "deeply" (Stevick, 1976).

to the Affective Filter Hypothesis, acquirers in a less than optimal affective state will have a filter, or mental block, preventing them from utilizing input fully for further language acquisition. If they are anxious, "on the defensive," or not motivated, they may understand the input, but the input will not enter the "language acquisition device." Figure 2 illustrates the operation of the filter.

The Causative Variable in Second Language Acquisition

We can summarize the five hypotheses with a single claim: People acquire second languages when they obtain comprehensible input and when their affective filters are low enough to allow the input in. In other words, comprehensible input is the only causative variable in second language acquisition. All other factors thought to encourage or cause second language acquisition only work when they are related to comprehensible input.

This hypothesis resolves many problems in the professional literature. For example, some studies seem to show that language teaching is beneficial, while others show that real-world use of the second language is superior [for a review, see Krashen, 1982(b)]. This conflict is resolved by positing that language teaching helps second language acquisition by providing comprehensible input. It seems that language teaching is most efficient for students who have no other source of comprehensible input, that is, foreign language students who have no chance to interact with speakers of the target language and beginners who are not yet advanced enough to understand natural second language input outside class. Language teaching is of less value when rich sources of comprehensible input are available, e.g., for the intermediate students living in the country where the language is spoken.

The effects of *age* on second language acquisition also reduce down to comprehensible input plus the affective filter. The professional literature consistently supports these generalizations about age and second language acquisition: (1) Older acquirers progress faster in earlier stages (adults are faster than children; older children acquire faster than younger children), but (2) children outperform adults in the long run (Krashen *et al.,* 1979). It usually takes children about six months to one year to catch up to older acquirers (Snow and Hoefnagel-Hohle, 1978).

A possible explanation for these findings is as follows: Older acquirers are faster because they can use production strategies younger acquirers do not usually

TABLE 3   Age differences in second language acquisition

1. Older acquirers are faster in the early stages of second language acquisition because:
   a. They are better at obtaining comprehensible input (conversational management).
   b. They have superior knowledge of the world, which helps to make input comprehensible.
   c. They can participate in conversation earlier, via use of first language syntax.
2. Younger acquirers tend to attain higher levels of proficiency in second languages than adults in the long term due to a lower affective filter.

have. Specifically, older acquirers are able to "beat the system" and perform using a combination of the first language and the conscious grammar, as described earlier. While children also show occasional first language interference, adults appear to be more able to use the first language syntax as a strategy, and with their superior cognitive development, are better able to use the conscious grammar to bring their sentences into conformity with second language patterns. A good "learner" can use a combination of the first language and monitor to begin speaking fairly complex sentences very early, in a matter of hours. While this system has real drawbacks, i.e., it requires constant monitoring and vigilance, it allows the older acquirer to participate in conversation early and obtain more input.

Recent evidence also suggests (Scarcella and Higa, 1982) that older acquirers are more proficient at conversational management. While younger acquirers get what looks like simpler input, older performers are better able to make the input comprehensible; they ask native speakers for more help, are better at keeping the conversation going, etc.

Older acquirers also have the advantage of greater knowledge of the world—greater cognitive/academic language proficiency (CALP) (Cummins, 1980). This additional extralinguistic information gives older acquirers a greater chance to understand what they hear, both in and out of school.

An explanation for children's superiority in ultimate attainment is simply that the strength of the affective filter is sharply increased at puberty; adults may get sufficient quantities of input, but it does not all get in. The increase in filter strength at this time is due to the biological and cognitive changes the adolescent is going through at puberty [Elkind, 1970; Krashen, 1982(a)].

Table 3 summarizes explanations for age differences in second language acquisition.

SECOND LANGUAGE TEACHING

Before proceeding on to the implications of second language theory for bilingual education, it will be useful to examine the implications of theory for language teaching, since language teaching is usually considered one of the goals of bilingual education. While theory should not be the only element considered in language teaching practice [Krashen, 1982(b)], the five hypotheses given in the previous section have some very clear implications. They predict that any successful second language teaching program will have these characteristics:

1. It will supply input in the second language that is, first of all, comprehensible and, second, interesting and relevant to students. As discussed earlier, the goal of this input will not be to provide practice on specific points of grammar but to transmit messages of interest.
2. It will not force students to speak before they are ready and will be tolerant of errors in early speech. The theory implies that we improve in grammatical accuracy by obtaining more input, not by error correction. [Although error correction will work for some people (monitor users) some of the time (when they have time to think about form) and for some easy-to-learn rules.]
3. It will put grammar in its proper place. Some adults, and very few children, are able to use conscious grammar rules to increase the grammatical accuracy of their output; and even for these people, very strict conditions need to be met before the conscious knowledge of grammar can be applied, given the Monitor Hypothesis presented above. Children have very little capacity for conscious language learning and may also have little need for conscious learning, since they can come close to native speaker performance standards using acquisition alone.

Many different methods come very close to meeting these requirements. Asher's Total Physical Response Approach, Lozanov's Suggestopedia, Terrell's Natural Approach, and recent materials developed by Winitz are some examples [Stevick, 1980; Krashen, 1982(b)]. In addition, several non-methods also meet these requirements. For example, successful *conversation* with a speaker of the language you are trying to acquire may be the best lesson of all, as long as the speaker succeeds in modifying his or her speech so that you understand. According to the theory, acquirers profit directly not from what they themselves say, but from what native speakers say. Acquirer output makes an *indirect* contribution to acquisition by inviting comprehensible input. Also, pleasure reading or reading for content and intrinsic interest has the potential for supplying the necessary input for acquisition.

Subject Matter Teaching and Second Language Acquisition

Another clear potential source of comprehensible input is the subject matter classroom itself in which subject matter is taught using the second language as a medium of instruction (immersion classes).

Simply, the theory predicts that second language acquisition will occur in subject matter classes taught in the second language if the child can follow and understand the lesson. Language levels necessary for comprehension will differ, of course, for different subjects. It has been suggested, for example, that arithmetic does not require as much control of the second language as science. In the former, there is considerable extralinguistic help in understanding, fewer demands on students in terms of verbal responses, and a more restricted vocabulary (Cazden, 1979).

Applied linguistics research confirms this prediction and helps us see both the advantages and limitations of subject matter teaching as a means of encouraging second language acquisition. English-speaking immersion students, both in the United States and Canada, are in general able to follow the curriculum in a second language, that is, they learn subject matter as well as monolinguals do. Research has shown that they also do far better in acquiring the second language than students who study the second language only in formal classes. Researchers are careful to point out, however, that immersion students do not reach native-like levels in speaking and writing. Also, it takes several years for immersion students to attain these high levels of competence in the second language (see e.g., Lambert and Tucker, 1972; Swain, 1978, 1979). The classroom, thus, has its limits. Immersion students hear the language only from the teacher and not from peers. This may mean both a lack of certain kinds of input (conversational) and the existence of an affective filter.

Subject matter teaching, thus, has both advantages and limitations. It can provide comprehensible input and help second language acquisition; students exposed to the subject matter alone can achieve high levels of proficiency in certain kinds of second language usage. This takes time, however, and such students do not typically reach the native speaker level.

Before proceeding to implications, one major point about the success of immersion programs needs to be made. Cohen and Swain (1976) point out that one of the reasons immersion programs succeed, where some kinds of bilingual programs fail, is because the immersion students are "segregated." In early immersion, they note, "all kindergarten pupils are unilingual in the L1. In essence, the successful program starts out as a segregated one linguistically" (p. 47). This linguistic segregation raises the chances of students receiving comprehensible input. The presence of native speakers in a class (submersion) ensures that a good percentage of the language heard by the non-native speaker will be incomprehensible, since teachers naturally will gear much of their speech to the native speakers in a native to native rather than a native to non-native speaker register.

Cohen and Swain (1976) point out several other factors that, in our terms, lead to a lower affective filter in immersion programs. The linguistic segregation "eliminates the kind of ridicule that students exert on less proficient performers" (p. 47), teachers have positive expectations, and the program is voluntary. Also, "in kindergarten, the children are permitted to speak in the L1 until they are ready to speak in the L2" (p. 48). Thus, a silent period in L2 is allowed.

BILINGUAL EDUCATION AND SECOND LANGUAGE ACQUISITION

We are now prepared to deal with some of the questions and issues raised in the first section. To do this, we first need to consider what requirements any program must meet in order to promote second language acquisition. From what we have learned from second language acquisition theory, there seem to be two major requirements.

I. Provide Comprehensible Input in the Weaker Language

Clearly, this requirement does not mean merely being exposed to the second language. There is a tremendous difference between receiving comprehensible, meaningful input and simply hearing a language one does not understand. The former will help second language acquisition, while the latter is just noise. It remains noise no matter how much exposure is provided. According to the theory, a small amount of comprehensible input, even one hour per day, will do more for second language acquisition than massive amounts of incomprehensible input.

There are several possible sources of comprehensible input for NEP children. The one that we traditionally turn to is classes in ESL. Simply, the theory predicts that ESL will help to the extent that it supplies comprehensible input. Not all teaching methods do this; some, in fact, supply amazingly little comprehensible input in a second language (e.g., grammar-translation and audio-lingual type methods). Both theory and practical experience confirm that repetitive drill does very little for acquisition; and grammar approaches, shown to be ineffective for adults, are even less effective for small children. ESL can make a contribution when it supplies the necessary input to children who have few or no other sources of input (see Terrell, 1977, 1981 for some ideas on how this can be done).

A second source of comprehensible input for NEP children is interaction with other children outside of school, on the playground, and in the neighborhood. This can be an extremely rich source of input, and it may be the case that the availability of this source is responsible for the success of many people who succeeded without ESL or bilingual education.

It should be pointed out that even with informal playground interaction, acquisition of English or of any other language takes time. As mentioned earlier, children in informal environments typically show a silent period and may produce very little for several months. Thus, even under the best conditions, language acquisition is slow.

A third possible source of comprehensible input is subject matter, as discussed in the previous section. It will help second language acquisition if children understand enough of the second language to follow the lesson. Non-English proficient children, however, can make it to this level in "Sink or Swim" programs only if they get the comprehensible input somewhere else or if the linguistic level of the class is somehow lowered.

II. Maintain Subject Matter Education

A bilingual program needs to make sure that NEP children do not fall behind in subject matter. This entails, in many cases, instruction in subject matter using the first language as a medium of instruction. Contrary to the view of critics, this does not necessarily mean less acquisition of English as a second language. In fact, *it may mean more acquisition of English*. To see how this is so, we will describe what observance this requirement can do for NEP children.

First, the school system's basic responsibility is providing subject matter instruction so that NEP children can keep up and obtain the tools they need to live in and contribute to society. Second, subject matter instruction plays an important role in cognitive development. Children who fall behind in subject matter because they do not understand the language of instruction may also be missing the stimulation necessary for normal intellectual development.

The third reason is that subject matter knowledge and the cognitive/academic proficiency it encourages will help second language acquisition. It does this by giving children the context or background needed to understand academic input. In other words, children who are not behind in subject matter and who have normal cognitive development will simply understand more of what they hear, both in English language medium classes and in academic or intellectual discussions outside of class. If children understand more, they will acquire more of the language! Very simply, the more cognitively mature and knowledgeable children are about the *topic* of discussion, the better chance they have to acquire the language.

Anyone who has attempted to acquire a second language has had experiences that illustrate this phenomenon: We find it much easier to understand discussions of topics with which we are familiar and find it difficult to eavesdrop and come into conversations in the middle. (In my own case, I find it easy to read and understand discussions on familiar topics with my intermediate French and German, but I understand very little when I overhear a conversation in these languages.) This illustrates the powerful effect context and background knowledge have on our ability to understand a partially acquired language. The major point here is that understanding is a prerequisite for acquisition. Thus, the more context or background we can provide, the more acquisition will take place.

Children who are behind in subject matter and weak in the second language face double trouble. Their failure to understand will not only cause them to fall further behind but they will also fail to make progress in second language acquisition. Knowledge of subject matter, thus, has an indirect but very powerful effect on second language acquisition despite the fact that it may be provided in the students' first language.

Finally, it can be argued that maintaining subject matter, whether in the first or second language, leads to a better attitude toward school in general and higher self-esteem, factors that contribute to a lower affective filter and better acquisition of English, especially when English is presented in a school situation.

We can also suggest a third requirement for bilingual programs, not one motivated by considerations of second language acquisition but by independent motivations. As we shall see, this requirement may be met by programs that meet the first two requirements, at little or no additional cost.

III. Maintain and Develop Children's First Language

As with nearly all other issues in bilingual education, there is pro and con here as well. Some experts argue that we should make real efforts to maintain the first language. Reasons given include:

1. Speakers of languages other than English make a valuable contribution to our society. Since so few native English speakers successfully acquire a second language, it is foolish to waste this natural resource. Campbell expressed this view in a *Los Angeles Times* (September 5, 1980) interview:

[The] emphasis on "transition" means we will systematically eradicate foreign languages in elementary school, then spend millions to try to develop these same skills in high school and college. . . . That doesn't make much sense.

2. Maintaining the first language and culture of NEP children may help to build pride and counter negative attitudes members of a linguistic minority may have. There is evidence, in fact, that strongly suggests that those language acquirers who do not reject their own language and culture succeed better in second language acquisition than those who have negative attitudes toward their own group (Gardner and Lambert, 1972).

3. Cummins (1978; 1980) argues that in order to keep up in subject matter and maintain normal cognitive development, students need to develop high levels of first language competence. Specifically, they need to develop not only basic interpersonal and communicative skills in the first language (termed BICS) but also "cognitive competence," the ability to "use language effectively as an instrument of thought and represent cognitive operations by means of language" (Cummins, 1978, p. 397). A lack of development of this aspect of first language competence may explain problems some minority children have in school. When the first language is not used extensively and promoted at home, and is not supported at school, low first language skills, according to Cummins, can exert "a limiting effect" on the development of the second language. Majority language children in immersion programs do not have this problem, since their language is highly developed outside school (Cummins, 1978).

Cummins argues that education in the first language develops CALP (Cognitive/ Academic Language Proficiency). CALP developed in one language contributes to CALP in any other, according to Cummins; that is, someone who is able to use Spanish for academic purposes will have developed an ability that will be useful in using any other language for academic purposes.

Arguments against first language maintenance have, in general, attempted to counter any of the above arguments but usually insist that since English is the official language of the United States, taxpayers should not have to support the maintenance or development of minority languages.

Another Look at the Options

We can now ask to what extent different programs meet the conditions described in the previous section. In this section, we will see that both theoretical predictions and empirical evidence show that some programs do satisfy the requirements while others do not and that this success or the lack of it depends not only on the program but also on the characteristics of the students. Most important, it will show that research exists, is not conflicting, and that real generalizations can be made about what works and what does not work in bilingual education. Table 4 presents this analysis.

1. We first consider submersion, or "Sink or Swim" programs. According to Table 4, "Sink or Swim" will satisfy the first requirement by providing

TABLE 4 Requirements to be met by programs for NEP children and current options

Requirements for Programs (predicted by theory)	Submersion ("sink or swim")			Immersion		Bilingual Education	
	Only	+ Informal CI	+ ESL	Majority Child	Minority	Concurrent Translation	Ideal Bilingual
1. Comprehensible input in weaker language.	no	yes	yes[b]	yes	yes[c]	no[d]	yes[e]
2. Maintain subject matter.	no	?[a]	?[a]	yes	yes[c]	?[f]	yes
Additional: 3. Maintain and develop first language.	no	no	no	yes	no	?[f]	yes

a: This program will work if second language ability grows fast enough to reach subject matter threshold before children are too far behind.

b: Yes, if the ESL method supplies comprehensible input.

c: *De facto* immersion programs do not succeed as well as bilingual education, however. May be due to attitudes, teacher expectations, low development of first language, and inappropriate materials.

d: Students tune out weaker language in concurrent translation programs (Legarreta, 1979).

e: Yes, if second language skills are adequate for those classes taught in the second language.

f: Will not succeed unless there is adequate input in the second language.

CI = Comprehensible Input

Ideal Bilingual = Subject matter in primary language, plus comprehensible input in English, either as ESL and/or subject matter instruction in comprehensible English.

comprehensible input in the weaker language only when extra ESL is provided (assuming a form of ESL that indeed provides comprehensible input) and/or when children have sufficient contact with input from the outside. In and of itself, "Sink or Swim" may not meet the first requirement, and children in such situations are in danger of not getting the input needed to acquire English. Such situations clearly exist in submersion programs that include children living in *barrios* where there is little if any social interaction among NEP and native English-speaking children.

The second requirement can only be met by "Sink or Swim" if the children's linguistic competence in English develops quickly enough. Children in "Sink or Swim" are playing a dangerous game of catch-up, hoping their competence in English will be high enough to do school work before they are hopelessly behind in subject matter. "Sink or Swim," even under the best conditions, is a risk.

No "Sink or Swim" program, by definition, attempts to meet the third requirement, development of the first language.

2. Immersion programs for majority children do meet all conditions. As discussed earlier, immersion programs have a better chance of supplying comprehensible input in subject matter classes than do "Sink or Swim" programs. Since all children are at the same linguistic level, there is less of a tendency to speak over the comprehension level of the students. This helps to satisfy the first and second requirements. The empirical evidence from the research programs evaluating immersion classes done over the last decade confirms that immersion children develop high levels of competence in the second language and do as well as monolinguals in subject matter.

Immersion programs for majority students also meet the third requirement through use of language arts classes in the first language. Also, many programs provide for increasing use of the first language as a medium of instruction as children progress in school. Of great importance in meeting this requirement is that in immersion programs for majority students, children's first language is the language of the country, home, and playground; there is little chance that this language will be assigned a lower status.

One could argue that a solution for NEP children is an adaptation of the immersion model. This would entail a completely separate curriculum, all taught in English, to groups consisting only of NEP children. Assuming all children start at the same time and on an equal footing with respect to English competence, it would appear to have the linguistic advantage of having a better chance of supplying comprehensible input as compared to "Sink or Swim." Thus, theoretically, we could expect progress both in language acquisition (first requirement) and subject matter (second requirement) even if little or no contact with English-speaking children outside of school was possible. Judging from reports from majority immersion, we would not expect completely native-like English.

It can be maintained, however, that many "Sink or Swim" programs are already *de facto* immersion programs in that they often involve a majority of NEP children and, in some cases, are composed entirely of NEP children (e.g., in certain inner city areas and on American Indian reservations). These programs do not report overwhelming success. There may be good reasons why, however, reasons that explain why minority-child immersion may look good on paper but may not always work.

First, NEP students who enter immersion programs late will face nearly the same problems they face in "Sink or Swim"; they will not understand and may thus fall behind in subject matter and not improve in English. (Late entering bilingual education students will not have this problem; they can be taught in the first language at least until their English develops sufficiently.)

Also, minority immersion teachers may not have the same kinds of expectations as do majority immersion teachers. They may be less able or willing to make input comprehensible and may set higher standards for second language acquisition than are possible under the circumstances. As Cohen (1976) points out, we have a double standard:

> People applaud a majority group child when he can say a few words in the minority language (e.g., at the beginning of an immersion program) and yet they impatiently demand more English from the minority group child. (p. 85)

Thus, many *de facto* immersion programs look more like "Sink or Swim," with inappropriate materials and input that is too complex and incomprehensible.

3. We turn now to the programs categorized as Bilingual Education in Table 4. Let us first consider the program labeled concurrent translation. In this kind of program, concepts are explained in one language and then repeated in the second. This kind of program may not meet the first requirement for the simple reason that children need not pay attention to the explanation in the second or weaker language, and there is no motivation for teachers to attempt to simplify explanations in the second language. Legarreta (1979) notes that in the concurrent translation program, "Teachers reported that Hispanic students tune out the English and wait to hear the material explained in Spanish" (p. 533). (This phenomenon also predicts, and correctly I think, the failure of bilingual TV to teach the second language. In many programs, a given character will speak either Spanish or English, but it is quite possible to follow the story line by attending only to one language. Similarly, it predicts that Americans will not acquire centigrade temperature systems from the practice of announcing the temperature in both centigrade and fahrenheit. Most people will simply listen to the version they understand.) Concurrent translation can theoretically meet the second and third requirements, however, since subject matter can be explained in the first language and continued use of the L1 helps to ensure its maintenance. In practice, however, concurrent translation often fails to meet these requirements. This is because, despite its intentions, concurrent translation input in many programs often is incomprehensible, most materials are in English, and primary language input often is provided by under-trained aides or Anglophone teachers who have not fully mastered the children's first language.

The Ideal Bilingual program, shown in Table 4, is one in which subject matter it taught in the primary language and some source of comprehensible input in the second language is supplied. This can be in the form of ESL or comprehensible subject matter instruction using English (as in the balanced bilingual programs discussed earlier). Such programs have the potential for satisfying all three requirements, even for children who have little access to English outside of school. Balanced bilingual programs will be successful according to the predictions of the theory, especially if the subject matter classes given in the second language are those where more extra-linguistic context is available to aid comprehension (e.g., math), while those dealing with more abstract topics—topics that typically employ fewer physical props (e.g., social science and language arts)—are taught at first in the primary language (Cazden, 1979).

Empirical Evidence

Our analysis based on the three requirements derived from language acquisition theory brings us to these conclusions:

1. "Sink or Swim" programs will not be effective for children with no extra source of comprehensible input.
2. Adding ESL to "Sink or Swim" will help but will not be as effective as bilingual education in encouraging acquisition of English.
3. Bilingual programs in which subject matter is taught in the first language, and a source of comprehensible input is provided in the second language, whether ESL or not, will succeed best.

Despite years of discussion of bilingual education in the professional literature and many studies of different aspects of bilingualism, little research speaks directly to these three predictions. The research that is available, however, is fully consistent with them.

Legarreta (1979) examined the acquisition of English in kindergarten children in three kinds of bilingual programs (balanced, concurrent translation, and concurrent translation + ESL) and two kinds of "Sink or Swim" programs [with and without ESL where the ESL component consisted of "daily, sequenced lessons in English structure and use, presented orally to small groups" (p. 523)]. The overall exposure time was seven months—relatively short for this kind of study, as Swain (1979) points out—and the number of subjects involved was not large. The results, however, are very interesting.

1. Children in all bilingual education programs outperformed "Sink or Swim" children in listening comprehension and conversational competence[2] tests of English, despite the fact that the "Sink or Swim" children had more exposure to English.
2. The balanced bilingual program produced the greatest overall gains in both the second language and the first language (Spanish).
3. "Sink or Swim" with ESL outperformed "Sink or Swim" without ESL on listening comprehension testing but not on the test of conversational competence.

---

[2] The test of conversational competence asked children to use the language in real communication; it thus demands more than knowledge of vocabulary and grammar but also tests abilities such as "the ability to be only as explicit as a situation demands, to elaborate, to make inferences about a situation, to be sensitive to social rules of discourse . . ." (Legarreta, 1979, p. 525).

Legarreta (1979) concludes that the use of audio-lingual style ESL training is "marginally facilitative" (p. 534), while "an alternate immersion bilingual program, with balanced Spanish and English input, really facilitates both Spanish and English acquisition" (p. 534). This appears to be so, but her data support a deeper generalization: Bilingual programs will work when they supply comprehensible input in the second language and adequate, comprehensible subject matter instruction in either language. The balanced program does this, but so do other versions.

Rosier and Farella (1976) report results from a different context that conform to the same underlying principles. They report of the success of bilingual education for Navajo children at the Rock Point Community School in the heart of the Navajo reservation. In 1960, according to Vorih and Rosier (1978), Rock Point ranked at the bottom of eight Indian schools in student achievement. The introduction of intensive ESL in 1963 helped somewhat, but Rock Point sixth graders were still two years behind national norms. In 1967, bilingual education was introduced, with kindergarten children receiving 70 percent of their instruction in Navajo and first and second graders receiving 50 percent in Navajo. Third through sixth graders had 75 percent of their instruction in English. English is taught in early grades "by TESL methods" (Vorih and Rosier, 1978, p. 264). The program can thus be classified as Bilingual Education + ESL.

Analysis of the Rock Point program confirms the validity of our requirements: Students in the bilingual program, with subject matter in the first language, outperformed non-bilingual education students on a reading test of English. Again, the bilingual students actually had *less* exposure to English but apparently acquired more, confirming that it is comprehensible input and not mere exposure that counts.

Some as yet unpublished research, cited by Cummins (1980), provides even more confirmation. As Cummins (1980) reports it:

> Carey and Cummins (1979) reported that grade 5 children from French-speaking home backgrounds in the Edmonton Catholic School System bilingual program [Canada] (80% French, 20% English from K-12) performed at an equivalent level in English skills to anglophone children of the same IQ in either the bilingual or regular English programs. A similar finding is reported in a large-scale study carried out by Hébert et al. (1976) among grades 3, 6 and 9 francophone students in Manitoba. At all grade levels there was a significant positive relationship between percentage of instruction in French (PIF) and French achievement, but no relationship between PIF and English achievement. In other words, francophone students receiving 80% instruction in French and 20% instruction in English did just as well in English as students receiving 80% instruction in English and 20% in French. (p. 184)

CONCLUSIONS

We are now ready to return to the issues raised in the first section of this paper and attempt to give some answers.

1. Does Bilingual Education Retard the Development of English as a Second Language?

Both theory and empirical research tell us that proper bilingual education need not retard the development of second language competence and should, in fact, promote it. Classes taught in the first language help children grow in subject matter knowledge and stimulate cognitive development, which in turn helps second language acquisition by providing children with the extra-linguistic context necessary for comprehension.

2. Are "Sink or Swim" (Submersion) and/or ESL Methods Better?

Obviously, "Sink or Swim" children have more exposure to English, but they do not necessarily have more comprehensible input; it is comprehensible input, not merely "heard" language, that makes language acquisition happen. Thus, "Sink or Swim" classes, at worst, may be providing children only with noise. The results of this are doubly tragic: Children will fall behind in subject matter and will not acquire the second language.

"Sink or Swim" with ESL will fare somewhat better but will work only if children acquire English fast enough, before they are hopelessly behind in subject matter. It may be that in most cases where "Sink or Swim" worked, children had rich comprehensible input from playmates outside the classroom.

3. How Should ESL Be Taught?

Second language acquisition research strongly suggests that methodology *per se* is not the issue: By whatever name, children need comprehensible input to acquire English. This can come in the form of ESL classes taught according to a method that provides such input (e.g., Terrell's Natural Approach) or subject matter taught in comprehensible English.

4. Is There a Place for Immersion for NEP Children?

Theoretically, immersion for NEP children appears to meet the three requirements. Yet, results of *de facto* immersion programs in the United States are not encouraging. This could be due to several factors, including inadequate development of the first language, as suggested by Cummins (1978), differing teacher expectations, the failure of late-entering students to obtain comprehensible input, and inappropriate materials.

5. Which Bilingual Education Options Are Better for Language Acquisition?

There are several bilingual education options that will satisfy the requirements given in Table 4 and earlier in the paper. Balanced bilingual education programs will do this as long as those subjects taught in the second language are comprehensible. There is nothing magic, however, in the 50 percent figure: It need not be the case that exactly one-half of the program be in one language and one half in the other. What counts is that the requirements are met and that NEP students receive enough comprehensible input to improve in their weaker language. This has happened with as little as 20 percent in the second language in some programs.

Several issues of course remain unsolved, and in a real sense they always will be. As is typical of scientific reasoning, we have discussed hypotheses and some evidence that supports them. We have not provided proof, nor can we. What we have tried to show is that there is substantial information available about how language is acquired, that it is certainly enough to formulate hypotheses, that these hypotheses shed light on some of the basic issues in bilingual education, and that the field is not in a state of helpless confusion. Researchers are evaluating children's progress, adding to their knowledge of language acquisition, and using this knowledge to better serve the children they study and those who will come after them.

REFERENCES

Brown, R., Courtney Cazden, and U. Bellugi. "The Child's Grammar from I to III," *Studies in Child Language Development,* eds., C. Ferguson, and D. Slobin. New York: Holt, Rinehart and Winston, 1973, pp. 295-333.

Campbell, Russell. *Los Angeles Times,* September 5, 1980.

Cazden, Courtney B. "Curriculum/Language Context for Bilingual Education," *Language Development in a Bilingual Setting,* ed., Eugene J. Brière. Los Angeles, California: National Dissemination and Assessment Center, California State University, Los Angeles, 1979, pp. 129-138.

Cohen, Andrew D. "The Case for Partial or Total Immersion Education," *The Bilingual Child,* ed., António Simões. New York: Academic Press, 1976, pp. 65-89.

———, and Merrill Swain. "Bilingual Education: The 'Immersion' Model in the North American Context," *TESOL Quarterly,* X, No. 1 (March, 1976), 45-53.

Cummins, James. "The Cross-Lingual Dimensions of Language Proficiency: Implications for Bilingual Education and the Optimal Age Issue," *TESOL Quarterly,* XIV, No. 2 (June, 1980), 175-187.

———. "Educational Implications of Mother Tongue Maintenance in Minority Language Groups," *The Canadian Modern Language Review,* XXXIV (1978), 395-416.

Dulay, Heidi C., and Marina K. Burt. "Remarks on Creativity in Second Language Acquisition," *Viewpoints on English as a Second Language,* eds., Marina K. Burt, Heidi C. Dulay, and M. Finnochiaro. New York: Regents, 1977, pp. 95-126.

———. "Some Guidelines for the Assessment of Oral Language Proficiency and Dominance," *TESOL Quarterly,* XII, No. 2 (June, 1978), 177-192.

———, ———, and Stephen Krashen. *The Second Language.* New York: Oxford University Press, 1982.

Elkind, David. *Children and Adolescents: Interpretive Essays on Jean Piaget.* New York: Oxford University Press, 1970.

Gardner, Robert C., and Wallace E. Lambert. *Attitudes and Motivation in Second Language Learning.* Rowley, Massachusetts: Newbury House, 1972.

Hatch, Evelyn M. "Discourse Analysis and Second Language Acquisition," *Second Language Acquisition: A Book of Readings,* ed., E. Hatch. Rowley, Massachusetts: Newbury House, 1978.

Krashen, Stephen. "Accounting for Child-Adult Differences in Second Language Rate and Attainment," *Child-Adult Differences in Second Language Acquisition,* eds., Stephen Krashen, R. Scarcella, and M. Long. Rowley, Massachusetts: Newbury House, 1982(a).

———. *Principles and Practice in Second Language Acquisition.* New York: Pergamon Press, 1982(b).

———. *Second Language Acquisition and Second Language Learning.* London: Pergamon Press, 1981.

———, Michael A. Long, and Robin C. Scarcella. "Age, Rate and Eventual Attainment in Second Language Acquisition," *TESOL Quarterly,* XIII, No. 4 (December, 1979), 573–582.

Lambert, Wallace E., and G. Richard Tucker. *Bilingual Education of Children: The St. Lambert Experiment.* Rowley, Massachusetts: Newbury House, 1972.

Legarreta, Dorothy. "The Effects of Program Models on Language Acquisition by Spanish-Speaking Children," *TESOL Quarterly,* XIII, No. 4 (December, 1979), 521–534.

Lopez, Rosa Maria. *Los Angeles Times,* September 19, 1980.

*Los Angeles Times, Septembe*r 19, 1980.

Newmark, L. "How Not to Interfere with Language Learning," *International Review of American Linguistics,* XL (1966), 77–83.

Rosier, Paul, and Merilyn Farella. "Bilingual Education at Rock Point—Some Early Results," *TESOL Quarterly,* X, No. 4 (December, 1976), 379–388.

Scarcella, Robin, and C. Higa. "Input and Age Differences in Second Language Acquisition," *Child-Adult Differences in Second Language Acquisition,* eds., Stephen Krashen, Robin Scarcella, and Michael A. Long. Rowley, Massachusetts: Newbury House, 1982.

Selinker, Larry, Merrill Swain, and Guy Dumas. "The Interlanguage Hypothesis Extended to Children," *Language Learning,* XXV, No. 1 (June, 1975), 139–152.

Snow, Catherine E., and Marian Hoefnagel-Hohle. "The Critical Period for Language Acquisition: Evidence from Second Language Learning," *Child Development,* XLIX, No. 4 (December, 1978), 1114–1128.

Stevick, Earl W. *Memory, Meaning, and Method.* Rowley, Massachusetts: Newbury House, 1976.

Stevick, Earl W. *Teaching Languages: A Way and Ways.* Rowley, MA: Newbury House, 1980.

Swain, Merrill. "Bilingual Education: Research and Its Implications," *On TESOL '79,* eds., C. Yorio, K. Perkins, and J. Schachter. Washington, D.C.: TESOL, 1979.

———. "French Immersion: Early, Late, or Partial?" *Canadian Modern Language Review,* XXXIV (May, 1978), 577–585.

Terrell, Tracy D. "The Natural Approach in Bilingual Education," *Schooling and Language Minority Students: A Theoretical Framework.* Los Angeles, California: Evaluation, Dissemination and Assessment Center, California State University, Los Angeles, 1981.

———. "A Natural Approach to Second Language Acquisition and Learning," *Modern Language Journal,* LXI, No. 7 (November, 1977), 325–337.

Trombley, William. "Bilingual Education: Even the Experts Are Confused," *Los Angeles Times,* September 7, 1980a.

———. "Is Bilingual Education Able to Do Its Job?" *Los Angeles Times,* September 4, 1980b.

Vorih, Lillian, and Paul Rosier. "Rock Point Community School: An Example of a Navajo-English Bilingual Elementary School Program," *TESOL Quarterly,* XII, No. 3 (September, 1978), 263–269.

THEORY AND IMPLICATIONS

1. What underlying issues do you think are involved in the choice between those bilingual programs that enable students to study subject matter in their first language while their weaker language skills catch up and those programs that focus only on learning English?

2. Immersion and submersion affect different populations. Why do you think this distinction is so important, when the principles of language learning seem broadly the same?

3. Krashen distinguishes between acquisition and learning. Do you think this distinction appears clear or blurred? Do you think that these processes are always antithetical? Could they be used together in the classroom? Explain your answers.

4. Krashen implies that conscious learning does not turn into unconscious acquisition for several reasons: because many L2 students who know all the rules cannot speak the language, because many have acquired an L2 without ever learning the rules, and because nobody knows all the rules. Do you think these arguments prove conclusively that learning never turns into acquisition? Why?

5. In you own experience, what role does the monitor have in learning a second language? Does it always affect accuracy? Does it ever affect fluency or "communicative competence"? Explain.

6. The concept of the monitor has come under attack in recent years: Concentration on the rules of grammar does not always improve L2 accuracy, and under normal conditions L2 acquirers hardly ever use the monitor. Thus critics question what role the monitor has in language acquisition. Do you agree with this criticism? Is the monitor a useless concept?

7. Krashen's input hypothesis depends on the notion that acquirers move from one stage to the next by understanding input containing i (our current level) + 1 (the next level along the natural order). Critics claim that Krashen isn't very clear about how this happens or how one determines what is i + 1 for a particular L2 student. Reexamine his explanations and determine how serious these criticisms are.

8. What implications do Krashen's five hypotheses have for assessing bilingual and other programs? What other criteria might also be important for such assessments?

9. What are the principal applications of Krashen's research for the classroom?

PROFESSIONAL CONCERNS

1. Write a letter to parents defending the bilingual education program in your hypothetical school. Explain to them that this program will not reduce or delay their children's L2 learning but will enhance it. Try to address the arguments that you assume will be made against your view.

2. Write a letter to all teachers in your school explaining what attitude toward L1 errors you think they should express, using and explaining such concepts as comprehensible input, CALP versus BICS, acquisition versus learning, and affective filter.

3. Write a letter to the editor of your local newspaper defending the language "maintenance" programs as opposed to transitional programs.

4. Write a formal paper for a professional journal in which you raise questions and criticisms about Krashen's hypotheses and key distinctions.

A Chinese Child's Acquisition of English*

JOSEPH HUANG AND EVELYN HATCH

"A Chinese Child's Acquisition of English" extends those studies that emphasize universal language processes, but also includes specific social factors. It confirms the correspondence between first and second language acquisition by showing that the child Paul moved from simple to more sophisticated rules based on his growing acquisition of English syntax. Huang and Hatch's emphasis on innate, sequential processes indicates their psycholinguistic perspective and explains Paul's language in terms of interlingual, developmental errors.

This essay introduces social factors by correlating teacher and friend input with Paul's output and by investigating Paul's use of imitation as a means of social response. Most important, however, it provides stage-by-stage analysis of the movement from imitation to rule formation: from immediately echoed restatements, to repetition in later situations, to the breaking up and recombining of sentence parts indicating rule formation. In so doing, it clarifies the relationship between rule formation and imitation, suggesting ways for teachers to decide when a student's utterance reflects rule-based understanding and when it is "unanalyzed" imitated speech. Paradoxically, "ill-formedness" or error indicates rule-based or analyzed speech, whereas "well-formedness" likely indicates unanalyzed, memorized speech. This reversal flies in the face of teachers' expectations that correctness measures learning.

Much has been written about how children acquire language. But so far the literature refers either to first language acquisition or to the simultaneous acquisition of two languages. Since circumstances surrounding a child's acquisition of a second language are clearly different from those of his first language, we felt that much could be learned by observing Paul Chen, a Chinese child who arrived in Los Angeles on December 13, 1969, as he acquired English as a second language.

Before Paul left Taiwan with his grandmother, he spoke only Taiwanese; he watched only Taiwanese TV programs; he had no exposure to English. It is likely that he first heard English during his air trip to Los Angeles. In Los Angeles, Paul lived with his grandmother, his parents (both of whom worked during the day), and his three-year-old brother. The two boys spent the day in the care of their maternal grandmother who did not speak English. They played at home; they were not encouraged to play with other children in the neighborhood. While there was a television set in the home, neither the grandmother nor the children watched it. Taiwanese was the language spoken in the home.

One month later, when Paul was 5 years, 1 month old, he was enrolled in a play-school with American children. For a four and a half month period (the 19-week period from January 22 to June 6) observational data was collected at the

---

* Huang, J., and E. Hatch, "A Chinese Child's Acquisition of English," in *Second Language Acquisition: A Book of Readings,* 1978, Newbury House. Reprinted by permission of the author.

school, 5 mornings a week from 9:00 to 11:30. In addition, there were 13 recorded sessions on weekends which totaled an additional 14 hours of data. Notes were also taken on utterances the informant made in the car on the way to and from school.

It seems important to emphasize the close observation throughout the study. Since the investigator (hereafter JH) was with Paul at all times when he could be exposed to English, exact information on time and order of acquisition of utterances could easily be established. The only other possible exposure to English would be with the parents during the evening. While they customarily spoke no English at home, it seems unlikely that they never spoke to Paul in English once he began to acquire the language.

The playschool schedule involved $1\frac{1}{2}$ hours of classroom activities, the rest of the morning being spent on the playground. Paul could easily participate during the classroom period (dancing, playing games, playing with toys, "singing," art work, and listening to stories) by observing and copying the activities of the other children. Language was not necessary. Indeed, the teacher did most of the talking. Therefore, he neither had the need nor the opportunity to speak. On the playground, the opportunity to talk was unlimited. The investigator was always within hearing distance both on the playground and during the classroom period, taking careful notes on Paul's utterances and his nonverbal responses to remarks of those around him. All events were noted as completely as time permitted in order to clarify the situational context. All notes and tapes were transcribed in regular orthography.

A number of questions had to be taken into consideration almost immediately in summarizing and analyzing the data if a true picture of language acquisition was to be obtained. For example, if during the first few days, Paul said "Mary had a little lamb," did he know the structure or how much did he know about it? Did he know the words or morphemes in the sentence or how many of them did he know? Did he know the meaning of the sentence, or how much did he know about it? It should be no surprise if he knew nothing about the structure and possibly nothing about the meaning for he might happen to repeat it in an echolalic fashion after the teacher without knowing anything about it at all. But it might also be possible that he had happened to meet a girl named Mary and thus knew what "Mary" was; that his mother happened to have shown him a picture of lambs and had taught him the word "lamb" without our knowing it. And, finally, someone might have paraphrased the sentence for him in his first language. All of these are highly unlikely but had to be taken into consideration in examining the data. Another question which had to be posed was: could he use or understand other sentences of similar structure? For example, was he responsive to, or could he say "I have a little lamb" or "Mary had a little dog." In other words, what evidence was there to indicate any knowledge of English in either the comprehension or production data? In the first month of the study, the analysis focused on these questions.

Paul's prompt non-verbal responses to verbal commands were frequently misleading. For example, on his second day at school, when his teacher (hereafter E) said, "Paul, would you like to sit there?" he smiled and sat down immediately. If he responded to any verbal cue at all it would be to "Paul." More likely he saw the other children seating themselves and E pointing to a chair as she spoke to him. His response was the expected one and could not be taken as evidence of sentence comprehension. He might also have been responding to intonation, though it seems unlikely in this case. During the first day at school, Paul nodded when E said, "Are you through now?" with an exaggerated rising intonation. Exaggeration was necessary to get this response at the beginning of the study. For example, after Paul returned from toilet, he was asked, "Have you washed your hands?" He gave no response. Yet, when the question was repeated later with exaggerated rising intonation, he responded immediately with a nod. Sometimes what might be considered a response to verbal command was, in fact, just something he happened to be in the act of doing. For instance, having parked the car, JH said "Open the door" and Paul moved to the door, opened it, and got out. But rather than Paul understanding the utterance and acting on it, JH himself, was actually labeling an act Paul would have performed anyway.

Global comprehension, however, was almost always quite clear. In the third day of the observation, Paul began muttering, "Get out of here" to himself. On the way home, he asked what it meant. When JH, instead of telling him, asked what had happened, Paul replied that a boy had said "ma-ai-den-me chia la" (don't be/stay here) to him. A day later Paul was on a tricycle. Another child, M., holding onto the handle bars, kept bothering him. In exasperation Paul shouted, "Get out of here!" Paul had learned the utterance as an unanalyzed unit. He knew the meaning of none of the words separately. When asked about the words, his response each time was "m-chai" (I don't know). Yet he understood its meaning in a global sense, stored it in memory, and recalled it for use in the appropriate situation.

There is no doubt that Paul learned words, phrases, and greetings by imitation (Table 1). In the first three weeks, most of these were imperatives, perhaps because they were used with great frequency in both teacher and peer language: "Get out of here! Let's go! Don't do that! Don't touch!" Statements said frequently, such as "It's time to eat and drink" (said every day before snack time) were also imitated. Frequency seems to be one clue as to which utterances would be imitated.

It was almost always true that once he had "memorized" such utterances, Paul used them either in identical situations or closely similar ones. Occasionally, Paul misinterpreted utterances. For example, after learning "good-bye" he heard and repeated "Good-bye, see you tomorrow" which he then produced, regardless of situation, as an extended form of good-bye.

Another example of wrong meaning assignment was "I'm finished" which Paul interpreted as "ngwa me lei-ke ah" (I want to go). One day, Paul and M. were doing easel painting. M. finished first, turned to E. and said, "I'm finished." When E. said, "Okay, you can go," M. took off her smock, put it away and went to play. After that, when he finished too, Paul said, "I'm finished," and was treated in the same way. His misunderstanding was not corrected but it is interesting that Paul used this structure only in the context of painting. Perhaps this is because the language cue was not recognized well enough to be separated from the specific situation. That is, in the first stage of learning, utterances were usually learned in conjunction with a repeated situation. It is possible that he felt that this "go" utterance applied only in this particular situation. Of course, it wasn't long before

TABLE 1   Imitation and rule formation examples

Week	Imitation	Rule Formed Utterances
2	Get out of here.*	
4	It's time to eat and drink* Let's go. Don't do that. Don't touch.	
6	Are you ready? See you tomorrow. Excuse me. Hold my hand.* Kenny, sit down.	This +++ kite. Yeah, that +++ bus. Ball +++ no.
7	Are you going too?* It's time to go home.* Here we go.* Scoot over.*	This +++ money? Paper +++ this. Cow +++ this. Mother +++ no. Tree +++ no. No +++ ball. Wash hand? Two cat.
8	I'll see you. You shut up. What do you like? Hi, how are you?* We are going home.	Kenny car. This good. This ball? This +++ boat. This +++ paper. No ice cream. No candy. Ball doggy?
9	How are you doing?* This is mine.	No money. No turtle. No more truck. Paul +++ baby. This +++ freeway. This not box.
10	Get out of here. Scoot over. All the birds up in the tree now that spring is coming . . . (singing)	

* = immediate repetition of another's speech, but later used in appropriate situations

he corrected his interpretation. By the end of the study he used "I'm finished" appropriately in many different circumstances.

This discussion of the problems of analysis may give an inaccurate picture of Paul's ability to imitate utterances of considerable length, to store and recall them for use in appropriate situations. In fact, he was so talented at mimicry, both verbal and non-verbal, that without careful checking in a variety of ways, it appeared that he understood almost everything that was said to him (see Table 1).

For the first month of observation, imitation appeared to be the sole method of language learning. If it were the only way, Paul would not have gotten very far. While he was very talented, it's unlikely that he could have memorized all the sentences he needed for communication, let alone associate them with the right contexts in which to use them.

It was no real surprise then, in the second month of observation, to find a second kind of utterance which clearly was not based on imitation. On March 3, Paul produced the utterance: "This +++ kite," the first indication of development of his own syntactic system for English. More examples of two-word utterances followed during the next few days. These data brought with them a new set of questions to be answered: 1. What is the difference between a sentence learned by imitation and an utterance formed through Paul's own syntactic system? What are the criteria for judging whether an utterance is the former or the latter?

2. Was imitation always the strategy applied first to produce new sentence types?
3. Did imitation continue to apply after he started his own syntactic system?
4. Did Paul's developing syntactic system reflect Taiwanese interference?

As mentioned earlier, Paul's imitated sentences were grammatical (he sounded like a native-speaker of English), and he was not aware of the smaller units within such utterances. He made no attempt to break up these sentences and recombine words into new sentences during the first month. While he said, "It's time to eat and drink" along with other children as juice and crackers were put on the table, he didn't say "It's time to" anything else. Conversely, it could be said that the criteria for judging utterances as of his own rule-formation, were familiarity with the smaller units and ill-formedness.

The first utterances of his own syntactic system (see Table 1) were: "This +++ kite." "Yeah, that +++ bus." "This +++ car." There is a pause between the two words and each is equally stressed so that it sounds neither like "this kite" in the sentence "This kite is bigger than that one" nor "I bought this kite yesterday." There is a distinct juncture between the two words with falling intonation on each word.

The first problem is to prove that the omission in these utterances is not simply due to faulty imitation. The most striking evidence is that Paul had already shown himself to be a flawless imitator. He did not omit the copula or article in such imitations as "If you have *a* nickel" or "All *the* birds sing up in *the* tree" or "Tha*t's* all right." He was clearly capable of hearing and reproducing word final consonant clusters and unstressed words. The fact that he paused between the two words "That +++ bus" indicates it is not an imitation of some utterance like "That's a bus." Moreover, none of the children in the playschool used the sort of two-word utterances with internal pause that Paul was producing. There is no possibility that Paul was imitating anyone else. He had no contact with children learning English as a first language who might be at the "two-word utterance" stage described by Bellugi, Braine, Bloom, and others, where sentences identical to Paul's would be typical.

Another problem was the possibility that these utterances were evidence that he was simply plugging English words into his first language system, a sort of reflexification process. The fact was that in Paul's Taiwanese dialect, the omission of the copula in the sentence $NP_1 + cop + NPx_2$ where NP_1 is a demonstrative pronoun is acceptable. However, in his dialect (that spoken in Southern Taiwan) the omission of the copula is optional in such sentences. Furthermore, the copula (*shi*) can only be deleted in affirmative sentences. And, it cannot be deleted where NP_1 is a proper N or a personal pronoun: Table 2 shows examples from Taiwanese, the predicted form if Paul were using Taiwanese syntax, and Paul's utterances. Paul did not follow the predicted forms. Two further points made us sure that these were not examples of Taiwanese interference. First, Paul's parents did not omit the copula in any of these forms, and felt there was something unacceptable about copula deletion *chen dzu* even where it was a grammatical optional form; secondly, the one time Paul was observed deleting the copula in Taiwanese, there was no pause between the two NP's.

We felt justified, then, in claiming that Paul, like American children learning English as a first language, was beginning to develop his own English syntactic

TABLE 2   Predicted two-word utterances based on Taiwanese

Taiwanese + Translation		Predicted English Form	Paul's Utterance
NP1 = demonstrative pronoun			
cheh shi dzu	This (is) book.	This kite.	this +++ kite
cheh dzu			
heh shi dzu	That (is) book.	That baby.	that +++ baby
he dzu			
cheh m shi dzu	This not is book.	This not is freeway.	this +++ not freeway
*che m dzu			
heh m shi dzu	That not is book.	That not is Brent.	that +++ not Brent
*heh m dzu			
NP2 = personal pronoun			
ni shi sien-sen	You are teacher.	You are Edmond.	you +++ Edmond
*ni sien-sen			
ngwa m shi sien-sen	You not are teacher.	You not are truck.	you +++ not truck
*ngwa m sien-sen			
NP1 = proper noun			
Bun-dao shi ngin-nan	Bundao is boy.	Bozo is clown.	Bozo +++ clown
*Bun-dao ngin-nan			
Bun-dao m shi ngin-nan	Bundao not is boy.	Brent not is baby.	Brent +++ not baby
*Bun-dao m ngin-nan			

* = ungrammatical sentence

system. In the literature on first language acquisition, the two-word utterance has been explained in a number of ways. One explanation is that memory span and physical ability are not developed enough for the child to produce more than two words in a string. However, in this study, we have similar data even though Paul obviously had the physiological ability and the memory necessary to repeat much longer utterances. For example, at the same time he said "This +++ kite" he could also say such things as "Okay, this is your turn" or "I want to open the window." And of course, he spoke much longer sentences in Taiwanese.

As in the literature on first language acquisition, it was frequently difficult to establish the exact meaning of Paul's rule-formation utterances. For example "ball +++ doggy?" might mean the ball belonged to the doggy or it might be a question as to whether or not Paul could give the ball to the doggy. The tapes, even with context given, do not always help in clarifying meaning:

JH: Throw the ball to me. (P does.) Good. Now give it to Joe.

P: Joe, this +++ ball? Ball +++ doggy?

JH: No.

The following transcription shows the confusion even more clearly:

P: Lookit. (He had written his name and wanted JH to look at it.)

JH: Now, Paul.

P: You +++ Joe, Okay?

JH: Right. My name is Joe. Do you want me to write down my name?

P: Yeah.

The response shows that JH does not know the relationship between "You +++ Joe, okay?"—"You are Joe, okay?" or "You write 'Joe,' okay?" so he responded to both and both were accepted by Paul.

Paul quickly moved on from the two-word stage to more sophisticated rules. While a full report of Paul's second language acquisition is beyond the scope of this paper, Table 1 gives some notion of this development. Table 3 shows one part of his syntactic system: the development of interrogative structures through both imitation and rule formation techniques.

Before discussing Paul's interrogative structures, it might be wise to look at the input of questions asked him by peers and adults. During the first month, few questions were asked him. His responses were cued, as discussed earlier, by intonation, gestures, and context. During the second month, he was deluged with

TABLE 3 Production of question forms

Stage 1

X: Table? This? Walk? Wash hands? Two cat?

A_1 Question repetition
What do you like? How are you doing? What are you doing? What's my name?

B_1 Questions learned via imitation
Are you ready? Are you going too? Hi, how are you? What? What's that? What's your name? Where's Bobby? Which way?

C_1 Rule application. (Q = rising intonation)
This +++ slipper? Joe, this +++ ball? Ball +++ doggy? Okay? Fish +++ see?

Stage 2

A_2 Question repetition
Which one? Where are you going?

B_2 Questions learned via imitation
What's this? Whose is this? This one? That one? What now?

C_3 Rule application (Q = rising intonation; where's, what's, whose are question markers, "okay" is a tag question marker)

a   This +++ orange? This +++ you? This +++ not truck? This +++ yours book?

b   Where's Kenny? Where's pen? Where's car? Where's Teddy's car? Whose truck?

c   This is my book? This is jacket? This is flower?

Stage 3

B_3 May I be excused?

C   Rule application (addition of can questions, how many, color, and be-inversion)

a   Can K have some juice? Teddy, can I play? Can I write my name? Jim, can you play with the ball?

b   You put the belt on? You see a flag? B is a boy? You want this one?

c   Is this yours house? Are you a good boy? What am I doing?

"What's this/that?" and "Is this a *Noun?*" questions. He responded to these by nodding or shaking his head, saying yes, no, I don't know, or supplying a noun.

Three other question forms appeared with great frequency.

1. The "do you want" (d'yawana) question:

$$
\text{Do you want to} \left\{ \begin{array}{l} \text{go home} \\ \text{take off your jacket} \\ \text{make a picture} \\ \text{help us} \\ \text{eat that} \\ \text{fall down} \end{array} \right\} ?
$$

2. The "can you" (kə̃nyə) question:

$$
\text{Can you} \left\{ \begin{array}{l} \text{kick it} \\ \text{button it up} \\ \text{drive a truck} \\ \text{say "teacher"} \\ \text{see K over there} \end{array} \right\} ?
$$

It is doubtful if Paul responded to the "do you want" or "can you" signal. He only needed the intonation to know that it was a question. The rest of the utterance was exactly the same as the imperatives that formed the largest part of the language input.

3. The "where's _____?" question. This is labeled as "where's" rather than "where" since it always occurred with the copula contracted

$$
\text{"Where's} \left\{ \begin{array}{l} \text{the} \\ \text{your} \end{array} \right\} \text{NOUN?"}
$$

To these questions, Paul customarily repeated the noun and found it or pointed to it.

"Okay" was used as a tag question during this period (e.g., "You just listen, okay?").

During the first stage (months 1 and 2) Paul responded appropriately to most questions including less frequent *which, who,* and *whose* questions. He also showed that he did not understand the following questions:

3/22 If it isn't a balloon, what is it? (no response)

3/22 Paul, tell us what you're doing? (no response)

One yes/no question was not understood, though it's not clear whether it was a vocabulary problem with "through" or the question form that he misunderstood (he answered other "are you" questions quickly and accurately).

3/1 Paul, are you through now? (looks puzzled)
   Are you through with the ball? (Through?)
   Are you through with it? (Yah.)

During the third month (labeled stage 2) Paul continued to be barraged with "What's this/that?" and Is this a *Noun?* questions, "do you want" and "can you?" questions. *Who/whose* questions were asked more frequently. The most dramatic increase was in the number of "What are you doing?" questions and the "Are you *verb*ing" prompt. Many of these were in an attempt to see if he had acquired the present continuous verb forms, but they also seemed to occur much more frequently in natural conversations than previously. The "How many" question was also added as Paul quickly learned English numbers.

Questions were responded to appropriately with few exceptions. However, Paul had also learned to evade questions by ignoring them, changing the subject or saying "I don't know.":

What happened to your face there? (I don't know.)
What happened? (No.)
Where are you going? (no response)
Where are you going? (no response)
Where did you go? (no response)
Did you go outside? (No.)

One *why* question, a negative, also appears in the data and it was not responded to: Why don't you go to the fence? Questions asked during this second stage included: yes/no, do-inversion, can-inversion, what-doing, where, who-whose, how many, which, why, and tag questions with "okay."

In the final month, the complexity of all questions increased markedly. For example, *what*-questions included the following:

What's this/that?
What's the time now? (It's time to go.)
What's the baby doing? (Sleep. Sleeping.)
What are you going to take home? (This and this.)
What is it that you want? (I want this, please.)

Would questions suddenly increased, largely replacing *can*:

Paul, would you $\left\{\begin{array}{l}\text{give me one please}\\\text{come and sit here}\\\text{teach her how to write your name}\\\text{help E}\end{array}\right\}$?

Perhaps no one doubted his ability any longer so that *can you* questions no longer seemed as appropriate as *would you.*

With few exceptions, all questions were responded to appropriately. Color questions were new:

5/10 Is this whistle black? (no response)

5/10 What color is this? (no response)

However, ten days later he could respond to such question forms:

5/20 Is this table dirty? (Yes. Dirty.)

5/20 What color is M using? (Yellow)

5/20 What color are you going to use? (I want red.)

Why questions were still not responded to:

E: Why did you give your picture to me? (no response)

Do you want me to keep it? (Yes.)

It is possible that Paul did not understand the why/because relationship even though he had the concept in his first language. It might also be that he simply had no definite reason in mind when asked "why" by various peers and adults.

If-then conditionals were responded to with great accuracy, surprisingly enough:

JH: Ask E if you can have this one.

P: E, can I have this one?

JIM: If I give Paul one and give Joe one then how many will you have?

P: One.

JH: Can you write your name if you don't have a pencil?

P: No.

Turning then to Paul's production of questions, Table 3 shows the data divided into three stages: stage one being months 1 and 2; stage 2, month 3; and stage 3, month 4.

In stage one, Paul immediately identified rising intonation as a question signal. Utterances listed under X in Table 3 are words repeated from statements made to him but with rising intonation.

JIM: Take the pencil. (Paul: Pencil?)

JIM: No, Paul, this way, please, this way. (This way?)

JH: Paul, have you washed your hands? (P: Wash hands?)

In the table, A1 utterances are echoed questions which he repeated immediately after someone asked him the question. Usually he did not understand the question. Later, however, some of the questions he repeated earlier occur under

B1. That is, he remembered the questions and used them appropriately later (usually after hearing them in context a number of times).

The utterances under C1 are questions which Paul formed himself. The rule at stage one is that questions are formed by adding rising intonation to statements: "This +++ ball?"

Stage 2 covers the third month of observation. It is difficult to find many direct imitations of questions. He did mutter "whose? whose?" to himself after being asked a "whose" question, but "Whose" questions also appeared in his delayed imitation questions as well (B2). It is also difficult to separate B2 and C2 questions. In addition to the "This +++ ball?" question type, Paul added "What's" and "Where's" questions. He did not go through the "What +++ this?" or "Where +++ Bobby?" typical of first language acquisition of English. The copula was never deleted. Since he heard so many "what's" and "where's" questions, it appears he learned these by imitation and the *'s* was not the copula but part of the interrogative word. While he learned the question form by imitation, he soon began substituting new nouns freely following the interrogative marker. Evidence that the "where's" question also involved his own rule-formation rather than just straight memorization is the missing article in the questions:

$$\text{Where's} \begin{Bmatrix} \text{pen} \\ \text{car} \\ \text{turtle} \end{Bmatrix} ?$$

While he learned to form such questions by a combination of imitation and rule-formation, it is clear that they were learned as non-transformational routines. He did not go through a stage of learning to front the interrogative word, then acquire subject-verb inversion, then contract the copula.

The copula began to appear in his "This +++ kite" sentences at the very end of this stage. It appeared in both statement and questions:

This yours book?- - -This *is* my school?
This *is* yours school?

At this point the contracted *'s* on "where's" and "what's" questions was also separated:

Where's ball?- - -Where *is* ball?
Where *is* my hot-wheel?

Only at this point could we be sure that the *'s* ending was not just part of the interrogative word.

In the final period of the study, the rules of stages 1 and 2 continued. Rising intonation had been the most powerful strategy for question formation up to this point but during the month gradually more and more subject-verb inversion took place.

As mentioned before, *where's, what's, whose* questions were learned as inverted forms to begin with. *Can* questions, with can-inversion, were also learned this way. Again, Paul did not pass through a non-inverted stage. He did not say such things as "I can play?" He had, of course, been subjected to three months of "can you/can I?" questions so again, it is not surprising that this word order was learned via imitation.

Since *can, where's,* and *what's* questions were learned in this manner, it is a puzzle why other questions involving inversion were not imitated too. Paul was asked many "do you . . . ?" "Are you . . . ?" "Is this . . . ?" questions daily. He never imitated a "do you . . . ?" question. He persisted in using rising intonation for all questions with *be* or requiring *do*-support:

You don't want to go?

This is my name?

Jim is coming too?

He did imitate "are you . . . ?" questions; in fact, his first question was an imitated "Are you ready?" Yet he did not generalize from his imitated questions with copula inversion. Instead he went through three stages of rules: 1. rising intonation "This +++ kite?" 2. copula addition "This is flower?" 3. copula inversion "Is this yours house?"

There seems to be no ready answer as to why some questions were learned by imitation and others were not. Perhaps there is something particularly difficult about recognizing the copula and do-support in English (and not about recognizing *can,* and the interrogative words). Slobin has suggested that grammatical markers carrying some semantic content will be learned earlier than those with little, if any, semantic function. Perhaps this is a possible explanation for slow acquisition of the copula and do-inversion rules.

Again, the production data seems to underrate Paul's ability to communicate with question and response. At the end of the study it appeared that his language was indistinguishable from that of the American children with whom he played. No attempt was made to elicit do-inversion questions from him but he responded to them and to much more complicated question forms with ease.

The question forms show that Paul used two main strategies in learning his second language: imitation and rule formation. It also showed that the two strategies overlapped once he began to recognize segments of sentences which he had originally learned as single units.

Paul's language development differed from that of a child learning a first language in some important aspects. He already had experience with one natural language system and this helped him in the analysis of meaning and of syntax. He was capable, as younger children are not, of imitating amazingly complex sentences almost from the start and to attach a global meaning to them. It took Paul four months to learn as much language as a child would normally learn in two or three years. In 19 weeks Paul learned a second language without formal "language classes." And he learned it with much less exposure to English than first language learners normally get.

At the end of the nineteen weeks, our appreciation of the child's ability to learn language without formal instruction had increased tremendously. We also appreciated how difficult it is to find answers to such questions as: How is a child able to hear, repeat, store, and recall sentences of considerable length and complexity with perfect phonetic detail when imitating sentences in the new language? How can he recall these utterances in the appropriate context seemingly without effort? How does he recognize the structure of the new language as different from that of his first language? Why doesn't he simply treat the new language as new vocabulary to be plugged into the syntax he has already created for his first language? Why are some structures in the new language learned by imitation while other similar structures are not? As in most basic research, our knowledge has increased in that we have identified a number of questions for which we have no immediate answer. Much more data will have to be examined in order to find answers and to place the questions in their respective places in the study of second language acquisition.

THEORY AND IMPLICATIONS

1. How does this reading modify your view of the role of imitation in language learning? Does it conflict with views in earlier readings or is it complementary? Explain.
2. Given that such factors as intonation and use of here-and-now contextual clues influence language learning, what is the problem with assuming an immediate correspondence between such clues and language output?
3. What clues indicate the development of a child's own syntactic system through rule formation? Do you think we need to postulate a language acquisition device to account for such development? Why?
4. The ill-formedness of Paul's syntax actually indicates his increasing use of rule formation. What implications do you see in this fact for teachers' response to error?
5. The arguments for Paul's developing his own grammar and not simply illustrating interference from Taiwanese are based on a comparison of Taiwanese rules and Paul's English production (Table 2). Looking carefully at the evidence, explain how Paul did not use the forms predicted by a theory of interference. Do you think this evidence rules out interference completely? Explain.
6. How is Paul's development of L2 syntax like and unlike the development of L1 syntax?
7. What sources of error does Paul illustrate other than overgeneralization? Are there any pedagogical implications that derive from these sources?

PROFESSIONAL CONCERNS

1. Which interference theory and L1 theory assumptions about how children acquire a second language does this case study refute? How? Explain in a professional journal.
2. Write a letter to your principal or other interested party on the complexity of an L2 acquirer's use of imitation and rule formation. Indicate why your reader should be interested in such information.

Underachievement Among Minority Students*

JIM CUMMINS

Jim Cummins is a major spokesperson for minority language children. This reading, from his book Bilingualism and Special Education, *distinguishes between factors that do and do not contribute to minority children's underachievement. It explains Cummins's key threshold hypothesis and his criticism of the home-school mismatch theory and insufficient exposure theory. Concerned with the relationship between bilingualism and academic success, he reviews earlier research on bilingualism, which in the 1960s was considered a source of academic confusion and difficulty. He cites more recent studies, most of which show positive correlations between bilingualism and intellectual development. In arguing that factors other than bilingualism cause underachievement, in particular social and educational factors, Cummins familiarizes readers with such important distinctions as Lambert's "subtractive" versus "additive" bilingualism and Ogbu's "autonomous," "caste," and "immigrant" minorities.*

Although much research now supports Cummins's work, his theories remain hypothetical and in some cases openly challenged. In particular, his theory of a higher threshold of language proficiency (specific level for generating cognitive benefits) and the implication that the threshold causes competence are unsubstantiated; some research indicates that cognitive benefits accrue before Cummins's threshold. Other research challenges his notion that universal cognitive faculties affect the development of literacy across languages. Nonetheless, Cummins's views have had immense impact: They support development of strong first language skills; they have changed reclassification criteria for transferring students from bilingual to English-only programs and placement criteria for avoiding relegating minority students to remedial classes; and they have contributed to the development of a new theoretical framework for bilingual education based on a distinction between communicative competence and cognitive academic competence. Indirectly, his theories have underscored the need for whole task (not discrete skill) approaches to teaching minority students, especially those with learning problems.

In more recent work Cummins has emphasized the importance of addressing social power relationships, to help minority students take control of their education. Thus, he continues to integrate cognitive theories and social factors.

A considerable number of explanatory hypotheses have been suggested to account for the underachievement of minority students. For example, minority underachievement has been regarded as a function of (a) bilingualism, (b) lack of exposure to the school language, (c) linguistic mismatch between home and

---

* Cummins, J., "Underachievement Among Minority Students," in *Bilingualism and Special Education*, 1984, Multilingual Matters, Ltd., Avon, England. Reprinted by permission of the publisher.

school, (d) cultural mismatch between home and school, (e) inferior quality of education provided to minority students, (f) factors associated with socio-economic status, and (g) disrupted patterns of inter-generational cultural transmission as a result of majority-minority group status relations.

Many of these variables are undoubtedly related to patterns of minority group achievement. For example, minority children are unlikely to perform adequately in English if their exposure to English has been minimal. However, few of these variables, considered in isolation, provide a firm basis for educational policy decisions. This is because, for the most part, their effects are not consistent across different contexts as a result of their interactions with other variables. It will be suggested, however, that although no completely satisfactory theory is currently available, it is possible to resolve many of the apparent inconsistencies in the data and that a partial basis for educational policy with regard to minority students can be provided. Each of the proposed explanatory constructs are considered in turn.

BILINGUALISM AS AN EXPLANATORY VARIABLE

The Myth of Bilingual Handicaps

In the United States, many minority children with severe academic difficulties are educated in monolingual English programs on the recommendation of special education personnel because it is felt that these children's learning problems will be further complicated if they are required to cope with two languages of instruction. The assumption is similar to that stated in a brief by the Association of (English-speaking) Catholic Principals of Montreal (1969) opposing the spread of French immersion programs:

> We are of the opinion that the average child cannot cope with two languages of instruction and to try to do so leads to insecurity, language interference, and academic retardation (quoted in Lambert & Tucker, 1972: 5).

This opinion is more than just an intuitive assumption. In fact, it draws on the findings of a large body of research conducted in a variety of contexts since the 1920s which suggested that bilingualism exerted a negative influence on children's academic development. The image of bilingualism as a negative force in children's development was especially common prior to the 1960s when most teachers of minority language children saw bilingualism almost as a disease which not only caused confusion in children's thinking but also prevented them from becoming "good Americans" or "good Canadians." Therefore, they felt that a precondition for teaching children the school language was the eradication of their bilingualism. Thus, children were often punished for speaking their L1 in school and were made to feel ashamed of their own language and cultural background. It is not surprising that research studies conducted during this period often found that bilingual children did poorly at school and many experienced emotional conflicts. Children were made to feel that it was necessary to reject the home culture in order to belong to the majority culture and often ended up unable to identify fully with either cultural group.

Most of the studies carried out prior to the 1960s involved minority group bilinguals and investigators tended to interpret the research findings as though "bilingualism" were the independent variable which led directly to a variety of unfortunate consequences. Jensen (1962a) summarized the findings of the early "negative" studies as follows:

> Many observers and investigators conclude that childhood bilingualism, forced or voluntary, results in many disadvantages. Numerous handicaps may accrue to the individual in his speech development, overall language development, intellectual and educational progress, and emotional stability. In addition, society may suffer many disadvantages. (1962a: 133)

The specific intellectual, educational and personal disadvantages of childhood bilingualism, according to more than 200 studies reviewed by Jensen, are summarized in the following extracts:

> *(a) intellectual development:*
> It is said that the bilingual child will tend to learn only by imitation and rote, that he will frequently suffer mental fatigue, and that his originality of thought will be impaired. He will be handicapped on intelligence tests, especially on those demanding language facility. (1962a: 135)

> *(b) educational progress:*
> His interest and aptitude in language learning will be adversely affected. He may become handicapped in reading and studying in general . . . His interest, initiative and responsiveness in class may decline, and he may develop an inadequate adjustment to school and education in general, which in turn may result in his prematurely dropping out of school. (1962a: 136)

> *(c) personal adjustment:*
> Losing his self-confidence and sense of security, he may develop extreme introversion and shyness or he may become very aggressive and antisocial. He may become schizophrenic, for most bilinguals, according to Christophersen (1948, p. 9), feel a "pull in opposite directions which threatens the unity of their personality." Much of the emotional stress and tension will center in the family. After being exposed to a second language in school, the child may develop a sense of shame and guilt regarding the language of his family and may direct this into feelings of arrogance, contempt, hatred, rejection and avoidance towards his parents. (1962a: 136)

Other reviews of the early literature on the consequences of bilingualism note similar trends in the findings (e.g. Darcy, 1953; Diebold, 1968; Macnamara, 1966; Vildomec, 1963). Vildomec (1963: 32) even mentions some investigations which claimed that bilinguals were morally untrustworthy! Although a handful of studies suggested some positive consequences as a result of childhood bilingualism (see e.g. Vernon Jensen, 1962b), the overwhelming trend was in the opposite direction.

To most current investigators these negative findings have little credibility because of severe methodological problems in a large majority of studies. Failure to control for factors such as SES [Socioeconomic Status], urban-rural differences and language of testing render most of the findings uninterpretable (see e.g. Cummins, 1976; Peal & Lambert, 1962). Nevertheless, many of these early negative findings have a contemporary ring. For example, a considerable number of studies have reported lower performance on verbal IQ tests by minority language students, whether tested in L1 or L2 (see e.g. Kaufman, 1979 for a review; also Novak, 1973); the poor academic performance of many minority language students has been widely documented (e.g. Coleman *et al.,* 1966; Skutnabb-Kangas & Toukomaa, 1976), and severe problems of adjustment among minority students are often observed by educators and social workers (see e.g. Coehlo, 1976; Duran, 1978). The point at issue is not so much the presence of these phenomena in some (but by no means all) bilingual learning situations but rather their attribution to bilingualism *per se,* instead of to the social and educational conditions under which minority students acquire their two languages.

The fact that educators and researchers were so ready to make minority children's bilingualism the scapegoat for their academic difficulties can be understood in the context of the "Anglo-conformity"/melting pot philosophy which pervaded North American schools until recently. The commitment to assimilation of minorities was so strong that the school treatment of minority students was taken for granted and not subjected to scrutiny in relation to students' academic, intellectual or personal difficulties. These difficulties were usually attributed to some deficiency within the child. Various "scientific" explanations were suggested as to why minority students tended to perform poorly at school; for example, confusion in thinking due to bilingualism, cultural deprivation and even genetic inferiority. Research showing that bilingual children performed lower on verbal IQ tests than monolingual children was interpreted by many researchers and educators to mean that there is only so much space or capacity available in our brains for language; therefore, if we divide that space between two languages, neither language will develop properly and intellectual confusion will result. This self-perpetuating pattern of "blaming the victim" (Ryan, 1972), is outlined in Table 1.[1]

Bilingualism as a Positive Force in Children's Academic Development

A large majority of studies carried out since the Peal & Lambert study in 1962 have consistently reported cognitive advantages associated with bilingualism. For example, children in French immersion programs in Canada have been found to

TABLE 1 Blaming the victim in minority language education*

A. *Overt Aim*	*Covert Aim*	D.	*Outcomes*
Teach English to minority children in order to create a harmonious society with equal opportunity for all	Anglicize minority children because linguistic and cultural diversity are seen as a threat to social cohesion		—The failure of these efforts only serves to reinforce the myth of minority group deficiencies
		—Even more intense efforts by the school to eradicate the deficiencies inherent in minority children	
B. *Method*	*Justification*	C. *Results*	*"Scientific" Explanation*
Prohibit use of L1 in schools and make children reject their own culture and language in order to identify with majority English group	1. L1 should be eradicated because it will interfere with the learning of English; 2. Identification with L1 culture will reduce child's ability to identify with English-speaking culture	1. Shame in L1 language and culture 2. Replacement of L1 by L2 3. School failure among many children	1. Bilingualism causes confusion in thinking, emotional insecurity and school failure 2. Minority group children are "culturally deprived" (almost by definition since they are not Anglos) 3. Some minority language groups are genetically inferior (common theory in the U.S. in 1920s and 1930s).

* This table reflects the assumptions of North American school systems in the first half of this century. However, similar assumptions have been made about minority language children in the school systems of many other countries.

perform better than comparison groups in some academic and cognitive skills (see Swain & Lapkin, 1982). A positive association has also been found between bilingualism and aspects of both cognitive flexibility (Balkan, 1970; Duncan & De Avila, 1979; Hakuta & Diaz, 1983; Kessler & Quinn, 1980; Mohanty, 1982) and divergent or "creative" thinking abilities (Cummins & Gulutsan, 1974; Scott, 1973) and some studies have reported that bilingual children are more advanced in general intellectual development than are unilingual children (Bain, 1975; Liedke & Nelson, 1968; Peal & Lambert, 1962). There is also evidence that bilingual children are better able to analyze linguistic meaning and are more sensitive to aspects of interpersonal communication than unilingual children (Bain, 1975; Bain & Yu, 1980; Ben-Zeev, 1977a, 1977b; Cummins, 1978a; Cummins & Mulcahy, 1978; Feldman & Shen, 1971; Genesee, Tucker & Lambert, 1975; Ianco-Worall, 1972; Merino, 1983; Rueda, 1983).

In their analysis of neuropsychological research on "The Bilingual Brain," Albert & Obler (1979) conclude that

> Bilinguals mature earlier than monolinguals both in terms of cerebral lateralization for language and in acquiring skills for linguistic abstraction. Bilinguals have better developed auditory language skills than monolinguals, but there is no clear evidence that they differ from monolinguals in written skills. (1979: 248)

These trends in the research are not at all surprising when one considers that bilingual children have been exposed to considerably more "training" in analyzing and interpreting language than unilingual children. The possibility of a greater analytic orientation to language in bilingual children is consistent with the view of Vygotsky (1962) who argued that being able to express the same thought in different languages will enable the child to "see his language as one particular system among many, to view its phenomena under more general categories, and this leads to awareness of his linguistic operations" (p. 110). Lambert & Tucker (1972) argued that a similar process was likely to operate among children in immersion programs. They suggested that as children develop high level bilingual skills they are likely to practice a form of "incipient contrastive linguistics" by comparing the syntax and vocabulary of their two languages.

It should be pointed out that the validity of these recent "positive" findings is not accepted by all investigators. McNab (1979), for example, has criticized research design, control variables and sample selection procedures in several of these studies. McLaughlin (1984) takes an intermediate position in a recent comprehensive review, arguing that although bilinguals appear to experience linguistic advantages, the evidence for cognitive advantages is inconclusive:

> It seems clear that the child who has mastered two languages has a linguistic advantage over the monolingual child. Bilingual children become aware that there are two ways of saying the same thing. But does this sensitivity to the lexical and formal aspects of language generalize to cognitive functioning? There is no conclusive answer to this

question—mainly because it has proven so difficult to apply the necessary controls in research.

McLaughlin's conclusion is consistent with the findings of Rueda's (1983) study among mildly retarded bilingual and monolingual students matched for IQ (mean age approximately 12 years). Rueda reported that the bilingual students had developed a greater awareness of some metalinguistic aspects of language but no differences were found on Piagetian measures of cognitive development. This latter finding is not entirely surprising in view of the fact that bilingual and monolingual students were matched on IQ.

In short, there is evidence for some subtle metalinguistic advantages associated with bilingualism but the extent to which these give rise to generalized *cognitive* advantages has not been adequately resolved.[2] In the next section the conditions under which bilingualism is associated with different linguistic and cognitive outcomes are examined.

Additive and Subtractive Bilingualism and the Threshold Hypothesis

Lambert (1975) pointed out that a large majority of early studies were carried out with immigrant or minority language children whose L1 was gradually being replaced by a dominant and more prestigious L2. He terms the resulting form of bilingualism "subtractive" in that bilingual children's proficiency in their two languages at any point in time is likely to reflect some stage in the subtraction of L1 and its replacement by L2. Some research studies (Skutnabb-Kangas & Toukomaa, 1976) suggest that proficiency in L1 declines more rapidly than L2 proficiency is developed; however, considerable variation across social and educational contexts is likely in this regard. For present purposes, it is sufficient to note the subtractive character of the bilingualism developed by minority students who tend to experience academic difficulties and the fact that among these students proficiency in *both* languages is likely to be less well developed in some respects than among native speakers of each.

Lambert contrasts the subtractive bilingualism of many minority language children with the "additive" bilingualism generally achieved by children whose L1 is dominant and prestigious and in no danger of replacement by L2. The bilingualism of these children (e.g. anglophone children in French immersion programs) is termed "additive" since another socially relevant language is being added to the bilingual's repertory of skills at no cost to proficiency in L1. In addition to children from dominant language backgrounds, children from subordinate language backgrounds can also develop an additive form of bilingualism when their L1 is strongly promoted in the school. A large majority of studies reporting cognitive advantages associated with bilingualism have been carried out in contexts where children have attained an additive form of bilingualism, that is, relatively high levels of proficiency in both languages.

This analysis suggests that the levels of proficiency bilingual children attain in their two languages may be an important intervening variable mediating the effects of bilingualism on children's cognitive and academic development. Specifically, it has been hypothesized that there may be threshold levels of linguistic proficiency bilingual children must attain in order to avoid cognitive deficits and allow the potentially beneficial aspects of becoming bilingual to influence cognitive growth. The threshold hypothesis assumes that those aspects of bilingualism that might positively influence cognitive growth are unlikely to come into effect until children have attained a certain minimum or threshold level of proficiency in the second language. Similarly, if bilingual children attain only a very low level of proficiency in one or both of their languages, their long-term interaction with their academic environment through these languages, both in terms of input and output, is likely to be impoverished.[3]

The form of the threshold hypothesis that seems to be most consistent with the available data is that there are two thresholds (Cummins, 1976; Toukomaa & Skutnabb-Kangas, 1977). The attainment of a lower threshold level of bilingual proficiency would be sufficient to avoid any negative effects; but the attainment of a second, higher level of bilingual proficiency might be necessary to lead to accelerated cognitive growth.

Since this hypothesis was originally formulated (Cummins, 1976), several studies have reported findings consistent with its general tenets (Cummins & Mulcahy, 1978; Duncan & DeAvila, 1979; Hakuta & Diaz, 1983; Kessler & Quinn, 1980). Duncan & DeAvila (1979), for example, found that minority students who had developed high levels of L1 and L2 proficiency (proficient bilinguals) performed significantly better than monolinguals and other sub-groups of bilinguals (partial [i.e. high in one language] and limited [i.e. low in both languages] bilinguals) on a battery of cognitive tasks. Kessler & Quinn (1980) found that Hispanic bilingual students who had been in a bilingual programme performed significantly better than monolinguals on a science problem-solving task, while Cummins & Mulcahy (1978) found that Ukrainian–English bilingual students who spoke Ukrainian at home and received 50% instruction through Ukrainian were better able to detect ambiguities in English sentence structure than were monolingual English-speaking students. Hakuta & Diaz carried out a longitudinal study among Hispanic kindergarten and grade 1 students in a transitional bilingual program in order to assess both the extent to which level of bilingual proficiency was related to non-verbal intellectual development (measured by Raven's Progressive Matrices) and the direction of causality if a relationship were found. Their findings suggested that level of bilingual proficiency positively influenced rate of intellectual development.

Although the threshold hypothesis is generally consistent with the research data and has had considerable heuristic impact, it does not elaborate on the nature of the language proficiencies that comprise the thresholds nor on the relationships that exist between the development of L1 and L2 proficiency. These issues are considered in the next chapter.

In summary, the research findings clearly refute the assumption that bilingualism *per se* is a cause of minority students' academic difficulties. Rather, it is the failure to develop students' L1 for conceptual and analytic thought that contributes to "cognitive confusion." When minority students' L1 proficiency is strongly promoted by the school program, the resulting additive bilingualism appears to entail some subtle linguistic and possibly cognitive benefits.

For special educators concerned with minority students whose academic self-concept is frequently low, it is particularly important to communicate effectively to them that their bilingualism is a special achievement to be valued and developed. Unfortunately, it has frequently been the case that special educators have contributed to the development of subtractive bilingualism by communicating the opposite message to minority students and by recommending that they be educated exclusively through their weaker language (English).

PATTERNS OF EXPOSURE TO THE SCHOOL LANGUAGE

The opposing conventional wisdoms around which the bilingual education debate in the United States has revolved can be termed the "maximum exposure" and "linguistic mismatch" assumptions. The first assumption is frequently invoked against bilingual education for minority students and consists of the argument that limited English proficient students need as much exposure to English as possible. The second assumption is that a home-school language switch or "linguistic mismatch" will almost inevitably result in academic retardation since children cannot learn in a language they do not understand. Paradoxically, although the linguistic mismatch assumption is used to argue for bilingual education, it could equally be used by opponents of bilingual education to argue that minority parents should be encouraged to switch to English in the home, thereby increasing exposure to English and eliminating linguistic mismatch.

Despite the obvious intuitive appeal of each of these theoretical assumptions, they are refuted, as general principles, by an enormous amount of research evidence. There are many examples of successful academic development under home-school language switch conditions and virtually all the empirical data show that there is no direct relationship between exposure to the majority language in a bilingual program and achievement in that language. Similarly, data regarding language use in the homes of bilingual children refute both the maximum exposure and linguistic mismatch assumptions. The data from bilingual program evaluations and home language use studies are briefly considered in turn.

Bilingual Program Evaluations

Currently, there are more than 100,000 Canadian students in various kinds of French immersion programs in which a large proportion of initial instructional time is spent through the medium of students' second language, i.e. French. Evaluations from across Canada have consistently shown that although immersion students tend to lag behind their monolingual peers in English language arts until formal English instruction is introduced, they very quickly catch up and may even surpass their peers by grade 5 or 6 (see Swain & Lapkin, 1982).

The immersion data refute both the linguistic mismatch and maximum exposure assumptions, the former because students perform well academically under home-school language switch conditions, and the latter because there is no relationship between the amount of instruction through English and achievement in English.

Similarly, evaluations of bilingual programs for minority students in Canada (see Cummins, 1983 for a review), the United States (reviewed by Baker & de Kanter, 1981; Troike, 1978), Sweden (e.g. Löfgren & Ouvinen-Birgerstam, 1982), Ireland (Cummins, 1978b), Holland (Altena & Appel, 1982), Wales (Wijnstra, 1980), Australia (Gale, McClay, Christie & Harris, 1981), Mexico (Modiano, 1968) and many other countries report that students taught through a minority language for all or part of the school day perform at least as well (and in many cases better) in majority language academic skills as equivalent students taught through the majority language for all or most of the school day. In some cases there is a slight initial lag in the development of majority language academic skills but this usually disappears by the middle grades of elementary school and in many cases the bilingually-instructed students have shown superior performance by the end of elementary school (see Cummins, 1983, and Troike, 1978, for reviews).

In short, the evaluation data clearly show the inadequacy of the maximum exposure and linguistic mismatch hypotheses. That these two conventional wisdoms continue to dominate the U.S. bilingual education debate is a sad reflection on the disjunction between policy and research. As pointed out earlier, a major reason for this disjunction is that the role of theory has been forgotten.

L1 Development in the Home

Several studies show that the use of a minority language in the home is not, in itself, a handicap to children's academic progress (Carey & Cummins, 1983; Cummins & Mulcahy, 1978; Dolson, 1984; National Assessment of Educational Progress, 1983a; Spence, Mishra & Ghozeil, 1971; Yee & Laforge, 1974). This fact is evident from the pattern of findings in the Toronto Board surveys discussed earlier. There is evidence, in fact, that in some situations exclusive use of the majority language in the home may be associated with poor academic progress in that language (e.g. Bhatnagar, 1980; Chesarek, 1981). Bhatnagar, for example, examined the academic progress of 171 Italian immigrant children in English language elementary schools in Montreal and 102 in French language schools in relation to language spoken at home and with friends and siblings. He summarized his findings as follows:

> The results reported here do not support the popular assumption that the more immigrant children speak the local language the better their adjustment to the host culture. It is interesting to note that immigrant children who used Italian and a Canadian language interchangeably were better even at English or French, or both the spoken and written variety, than children who used English or French all the time. . . . Language retention . . . should lead to higher academic adjustment, better facility in the host language, and better social relations of immigrant children. (1980: 153–155)

Bhatnagar (1980) also reported that immigrant students who used L1 exclusively with parents and siblings also performed significantly worse than those who used both L1 and L2. However, it seems likely that this finding can be attributed to the fact that only those students who had immigrated relatively recently would use L1 exclusively. Length of residence is not considered in Bhatnagar's study, but there is considerable research documentation (see, for example, Skutnabb-Kangas, 1984) about how rapidly a switch to the majority language occurs among siblings.

A recent National Assessment of Educational Progress (NAEP) (1983a) study provides the most comprehensive data on the implications of speaking a minority language in the home. It was found that although students from other-language dominant homes tended to lag behind students from English-dominant homes in reading achievement, the pattern of findings could not be attributed to any simple relationship between linguistic mismatch and achievement. The trends in the data are summarized in the NAEP Newsletter (1983b: 3):

> . . . some students from homes where English is not spoken often are much better readers than others. And some, in fact, read better than many students from English-dominant homes . . . Consequences of coming from an other-language-dominant home are not the same for students of different racial and ethnic backgrounds . . .
>
> White youngsters from other-language-dominant homes have a strike against them when it comes to reading skills. At age 17, these pupils are about 5 percentage points below whites from English-speaking homes in reading performance.
>
> For Hispanos, however, language spoken in the home doesn't appear to make much difference in reading abilities. For 17-year-olds, students from both other-language-dominant and English-speaking homes lagged about 9 percentage points behind the nation in reading skills.

The complexity of the interactions between home language use and other variables can be seen in the results presented by Yee & Laforge (1974). Their study of 53 American-born Chinese 9- and 10-year olds in San Francisco revealed that the more exposure to and emphasis on Chinese outside the home (e.g. closeness of home to Chinatown, attendance at Chinese school), the better students performed on the English WISC. Amount of English use in the home was unrelated to WISC scores.

Dolson (1984) investigated the academic performance of 108 Hispanic student in grades 5 and 6 in relation to the extent that Spanish had been maintained as the major home language. He reported significantly poorer academic performance on 5 out of 10 scholastic measures among students who had switched to English as the main home language (subtractive bilinguals) in comparison to students who had maintained Spanish as the main home language (additive bilinguals).

These findings also show the inadequacy of attempts to explain minority students' achievement solely by means of "acculturation" (e.g. Troike, 1984). If acculturation to the values and norms of the majority culture were the primary causal factor, then we would expect to find that students who made more use of the majority language would perform better. Clearly, this is not the case.

In conclusion, the evaluation and research data reviewed above clearly refute both the "maximum exposure" and "linguistic mismatch" hypotheses with regard to the causes of minority student underachievement. This does not mean that exposure to a language is unimportant nor that it is not more difficult to learn through the medium of a second language than through one's first language; rather, the data show that the influence of exposure and linguistic mismatch is considerably modified by other factors, such that predictions about the influence of these factors *in isolation* are not possible.

The data reviewed have some obvious implications for special educators. First, there is no evidence that minority students who are academically "at risk" experience difficulty coping with two languages of instruction. The opposite, in fact, appears to be the case (e.g. Bruck, 1982; Malherbe, 1946). Similarly, there is no justification for encouraging minority parents to use more English in the home. Not only is a switch to English unnecessary, it can easily backfire by lowering the quality of parent-child interaction in the home and exposing the children to poor models of English.

In the next section educational influences on minority students' academic difficulties are reviewed. We are concerned primarily with the differential quality of instruction that may be offered to minority students in contrast to majority students and also with educators' failure to adjust instruction to minority students' styles of participation in learning tasks.

EDUCATIONAL TREATMENT: QUALITY AND CULTURAL MISMATCH

Quality

A large number of studies have shown that teachers tend to use positive inter-actions more frequently with students whom they perceive as high achievers than with students perceived as low achievers (e.g. Good & Brophy, 1971; Kerman, Kimball & Martin, 1980; McDermott, 1978; Rist, 1970). Good & Brophy, for example, reported that grade 1 students perceived by the teacher as low achievers received fewer reading turns in reading groups, fewer opportunities to answer questions and fewer opportunities to recite. Students perceived as high achieving received more praise and less criticism than the perceived low achievers.

In view of the fact that minority students are frequently perceived as low achievers (e.g. Fram & Crawford, 1972), it is not surprising that they are also reported to experience less positive interactions with teachers than majority group students. A large-scale study conducted by the U.S. Commission on Civil Rights (1973) reported that majority students were praised or encouraged 36% more often than Mexican–American students and their classroom contributions were used or built upon 40% more frequently than those of Mexican–American students. In all positive categories the majority students experienced more interaction whereas the minority students experienced more interaction only with respect to criticism and being given directions.

In discussing these findings the California State Department of Education (1982) suggests as a general principle affecting minority student achievement that

> The perceived status of students affects the interactions between teachers and students and among the students themselves. In turn, student outcomes are affected. (p. 18)

Teacher assumptions about students' proficiency in English can also inadvertently affect the quality of instruction. This is illustrated by the micro-ethnographic study of reading instruction carried out by Moll and his colleagues (Moll, 1981) in the context of a team-taught maintenance bilingual program. A considerable emphasis on higher-level comprehension-oriented literacy activities (e.g. inferring from the text, analyzing content, writing book reports) was observed among the high ability reading group in the Spanish lesson. In the English classroom, on the other hand, students were

> made to focus primarily on the mechanical tasks of practicing decoding skills, word sounds or lexical meaning. Practically absent are key activities that promote reading *comprehension* and help the students learn how to *communicate their knowledge* of content. (1981: 439)

Moll suggests that a likely source of the problem is that the English teacher was confounding pronunciation and decoding problems.

> The teacher seems to be assuming that decoding is a prerequisite to comprehension and that correct pronunciation is the best index of decoding. The implicit theory guiding instruction is that correct pronunciation (decoding) must precede comprehension (cf. Goodman, Goodman and Flores, 1979). Consequently, the teacher organizes the lessons to provide the children with the necessary time on the task to help them practice pronunciation, phonics, and other aspects of language learning such as lexical meaning. In so doing, higher order (comprehension) reading skills are structured out of the lessons' interactions. (1981: 440)

These findings suggest that students perceived as "learning disabled" or of low academic ability are frequently subjected to reading instruction which focuses on single word decoding rather than on the meaning of longer segments of text (see Guthrie & Hall, 1983 for a more detailed review of micro-ethnographic studies in this area).

In summary, the inferior instruction often experienced by low status students is likely to contribute to minority students' academic difficulties. It is not, however, capable of accounting for the differential achievement of different minority groups. For example, until recently, Asian–American students have had as low status as any other minority group but have achieved well academically.

During the past decade, their status appears to have been elevated as a result of greater awareness on the part of teachers and the general public of their relatively high achievement.

Cultural Mismatch

Cultural mismatch between home and school came to prominence as a possible explanation for the academic difficulties of many minority students with Susan Phillips' (1972) study of home and school interaction patterns among students in the Warm Springs Indian reserve. Phillips introduced the notion of "participant structure" to refer to the implicit rules governing patterns of interaction in particular situations. Within a classroom, for example, different participant structures or implicit rules will govern behavior such as speaking and turn-taking in whole-group instruction, small-group instruction and seatwork. Phillips (1972) and many subsequent investigators (e.g. Au, 1980; Cook-Gumperz, Gumperz & Simons, 1981; Guthrie, 1981; McDermott, 1978; Mohatt & Erickson, 1981; Wong Fillmore, 1983) have shown significant disjunctions between the typical participant structures minority children employ in their communities outside school and those required in the school by teachers from the dominant group culture.

The results of the KEEP experience in Hawaii provide the most impressive demonstration to-date of the positive effects of changing the organization of interaction within the school context to increase its compatibility with the minority culture participant structures (Au, 1980; Au & Jordan, 1981). This project, however, also shows how difficult it often is to identify the relevant cultural/ linguistic discontinuities in that many years of ethnographic work in the community and educational "trial-and-error" were spent prior to uncovering the specific participant structures whose mismatch between home and school was impeding Native Hawaiian children's academic development.

Guthrie & Hall (1983) make a similar point in concluding their review of research on the "cultural mismatch" hypothesis:

> As for the question of language discontinuity on a cultural level, much of the recent research points in the direction of the cultural mismatch hypothesis. The work described here suggests that cultural differences in language use do exist; the difficulty lies in identifying them. Because these differences are subtle and largely unconscious they are not available to the casual, or even interested, observer. (1983: 73)

If the notion of "cultural mismatch" is relevant to explaining the differences in achievement between minority group students reviewed earlier, then comparisons of the participant structures of Chinese and Hispanic students should reveal important findings. An in-depth investigation of these differences and their educational implications has recently been carried out by Lily Wong Fillmore and her colleagues (Wong Fillmore, 1983). Parental interviews revealed that Mexican–American parents (in the San Francisco area) wanted their children to be happy and respected as human beings whereas success in life was more of a priority for Chinese parents. Observation of children's classroom interaction patterns over a period of several years showed significant group differences. The Mexican–American children tended to be very socially mature compared to the Chinese. Within a couple of months of starting grade 1 they had a coherent social organization and were capable of getting things done cooperatively in small groups. By contrast, Chinese children tended to orient themselves to adults and to compete with each other for adult approval.

The findings of Wong Fillmore's study suggest that the peer orientation of the Mexican–American students compared to the Chinese adult orientation is an important factor in accounting for the differential achievement patterns of these two groups. According to Wong Fillmore (1983), the Chinese students were so anxious to please the teacher that they were prepared to strive for perfection in carrying out teacher-assigned tasks, no matter how dull or boring. Mexican–American students, on the other hand, would carry out teacher assignments that were not highly motivating, but without the intensity of involvement shown by the Chinese students.

Wong Fillmore relates these patterns of classroom behavior to differences in socialization between Chinese and Mexican–American homes. Specifically, she suggests that the use of shame as a mechanism to promote conformity to adult expectations in Chinese homes has a powerful effect in motivating children to succeed in school and to tolerate teacher-set tasks that in themselves may not make much sense to the student. Mexican–American students, on the other hand, tend to be given considerable responsibility in the home (e.g. to look after baby) and are less tolerant of tasks whose purpose they do not appreciate.

Although based on detailed parental interviews and ethnographic work in both communities, these characterizations must, at this stage, be regarded as hypotheses. Their validity is supported, however, by the predictable effects of different classroom organizations on children's achievement. Chinese students tended to thrive in a highly structured classroom where teacher expectations were clearly stated. Mexican–American students, on the other hand, did better in a less structured situation which provided more opportunities for small-group work.

In summary, cultural mismatch appears to be a significant contributor to minority student underachievement in many situations. It is difficult, however, to generalize about the effects of this factor because, almost by definition, the specific form of mismatch is likely to vary across different cultural groups and even among subgroups within a minority culture. Cultural factors are also likely to interact with other causal variables such as educational quality and broader societal factors. However, the demonstrated operation of cultural mismatch in a variety of minority group learning situations should cause educators and policy-makers to exercise caution in accepting plausible but greatly oversimplified explanations of minority students' academic difficulties (e.g. linguistic mismatch).

THE SOCIETAL ROOTS OF MINORITY STUDENTS' EDUCATIONAL FAILURE

Thus far in this chapter we have seen that minority students show a complex pattern of educational achievement, some groups tending to perform better than equivalent students from the majority group while others perform considerably worse. This variation in itself demonstrates that there is no one simple explanation for the educational failure of certain minority groups. Detailed examination of the effects of variables such as home-school language switching, differential exposure to L2, and bilingualism confirm the fact that none of these variables, by themselves, can account for the data. There is, however, evidence that bilingual language proficiency may operate as an intervening variable which contributes to the differential cognitive and academic outcomes observed in different bilingual learning situations. In this regard, preliminary evidence is consistent with predictions derived from the threshold hypothesis which appears to have at least heuristic value as a theoretical construct for partially integrating the research findings.

Patterns of bilingualism, however, cannot be regarded as fundamental causal variables since they are determined by educational and social factors. There is strong evidence that in many situations educational factors contribute to minority students' academic difficulties. However, at this stage, neither the inferior quality of education nor the home-school cultural mismatch which many minority students experience appears to provide a complete explanation of minority students' achievement patterns. For one thing, the influence of the societal context on the educational treatment itself needs to be examined and also educational variables are likely to interact in complex ways with both individual and social variables. Currently, there exists no general theory or set of hypotheses based only on educational variables that claims to account for the complex patterns of minority student achievement.

Thus, we turn to an examination of the role of broader social factors, To recapitulate, some of the main trends to be explained are as follows: In the United States, Native and Hispanic students (with the exception of Cubans) tend to perform considerably worse than some other groups (e.g. Asian students) and at a similar level to Blacks. In Canada, Franco-Ontarian students show very poor performance in L2-only programs whereas most Canadian-born children of recent immigrant groups have tended in the past to perform as well as or better than equivalent SES Anglo students. The extremely low academic performance of Finnish students in Sweden has also been documented (e.g. Paulston, 1983; Skutnabb-Kangas & Toukomaa, 1976), but, by contrast, Finnish immigrant students in Australia are reported to perform well academically (Troike, 1978). Children of migrant workers in Northern Europe (e.g. Turkish children in West Germany) are also reported to show extremely high rates of school failure (see e.g. Rist, 1979; Skutnabb-Kangas, 1984).

This variation in patterns of minority student performance suggests that social variables are at work. Other research data reinforce this contention. Skutnabb-Kangas & Toukomaa (1976), for example, reported that despite considerably less exposure to Swedish, Finnish children who immigrated to Sweden at the age of 10-12 appeared to have better academic prospects that Finnish students who were either born in Sweden or immigrated at younger ages. A similar pattern has been reported for Hispanic students in the United States (see Cummins, 1981a, for a review). Skutnabb-Kangas & Toukomaa attribute their finding to the better developed L1 proficiency of the older immigrant students. However, the inadequacy of psycho-educational variables alone can be seen in the fact that very different patterns of performance have been reported for immigrant students in the Toronto Board of Education, in Canada. Minority students born in Canada succeeded in attaining or exceeding academic grade expectations. Similarly, immigrant students who arrived in Canada before the age of six attained grade norms and appeared to have better academic prospects than students who arrived at older ages (see Cummins, 1981b).

The difference between both the Swedish and U.S. data on the one hand, and the Toronto data on the other, suggests that the societal context radically alters the effects of variables such as length of residence (i.e. exposure to L2, "acculturation") and age on arrival on academic achievement of minority students in L2-only programmes.

An obvious initial question is whether SES can explain the observed pattern of findings, as recently suggested by Rosenthal *et al.* (1981). Although variables associated with SES are likely to contribute to minority students' underachievement in many contexts, SES alone cannot explain the differences between the Canadian and Swedish/U.S. patterns of minority group achievement since all students in these studies were low SES, nor can it explain the vast differences among minority groups of the same SES in the Toronto Board data.

Three related societal constructs have been independently suggested to account for the data. These are the notion of "bicultural ambivalence" (Cummins, 1981a), Ogbu's (1978) distinction between "caste" and "immigrant" minorities, and Feuerstein's (1979) concept of "cultural deprivation" by which he refers to a disrupted process of inter-generational cultural transmission.

Bicultural Ambivalence

The notion of bicultural ambivalence was suggested on the basis of an examination of the common characteristics of the contexts in which certain minority group students experience academic difficulties. One common characteristic appeared to be a pattern of ambivalence or hostility toward the majority cultural group and insecurity or even shame about the home language and culture. Consider, for example, the following description of Finnish immigrants in Sweden given by Heyman (1973), a Swedish researcher:

> Many Finns in Sweden feel an aversion, and sometimes even hostility, towards the Swedish language and refuse to learn it or learn it under protest. There is repeated evidence of this, as there is, on the other hand, of Finnish people—children and adults—who are ashamed of their Finnish language and do not allow it to live and develop (quoted in Skutnabb-Kangas & Toukomaa, 1976: 29)

The attitudes of Finns towards Swedes are clearly not independent of the fact that Finnish is regarded as a very low status language in Sweden and Swedes tend to have negative views of Finns. By contrast, in Australia, where Finnish students perform well, Finns are regarded as a high status group (Troike, 1978). There is also considerable documentation (e.g. Mougeon & Canale, 1978-79) that many Franco-Ontarian students tend to have low self-esteem, regard their own dialect of French as inferior and show low aspirations for social and economic mobility in the majority culture.

This pattern of "bicultural ambivalence" is also evident among Black, Mexican–American and Native students in the United States and can be clearly linked to historical patterns of segregation and discrimination (see Carter, 1970). In the U.S. *v.* Texas (1981) decision, for example, it was pointed out that while many of the overt forms of discrimination against Mexican–Americans had been eliminated

> the long history of prejudice and discrimination remains a significant obstacle to equal educational opportunity for these children. The deep sense of inferiority, cultural isolation, and acceptance of failure, instilled in a people by generations of subjugation, cannot be eradicated merely by integrating the schools and repealing the 'no Spanish' statutes. (1981: 14)

Thus, when the insecurity and ambivalence of some groups is reinforced by the linguistic and cultural message conveyed by the school, it is not surprising that students fulfill their preordained role in the system and "mentally withdraw" (Carter, 1970) from academic tasks.

The hypothesis of "bicultural ambivalence" can also help explain why Mexican–American and Finnish immigrant students who immigrate after several years of schooling in the home country appear to have better academic prospects than minority children born in the U.S. or Sweden, despite much less exposure to English (Carter, 1970; Cummins, 1981a; Skutnabb-Kangas & Toukomaa, 1976). The fact that the older immigrant students have not internalized the majority group's perception of them as inferior, together with their better developed L1 academic skills, can account for their superior long-term academic performance in comparison to students born into a minority setting.

At this stage it is necessary to ask why some groups of minority students appear to be characterized by a pattern of bicultural ambivalence while others enjoy relatively high status within the majority culture and are also confident in their ethnic identity. The analysis of minority student academic failure provided by John Ogbu (1978), a Nigerian-born anthropologist based in the University of California, Berkeley, appears to go some way towards answering this question and accounting for the patterns of minority group achievement described earlier.

Immigrant and Caste Minorities

Ogbu first distinguishes between three types of minority groups, namely, autonomous, caste and immigrant minorities. Autonomous groups possess a distinct racial, ethnic, religious, linguistic or cultural identity and are generally not subordinated economically or politically to the dominant group. Jews and Mormons are current examples of autonomous groups in the United States.

Caste minorities, on the other hand, are usually regarded by the dominant group as inherently inferior in most respects. Their post-educational opportunities are restricted to the least desirable social and occupational roles and their failure to ascend the socio-economic ladder is attributed to inherent characteristics of the group (e.g. "innate intelligence," "cultural deprivation," "bilingualism"). Ogbu identifies Black, Native Indian and Hispanic groups (with the exception of Cubans) in the United States as caste minorities and attributes their school failure to inferior education combined with the perception by the group of post-school economic barriers ("job ceiling") which limit the rewards to be gained from formal education. The perception of powerlessness or lack of mastery over their own fate may influence the patterns of parent-child interaction and the consequent cognitive, linguistic and motivational styles parents transmit to their children. Ogbu points out that

> caste minority children naturally acquire the linguistic, cognitive, motivational, and other skills or personal attributes adaptive to their adult roles. These skills may promote their failure in the dominant group's type of school success, but in that very way schooling improves their adaptability to the menial social and occupational roles they will play as adults. (1978: 41)

Ogbu's analysis of the genesis of low school achievement among caste minorities in the United States is supported by the identification of similar patterns among caste groups in Britain (West Indians), New Zealand (Maoris), India (the scheduled castes), Japan (Buraku outcastes), and Israel (Oriental Jews). The essential characteristics Ogbu attributes to caste minorities are similar to those included in the notion of bicultural ambivalence, namely a sense of inferiority about self combined with low motivation to participate and succeed economically in the mainstream culture.

The third type of minority group, immigrant minorities, differs from most caste minorities in that they have moved into a host society more or less voluntarily and tend to have instrumental attitudes towards the host society and its institutions. They tend to be less affected by the ideology of dominant group superiority than are caste minorities and, despite discrimination, often their lot appears very good compared to that of their reference group in the homeland. Ogbu gives Chinese and Japanese as examples of immigrant groups in the United States. He also points out that the status of minority groups may change. For example, immigrant minorities may develop into autonomous or caste minorities.

Ogbu's description of immigrant minorities clearly characterizes the minority groups identified as academically successful in the two Toronto Board surveys. Parents immigrated to Canada in order to better their social and economic life prospects and usually have extremely high aspirations for their children's educational success. This appears particularly so for the Chinese parents who are reported to value education highly and to strongly encourage not only their children's academic development but also their pride in Chinese identity.

The explanatory power of Ogbu's distinction between caste and immigrant minorities is illustrated by its ability to account for the much lower level of academic class placement for the Franco–Ontarian group as compared to the recent immigrant students born in Canada. The Franco-Ontarian group has all the essential characteristics Ogbu attributes to caste minorities (see, e.g. Churchill, 1978–79) and this is reflected in its relatively poor academic performance and low post-school economic and social mobility. The pattern outlined cannot be explained by linguistic, cultural, socio-economic or pedagogical variables, either individually or collectively, but the distinction between caste and immigrant minorities does appear to go some way towards accounting for the data. As Ogbu (1983) points out, the distinction can also account for the fact that Buraku outcastes in Japan experience persistent disproportionate school failure yet in the United States (where they constitute an immigrant minority group) the same Burakus are doing as well as other Japanese–Americans at school.

Within this framework one of the reasons why some bilingual programs have been highly successful in helping to reverse minority students' pattern of academic failure is that by validating the cultural identity of the students (as well as of the community), they reduce students' ambivalence towards the majority language and culture.

In summary, while not denying that factors associated with SES and language/cultural differences do represent real impediments to academic and economic success, Ogbu's analysis helps account for the fact that some minority groups have overcome these difficulties whereas others have been locked into a caste system in which schools have used language and cultural differences as tools to perpetuate inequalities (Carter & Segura, 1979). This has given rise to subtractive forms of bilingualism, involving low levels of L1 and L2 academic proficiency which, in turn, has limited minority students' ability to profit fully from instruction.

At this stage, a limitation of Ogbu's theory is the vagueness of the criteria used to define caste and immigrant minorities. While the distinction appears extremely useful on a *post hoc* basis in accounting for patterns in the data, it is not sufficiently specific as yet to make fully accurate *predictions* about minority student achievement. For example, the characteristics of Jewish and Chinese immigrant students that allowed them to succeed academically in the U.S. despite strong discrimination are still a matter of speculation. Although Ogbu's speculations in this regard are plausible, the final word has not yet been said on the interactions among the many variables (social, educational and psychological) subsumed under the caste and immigrant minority distinction.

"Cultural Deprivation" and Mediated Learning

On the basis of many years of clinical research in Israel on the academic adjustment of children labeled as "retarded," many of whom were immigrants, Reuven Feuerstein (1979) developed both a procedure for assessing the child's learning potential and also pedagogical techniques of "instrumental enrichment" which, he reports, have met with dramatic success in improving adolescent children's cognitive and academic functioning. Here we are primarily concerned with the theoretical constructs he has proposed to explain the academic difficulties of minority students.

Central to Feuerstein's theory is a potentially controversial distinction between "cultural difference" and "cultural deprivation." Culturally different students are those who come from a cultural background different from that of the dominant group but whose adaptive capacities are well-developed as a result of strong cultural transmission within their own group. Although these students may well show low levels of manifest cognitive functioning when confronted with task requirements (e.g. on a test or in the classroom) that vary from the expectations of their own familiar culture, these difficulties may be overcome relatively easily because of the self-confidence and cognitive/linguistic foundation that their interaction with adults in their own culture has established. Feuerstein expresses the characteristics of cultural difference as follows:

> The individual who has learned to function within his own culture has learned to adapt and become modified. This modifiability, while developed and expressed within the context of a particular culture, is of much general adaptive value because it has established the prerequisites for learning and continued modifiability. (1979: 39)

By contrast, Feuerstein regards the culturally deprived as "an individual or a group that has become alienated from its own culture." This alienation can be produced by a variety of sociological, economic or cultural factors but is always "reflected in a disruption of intergenerational transmission and mediational processes." It is important to note that Feuerstein is using the term "cultural deprivation" in a way that is very different from its usual meaning. Specifically, the concept

> refers to an *intrinsic* (emphasis original) criterion of the specific culture, namely, the lack of the process inherent to the concept of culture itself: intergenerational transmission. This differs from the usually accepted meaning of the term "cultural deprivation," which refers to an extrinsic criterion by which the culture of certain ethnic subgroups is considered as depriving their members, thereby negatively affecting their cognitive capacities. As we define it, however, culture can never be viewed as a depriving factor. (1979: 39)

Consistent with this definition, many of the "culturally deprived" students whose cognitive functioning showed major improvements subsequent to dynamic assessment and appropriate intervention came from middle-class dominant cultural backgrounds.

Contrary to the impression conveyed by static measurement procedures, the condition of culturally deprived children is not immutable or fixed. According to Feuerstein, the cognitive impairments of the culturally deprived do not reflect any real lack of capacity "but rather ineffective attitudes, faulty work habits, and inadequate modes of thinking—in other words, functions that can be trained to operate more adequately" (1979: 70).

The immediate causal factor underlying cultural deprivation is inadequate and insufficient mediated learning experience. This is defined as

> the interactional processes between the developing human organism and an experienced, intentioned adult who, by interposing himself between the child and external sources of stimulation, "mediates" the world to the child by framing, selecting, focusing, and feeding back environmental

experiences in such a way as to produce in him appropriate learning
sets and habits. (1979: 71)

Feuerstein points out that although a variety of factors may give rise to insufficient
mediated learning (e.g. emotional disturbance among adults, sociopolitical disruption
in the life style of minority groups), the inevitable result is cultural deprivation.

The distinction between "cultural difference" and "cultural deprivation" is
similar in many respects to Ogbu's (1978) distinction between immigrant and
caste minorities, although Ogbu's distinction is sociological in nature whereas
Feuerstein's is primarily psychological. Both theorists are concerned to explain
the differential pattern of academic achievement of minority group students, but
Feuerstein's focus is on insufficient mediated learning experiences as the most
immediate determinant of retarded performance, whereas Ogbu focuses on the
socio-historical factors which give rise to, among other things, patterns of adult-
child interaction that prepare children for their pre-ordained subordinate role in
the social and economic system.

In short, Feuerstein's characterization of the "culturally deprived" as those
individuals or groups who have become alienated from their own culture is clearly
compatible with Ogbu's notion of a "caste minority," as well as with the notion
of "bicultural ambivalence." Differences in patterns of intergenerational cultural
transmission also appear to elucidate, to some extent, the relatively better
academic prospects of certain groups of minority students who immigrate after
several years of education in the home country, as compared to those who are
born in the host country. The fact that a very different pattern emerges among
the minority students in the Toronto Board who were born in Canada is also
readily interpretable in terms of cultural transmission processes.

However, Feuerstein's use of the term "cultural deprivation" is unfortunate
because, despite his care in distinguishing his understanding of the term from
its more usual meaning, he is still likely to be accused of proposing a "deficit"
view of minority student underachievement (see Edelsky *et al.,* 1983; and
response by Cummins & Swain, 1983). Certainly, in this regard, legitimate issues
can be raised and there is an obvious need to clarify the distinction. Thus, some
commentators might interpret Feuerstein as suggesting that Mexican–American
and Black students tend to experience disproportionate school failure because
they are "culturally deprived" as a result of insufficient mediated learning
experiences in the home. By contrast, a more charitable (and, I believe, accurate)
interpretation of Feuerstein's position is that *some* of these minority students,
as well as some dominant group students, do experience academic difficulty as
a result of what he terms "cultural deprivation" in combination with inappropriate
educational treatment. However, a large number also experience difficulty solely
because the school responds inappropriately to their cultural difference.

The basis for Feuerstein's notion of "cultural deprivation" appears difficult to
dispute; namely, that there are substantial *individual* differences in the quality and
quantity of adult-child interaction (not necessarily between different ethnic and SES
groups—see Wells, 1981) and that the resulting differences in mediated learning experiences are relevant to children's cognitive and academic development

(e.g. Vygotsky, 1962). However, the term unfortunately suggests that "deprivation" is a phenomenon that characterizes some cultural minorities and thus it may have the effect of obscuring the relevance of Feuerstein's distinction. It would have been preferable to have used a more neutral term to describe the process of disrupted intergenerational transmission.

CONCLUSION

The preceding review suggests that the related notions of "bicultural ambivalence," "caste" minority status, and "cultural deprivation" (in Feuerstein's sense), appear relevant to explaining patterns of minority student achievement. Data which are not readily amenable to either psychological or education explanations (e.g. poor academic performance by Franco–Ontarian students), can be interpreted within the theoretical context provided by these societal factors. An implication is that the determinants of what presents itself as a "learning disability" when viewed through psycho-educational lens may be considerably more complex than assumed by the psychologist or special educator.

However, we are still a considerable distance from a comprehensive theory of minority student underachievement because the interactions among social, educational, psychological and linguistic factors remain to be specified. At the same time it is important to articulate those aspects of the total picture that have become clear and whose policy implications we can state with some degree of confidence.

In the first place current policy-making with respect to the education of minority students in the United States is based on demonstrably inadequate theoretical constructs. Neither the linguistic mismatch hypothesis assumed by many proponents of bilingual education nor the maximum exposure hypothesis promoted by advocates of "English immersion" can account for the observed data.

Unintentional differences in quality of educational treatment as well as subtle mismatches between the minority child's social interaction patterns and those required by the school appear to be important contributors to minority students' underachievement. A greater sensitivity on the part of teachers to the potential for this type of unconscious discrimination and/or mismatch in participant structures is certainly to be recommended. This clearly applies as much to special education teachers as to those in mainstream classrooms.

The patterns of minority student academic achievement also seem to be conditioned by broader societal variables related to status relations between minority and majority groups. It was suggested that these societal variables influence adult-child interaction both in the home and school. In this regard, the theoretical constructs proposed appear to have implications for the development and consequences of minority children's bilingualism. Specifically, in Feuerstein's terms, the good academic prospects (or "generalized modifiability") which characterize culturally different students as a result of the strong intergenerational transmission processes within their own culture, are compatible with the hypothesis that cognitive/academic skills can transfer readily across languages or cultural contexts (e.g. Cummins, 1981b). The importance of strong promotion both in home and school of minority students' L1 proficiency and cultural identity is also supported by the notions of bicultural ambivalence, caste minority status and cultural difference/deprivation. In short, a general hypothesis that emerges from these three independent theoretical positions is that children's cognitive and academic development is a direct function of their interaction with adults both in the home and school and whatever can be done to validate and strengthen this process of cultural transmission is likely to contribute to children's overall personal and intellectual growth.

NOTES

1. In many contexts minority students were frequently punished for speaking their L1 in school. The "Welsh not" which came into existence after the 1870 Education Act in Britain represents a particularly vicious example of an attempt to eradicate a subordinate language through physical punishment of children. Any child heard speaking Welsh in school had a wooden halter placed over his or her shoulders. If that child heard another child speaking Welsh he or she could transfer the "Welsh not" to the other child. The child carrying this halter at the end of the day was caned (Evans, 1978). Richard Llewellyn gives an account of this type of punishment in his auto-biographical novel *How Green Was My Valley:*

    > I heard crying in the infants' school as though a child had fallen and the voice came nearer and fell flat upon the air as a small girl came through the door and walked a couple of steps towards us . . . About her neck a piece of new cord, and from the cord, a board that hung to her shins and cut her as she walked. Chalked on the board, in the fist of Mr. Elijah Jonas-Sessions, I must not speak Welsh in school . . . And the board dragged her down, for she was small, and the cord rasped the flesh on her neck, and there were marks upon her shins where the edge of the board had cut. (Llewellyn, 1968: 267)

2. Anecdotal evidence provides perhaps more convincing support than formal research studies for the notion that bilingualism can promote greater metalinguistic awareness. Two examples from my daughter, then a grade 3 French immersion student, illustrate this. In the car one evening I used the word "perceive" and she asked what it meant; I told her its meaning was similar to "see" as in "I see/perceive that house over there." Her response was "Oh, it's like 'apercevoir'." Later that same evening, also in the car, the radio announcer said something to the effect that in the next hour they would have music by Mozart and also poems by Percy Shelley. My daughter, out of the blue, said "Percy cottage." In response to my blank stare she explained the sequence: "Percy Shelley—Percy châlet (French word for cottage)—Percy cottage." Many other examples of bilingual children's word-play are provided by Heller (1983).

3. In two articles (Cummins, 1978a, 1979a) I used the term "semilingualism" with reference to the lower threshold level of bilingual proficiency. Later, I repudiated the use of the term on the grounds that it tended to be misunderstood and had pejorative connotations (Cummins, 1979b). The emotional debates that have taken place in both Europe and North America on whether "semilingualism" exists appear both misdirected and futile. Investigators who have used the term explicitly identify it with cognitive

and academic functions of language and discuss its role as an intervening variable determined by social and educational factors (e.g. Skutnabb-Kangas & Toukomaa, 1976). Those who reject the concept of semilingualism rarely analyze what they mean by "language proficiency" nor acknowledge the obvious fact that even in a middle-class monolingual context there are huge individual differences in academic aspects of language proficiency (e.g. range of vocabulary-concept knowledge, reading ability). In bilingual situations individual differences in both L1 and L2 academic skills are equally apparent, and there is no logical reason why one might not choose an arbitrary cut-off point and term the proficiencies below that level "semilingualism."

However, there are compelling social and ethical reasons why the term semilingualism should be avoided. First, to many educators and academics it connotes a deficit view of minority children in which children's academic underachievement is attributed to their "semilingualism," thereby deflecting attention from social and educational variables. In other words, use of the term risks making one more psycho-educational variable (e.g. retardation, learning disability) the scapegoat for schools' failure to educate minority children (see for example Edelsky *et al.,* 1983; Paulston, 1983).

Another reason for eliminating the term from academic discussion is that it inevitably leads to conflict and misunderstanding between investigators whose actual positions are often very similar. The energy could be much better spent co-operating in trying to effect educational changes. Thus, despite the fact that the construct is, in principle, defensible and follows logically from the acknowledgment that there are individual differences among bilinguals in L1 and L2, its use is extremely ill-advised.

REFERENCES

Albert, M. L. & Obler, L. K. 1979, *The Bilingual Brain.* New York: Academic Press.

Altena, N. & Appel, R. 1982, Mother tongue teaching and the acquisition of Dutch by Turkish and Moroccan immigrant workers' children. *Journal of Multilingual and Multicultural Development,* 3, 315–22.

Association of Catholic Principals of Montreal. 1969, A brief to the commission of inquiry on the position of the French language and on language rights in Quebec. Montreal, June.

Au, K. H. 1980, Participant structures in a reading lesson with Hawaiian children. Analysis of a culturally appropriate instructional event. *Anthropology and Education Quarterly,* 11, 91–115.

Au, K. H. & Jordan, C. 1981, Teaching reading to Hawaiian children: Finding a culturally appropriate solution. In H. Trueba, G. P. Guthrie, & K. H. Au (eds), *Culture and the Bilingual Classroom: Studies in Classroom Ethnography.* Rowley, Mass.: Newbury House.

Bain, B. C. 1975, Toward an integration of Piaget and Vygotsky: Bilingual considerations. *Linguistics,* 160, 5–20.

Bain, B. C. & Yu, A. 1980, Cognitive consequences of raising children bilingually: "One parent, one language." *Canadian Journal of Psychology,* 34, 304–13.

Baker, K. A. & de Kanter, A. A. 1981, *Effectiveness of Bilingual Education: A Review of the Literature.* Washington, D.C.: Office of Planning and Budget, U.S. Department of Education.

Balkan, L. 1970, *Les Effets du Bilingualisme Francais–Anglais sur les Aptitudes Intellectuelles.* Bruxelles: Aimav.

Ben-Zeev, S. 1977a, The influence of bilingualism on cognitive development and cognitive strategy. *Child Development,* 48, 1009–18.

———— 1977b, The effect of Spanish-English bilingualism in children from less privileged neighborhoods on cognitive development and cognitive strategy. *Working Papers on Bilingualism*, No. 14, 83-122.

Bhatnagar, J. 1980, Linguistic behaviour and adjustment of immigrant children in French and English schools in Montreal. *International Review of Applied Psychology*, 29, 141-59,

Bruck, M. 1982, Language impaired children's performance in an additive bilingual education program. *Applied Psycholinguistics*, 3, 45-60.

California State Department of Education. 1982, *Basic Principles for the Education of Language-Minority Students: An Overview*. Sacramento: California State Department of Education.

Carey, S. T. & Cummins, J. 1983, Achievement, behavioral correlates and teachers' perceptions of Francophone and Anglophone Immersion Students. *Alberta Journal of Educational Research*, 29, 159-67.

Carter, T. P. 1970, *Mexican-Americans in School: A History of Educational Neglect*. New York: College Entrance Examination Board.

Carter, T. P. & Segura, R. D. 1979, *Mexican-Americans in School: A Decade of Change*. New York: College Entrance Examination Board.

Chesarek, S. 1981, Cognitive consequences of home or school education in a limited second language: A case study in the Crow Indian community. Paper presented at the Language Proficiency Assessment Symposium, Airlie House, Virginia, March, 1981.

Churchill, S. 1978-79, So why aren't the French ever satisfied? *Interchange*, 9, 56-59.

Coehlo, A. M. 1976, *Conflicts and Adjustments of Portuguese Youth in School, Home and Community*. Toronto: Ministry of Culture and Recreation, Ontario.

Coleman, J. S., Campbell, E. Q., Hobson, C. J., McPartland, J., Mood, A. M., Weinfeld, F. D., & York, R. L. 1966, *Equality of Educational Opportunity*. Washington, D.C.: Department of Health, Education and Welfare, Office of Education.

Cook-Gumperz, J., Gumperz, J. & Simons, H. 1981, *Final Report of School/Home Ethnography Project*. Washington, D.C.: National Institute of Education.

Cummins, J. 1976, The influence of bilingualism on cognitive growth: A synthesis of research findings and explanatory hypotheses. W*orking Papers on Bilingualism*, No. 9, 1-43.

———— 1978a, The cognitive development of children in immersion programs. *The Canadian Modern Language Review*, 34, 855-83.

———— 1978b, Immersion programs: The Irish experience. *International Review of Education*, 24, 273-82.

———— 1979a, Linguistic interdependence and the educational development of bilingual children. *Review of Educational Research*, 49, 222-51.

———— 1979b, Cognitive/academic language proficiency, linguistic interdependence, the optimum age question and some other matters. *Working Papers on Bilingualism*, No. 19, 121-29.

———— 1981a, The role of primary language development in promoting educational success for language minority students. In California State Department of Education, *Schooling and Language Minority Students: A Theoretical Framework*. Los Angeles: Evaluation, Dissemination and Assessment Center.

———— 1981b, Age on arrival and immigrant second language learning in Canada: A reassessment. *Applied Linguistics*, 2, 132-49.

———— 1983, *Heritage Language Education: A Literature Review*. Toronto: Ministry of Education, Ontario.

Cummins, J. & Gulutsan, M. 1974, Some effects of bilingualism on cognitive functioning. In S. Carey (ed.), *Bilingualism, Biculturalism and Education.* Edmonton: University of Alberta Press.

Cummins, J. & Mulcahy, R. 1978, Orientation to language in Ukrainian–English bilingual children. *Child Development,* 49, 1239–42.

Cummins, J. & Swain, M. 1983, Analysis-by-rhetoric: Reading the test or the readers' own projections? A reply to Edelsky *et al., Applied Linguistics,* 4, 23–41.

Darcy, N. T. 1953, A review of the literature on the effects of bilingualism on the measurement of intelligence. *Journal of Genetic Psychology,* 82, 21–57.

Diebold, A. R. 1968, The consequences of early bilingualism in cognitive development and personality formation. In E. Norbeck, D. Price-Williams, & W. M. McCord (eds), *The Study of Personality.* New York: Holt, Rinehart & Winston.

Dolson, D. 1984, *The Influence of Various Home Bilingual Environments on the Academic Achievement, Language Development, and Psychosocial Adjustment of Fifth and Sixth Grade Hispanic Students.* Unpublished doctoral dissertation, The University of San Francisco.

Duncan, S. E. & DeAvila, E. A. 1979, Bilingualism and cognition: Some recent findings. *NABE Journal,* 4, 15–50.

Duran, M. S. 1978, Working with Spanish-speaking Latin American students in Toronto. *TESL TALK,* 9, 27–31.

Edelsky, C., Hudelson, S., Flores, B., Barkin, F., Altweger, B. and Jilbert, K. 1983, Semi-lingualism and language deficit. *Applied Linguistics,* 4, 1–22.

Evans, E. 1978, Welsh (Cymraeg). In C. V. James (ed.), *The Older Mother Tongues of the United Kingdom.* London: Centre for Information on Language Teaching and Research.

Feldman, C. & Shen, M. 1971, Some language-related cognitive advantages of bilingual five-year-olds. *Journal of Genetic Psychology,* 118, 235–44.

Feuerstein, R. 1979, *The Dynamic Assessment of Retarded Performers: The Learning Potential Assessment Device, Theory, Instruments, and Techniques.* Baltimore: University Park Press.

Fram, I. & Crawford, P. 1972, An examination of the relationship between sex, birth date, and English-as-a second language and teachers' predictions of academic success. Research report, North York Board of Education. (ONOO494).

Gale, K., McClay, D., Christie, M. & Harris, S. 1981, Academic achievement in the Milingimbi bilingual education program. *TESOL Quarterly,* 15, 297–314.

Genesee, F., Tucker, G. R. & Lambert, W. E. 1975, Communication skills of bilingual children. *Child Development,* 46, 1013–18.

Good, T. L. & Brophy, J. E. 1971, Analyzing classroom interaction: A more powerful alternative. *Educational Technology,* 11, 36–40.

Goodman, K., Goodman, Y. & Flores, B. 1979, *Reading in the Bilingual Classroom: Literacy and Biliteracy.* Rosslyn, Virginia: National Clearinghouse for Bilingual Education.

Guthrie, L. F. 1981, *The Task Variable in Children's Language Use: Cultural and Situational Differences.* Unpublished doctoral dissertation, University of Illinois at Urbana-Champaign.

Guthrie, L. F. & Hall, W. S. 1983, Continuity/discontinuity in the function and use of language. In E. Gordon (ed.), *Review of Research in Education. Vol. 10.* Itasca, Illinois: F. E. Peacock.

Hakuta, K. & Diaz, R. M. 1983, The relationship between degree of bilingualism and cognitive ability: A critical discussion and some new longitudinal data. In K. E. Nelson (ed.), *Children's Language.* Hillsdale, New Jersey: Lawrence Erlbaum Associates.

Heller, M. 1983, The social meaning of French and English in a French language school. Unpublished research report, The Ontario Institute for Studies in Education.

Heyman, A. G. 1973, *Invandrarbarn. Studiehangleding.* Stockholms invandrarnamnd.

Ianco-Worrall, A. 1972, Bilingualism and cognitive development. *Child Development,* 43, 1390–1400.

Jensen, J. V. 1962a, Effects of childhood bilingualism, I. *Elementary English,* 39, 132–43.
——— 1962b, Effects of childhood bilingualism, II. *Elementary English,* 39, 358–66.

Kaufman, A. S. 1979, *Intelligent Testing with the WISC-R.* New York: Wiley.

Kerman, S., Kimball, T. & Martin, M. 1980, *Teacher Expectations and Student Achievement.* Downey, California: Office of the Los Angeles County Superintendent of Schools.

Kessler, C. & Quinn, M. E. 1980, Positive effects of bilingualism on science problem-solving abilities. In J. E. Alatis (ed). *Georgetown University Round Table on Languages and Linguistics,* 1980. Washington, D.C.: Georgetown University Press.

Lambert, W. E. 1975, Culture and language as factors in learning and education. In A. Wolfgang (ed.), *Education of Immigrant Students.* Toronto: The Ontario Institute for Studies in Education.

Lambert, W. E. & Tucker, G. R. 1972, *Bilingual Education of Children: The St. Lambert Experiment,* Rowley, Mass.: Newbury House.

Liedke, W. W. & Nelson, L. D. 1968, Concept formation and bilingualism. *Alberta Journal of Education Research,* 14, 225–32.

Llewellyn, R. 1968, *How Green Was My Valley.* Toronto: Signet.

Löfgren, H. & Ouvinen-Birgerstam, P. 1982, A bilingual model for the teaching of immigrant children. *Journal of Multilingual and Multicultural Development.* 3, 323–31.

Macnamara, J. 1966, *Bilingualism and Primary Education.* Edinburgh: Edinburgh University Press.

Malherbe, E. G. 1946, *The Bilingual School.* Johannesburg: Bilingual School Association.

McDermott, R. P. 1978, Relating and learning: An analysis of two classroom reading groups. In R. Shuy (ed.), *Linguistics and Reading.* Rowley, Mass.: Newbury House.

McLaughlin, B. 1984, Early bilingualism: Methodological and theoretical issues. In Y. Lebrun and M. Paradis (eds), *Early bilingualism and child development.* Amsterdam: Swets and Zeitlinger.

McNab, G. 1979, Cognition and bilingualism: A reanalysis of studies. *Linguistics,* 17, 231–55.

Merino, R. 1983, The Effects of L1 and L2 Instruction on the Metalinguistic Awareness of Spanish-speaking Children. Unpublished dissertation, University of the Pacific.

Modiano, N. 1968, National or mother tongue language in beginning reading: A comparative study. *Research in the Teaching of English,* 2, 32–43.

Mohanty, A. K. 1982, Bilingualism among Kond tribals in Orissa (India): Consequences, issues and implications. Unpublished research report, Uktal University.

Mohatt, G. & Erickson, F. 1981, Cultural differences in teaching styles in an Odawa school: A sociolinguistic approach. In H. T. Trueba, G. P. Guthrie & K. H. Au (eds), *Culture and the Bilingual Classroom: Studies in Classroom Ethnography.* Rowley, Mass.: Newbury House.

Moll, L. C. 1981, The microethnographic study of bilingual schooling. In R. V. Padilla (ed.), *Ethnoperspectives in Bilingual Education Research, Volume III. Bilingual Education Technology.* Ypsilanti, Michigan: Department of Foreign Languages and Bilingual Studies.

Mougeon, R. & Canale, M. 1978–79, Maintenance of French in Ontario: Is education in French enough? *Interchange,* 9, 30–39.

National Assessment of Educational Progress. 1983a, *Students from Homes in Which English Is Not the Dominant Language: Who Are They and How Well Do They Read?* No. 11-R-50. Denver: Education Commission of the States.

———— 1983b, Newsletter, 16, No. 1, Winter.

Novak, C. 1973, *Intellectual Assessment of Bilingual Italian Immigrant Children in Their Native Language*. Unpublished master's thesis, University of Toronto.

Ogbu, J. U. 1978, *Minority Education and Caste*. New York: Academic Press.

———— 1983, Minority status and schooling in plural societies. *Comparative Education Review*, 27, 168–90.

Paulston, C. B. 1983, *Swedish Research and Debate about Bilingualism*. Stockholm: National Swedish Board of Education.

Peal, E. & Lambert, W. E. 1962, The relation of bilingualism to intelligence. *Psychological Monographs*, 76, No. 546.

Phillips, S. 1972, Participant structures and communicative competence: Warm springs children in community and classroom. In C. Cazden, D. Hymes, & V. J. John (eds), *Functions of Language in the Classroom*. New York: Teachers' College Press.

Rist, R. C. 1970, Student social class and teacher expectations: The self-fulfilling prophecy in ghetto education. *Harvard Educational Review*, 40, 411–51.

———— 1979, On the education of guest-worker children in Germany: A comparative study of policies and programs in Bavaria and Berlin. *School Review*, 87, 242–68.

Rosenthal, A. S., Milne, A., Ginsburg, A. & Baker, K. 1981, *A Comparison of the Effects of Language Background and Socioeconomic Status on Achievement among Elementary School Students*. Washington, D.C.: Applied Urbanetics, Inc.

Rueda, R. 1983, Metalinguistic awareness in monolingual and bilingual mildly retarded children. *NABE Journal*, 8, 55–68.

Ryan, W. 1972, *Blaming the Victim*. New York: Vintage.

Scott, S. 1973, The relation of divergent thinking to bilingualism: Cause or effect? Unpublished research report, McGill University.

Skutnabb-Kangas, T. 1984, *Bilingualism or Not: The Education of Minorities*. Clevedon, England: Multilingual Matters Ltd.

Skutnabb-Kangas, T. & Toukomaa, P. 1976, *Teaching Migrant Children's Mother Tongue and Learning the Language of the Host Country in the Context of the Socio-Cultural Situation of the Migrant Family*. Helsinki: The Finnish National Commission for UNESCO.

Spence, A. G., Mishra, S. P. & Ghozeil, S. 1971, Home language and performance on standardized tests. *Elementary School Journal*, 71, 309–13.

Swain, M. & Lapkin, S. 1982, *Evaluating Bilingual Education: A Canadian Case Study*. Clevedon, England: Multilingual Matters Ltd.

Toukomaa, P. & Skutnabb-Kangas, T. 1977, *The Intensive Teaching of the Mother Tongue to Migrant Children of Pre-School Age and Children in the Lower Level of Comprehensive School*. Helsinki: The Finnish National Commission for UNESCO.

Troike, R. 1978, Research evidence for the effectiveness of bilingual education. *NABE Journal*, 3, 13–24.

———— 1984, SCALP: Social and cultural aspects of language proficiency. In C. Rivera (ed.), *Language Proficiency and Academic Achievement*. Clevedon, England: Multilingual Matters Ltd.

United States v. State of Texas. 1981, Civil Action No. 5281 (Bilingual Education). Memorandum Opinion.

U.S. Commission on Civil Rights. 1973, *Teachers and Students: Differences in Teacher Interaction with Mexican–American and Anglo Students.* Washington, D.C.: U.S. Government Printing Office.

Vildomec, V. 1963, *Multilingualism.* Leyden: A. W. Sythoff.

Vygotsky, L. S. 1962, *Thought and language.* Cambridge, Mass.: M.I.T. Press.

Wells, G. 1981, *Learning through interaction: The study of language development.* Cambridge: Cambridge University Press.

Wijnstra, J. M. 1980, Attainment in English in the schools of Wales. *International Review of Applied Psychology,* 29, 61–74.

Wong Fillmore, L. 1983, The language learner as an individual: Implications of research on individual differences for the ESL teacher. In M. A. Clarke and J. Handscombe (eds), *On TESOL '82: Pacific perspectives on language learning and teaching.* Washington, D.C.: TESOL.

Yee, L. Y. & Laforge, R. 1974, Relationship between mental abilities, social class, and exposure to English in Chinese fourth graders. *Journal of Educational Psychology,* 66, 826–34.

THEORY AND IMPLICATIONS

1. What arguments do you find to be most convincing concerning the benefits of bilingualism? Why?

2. Why do you suppose educators were so ready to make minority children's bilingualism the "scapegoat for their academic difficulties"? Do you think it is just "Anglo-conformity"? What else could it be?

3. What "metalinguistic" advantages can you recall from your own experience learning a second language?

4. The idea of a certain minimum or threshold level of proficiency has been criticized. One criticism is that the benefits may accrue before Cummins's minimum level. What might be some of the other problems with the concept?

5. Why are the bilingual program evaluations so helpful in assessing the cause of minority-language children's underachievement?

6. Many educators think that parents' use of the minority language in the home handicaps their children. What are some of the negative implications of this assumption?

7. Educators often assess language difficulties incorrectly. What signs of deficiency might easily be misinterpreted? Where do educators most need to be careful with assessments?

8. Why are Ogbu's distinctions important? How do they complement the theory of additive versus subtractive bilingualism?

9. The distinction between context-reduced and context-dependent or -embedded language has generated controversy. Some researchers suggests that language is always context-embedded—even writing, which supposedly aims at being context-independent. Do you think that language can be sometimes more and sometimes less dependent on context? Explain.

10. What general implications for teaching does this research offer?

PROFESSIONAL CONCERNS

1. Cummins's theories have had an immense impact on the education of minority students. Explain to a skeptical professional why the theoretical constructs Cummins offers, however problematic, have so much power to reshape educators' thinking about language minority students.

2. Write a letter to a colleague who has expressed disgust with the mistakes her minority-language students make. Perhaps locate an essay written by a minority-language student and fabricate a typical teacher response provoked by such disgust. Write a gently argumentative reply to this colleague in which you analyze the students' mistakes and provide an explanation in terms of Cummins's theories.

The Cognitive Academic Language Learning Approach*

ANNA UHL CHAMOT AND J. MICHAEL O'MALLEY

"The Cognitive Academic Language Learning Approach" offers concrete suggestions to implement Cummins's emphasis on academic proficiency. As research points increasingly to academic deficits experienced by L2 learners, studies like this one help teachers to make an important distinction: Language is not *a superficial skill acquired in a quick-fix ESL class stressing rule memorization and application; rather, it involves complex "procedures" with endless possibilities of combination. Procedures are not isolated skills but methods for approaching the task as a whole. To develop these procedures fully, L2 learners must use language to master subject matter, not simply to demonstrate rule mastery. Thus teachers need to devise a content-based curriculum that allows for the slow accretion of procedural skills.*

This distinction between rules and procedures also surfaces in Mike Rose's important work on writer's block ("Rigid Rules, Inflexible Plans, and the Stifling of Language: A Cognitivist Analysis of Writer's Block," College Composition and Communication, *Vol. 31, No. 4, Dec. 1980). Inflexible rules like "Have a thesis before writing the paper" can distort the writing process; they demand error-free performance of a single step before further steps can be taken. To the contrary, the procedural approach described by Chamot and O'Malley stresses that learners need "to perform complete sequences of the procedure, no matter how inexpertly." This encapsulates one of the central controversies in language arts: whole language versus discrete skills approaches.*

---

* Chamot, A. U. and J. M. O'Malley, "The Cognitive Academic Language Learning Approach," in *When They Can't All Speak English: Integrating The ESL Student into the Regular Classroom,* Pat Rigg and Virginia G. Allen, editors. Copyright © 1989 by the National Council of Teachers of English. Reprinted with permission.

The methods offered here can be used in both an ESL program and an English-only or monolingual classroom comprising many ESL students. The practical suggestions for developing academic language skills should be useful to all teachers addressing nonnative speakers of English.

INTRODUCTION

This [reading] provides suggestions to elementary classroom teachers and secondary English and reading teachers on ways in which they can help their second-language students achieve greater success in content-area subjects. Mainstream teachers have an important role in furthering the education of ESL students in their classrooms, both in identifying and overcoming any difficulties these students may experience and in capitalizing on their background as a resource to other students. First, we will explain some of the reasons second-language students encounter academic difficulties related to both language and prior educational experiences. Then we will describe an instructional system designed to develop the academic language skills and learning strategies of these students in ESL classes, and show how many of the same techniques can be used by classroom teachers to further the academic development of their ESL students. Finally, we will present a lesson plan model that can be used to improve the academic competence of both first- and second-language speakers in a mainstream classroom.

BACKGROUND

When students speaking little or no English first enter school, they are usually placed in a language program to develop English skills for one or more years. Two general types of program are available to these students: English-as-a-second-language (ESL) and bilingual programs. In ESL programs, students receive intensive instruction in English-language skills for part of the day and spend the remainder in their regular classroom. In bilingual programs, students also receive ESL instruction, but the remainder of the day is spent in basic skills instruction in the native language. The rationale for bilingual programs is that skills such as reading and problem solving are transferable across languages; by providing instruction in a language that students can understand, greater progress may be achieved in the long run. Second-language students, whether in an ESL or a bilingual program, leave the program as soon as they demonstrate a level of proficiency in English that teachers and test performance indicate will allow them to function successfully in the all-English mainstream curriculum. Deciding exactly when a student has reached an adequate level of English proficiency is a difficulty faced in both ESL and bilingual programs. The most frequently used language proficiency tests tap social, interactive, and basic literacy skills, only a small portion of the total array of language skills required in academic subject areas.

Of the minority-language background students entering mainstream classrooms after a bilingual or ESL program, some will have already learned English and some basic skills well enough to make satisfactory progress in their schooling.

But many of these students will still have problems learning in English and will encounter serious difficulties with the academic subjects. The record shows high dropout rates for such students (Bennett 1986; Duran 1983; O'Malley and Schmitt 1987), with the result that they are denied opportunities for participating successfully in our society.

Researchers have attributed many of the difficulties encountered by ESL students in mainstream classrooms to differences between the type of language used for ordinary social conversation and the type of language used for academic purposes, and the fact that these academic language skills take considerably longer to develop than social language skills (Collier 1987; Cummins 1983; Saville-Troike 1984). Cummins (1981) analyzed the school records of 1,200 immigrant minority-language students in Canada, and found that while most developed social inter-active skills in English in about two years, five to seven years were needed before students were able to use academic language appropriate to their grade level.

A recent study confirmed Cummins's findings and provided additional information about the relationships between age of arrival and amount of previous education on school achievement by immigrant students in the United States. Collier (1987) examined the standardized achievement test scores of over 1,500 immigrant students who had been mainstreamed after completing an ESL program. These students, with the exception of five- to seven-year-olds, had been at grade level in their native countries when they arrived in the United States of America. Collier found that immigrant students entering school between the ages of eight and eleven needed four to five years to reach an average score at the fiftieth percentile on nationally standardized tests of reading, language arts, science, and social studies. These eight- to eleven-year-olds needed the least time to become moderately successful in mainstream instruction, as evidenced by standardized test scores. Students entering school at ages five to seven without initial primary education in their native countries were less advanced academically than the older group. For these younger students, a period of five to eight years was needed to reach the same standardized test norms. At greatest academic risk were students who had arrived in the United States at age twelve or older. These middle and secondary school students were only at about the fortieth percentile on most tests after four to five years of instruction, which included both ESL and regular classroom instruction. Collier indicates that the heavy cognitive and academic language demands which students encounter in the secondary school make it difficult for them to catch up, and states that secondary students are most in need of content-area instruction (rather than only intensive English-language instruction).

Close collaboration between classroom and language specialist (ESL and bilingual) teachers is essential in meeting the educational needs of these students. Language development does not stop when students are not in ESL classes. All teachers need to work together to ensure that language skills are developed throughout the school day. Minority-language students may need more time than is usually provided for them to develop academic language skills in English in bilingual and ESL programs. In many cases, ESL students may also need help in how to learn academic content. Because of the attention devoted to language at the beginning level of ESL instruction, students may have had limited opportunities to develop effective learning strategies and study skills. Also, unless students have been in a content-based ESL class or maintained their subject matter development through instruction in their own languages, they can be expected to have significant gaps in content-area knowledge and skills. For these reasons, classroom teachers with students who are either in an ESL or bilingual program for part of the day or have recently exited from such a program need to continue to develop language skills and learning strategies in all areas of the curriculum. In the next section, we describe an instructional approach that can be used to teach language across the curriculum and to provide direct instruction in the use of learning strategies for all subjects.

THE COGNITIVE ACADEMIC LANGUAGE LEARNING APPROACH

The Cognitive Academic Language Learning Approach (CALLA) is an instructional system designed to develop academic language skills in English for students in upper elementary and secondary schools. CALLA (pronounced *kala*) is intended for three types of ESL students (Chamot and O'Malley 1987):

- students who have developed social communicative skills through ESL or exposure to an English-speaking environment, but have not developed academic language skills appropriate to their grade level
- students exiting from bilingual programs who need assistance in transferring concepts and skills learned in their native language to English
- bilingual English-dominant students who are even less academically proficient in their native language than in English, and need to develop academic English language skills

The CALLA instructional system consists of three components: a content-based curriculum appropriate to the students' grade/developmental level; academic language development activities; and instruction and practice in using learning strategies. CALLA was originally designed as a transitional ESL program for students at intermediate and advanced levels of English proficiency, but the instructional techniques we advocate can be effectively used by mainstream teachers with second-language students in their rooms.

CALLA is based on theory, research, and practice. In this chapter, an overview of the theoretical model underlying CALLA is described first. Next, a discussion of the three components of CALLA and how each can be developed by the classroom teacher is presented. Finally, a lesson plan model focusing on the development of academic language skills and concepts in English is described.

Theoretical Model

CALLA is based on a theory which suggests that language is a complex cognitive skill, similar in many respects to other complex cognitive skills (such as reading for comprehension, writing, and problem solving in mathematics). The theory indicates that learning a language is similar to learning any other complex cognitive skill; that is, learning a language has more in common with learning complex cognitive skills than it does with learning facts, isolated pieces of information, or even meaningful texts. Therefore, many of the techniques that classroom teachers use in teaching other complex skills will apply directly to teaching the ESL learner. In this section, we identify four aspects of complex cognitive skills, and then derive implications for teaching.

First, complex cognitive skills consist of procedures (Anderson 1985). These procedures are based on complex sequences or steps that learners begin to master gradually as they compile larger units of the skill. As in learning the procedures to perform a borrow and carry operation in mathematics, students may learn the procedures for a language skill such as regular and irregular pluralization.

Second, it takes a very long time to master complex cognitive skills. In language learning, the procedures are so complex, and the possibilities of combinations are so limitless, that achieving mastery level performance of the skill may easily take several years (Collier 1987; Cummins 1983; Saville-Troike 1984).

Third, any complex skill is best learned when the learner can try to perform complete sequences of the procedure, no matter how inexpertly, and receive cued feedback upon encountering difficulties (Gagné 1986). This is in contrast to learning a set of rules, rehearsing and repeating the rules until they are committed to memory, and then attempting to use the rules as a guide to performance. The best feedback in second-language acquisition is immediate and responds to the learner's intended meaning, rather than to any errors committed in the attempt to communicate. Feedback that is based on the success of meaningful communication may be provided by other students as well as by the teacher.

Fourth, it may be difficult to transfer a complex skill learned in one environment to another environment or to a different linguistic task. For example, ESL students may comprehend present progressive constructions (I am _____ ing) quite well when they hear or read them, but still say "I am go" or "I going."

These aspects have implications for teaching. One implication is that second-language development may progress most effectively when learners can use the language on the type of materials for which they are expected to demonstrate mastery. This is why we recommend using authentic content-related materials in a content-based ESL classroom to prepare students for the same type of materials in a regular classroom. A second implication is that the learner needs to receive immediate feedback, and since the teacher cannot give every student immediate feedback on every utterance, the teacher should use peer tutoring in cooperative learning situations with students whose English proficiency is at varying levels. A third implication is that the teacher should make sure that all four language areas of writing, listening, speaking, reading—are included in every lesson and in every content area. This addresses, at least in part, the problem of transfer.

The Three Components of CALLA

The three components of CALLA (grade-appropriate content, academic language development, and learning strategy instruction) are integrated into an instructional system which teaches ESL students how to use the language and learning strategies that they need for success in academic areas of the curriculum. Although CALLA was originally designed as a transitional ESL program, the educational principles of CALLA can be applied to mainstream classrooms with both native- and non-native-English-speaking students. This is because CALLA is based on research about how students learn both concepts and skills—whatever the language. Teaching students how to learn more efficiently by applying appropriate learning strategies including language activities in all areas of the curriculum is, we believe, beneficial to all students, not just ESL students.

The Content-based Curriculum. When CALLA is taught in an ESL program, the curriculum is carefully aligned with the all-English curriculum that students will eventually enter, so that practice is provided with a selection of the actual topics students will encounter in the mainstream classes. The intent is not to duplicate the mainstream curriculum, but to prepare the students to enter that curriculum, one subject at a time. We recommend that different subjects be phased in the following sequence: first science, then mathematics, then social studies, and finally language arts (literature and composition, not ESL).

Why do we recommend moving the ESL student gradually into the curriculum? We recommend beginning with science because by using a discovery approach to science, teachers can provide hands-on activities, which are so important for the ESL speaker. The next subject, mathematics, is highly abstract in the upper grades, and uses more restricted language than science. The third subject, social studies, has heavy reading and writing demands as well as potentially unfamiliar cultural information. Language arts is introduced last because grade-appropriate literature and composition are often the most difficult for ESL students; not only is a high level of English required, but so is a shared background of cultural assumptions. In a CALLA classroom, content topics are carefully selected to represent both authentic topics at grade level and high priority topics within the curriculum. Classroom teachers can work closely with ESL and bilingual teachers, sharing their content objectives and major topics of study, so that common curricular objectives can be taught by both mainstream and language specialist teachers.

A common reaction to the less-than-fluent English of a student is to teach content from a lower grade level and to expect only lower-level cognitive skills, such as simple recall. CALLA demands the opposite. ESL students need to learn content that is appropriate to their developmental level and prior educational experience, and higher-level thinking skills are as much to be expected from them as from any student. Teachers should ask higher-order questions and evaluate responses on the basis of the ideas expressed, rather than on the correctness of English. Rather than watering down content for second-language students, teachers can make challenging content comprehensible by providing additional contextual support through demonstrations, visuals, and hands-on experiences. Also, teachers can help students apply learning strategies in order to understand and remember the content presented. Suggestions for doing this are presented later in this chapter.

Academic Language Development. In CALLA's second component, students practice using English as a tool for learning academic subject matter. These academic language skills may or may not have been developed in the first language, so students may either need instruction on how to transfer previously learned skills to English, or may need to learn academic language for the first time.

Why should academic language be particularly difficult for ESL students? There are two factors, according to Cummins (1981, 1983), that affect language comprehension: context and cognitive complexity. Language that is most comprehensible takes place in a here-and-now context that is rich in both nonverbal cues (such as concrete objects, visual aids, and gestures) and in opportunities to interact with people and things. For example, a child has a good chance of understanding the term *red ball* when she and a friend are playing with several toys and the friend points and asks her to "throw the red ball." Her chance of understanding this highly contextualized term is much less when she is asked to look at a workbook page with three circles, and is told that the one in the middle is a red ball.

The language of classrooms is sometimes called "decontextualized" because often the language does not refer to hands-on activities, but to ideas and events that are far removed from the immediate setting. Furthermore, the language of classrooms is often complex and requires manipulation of difficult concepts, especially in content areas. Thus, academic language is both decontextualized and high in cognitive complexity. The schooling process gradually develops in children the skills necessary to use this sort of academic language though the use of contextual supports for meaning in the early grades. But when ESL children enter mainstream classes at the upper elementary or secondary level, they may not be able to manipulate academic concepts in English in a decontextualized instructional setting.

ESL students can begin developing academic language skills in English through cognitively demanding activities in which comprehension is assisted by contextual support. Some of these activities include (Chamot and O'Malley 1987):

Developing an academic vocabulary in different content areas.

Understanding academic presentations accompanied by visuals and demonstrations.

Participating in hands-on science activities.

Using manipulatives to discuss and solve math word-problems.

Making models, maps, graphs, and charts in social studies.

Participating in academic discussions and making brief oral presentations.

Understanding written texts through discussion, demonstration, and visuals.

Using standard formats as supportive structures for writing simple reports in science and social studies.

Answering higher-level questions orally.

These and similar content-based language activities provide opportunities for ESL students to develop academic language proficiency in English while participating in mainstream classrooms. The language arts and English teacher can assist this development by including in their classes materials and concepts drawn from the content areas. For example, some reading exercises might include skimming a scientific article, scanning a mathematics word-problem, and taking notes on a chapter in a social studies textbook. Writing activities could include additional expository writing related to content areas, so that students learn how to organize a science laboratory report and how to do library research for a history paper.

Learning Strategy Instruction. The third and central component in CALLA is instruction in learning strategies. This is a cognitive approach to teaching that assists students by identifying and teaching conscious techniques that facilitate learning both language and content. We have four main reasons for advocating this sort of instruction (Chamot and O'Malley 1987):

1. Mentally active learners are better learners. Students who organize new information and consciously relate it to existing knowledge should have more cognitive linkages to assist comprehension and recall than do students who approach each new task as something to be memorized by rote learning.
2. Strategies can be taught. Students who are taught to use strategies and provided with sufficient practice in using them will learn more effectively than students who have had no experience with learning strategies.
3. Learning strategies transfer to new tasks. Once students have become accustomed to using learning strategies, they will use them on new tasks that are similar to the learning activities on which they were initially trained.
4. Academic language learning is more effective with learning strategies. Academic language learning among students of ESL is governed by some of the same principles that govern reading and problem solving among native English speakers.

Many older ESL students may have developed learning strategies attuned to educational experiences in their native countries. For example, in an educational system that places a high value on assimilation of facts, students might learn highly effective rote memorization strategies. Other strategies, however, are needed for integrative language tasks such as reading for information, explaining a process, or developing a report. Many students, whether proficient in English or not, need direct instruction and extensive practice in using learning strategies appropriate to different types of academic tasks. Teachers who have used CALLA in classes with both mainstream and ESL students report that instruction in learning strategies is as beneficial to native speakers of English as it is to students learning English as another language.

Teaching ESL students to use conscious learning strategies can accomplish three important goals: learning language, learning through language, and learning to learn. Studies that have taught English-speaking students to use learning strategies to improve their reading comprehension and their ability to solve problems in math and science have demonstrated that learning strategy instruction can be successful (Romberg and Carpenter 1986; Weinstein and Meyer 1986; White and Tisher 1986). In extending this research to second-language learners, we have concluded that learning strategies seem to be as effective for learning language as they are for learning in other areas. Good language learners use many different learning strategies, often in quite intricate ways, to help them understand and remember new information, whereas less effective learners have fewer strategies and apply them infrequently or inappropriately (O'Malley, Chamot, and Kupper, 1987).

We have identified three major types of learning strategies used by students (O'Malley et al. 1985a):

Metacognitive strategies, which involve executive processes in planning for learning, monitoring one's comprehension and production, and evaluating how well one has achieved a learning objective.

Cognitive strategies, in which the learner interacts with the material to be learned by manipulating it mentally (as in making mental images, or elaborating on previously acquired concepts or skills) or physically (as in grouping items to be learned in meaningful categories, or taking notes on important information to be remembered).

Social-affective strategies, in which the learner either interacts with another person in order to assist learning, as in cooperation or asking questions for clarification, or uses some kind of affective control to assist a learning task.

In studying learning strategies used in different contexts, we have come to the conclusion that a group of general learning strategies may be of particular use for ESL students who are learning both language and content (Chamot and O'Malley 1987). Figure 1 lists and defines this group of learning strategies.

Some of the learning strategies in Figure 1 are often thought of as study skills. Study skills describe overt behavior, such as taking notes, writing summaries, or using reference materials, while learning strategies generally pertain to unobservable mental processes. Students need to learn study skills, the overt behavior associated with learning strategies, and they also need to learn to use nonobservable strategies, such as monitoring for comprehension, elaboration of prior knowledge, and inferencing. Learning strategies can be defined, then, as how a person thinks and acts to complete a task.

A good way to initiate learning strategy instruction is to find out what strategies students are already using for different learning activities. Teachers can interview students about ways they approach specific classroom tasks and can also have students "think aloud" as they take turns working on a task. These two activities can help students become more aware of the mental processes they engage in when approaching and solving a problem, and can help teachers diagnose learning strategy needs. After identifying strategies that students are already using, teachers can use the strategy list in Figure 1 to select, model, and provide practice with additional strategies.

In summary, learning strategy instruction can play an important role in teaching both ESL and native-English-speaking students by showing them how to apply effective learning techniques to language and content learning.

Metacognitive Strategies

Advance Organization	Previewing the main ideas and concepts of the material to be learned, often by skimming the text for the organizing principle.
Organizational Planning	Planning the parts, sequence, main ideas, or language functions to be expressed orally or in writing.
Selective Attention	Deciding in advance to attend to specific aspects of input, often by scanning for key words, concepts, and/or linguistic markers.
Self-monitoring	Checking one's comprehension during listening or reading, or checking the accuracy and/or appropriateness of one's oral or written production while it is taking place.
Self-evaluation	Judging how well one has accomplished a learning activity after it has been completed.

Cognitive Strategies

Resourcing	Using target-language reference materials such as dictionaries, encyclopedias, or textbooks.
Grouping	Classifying words, terminology, or concepts according to their attributes.
Note-taking	Writing down key words and concepts in abbreviated verbal, graphic, or numerical form during a listening or reading activity.
Summarizing	Making a mental or written summary of information gained through listening or reading.
Deduction/Induction	Applying rules to understand or produce the second language, or making up rules based on language analysis.
Imagery	Using visual images (either mental or actual) to understand and remember new information.
Auditory Representation	Playing back in one's mind the sound of a word, phrase, or longer language sequence.
Elaboration	Relating new information to prior knowledge, relating different parts of new information to each other, or making meaningful personal associations to the new information.
Transfer	Using previous linguistic knowledge or prior skills to assist comprehension or production.
Inferencing	Using information in an oral or written text to guess meanings, predict outcomes, or complete missing parts.

Social-Affective Strategies

Questioning for Clarification	Eliciting from a teacher or peer additional explanation, rephrasing, examples, or verification.
Cooperation	Working together with peers to solve a problem, pool information, check a learning task, model a language activity, or get feedback from an oral presentation.
Self-talk	Reducing anxiety by using mental techniques that make one feel competent to do the learning task.

FIGURE 1   Learning strategy definitions (Chamot and O'Malley 1987)

PLANNING A CALLA LESSON

In order to integrate the three components of CALLA into an instructional plan, we have developed a lesson plan model that incorporates learning strategy instruction, content-area topics, and language development activities. In this plan, learning strategy instruction is embedded into daily lessons so that it becomes an integral part of the regular class routine, rather than a supplementary activity. In this way, both second-language and proficient English-speaking students have opportunities to practice the strategies on actual lessons, and use of the strategies becomes part of the class requirements. At first, teachers show students how to use the strategies, often by modeling, and then continue to remind students to use them. Later, teachers remind students less frequently so that they can begin to use strategies independently. Discussion of learning strategies that different students find effective should be ongoing in a CALLA classroom.

CALLA lessons are useful for all students because all students can profit from the integration of language and content and the development of effective learning strategies.

CALLA lessons include both teacher-directed and learner-centered activities. Each CALLA lesson plan is divided into five phases. These are: preparation, presentation, practice, evaluation, and expansion activities. These brief descriptions of each phase indicate how content topics, academic language skills, and learning strategies can be developed in a CALLA lesson.

Preparation

In the preparation phase of the lesson, the teacher finds out what students already know about the concepts to be presented and practiced, what gaps in prior knowledge need to be addressed, and how students have been taught to approach a particular type of learning activity or content area. At the same time, students have the opportunity to remember and value their prior knowledge as they begin to connect it to the lesson topic. Another valuable aspect of this initial discussion is that students can share their different approaches to completing the task. In the preparation phase, the teacher should check essential vocabulary needed for the lesson and, if necessary, develop labels in English for concepts known in the native language.

The learning strategies commonly practiced in the preparation phase are advance organization (students preview the lesson) and elaboration (students recall relevant prior knowledge).

Presentation

In the presentation phase of the lesson, new information is presented and explained to students in English that is supported by contextual clues, such as demonstrations and visuals. Teachers need to make sure that ESL students are comprehending the new information so that they will be able to practice it accurately in the next phase of the lesson. The following suggestions can help the classroom teacher present information that is comprehensible to their ESL students as well as their native-English-speaking students.

- Monitor your own language for clarity, precision, pace, and word choice. When presenting key vocabulary and concepts, define, paraphrase, and give an example.
- Contextualize the language used during presentation of new information (either by the teacher, the text, or other information source) by using concrete objects, pictures, manipulatives, demonstration, miming.
- Use the chalkboard to provide visual backup to the information presented by writing key words and concepts, drawing graphs and charts, or graphically indicating relationships.
- Group students homogeneously for presentation of especially difficult or language-demanding information, and provide additional explanation and illustrations to ESL students.
- Group students heterogeneously for small-group cooperative learning in order to maximize interaction between students, and provide extra incentives for group performance.
- Maintain a supportive affective climate for ESL students by responding to intended meaning (even when expressed in inaccurate English), showing interest in and respect for students' home culture, and involving ESL students in class activities with native-English-speaking students.
- Encourage ESL students to ask questions for clarification when they do not understand; model appropriate questions when necessary; and provide specific guidelines for classroom participation.
- Ask ESL students higher-level questions about the material presented rather than only factual recall questions.

Some of the learning strategies practiced in this phase are: selective attention (attending to or scanning for key ideas), self-monitoring (students check their degree of comprehension), inferencing (guessing meaning from context), note-taking, imagery (imagining descriptions or events presented), and questioning for clarification.

Practice

The practice phase of the lesson is learner-centered, as students engage in hands-on activities to practice the new information they were exposed to in the presentation phase, and the teacher now acts as facilitator. A variety of types of practice should be provided so that students can assimilate the new information and use it in different ways. Cooperative learning in heterogeneous teams is particularly effective during the practice phase, as students can work together in small groups to clarify their understanding of the information previously presented. ESL students can profit from working in small groups with native

English speakers, who can serve both as language models and tutors. The learning strategies typically practiced in this phase of the CALLA lesson are: self-monitoring (students check their language production), organizational planning (planning how to develop an oral or written report or composition), resourcing (using reference materials), grouping (classifying concepts, events, terminology), summarizing, deduction, imagery (making sketches, diagrams, charts), auditory representation (mentally playing back information presented by the teacher), elaboration, inferencing, cooperation (working with peers), and questioning for clarification.

Evaluation

In the evaluation phase of the lesson, students check the level of their performance so that they can gain an understanding of what they have learned and any areas that need review. Evaluation activities can be individual, cooperative, or teacher-directed. Teachers can assess higher-level comprehension by focusing on the meaning of student answers rather than on their grammatical correctness. Learning strategies practiced in the evaluation phase of a CALLA lesson are: self-evaluation, elaboration, questioning for clarification, cooperation, and self-talk (assuring one's self of one's ability to accomplish the task).

Expansion

In the expansion phase of the lesson, students are given a variety of opportunities to think about the new concepts and skills they have learned, integrate them into their existing knowledge frameworks, make real-world applications, and continue to develop academic language. This phase also provides the opportunity to exercise higher-order thinking skills such as inferring new applications of a concept, analyzing the components of a learning activity, drawing parallels with other concepts, and evaluating the importance of a concept or new skill. Some expansion phase CALLA lessons ask students to interview family members about parallels in their native culture to topics presented in class. These home interviews will probably be conducted in the native language, but are then reported in class in English. By finding opportunities to include information about ESL students' cultural and linguistic background in class activities, classroom teachers not only assist in the development of positive self-concept but also provide native-English-speaking students with valuable multicultural experiences. In the expansion phase of a CALLA lesson, any combination of learning strategies appropriate to the activities can be practiced.

The CALLA lesson plan allows for flexibility and different types of activities. We recommend cooperative learning activities for part of each lesson because cooperation not only improves student performance, it also provides additional opportunities for students to use academic language skills for a learning task. The five phases of a CALLA lesson will vary in duration depending on the lesson topic and the extent of students' prior knowledge. The structure of a CALLA lesson helps ensure that students have many opportunities to practice learning strategies and to use academic language skills as they work on grade-appropriate content. Finally, CALLA lessons are organized to facilitate a learner-centered classroom in which all activities are designed to meet student needs and to help students become aware of themselves as mentally active and competent learners.

CONCLUSION

We have described some of the major language-related difficulties that ESL students encounter in mainstream classrooms and have suggested ways in which classroom teachers can assist minority-language students to continue their English language development across the curriculum.

First and most important, we have suggested that classroom teachers need to collaborate closely with language specialist teachers in planning educational activities for ESL students. Classroom teachers can provide assistance to language specialist teachers by sharing with them the major curriculum objectives of the subject(s) they teach, so that these same objectives can be addressed in the ESL or bilingual program. Classroom teachers can also benefit from suggestions and ideas that language specialist teachers can provide on integrating language development activities in all areas of the curriculum. Finally, both mainstream and language specialist teachers need to work together to develop specific instruction on learning strategies for all students, with the ultimate aim of creating autonomous learners.

REFERENCES

Anderson, J. R. 1985. *Cognitive Psychology and Its Implications.* 2d ed. New York: W. H. Freeman.

Bennett, W. J. 1986. *The Condition of Bilingual Education in the Nation, 1986: A Report from the Secretary of Education to the President and the Congress.* Washington, D.C.: Department of Education.

Chamot, A. U., and J. M. O'Malley. 1987. The Cognitive Academic Language Learning Approach: A Bridge to the Mainstream. *TESOL Quarterly* 21 (2): 227–49.

Collier, V. P. 1987. Age and Rate of Acquisition of Cognitive-Academic Second Language Proficiency. Paper presented at the annual meeting of the American Education Research Association, Washington, D.C.

Cummins, J. 1981. The Role of Primary Language Development in Promoting Educational Success for Language Minority Students. In *Schooling and Language Minority Students: A Theoretical Framework.* Los Angeles: California State University, Evaluation, Dissemination, and Assessment Center.

———. 1983. Conceptual and Linguistic Foundations of Language Assessment. In *Issues of Language Assessment Volume II: Language Assessment and Curriculum Planning,* edited by S. S. Seidner. Wheaton, Md.: National Clearinghouse for Bilingual Education.

Duran, R. 1983. *Hispanics' Education and Background: Predictors of College Achievement.* New York: College Entrance Examination Board.

Gagné, E. D. 1986. *The Cognitive Psychology of School Learning.* Boston: Little, Brown.

O'Malley, J. M., A. U. Chamot, and L. Kupper. 1987. Listening Comprehension Strategies in Second Language Acquisition. *Applied Linguistics,* vol. 10.

O'Malley, J. M., A. U. Chamot, G. Stewner-Manzanares, L. Kupper, and R. P. Russo. 1985a. Learning Strategies Used by Beginning and Intermediate ESL Students. *Language Learning* 35 (1): 21–40.
———. 1985b. Learning Strategy Applications with Students of English as a Second Language. *TESOL Quarterly* 19 (3): 557–84.
O'Malley, J. M., and C. Schmitt. 1987. *Academic Growth of High School Age Hispanic Students in the United States.* Washington, D.C.: Center for Education Statistics, U.S. Department of Education.
Romberg, R. T., and T. P. Carpenter. 1986. Research on Teaching and Learning Mathematics. In *Handbook of Research on Teaching,* 3d ed., edited by M. C. Wittrock. New York: Macmillan.
Saville-Troike, M. 1984. What Really Matters in Second Language Learning for Academic Achievement? *TESOL Quarterly* 18 (2): 199–219.
Weinstein, C. E., and R. E. Mayer. 1986. The Teaching of Learning Strategies. In *Handbook of Research on Teaching,* 3d ed., edited by M. C. Wittrock. New York: MacMillan.
White, R. T., and R. P. Tisher. 1986. Research on Natural Sciences. In *Handbook of Research on Teaching,* 3d ed., edited by M. C. Wittrock. New York: MacMillan.

THEORY AND IMPLICATIONS

1. What theories that you have read on L2 acquisition do these methods support? How?

2. Choose a grade level and decide what kind of academic vocabulary you think L2 students should develop for a particular content area. Defend your choice.

3. Can you think of possible hands-on science activities that would be appropriate for different grade levels?

4. What kinds of manipulatives would you use "to discuss and solve math word-problems" for a particular grade level?

5. What do you think Chamot and O'Malley mean by "higher level" questions? What kinds of questions are "higher level"?

6. Devise a lesson for a class you anticipate teaching. What metacognitive, cognitive, and/ or social-affective strategies might be developed for it? How?

7. The distinction between rules and procedures has important implications for language teaching. What do you think these are? Explain.

8. Some of the learning strategies from cognitive psychology have been criticized for being overly general when applied to language learning. Do you think that they are still helpful? Why or why not?

9. How might it be more difficult to implement CALLA in high school classes than in elementary-level classes?

PROFESSIONAL CONCERNS

1. The theory presented here depends on the idea that L2 students need to perform "complete sequences," not isolated activities. Write a position paper for your department or a more speculative paper for your classmates. Try to define what this notion of

"complete sequences" might mean for a particular subject; include how you think feedback might then take place.

2. Chamot and O'Malley state that instruction in learning strategies is as "beneficial to native speakers of English as it is to students learning English as another language." In a letter to your principal, defend your use of CALLA in the classroom. Make explicit references to what you would do and why you would do it. You especially need to detail the explicit benefits to native speakers.

3. Write a paper in which you explain how tenets of CALLA accord with L2 theories you have read.

chapter 3

Acquiring a Second Language: A Sociolinguistic Approach

THE ISSUES

This is the second of two chapters on second language acquisition, one that raises different issues from the psycholinguistic research of the previous chapter. Sociolinguists ask whether or not social factors can account for language acquisition, such as for the early use of *ing* endings. And, examining broad contexts to search for differences, they ask whether all L2 students learn the same way and at the same rate. Thus sociolinguists account for other variables, some of which increase the complexity of the research. For instance, whereas the psychologist S. P. Corder admittedly excludes motivation as a factor in learners' errors, holding motivation constant in order to prove that L2 learners' errors are not caused by interference, sociolinguists include such variables.

The field of sociolinguistics looks at social forces like learning environments, social purposes, motivation, and teaching methods. It does not raise questions about universals or try to describe intrinsic difficulty levels among grammatical features. Significantly, both fields offer extensive practical applications for teachers. But whereas psycholinguistic research suggests that teachers devise a broadly interactive learning environment, sociolinguistic studies stress the importance of specific social contexts and teaching strategies to increase motivation, hasten acquisition, and develop academic competence in the L2.

PRINCIPLES OF LANGUAGE ACQUISITION—A SOCIAL PERSPECTIVE

A social perspective of L2 acquisition broadens grammatical concerns of linguists to include such variables as motivation, social constraints, rules of conversation, and language roles and play. It de-emphasizes innate processes and thus downplays similarities between L1 and L2 learning strategies; instead it emphasizes differences between L1 and L2 situations and strategies. Therefore, although all children are highly motivated to learn L1, not all are equally motivated to learn L2. And even if children are equally motivated, they may do so at widely different rates, depending on personality and social access. What is learned comprises social meanings, not simply grammatical forms. Thus, whereas psycholinguists focus on individual morphemes and grammatical units, sociolinguists typically look at larger conversational or discourse units.

Psycholinguists and sociolinguists share the same concerns for reducing bias, recognizing ethnic diversity, changing teacher attitudes, and implementing appropriate classroom pedagogies, but their different emphases shape these issues differently. Although both stress the need for interaction, extensive comprehensible input, and an environment for active rule hypothesizing, a social view suggests attention to individual student needs, especially motivation, language history, and the creation of social roles in the classroom. How language is used within specific contexts for specific purposes becomes important in students' learning the meaning of words, not simply their grammatical forms. Thus a social perspective stresses learning that is not necessarily innate or achieved in a preset sequence; it is learning in the social context.

Given the complexity of social factors, the issue of L2 errors becomes equally complex. The range of errors for L2 acquirers is very large, far greater than for dialect speakers, whose language reflects well-established community standards. Lacking such standards, L2 errors are sensitive to such widely varying influences as personality, motivation, and learning strategies. The errors themselves reflect competencies, as psycholinguistic studies show, but their perpetuation (fossilization) reflects complex social factors.

PROFESSIONAL APPLICATIONS

Introducing this chapter are readings on our language heritage and on laws affecting language minorities. These readings are more generally social than sociolinguistic, but they raise language issues central to our society as a whole. Teachers benefit from the background information provided by such studies. Understanding the language history and laws regarding second language learners provides a context for teaching decisions and gives teachers the knowledge of legal and social history they need to defend their practices. Parents cannot claim "English only" in the face of U.S. language history; nor can they claim that enhancing L1 while teaching L2 increases national divisiveness when it has not done so in the past. When parents complain about the funds diverted to bilingual programs, teachers can cite laws and cases that make such programs necessary.

The more sociolinguistic readings that follow these broad readings indicate how social factors can interact with cognitive factors. Understanding the important social variables affecting L2 learners particularly helps teachers to shape their classroom environment and curriculum. The studies recommend that teachers use functional materials with clear social uses and build on children's social skills, enhancing acquisition by using their motivations to converse, to play, and to gain social ends. Specifically, teachers can encourage collaboration, role play, and dramatization, which build students' confidence. Defining social roles for students other than that of passive listener—roles such as collaborator, teacher, expert, or critic—enhances language acquisition.

OVERVIEW OF THE READINGS

The essays selected here attempt to give context and scope to the issues of language acquisition raised in the previous chapter. First, to offer the broadest social perspective, they offer a historical overview of U.S. language policy and law. The first two readings, Shirley Brice Heath's "English in Our Language Heritage" and Sau-ling Cynthia Wong's "Educational Rights of Language Minorities," offer historical overviews of language attitudes, laws, and teaching in the United States. Heath's essay should surprise many who assume that the United States has held an "English only" policy since the Revolution. Wong's focus on U.S. legal history provides useful information about specific legal mandates addressing language problems. Together these essays offer important contexts for sociolinguistic theory that affect other variables, such as motivation and opportunity for social interaction.

The next two readings emphasize, in different ways, the importance of social interaction. "A Look at Process in Child Second-Language Acquisition," by Evelyn Hatch, Sabrina Peck, and Judy Wagner-Gough, show that the rules of conversation account for the set order of acquisition that psycholinguists attribute to innate factors. Through conversation, children learn discourse formulas as well as grammar, which thus implies the importance of social access and personality. Similarly, Lily Wong Fillmore's "Individual Differences in Second Language Acquisition" addresses broad social factors of personality, motivation, and social interactions as they affect individual rates of acquisition. In her study, those children who identified with English speakers and used the language to make friends, play-act, or express themselves acquired English faster than those who did not, regardless of stated motivation. Thus not only are L2 processes different from L1 processes, but individual L2 learners differ widely as well.

The last essay, Donna Johnson's "ESL Children as Teachers: A Social View of Second Language Use," offers the practical implications of a social perspective. She stresses the need for functional approaches to teaching L2 acquirers, approaches that call for new roles and purposes such as those created through peer tutoring.

English in Our Language Heritage*

SHIRLEY BRICE HEATH

"English in our Language Heritage" chronicles immigration patterns and language attitudes in the United States, offering a needed historical perspective on current debates about maintenance versus suppression of the native language, and a history of the legal decisions made with respect to language. Specifically it shows that English has never been made the legal language of this country, that one's native language has traditionally been held a human right, and that the early public schools taught subject matter in the immigrant language. Indeed until the 1920s, individual settlements used religious education and economic institutions to maintain their native tongue.

Despite this insistence on language maintenance, standard English has long been viewed as a necessity, and correctness of standard English has always been highly valued. We can thus conclude that the debates today over bilingualism versus monolingualism, and language variety and cultural rights versus standard English correctness, resemble earlier debates in U.S. history. For over two centuries, Americans have looked at these issues with double vision.

Knowledge of language history helps teachers to respond to typical parents' views that immigrants have always had to learn English, that the most effective way to learn is through maximum exposure, and that language maintenance programs delay or impede progress in English. This knowledge also helps them to contend with parents' angry feelings that scarce public funds are being diverted to counterproductive bilingual education programs.

Teachers can respond to such criticism by recalling early immigrants' insistence on maintaining their native language; perceived as a human right, language choice was identified with religious and political freedoms. Furthermore teachers can note that immigrants' experience of learning two languages did not impede the learning of one. Indeed early settlers strove to teach their children English, even while the language of the home and community was the unquestioned first language. Therefore, our English heritage provides no evidence that elimination of L1 through submersion in English results in better acquisition of English.

The Constitution of the USA contains no reference to choice of a national language. Early national leaders chose not to identify one language as the official or national standard. The legacy of the colonial and Revolutionary periods includes tolerance of diverse languages and the absence of official selection of a specific language for use among the indigenous or a linguistic norm to be achieved by immigrants.

Some early national leaders, such as John Adams, proposed a national academy to regulate and standardize English, but these efforts were rejected as

---

* Heath, S. B., "English in Our Language Heritage" in Ferguson and Heath: *Language in the USA*. Copyright © 1981. Reprinted with the permission of Cambridge University Press.

out of keeping with the spirit of liberty in the United States (Read 1936; Heath 1976). Noah Webster's prolific and energetic writings on the language of America (1789) helped keep the goal of a national language in the public eye in the first half century of nationhood. His grammar, sold about the country in company with his blue-backed speller and the Bible, helped set the mood for the American public to embrace the commercially published dictionary as an authority on language correctness. The public schools promised to all an "English" education, understood to be the study of English grammar and spelling, and the achievement of skills in composition, reading, and mathematics. Public education promoted the vision of a Standard American English, which those who would mark themselves as social-minded and civic-conscious individuals should acquire.

The legacy of the language situation in the United States is, therefore, the rejection of an official choice of a national language or national institutions to regulate language decisions related to spelling, pronunciation, technical vocabulary, or grammar. Yet Americans overwhelmingly believe that English is the national tongue and that correctness in spelling, pronunciation, word choice, and usage, as well as facility in reading and writing English, are desirable goals for every U.S. citizen. Nevertheless, numerous diverse languages and varieties of English have been maintained in communities across the United States, and there has never been federal legislation to eliminate them. Government funding has in recent decades supported the teaching of foreign languages. These seeming contradictions have been played out in the past as well as in the present period, when BILINGUAL EDUCATION, the linguistic and cultural diversity of the USA, and cries for basic skills in teaching and writing English seem to tug the future of English in the United States in different directions.

Linguistic diversity was not unusual in colonial and early national America. Classical and modern languages played critical roles in the social and political life of the early nation. Separate settlements within the United States maintained their native tongues in religious, educational, and economic institutions; newspapers, schools, and societies provided instructional support for diverse languages. The use of these languages was encouraged, and intellectual leaders valued different languages for both their practical and their symbolic purposes. Throughout the nineteenth century, a bilingual tradition existed in public and private schools, newspapers, and religious and social institutions. It was not until the late nineteenth century and the first half of the twentieth century that legal, social, and political forces strongly opposed maintenance of languages other than English. Only then was a monolingual English tradition mandated in some states and espoused as both natural and national. During the 1920s, legal and social forces restricted the use and teaching of foreign languages, especially German. Since the 1960s, linguistic minorities among widely varying ethnic groups have stressed the multilingual, multicultural nature of the national society. These minorities have pointed out the necessity of bilingualism in education, judicial matters, and the world of work. These efforts to revitalize the bilingual tradition in the United States have brought forth questions regarding the historic and current role of linguistic uniformity in national unity and the place of English in our language heritage.

SOLUTIONS TO THE CONTRADICTIONS?

In 1855, a London publication squarely faced the issue of the future language of the United States:

> Does the supremacy of the English language in the United States run any serious risk? Considering the great, and every year increasing number of continental emigrants who bring with them their languages and associations—considering that the Americans of Anglo-Saxon descent do not exceed *one-third* of the whole population, if indeed, they amount to that—is there no danger that, in course of time, the English tongue may be compelled to yield a part of its ground, and be in some regions, at least, supplanted? And, may not present or future tendencies to widen the political separation of the two countries [England and the USA] have some further effect on this, their great common bond of union? (Bristed 1855: 75)

Early in the twentieth century, the possibility of language diversity leading to political separation was once again raised. However, this time the question centered not on the issue of England and the United States losing the bond of a common tongue, but on the possibility of a national split within the United States. Numerous discussions of language and nation suggested that without a forceful language policy establishing English as the national language *and* restricting the teaching of other languages, the United States would be fragmented into linguistic minorities seeking to establish their own separate states.

> A cleavage in the language now would mean to us a cleavage of the nation in its most vulnerable if not in its most essential part. That, no matter what our origin, no real American can desire; for it is not a question whether we are to be part German or part English. We might survive with the national spirit cut in two; but should our German born citizens be successful in making German co-equal with English in our public schools, the Bohemians, who hate the very sound of the German language, will demand a similar chance for the Czesch [*sic*] tongue, and they know how to fight for what they want. (Steiner 1916: 102–3)

The author further warned that Hungarians, Finns, Scandinavians, and other language groups would "clamor for the same privilege," and when that happened, "we may at once say good-bye to the unity of the United States." The purge of foreign languages was to extend from classrooms to concert halls; no teacher should instruct in a foreign tongue; no singer should perform in any language other than English.

Since the 1960s, the possibility of a linguistically divided nation has been discussed with great fervor and frequency. Not surprisingly, the solutions currently offered are similar to those made periodically over the past two hundred years. In response to the BILINGUAL EDUCATION ACT designed to provide bilingual education for children whose MOTHER TONGUE was a language other than English, and sub-sequent laws extending and amending this Act, numerous discussions pointing out the possibility of a divided nation have appeared in the press, in court cases, and on the platforms of local parent-teacher organizations. Editorials have suggested that the current encouragement of bilingual education will take the USA on a road to cultural, economic, and political divisiveness. Parents of children who come to school without English have been characterized as lazy, un-American, and undeserving of American citizenship (e.g. Cuneo 1975).

As is so often the case, easy interpretations from selected historical facts and rigid arguments such as those cited about equating linguistic and national unity do not bear up under comprehensive examination of the history of debates over language heritage. The question of the future of language as a national symbol and means of unification in the United States has been a frequent topic of debate with respect to one or another issue throughout the history of the country. In every case, language itself was not the central issue of debate, but became a focus of arguments made for political, social, or economic purposes.

During the colonial period, Latin, Greek, and Hebrew were debated as the languages of elitism, intellectual pursuits, and mental discipline. In 1743, an unknown citizen of the American colonies argued that English was in peril for those who knew "common sense in *English* only" (*American Magazine and Historical Chronicle* 1743–4: i). He felt exaggerated emphases on Latin and Greek and heavy Classical ornamentation of English threatened the future of language for the colonies' citizens. Those who felt that English and other modern languages were more practical often exaggerated the Classicists' arguments and led readers of early American periodicals to believe that those who favored the Classical languages proposed them as UNIVERSAL LANGUAGES to supplant all others. To this point, those who favored English and other modern languages made an argument familiar in pedagogical and linguistic circles today: "The only purpose of language is to convey ideas: if modern speech does this, it is complete: if it does not, it is no language" (*American Museum or Repository* 1798: iii). No doubt, fear of the over-zealous promotion of the Classical languages and their extension helped promote the legend that a legislator proposed the United States assert its linguistic independence by adopting either Hebrew or Greek as the national language. Attention to the pronunciation of Latin and Greek was an interest of Thomas Jefferson's, and some of his correspondence to scholars of Classical languages could be interpreted as favoring the extension of Greek in the USA (Wright 1943: 223–33).

Modern languages other than English also appear in debates and folk legends about a national language for the USA. Sir Herbert Croft, a British etymologist, reported in a letter of 1797 that Americans had proposed during the Revolutionary period the idea of "revenging themselves upon England by rejecting its language and adopting that of France" (Croft 1797; Spurlin 1976). The most long-lasting and widespread legend is one which claims that German almost became the national language in 1794, and only one vote in the House of Representatives saved future generations from having to learn German instead of English. This "Muhlenberg legend" refers to a request from Virginia Germans that some laws of the United States be issued in German as well as English, as was done with many documents at the time. A Congressional committee favored the proposal, but when the issue came to a vote in the House, it was rejected 42 to 41. Frederick August Muhlenberg may have cast the deciding negative vote, but that cannot be determined from Congressional records (Lohr 1962; Kloss 1966). The legend was picked up by British and American journalists, passed on in a distorted and inaccurate form, and refurbished in the second half of the nineteenth century to remind Americans that Germans might once again muster sufficient power to turn around the language choice of the United States.

SOCIAL, POLITICAL, AND IDEOLOGICAL FACTORS

The centrality of language in social, political, and ideological issues accounts for both the frequency and intensity of language heritage debates. When Benjamin Franklin lashed out against the Germans in Pennsylvania in 1753, he feared their language would soon dominate the state. Of the Pennsylvania Germans, Franklin wrote:

> Those who come hither are generally the most stupid of their own nation, and as ignorance is often attended with credulity when knavery would mislead it, and with suspicion when honesty would set it right: and as few of the English would understand the German language and so cannot address them either from the press or pulpit, it is almost impossible to remove any prejudices they may entertain. Their clergy have very little influence on the people, who seem to take pleasure in abusing and discharging the minister on every trivial occasion. Not being used to liberty, they know not how to make a modest use of it. (Franklin 1959: IV, 483–4)

Placing Franklin's pejorative statements in the context of political issues of the times indicates that they were motivated by his resentment of the Germans' domination of local elections and his fear that they would not support his choice for colonial governor. Franklin's comments also point out the willingness of speakers of one language to accuse speakers of other languages of immorality, unpredictability, and untrustworthiness. Throughout the history of the United States, whenever speakers of varieties of English or other languages have been viewed as politically, socially, or economically threatening, their language has become a focus for arguments in favor of both restrictions of their use and imposition of Standard English.

Ideological or political views about the status of a particular language may arise in response to issues which have no direct or necessary relation to language. Within these motivations, language may be considered a tool or a symbol, and politicians may not concern themselves with changing the language itself, but rather with promoting it for status achievement and extension to speakers of other languages. For example, within the United States, ideological adherence to English has been supported by the ideal of "a perfect Union," a coming together of diverse peoples in a creative force. Individuals, groups, and the national government have promoted the idea at different times throughout our history that speaking the same language would ensure uniformity of other behavioral traits, such as morality, patriotism, and logical thinking.

ROLES FOR FOREIGN LANGUAGES

During the colonial and early national periods, foreign language maintenance was an issue for churches, local politicians, educators, and special interest groups. In urban areas, speakers of foreign languages formed societies to promote the use of their native language as they developed ways of caring for orphans, widows, and children of families who could not afford to send their children abroad for education. For example, the German Friendly Society of Charleston, South Carolina required that its members speak German in the late 1700s. Individuals were supposed to maintain their knowledge of foreign languages through individual study, or with minimal help from such primary associates as they could find. Colonial and early national newspapers abounded with advertisements placed by individuals who would give instruction in foreign languages in their home or in the home of the pupil. A typical advertisement read: "A Young Frenchman, who has been resident about seven months in this town, has a desire to make himself useful to the publick—and believes he can be so in no other way so well as in the instruction of the youth of both sexes in the French language" (*Massachusetts Spy* April 19, 1772).

Arguments over the advantages of modern languages versus the Classical languages ran the gamut from the serious to the sublime and were often summarized in exaggerated terms by modern language instructors. One overly anxious tutor of German included in the advertisement of his services:

> This being the original language of Europe, for which, as from the Celtic, its oldest dialect, the Greeks and Latins borrowed many hundreds of their words, as Sir Richard Steele observes in his English grammar; therefore, it is of greater antiquity than those of the Greeks and Romans—and as being the mother tongue, or the origin and source of the French and English, the radical knowledge, of these languages depend on it. (*Aurora General Advertiser,* Philadelphia, January 2, 1794: 9)

Bookkeepers who kept records in French advertised their services. Public brokers and translators were available for numerous languages.

There was, in addition, a keen interest among readers of early American periodicals in the language affairs of countries abroad. When the French circulated a petition asking that the language of public monuments be shifted from Latin to French, the petition was widely published in newspapers of the United States. Excerpts from the constitutions, scientific reports, and literature of the French were particularly widely distributed in American periodicals. General articles about language appeared frequently, and often asserted the equal value of all languages: "Sense is Sense in all Languages" and "in Point of Invention, all Men are on a Par" (*American Magazine and Historical Chronicle* 1743–4: vol. 1, 1745: vol. 2).

For some groups of the society, self-instruction in foreign languages was expected behavior; moreover, learning to read another language was viewed as a relatively simple task. Foreign languages were tools used to obtain knowledge not accessible in English. Many asserted both the ease and necessity of learning foreign languages. For example, Thomas Jefferson urged his daughter to read French daily, and he suggested to young correspondents that a speaking knowledge of French be acquired in Canada. He judged learning French "absolutely essential" and Spanish vitally important, because of both diplomatic interchanges and the history of Spanish influence in the New World. Jefferson himself learned Spanish by reading *Don Quixote* with the help of a grammar and dictionary. Self-education in foreign languages was also promoted for special vocational purposes. An 1834 grammar purporting to give in German and English colloquial phrases on every topic necessary to maintain conversation noted: "The prevalence of the German language in many parts of the United States should form a powerful inducement for men in every situation of life to become, at least partially acquainted with it. To the man of business, especially, a knowledge of the German tongue is of the first importance, as it will greatly facilitate his intercourse with a very valuable part of our population" (Ehrenfried 1834). Printers were recommended not only for their skills in printing, but also their knowledge of foreign languages. Most of the individuals learning modern languages other than English during the eighteenth and early nineteenth centuries were self-instructed and interested primarily in acquiring reading knowledge of the languages for either general information or specific career plans.

Institutions which provided instruction in languages other than English and the Classical languages focused primarily on retention of foreign languages for in-group maintenance or religious support. The family and religion were the primary institutions which supported use of the native languages of immigrant groups. Children learned to read from religious materials and were called on to display their school learning in understanding and contributing to aspects of church-related and community-centered activities. Children learned formal stylistic norms as well as characteristic features of the language used in religious settings— specialized vocabulary and formulaic utterances. They were expected to recognize differences between the style of language used in church services and that used in daily communications. Individuals and groups came to associate retention of their language with religious maintenance, and not until late in the nineteenth century was this connection broken for many religious groups. Some, such as the Hutterite and Amish, retain use of their language in worship services and community activities today. As churches began to realize the youth of their congregations would increasingly insist on the use of English in services, religious leaders sought other means to preserve their culture and language. Schools and newspapers gradually took over this service. Pastors and lay people feared that those who knew religious language in only their mother tongue would have no opportunities for meaningful worship if all churches went to English only. After

1900, shifts to English became more frequent, as children received catechism instruction in English, and national religious meetings allowed the use of English.

THE LANGUAGE(S) OF EDUCATION

By the mid-nineteenth century, educators were calling for a common school system which would make education available to the youth of America. The social bases of education did not appeal uniformly to all Americans; the removal of education as a responsibility of the individual and his family, and the establishment of the power of the state to tax a citizen's property for school support caused numerous difficulties for the early schools. The society was not homogeneous, and establishment of nonsectarian, publicly supported schools open and free to all children raised almost immediately the question of diversities in the classroom. It was necessary during the decades of the 1860s, 1870s, and 1880s to recruit students for schools. Opportunities for work and home responsibilities were more favorable and profitable settings for children of these decades than were schools. Political leaders and school personnel had to admit to the need to recruit students and to impress parents with the merits of compulsory attendance and public schooling.

Immigrants were thus looked upon during this period as potential clients to be courted and accommodated. In particular, the public schools wanted to draw children away from private academies where instruction was frequently given in languages other than English. A case study of Wisconsin's development of public instruction illustrates this trend (Jorgenson 1956). In 1847, the state convention heard requests that provision be made for free schools. A German-born member of the convention proposed that districts having large numbers of foreign-born settlers be allowed to offer instruction in languages other than English. The convention adopted the resolution. In a state where more than a third of the population was foreign born, such a concession seemed hardly necessary for specific notice. Each nationality group—Norwegians, Poles, Dutch, Swiss, or Germans—tended to establish its own community. In some of these, the mother tongue was used in public schools. What must have been merely nominal laws were passed in 1848, 1849, and 1854, stipulating that certain subjects in public schools were to be taught in English. Compliance with the laws was impossible in most settlements, and school personnel in communities worked without interference to ensure that the native tongue of their constituents was maintained in the schools. Proof of this practice is evidenced by reaction to the Bennett Law, passed in Wisconsin in 1889.

Proposed primarily to restrict child labor and to provide for compulsory school attendance annually for all children between the ages of seven and fourteen for not less than twelve weeks, the Bennett Law contained one section which stipulated that instruction be given in the English language. Passed without a dissenting vote, the law was received with severe hostility in German communities throughout the state. Parochial schools could no longer conduct their classes primarily in German, and public schools which had been doing so might now be more closely watched than before. The law was repealed in the legislative session of 1891. However, in Wisconsin, as elsewhere across the nation, in the next two decades, religious schools declined in number, and public schools increased in both enrollment size and influence (Billigmeier 1974).

In particular, in the middle decades of the nineteenth century, urban school systems were becoming more centralized and more conscious of their particular responsibilities to immigrants. Political leaders supported recruitment of immigrant children to public schools, and argued that education of the young would influence parents to make wise political choices. Moreover, there was ready recognition of the value of knowledge of multiple languages in education. In 1870, the U.S. Commissioner of Education stressed this point in his assessment of the national language situation: "the German language has actually become the second language of our Republic, and a knowledge of German is now considered essential to a finished education" (cited in Zeydel 1964: 345). Cleveland, St. Louis, and Milwaukee were among those urban school systems which provided for instruction in the students' first language or offered dual-language classes. Kluwin's (forthcoming) study of the Cleveland schools provides important data and interpretive analysis of school leaders' reasons for maintaining the languages of immigrant children in the elementary programs of the school system. Cleveland's superintendent during the 1870s was not afraid to announce that though certainly English was the "language of our country, it was only natural for German-speaking groups to keep their own language as a bond of common experiences, past and present." In 1871, Louis L. Klemm was appointed supervisor of German instruction in the elementary schools of Cleveland. Klemm focused on provision of kindergarten experience for immigrant children, teacher training, foreign language teaching methods, and organization of a network of German and German–English teachers for mutual exchange of material and techniques. Klemm argued that society had the responsibility of enabling immigrants to recognize and avail themselves of educational opportunities for their children; he did not place blame on the immigrant for not assimilating solely through his own motivation.

Klemm advocated adoption of pedagogical methods used in Germany, and he imported books from Germany in order that elementary teachers might have ready access to sources of innovative instructional methods. He urged a comparative grammar approach in the teaching of English and German, and he recommended that attention to both languages be given in classes across the curriculum. The German language should not be reserved solely for basic literacy skills or social studies, but its use should be incorporated in the teaching of various subjects and across different functions of language usage. Regarding the relation between ethnicity and language, Klemm pointed out that the mixture of two peoples, Anglo-Saxon and German, would provide a creative force in the American society, and the bond of a common culture would be built while both languages were maintained. Klemm extended the German language into high schools, with the goal of better preparing German language teachers for the elementary system. Believing that foreign languages were best learned at an early age, Klemm proposed that only those native English speakers who had been part of the dual-language program at the elementary level be admitted to the high school classes of German.

By the 1890s, the public schools of Cleveland, San Francisco, and New York were beginning to meet their quotas for filling classrooms, and accommodation of the special needs of immigrant children no longer seemed as important as it had several decades earlier (Kluwin, forthcoming). Moreover, political forces were stirring up fears of "the foreign element" within the national population, and proposals were made to limit and restrict immigration. Language and literacy became foci for restriction. In 1897, President Grover Cleveland returned without approval to the House of Representatives a bill which excluded from admission to the United States "All persons physically capable and over sixteen years of age who cannot read and write the English language or some other language . . ." Cleveland viewed this restriction as "harsh and oppressive." Taft and Wilson vetoed similar bills (Davis 1920: 377) before one passed over Wilson's veto in 1917.

Concerns similar to the move to restrict immigration influenced changes in naturalization requirements. Before 1906, there was no prerequisite in naturalization laws that an alien either speak or be literate in English. However, the Nationality Act of 1906 required that an alien speak English in order to become naturalized. This requirement was codified in the Nationality Act of 1940 and extended to include demonstration of an ability to read and write English in the Internal Security Act of 1950 (Leibowitz 1976).

In the early decades of the twentieth century, educators and politicians included adults in their language teaching programs. Evening classes offered adults opportunities to acquire literacy and a speaking knowledge of English. Each city had its own policy, and in many cases private evening schools and individuals offered miraculous language conversion for immigrants at high prices. After 1915, licensing of evening schools and closer control of standards for the teaching of English and civics were accomplished in several cities. In addition, some individuals argued that adult immigrants should be able to study reading and writing through their native language. Jane Addams, the social reformer, pointed out that many older men and women never would learn English, but would need information in their own languages about coping with daily problems of living and managing families in American cities (Abbott 1917). Ironically, guides offering advice on many of these problems to immigrant populations were published *in English.* Public libraries in some cities supplied books in the languages of the immigrants, but information on specific problems such as the city's water and milk supply, sanitary regulations, or labor laws was not available in languages other than English during the first decades of the twentieth century.

Another approach to spreading English among the immigrant populations was the recognition that the school could not be the sole agent of Americanization. The superintendent of the Boston public schools pointed out in 1910 that out of the thirteen million immigrants in the United States, three million spoke no English. The majority of these were past school age, and linked use of their native tongue with practice of their religious freedoms. The superintendent noted that "Religious devotion and feeling are inextricably bound up with the native language, so that in spite of any lack of intention on our part, when we begin to propose compulsion about language, we probably seem to the foreigner to infringe upon religious rights" (Davis 1920: 584).

In a remarkable effort at comparative social science inquiry, the superintendent reviewed the language policies of Switzerland and the Austro-Hungarian empire and concluded "the mere imposition of language cannot bring about automatically nationalization, a fact which uncompromising advocates of compulsion in this country should note" (Davis 1920: 586). He concluded that the language policy of the United States had, through its very inadequacy, been successful, because it had depended in the past on the motivations of the learners. Immigrants had been highly resourceful in hiring themselves out as groups working under an interpreter in foundries, stockyards, and construction projects. "Gang work" in employment and efforts to learn about city transportation systems, labor laws, and union practices had provided means by which immigrants were cushioned through group efforts to acquire English for necessary functions. The Boston school superintendent warned against forced subjugation of immigrants to a nationalize-through-language program; language is a "right which even *might* may not take away . . . a fundamental right which no constitution of men may remove" (Davis 1920: 587). The language policy choice for the United States in its program of Americanization was simple:

> Shall we insist that the stranger who has joined our membership shall by law and compulsion acquire our language, conform to our major customs, become naturalized, renounce all prior allegiance, or shall we attempt to persuade him to adopt American customs and to use our language, by pointing out the moral obligation, by furnishing convenient means in the way of free instruction, and perhaps by granting privileges which may be withheld from the non-citizen? (Davis 1920: 588)

Language choice had to be in response to social, religious, and economic, as well as political issues. Americanization and the ideological role of English in political concerns were not nearly so important in a basic sense as socio-economic issues. For example, industry was increasingly encountering difficulties with safety-first campaigns and problems of labor turnover. New state compulsory compensation laws were making employers liable for accidents which occurred as a result of immigrants' inability to read signs or understand about machinery operations. Long-standing immunity from costs and damages based on the common law procedure involving the principle of contributory negligence had given way to unavoidable payments by employers. Laborers' knowledge of English and acquisition of minimal literacy skills became economic assets to employers. Furthermore, non-English-speaking employees moved from job to job rapidly, and companies began to emphasize the positive correlation between time on the job and knowledge of English among immigrant workers (Abbott 1917). Handbooks for immigrants warned:

> English is absolutely indispensable to the workman. He needs it in order to find work. He needs it to take direction and have his work explained. He needs it unless he is willing to work for the smallest wages with no hope of increase. He needs it when he is in difficulties to avoid interested [exploitative] helpers. He needs it to protect himself without

requiring the help of the law. He needs it to understand words of warning and keep out of danger, for every year hundreds of immigrants are
hurt or killed in America, because they do not understand the shouts
of warning, or do not know how to read danger signals, when a few
English words might have saved their lives. (Carr 1912: 14)

Citizenship and Americanization as reasons to acquire English paled beside such
realistic and basic reasons as personal safety, economic support, and social
security. As industries became more involved with the need for immigrants to
learn English, they also provided means. Newly arrived immigrants were established temporarily in the homes of English speakers who helped provide transition
skills in coping with daily routines of city and factory life. Labor unions actively
recruited White immigrants in the hope of reducing rivalries among groups and
of breaking down boundaries of ethnicity and language.

    These practical measures came to be reinforced by the growing xenophobia
of the period from 1920 through the 1940s, when repressive measures against
German, Japanese, and Chinese speakers were supported by state and local
institutions as well as laws. In the period from 1917 to 1923, states removed
laws tolerating instruction in languages other than English from their codes and
prohibited the teaching of foreign languages. Court cases challenged these laws,
as in Meyer *v.* Nebraska (1923), when a teacher was convicted for giving German
instruction in a private school. The Nebraska supreme court affirmed a fear
of ethnic boundary maintenance and its relationships to use of languages other
than English:

    The legislature had seen the baneful effects of permitting foreigners,
who had taken residence in this country, to rear and educate their
children in the language of their native land. The result of that condition was found to be inimical to our own safety. To allow the children
of foreigners, who had emigrated here, to be taught from early childhood the language of the country of their parents was to rear them
with that language as the mother tongue. It was to educate them so
that they must always think in that language, and, as a consequence,
naturally inculcate in them the ideas and sentiments foreign to the best
interests of this country. The statute, therefore, was intended not only
to require that the education of all children be conducted in the
English language, but that, until they had grown into that language and
until it had become a part of them, they should not in the schools be
taught any other language. (Meyer *v.* Nebraska, 262 U.S. 390: 397–8)

The Supreme Court overturned the conviction of the lower courts by ruling that
a teacher's right to teach and a parent's right to engage him were protected by
the Fourteenth Amendment. The attempt by the Nebraska legislature to interfere

with the "calling of modern language teachers" and to spread fear of foreign tongues as perils to public safety were specifically rebuked. However, the Court stated that it did not question the power of the state to compel attendance in school and to require that instruction be given in English. With respect to several other state cases on school regulation in the 1920s, the Supreme Court ruled that requiring the language of instruction to be English in a state or territory of the United States was constitutional, but restriction of secondary language efforts by ethnic groups was unconstitutional (Leibowitz 1970, 1971, 1976).

With the Civil Rights Act of 1964 as background, federal legislators who debated the Bilingual Education Act in 1967 seemed to recognize the educational role of languages other than English for ethnic groups in the United States as had been the case occasionally in the early part of the century. Individual states, such as Massachusetts, California, New Mexico, and Texas also passed statutes favoring bilingual education. In the Lau *v.* Nichols case (1970–4), the courts had to face the issue of language with respect to whether or not Chinese-speaking students received equal educational opportunity when they were taught in a language they could not understand. Title VI of the Civil Rights Act of 1964 prohibited exclusion from participation in federally funded programs of any person "on the ground of race, color or national origin." The Bilingual Education Act of 1968 defined bilingual–bicultural education and established funding for programs for "children of limited English-speaking ability." By the early 1970s, most of the school districts of the United States were receiving federal monies, and control over language policies and other educational issues which had in the nineteenth century resided in local school boards, had shifted to administrators assessing districts' needs for federal funds. Therefore, as a condition for receiving federal aid, school districts had to take "affirmative steps to rectify the language deficiency of national-origin minority group students" unable to speak and understand English (Teitelbaum and Hiller 1977).

Chinese students in San Francisco argued that they did not receive an equal educational opportunity in schools where they could not understand the language of instruction. Relying in part on Meyer *v.* Nebraska, the lower court ruled that uniform use of English did not constitute unlawful discrimination. The Supreme Court overturned the decision, ruling that under state-imposed standards which required school attendance, mandated use of the English language, and required fluency in English as a prerequisite to high school graduation, the Chinese students were not receiving equal treatment under Title VI of the 1964 Civil Rights Act. Ramifications of this decision and guidelines for compliance with it have increasingly raised the issue of ethnic boundary maintenance and relations between language and ethnicity. Discrimination has generally been identified in terms of differential treatment. In Lau *v.* Nichols, the failure to differentiate the language of instruction for Chinese students was judged to be discriminatory. Applications of the decision have most consistently affected educational policies for Spanish speakers in the Southwest, California, Florida, and New York. Other ethnic groups are now asking to be identified as "linguistic minorities" and to have public services and education made available to them in their own languages.

IMPLICATIONS OF OUR LANGUAGE HERITAGE

Currently, the majority of U.S. citizens do not seem to see the Bilingual Education Act as reviving a valuable tradition we have lost, but rather as an aberration in American history. Maintenance of the Anglo tradition and Americanization in language have seemed to most Americans both natural and national; most Americans view English as the "natural" choice, one which contributes to the national good. When particular groups now speak out for extensions of bilingualism in American society and emphasize the disparity of opportunities which exist between those who speak English and those who do not, many citizens become nervous over the possibility of political schisms. Historical accounts of the place of English in the language heritage of the United States should reassure those who believe language and ethnic maintenance in the United States has to lead to cultural or political divisions.

The language heritage of the United States is complex, and the status of English has been achieved through social and economic forces which shaped educational and labor practices and policies to promote English. Historical and literary accounts (e.g. Fairchild 1926) portray English as the implicit, if not the explicit, choice for the national language. National leaders have never considered in any concrete way such questions as the means for determining a standard norm of English, formulating policy with regard to tolerance or promotion of other languages, and implementing language choices in schools, business, law courts, and voting procedures. One observer has noted that this absence of attention to a specific language policy in the United States has created "one of history's little ironies": "no polyglot empire of the old world has dared be as ruthless in imposing a single language upon its whole population as was the liberal republic 'dedicated to the proposition that all men are created equal'" (Johnson 1949: 118–19). It has been proposed that the absence of compulsion is an indirect, but nevertheless strong, motivation for immigrants to learn English. For example, if Germans wished to speak German, they did so for internal group purposes; they broke no law in doing so. Therefore, if they rejected English and handicapped themselves economically, they did not have "the inner consolation of feeling that they defied tyrannous authority" (Johnson 1949: 119). Haugen (1966: 11–12) has noted that the lack of specificity regarding language choice and change at the national level and the emphasis on "individual enterprise" in these matters have effectively precluded either active opposition to the language attitudes and practices of those in power or proposals for legal reforms of U.S. language policy.

The place of English among other languages and the type of English to be used have been shaped by socio-economic forces in the United States. Without the force of law, institutions and individuals have alternately permitted, restricted, and promoted the use of languages other than English. Access to the wider society outside one's own primary group has, however, consistently been dependent on knowledge of English, and upward mobility in that society has called for facility in using a standard variety of English. The central themes of our language heritage have been the legal tolerance of other languages, a consensual high value placed on the ability to use English, and general recognition of Standard American English as a means and mark of socio-economic advancement.

FURTHER READING

The role of English in the language heritage of the USA is generally treated in one of two contexts: with respect to the history of language policies and bilingual education, or with respect to the evolution of American English as a viable language. Kloss 1977 is the most complete account of legal decisions, local policies, and state and federal legislation on the uses of languages other than English. Kloss opens to the scholar a multitude of primary sources, laws, town council meetings, and church records, etc. on the uses of languages other than English throughout U.S. history. General accounts of the history of bilingual education in the United States appear in Andersson 1969 and Andersson and Boyer 1970.

Books on American English have long been among those books on language with which the general reader is most familiar. H. L. Mencken's various editions and supplements (1919-48 and 1977) provide both substantive and humorous details on how American English came to be defined. C. Merton Babcock's reader, *The Ordeal of American English* (1961), consists of primary sources reflecting evolving views of a "standard" American English. Students in a variety of English courses have read Marckwardt's *American English* with pleasure since 1958. Laird's *Language in America* (1970) is a very readable, highly informative treatment of such topics as immigrant languages and the "linguistic growing pains" of American English. Dillard 1975 provides in his history of English in America treatment of these topics as well as discussion of the effect English in America has had on the use of English as a world language. Dohan 1974 and Dillard 1976a reflect the fascination Americans have always had with words, where they came from, and how they have developed meanings in their uses in the United States. Flexner 1976 presents the American language through American history in a book expressly designed for the lay reader. Notions of "good English" throughout the nation's history are traced in Finegan 1980.

REFERENCES

Abbott, Grace. 1917. *The Immigrant and the Community.* New York: Century.

Andersson, Theodore. 1969. *Foreign Languages in the Elementary School: a struggle against mediocrity.* Austin, TX: University of Texas Press.

Andersson, Theodore and Mildred Boyer, eds. 1970. *Bilingual Schooling in the United States.* 2 vols. Washington, DC: U.S. Government Printing Office.

Billigmeier, Robert Henry. 1974. *Americans from Germany: a study in cultural diversity.* Belmont, CA: Wadsworth.

Bristed, Charles Astor. 1855. The English language in America. In *Cambridge Essays.* London: Parker.

Carr, John Foster. 1912. *Guide to the United States for the Jewish Immigrant:* New York. Connecticut Daughters of the American Revolution.

Croft, Sir Herbert. 1797. *A Letter, from Germany to the Princess Royal of England: on the English and German Languages.* Hamburgh, Fuche.

Cuneo, Ernest. 1975. *Bilingual Teaching Is a Grave Error.* Long Island Press (June 19).

Davis, Philip. 1920. *Immigration and Americanization: selected readings.* Boston: Ginn.

Dillard, J. L. 1975. *All American English: a history of the English language in America.* New York: Random House.

———. 1976. *American Talk: where our words came from.* New York: Random House.

Dohan, Mary Helen. 1974. *Our Own Words.* New York: Knopf.

Ehrenfried, Joseph. 1834. *Colloquial Phrases and Dialogues in German and English.* Philadelphia: J. A. Speel.

Fairchild, Henry Pratt. 1926. *The Melting-Pot Mistake.* Boston: Little, Brown.

Finegan, Edward. 1980. *Attitudes toward English Usage: the history of a war of words.* New York: Teachers College Press.

Flexner, Stuart Berg. 1976. *I Hear America Talking: an illustrated treasury of American words and phrases.* New York: Van Nostrand.

Franklin, Benjamin. 1959. *Papers of . . .* 21 vols. Leonard W. Labaree, ed. New Haven, CT: Yale University Press.

Haugen, Einar. 1966. *Language Conflict and Language Planning: the case of modern Norwegian.* Cambridge: Harvard University Press.

Heath, Shirley Brice. 1976. A national language academy? Debate in the new nation. *International Journal of the Sociology of Language* 11: 9-43.

Johnson, Gerald W. 1949. *Our English Heritage.* Philadelphia: J. P. Lippincott.

Jorgenson, Lloyd P. 1956. *The Founding of Public Education in Wisconsin.* Madison. WI: State Historical Society of Wisconsin.

Kloss, Heinz. 1966. *Excerpts from the National Minority Laws of the United States of America.* Honolulu: East-West Center.

———. 177. *The American Bilingual Tradition.* Rowley, MA: Newbury House.

Kluwin, Mary Bridget. Forthcoming. Coping with Language and Cultural Diversity: a study of changing language instruction policy from 1860 to 1930 in three American cities. Ph.D. dissertation, Stanford University.

Leibowitz, Arnold H. 1970. English literacy: legal sanction for discrimination. *Revista Juridica de la Universidad de Puerto Rico* 39: 313-400.

———. 1971. *Educational Policy and Political Acceptance: the imposition of English as the language of instruction in American schools.* Washington, DC: ERIC/CAL.

———. 1976. Language and the law: the exercise of power through official designation of language. In *Language and Politics.* W. M. O'Barr and J. F. O'Barr, eds. The Hague: Mouton.

Lohr, O. 1962. *Deutschland und Ubersee.* Herrenalb: Erdmann.

Menken, H. L. 1919. *The American Language.* New York: Knopf.

———. 1921. *The American Language,* Rev. ed. New York: Knopf.

———. 1923. *The American Language,* 3rd. ed. New York: Knopf.

———. 1936. *The American Language,* 4th. ed. New York: Knopf.

———. 1977. *The American Language,* 1-volume abridged ed. R. I. McDavid, Jr. (ed.) New York: Knopf.

Read, Allen Walker. 1936. American Projects for an academy to regulate speech. *Publications of the Modern Language Association* 51: 1141-79.

Spurlin, Paul M. 1976. The Founding Fathers and the French Language. *The Modern Language Journal* 60: 85-97.

Steiner, Edward A. 1916. *Nationalizing America.* New York: Fleming H. Revell Co.

Teitelbaum, Herbert and R. J. Hiller. 1977. Bilingual education: the legal mandate. *Harvard Educational Review* 47: 138-72.

Webster, Noah. 1789. *Dissertations on the English Language.* Boston: Isiah Thomas.

Wright, Louis B. 1943. Thomas Jefferson and the Classics. *Proceedings of the American Philosophical Society* 87: 223–33.

Zeydel, Edwin H. 1964. The teaching of German in the United States from colonial times to the present. *The German Quarterly* 37: 315–92. Also in *Reports of Surveys and Studies in the Teaching of Modern Foreign Languages.* New York: Modern Language Association.

THEORY AND IMPLICATIONS

1. A central argument for the establishment of a national language concerns national unity. Do you think that having various spoken languages necessarily contributes to divisiveness? Discuss.

2. What history of first language tolerance is reflected in the 1968 Bilingual Education Act? Does that history affect your views of the importance of the act? How?

3. Do you think that the arguments made in the eighteenth and nineteenth centuries for or against "English only" reflect similar arguments made today? How so?

4. There is a tendency today, as in the past, to exaggerate positions and promote false fears about the effect of certain language views. Discuss.

5. Why has the United States not established a law recognizing English as the official language of the United States? Do you think it ever will? Why?

6. How has the changing role of the public school affected language values in this country? What current controversies over public schooling may yet affect language values? How?

7. How has the conflict between language maintenance and language suppression changed but also stayed the same since this country was founded? Why?

PROFESSIONAL CONCERNS

1. Using our language history, argue for what you think the role of public schools should be with regard to the teaching of English. Choose some rhetorical situation pertinent to you. For instance, you might assume you are writing this piece as an editorial in a newspaper, addressing a general audience. Or, you can write a formal paper as a student in a class. Or, you can address other teachers.

2. Present an explanation in writing to your English Department or to any other specified audience on the history and intention of the Bilingual Education Act of 1968. How is it reviving a valuable tradition in U.S. history?

3. Respond to an angry parent's claim that you are overly tolerant of students who speak Spanish to one another during group work and who use Spanish to develop their essay ideas. The parent claims that English is the language of this country and that only English rightfully belongs in the schools.

4. Explain to a sympathetic group of future teachers how the problems of maintenance and suppression are manifested today, perhaps in classrooms you have encountered.

Educational Rights of Language Minorities*

Sau-ling Cynthia Wong†

"Educational Rights of Language Minorities" presents the history of legal issues, decisions, and laws concerning language rights. This legal background is important to teachers who encounter parents, administrators, and members of the general public who resent the many programs devoted to educating language minorities. A familiarity with the laws can often defuse needless arguments about natives versus foreigners, about "extras" one group is receiving over others, and about the effectiveness of programs. Second language learning theory and practice can never be divorced from the political assumptions and laws that surround them. The theories inform the laws, but the laws then make possible the implementation of the theories. With respect to language rights, no teacher should be ignorant of the major decisions and the arguments on which they are founded.

The important question Wong asks is whether or not submersion ("sink or swim," or simply placing language minority students in regular classes) is justified by law. Most of the cases tried conclude that submersion is not a method but rather the absence of one. The cases were tried to see if some form of "language education services" was required for language minority students. Wong explores what those language rights are and how they are justified under law.

. . . This chapter attempts to clarify some major legal issues regarding the rights of language minorities to receive language education services.

(The phrase "language education services," which is not a legal term, I have coined to refer to publicly funded programs related to the language education of minorities. It is preferred over possible alternatives such as "language assistance," "language remediation," or "special language programs," which all connote something "extra" given to minorities. Since the very issue under discussion is what minority school children are entitled by law to receive, such connotations are to be avoided.)

Because of the virtually inevitable emotional component in exchanges over language issues, what a group feels to be its "rights" regarding language may bear only a tenuous relationship to the much more precise and technical concept of "language rights" upheld in law. Thus, in a sense, a clarification of the nature of educational rights for linguistic minorities will be useful only to those who,

---

* Wong, S. C., "Educational Rights of Language Minorities," in S. L. McKay: *Language Diversity, Problem or Resource,* Heinle & Heinle. Reprinted by permission.

† I would like to thank the following people for the generous help they have given me on the research for this chapter: Carolyn Patty Blum, Ray Frank, Paula Gillett, Rachel Moran, Jeff Numberg, Anne Okahana, John D. Trasvina, Evelyn P. Walters, Michael J. Wong, and the staff of the Asian Law Caucus in Oakland and the Immigrant Law Resource Center at the Stanford Law School.

predisposed to take a more dispassionate view of the subject, already feel the need for such a clarification, which is to say that it will be of limited value in influencing the turn of larger political events. Still, responsible individual decisions concerning language issues cannot be made without knowledge of how language rights have been shaped by the evolving U.S. legal tradition. In particular, teachers and administrators charged with language education, if only out of concern for their livelihood, need to be informed about how their work fits into the overall language policy of this nation.[1]

The term language minorities covers groups with varied citizenship status, settlement history, and "track record" of language maintenance, all of which affect a group's precise degree of entitlement; the legal literature on language education services is voluminous and often inconclusive. In a chapter of this length, it would be difficult to give an in-depth review of all relevant aspects of educational rights. For the sake of simplicity, we will restrict the discussion to two main questions: *Is submersion justified by law? And if not, are language minorities entitled to bilingual education?*

Since submersion means simply placing language-minority children in regular classrooms with speakers of the majority language, the question is really another way of asking whether the children are entitled to any kind of language education service. The phrasing chosen here, however, has the advantage of drawing attention to the legality of a so-called "method," touted by many English-only proponents, that is in fact a "nonmethod." As for the second question, the chosen phrasing has the advantage of placing in the background many questions (e.g., on the pedagogical soundness or feasibility of various methods) that, although relevant, are not questions of entitlement. If a group is legally entitled to bilingual education, it has to be provided, however controversial or difficult the implementation. Only after the entitlement issue is settled can we begin to focus on the other questions.

SOME PRELIMINARY CLARIFICATIONS

Before focusing on the two major questions of entitlement concerning submersion and bilingual education, it might be helpful to examine some common perceptions of and arguments against the educational rights of language minorities in the United States.

Public debates on the educational rights of language minorities are often colored by an "us vs. them" tone: "foreigners" are those who "talk funny," "can't speak English properly," "don't belong in this country." One reason for this attitude is that for an ingroup intent on containing a perceived threat to its privileged status, language is a particularly felicitous device for targeting outsiders, since the ingroup members' acquisition of their first language is reassuringly unrelated to individual merit (the achievement of which can be used to support an outsider's demand for admission to the ingroup). On this point, it is important to remember that, as Waggoner's statistics show, many language minorities are native-born citizens; that immigrants are legally admitted and are taxpayers just as much as citizens; and that, even for the children of illegal immigrants, there may be some legally guaranteed rights to receive a public education (see below). Without such an awareness, the issue would easily become clouded, turning into a pitting of the usurping, freeloading "foreigners" against the responsible but victimized "taxpayers."

In casual usage, the term "foreign student" is commonly used to refer to any student who is not native English-speaking; even legal scholars like Farrell (1983:70) use the term in this loose sense. The practice is unfortunate in that it creates confusion in the public's mind between students who are permanent members of this society—more appropriately designated as "immigrant students"—and "foreign students" proper: those temporarily in the United States on F-1 visas (student visas) for educational purposes only. The former group, when erroneously named "foreign," are often unjustly seen as rivals to "American children," siphoning away resources their parents supposedly did not pay for and allegedly lowering the quality of education for the latter. Actually, the everyday term "foreigner" is not precise enough to capture the various degrees of entitlement enjoyed by subgroups of linguistic minorities.

Awareness of the residency and citizenship status of language minorities is also important when one encounters attacks on immigrant language rights made in the form of what Kloss (1971:255–256) calls the "tacit compact" and "take-and-give" arguments, namely, that in deciding to emigrate, the immigrant has tacitly given up any claim to his or her language and has in effect agreed to exchange it for benefits obtained in the adopted land. It should be noted that, first, immigrants are already contributing to their new country by working, buying goods and services, and in particular paying taxes (which would make them taxpayers instead of "outsiders" or "foreigners" taking advantage of taxpayers). Second, in U.S. immigration laws, giving up one's language for English is not stipulated as a condition for immigration; it would not be reasonable, subsequent to admitting immigrants on some other bases, to accuse them of not having held up their end of the bargain when they cannot demonstrate English proficiency to the satisfaction of native English speakers (see the arguments in Beck 1975:6–7).

In addition to the "tacit compact" and "take-and-give"[2] theories referred to above, what may be called the "we were here first" argument has frequently been advanced to curtail ethnic language use or deny English-language assistance to groups perceived as "newcomers." The reasoning is that "newcomers" should conform to the long-time inhabitants of the land. As Molesky's historical overview amply demonstrates, however, English speakers were *not* "here first" relative to a significant number of linguistic minorities.

Finally, we may attempt to understand the issue of entitlement using a well-known concept in the literature on language rights: "tolerance-oriented" vs. "promotion-oriented rights" (Kloss 1971). Since educational rights concerning language education services are specific instances of language rights, they too fall under the terms of Kloss's system. Proposing that the allocation of language rights be based on how successful a group has been in maintaining its ethnic language, he distinguishes two kinds of language rights: "tolerance-oriented rights" and "promotion-oriented rights." Briefly stated, the former are rights to use the minority language in home and communal life, such as attending private language schools or publishing commercial ethnic language newspapers, where public funding is not used. The latter involve government use of public resources for the benefit of those using the minority language, such as translation of laws, bilingual ballots, or purchase of ethnic language books in public libraries. Kloss argues that it would be reasonable to expect a group to have a strong "track record" in language maintenance, that is, to demonstrate the ability to maintain its language beyond the third generation, before granting it promotion-oriented rights. If language maintenance were a passing fancy or a doomed enterprise rather than a successful long-term commitment, it would not be sensible to allocate public resources for it.

Kloss's distinction of these two kinds of rights is a useful one in general. However, it may be problematic under certain circumstances. Given current U.S. immigration trends, certain long-standing ethnic groups will experience a constant influx of speakers of the ethnic languages; these, along with the native-born population, will be labeled as belonging to the same language minority. In such cases, while the group *taken as a whole* may show maintenance beyond the third generation, the success is due mainly to immigration and the precise status of its "track record" is obscured. As the case of Chinese language reten-tiveness shows, even with massive empirical data it is not always easy to disentangle the effects of continued immigration from those of successful intergenerational transmission of the language (which seems to be Kloss's concept of maintenance).

Furthermore, the term "promotion" is not entirely satisfactory, since it connotes an active enhancement of the minority language's status or its speakers' influence. It is true that connotations do not affect how law is interpreted in the judicial system, but they do cloud the issue when the technical terminology, retaining only part of its meaning, is used in discussions among nonexperts in law. While language education services intended to ease transition into the English-speaking mainstream technically qualify as "promotion," in effect they may only serve to bring disadvantaged minorities up to par with speakers of the majority language and may have little long-term effect on the strength of the minority languages used. The current controversy over bilingual education for Spanish speakers stems partly from a perception that maintenance is the *aim* (rather than the unintended *effect*) of the programs, and that the presence of students who do maintain their ethnic language proves that it has been unfairly "promoted." In other words, any failures of transitional programs are cited as if they were the successes of maintenance programs. The case of immersion education, which suggests that sometimes "maintenance" of the minority language is the best kind of "transition" into mainstream society, further complicates the issue. Thus the dividing line between "transition" and "maintenance" is not always clear. Without a firm definition of "maintenance," the question of what constitutes "promotion" itself becomes harder to answer. Still, Kloss's scheme is useful under most circumstances and is widely accepted in the literature on language policy.

With the above clarifications in mind, we may now take a closer look at educational rights for language minorities.

OVERVIEW OF ENTITLEMENT ISSUES IN LANGUAGE EDUCATION SERVICES FOR MINORITIES

Table 1 gives an overview of the various possible legal grounds on which language minorities may be able to claim language education services. Due to space limitation, we will cover only the more important level, the federal level (if federal and state laws conflict, the former overrides the latter; see Macías 1979:90). The legal grounds at the federal level are further divided into "constitutional" and "statutory" components. The three items in bold type, one constitutional and two statutory, with the exact texts of their relevant portions given, are the most frequently appealed-to principles on which claims to language education services are made. They are the equal protection clause of the Fourteenth Amendment (often abbreviated to "the equal protection clause"); Title VI of the Civil Rights Act of 1964 (often abbreviated to "Title VI"); and the Equal Educational Opportunities Act of 1974, Section 1703(f) (often abbreviated to "the EEOP"). Title VII of the Elementary and Secondary Education Act (ESEA), although frequently associated with bilingual education, will not apply if the state does not receive federal funds (Grubb 1974:62); it is more a piece of legislation to provide funding

TABLE 1 Possible legal grounds on which language minorities may be able to claim language education services

Federal
  Constitutional
   Equal protection clause of the Fourteenth Amendment
   "No state shall . . . deny to any person within its jurisdiction the equal protection of the laws." (Section 1)
     Related: Due process clause
     "No state shall . . . deprive any person of life, liberty or property, without due process of law." (Section 1)
  Statutory
   Title VI of the Civil Rights Act of 1964
   "No person in the United States shall, on the ground of race, color, or national origin, be excluded from participation in, be denied the benefits of, or be subjected to discrimination under any program or activity receiving Federal financial assistance." (Section 601)
     Related: "May 25 Memorandum" of 1970
     "Where inability to speak and understand the English language excludes national origin–minority group children from effective participation in the educational programs offered by a school district, the district must take affirmative steps to rectify the language deficiency in order to open its instructional programs to these students."
     Related: "Lau Remedies" of 1975
   The Equal Educational Opportunities Act (EEOA) of 1974
   "No state shall deny equal educational opportunity to an individual on account of his or her race, color, sex, or national origin, by . . . the failure of an educational agency to take appropriate action to overcome language barriers that impede equal participation by its students in the instructional programs." (Section 1703(f))
   Title VII of the Elementary and Secondary Education Act (ESEA), 1968, 1974, 1978, 1984
  State
   Certain state constitutions
   Certain state statutes permitting or mandating language education services

TABLE 2 Language education services for language minorities: Entitlement issues: Is submersion justified by law? If not, are language minorities entitled to bilingual education?

Possible Legal Basis	Issues	Relevant Major Court Cases
Constitutional		
Equal protection clause	Equality of access vs. outcome	*Brown* v. *Board of Education* 1954
	Discriminatory intent vs. impact	*Washington* v. *Davis* 1976
	Fundamental right	*San Antonio Indep. School District* v. *Rodriguez* 1973
	Suspect classification	*San Antonio Indep. School District* v. *Rodriguez* 1973
	Compelling state interest	*Plyler* v. *Doe* 1982
Statutory		
Title VI of Civil Rights Act 1964	Equality of access vs. outcome	*Lau* v. *Nichols* 1974
	Discriminatory intent vs. impact	*Lau* v. *Nichols* 1974 *Regents of U. Cal.* v. *Bakke* 1978
	Substantial numbers	*Lau* v. *Nichols* 1974
	Desegregation	*Keyes* v. *School District No. 1, Denver, Colorado* 1976
Section 1703(f) of Equal Educational Opportunities Act 1974	Equality of access vs. outcome	*Castaneda* v. *Pickard* 1981
	Discriminatory intent vs. impact	
	"Appropriate action"	*Castaneda* v. *Pickard* 1981

Conclusion: The law does not justify submersion, but neither does it create entitlement for bilingual education

than entitlement. Thus it will not be discussed here. Interested readers are referred to Fernández (1987) for an overview of Title VII.

Table 2 summarizes entitlement issues concerning language education services for minorities, listing the legal bases cited, the legal concepts at stake, and key court decisions that have shaped answers to our two questions.

This chapter will not discuss language rights in terms of international law. Although several documents of international law do recognize the language rights of the minorities, the United States did not ratify some of them, and there are also problems with interpretation and implementation (Macías 1979:86–91; Marshall 1986:18–19).

THE EQUAL PROTECTION CLAUSE OF THE FOURTEENTH AMENDMENT

The equal protection clause is the portion of the Constitution most frequently cited to establish claims for language education services for minorities. Some legal scholars have also appealed to the due process clause to argue that by compelling minority children to attend school without providing language education services, one is in effect depriving them of physical liberty as well as the liberty to acquire useful knowledge (based on the 1923 *Meyer* v. *Nebraska* Supreme Court decision) (Grubb 1974:88–91). However, traditionally these arguments have not been important in affecting court decisions.

The Concept of "Equality"

The equal protection clause applies only to "state action," not private action (Johnson 1974:957). The concept of "equality" has "never been adequately defined as a philosophical concept, much less as a legal concept" (Johnson 1974:965). In the area of education, "traditionally, the courts have found a denial of equal protection only where the state has made *different* provisions for similarly situated citizens without adequate justification" (Grubb 1974:71); the classic example of this principle is the 1954 *Brown* v. *Board of Education* Supreme Court decision that ended segregation. As we will see, however, in the case of language-minority children, if no language education services are provided (i.e., in a submersion situation), we would have a group receiving what is on the face similar treatment, but experiencing markedly different results (Grubb 1974:58). In such a case, a "proportional or consequential theory of equality" has been proposed (Grubb 1974:72); its criterion is whether a group has been denied equal protection because it bears a disproportionate share of the measure's impact. The main issues here are (1) equality of access vs. equality of outcome, and (2) discriminatory intent vs. discriminatory impact. Let us turn now to how the judiciary stands on these issues.

Discriminatory Intent?

It is, of course, impossible to run an educational system without distinguishing between and classifying students in some way; the question then arises of when a classificatory scheme is acceptable and when it becomes discriminatory against a particular group. In determining whether the equal protection clause has been violated, it has been customary to examine, first, to see if the classification is "rationally related" (i.e., not arbitrary) to the purpose of a formally neutral program. If that is the case, the judiciary will normally uphold the program even if its impact is discriminatory (Grubb 1974:81–82). The burden would be on the plaintiff to demonstrate that there has been discriminatory intent. The 1976 *Washington* v. *Davis* Supreme Court decision rules that even with disproportionate racial impact, discriminatory intent must be proven (Farrell 1983:75–76). In the context of minority language education, we might note that in trying to establish claims to language education services for children from a recent immigrant group, it would be difficult to demonstrate discriminatory intent because the group's history in this country is so short (Dobray 1984:269; McFadden 1983:25).

Judicial restraint normally prevails when a program is formally neutral. However, if the state action "either impairs a fundamental right or distinguishes a suspect class," the burden of justification would be on the state to show that a "compelling state interest" is at stake, so that it has been necessary to violate a "fundamental right" or distinguish a "suspect class" (Grubb 1974:83; Johnson 1974:958). In such instances, a merely rational relationship between purpose and classification has been insufficient to uphold the measure in question, and decision has been based on a balancing of societal benefit against individual harm (Grubb 1974:83).

Fundamental Right

What, then, is a fundamental right? And is the right to education a fundamental right? Fundamental rights have been variously defined as rights "implicit in a concept of ordered liberty" (Dobray 1984:258) or rights based on "natural law" (such as the rights to procreate and to travel) (Johnson 1974:960-1). For all practical purposes, a fundamental right is best defined as one "explicitly or implicitly guaranteed by the Constitution" (Johnson 1974:960-961). Although legal scholars have argued for education as a fundamental right because of its value to society and its importance for protecting other rights (e.g., free speech, voting), the courts thus far have explicitly ruled that the right to an education is *not* guaranteed by the Constitution.

The landmark case concerning the status of education as a right is *San Antonio Independent School District* v. *Rodriguez* (1973). In this case, the Texas system of financing public schools through local property taxes, which resulted in great disparities between school districts, was challenged (Farrell 1983:72). The Supreme Court upheld the system. While acknowledging the relationship of education to First Amendment freedoms and the franchise, the Court also stated: "Education . . . is not among the rights afforded explicit protection under our Federal Constitution. Nor do we find any basis for saying it is implicitly so protected" (cited in Johnson 1974:975; see also Farrell 1983:72ff for details). If education itself is not a fundamental right, it follows that language education services are not constitutionally guaranteed. It would also follow that submersion would not violate a fundamental right. (Note that the 1974 *Lau* v. *Nichols* Supreme Court decision, one of the best known in the area of minority language education issues, was *not* decided on constitutional but on statutory grounds, specifically Title VI. See discussion below.)

Before we leave the question of fundamental right, however, two more points must be noted. In a dissenting opinion to the *San Antonio Independent School District* v. *Rodriguez* decision, Justice Marshall pointed out that "the Constitution neither mentions nor implies the right to privacy, the right to interstate travel, the right to participate in state elections, the right to procreate, all of which have been held to be fundamental" (cited in Johnson 1974:976). Thus, as the American legal tradition evolves, education may one day come to be regarded as a fundamental right. Moreover, an aside to the *San Antonio* case leaves the question open as to whether "a system which failed to provide some identifiable quantum of education" would in fact be denying its students a fundamental right (Farrell 1983:73; McFadden 1983:25; Dobray 1984:259). In other words, while education itself is not asserted to be a fundamental right, total denial of education may constitute the denial of a fundamental right. Non-English-speaking language-minority children in submersion classes may arguably be seen as suffering from a total denial of education. Again, since *Lau* v. *Nichols* avoided the constitutional issue altogether, at this point it is still unclear whether such an interpretation would hold. We may safely say, however, that the question of whether education is a fundamental right is far from closed.

Suspect Class

Suspect classification could be based on race, national origin, alienage (i.e., legal status as an alien) (Johnson 1974:961), as well as sex and illegitimacy (Johnson 1974:990–991), which are all characteristics beyond the choice and control of the individuals so classified. Classification on the basis of these characteristics has been struck down as reasons for discrimination. The question for the language education of minorities is whether a suspect class is involved. If so, the authorities responsible for a given program would have to demonstrate a state interest compelling enough to justify the classification. If not, the principle of judicial restraint would cause the courts to uphold a formally neutral educational program.

It is true that language, unlike characteristics such as race, is not immutable (Grubb 1974:84): language can be learned and changed. In this sense, limited-English-proficient (LEP) and non-English-proficient (NEP) students from a minority language group do not form a suspect class. On the other hand, in many cases language and race or national origin are intimately related (Johnson 1974:980); the relationship may be so close that "separation is meaningless in practice" (Grubb 1974:84). Moreover, being LEP or NEP involves "disabilities beyond [the children's] control" (Dobray 1984:265–266); "a bilingual child cannot select a language" (Johnson 1974:975). In addition, the *San Antonio Independent School District* v. *Rodriguez* decision further characterizes a suspect class as being saddled by disabilities, subjected to a history of purposeful unequal treatment, and politically powerless, to such an extent that "extraordinary protection from majoritarian political powers" is called for (cited in Johnson 1974:979). Language-minority children could fit such a description (Grubb 1974:79). Finally, from a second language acquisition perspective, language is really not as "mutable" as popularly believed; accents, morphological errors, and other features often persist in spite of the best efforts of the individual. Overall, a case may be made to challenge the denial of language education services by demonstrating suspect classification in the case of LEP and NEP children.

Compelling State Interest

Although education is not a fundamental right, the judicial system has come to recognize that it occupies a special status, so that failure to provide education must be subjected to more stringent demands for justification.

In the 1982 *Plyler* v. *Doe* Supreme Court decision, involving the question of whether the state of Texas had to give the children of illegal aliens an education, the Court reiterated that education is not a fundamental right. (Note that this is so even though the state was considering absolute denial of education.) At the same time, it also recognized that education is more than just another governmental benefit, because of its important role as socializing agent and sustainer of the nation's political and cultural heritage (Farrell 1983:80). As a result, rather than allowing the state to justify its classification by relating it rationally to a purpose, the Court required it to show a "compelling state interest" (Farrell 1983:80). In the *Plyler* v. *Doe* case, fiscal restraint, local autonomy, and the desire for a homogeneous society were all rejected as "compelling state interests" (Dobray 1984:276). The Court noted that denying an education to the children of illegal aliens has imposed "a lifetime hardship on a discrete class of children not accountable for their disabling status" (Dobray 1983:276), and ordered Texas to provide an education to the children of illegal aliens.

Because of the many parallels between the children of illegal aliens and LEP and NEP children from language-minority groups, such as disabilities beyond their control and disfavored status in American society (Dobray 1984:276), it is likely that a claim for language education services can be established based on arguments similar to those used in the *Plyler* v. *Doe* case. "A school district that failed to provide any remedial programs for language-deficient students would have a very difficult time finding state purposes sufficiently substantial to justify this exclusion from participation" (Farrell 1983:80). For example, an argument that submersion saves the school district money that can then be applied to benefit "everybody" will not carry weight in the courts.

TITLE VI OF THE CIVIL RIGHTS ACT OF 1964

Title VI, as Table 1 shows, prohibits discrimination on the basis of race, color, or national origin in federally funded programs. The so-called "May 25 memorandum" extends protection to language-minority children, specifically barring assignment of such children to retarded classes and tracking or ability grouping based on language (Rotberg 1982:151). (As Johnson 1974:947 and McFadden 1983:8 point out, placement of Mexican American children in classes for the "educable mentally retarded" was once commonly practiced in the American school system.)

Lau *v.* Nichols (1974)

Title VI is the basis for a landmark decision, *Lau* v. *Nichols* (1974). In 1970, Kinney Kinmon Lau and 12 NEP Chinese American students—over half of whom were American-born—filed a class action suit on behalf of Chinese-speaking students in the San Francisco Unified School District, charging that they were being denied an education because of a lack of special English classes with bilingual teachers (Wang 1976:240–241). The case reached the Supreme Court which in 1974 ruled in favor of the plaintiffs.

The Court noted: "Simple justice requires that public funds to which all taxpayers of all races contribute not be spent in any fashion which encourages, entrenches, subsidizes, or results in racial discrimination." Moreover,

[T]here is no equality of treatment merely by providing students with the same facilities, textbooks, teachers, and curriculum; for students who do not understand English are effectively foreclosed from any meaningful education.

Basic English skills are at the very core of what these public schools teach. Imposition of a requirement that, before a child can effectively participate in the educational program, he must already have acquired those basic skills is to make a mockery of public education. We know that those who do not understand English are certain to find their classroom experiences wholly incomprehensible and in no way meaningful.

The Court ordered "appropriate relief," although it did not specify a particular method (quotations from the *Lau* decision are from the summary in Leibowitz 1982:131–135).

Significance of the *Lau* decision

The *Lau* decision, as Landry (1983:369) notes, is "just as important for what it did not say as for what it did say." It is therefore imperative to have a clear understanding of what the case implies on the issue of entitlement to language education services.

The *Lau* decision did not clarify the status of education in general, and language education services in particular, as a constitutionally guaranteed right. In fact, the Court scrupulously avoided a constitutional argument and instead relied on a statutory one (Title VI) to determine the plaintiff's claim to language education services. "It is tempting to say that somehow the *Lau* decision created some language rights for the plaintiffs, but it did not" (Macías 1979:92). Thus the question of whether education is a fundamental right is as yet unsettled.

The *Lau* decision did differentiate equality of access from equality of outcome. The Court rejected the defendant's argument that the Chinese-speaking students were treated equally because they were in the same classrooms, using the same books, being taught by the same teachers, etc. In other words, submersion was determined to be neutral on the surface but discriminatory in fact (Dobray 1984:266).

The *Lau* decision did not require showing of discriminatory intent and accepted disproportionate impact as sufficient proof of discrimination, stating: "discrimination is barred which has that *effect* even though no purposeful design is present" (Leibowitz 1982:133). In other words, it reflected the "proportional or consequential theory of equality" mentioned earlier. (But see below for recent developments on this issue.) However, two of the Justices emphasized that numbers were "at the heart of the case" (Macías 1979:92): "even if Title VI may be violated without the presence of a discriminatory intent, . . . remedial relief may be appropriate only when a significant number of limited English-speaking students are denied an equal opportunity" (Dobray 1984:283). The question of what constitutes a sufficiently substantial number to trigger relief is difficult to determine (Farrell 1983:106–107), and so far lower court decisions have given the concept conflicting interpretations (Dobray 1984:279).

The *Lau* decision did not create a right to receive bilingual education. Much of the confusion on this question arose from the so-called "Lau Remedies" or "Lau Guidelines," which were issued in 1975 on the basis of, but were *not* part of, the 1974 Supreme Court decision. Regarding appropriate relief, the Supreme Court simply stated: "Teaching English to the students of Chinese ancestry who did not speak the language is one choice. Giving instruction to this group in Chinese is another. There may be others" (cited in Rotberg 1982:151). The "Lau Remedies," in contrast, went further to call for bilingual education instead of English as a second language (ESL), maintenance of the minority language as a program goal, and cultural components (Rotberg 1982:152–154). These requirements were stringent, often unworkable (Rotberg 1982:152–154; Farrell 1983:85–86), and came under much criticism (Fernández 1987). It should be noted that the "Lau Remedies" had no statutory status (Dobray 1984:281–282) and could not, strictly speaking, prohibit ESL and require bilingual–bicultural education (Fernández 1987). Nevertheless, between 1975 and 1980, over 400 school districts negotiated "compliance agreements" with the Office of Civil Rights, many of which contained bilingual education provisions in the spirit of the "Lau Remedies" (Fernández 1987).

Ironically, in some cases, setting up bilingual education programs may conflict with another provision of the law protecting minorities: desegregation. "Whereas *Brown* v. *Board of Education* clearly forbids the maintenance of separate educational facilities for minority children, bilingual programs by their very nature tend to segregate language minority students during a large part of the school day" (McFadden 1983:17). In the 1976 *Keyes* v. *School District No. 1, Denver, Colorado* decision, a lower court ruled that desegregation should take precedence over bilingual education when the two conflict (McFadden 1983:17). Landry (1983:372) proposes that such conflicts be resolved by determining, in a given school community, whether protection of language rights or protection against racial discrimination is "the most pressing need"; in practice, however, assessing the relative urgency of the needs is problematic. The courts have by no means been unanimous on this issue, but "most courts have not seen the two philosophies as incompatible" (McFadden 1983:19).

Developments Since Lau

Diminishing Federal Role in Minority Language Education. In 1980, a new set of "Lau regulations" were proposed that would have had the force of law; however, they were withdrawn in 1981 (Rotberg 1982:154; Farrell 1983:86). Fernández (1987:102) notes:

> By 1981, any hope of enacting enforceable rules focusing on LEP students had vanished. The push for local control and decentralization

meant that the federal government was relinquishing its more active pre-1981 role in the area of education. . . . The Department of Education reverted to the May 25 memorandum and to the language of the *Lau* decision . . . as the basis for enforcement by the OCR [Office of Civil Rights], a practice that continues to this day.

As Seidner and Seidner (1983) suggest, the 1980s are a period of conservatism when bilingual education will be viewed in an increasingly unfavorable light by the Administration. Choice of language education service programs is likely to be left more and more to the local school districts, yet on this matter the law has offered a confusing array of precedents, with some lower court decisions requiring bilingual education and some requiring ESL (see review in Farrell 1983:77–89).

Recent Emphasis on Discriminatory Intent   Since *Lau*, another landmark Supreme Court decision in the area of education has raised "serious doubts concerning the correctness of what appeared to be the premise of [the *Lau* decision]" (Farrell 1983:87). In its 1978 decision on the *Regents of the University of California* v. *Bakke* case, in which a white applicant to medical school sued the University of California claiming that affirmative action constituted "reverse discrimination," the Supreme Court ruled that the Constitution was coextensive with Title VI and that Title VI would prohibit only *intentional* discrimination (Farrell 1983:87). This might force a radical reassessment of the significance of the *Lau* decision. In the meantime, however, *Lau* still stands.

THE EQUAL EDUCATIONAL OPPORTUNITIES ACT OF 1974

Finally, claims to language education services may be based on Section 1703(f) of the EEOA. As Table 1 shows, the relevant portion of the EEOA text is very similar to that of Title VI, except for the inclusion of "sex" in the phrase prohibiting discrimination, and the term "appropriate action to overcome language barriers." The issues raised by EEOA are also very similar to those raised by both the equal protection clause and Title VI.

Again, equality of access vs. equality of outcome is one of the points of contention. Johnson, in clarifying these concepts, suggests that the latter is harder to measure and is not as useful as the former (1974:969). He adds, however, that access must not be taken to mean merely physical access, which is the bare minimum. Rather, citing a 1950 court decision, *Sweatt* v. *Painter,* he points out that students should have access to the "interplay of ideas and the exchange of views" (971). A language barrier can be said to occur "at the lower end of the access continuum, is readily recognizable, and is readily remedied" (971). It is thus a "justiciable issue."

Discriminatory intent vs. discriminatory effect is again an issue to consider in deciding whether the EEOA has been violated. In a 1981 decision on the *Castaneda* v. *Pickard* case (see Leibowitz 1982:192–218 for a summary), a lower court ruled that there was no need to prove discriminatory intent (Farrell 1983:94; McFadden 1983:15; Dobray 1984:284).

The EEOA is, nevertheless, not identical to other possible legal justifications for language education services because of its "appropriate action" clause. This clause proved to be important in the *Castaneda* case, where the court devised a three-prong test to determine whether the language education services then being provided constituted "appropriate action" (Dobray 1984:287–288; Farrell 1983:95–97): the challenged program must be informed by a sound educational theory, implemented effectively with sufficient resources, and, after a reasonable period of trial, evaluated as being able to overcome the students' language barrier. In other words, "[m]ere good faith efforts are insufficient" (Farrell 1983:96). Thus Section 1703(f) of the EEOA "has been generally interpreted by courts to require that school districts take *effective* action to overcome language barriers, whether or not there has been discriminatory intent on the part of school officials" (McFadden 1983:26; original italics).

"Appropriate action" is not specifically identified with bilingual education (Dobray 1984:285). ESL, for example, is also based on sound educational theory, can be adequately implemented, and can therefore satisfy the first two parts of the three-prong test. However, if it can be convincingly demonstrated that upon evaluation, ESL has not produced the desired results, a claim for bilingual education can be made (Farrell 1983:100). "Prevailing on the liability issue may be easier for plaintiffs under the EEOA than under the Constitution or Title VI" (Dobray 1984:285).

CONCLUSION

After the above review of the major possible legal bases on which claims to language education services for language minorities may be made, we are now ready to return to the two central questions of entitlement: Is submersion justifiable by law? And if not, are language minorities entitled to bilingual education?

The answer to the first question is "No." Although the legal tradition thus far has not considered education a fundamental right, and although the *Lau* decision avoids the constitutional issue, absence of language education services (i.e., submersion) approaches total denial of education and may constitute a violation of a fundamental right. Moreover, a suspect classification may be involved, and compelling state interest for it is difficult to establish. The *Lau* decision provides protection against submersion on the basis of Title VI. Even if *Lau* were someday to be overturned because of a post-*Bakke* emphasis on demonstration of discriminatory intent, the EEOA would still suggest an adequate basis for requiring effective "appropriate action" to remove the language barrier.

As for the second question on bilingual education, the answer is also "No." *Lau* did not specify the type of language education service the challenged school district was to supply. Neither did the EEOA. Bilingual education, like ESL, is, according to the law, only one possible kind of "appropriate action"; only when ESL can be shown to be ineffective upon evaluation can a claim for bilingual education be made. What needs to be borne in mind, however, is that submersion and bilingual education, though often portrayed in public debates as the only two alternatives, simply refer to absence of all language education service on the one hand, and a particular type of it on the other. There are other choices, such as ESL, to which language minority children *are* legally entitled. One should not be misled by the terms of the existing public debate into thinking that since bilingual education is not mandated by law, submersion is the only alternative.

A lower court judge, commenting on the *Lau* case, described LEP and NEP language-minority children as being "separated from their English-speaking peers" not by "walls of brick and mortar, but [by] the language barrier" (cited in Grubb 1974:52). The recent English-only movement, in promoting submersion as an allegedly effective, cheap, fair, and patriotic means of educating LEP and NEP students, is threatening to strengthen, not weaken, this invisible language barrier. To help protect the welfare of the nation's many language-minority children, it is important for all those concerned, language education professionals and ordinary citizens alike, to be acquainted with both the historical context and current status of language rights.

NOTES

1. Judd (1987:15) notes: "ESOL [English as a Second Other Language] instruction . . . is part of the country's general language policy. . . . ESOL teaching and teachers are not only affected by the political processes; we are also part of that process. . . . We may choose on an individual level to remain apart from partisan politics, but we cannot claim that we are above politics or beyond its grasp. As educators implementing approved governmental policies, we are a part of that system."
2. The two other commonly used arguments against the language rights of immigrant groups, examined and refuted in Kloss (1971), are the so-called "antighettoization" theory and "national unity" theory. The former states that imposition of the majority language is necessary for the good of the minorities, to enable them to escape the ethnic ghetto. The latter states that allowing immigrant language rights endangers national unity. Both these arguments overlook the fact that language is often merely an excuse for rationalizing or perpetuating existing inequities between the majority and the minorities.

REFERENCES

Beck, C. 1975. Is immigrant education only for immigrants? In A. Wolfgang (ed.), *Education for Immigration Students: Issues and Answers*. Toronto: Ontario Institute for Studies in Education, 5-18.

Dobray, D. 1984. Constitutional and statutory rights to remedial language instruction: Variable degrees of uncertainty. *St. Mary's Law Journal* 15, 253-297.

Farrell, R. C. 1983. Bilingual education: The extent of an entitlement. *GMU [George Mason University] Law Review* 6:1, 69-110.

Fernández, R. R. 1987. Legislation, regulation, and litigation: The origins and evolution of public policy on bilingual education in the United States. In W. A. Van Horne and T. V. Tonnesen (eds.), *Ethnicity and Language.* Milwaukee, WI: University of Wisconsin System Institute on Race and Ethnicity, 90-123.

Grubb, E. B. 1974. Breaking the language barrier: The right to bilingual education. *Harvard Civil Rights-Civil Liberties Law Review* 9, 52-94.

Johnson, W. E. 1974. The constitutional right of bilingual children to an equal educational opportunity. *Southern California Law Review* 47, 943-997.

Judd, E. 1987. Teaching English to speakers of other languages: A political act and a moral question. *TESOL Newsletter* (February), 15-16.

Kloss, H. 1971. The language rights of immigrant groups. *International Migration Review* 5, 250-268.

Landry, W. J. 1983. Future Lau regulation: Conflict between language rights and racial nondiscrimination. In R. V. Padilla (ed.), *Theory, Technology and Public Policy on Bilingual Education.* Rosslyn, VA: National Clearinghouse for Bilingual Education, 365-376.

Leibowitz, A. H. 1982. *Federal Recognition of the Rights of Minority Language Groups.* Rosslyn, VA: National Clearinghouse for Bilingual Education.

Macías, R. F. 1979. Language choice and human rights in the United States. In J. Alatis and G. R. Tucker, (eds.), *Language in Public Life: Georgetown Round Table on Languages and Linguistics 1979.* Washington, D.C.: Georgetown University Press, 86-101.

Marshall, D. F. 1986. The question of an official language: Language rights and the English Language Amendment. *International Journal of the Sociology of Language* 60, 7-75.

McFadden, B. J. 1983. Bilingual education and the law. *Journal of Law and Education* 12:1, 1-27.

Rotberg, I. C. 1982. Some legal and research considerations in establishing federal policy in bilingual education. *Harvard Educational Review* 52, 149-168.

Seidner, S. S. and Seidner, M. M. 1983. In the wake of conservative reaction: An analysis. In R. V. Padilla (ed.), *Theory, Technology and Public Policy on Bilingual Education.* Rosslyn, VA: National Clearinghouse for Bilingual Education, 327-349.

Wang, L. L.-C. 1976. *Lau v. Nichols:* History of a struggle for equal and quality education. In E. Gee (ed.), *Counterpoint: Perspectives on Asian America.* Los Angeles: Asian American Studies Center, University of California, Los Angeles.

THEORY AND IMPLICATIONS

1. Wong describes some of the myths about nonnative English speakers. Of the explanations offered, which do you think most accounts for these myths? Why?

2. Why do you think that the "tacit compact" and "give and take" theories are so compelling to many Americans?

3. Why is the Equal Protection clause of the Fourteenth Amendment so difficult to apply? Which elements of that clause do you think allow bilingual education proponents the strongest case? Why?

4. Why do you think the arguments for "compelling state interest" that Texas put forth for denying education to the children of illegal aliens were rejected?

5. Distinguishing a "suspect class" has become important in trying cases under the Equal Protection clause of the Fourteenth Amendment. It can be argued that, like sex or race, language is beyond the choice of the individual, is linked to race and background, and is not changeable. However, others can argue that language is changeable, and thus nonnative speakers are not a "suspect class." How could you counter this last argument?

6. Why is the *Lau v. Nichols* case so important? Why is it so hard to apply?

7. How are tolerance-oriented rights and promotion-oriented rights often confused?

8. Wong makes the point that teachers need to be aware of the residency and citizenship status of language minorities. How does this apply to you in your teaching or to teachers and students with whom you are familiar?

9. Why is the teaching of minority-language students necessarily a political act? Explain.

PROFESSIONAL CONCERNS

1. Why do you suppose that in U.S. law, a national language was never stipulated? Do you think it would be a good idea to have one? Write your opinion to members of your class. Or, write an editorial expressing your views in a newspaper.

2. How are teachers particularly affected by the language policy of our nation? How can they help affect it? In a formal essay, argue for your views. Or, write an article for a teacher's journal that expresses your views.

3. For a newspaper editorial, write an argument for submersion as you think those who favor it might argue. Rely on legal as well as common-sense arguments.

4. Look at the dissenting opinion in the case of *San Antonio Independent School District v. Rodriguez.* How might education become a right guaranteed by the constitution? Present your views on language issues and the law as a speculative article for a teachers' newsletter.

5. Arguments over tolerance-oriented rights versus promotion-oriented rights continue to plague educators. Determine which views underlie some of the arguments presented in the media or in school policy statements. Write a short essay analyzing these views. Or, write an article analyzing these views for a teachers' newsletter or journal.

A Look at Process in Child Second-Language Acquisition*

EVELYN HATCH, SABRINA PECK, AND JUDY WAGNER-GOUGH

"A Look at Process in Child Second-Language Acquisition" incorporates cognitive insights within a larger framework of social interaction. It builds on Corder's and Krashen's concern that all language learning involves active hypothesizing

---

* Hatch, E., S. Peck, and J. Wagner-Gough, "A Look at Process in Child Second-Language Acquisition," *Developmental Pragmatics,* edited by Elinor Ochs and Bambi B. Schieffelin. Copyright © 1979 by Academic Press, Inc.

of rules (the broadest ones first) and that learning necessarily involves error; indeed, the examples in this study show children gradually analyzing rules, making mistakes, and refining their rules. Hatch, Peck, and Wagner-Gough, however, emphasize conversational requirements rather than cognitive processes as the key determinants of acquisition. Children do not simply acquire morphemes (e.g., ed, ing, s) *in a set order because of inherent difficulty; they acquire them in a set order because conversational demands require the use of those morphemes. Furthermore children do not first acquire structures (one word, two words, etc.) and then apply them as situations demand; instead their conversational situations determine the kind, frequency, and order of syntactic forms acquired. Hatch, Peck, and Wagner-Gough investigate conversational interactions, not simply forms used in isolation.*

This essay focuses on the importance of social factors: input frequency, the rules of conversation, and the limited options for discussing a topic. The syntactic forms that language acquirers use reflect attempts to get another's attention, nominate a topic, make a relevant reply, and take turns—requirements that ensure a high frequency of what, where, whose, and what-is-he/she-doing questions and answers. These question-and-answer forms are acquired early not because of inherent simplicity but because conversation requires them. And even one-word utterances are not simply primitive syntax used only to identify objects, but are also a situationally complex means of nominating a topic for further elaboration.

Interestingly, the focus on social factors newly defines the role of imitation in language acquisition. Recent research focusing on morpheme acquisition, in its criticism of stimulus-response theories, dismisses imitation as a language learning strategy. In conversation analysis, however, imitation reappears as a social strategy that is helpful in rule formation. To meet conversational requirements, children juxtapose chunks of imitated speech, then apply the rule of deletion; or they incorporate memorized chunks into rule-generated patterns they have already mastered, creating errors that teachers can anticipate. In both cases, repetition of memorized patterns plays a central role, one not recognized in first language acquisition research and overlooked in much of second language acquisition research. Hatch, Peck, and Wagner-Gough clarify how such strategies allow the learner to participate in conversation and thus gain the needed here-and-now input for hypothesizing rules. What is important to learners is that they keep the conversation going, however error-prone the utterance.

Recently, researchers in second-language acquisition (as in first) have turned to conversational analysis as a valuable methodology for the study of language development. Though we are, of course, interested in the emergence of specific syntactic forms in speech the learner produces, it is perhaps even more interesting to see what can be discovered about the acquisition process itself from the study of conversations.

This chapter will review the findings from a series of papers (Hatch, 1975, 1976; Peck, 1976; and Wagner-Gough and Hatch, 1975) on second-language acquisition. The findings will be discussed as evidence for the following three claims:

1. The frequency of specific syntactic forms in the speech directed to the learner influences the language forms he produces. The forms themselves and the frequency can be accounted for by basic rules of conversation.
2. Conversations provide the learner with large units which are incorporated into sentence construction.
3. Though child-adult conversations and child-child play conversations provide the learner with highly predictable and repetitious input based on the here-and-now principle, child-child language-play conversations provide the acquirer with a rich, if possibly confusing, variety of input. The learner appears to benefit from each but in different ways.

FREQUENCY AND CONVERSATION RULES

An analysis of data from Huang's (1970) study of a Taiwanese child, Paul, as he learned English, showed that the language addressed to this 5-year-old learner fell into three categories in the initial 2 months: imperatives (46%), yes/no questions and WH-questions which requested information on identity and location (40%), and statements (14%). Paul's own speech contained formulas borrowed from those in the input. For example, he quickly learned to produce *What's this* and *Where's the NP,* the two WH-questions most frequently asked of him. He also controlled a repertoire of explosive imperatives such as *You shut up* and *Don't do that,* which are common sentences on the playground of any nursery school. These were supplemented with more sociable formulae such as *Thank you* and *How are you doing?*. Further examples are displayed in Table 1.

It is not enough, however, to simply look at input and at frequency. Examining the corpus as a whole and looking at the interactions that take place within conversations can show us how that interaction determines frequency of forms.

What does the child need to do in order to talk with others? First, he must get the attention of the person with whom he wishes to talk. This can be accomplished in nonverbal ways or through verbal gestures:

PAUL: (to Kenny) *You-you-you-you!*   PAUL: *Oh-oh!*
K: *Huh?*   J: *What?*
PAUL: *I-see-you Kenny*   PAUL: *This*

Once the learner has secured the attention of his conversation partner, the second task is to get the partner to attend to the topic of discourse. He can do this by pointing or he may use other deitics:

PAUL: *Lookit*   PAUL: *oh-oh!*
J: *What?*   J: *What?*
PAUL: *ball*   PAUL: *that* [points at box]

If one can accept that a call for attention (*oh-oh, lookit,* etc.), a pointing out of a topic (*this,* etc.), and the learner's and partner's identifying remarks

TABLE 1 Effect of input frequency on production

Input	Production		
	Stage 1	Stage 2	Stage 3
Stage 1: Question (40% of Input)			
1. What's this? What is it? (51) →	What's this?		
2. Is this a NOUN? (35)	This +++ ball? / Table? →	This is book? / This is jacket? →	Is this yours house? / Are you a good boy? ("only" examples)
3. Where's the NOUN? (32) →	Where's the NOUN? →	Where's K? / Where's pen? →	Where's (the) NOUN?
4. Do you want to VERB? (11)	– – – – –		
5. CAN you VERB? (11)	– – – – –		Can I play? / Can I write my name?
6. Okay? (tag question) (6) →	Okay? →	you sit down, okay? / I'm going, okay?	
Stage 1: Imperatives (46%)			
Don't!	Don't!		
Don't do it! Don't do that!	Don't do that!		
Get out of here!	You shut up!		
Give it to me!	Get out of here!		
Show me your hands!	Say see!		
Stage 1: Statements (14%)			
(Very) good.	Very good.		
This is NOUN.	This +++ NOUN.	This is NOUN.	This is (a) NOUN.
Okay.	Okay.		
That's it.	Thank you.		
There.	I see you.		

served to nominate a topic for conversation, then we have accounted for the presence of such utterances as *This* +++ NOUN in the early data. That is, this particular structure evolves out of conversation rules for nominating topics.

While the output data of the learner is shaped by the rules of conversation, the adult input is also constrained by the same rules. The partner must, by the rules of conversation, "make a relevant reply." There are few directly relevant replies to be made to the kinds of topics the child nominates. For example, if the child nominates *this,* pointing to a fish in a fish tank, the child and adult seem to talk about *this* as a topic in a very few, very limited ways: *What? Fish. What's this? A fish. Where's the fish? Whose fish is that? Is it yours? How many fish are there? What color is it? What's the fish doing? It's swimming. Can he swim? No, it's not a fish.* There are not many other possibilities. And precisely these questions and responses to the topic can account for the order of acquisition in AUX development and in morphology that have been discussed at length in the literature (e.g., Dulay and Burt, 1974; Hatch, 1974). It gives us a high frequency for COP sentences, plurals and the ING progressive (the forms first acquired according to morpheme studies of both first and second language learners).

The rules of conversation put the adult under two constraints as to what is a relevant reply: *(a)* what information about *this* is shared by adult and child, and *(b)* what are the attributes of *this* that one can talk about. The first constraint prevents the adult from launching into a tirade against pet stores: the second gives us a high frequency for what, where, whose, what doing, or is X VerbING questions. The rules of conversation, then, put constraints on questions which explain their frequency in the input. That the child then uses (and eventually acquires) these same questions first in the data collected in adult-child discourse should not be surprising.

INCORPORATION OF LARGE UNITS

The child acquiring a second language after having his first language development well under way is able to repeat large chunks of the language and is also able to store and retrieve sequences which he hears frequently or which delight him in some special way (e.g., songs, expressions such as *okey-dokey, I can beat you up*). This ability serves him well in two ways. It gives him chunks of language which he can use in taking a turn in conversations and it gives him large units from which to abstract his set of rules for the new language.

While repetition and chunk learning of forumulae is a commonly discussed phenomenon, what is especially interesting about it is the subsequent impact these formulae have on rule formation. Conversations between Homer, an Iranian 5-year-old, and native speakers of English show that incorporation was an important strategy for learning the new language. Sometimes this was immediate as in (Wagner-Gough, 1975):

M: *Come here.*   M: *Don't do that!*
HOMER: *No come here.* [= I won't]   HOMER: *Okay don't do that.*

J: *Where are you going?*
HOMER: *Where are you going is house.*

Sometimes a pattern was stored for later incorporation:

E: *Which one?*
HOMER: *I'll show you is that one. Which one is that one.*

Homer's most pervasive use of incorporation appeared in WH-patterns, some of which are listed below.

> *What is this truck.* [= This is a truck.]
> *What this is Homer.* [= This is Homer.]
> *What is this is?* [= What is this?]
> *What this is?* [= What is this?]

The process by which Homer formed these patterns appears to be as follows.

1. He juxtaposed related units of conversation (question and answer), then applied deletions to related units within each phrase.
2. Deletions were randomly applied:
   a. Sometimes the amalgamated pattern *What is this this is* NP became *What this is* NP, as evidence of *is this* deletion:
      > *What this is Homer.*
      > *What this is airplane.*
   b. Sometimes *this is* deletion occurred and the pattern became *What is this NP:*
      > *What is this airplane.*
      > *What is this screaming.*
   c. Sometimes only *this* was deleted, giving *What is this is NP:*
      > *What is this is car.*
   d. Homer sometimes deleted the NP and either *is this, this is* or *this* when asking a question:
      > *What is this?*
      > *What this is?*
      > *What is this is?*

These incorporated patterns tell us something about process strategies in language learning. Homer's rules for both WH-questions and statements were derived from the combined question-answer patterns of conversations. Therefore, Homer was focusing on and processing much more than isolated sentence units of speech. Instead, he was sorting through and storing linguistic information which he received in conversations.

Scollon (1974), R. Clark (1974), and others have also found evidence of incorporation rules in the language of the children they have studied. Clark contends that much of children's speech consists of prepackaged routines, incorporated from adults' speech without being internally analyzed. Certainly these findings suggest that an analysis of language learning based solely on sentence grammars may not capture the essence of the process.

The second-language learner's ability to repeat large chunks of the language also serves him well in conversations. To take a turn in conversations, he can, in fact, use the input he has just heard, whether he has understood it or not. Repetition is appropriate behavior in a large variety of speech acts the child participates in.

Data collected in the classroom by Young (1974) provides us with examples of Spanish-speaking acquirers of English using repetition for a variety of conversational functions (NS = native speaker).

NS: *I got a real gun.*

ENRIQUE: *I got a real gun.*

ADULT: *A real what?*

ENRIQUE: *Real gun. Go like dat.* [gun noises]

NS: *You gotta parachute?*

ENRIQUE: *Hey, yeh. Gotta parachute.*

ADULT: *What's a parachute?*

NS: *It have a man go down.*

ENRIQUE: *Yeh XXX go down, down, down, down, down.*

NS: *Hey, he do more better 'n you.*

ENRIQUE: *He do more better 'n you.*

NS: *I can—*

ENRIQUE: *—I can do more XXX. Lookit. No more better 'n me. Lookit. Look what is. Dumb. Lookit.* [Sings:] *dumb, dumb, dumb.*

In much of child-child conversation, repetition is exactly what is called for. Even in threats, repetition is an important part of the speech act:

NS: [at swings] *I can beat your brother up. I can beat him up.*

ENRIQUE: *You can beat him, huh. I can beat him to my party 'n you can beat him 'n you can beat my brother. He beat you up. You XXX it. I can beat you up!*

In this last example, it appears that if there is no gradual build up of traded insults, the child must sustain what he says over a longer period of time and gradually build volume so that the final threat is said both at higher pitch and with greater intensity. Therefore, the materials that lead up to the final *I can beat you up* do not have to make strict sense though it incorporates repetition of the original boast of the native speaker.

The learner's ability to use frequently heard formulae and to repeat large chunks of the input give him quick entry into the communicative aspect of language learning, an advantage not shared by the adult second-language learner.

INPUT TO CHILD SECOND-LANGUAGE LEARNERS

At first glance, the input to child learners in child-child conversations appears to be almost as varied as that addressed to adult second-language learners. Peck (1976), however, has categorized such conversations into two types: language during play and language play, a categorization that allows us to see important differences in such input.

LANGUAGE DURING PLAY

Children's play often contains language that is highly predictable, repetitious, and well contextualized, and as such is ideal for the learner. There are certain routines for setting up the rules of a game or play situation (e.g., *You throw it to him. The king can go here. I'll be the doctor.*) and for arguing about one's own version of the rules, should a dispute arise (e.g., *My turn! You have to go like that.*), and these utterances are often accompanied by gestures and pointing. Once the game has begun, there is often a small set of structurally and semantically similar utterances which can be used for commenting on the play (e.g., *You throw to her. One here and one here. Ha! Very simple!*) or as integral parts of the game (*Do you have any tens?*), and, again, for maintaining the rules which have supposedly been agreed on (e.g., *No, this just going like this. You can't do that. Not to him—to him!*).

The language of play can be exceedingly clear to the learner not only because it is tied to the situation and therefore follows the here-and-now principle, but because it is often repeated many times. If the two children work together in setting up the rules and roles of a game or play situation, the resultant language in that situation will perhaps be even more predictable to the acquirer.

While it is true that native speakers do correct errors of fact in fast-paced play situations, the acquirer can easily ignore most of these corrections (Peck, 1976).

WIGBERTO: *No, I* ⌈ *throw* ⌉ *it to him, you throw*
NS 1:   ⌊ *to her* ⌋
WIGBERTO: *it to him, /id/ you:*
NS 1: [shriek:] *No!*
WIGBERTO: ⌈ [loud:] *y you—y you* ⌉ *throw it to him!*
NS 2:   ⌊ *We're not boys!*   ⌋
NS 3: *No!*
NS 2: [shrill:] *No!*
NS 3: *Throw it to her!*
WIGBERTO: *I throw it to him.*

It is probable that in some kinds of games (catch, chess, etc.) language is not even necessary for the progress of the game itself, so that the learner is in a low-anxiety situation in which any correction or teasing by the native speaker, even of matters of fact, can be ignored.

LANGUAGE PLAY

In language play, the native speaker may provide the acquirer with a rich and possibly confusing variety of input. Peck (1978) described conversations between two 7-year olds, a native speaker of English, and a Spanish speaker who was acquiring English. The native speaker initiated many episodes of language play, much of it seemingly to correct or tease the learner. He imitated the acquirer's pronunciation (e.g., /sImpl/ for "simple," /gœmərə/ for "camera") and varied the learner's nonstandard syntactic patterns (Peck, 1978).

ANGEL: *No, your are enjoy.*
         [Two utterances intervene.]
NS: I—I'm enjoy—what about your enjoy?

He sang, whispered, shouted, made sound effects, used a singsong intonation, or made up his own versions of tunes. According to his own free associations, which were sometimes probably touched off by the sound or structure of the acquirer's words, he recited nursery rhymes and pieces of advertisements. He sang songs that both boys knew from school, as well as songs that the learner did not know, and parodies of songs. Much of the input to the learner, then, had no relation to any object or activity in the room (did not conform to the here-and-now principle). Because of this, the child learner probably did not understand the meaning of much of it. However, the learner was still able to take turns in conversation because the rules called for attention to sound and structure over meaning (Peck, 1976).

NS: *Do that, do what, D'* [6x]*—Umm Da* [4x]
ANGEL: [making up a tune:] *My Daddy's in Mexico.*

The native speaker may likewise ignore many of the acquirer's requests for clarification.

NS: [part of utterance omitted] *You know what you just did? Gave me a clue.*
     Thank you ve'—very **not** *much.*
ANGEL: *Not much? Why* ⎡*not much?*⎤
NS: ⎣*Not much.*⎦

Although the input during language play may be semantically opaque for the acquirer and frustrating if he gets tired of being teased, it also gives him opportunities to play with the words and sounds of the language and to tease. For these reasons the learner himself may initiate language play.

NS: *You know what?*
ANGEL: *You know why?*

NS: *You know why?* [frustrated with the puzzle:] *Oh!*
ANGEL: [starting to laugh] *You know why—you/not/why?*

In summary, in play with other children, child second-language learners have the advantage of receiving input which is highly understandable in the context of the game, often repeated, and therefore containing, perhaps, many utterances which are structurally and semantically similar. In language play, on the other hand, the native speaker's input may be almost meaningless to the acquirer but perhaps useful in the opportunities for phonological and pattern practice that it can offer, as well as for additional conversational practice.

CONCLUDING REMARKS

Conversational analysis allows us to look at process in second-language learning. We have found that, in exchanges with adults, the child is continually bombarded with questions, primarily with questions of identification and elaboration. These are what, where, whose, or what-doing questions. The questions ask the child to clarify and enlarge on the topics that he or the adult nominates. The questions are constrained by what is shared by both speakers in terms of objects present in the immediate environment, ongoing actions, and assumed prior knowledge. The questions asked the child require him to give new information in an order specified by the adult. This ordering may force the child to put constituents into an order which provides the precursor to more formal syntactic arrangements. Further, the frequency of the question forms used by the adult is reflected in the order of acquisition that we have found for question formation for the child. From the adult, the learner receives input that is, then, simplified to fit the here-and-now principle. The here-and-now aspect makes the meaning of the input obvious for the learner.

From the conversations he participates in with other children, the learner receives at least two distinctly different kinds of input. In play the input agrees with the here-and-now principle. Play contextualizes the language. In addition, play routines are repeated over and over in the course of the game. In certain ways (contextualized and predictable) the input in child-child conversations during play is similar to adult-child conversations. The major difference, perhaps, is that it is not based on question and answer turn-taking.

In contrast, language-play conversations of children are highly unpredictable. The native speaker child has a vast repertoire of associations that he can launch at any moment (e.g., from "pieces" to "pizzas" to "pepsi" to the pepsi cola commercial song). While the meaning of such associations must be opaque for the learner, he can still participate by echoing parts of what he hears and making his own associations.

The learner of a second language is able to repeat, store, and retrieve large chunks of the new language. For example, one of the first utterances of Huang's subject was *Are you ready?* He used this question appropriately in context, but it was not until many months later that such questions appeared in an analyzed form in his language. This ability to use large chunks of the language appropriately gives the learner two advantages: He can take a turn in conversations by using these formulae, and he can use these chunks—juxtaposing them to form new utterances, breaking them down as parts of them are analyzed, and recombining them in a variety of ways—to form his own syntactic rules.

In investigating second-language acquisition in the past, we have concentrated on speech production of subjects, most frequently on the order of acquisition of a small set of morphemes. While we have found some regularity in language development, we have been unable to construct a satisfactory model to describe the process by which language is learned. Our lack of a model may, in part, be due to our interest in research that isolates language form from the context in which it occurs. Our hope is that in looking at conversations we will begin to understand something more of that process.

REFERENCES

Clark, R. 1974. Performing without competence. *Journal of Child Language,* 1, 1–10.

Dulay, H., and Burt, M. 1974. A new perspective on the creative construction process in child language acquisition. *Working Papers on Bilingualism,* 4, 71, 97.

Hatch, E. 1974. Second language universals? *Working Papers on Bilingualism.* OISE, Toronto. 3, 1–17.

———. 1975. The analysis of discourse in second language learning. Paper presented at the UCLA-USC Second Language Acquisition Forum.

———. 1976. Discourse analysis and second language acquisition. Paper presented at the HAFSA Convention in San Diego.

Huang, J. 1970. A Chinese child's acquisition of English syntax. Unpublished M.A. thesis, UCLA.

Peck, S. 1976. Play in child second language acquisition. Paper presented at the UCLA-USC Second Language Acquisition Forum.

———. 1978. Child-child discourse in second language acquisition. In E. Hatch, Ed., *Second language acquisition.* Massachusetts: Newbury House.

Scollon, R. 1974. One child's language from one to two: The origins of construction. Unpublished Ph.D. dissertation. University of Hawaii.

Wagner-Gough, J. 1975. Comparative studies in second language learning. Center for Applied Linguistics. CAL-ERIC CLL Series on Languages and Linguistics, no. 26.

Wagner-Gough, J., and Hatch, E. 1975. The importance of input data in second language acquisition studies. *Language Learning,* 25, 297–307.

Young, D. 1974. The acquisition of English syntax by three Spanish-speaking children. Unpublished M.A. thesis, UCLA.

THEORY AND IMPLICATIONS

1. Why must researchers look to conversational patterns, not just isolated units of speech, to understand the acquisition process?

2. Do you think that the positive view of imitation revealed here contradicts cognitivists' views of imitation as not furthering language acquisition? How might the views be reconciled?

3. How do the rules of conversation account for the rules of syntax that are learned first? Is there clearly a causal relationship? What questions still need to be answered about this process?

4. Given that most first and second language acquisition studies emphasize analyzed or rule-formed speech, why is recognition of the use of a formula important?

5. What syntactic errors and inappropriate usages do you think the new L2 speaker must be willing to make in order to converse? What do these errors show about language acquisition?

6. Do you think that the processes of incorporation and deletion that L2 acquirers use in conversation have cognitive as well as social dimensions? If so, do you think that you can predict errors from such processes? Would grammar correction address such errors? Explain your answers.

7. In the examples of Homer's use of incorporation, the deletions appear random. Yet the underlying process appears very systematic. From the perspective of Homer's processing of question-answer patterns of conversations, how were they systematic? What do the errors suggest about Homer's increasing conversational competence?

8. Why is language during play that employs both analyzed and unanalyzed patterns so helpful for L2 acquirers? What is different but equally helpful about language play?

9. Little in the literature of L2 investigates language play. What other uses could such investigations have?

PROFESSIONAL CONCERNS

1. Explain to another teacher who insists on "good grammar" why a student of hers makes the kind of redundancy errors he does. Use this occasion as an opportunity to justify the need for analyzing interactions between students to understand the origins of many unusual L2 errors.

2. Explain the need to look at social processes to a linguist who believes that all language learning is based on innate processes. As part of your argument, show how the acquisition of the pattern "X is VERBing" (present participle) is learned early not just because the form is very regular but also because it is used so often in typical L2 child and adult interactions.

3. Compose a five-minute training workshop for other teachers based on insights from this study.

4. Argue for the importance of looking at conversational competence as central to L2 acquisition. Assume an audience of administrators or other teachers.

Individual Differences in Second Language Acquisition*

LILY WONG FILLMORE

"Individual Differences in Second Language Acquisition" extends the investigation of social factors affecting L2 acquisition. It is a longitudinal, rather than a cross-sectional, study that follows five children over the course of a year. Although not originally intended to do so, it emphasizes differences among L2 acquirers, revealing that one child had accomplished in three months what others would take a year and beyond to accomplish. It is one of the first studies to isolate variables including gender, personality, and motivation, suggesting a wide interplay of social, personal, and linguistic factors.

Most important, Fillmore's study moves beyond conversation to describe the social world of the L2 acquirer, vivifying the various possible reactions of different L2 students to the daunting task of establishing social relations. It is not just exposure to conversation or the rules of conversation that affect acquisition, but also children's roles, need for acceptance, ability to establish friendships, and games. Like Krashen, Fillmore acknowledges that children unconsciously form rules while they think they are doing something else; but she also stresses that the particular "something else" they think they are doing proves to be a key variable.

This study also has important implications for pedagogy. First, it suggests that teachers should provide language "embedded in current, interest-holding activities over which learners ha[ve] already acquired some mastery, and from which they ha[ve] already received social rewards." By this, Fillmore means a focus on content or communication among friends, not specific language instructions. Second, she helps teachers to understand sources of error other than overgeneralization, such as children's use of imitated structures in inappropriate settings. Imitated structures are here seen not as secondary to rule formation, as in the Huang and Hatch study, but as primary to rule formation. This study thus emphasizes broad, differential social factors over uniform cognitive ones, accounting for great differences among L2 acquirers.

Because this classic study is based on only a few cases, it has been open to criticism in recent years for overgeneralization. Some researchers have found Nora, Fillmore's "star" learner, an exception; others have offered studies indicating that Nora's "integrative motivation"—her desire to be with and like Anglos—was not necessarily the cause of her spectacular success in learning English. Despite these criticisms, Fillmore's study remains a focal point for discussions of individual differences among L2 learners.

---

* Fillmore, L. W., "Individual Differences in Second Language Acquisition," in *Individual Difference in Language Ability and Language Behavior,* edited by Charles J. Fillmore, Daniel Kempler, and William S.-Y. Wang. Copyright © 1979 by Academic Press, Inc.

There is some difference of opinion concerning the role of individual differences in second language acquisition. One view is that individual variation is an all-important factor—one which differentiates the process of second language acquisition from that of first language acquisition. This position has been widely held by investigators who are interested in the acquisition process principally as it occurs in adolescents or adults learning foreign languages in formal classroom settings. In such settings, it is apparent that individuals vary greatly in the ease and success with which they are able to handle the learning of new languages, and hence, it is argued that second language learning must therefore be different from first language learning. Whereas first language acquisition is quite uniform across populations in terms of developmental scheduling, the strategies used to achieve it, and the control over the language which is ultimately achieved, there is considerable variation among individuals in the ability to acquire second languages. Some individuals seem to acquire languages after the first with ease, and they manage to achieve a degree of mastery over the new languages comparable to the control they have over their first language in a relatively short time. Others find it quite difficult to learn later languages, to learn them as well as the first, or to do so at all without a great deal of conscious effort. Much of the research activities on second language acquisition until recently was aimed at finding explanations for this apparent variability. The favored explanations have centered on variations in learner characteristics such as motivation, attitudes, and language learning aptitude; and the research linking these characteristics to variation in language learning ability has been carried out largely on late adolescent and adult students of foreign languages with formal tests of achievement used as criterion measures. The investigations of Wallace Lambert and R. C. Gardner on the role of attitudes and motivations (Lambert *et al.,* 1962; Gardner and Lambert, 1972) and those of John Carroll (1963) on language learning aptitude have been particularly important in this regard.

The second and opposing view is that individual variation plays no greater a role in the acquisition of second languages than it does in the learning of first languages—that is to say, its role, if any, is trivial. This position is taken by more recent investigators who have been looking at the acquisition of second languages by relatively young children in naturalistic settings where the language is not taught explicitly. The goal of these investigators is to demonstrate that the same processes which account for the learning of first languages are also responsible for the learning of later ones. Thus they look for evidence of acquisitional procedures and developmental schedules which resemble those found in first language learning, and they attempt to infer the existence of the same uniformity in acquisition that has been claimed in first language learning. Any evidence of individual variation among second language learners tends to get overlooked—partly because of the orientation of these investigators, and partly because much of their research has been carried out as single-subject case studies which attempt to map the developmental course of second language acquisition in individuals (e.g., Huang, 1971; Hakuta, 1976; and Milon, 1974), or as cross-sectional studies of a relatively large number of subjects tested on a one-shot basis, which attempt to establish statistical evidence of uniformity in the developmental sequence of a small number of specific grammatical items or processes (e.g., Dulay and Burt, 1974; Chun and Politzer, 1975; and Fathman, 1975).

In the case of the cross-sectional studies, the objective is to establish norms, and therefore, the statistical measures typically used are those which are not especially sensitive to variation: What variation there is manages to get lost with little difficulty in the statistical manipulations. The single-case studies, of course, do not yield any evidence of variation, since in order to show variation, there must be comparison—and in such studies, there is nothing to compare. Nor have attempts to compare findings across studies been especially fruitful since, in general, such studies tend to be noncomparable with respect to their subjects (in age, first language background, or circumstances under which the second language was being learned), the type of data used, the way they were collected, and the methods used to analyze the data.

And so it is that the issue of individual variation is rarely discussed in studies of childhood second language acquisition, this despite the fact that even the most casual observations of the language performance of any group of children in the process of learning a second language naturalistically or otherwise would reveal considerable variation in the rate and ease at which they are managing the learning of it, and in how well they are able to use the language they are learning. But because researchers are more interested in discovering what is universal about the acquisition process than in knowing whether the process might vary in individuals, the question is never discussed, or even raised.

In my own research on second language acquisition (Fillmore, 1976), I was not looking for individual differences either, but the research design I used would not permit me to ignore evidence of variation, as I might have been able to do had I limited myself to a sane single-subject case study or a tidy cross-sectional study. Instead, I did a longitudinal study of five subjects, tracking their second language development (English) for the period of one school year. But while the comparisons of the speech development of the five children during that year would have yielded evidence of variation, comparisons alone would not have revealed the factors which produced that variation, nor the manner in which those factors managed to affect the language learning of each child. This was done by another fortuitous aspect of the research design: I paired the five subjects who were Spanish-speakers with five English-speaking friends for observations. The five subjects and their friends shared no common language at first, and my purpose in observing the children in pairs was to discover what social processes might be involved when children who need to learn a new language come into contact with those from whom they are to learn it—but with whom they can not communicate easily. A language can be learned only if there is input of the proper sort—for the child second language learner, this is language as it is used in social situations which make sense, and in which the learner is himself involved. To get this kind of input, the typical second language learner must play an active role in inviting interaction from the speakers of the language, and in maintaining contact once it is established. Since all of this must be managed at a time when the learner cannot communicate with those from whom he is to learn the language, he needs some very special social skills. These social issues were at least as important as the cognitive issues I hoped to examine, and I wanted to discover what sorts of strategies the children would need to apply in order to handle the problem of making social contact. Thus I observed the subjects, not as they responded to me in elicitation sessions, but as they interacted and played with age-mates. It was in the course of these play sessions that the children revealed the impressive ways in which they were individuals, and which specific characteristics affected the way they approached the task of learning a second language.

Each of the five pairs of children—a Spanish-speaker and his or her English-speaking friend—was observed at play one hour each week in a playroom which was stocked with school materials and toys. These play sessions were audio-recorded, and written records were also kept of the children's interaction during these sessions. The audiotapes were all transcribed, and in all, there were 106 hours of transcribed conversations which served as the data for this study. The five Spanish-speaking subjects were all newly arrived from Mexico, and spoke no English at the beginning of the study period. All five were the children of farmworkers, and their parents planned to stay in the area where there was promise of year-around work. There were three boys and two girls: The youngest was Nora who was 5:7 and in kindergarten; Ana who was 6:5, Alej who was 6:9, and Juan who was 7:3 were all in the first grade; Jesus at 6:11 was in the second grade. Juan and Jesus had each had a year of school in Mexico before coming to California, but for the others, the study year was the first year of school. Two of the boys, Juan and Alej, were in the same class, but otherwise, the children were in different classrooms. None of the children received any formal language instruction during the study year. The source of their learning was the language used by their teachers and classmates.

Each of the English-speaking friends was close in age to the subject with whom he or she was paired, and attended the same classrooms as the subject. All but one were "anglos." The one exception was Juan's friend, Carlos. Carlos was a Mexican-American bilingual child, and he represented the only departure from the original plan of pairing the subjects with English monolingual friends. The reason for the departure was that Juan refused to have anything to do with English-speakers, and would only play silently beside the ones I attempted to pair him with for the purposes of the study. Carlos was Juan's own choice—and I thought it only fair that he should have a self-selected friend as the others did, especially after a month and a half of no success in trying to match him up with an English-speaker. Otherwise, the friends were self-selected, and while the study had the effect of prolonging friendships which might have been more temporary, the friendships between the Spanish and English-speakers were genuine enough, and reflected the social life of the children outside the Playroom during the school day and year.

The criteria for selecting the Spanish-speaking subjects were several—besides having an anglophone friend with whom he or she could be paired for the study, each had the following characteristics as far as could be determined through observations and without tests: (*a*) a reasonably outgoing personality; (*b*) normal first language development and fairly clear articulation; (*c*) normal intellect (i.e., was reasonably alert); and (*d*) parents who were willing to give assurances that they intended to stay in the community for at least the year. The object was to select five children who were as "ordinary" as possible, so that their second language might be offered as representative of other children their age, and from a similar linguistic and cultural background. I expected that the second language development of the five would be fairly uniform after 9 months of exposure to the new language as it was used in the classroom and in the playground by their teachers and classmates. But the results were quite different.

By the end of 3 months of observations, it became quite clear that there would be enormous differences among the five children in what they would achieve during the study year. In fact, after just 3 months of exposure, one child, Nora, had already learned more—or at least she was producing better-formed and more varied sentences—than two of the others, Juan and Jesus, would be able to manage by the end of the study period. And by the end of the study period, Nora herself was speaking English as well as her friends who came from bilingual homes, and very nearly as well as her English monolingual friends. In order to achieve the same degree of proficiency, the others in the study would need at least another year of exposure, and at the rate that Juan and Jesus were progressing, even two. This was the principal manifestation of individual differences in the data. It showed up in the records of the children's speech performance as differences in ease and rate of development rather than in acquisitional procedures—but these differences were related to the children's cognitive approaches to the learning task in interesting ways. In fact, the individual differences found among the five learners in this study had to do with the way in which the cognitive and social factors of language acquisition interact together. But before this can be described or shown, I will need to discuss what I found about the cognitive and social problems in second language learning, and of the strategies the children employed in dealing with these problems.

COGNITIVE AND SOCIAL STRATEGIES IN SECOND LANGUAGE LEARNING

The cognitive problem facing the second language learner is an immense one— he has everything to learn about the language, and little to work with, save a general awareness of how languages function, based on his first language experience. Thus he must approach this task with some strategies in hand. For starters, however, the first strategies that occur to him for dealing with language learning have nothing to do with learning a language. It is safe to say that none of the five children in this study approached the task as if they knew that is what they were doing. Instead, they seemed more aware of the problem of establishing social relations with the children who spoke that language. As pointed out earlier, language cannot be learned without input, and to get input of the right sort, the learner needs exposure to the language as it is used in social situations which involve him. To get into these social situations in the first place, and to establish a relationship with the speakers of the language so they are willing to provide the necessary input to him, the learner needs some special social strategies. And since all of this is to be accomplished at a time when he has little or no language in common with these people, the learner has a very sticky and circular problem on his hand. So the social problem in second language learning reduces to two major issues: How to get along for a while without a common language, and how to get your friends to want to help you learn theirs.

The cognitive problems are much more complex: Before the structures of the new language can be learned, the learner needs first to comprehend them. Second, he needs somehow to gain entry into the language, and then to figure out how the pieces of it fit together. Furthermore, he has somehow to develop fluency in the language, and to ferret out its structural details, so that his version of it matches the one spoken by the people around him. But while the children were quite aware of the social problems facing them, they appeared quite unconcerned about the cognitive ones. Perhaps they understood the social issues better, since the social ones had more direct relevance to them. They never seemed particularly motivated to learn the new language as they were to get along with the people who spoke it. Juan was the exception in this regard; he was not interested in associating with the English speakers, and the result was that he learned less than any of the others during the study year. But it was not for lack of interest in the learning of the new language, nor for want of trying: He frequently asked how one said this or that in English, repeated things he heard people saying, and he seemed to try hard to remember what he learned. But he truly did not care much to socialize with the people who spoke the language, and hence, he had little reason to use what he was learning. The other four children were far more interested in making friends than they were in learning any language, and they learned considerably more than Juan during the year.

To deal with the task of learning a language which they were largely unconcerned about learning, the children had to have some rather special cognitive and social strategies. The strategies which were revealed through the interactional and linguistic records of the children are summarized in Table 1. These strategies are phrased as maxims that the children might have formulated for themselves, following the convention used by Slobin in discussing the operational principles of children in first language acquisition (1973). The

TABLE 1 Cognitive and social strategies

Social Strategies	Cognitive Strategies
S-1: Join a group and act as if you understand what's going on, even if you don't.	C-1: Assume that what people are saying is directly relevant to the situation at hand, or to what they or you are experiencing. Metastrategy: Guess!
S-2: Give the impression—with a few well-chosen words—that you can speak the language.	C-2: Get some expressions you understand, and start talking.
	C-3: Look for recurring parts in the formulas you know.
S-3: Count on your friends for help.	C-4: Make the most of what you've got.
	C-5: Work on big things first; save the details for later.

cognitive and social strategies are presented together because it is difficult to separate them. They are presented this way to show how the social strategies relate to the cognitive ones, and in a way that might be taken as providing the motivation for several of the most important cognitive strategies.

The first social strategy is one which gets the learner into a position in which he is able to learn the language:

> S-1: *Join a group and act as if you understand what's going on, even if you don't.*

Ordinarily, it is up to the learner to invite interaction. He is the "outsider" and he must somehow give the impression that he is worth talking to before the speakers are willing to have him join the group. The way the learner does this is to behave as if he understands, although obviously in the early stages of language learning, he will understand little. This means that he must pay attention to what is going on, and guess at what people are saying on the basis of contextual information.

This strategy worked because it had an important effect on the friends of the learners. The learners behaved as if they understood what was going on; the friends, believing that the learners understood them, included them in their conversations. Nevertheless, while the English-speaking friends believed that the learners understood English, they also recognized that their comprehension was limited, perhaps in the way one understands that the comprehension of younger or less experienced people is likely to be limited, and they therefore modified their language use accordingly. The crucial factor was this: Because the friends believed that the learners could understand them, and that communication between them was possible, they included them in activities and conversations, and this allowed the learners to assume roles in social situations and activities that made sense to them, and gave them an opportunity to observe and acquire the kind of language children use in these activities, despite their initial inability to speak or understand the language.

This, then, is the motivation for applying the first of the cognitive strategies:

> C-1: *Assume that what people are saying is directly relevant to the situation at hand, or to what they or you are experiencing. Metastrategy: GUESS!*

The first social strategy constitutes the learner's motivation for making the effort to figure out what is being said; its related cognitive strategy (C-1) constitutes the plan that enables the learner to begin comprehending the language used around him—the necessary first step in language learning. The use of situational information for speech interpretation is a very important strategy, one which the learners provided ample evidence of using. An obvious kind of language use in the classroom which lends itself to easy interpretation is the use of speech routines such as *It's time to clean-up now. Who's buying lunch in the cafeteria today? Let's line up for recess. Let's see which table can sit-up the straightest!* Such utterances through repeated or routine use quickly become associated with their related activities, and thus, can be readily interpreted and comprehended. However, the great majority of utterances produced in a day in the classroom or playground are not routine, but are situationally anchored nevertheless, whether they are formulaic or propositional. By paying close attention to what is going on when they are spoken, the learner can interpret with fair accuracy what is being said. Of course, not every instance of language use lends itself to interpretation this way, and there were many times, obviously, when the children did not know what was going on. Still, the daily experience of a child in the classroom and in the playground contains ample occasions when the situation provides the means for figuring out rather easily what people must be saying.

The second social strategy has to do with maintaining social contact once it has been established:

S-2: *Give the impression—with a few well-chosen words—that you can speak the language.*

If the desire to join a social group whose language the learner does not speak is the social motivation for using contextual information to figure out what people are saying, then the desire to maintain contact and to sustain social relations with members of the group is the motivation to begin using the language. The learner cannot continue for long his charade of "knowing" the language without giving evidence of being able to speak it as well. What he must do is to acquire some language which will give the impression of ability to speak it, so that his friends will keep trying to communicate with him. This is accomplished through the use of the second cognitive strategy which gives the learner the needed entry into the new language:

C-2: *Get some expressions you understand, and start talking.*

The children in this study applied strategy C-2 by picking up formulaic expressions—expressions which were acquired and used as unanalyzed wholes. This strategy is extremely important since it allows the learner to use and become familiar with the language long before he knows anything about its structure, and before he can create any sentences in the language himself. There was a striking similarity among the five subjects in the acquisition and use of formulaic expressions.

All five quickly acquired repertories of expressions which they knew how to use more or less appropriately, and put them to immediate and frequent use. The phrases they learned were those they found most useful—expressions which helped them to appear to know what was going on (e.g., *Oh yeah? Hey, what's going on here? So what? No fighting, now.*), to participate in games and play activities (e.g., *You wanna play? It's my turn. Me first. No fair!*), and to request information, confirmation, and clarification from their friends (e.g., *How do you do this? What's happening? Is this one all right? What did you say?* and *I don't understand.*). The following are just a few of the typical formulas found in the spontaneous speech records of the children:

Lookit.	*I wanna play.*	*Liar, panzón fire.*
Wait a minute.	*Do you wanna play?*	*It's time to clean up.*
Lemme see.	*Whaddya wanna do?*	*OK, you be the X,*
Gimme.	*I gotta hurry up.*	*I'll be the Y.*
Let's go.	*I get 2 turns.*	*I tell you what to do.*
I don't care.	*Whose turn is it?*	*Shaddup your mouth.*
I dunno.	*You have to do it this way.*	*Beat it.*
You know what?	*I'm gonna tell on you.*	*Knock it off.*

This kind of language was extremely important, because it permitted the learners to continue participating in activities which provided contexts for the learning of new material. This new material was learnable and memorable by virtue of being embedded in current, interest-holding activities over which the learners had already acquired some mastery, and from which they had already received social rewards. Without doubt, the process would have been far less successful if the children had been only passive observers, rather than active participants. In order to make the progress they did, they needed to be in a position to discover under what pragmatic conditions particular utterances could appropriately be uttered, and they needed to be able to test their conclusions by using these utterances and getting feedback from their interlocutors to confirm whether they had guessed rightly or not. A good part of learning a language involves this kind of feedback. If the learner is not trying out his newly acquired language, he is not in a position to distinguish right guesses from wrong ones and thus discover what he needs to learn.

Other researchers (such as Huang, 1971; Hakuta, 1976) have observed the use of such language in second language learners. Huang has suggested that imitation may be a secondary strategy for language acquisition which is used in conjunction with the primary one of "rule formation" and acquisition. The point which has been missed so far is that the strategy of acquiring formulaic speech is central to the learning of language: Indeed, it is this step that puts the learner in a position to perform the analysis which is necessary for language learning. Formulaic speech in this study turned out to be important not only because it permitted the children to begin speaking the language long before they knew how it was structured, but also because the formulas the children learned and used constituted the linguistic material on which a large part of the analytical activities involved in language learning could be carried out. These formulas were generally expressions which were highly situational in use, and could be learned and used with the learner knowing nothing about their internal structures. In general, they were used as invariant forms, and the children had a fairly good idea of the appropriateness conditions for their use. Once in the learner's speech repertory, they became familiar, and therefore could be compared with other utterances in the repertory as well as with those produced by other speakers. Their function in the language learning process, then, is not only social, but cognitive too, since they provided the data on which the children were to perform their analytical activities in figuring out the structure of the language.

This, then, is the third cognitive strategy:

C-3: *Look for recurring parts in the formulas you know.*

There are two ways in which the learner begins to analyze the formulaic expressions in his repertory. The first involves noticing how parts of expressions used by others vary in accordance with changes in the speech situation in which they occur. The second involves noticing which parts of these formulaic expressions are like parts of other utterances the learner knows or hears, or noticing variations of these utterances in the speech of others. For example, Nora had in her speech repertory two related formulas: *I wanna play wi' dese* and *I don' wanna do dese.* No doubt the similarity of these expressions allowed her to discover that the constituents following *wanna* were interchangeable, and that she could also say *I don' wanna play wi' dese* and *I wanna do dese.* As soon as she realized that these phrases were interchangeable, she was on her way to discovering that similar phrases could be inserted. At that point, these formulas became formulaic frames with analyzed slots: *I wanna X/X=VP* and *I don' wanna X/X=VP,* that is, where other verb phrases (VP) can be inserted into the slot represented by X.

Through a gradual process of figuring out which parts of the formulas in their speech repertories could be varied, the children were able to free the constituents in many of them to become units in productive constructions. In the above formulas, the phrase *play wi' X/X=NP* became a formulaic verb phrase unit which could be used in the verb phrase slot of other frames such as *Le's X/X=VP* (e.g., *Le's play wi' that one*) and in productive constructions as well: *She's play wi' dese.* Thus the analytical process carried out on formulas yielded formulaic frames with abstract slots representing constituent types which could substitute in them, and it also freed constituent parts of the formula to function in other constructions either as formulaic units or as wholly analyzed items. Finally, when all of the constituents of the formula have become freed from the original construction, what the learner has left is an abstract structure consisting of a pattern or rules by which he can construct like utterances.

The formula-based analytical process just outlined was repeated in case after case of the children's spontaneous data. A particularly clear example of it can be seen in the evolution of a formula in Nora's speech record, *How do you do dese?* Table 2 summarizes the developmental course of this expression over time, as it evolved from a wholly unanalyzed formula into a productive construction.

Nora first acquired this useful question during the second quarter of the study year which is designated Time 2 on the table, and she used it frequently, but only in the form, *How do you do dese?* Early in the next quarter, Time 3, she began appending noun phrases or preposition phrases to the formula: *How do you do dese X/X=NP, PP.* At this point the phrase itself was as yet unanalyzed, but was nevertheless being treated as a sentence frame with a noun phrase (NP) or a preposition phrase (PP) slot appended to it:

> *How do you do dese September por mañana?*
> *How do you do dese flower power?*

TABLE 2   How do you do dese—from formula to productive speech (Nora)

Structure	Examples
Time 2 Wh[F]: *How do you do dese?*	*How do you do dese?*
Time 3–4 Wh[Fx]: *How do you do dese(X)/* *X = NP,PP*	*How do you do dese?* *How do you do dese September por mañana?* *How do you do dese flower power?* *How do you do dese little tortillas?* *How do you do dese in English?*

Wh[Fx]: *How do you* ⎫
       How did you ⎬ *X/X = VP*
	How do you make a little gallenas? (= ballenas)
	*How do you like to be cookie cutter? (= How
	   would you . . .)*
	How do you like to be a shrarks?
	How do you make the flower?
	How do you gonna make dese?
	How do you gonna do dese in English?
	How did you make it?
	How did you lost it?

Time 4
Wh[Fx]: *How do* ⎫
       How does ⎬ *X/X = Clause*
       How did ⎭
	How do cut it?
	How do make it?
	How does this color is?
	How did dese work? (= How does this work?)

Wh[S]: *HOW is freed, preposed*	*Because when I call him, how I put the number? (= How will I dial his number?)* *How you make it?* *How will take off paste?*

> *How do you do dese little tortillas?*
> *How do you do dese in English?*

Soon afterwards, the constituent following *you* became analyzed when Nora realized that she could substitute other verb phrases in that slot: *How do you X/X=VP.* With this frame, she produced questions such as

> *How do you like to be a cookie cutter?*
> *How do you make the flower?*
> *How do you gonna make dese?*

A second version of this formulaic frame was acquired, perhaps based directly on questions produced by others: *How did you X/X = VP.* With it she produced questions of the following sort:

> *How did you lost it?*
> *How did you make it?*

Nora was able to pick up variant forms rather quickly, and once she had some version of an expression in her speech repertory she would manage to find several others like it. In the fourth quarter (Time 4), the formulaic frame showed signs of further analysis—this time up to the auxiliary *do:*

$$\left.\begin{array}{l} \textit{How do} \\ \textit{How did} \end{array}\right\} \; \textit{X/X = Clause}$$

This frame took a clause in the analyzed slot, and the frame itself might have been regarded as a question-word unit which could be preposed to a clause to be questioned:

How did dese work?
How do cut it?
How does this color is?

In the final step, the question word was freed completely, and was used as a question word like the others in Nora's repertory of wh-forms, which could be used productively according to her current tactics for producing questions. These tactics included the selection of *how* as a manner adverb, and the positioning of interrogative words in front of the clause, but did not yet include *do* insertion or auxiliary inversion, as we see in the following:

Because when I call him, how I put the number?
How you make it?
How will take off paste?

Thus we see the formulaic question *How do you do dese?* becoming increasingly analyzed until only the question word remains. At that point, *how* questions were productive, but they lacked the detailed refinements which required further analysis. Having the auxiliary *do* in the formulaic frames and recognizing that it usually followed the question word directly would surely aid the learner in figuring out the rules which take care of those details, but at the point where the study ended, there was no evidence that these final steps in the analysis were being taken. Looking at this data without the time periods specified, we might have guessed that the developmental course went the opposite direction—from the less well-formed versions to the well-formed ones at the top. Indeed, this would have been the case if the acquisitional procedure had been a gradual sorting out of the rules whereby the learner was able to structure the utterances herself. Instead, the procedure was one which might be described as "speak now, learn later."

Eventually, through the use of these analytical procedures, the learner is freed from his dependence on strictly formulaic speech. For a long while, however, much of his speech will consist of formulas or be constructed of formulaic units according to rules which are being derived through the analytical procedures described above.

The fourth cognitive strategy is one which permits the learner to develop fluency in the new language, and it is also related to the second social strategy (S-2):

C-4: *Make the most of what you've got.*

There was, in the speech records of the children, much evidence of application of the strategy of making the greatest use of whatever is already known. During the acquisition period, the children's repertories of forms and structures were limited. Their communicative needs far exceeded their current knowledge of the language. One way in which the children were affected by this discrepancy between what they wanted to say and their ability to say it was that they tended to limit what they talked about. However, if they had in their speech repertories expressions which could somehow be stretched to perform the communicative functions they had in mind, they were very likely to use them. Evidence of their following this strategy can be seen in the numerous instances of semantic extension found in the speech records. Ana, for example, used the phrase *putting in a hat* to locate objects on surfaces, as in *X is on Y.* Juan used the word *sangwish* to refer to food in general. Alej used the phrase *no good* as the adjective *dead,* and *gotcha* as the verb *kill* (e.g., *Bang, dese one no good,* i.e., *This one is dead;* and *Hey look, you gotcha one cowboy,* i.e., *You've killed one cowboy*). Similarly, he used the question formulas *Wha' happen?* and *Wha'sa matter?* to perform a variety of interrogative functions—in fact, almost anything he wanted to ask.

Other evidence of this strategy is found in the children's inclination to make frequent and overly generous use of forms they had, sometimes appropriately, and sometimes not. Thus, as we can see in the following text, when Nora acquired the form *anyway,* she attempted to use it in as many sentences as she possibly could:

(We were drawing pictures—Nora was working on a fish, and Heidi a flower:)

NORA: *Anyway I making a fitching.*

OBSERVER: *A what?*

NORA: *Anyway a fitching.*

OBSERVER: *Are you?*

NORA: (Looking over at Heidi's flower) *Yeah, I making a flower.*

HEIDI: *I'm making a flower power.*

NORA: *How do you make a flower power?*

HEIDI: (Looks at Nora's picture which is clearly a fish) *That's not a flower.*

NORA: *Yeah it is.*

HEIDI: *What is that anyway?*

NORA: *Anyway a flower. That what is that anyway.*

HEIDI: *That sure doesn't look like a flower to me.*

NORA: *But to me it looks like a flower, and to you, don't looks a flower, and to me, yeah! And you're a cookie cutter, and how do you like to be a cookie cutter? How do you like to be a cookie cutter?* (Sings) *How do you like to be a cookie cutter?*

(Observational Records, March 16)

The strategy of making the most out of whatever has been learned has important consequences for the development of language. Nora's practice with adverb forms such as *anyway* established a slot within the sentence structure for them, and allowed her to notice and quickly acquire a large variety of similar forms. The other payoff is in the development of fluency. If the learner were to stop speaking each time he realized he did not have the appropriate word to insert in his sentence, rather than to take the most appropriate form in his repertory and let it substitute for the item he did not have, he would be far less fluent. This is especially clear in sentences such as Alej's *You gotcha one cowboy* where the formula *gotcha* as in *I gotcha!* is pressed into service as the verb *kill* which he apparently did not have or could not remember, and in sentences of his such as *C'mon me you house* where *c'mon* functions as the verb *come.*

This latter sentence of Alej's illustrates another way in which the learners tried to make the most of what they had. In the early acquisition period, they were all handicapped by having no easy way to structure sentences to express themselves propositionally. Until they learned how sentences were put together in the new language, either they were limited to what they could say with formulas, or they had to devise some sort of temporary makeshift pattern. Each of the children devised some idiosyncratic patterns for creating sentences using the speech units they had in their repertories. While these did not constitute major devices among their sentence producing tactics, still, they served a useful function. The goal, of course, was to communicate—and they had to do the best they could with what they had. Thus Alej devised a pattern with a pronominal noun phrase representing either a subject or indirect object preceded by a predicate which was generally a formulaic unit of one kind or another, as in *C'mon me you house* (=*I'll come to your house*), *C'mon me the shoe* (=*Won't you give me the shoes?*), and *What time you my house?* (=*What time are you coming to my house?*). Similarly, Ana produced sentences during Times 1 and 2 by stringing formulaic and lexical units together: *My sister—uh—come out—uh— dese—la quebró—dese,* and *Broke it—and my mother—said no—and my brother broke it.*

By making the best use of what they had, the children managed to get by quite nicely in English long before they actually knew very much. From the beginning, all of them tried to make the most of the English they knew. Juan, of course, said little or nothing in those early periods, since he did not care to communicate with the English-speakers with whom he had originally been paired. Still, what little he had to say to them, he generally said in English. In fact, the children resorted to Spanish only when their English failed them completely, even though they were all aware that they were free to use Spanish if they chose.

The fifth cognitive strategy is one which the children appeared to follow in the scheduling of their analytical activities which led eventually to learning the language. The task of learning a language is an impressively big one—there is everything to learn, and all of it is required for the creation of even very simple utterances, it seems. But obviously, the learner cannot deal with everything at once, and hence he needs a strategy for deciding what to work on first, and what to save for later. The strategy they followed was one which permitted them to make maximal use of what they had at any given point during the period of acquisition:

C-5: *Work on big things: save the details for later.*

All of the learners followed the first part of this strategy—only two of them got to the second part by the end of the study year. They were apparently dealing with major constituents first, and leaving the grammatical details to be worked out later. In fitting the major constituents into their sentences, the children generally followed English word order which they had ample opportunity to become familiar with through the use of the many formulaic utterances in their speech repertories. The process of gradual analysis by which parts of formulas become freed from their original frames yielded sentence patterns by which the learners could produce nonformulaic sentences. In the process, some of the grammatical morphemes and grammatical distinctions are unnoticed and lost. Therefore, when the learner begins producing his own constructions on the basis of the derived patterns, he does not include all of the details of the originals. We saw, for example, that Nora's productive *how* questions did not make use of the auxiliary *do,* although the original formula and all of her formulaic frames did. The function of the auxiliary in both questions and negatives was a detail that she would have to deal with later. This strategy makes a lot of sense considering what is involved in the task of learning a language. It would be an overwhelming task if one had to be concerned with all its aspects at once, and hence, it seems smart on the part of the learner to deal with the large problems first, and work on the details later. Once the learner has a basic grasp of the structural features of the language, he can focus better on the small ways in which his utterances differ from those produced by other speakers of the language. When that happens, he will be able to begin sorting out the detailed features.

The final strategy is a social one:

S-3: *Count on your friends for help.*

The acquisition of language, perhaps more than any other kind of learning activity, requires the participation of at least two parties—the learner, and someone who speaks the language already. Without the help and cooperation of friends, the children in the study would have learned little. The children's friends helped in many ways. First of all, there was their belief that the learners were capable of learning the language, and that they would succeed in learning it. There were numerous expressions of this belief, such as in the following conversation with Nora and a friend of hers a few weeks after the school year began:

OBSERVER: *¿Quieres hablar por el micrófono?*
    (=*Do you want to say something for the microphone?*)

NORA: *Sí. ¿Qúe digo? (=Sure. What shall I say?)*

OBSERVER: *Di, "hello".*

HEIDI: *She can't. She can't talk English.*

OBSERVER: *Oh, she can repeat. Say "hello".*

NORA: *No puedo. No puedo hablar en inglés.*
   (=I can't speak English)

OBSERVER: *Entonces, contéstame: ¿Cómo te llamas?*
   (In that case, answer me: What is your name?)

NORA: *Nora.*

HEIDI: *But she can say things like "Me don't speak English" and all that.*

OBSERVER: *Who taught her that?*

HEIDI: *I don't know. She just learned. She just caught up with us, I guess.*

(Observational Records, September 25)

Such expressions of faith proved to be more than mere goodwill: The friends acted on their belief. Because they believed that the learners could learn, the friends talked and interacted with them in ways that guaranteed that they would. They used gestures to aid in communication, but they did not limit their communication efforts to nonverbal modes. They simplified their speech, but in ways that aided learning rather than distorted the input that the children received. Most important, the friends included the learners in their activities, and it was in the context of these activities and relationships that the learners were able to get the exposure they needed to the new language in use.

Yet another way in which the cooperation of the friends was important was that they provided the learners with needed encouragement. From the beginning of the study year, the friends nearly always tried to make the most of the learners' efforts at speaking the language by figuring out what they were trying to say. The friends sometimes had to ask the learners what they meant, or to ask them to repeat something, in order to confirm their guesses. There were few genuine communication failures, however, since the friends were making use of contextual information to figure out what the learners were saying, and this contextual information was always relevant since the learners tended to limit their speech efforts to comments related to the activities at hand. It is a sign of their mutual success that the learners and their friends managed to get along well in endless hours of play throughout the school year.

The most vital kind of help friends gave the learners in this study was in the linguistic input they provided for the language learning effort. The language the friends used in playing with the learners can best be characterized as natural: Although there were simplification, careful contextualization, and repetitiveness, the language was, above all, very similar to the language children ordinarily use in playing with one another. It is not until it is examined closely and compared with the language spoken to others that the modifications the children made are revealed. One of the ways that the children modified their language use in talking to the learners had to do with limiting their speech topics to the activities at hand. In general, the friends tended to avoid talking to the learners about displaced events or topics. They discussed such matters with me from time to time, but it was clear that the speech effort was directed at me alone, and not at the learner.

SOURCES OF INDIVIDUAL DIFFERENCES IN SECOND LANGUAGE LEARNING

The individual differences found in the learning of a second language by the five children in this study had to do with the nature of the task, the sets of strategies they needed to apply in dealing with it, and the way certain personal characteristics such as language habits, motivations, social needs, and habitual approaches to problems affected the way they attacked it. They differed greatly in such characteristics, and in the course of the study year, it became quite apparent that it was the interaction of all these factors that produced the observed differences in the rate at which they learned the new language. One of the most critical ways in which they differed was in having the social skills required to make use of the social strategies which have been discussed. Before the learner could be in a position to exercise the cognitive strategies which would ultimately result in language learning, he needed to be in social contact with the speakers of the new language, but to do that, he needed some very special social skills.

This discussion of individual differences will focus on the ways the children differed in their approach to second language learning. It should be stated at the outset that these remarks are based strictly on the observations made during the study year, and that no independent measures of intelligence, personality, or language aptitude were administered to verify or support the comments which are made here. The children were not formally tested in these areas because none of the standard measures seemed appropriate for their age. Furthermore, the language they spoke was different from the one in which most tests have been prepared, and they came from a culture substantially different from that of the populations on which these tests have been normed.

With that caveat aside, it should be said that observational data of the sort gathered in this study can provide better insights into what children are like than any tests that might have been given. Children, when they are tested, sometimes behave in ways that they believe will please the tester, rather than as they might normally. Observations of naturalistic behavior over an extended period of time are, for this reason, more accurate, since "model behavior" is not likely to be sustained for long. Since play is the most natural medium of expression for children, much can be learned if they are observed at play over a period of time, as these children were. The children were observed at weekly intervals for the period of a school year as they interacted with friends. Over the course of the year, they revealed the impressive extent to which they differed in their feelings, attitudes, interests, and customary approaches to problems. By way of discussing these differences, I will review some of the observations made in the course of examining the children's speech records. Since Nora was the most successful learner, she will serve as the basis for comparison in much of this discussion.

The secret of Nora's spectacular success as a language learner can be found in the special combination of interests, inclinations, skills, temperament, needs, and motivations that comprised her personality. It seems that she was inclined to do just those things that promote language acquisition. She was strongly motivated to be associated with the English-speaking children in her classroom, and she sought them out to play with to an extent that none of the other children in the study did. In nearly all of the observations of her outside of the playroom in the first three periods of the study—whether in the classroom, cafeteria, or playground—she was with English-monolingual children. Since one-half of her classmates were Spanish-speakers (some monolingual like herself, others bilingual), it was more than a coincidence that she was seldom observed with these children with whom she might have interacted more easily. In fact, by the end of the study year, she was clearly identifying herself more as an English than as a Spanish-speaker. Note for example, her desire to exchange her name for a more English-sounding one in the following excerpt from an observational record:

(Beginning of the session. As usual, the girls are asked to record their names on the tape-recorder:)

OBSERVER: *Wait—say your name first.*

NORA: *Uh—*

OBSERVER: *You forgot?*

NORA: *N—un—*

OBSERVER: *What's your name?*

NORA: *Nora.* (English Pronunciation—[noɹə])

OBSERVER: *Nora?*

NELIA: *Nora!* (Spanish pronunciation—[nora])

NORA: *Nora!* (English)

OBSERVER: *Oh!*

NELIA: *Nora.* (Spanish)

OBSERVER: *'Scuse me, Nora.* (English)

NORA: *No—no, but my, my, but my mother tomorrow she's gonna give me another name, Lora.*

OBSERVER: *What? Lora? Is that what your mother's gonna do, Nora?*

NORA: *Um-hum. Lora.*

OBSERVER: *OK, so you wanna be—*

NORA: *Lora, Lora, not Nora* (Spanish).
   Teacher, teacher, but, but, you can call me, uh, by now, Orla.
                                        (Observational Records, May 23)

In contrast to Nora on this score, Juan avoided English-speakers almost altogether and was apparently uncomfortable around them. He preferred the company of those with whom he could communicate freely, and so he played only with other Spanish speakers or with bilingual children. The others—Alej, Jesus, and Ana—played with English speakers, but not exclusively. Alej and his friend, Kevin, played together a great deal, but usually with a larger group of boys. Most of the boys were bilingual, and in their games, both English and Spanish were spoken. Thus Alej was perhaps exposed to more Spanish than English. Kevin, his English-speaking friend, was unusual in this respect: He was the only one of the four English-speaking children in the study who associated almost exclusively with Spanish-speaking children. Jesus's friend Matthew was not ordinarily included in the games and activities of Jesus's principal group of playmates, who were all bilingual. Matthew was something of an "outsider": Jesus played with him from time to time in the playground, but Jesus's friends did not. When they played, Jesus's friends used both English and Spanish, but most of them were more inclined to speak English than Spanish. Jesus used what English he had, but mostly he spoke Spanish. Ana did not belong to any group at all. While she did not always get along well with Margot, her English speaking friend, still they seemed to be best friends, and either she played with Margot, in which case she used English, or she tagged along after her older sister, who spoke only Spanish.

And so only Nora put herself in a position to receive maximum exposure to the new language. Ana was in a somewhat similar position since, aside from her sister, she did not play with Spanish-speaking children at school. The difference between Nora and Ana was that where Nora had many friends, Ana had only Margot. And while Ana and Margot played together, they did not talk much. Furthermore, Ana played only with her siblings (who were Spanish-monolinguals) at home; whereas in addition to her brothers and sisters, Nora played with Heidi, who lived on the same block as she did. Thus Ana had far less exposure to English than Nora, both during and after school.

Another way in which Nora differed from the other children in the study was in her choice of play activities. Where the others—especially the boys— usually were involved in super-macho games that required little real talk, such as baseball, kickball, and marbles, Nora preferred activities that depended on verbalization. Her favorite ones involved dramatic play, and it was in the context of such games that she learned and was able to put to use the language she was picking up from her friends. She engaged in these play activities not only in the playroom but on the playground and in the classroom as well. And from her reports, this was how she and Heidi played together after school. Nora's interest in such games reflected her overall concern for social relations—the sort of dramatic play she and her friends customarily engaged in involved the taking of roles and the working out of relationships. They pretended to be teachers and students, mothers, fathers, and babies, doctors and nurses, and boyfriends and girlfriends. They conjured up problems and situations, all of which needed to be talked out, argued over, and resolved. These dramatic play situations were rather tame in comparison with Nora's real-life involvement with her friends. She had a tendency to develop intense relationships with her friends. Because of that, she was, once she had adequate command of the new language, constantly embroiled in one controversy after another, all of which required a great deal of verbal activity. In fact she wore out three friends during the study period. At 6 years of age, she was capable of becoming angry enough at her playmates to declare that she would have nothing more to do with them and actually follow through on her threat. Such was the fate of Heidi who from October to mid-March was her closest friend, of Nelia who was her friend from mid-March to May, and finally of Magda who was on her way out of Nora's circle of friends when the study year came to a close.

While the peer group was important to the other children, none seemed as caught up in its concerns as Nora. Ana, in fact, seemed to prefer the company of adults. When Margot was not around, she was at her sparkly best. Then she did not have to compete with Margot for my attention and she had an undivided audience for her stories and proposals. Both Nora and Ana had a great need to talk, but they were differently motivated. Nora's need stemmed from the more basic one of wanting to belong to the peer group; and communication was essential to the maintenance of relationships within it. Ana was less concerned with maintaining relationships with her age-mates than she was with communicating her problems and needs to adults. These were not matters she could share with friends her own age, and it is doubtful that she ever attempted to do so with Margot, since Margot was not particularly receptive or sympathetic to Ana's problems. Instead, she spent a lot of time talking with her teacher, who spoke only English, with the teacher's assistant, who spoke Spanish, and with me. Often on the days when I was at the school, Ana would visit me during recess and during the lunch hour just to talk. Of the two children, Nora's motivation for talking was the more profitable one for language learning purposes, since it placed her in precisely those situations in which the language spoken was most useful as input. Ana's adult friends could hardly have provided her with enough input of the right sort.

The other children were communicative, but they managed to suppress their need to communicate until they were with people with whom they could talk freely. With their English-speaking friends, the boys were able to limit themselves almost exclusively to talk which had to do with the activities they were engaged in at the moment. This, of course, was fine during the early stages of acquisition, but to go beyond the early stages they needed the opportunity of hearing and attempting to use more diversified language. Even in Spanish, the boys tended not to engage in conversations as such. Of the three, only Jesus did—but not frequently. The others were satisfied most of the time to limit their verbalizations, in English and in Spanish, to comments, responses, and sound effects which carried little informational weight. In general, Juan, Alej, and Jesus were more inhibited about using their new language than Nora and Ana were. Juan was the most cautious of all and rarely said anything in English unless he was quite sure of himself. Alej was less cautious, but still he sometimes mumbled what he had to say as if he was embarrassed or not sure of himself. Jesus gave the impression of having a great deal of confidence in what he was saying, but he seldom tried to communicate much in English beyond what he could say with formulas. Otherwise, he used Spanish or kept his thoughts to himself.

In contrast, Nora was quite uninhibited in her attempts at speaking the new language. After the first 2 months, she was able to get by almost exclusively with English, and from the first she was far more concerned with communication than with form. She used what she knew to say what she needed to say, and she usually made good enough sense. Ana, too, was quite uninhibited about using her new language, although she was somewhat more conscious of her limitations than Nora. Still, Ana was not particularly worried about how she sounded when she was speaking English. Both Nora and Ana were inclined to be experimental and playful in their efforts to speak English. Both engaged in syntactic play—a practice which resulted in the development of fluency and control over grammatical structures. Jesus, too, engaged in verbal play, but his was of a different sort. Where Nora and Ana took patterns and varied them by changing the words, Jesus took phrases and sang them repeatedly but with little variation. Compare, for example, Nora's syntactic play in

> *She said me that it wa' not too raining by she house.*
> *She said it wa' not too raining by she house.*
> *She said she not raining by she house.*

with Jesus's in

> *Somebody dance, somebody dance, somebody da, da, da!*
> *Somebody dance, dumbody dance, dumbody da, da, da!*

Nora's syntactic play is experimental in a way that is likely to result in better grammatical control, where Jesus's is not. He saw the possibility of playing with sounds, but apparently not with structures as Nora did. The syntactic play that Nora and Ana engaged in was indicative of their attention to structural matters. Nora was especially quick in figuring out which parts of the expressions in her repertory of formulas could be varied, and in analyzing them. Similarly, Ana could extrapolate patterns from the sentences she had in her repertory and produce endless variations on them, as she often did when she pretended to read from books. Consider the patterning, for example, which is apparent in these ersatz story-telling sentences:

> *She, the cat, she, what is this? A waterfly, ah, the cat she was playing with the waterfry—and the, the blue cat. What is this? Espider! spider, espider! espider and the cat, one day she was crying—the—what is this? What is this color? Black color—she was—what is—play wi' ji—What is dese color? 'Rown! 'Rown, 'rown cat. She wit' the laller. She run an' run an' run an' the res'—and the, what is this? What is this? A peeg? Pig! What is she doing? The dog, I can't do it. The dogs, she was playing. An' the dog she was playing with the, wi'—wit' da shoes. It's funny, huh? Doaks—she was playing in the grass—sapi! Eswans, she was playing in the water.* (Observational Records, March 27)

Nora's rapid analysis of formulas had a correlate in her disposition to figure out how toys, games, and gadgets were put together, and how they worked. She was constantly playing with things and taking them apart, and her doing so with linguistic structures was consistent with her overall approach to whatever she came across. Jesus, by contrast, was uninclined to disassemble his structures. In fact, he tended to maintain his expressions in the forms in which they were learned. While he (as did the others) eventually analyzed some of these formulaic expressions to get frames which could be used productively, still no one was as fast at doing this as Nora. Jesus's rigidity in dealing with linguistic structures was reflected in his general approach to new ideas. Once he thought he knew something, he found it difficult to change his mind. At least, he seldom admitted he was wrong, and it usually took an enormous amount of evidence to convince him that he was. For example, when he decided that *fitch* was the English word for *pigeon,* no amount of argument could convince him that he was wrong. Jesus liked to be right, and once he decided on any issue, he tended to protect his decision against change or modification. This was not a particularly profitable trait to have while learning a new language, since inflexibility can reduce the ability to see structural patterns and possibilities. There is no reason at all to believe that Jesus was less able to analyze than Nora or Ana—but his inclination to be inflexible in approaching new ideas and evidence slowed down his performance in those analytical activities which were essential to the language learning process.

Jesus, the audio records showed, was one of the best of the five children at mimicry. He had a talent for remembering and precisely reproducing formulaic expressions that he heard. Furthermore, he had a talent for recognizing and picking up memorable and useful expressions. But these abilities alone were insufficient for rapid progress in learning the new language. Alej was much poorer in these areas: He had difficulty remembering how expressions in the new language sounded, and an enormous difficulty reproducing them. He often garbled what he was saying so badly that it was nearly impossible to understand him. But despite his imprecision in hearing and reproducing sounds, he made greater actual progress than either Jesus or Juan did. Like Jesus, Juan was fairly good at remembering and reproducing utterances, but he did not make much use of these skills. Alej, on the other hand, made good and immediate use of whatever he learned and looked for ways to vary the expressions he had in his repertory. Thus he was able to make fairly rapid progress in learning the new language, and if he did not sound very authentically English-speaking, still he was able to express himself quite adequately by the end of the school year.

Juan had a one-step-at-a-time approach to language learning: That is, he tended to work on one kind of construction at a time, and seldom used anything until he was quite certain of its use. This is in sharp contrast to Nora's habit of putting whatever she learned to immediate use. Where Juan worked on one problem at a time and did not attempt to use what he was learning until he had most of the details worked out, Nora tended to work whatever she picked up into as many sentences as she could as a way of figuring out the potential uses of the new form. She learned to use vocatives, temporal adverbs, and tags by way of overusing them when they were first acquired. Juan's approach, of course, was much safer. He seldom said what he had not intended to say, as Nora sometimes did. However, his method was also much slower: He did not get the chance to say a fraction of what Nora was able to say—even if she was wrong now and then.

SUMMARY

In summary, the individual differences among the five children in the study had to do with the interaction between the nature of the task of learning a new language, the strategies that needed to be applied to the task, and the personal characteristics of the individuals involved. The children, it seems, were more or less equally endowed with the intellectual capacity to learn a new language— after all, they had already acquired one with comparable facility—but they were differently disposed to take the necessary steps to insure the learning of the second. Nora was particularly motivated by the desire to be a part of the social group that spoke the new language, and thus she sought out the company of the children she wanted to be with. At the other extreme, Juan avoided contact with people who did not speak his language. Thus Nora was in a position to learn the new language where Juan was not. That difference presumably had nothing to do with intellectual or cognitive capacity. It was solely a matter of social preference, and perhaps of social confidence as well. Furthermore, Nora and Ana tended to be playful and experimental with language, while Jesus was rather rigid and inflexible. Again, Nora's and Ana's proclivity permitted them to discover the structural possibilities in the new language, where Jesus was pretty much limited to the phrases he had in his repertory for much longer. Yet, the fact that Jesus did not analyze his expressions quickly and play with them cannot be taken as evidence that he was unable to do so. He eventually did analyze some of his expressions and was able to use the structures productively. It was not that he could not see the structural possibilities of the expressions in his repertory; he just was not looking for them.

To learn a language rapidly, it is perhaps most necessary to identify with the people who speak it, as Nora did. She not only wanted to be around English speakers, she wanted to be *like* them, and, therefore, she adopted their way of talking. The desire to be like the speakers of the new language was the motivation Nora needed to modify and adjust her speech according to their norms. By actively working to sound like them, she eventually was able to achieve just that goal. This, apparently, was not something the other children were as willing to do. While most of them were cordial and sociable with English speakers, no one else identified with them to the extent that Nora did, at least during the study year. The others will surely learn the language just as well as Nora did, even if it takes several years longer. One can hope that all five will maintain their individual identities while doing so.

REFERENCES

Carroll, J. B. Research on teaching foreign languages. In N. L. Gage (Ed.), *Handbook of research in teaching.* Chicago: Rand-McNally, 1963. Pp. 1060–1100.

Chun, J. A., and Politzer, R. L. A study of language acquisition in two bilingual schools. Final project report, School of Education, Stanford University, 1975.

Dulay, H. C. and Burt, M. K. Natural sequences in child second language acquisition. *Language Learning,* 1974, *24,* 37–54.

Fathman, A. K. Language background, age, and the acquisition of English structures. In M. K. Burt and H. C. Dulay (Eds.), *New directions in second language learning, teaching and bilingual education.* Washington, D.C.: TESOL, 1975. Pp. 33–43.

Fillmore, L. W. The second time around: Cognitive and social strategies in second language acquisition. Unpublished Doctoral dissertation, Stanford University, 1976.

Gardner, R. C., and Lambert, W. E. *Attitudes and motivations in second language learning.* Rowley, Massachusetts: Newbury House, 1972.

Hakuta, K. A case study of a Japanese child learning English as a second language. *Language Learning,* 1976, *26,* 321–351.

Huang, J. A Chinese child's acquisition of English syntax. Unpublished Master's thesis, UCLA, 1971.

Lambert, W. E., Gardner, R. C., Barik, H. C., and Turnstall, K. Attitudinal and cognitive aspects of intensive study of a second language. *Journal of Abnormal and Social Psychology,* 1962, *66,* 358–368.

Milon, J. P. The development of negation in English by a second language learner. TESOL QUARTERLY, 1974, *7,* 137–144.

Slobin, D. I. Cognitive prerequisities for the development of grammar. In C. A. Ferguson and D. I. Slobin, (Ed.), *Studies of child language development.* New York: Holt, Rinehart, and Winston, 1973.

THEORY AND IMPLICATIONS

1. What does this study add to the case study of Paul? What implications for language instruction does it have?

2. Does the study seem to emphasize similarities or differences between L1 and L2 acquisition? Why? What significance for instruction does this emphasis have?

3. Corder claims that to analyze L2 acquisition, you need to assume motivation. Fillmore clearly rejects this assumption. How do you think she would argue against Corder's view? How can teachers best increase motivation in the classroom?

4. Why do you think Fillmore separates cognitive and social demands when they seem so interrelated? Is this distinction useful in devising language lessons? Explain.

5. What is useful about phrasing the cognitive strategies as maxims that the learner might have used? Do they seem to oversimplify the task? Do the maxims have practical value in the classroom? Explain.

6. Does Fillmore's explanation of the relation between imitated (formulaic) and rule-formed structures in L2 acquisition add to Huang and Hatch's explanation? How?

7. The cognitive strategies children use ensure learning, yet also ensure error. Explain as Fillmore would why error is necessary.

8. Why is the issue of introducing personal characteristics so problematic? Why would such a study as this always be problematic? Are the implications for classroom instruction equally problematic?

9. Do you agree with the criticisms of this study summarized in the introduction? Explain.

PROFESSIONAL CONCERNS

1. Fillmore underscores the point that differences in L2 acquisition have nothing to do with deficiencies in intellectual capacities. Think of a situation in which such knowledge might be crucial and write a letter or a class position paper defending Fillmore's position.
2. Explain to a fellow teacher why you think that teachers need to see children's L2 acquisition through their eyes—what they are intent on doing—to understand their development.

ESL Children as Teachers: A Social View of Second Language Use*

DONNA JOHNSON†

"ESL Children as Teachers: A Social View of Second Language Use" offers practical advice, extending the theory of the previous readings, for teachers who are not specifically ESL teachers. It suggests ways of providing "comprehensible input," of encouraging ESL students to acquire language while they are doing something else, and of addressing individual differences. These methods should help ESL learners to feel that they can master and communicate important ideas in the language of the school. This essay should help non-language specialists to feel that they can be ESL teachers.

Johnson explains that language teaching need not be devoted to explicit language instruction and correction. Teachers need only be aware of the social structure affecting language and of how language can be used to minimize differences between native language and ESL students. Teachers should keep their focus on subject matter, not take "time out" to cope with ESL problems. The author thus exposes the misleading ideas about what ESL means, who teaches it, and what its content should be.

Johnson, like Fillmore, is concerned with the social aspects of second language acquisition, and especially with individual differences such as motivation. Her concern is for developing the nuances and subtleties of spoken rather than written discourse. She stresses the need to "engineer" meaningful exchanges, to put ESL students in control of exchanges, and to focus on content-based tasks and skills. Peer teaching appears to be a key method for enhancing language skills and maintaining appropriate content-level instruction.

---

* Johnson, D. M., "ESL Children as Teachers: A Social View of Second Language Use," *Language Arts*, February 1988. Copyright 1988 by the National Council of Teachers of English. Reprinted with Permission.

† I am grateful to Peter Fries for helpful comments on an earlier version of this manuscript.

Although the categories of field, tenor, and mode may seem cumbersome here, they suggest the kind of analysis of situation that teachers need to perform: Who are the people involved? What are their different perceptions of the activity's purpose? Who has status and control? Teachers often overlook these dynamics. The categories and questions these terms generate may help teachers to create the social conditions that Fillmore's study shows affect different acquisition rates. Teachers particularly need to ask how language can be made functional and comprehensible.

BACKGROUND

Who Does ESL?

It is becoming more widely accepted that promoting the development of English as a second language (ESL) is the responsibility of several of the teachers a child encounters in school rather than just the designated "ESL provider." Yet many regular classroom teachers feel, understandably, that they neither have the time nor the expertise to teach ESL and resist the suggestion that they should be involved. Part of their resistance is based in misconceptions about what the teaching of ESL involves.

Where's the ESL Part?

There is a great deal of confusion among teachers about what ESL instruction for children is, and many different ideas about what constitutes "teaching ESL." It is helpful, therefore, to start any discussion of ESL for children with a definition. The need for a general definition has become particularly apparent to me in teaching teachers in a university setting who work with students of all ages. Many teachers, especially elementary teachers, feel that they would not be "teaching language" if the teaching were not explicitly focused on language and if they were not doing grammar drills, working from vocabulary lists, and correcting most errors.

Because the terms "ESL classes" and "ESL programs" are written into federal and state law, it is important to define what ESL teaching is in a way that is not inextricably linked with any particular theoretical view of language learning or with any particular level of second language proficiency, and in a way that allows the kind of flexibility that good teachers need to be creative and innovative. I have asked my own graduate students this year to think of the teaching of ESL in the elementary school as the planning and organizing of events that are designed to promote the use and development of the second language (L2). This is a broad enough definition to encompass a wide range of things teachers can do throughout the school day to help students in their development of the L2. It helps a teacher to see that teaching ESL involves creating both the opportunity and the need to use English to do things at school.

Organizational Constraints on the Concept of Program

In the past, and in many schools today, ESL teaching has been somewhat constrained by the organizational structure of programs. ESL programs have been defined in terms of time, personnel, and linguistic content. Educators have conceptualized them as (1) the application of a structured commercial ESL curriculum to the students (2) by a designated ESL provider, often an aide, (3) in a situation, defined by time and location, that is identifiable in the organizational structure of the school. This structure for ESL is well entrenched, in part because it seems logical to many well-intentioned educators, and in part, because it demonstrates compliance with legal or funding requirements for services. But it is limited.

A PLAN FOR L2 DEVELOPMENT

Current theory and research suggest that the "ESL program" needs to be conceptualized as a flexible and dynamic plan for second language and literacy development that can operate in a variety of contexts—in bilingual classes, in multilingual classes, and across classroom boundaries. The plan should be built on concepts about how children use and learn language.

For children language is purposeful and meaningful and easy to learn when it meets functional needs. It is one realization of goal-directed activity. Children use written and oral language because they want to do things, to play with peers, to explore, to accomplish their goals in and out of the classroom.

It is the responsibility of teachers, then, to set up situations for L2 users such that there is a need to use the L2 to engage in activities that the child views as on the route to a goal. Such activities should provide successful experiences in communicating in a nonthreatening situation. Because language is learned through interaction, classroom activities should promote the kinds of meaningful interaction that enable children to understand the language of their peers and teachers with contextual support for figuring out meanings. In order to do this, pair and small group participation structures are essential (Miller 1982). ESL children need to interact with classmates who are fluent speakers of the L2 in order to develop a native-like control of that language (Wong Fillmore 1983). They need to be actively involved in instructional activities that allow them to interact freely in the course of working on mutually involving tasks that invite discussion, questioning, responding.

Opportunities for All?

This all sounds fine. But one of the important contributions of Wong Fillmore's (1983) research has been to show how widely students differ in their approaches to participating in the various kinds of classroom settings teachers provide. "Left on their own, students may not be inclined to interact in ways that are helpful from the standpoint of language learning" (Wong Fillmore 1986, p. 672). She points out that it takes planning and "social engineering" to make sure that active participation in second language is arranged. Children will learn a second language when it makes sense to them and as they have both the opportunity and the need to use it for functional purposes. So teachers need to create not only the opportunity but also the *need* to use L2, always in an environment oriented toward success. To provide rich and varied experiences using oral and written language we need to "nudge" children to use language in a variety of ways (Allen 1986) and support them as they take risks with language.

Richness in Spoken Language

The different ways of using spoken language in ESL classes for children have tended to be quite limited. Yet Halliday (1985) claims that language can be at its most complex in spontaneous spoken form. ". . . spoken language responds continually to the small but subtle changes in its environment, both verbal and nonverbal, and in so doing exhibits a rich pattern of semantic and hence also of grammatical variation that does not get explored in writing" (p. xxiv). He points out that while the complexity of writing lies in its vocabulary density, the complexity of spoken language is in its grammar. So involvement with a rich variety of speech events requires ESL children to draw on many of their linguistic resources. Swain (1985), emphasized the importance in negotiated L2 interaction of being pushed toward the delivery of messages that are conveyed precisely, coherently, and appropriately, of having the opportunity to try language out to see what works. Cathcart-Strong's (1986) study of kindergarten children in play situations indicates that when users of ESL have control in a situation, the quality of the native-speaker linguistic input they hear is especially high. All of this indicates that speech events in interaction with native, monolingual English speakers, in which the ESL child has some control, can provide rich language use experiences.

Teaching

One kind of experience that L2 users rarely have is using one of their languages to teach. Unfortunately children developing an additional language are often labeled as "Limited English Proficiency (LEP) children" and are more often than not viewed as having a language "problem." They are treated as passive students who need to be taught, and retaught, a new language. Rarely are they viewed as resources by peers and teachers, let alone competent experts and teachers. Some are very quiet in a large group and whole class settings (Miller 1982), adding to the notion that they have little competence. Research on dialogue journals (Sellevaag 1986) has shown, however, that some children who almost never talk in class, have much to express in a one-to-one interaction in which their communicative contributions are valued. Similarly we have found that seemingly shy and quiet users of ESL can and will successfully share their expertise with other children, using English, when an appropriate situation is set up for them. If the

ESL child has information that another child needs to accomplish a task and work toward a goal, then communication is motivated, needed, and "natural." In addition to linguistic, social, and affective benefits, teaching another child may also have cognitive benefits for learning in the content areas. Children will progress as they feel a sense of ownership of the content and language and a sense of confidence as a communicator in L2.

ESL CHILDREN AS KNOWERS AND TEACHERS

With these broad and ambitious goals in mind, we set out to create one specific way of structuring meaningful and functional interactions designed for L2 development. We felt that if teachers focused on content-based tasks and goals, and on organizing interaction, and made sure that it was all meaningful to the children, that language learning would take care of itself as a part of the interaction process. We also felt that we could even help promote friendships between ESL children and monolingual English users. Such friendships should give the ESL children one more social reason to use one of their two languages.

The basic idea of the technique is this. A small group of children are taught, in English, by their teacher, how to do an activity such as an art, science, or cooking project. After they have learned the process, each child is paired with a child who is not yet familiar with the activity. It is vital that these pairs be cross-language pairs. For example, a Spanish-speaking ESL child is paired with a compatible monolingual English user who does not know any Spanish. The ESL child takes the role of teacher and shows his or her partner how to do the project. The ESL child must use English to communicate with a partner who speaks only English. A need to communicate is created and the use of English becomes functional and oriented toward a goal—a completed project. The projects can be related to themes the children are exploring in class. Our children, who ranged from age five to eight and were involved in a summer program, made crystal gardens to explore science concepts, fruit salads, yarn drawings, and other science, art, cooking, and game projects.

FEATURES OF THE COMMUNICATIVE CONTEXT: SITUATION 1

In our research, which I summarize below, we found that this kind of peer teaching was effective for L2 vocabulary development and promoted social uses of the L2. What makes it work for language development and what makes it a functional ESL technique is the social structuring teachers do. I therefore will describe the process in a functional framework as a composite of two discourse situations that are linked and aimed toward a goal. I've chosen to use Halliday and Hasan's (1985) broad categories for describing the context of situation, since these are crucial to the functional theory of language behind the lesson structure.

The three broad aspects of the context of situation for L2 use here are: (1) the field of discourse: the nature of the social action, (2) the tenor of discourse: the nature of the participants, their statuses and roles, their permanent and temporary relationships, and (3) the mode of discourse: what part language is playing, its function in the context, the channel used. I will describe the context of situation for the preparation of peer teaching (Situation 1) and for the peer teaching process (Situation 2) using a science activity as an example. I will then discuss the importance of the link between the two situations.

Field

In Situation 1 the nature of the activity is the teaching of science content to children using objects and demonstrating a process. The science project is new to the children and appropriate for their developmental level and interests. It is important to note that the purposes of the activity from the teacher's perspective are different from the children's purposes. From the point of view of the children, this is a science activity. From the point of view of the teacher, this is most importantly a science activity, but one of its other purposes is to provide children an opportunity to use and to develop more control over the L2.

Tenor

The participants are the teacher and a small heterogeneous group of children who are interacting. The teacher leads and controls the direction of the interaction. Although some of the children are fluent users of English and some are not, their status as content learners in this situation is equal—they are all learning how to do a new activity. Their differences in English language proficiency and related status differences are minimized by the way the teacher uses language to teach.

Mode

Language is doing a job in a context here. The teacher is using English in sustained, connected discourse and focusing on the meaning of language, not its forms. The channel is spoken language. The teacher does most of the talking, providing comprehensible linguistic input (Krashen 1982) in a context of negotiated interaction. The language is comprehensible because it is functionally related to objects and actions in the immediate environment. The teacher is explaining, for example, commanding, suggesting, questioning in a way that children can understand because the language is task-oriented and directly linked to materials and actions. Children can figure out meanings from context. Meanings are negotiated as the teacher checks children's comprehension and the children ask questions or make comments in interaction with one another and the teacher. There is some natural vocabulary repetition because of the task-orientation and cohesiveness of the talk. It is important to note that the teacher's language use here is natural (not artificially simplified), but useful for L2 learning because children can link events to their realizations in language.

FEATURES OF THE INTERACTIVE CONTEXT: SITUATION 2

Field

In Situation 2 the nature of the social action is the teaching of the science activity, but now in a dyad of two children on their own. The teacher has stepped aside and is circulating about. The child teacher (in this case a girl) is a user of ESL and her peer audience is a fluent, monolingual English user who has not seen this activity before. From the point of view of both children this is a science project. From the point of view of the teacher, this is also functional, authentic L2 use that is contributing to L2 development. It's both science and ESL: content-based ESL or science that also works as ESL.

Tenor

In her teaching peer role, the ESL child comes into the situation bolstered with a certain degree of status because she has special expertise that her peer needs in order to complete the science task. Because this expertise needs to be shared, there is a powerful motivation for the two to communicate. An information gap must be bridged. The ESL child, then, has an expectant and cooperative audience that needs her. In this way the audience and purpose that make L2 use meaningful and functional are present. Communication is successful because the ESL child has come to the situation prepared with both the linguistic and the content knowledge she needs. With cumulative successful experiences as teachers, children build their confidence in using L2 and, even more importantly, their sense of control and personal power.

Mode

It is in Situation 2 that the ESL child tries out what she knows to see how it works. She draws on her linguistic resources supporting them with her non-linguistic resources, such as objects and actions, to try to make her intended meanings clear to her partner. She can see that she is in control and is making the L2 work for herself. She sees the powerful effects of what she says on what her partner does. Her partner helps in negotiating meaning by asking questions and performing actions. And when there are minor breakdowns in communication, the pair comes up with communication strategies to bridge the gap. The nature of this sustained conversational interaction is helping her extend her ability to use the L2 to accomplish her purposes. Subconsciously she probably evaluates her spoken discourse as successful in accomplishing her intentions.

CONNECTED DISCOURSE WORLDS

What links these two discourse worlds is the goal of seeing a peer complete the science activity and the teacher's expectation that all of this will occur. Children come to know that they must operate in related discourse worlds and each situation motivates the other as the entire process becomes familiar to them. While the teacher is first teaching a small group of students how to carry out a task, the teacher and the students are operating in the first discourse world. The children know, however, that they will later teach what they are learning to one of their peers. As they are engaged in Situation 1, they have the expectation that they will soon be operating in Situation 2. They may consciously or subconsciously imagine the second discourse situation. Graves (1983) refers to the excitement such an expectation can create as "the energy of anticipation." This term applies to ESL children as teachers because the children have done this whole process before and they soon learn to trust their ability to successfully teach another child using English. They can anticipate the impact of their information on their waiting peer audience. Just as this kind of "forward vision" can contribute to development in writing (Graves 1983, p. 160), it can also contribute to L2 users' growing sense of confidence in accomplishing things verbally through L2. This is because teachers have intentionally designed the conditions for successful and cumulative communicative experiences.

RESULTS OF AN EXPERIMENT

In a bilingual summer program for five to eight year olds we had the opportunity to try out this interaction structure. Our research team conducted a seven-week experiment (Johnson 1983) to compare the effects of participating in the peer teaching process with participating in the same activities only in a large group setting. In the control group the children did not have the opportunity to teach one another; rather, the teacher led the large group in the same set of art, science, and cooking activities. We predicted that those ESL children who taught others would derive two kinds of benefits: they would, in their free time, interact more in English with their monolingual English-speaking peers, and they would learn more English. Some of these predictions were borne out. While we found no significant differences in language proficiency as measured by a commercial test (DeAvila and Duncan 1977) or by functional measures of communicative competence (Johnson 1978), the peer teaching group made significantly greater growth in vocabulary comprehension (Dunn 1965). So peer teaching by ESL children was an effective way of promoting L2 vocabulary development.

   We were also interested in the effects of children's experience as teachers on their informal interactions with peers in English. We predicted that as a result of successful encounters teaching their monolingual English-speaking peers in English they would have more confidence and would develop stronger social relations with them. So we observed their language use (using the LUIS, Johnson & Hayes 1978) in informal, free-time settings for the length of the project. While we found only a few statistically significant differences between the two groups (using a variety of analyses on eight different interaction measures), we found that, over time, those ESL children who had engaged in peer teaching spoke more English with peers in their free time, while the control group children spoke less. These findings provide evidence, then, that the way teachers structure content-based L2 learning experiences can have an impact on the social envi-ronment that children create for themselves. After successful experiences teaching their peers, ESL children chose to use their English more to share in conversation with their monolingual peers.

CONCLUSION

A major part of teaching ESL to children involves setting up the social conditions that promote meaningful and purposeful use of English by children. Empowering ESL children to serve as teachers for their peers is one way to create functional and successful second language learning environments. The teacher's role in structuring such environments is critical, because some children who are learning English do not have access to, or do not actively participate in, the kinds of language-use situations that work for L2 development. For these children it is especially critical that teachers "nudge" them to use language to do a variety of things while at the same time setting up the conditions so that children will experience success.

I have used Halliday and Hasan's general framework to analyze the contexts of situation in the peer teaching process. This framework is based on a functional view of language, that language used by children is best understood in relation to its social context. How and why peer teaching works as one way of promoting ESL development can only be explained in terms of aspects of the context of situation. Particularly important are the characteristics of the participants, their role relationships, and how they act on others in their classroom environments.

This two-step procedure provides a functional structure for one specific type of content-based ESL lesson. The theory and research provide a principled basis for creating information gaps, for pairing children, and for empowering ESL children to use their L2 in a high-status role. The process provides not only opportunities to use the L2, but the need to actively use sustained L2 discourse to negotiate meaning with a peer and accomplish a goal. Children can see the results as they act on their environment. While our research dealt with spoken language, a similar social structure can work for writing or for combinations of writing and conversing. The peer teaching process can be one part of a series of activities related to a theme. For example, in our program, the making of salad worked well with five to eight year olds. Salad making could be part of a series of related activities such as those suggested by Allen (1986, p. 63). For teachers who must keep track of academic learning time, activities are multifunctional; they can be counted for the content area they address and for second language learning time.

As we attempt to move toward more integrated approaches to L2 develop-ment (Milk 1985), cooperation among ESL specialists and other teachers becomes important (Cazden 1986). Part of the role of the ESL specialist is to work with regular classroom teachers to show them how they can arrange activities and do the kind of "social engineering" necessary to allow L2 users to grow.

REFERENCES

Allen, V. G. "Developing Contexts to Support Second Language Acquisition." *Language Arts,* 63 (1986): 61-66.

Cazden, C. "ESL Teachers as Advocates for Children." In P. Rigg & D. S. Enright (Eds.), *Children and ESL: Integrating Perspectives.* Washington, DC: TESOL, 1986.

DeAvila, E., & S. Duncan. *Language Assessment Scales, Level I,* Second Edition. Corte Madera, CA: Linguametrics Group, 1977.

Dunn, L. M. *Peabody' Picture Vocabulary Test.* Circle Pines, MN: American Guidance Service, 1965.

Graves, D. *Writing: Teachers and Children at Work.* Exeter, NH: Heinemann, 1983.

Halliday, M. A. K. *Language, Context, and Text: Aspects of Language in a Social-Semiotic Perspective.* Victoria: Deaken University, 1985.

Johnson, D. M. "Natural Language Learning by Design: A Classroom Experiment in Social Interaction and Second Language Acquisition." *TESOL Quarterly, 17* (1983): 55-68.

————. *Child-Child Communication Test.* Unpublished test. Palo Alto, CA: School of Education, Stanford University, 1978.

Johnson, D. M., & Z. A. Hayes. *Language Use and Interaction System.* Unpublished observation system. Palo Alto, CA: School of Education, Stanford University, 1978.

Krashen, S. *Principles and Practice in Second Language Acquisition.* Oxford: Pergamon Press, 1982.

Milk, R. "The Changing Role of ESL in Bilingual Education." *TESOL Quarterly, 19* (1985): 657-670.

Sellevaag, L. "Writing and Reflecting on Writing." *Dialogue, 3* (1986): 5.

Swain, M. "Communicative Competence: Some Roles of Comprehensible Input and Comprehensible Output in Its Development." In S. M. Gass and C. G. Madden (Eds.), *Input in Second Language Acquisition.* Rowley, MA: Newbury House, 1985.

Wong Fillmore, L. "The Language Learner as an Individual: Implications of Research on Individual Differences for ESL Teachers." In M. A. Clark and J. Handscombe (Eds.), *On TESOL '82,* Washington, DC: TESOL, 1983.

THEORY AND IMPLICATIONS

1. Parents might see peer teaching as wasting their children's time. They might consider the repetition of instructions as mere repetition of knowledge. How would you argue that you are not slowing down the learning of the native speakers in the class in order to accommodate the nonnative speakers? What assumptions about the use of language and the acquisition of content knowledge would you use?

2. How do Johnson's methods show her commitment to Krashen's theories?

3. How might some of Johnson's ideas for spoken language development be applied to written language development?

4. How do the ideas for peer instruction build on Fillmore's ideas about individual differences?

such false premises, it is important that teachers understand and appreciate the particular rules and capabilities of nonstandard dialects.

This chapter examines one dialect in particular, Black English (BE), a pervasive social dialect that has often been viewed as illogical, truncated, and incapable of producing abstract thought. This focus on one dialect reveals the purposes, insights, principles, and methods of dialect study generally, all of which are applicable to other dialects that teachers will encounter. For instance, William Labov's study of BE reveals the main reason for dialect study—to counter bias— and shows how researchers, through faulty study design and a lack of linguistic knowledge, promoted the myth that nonstandard varieties of English were botched versions of the model standard form. BE speakers were labeled monosyllabic, illogical, and hobbled by a language with a "reduced" grammar, and were viewed as incapable of expressing abstract concepts because BE was considered overly dependent on context. A focus on BE helps us to examine how unfounded attributions arise and provides a key testing ground for teachers' concerns with "acceptability" and correctness.

The study of Black English reveals dialect principles applicable to all non-standard varieties. First, knowledge of the logical, rule-based nature of BE underscores the rule-based nature of all dialects. Second, knowledge of BE's unique evolution from a pidgin English into "Plantation Creole," paralleling the development of other creoles, confirms that all language varieties evolve independently and are not merely abbreviated versions of a standard form. Indeed BE's complex history belies the view that its speakers are merely imitating standard English. Third, knowledge of how BE can convey grammatical distinctions that SE cannot demonstrates that all varieties are linguistically equal, though different. Fourth, a knowledge of traditional BE discourse modes, which are rooted in a cultural heritage and evolving artistic conventions, reveals that all language varieties are more than just grammars; they also involve distinctive rhetorics.

A focus on Black English raises broad political and educational questions: What rights to their own language do BE speakers have? How much of the grammar of BE do teachers need to know? How should teachers of BE students respond to language variety? What attitudes and responses do even well-meaning and knowledgeable teachers display that might undermine the education of BE students? What are the underlying myths about BE and how are they promoted and institutionalized?

PRINCIPLES OF LANGUAGE VARIETY AND CHANGE

The study of Black English grammar and rhetoric reinforces a number of general language principles, many derived from first and second language acquisition studies. First, BE is clearly rule-based and systematic, and children learn it the way all children learn their first language: by hypothesizing rules. Second, just as the development of creoles out of pidgins may well illustrate universal language acquisition patterns and processes, so the development of BE out of pidgin English illustrates similar patterns and processes: BE forms like the double negative, found in most creoles, may reflect Bickerton's view that children are innately programmed to learn certain grammatical forms. Third, studies of BE's complex verb forms support the notion that BE contains a full complement of grammatical forms, supporting linguists' view that all children are preprogrammed to develop a full grammar, even when their only model is a pidgin. Finally, the study of BE discourse modes confirms that language varieties are socially based, with BE children developing storytelling and response patterns different from those of SE children.

PROFESSIONAL APPLICATIONS

The aforementioned principles have pedagogical implications. The teaching of standard English to BE speakers may need to draw, at least in part, on second language acquisition principles; speakers are learning a second code and need not relinquish the first. Because BE *is* a fully developed code, speakers are not making "mistakes" but instead are speaking in a rule-based system, their L1. Indeed some researchers argue that a method of instruction patterned after L2 acquisition models may prove very effective, with an emphasis on unconscious rule hypothe-sizing and interaction; given that the two dialects are very similar, such a method could be supplemented with direct instruction, for example, on explicit differ-ences in verb forms or differences in pronoun systems.

L2 models for teaching SE to BE speakers are also problematic, however: The "errors" of BE clearly differ from the "errors" that L2 speakers make. Whereas L2 errors are typically developmental approximations of the target language, BE errors are simply nonstandard forms supported and validated by community sanctions and restraints. Unlike L2 forms, BE forms reflect a successful model of communication within that community and are therefore not interpreted as errors by BE speakers. Add to the obvious communicative viability of BE the historical repression of African Americans and we can see how BE encourages African Americans to assume an identity of opposition. BE becomes a sign of ethnic loyalty, an identity established in opposition to mainstream language and culture. These problems of viability, identity, and resistance, particular to dialects, differ from those addressed by L2 models.

The pedagogical difficulty lies, then, in marking and rehearsing differences in dialects while validating not only the grammar but the discourse forms of BE. Teachers need to accept and encourage discourse forms, such as storytelling style, that differ from standard forms. Perhaps they can use dialect differences for class investigations of language as a way of teaching about language variety. Such investigations would ease parents' and teachers' fears that nonstandard examples would undermine the standard speakers' grammar; SE speakers will not "lose their grammar" through imitation.

Clearly the most important pedagogical implication lies in how teachers change their students' language attitudes. Teachers can tell students that BE is not wrong or incorrect but just another kind of language. In addition, they can convey the message that standard English is simply the "public" language needed to get jobs, communicate public information, and teach children. They can thus help to eradicate the bias associated with stigmatized dialects.

OVERVIEW OF THE READINGS

George Gadda's "Language Change in the History of English: Implications for Teachers" provides an abbreviated history of the English language and focuses on grammatical changes that reflect social and historical factors. It is illustrative rather than exhaustive, offering surprising examples of language change. Its purpose here is to demonstrate that language does change, that there is no "Golden Age" of English, and that accident and contingency are key factors in this change. These clarifications can help teachers to respond more flexibly to evidence of language change.

Jerrie Cobb Scott's "The King Case: Implications for Educators" discusses a legal case that determined whether or not the nonstandard dialect used by 11 black children "constituted a barrier to their education." The issue was not the intrinsic worth of a dialect but instead whether or not the social stigma, or attitudes, attached to that dialect constituted a learning barrier. Scott validates concerns expressed in the NCTE Policy Statement by identifying teachers' and parents' ignorance and bias toward BE as the source of students' low self-esteem, and offers some similar solutions. However, she seems to question the NCTE's optimistic assumption that more knowledge alone will change teachers' negative attitudes toward BE. Instead she offers a program for changing attitudes.

William Labov's classic "The Logic of Nonstandard English" explores the underlying myths and false research assumptions accounting for teachers' negative attitudes and pedagogies. First, it excoriates the research that blames black children's home life—its assumed lack of verbality—for black children's supposedly truncated language, BE. Second, it asks us to reassess our unthinking approval of middle-class verbal styles at the expense of lower-class verbal styles. And third, it introduces us to the logic of BE as both a grammatical and a rhetorical system.

"Forms of Things Unknown," from Geneva Smitherman's respected book *Talkin and Testifyin,* is an informative overview of Black English folklore and its "forms of discourse." Going beyond grammar, it addresses the discourse modes of BE speakers, including call-response, signification, tonal semantics, and narrative sequencing, and ties these modes to black culture. Smitherman thus expands the narrow focus on grammar we have seen so far, deepening our insights into the nature of language differences.

Language Change in the History of English: Implications for Teachers*

GEORGE GADDA

This essay describes some of the major changes in the English language. It demonstrates that the English we speak today differs significantly from the English of Chaucer, and looks and sounds nothing like the English before his

---

time. Invasions, migrations, dialect mixing, and word borrowings are all factors in language change. Some major changes, like the great vowel shift, remain unexplained, however; shifts do not always favor the dominant or prestige dialect. One of Gadda's examples shows the incorporation into the standard dialect of the once nonstandard s morpheme added to third-person singular verb forms, as in "he runs."

Gadda's essay is a consolidation of very complex and historically contingent changes. He provides teachers with an overview of the kinds, scale, and pervasiveness of these changes. He also emphasizes that awareness of these changes should help us to avoid the popular attitudes that language change is language decay, and that standard English as we know it has always been the standard. An appreciation for the diverse backgrounds of English is of particular importance in today's diverse classrooms.

The history of the English language is an enormous and technical subject—whole textbooks are devoted to tracing the language's development, whole monographs to exploring the evidence for theories about the dating or cause of a particular change in sound or syntax. The textbooks are primarily for English teachers and students of English literature—people who need to understand in some detail the ways in which the language of texts written by Chaucer or Shakespeare differs from the English we speak today. The monographs are for scholars— linguists who specialize in understanding how the language has changed. These treatments of the history of English are not likely to seem relevant to most teachers of other subjects, and the history of English itself may seem remote from their classroom concerns.

Nevertheless, it is important for all teachers to know something about the way in which English has become the language we use today. Recognizing how consistent radical change has been in the history of English—and how many forms that radical change has taken—should help all educators avoid the unfortunate popular attitude that sees all change in language as decay from a Golden Age of Good English located at some uncertain time in the past. They should understand that linguists view language change as inevitable. Further, knowing how significantly English has changed even in the last thousand years should help all educators realize that, although we must help all our students to control standard English in order to help them succeed in our society, we should do so with the knowledge that the language we teach and use is "standard" and prestigious in our time and place, not in a Platonic sense.

We will survey the history of English broadly but selectively. Our treatment is broad in that we pick up the development of our language well before it became English: we begin with some of the characteristics linguists have identified as those of Proto Indo-European, the ancestor of English spoken 5,000 years ago. Our treatment is selective in that it does not attempt to account for the development of all sounds and parts of speech in every period, but instead focuses on selected major developments that illustrate various kinds of language change. We also emphasize that, while some developments follow a consistent, predictable pattern through several periods, others are random, based as they are on external factors like conquest, migration, and cultural influence. If this interpretation of the history of English whets your appetite for more detail, the notes list a number of standard book-length treatments of the subject that you might consult.

PROTO-INDO-EUROPEAN

We have no records of the earliest stages of what has become English. Indeed, our earliest written records of a language closely related to English date from the fifth century AD, and our earliest sound recordings of English date from the early twentieth century. What we know of earlier stages of the language—before there are written records—comes from historical linguists' reconstructions of what earlier versions of the language had to be like to produce the various forms of words that still exist in related languages. They use this "algebra" of language to reconstruct the forms that words had to have existed in earlier languages in order for their sounds to change in systematic ways to produce the forms we have in various languages and dialects.

The earliest stage of our language that has been reconstructed is called Proto-Indo-European. Historical linguists believe that this language was spoken by a group of people who lived from about 3,000 to 2,000 BC in the area that is currently known as Georgia, in the former Soviet Union; they think so because almost all the languages descended from Proto-Indo-European share words like those for bear, salmon, and birch tree—words that name things that are all found only in the natural environment of that area. The Proto-Indo-European language was very different from what we know as English today. Two differences are particularly significant as the starting point for the later history of English: Proto-Indo-European was a language of many inflections (endings that indicate the tense and person of verbs, the case of nouns and adjectives, as so on); Proto-Indo-European was a language in which the stress moved from one syllable to another in different inflected forms of a single word.

If you have studied a language like Latin or Greek or German, you're aware that English has many fewer endings than they do. Those languages add endings to nouns and adjectives to show what function those words have in the sentence (as subject, direct object, object of a preposition, and so on); they add endings to verbs to indicate the tense (or time) of the action and to link them with the subject in person (first, second, or third) and number (singular and plural). With the exception of the -s on nouns to indicate plurals and possessives and the -s on present tense verbs that agree with singular subjects, English has lost the similar endings it once had. Proto-Indo-European, on the other hand, had even more endings than Latin, Greek, and German. Many of these endings were more than one syllable long.

In addition to having many long endings to indicate words' relations to each other, Proto-Indo-European shifted the stress or accent from one syllable to another of the same word when the inflection changed. In other words, in addition to adding endings to show what function a word had in its sentence, speakers of Indo-European also changed the syllable they stressed as they used the same word as the subject of one sentence and then the direct object of the next. This complexity can be found in some Indo-European languages to this day—Russian, for example, and other Slavic languages. Most of us, though, are accustomed to the stress remaining on only one syllable, no matter the word's ending or function in its sentence. To us Proto-Indo-European would seem almost unbelievably complex in its ways of signalling meaning by changes in words.

One reason we feel this way is that the history of English can in large part be seen as a progressive simplification of inflection. As we will soon see, one of the changes that defines the shift from Proto-Indo-European to Proto-Germanic is the fixing of stress on the first syllable, a development that helped cause the loss of endings in English.

PROTO-GERMANIC

The descendants of the people who spoke Proto-Indo-European gradually diffused in all directions from their presumed homeland in Georgia. As they formed self-contained groups, the sounds, forms, and structures of the language they had originally shared as Indo-Europeans began to differentiate in systematic ways within each group. One group went to the Indian subcontinent, and eventually developed the language we know as Sanskrit. One group went to the Mediterranean and eventually developed the languages we know as Latin and Greek. One group moved north and developed the language we know as Russian. And the ancestors of those who would come to speak English eventually settled in the vicinity of the North Sea and developed the language scholars have reconstructed as Proto-Germanic.

Proto-Germanic is the ancestor of modern German, English, Dutch, Swedish, Danish, and Norwegian. It dates from about 1,000 BC. Its grammatical system differed from that of Proto-Indo-European in several important ways.

The first of these concerns sounds. In all Germanic languages, consonants that all other descendants of Indo-European retain as the original *b, d, g, p* have become *p, t, k, f.* This change accounts for the fact that the English word *father* means the same thing as the Latin *pater* but differs in consonant. This change is known to linguists as Grimm's Law, in honor of the linguist and folklore collector—yes, Jacob Grimm of the Brothers Grimm—who first demonstrated it.

A second major change in all Germanic languages involves the verb system. We've noted before that in Proto-Indo-European verbs had endings to show different tenses. In Proto-Germanic, however, verbs had lost almost all those endings showing tense: as a result, in Proto-Germanic verbs had different inflections only for *present* and *past* tenses. To this day, verbs in Germanic languages have different forms only to designate present and past; in modern English, for example, we have inflectional differences only in pairs like *walk/walked.*

The third major change in Proto-Germanic also affects the verb system and tends to simplify it. The change is the development of what Jacob Grimm, who also identified this change, called the "weak preterite." In the grammatical terminology of the time "strong" verbs were those that change form internally to show differences in tense—verbs like "ring/rang/rung" in modern English. Today we think of these verbs as "irregular," and indeed we call them that when we introduce elementary school students to kinds of verbs. Historically, though, "regular" verbs were those that changed form internally as well as adding inflections to change tense. The ones we think of as "regular"—because they use what is now the most common English pattern—are historically irregular. And that historical irregularity began in Proto-Germanic, where for the first time some verbs began to form their past tense by adding a "d" or "t" sound to the present tense. An innovation then, this pattern is now so basic to native speakers' understanding of the way English works that, given a nonsense verb like "guunk" or a verb borrowed from another language, our immediate and unthinking impulse is to form its past tense by adding "-ed." The formerly "regular" verbs are the ones we teach as exceptions to the rule.

The fourth major change from Proto-Indo-European to Proto-Germanic is perhaps the one with the most important influence on the later development of English. In contrast to Proto-Indo-European, which we've said places stress on different syllables in different inflected forms of the same word, Proto-Germanic consistently placed stress on the first syllable in every word. Not only is this stress consistent, it's also strong. The strength of this tendency in English to accent words on their first syllables can be seen very clearly in the way speakers of British English make words they borrow from other languages conform to the patterns of English pronunciation. Although Americans often borrow the original pronunciation along with the word, speakers of British English use the accent and sound values of English to pronounce the words. For example, the French word "filet," pronounced "fi-lay" by the French and by Americans is pronounced "fill-it" by speakers of British English. Their accenting the word's first syllable shows how pervasive this tendency that began in Proto-Germanic still is in modern English.

OLD ENGLISH

The language we know as English today began to take shape in Britain once tribes speaking Germanic dialects began conquering and settling the island now divided into English, Scotland, and Wales. These tribes are generally known as the Angles, the Saxons, and the Jutes; they came from areas bordering the North Sea in what is today Germany and the Netherlands. The conventional date for the beginning of their conquest of the Celtish-speaking Britons who were already on the island, the date recorded by the Anglo-Saxon saint and scholar the Venerable Bede in his *Ecclesiastical History of the English People,* is AD 449.

Once they settled in Britain, the tribes did not speak a uniform language. Partly because they spoke related but distinct dialects before the migration and partly because new regional dialects developed in England itself, in the Old English period (449–1066) there were four major dialects—one in the north of English, one in the midlands, one in the southeast, and one in the southwest. Which dialect had the most importance and prestige depended on the political fortunes of the people who used it. In the early Old English period the most important dialect was that of the north; northern kingdoms were most powerful,

and the early texts that survive for linguists and historians to study come from
the north or have northern forms embedded in them. Later the most important
dialect was that of the southwest; this was the result of the political dominance
of King Alfred and his successors and of the writing and copying of books in
monasteries near the West Saxon capital of Winchester.

All these dialects shared many features, however. All used the present/past
system of verb inflection we've already described in Proto-Germanic; all used "ed"
endings to form the past tense of many verbs, although at this stage more verbs
still changed internal form in patterns like "ring/rang/rung;" all shared a strong
stress on words' first syllables. Like Proto-Indo-European and Proto-Germanic
before them, all these dialects also used what is now often called the continental
vowel system. That is, rather than pronouncing long vowels in stressed syllables
"ay-ee-ai-oh-yoo," as do native speakers of modern English, speakers of Old
English—like modern speakers of French, German, Italian—pronounced them "ah-
ay-ee-ah-oo." In the Old English period, speakers of English pronounced these
vowels in the way that speakers of all other languages descended from Proto-
Indo-European still do. This is only one of the features that makes Old English
sound like a foreign language to speakers of modern English.

Let's now look at a sample of Old English. We'll use the Lord's Prayer because,
as a text of great cultural prestige, it was translated and retranslated at every
period of our language's history. Because the Lord's Prayer is such a familiar text,
and because some words are recognizably related to modern words, we could
probably recognize this without a gloss. But we wouldn't understand it fully—
nor, if we heard it read, might we recognize it at all.

Fæder ure,
þu þe eart on heofonum,
si in nama gehalgod.
Tobecume in rice.
Gewuðe in willa on earðan swa swa on heofonum.

Urne gedæghwamlican hlaf syle us to dæg.
And forgyf us ure gyltas, swa swa we forgyfa urum glytendum.
And ne gelæd þu us on costnunge,
ac alys us of yfele. So lice.

Let's consider some features of Old English this passage illustrates. First, many
of the words are unfamiliar. Some are relatively easy to recognize when they're
identified—"nama" as "name," "willa" as "will," "eor an" as "earth," "heofonum" as
"heavens." Some become more recognizable when sound or spelling changes are
accounted for—"fæder" as "father," "hlaf" as "loaf," "yfele" as "evil." But many remain
unfamiliar because they are no longer in our language, having been replaced by
others, or because their forms have changed so radically: "þu" for "you," "gehalgod"
for "hallowed," "rice" for "kingdom," "gewurðe" for "become," "gedæghwamlican"
for "daily," "costnunge" for "temptation," "swa swa" for "just as," "so lice" for "amen."
The wordstock of Old English included a very few survivals from the language
of the conquered Britons, plus some borrowings from Latin; for the most part,

however, the words of Old English had developed within the language rather than being borrowed from outside.

Old English also had a more flexible word order than modern English. Because nouns, adjectives, and pronouns still changed endings to indicate their functions in the sentence, Old English speakers and writers had more options in word order than do speakers and writers of modern English. Possessive pronouns could come after the nouns they modified ("fæder ure"); for emphasis, verbs might come before their subjects ("*si* pin name gehalgod, *tobecume* . . . , *Gewurðe* . . .). A direct object could come before the verb it completes: the *-ne* ending on "urne," which cued speakers of Old English that this possessive pronoun is part of a direct object, allowed the speaker to put "our daily loaf" before its verb "give" ("syle"). Compare this freedom with the inflexibility of modern English word order, where changing "dog bites man" to "man bites dog" unavoidably reverses meaning.

The phrase "urne gedæghwamlican hlaf" illustrates another trait of Old English, one still seen in its relative modern German: a tendency to form words by compounding elements. The word "gedæghwamlican" is based on "dæg" ("day"); to that noun base are added syllables that change the noun to an adjective ("daily"). A similar process can be seen in "so lice," where the base noun "so" ("truth") becomes "true" with the addition of the adjective-forming "-lic" ("like") and then an adverb with "-e." Finally, the verb "syle" ("give") shows another way in which language can and does change over time. "Syle" is more immediately recognizable in its infinite form "sellan," from which we get the modern English "sell." Note, however, that "sell" now means to "exchange for money"; although this was one meaning possible in Old English, in this instance—and in usual Old English usage—the word's meaning was simply "to give" (without exchange). Even when a word remains in the language, over time there may be shifts in its meaning and in its uses.

MIDDLE ENGLISH

Just as the arrival of German tribes in Britain marks the beginning of Old English, the conventional beginning of Middle English is also an event in political history— the Norman Conquest of England in 1066. When William the Conqueror overcame Harold at the Battle of Hastings, he established a new social order in England. In the new order the governing classes did not share a variety of English with those they ruled. Instead, their language was the French the conquerors and governors who followed them used in the northern French province of Normandy. (It's worth noting, however, that this was the language the Normans had learned relatively recently—William was descended from Vikings who had conquered Normandy during the great Viking expansion of the ninth century.)

The Conquest had an enormous influence on the wordstock of English. Since French was the language of the royal court, the legal system, and all the rich and powerful landowners, the words they used to name the things and concepts in their spheres of influence usually replaced the native English equivalents. If the French word didn't replace the English equivalent, it usually entered the language as a near-synonym with a different—often more formal—connotation. This influx of French words was particularly concentrated in areas of government, law, religion, literature, and scholarship. The different social spheres in which French and English were used can be seen, as Sir Walter Scott's novel *Ivanhoe* points out, in the English names used for farmyard animals as opposed to the French names used for their meat at table: "cow" and "sow" (English) on the hoof, "beef" and "pork" (French) on the plate. Gradually words that were initially French became English as well as they were used by English speakers to name things that had before had other names in English, or that were entirely new. As a result, the vocabulary of today's English is much more heavily French and Latin in ultimate origin than it is English. Pick a sentence or two at random from something you're reading; if you check the etymologies of all the words in your dictionary, you're likely to find most of the words they use outside our core vocabulary are derived from Romance roots.

In contrast, the second principle change distinguishing Middle English from Old English is of internal origin. It is the loss of most inflections on nouns and adjectives, and the complementary increase in the importance of word order as a way of signalling meaning. Unlike the infusion of French vocabulary, whose beginning can be dated precisely in 1066, these changes were under way well before the Conquest; some manuscripts written before the year 1,000 show the changes related to this development almost completed, while some manuscripts a century later still preserve the Old English inflections much more fully. Whenever it occurred in different parts of English, the loss of distinct endings on nouns and adjectives made word order the most important way of showing grammatical relationships in Middle and modern English.

Ultimately, this change was caused by the strong stress on the first syllable we've already discussed as a characteristic of Germanic languages. Strong stress on first syllables preserved the vowels in them as distinct. That strong stress tended to reduce stress on syllables after the first, though, and as a result the vowels in them tended to be pronounced less distinctly. Late in the Old English period, the vowels in noun and adjective endings all came to be pronounced with a neutral vowel linguists call "schwa"—an "uh" sound produced in the middle of the mouth. This sound replaced short vowels like a, e, and u, whose differentiation had helped to signal different cases. Take, for example, the noun "hlaf" ("loaf"), which we've already touched on. In Old English it had six distinct forms:

	Singular	*Plural*
subject of sentence/direct object	hlaf	hlafas
possessive	hlafes	hlafa
indirect object/object of preposition	hlafe	hlafum

As all the ending vowels became "uh" rather than distinct a, e, u (and as the m of "hlafum" was lost), there were left only three forms—one with -s, one with

-e (the spelling of "uh"), one with no ending. Similar simplifications in other words reduced Old English nouns to something very close to the modern English noun infection of only two forms: loaf/loaves. Since grammatical function could no longer be understood from endings, word order became fixed—much like the word order of modern English. Both these changes can be seen in this fourteenth century version of the Lord's Prayer:

> Oure fadir that art in heuenes,
> halwid be thi name;
> Thy kingdom cuume to; be thi wille done as in heuen and in erthe;
> ʒif to vs this day oure breed ouer other substunce;
> And forʒeue to vs oure dettis, as we forzeue to oure dettours;
> And leed vs nat in to temptacioun, but delyuere vs fro yuel.
> Amen.

In comparison with the Old English version, much of the vocabulary here is French: "substance," "dettis," "dettours." In the last line the English "costnunge" has been replaced by the French "temptacioun," and the English "alys" by the French "delyuere." Notice also that in general the word order is closer to that of modern English: "oure" comes before "fadir"; "thy kingdom" comes before "cumme;" "ʒif to us" comes before "our breed." As a result of all the changes we've described, this version of the Lord's Prayer is one that a speaker of modern English can read with some confidence and understanding.

MODERN ENGLISH

The beginning of what linguists call modern English cannot be tied neatly to an event in political history. The changes that define modern English come from within the language and its speakers rather than outside. They happened between the death of Chaucer (c. 1400) and the start of Shakespeare's career (c. 1580), probably at different times in different parts of England.

The first of these changes is the final loss of the noun and adjective endings that remained from Middle English. As a result, the Middle English "name," which like its Old English ancestor "nama" had two syllables, in modern English came to have just one. During its history this word's pronunciation had thus changed from "nah-ma" to "nah-muh" to "naym." The final -e remains in spelling, but for us is only a signal that the vowel in the preceding syllable is long, not that it is a syllable by itself.

The second change that defines modern English has already been exemplified in the pronunciation "naym." We've already said that Old English used the continental system of pronouncing vowels in stressed syllables; Middle English did the same. Modern English, however, shows the result of what linguists call the Great Vowel Shift. In this change, all the long vowels and vowel combinations in stressed syllables changed their place in pronunciation. To oversimplify, each vowel moved up one position of articulation in the speaker's mouth; if the vowel was already pronounced at the top of the mouth, it moved toward the back of the mouth and became two linked sounds. This change was systematic; it affected all long vowels and diphthongs in stressed syllables.

Scholars don't know where this change in pronunciation originated, what caused it, or why it spread. Nevertheless, just as Proto-Germanic saw the systematic change in consonant pronunciation we call Grimm's Law, so early modern English saw this systematic change in vowel pronunciation. The changes we call Grimm's Law set Germanic languages apart from all other Indo-European languages; the Great Vowel Shift sets English apart from all other Indo-European languages, including all others in the Germanic family.

Two other important developments in early modern English illustrate yet another source of language change, one that has particular interest for us as teachers, especially teachers of students from a variety of dialects. The first development is the introduction of the third version plural pronouns in th-—"they, their, them." The second is the replacement of the historically appropriate third person singular verb form "he/she/it walk*eth*" with the form "walks." Both these changes stem ultimately from influence from yet another language—not French this time, but Old Norse.

How did this happen? We've said already that at various periods in its history different dialects of English have been the most prestigious, the "standard." In the Middle English and modern English periods that dialect has been the language of London, the seat of the royal court and the government. The English of London in the Middle English period was the direct ancestor of the English we speak today; many believe that the practice of government agencies, particularly the court of chancery, formed the basis for the written form of the modern language. But modern English also incorporates elements—the "th" pronouns and the -s ending—that in the early modern period entered London English through the language of immigrants to London from further north, from an area where people of Norse ancestry and culture had settled hundreds of years before.

We've already noted the expansion of the Vikings through the world in the ninth century; they invaded English as well as Normandy and many other places, including Russia. England's King Alref fought them for years, finally concluding a treaty with them in 886. This treaty allowed Viking settlement in a large area of midland and northern England called the "Danelaw." The Norse speakers who came there brought with them a language closely related to Old English, but with some distinct features that gradually became standard in the region. Among these distinctive features were versions of the pronouns "they/their/them" and the present tense third person singular verb ending "-s."

In the fourteenth century and after, merchants and others from the area that had been the Danelaw moved to the economic center of London. Clearly they brought their distinctive language with them—a language that to a speaker of London English would have seemed unusual, "non-standard." Over time, however, that same standard language replaced some of its own historically regular forms with borrowings from their language. Rather than continuing to use third person plural pronouns beginning with "h" (Old English "hie/her/hem," which became Middle English "hi/her/hem"), the standard language gradually replaced these pronouns with the Old Norse–derived "they/their/them." (One reason for the substitution may have been the greater distinctiveness of the "th" forms; in Middle English "her" means both "her" *and* "their," a fact that bewilders inexperienced readers of Chaucer.) There's no clear reason why "walks" should have replaced "walketh"; indeed, in many early modern English texts the two forms exist side by side. Eventually the "walks" form won out, as our own language today shows.

IMPLICATIONS FOR TEACHERS

All these developments are telling arguments against the popular view that language change is language decay, that there was a time when language was settled and perfect. As we have seen, the history of English is a history of perpetual and radical change—change so radical that our Old English sample, which comes from about a thousand years ago, would not be recognizable to most speakers of modern English as being English at all. It's also important to note that one ending that can be particularly troublesome for some learners of standard English—the -s ending in "walks," which does not exist in some dialects of modern English—ultimately comes from a language outside English, and entered the standard language from the speech of people who in their time were undoubtedly thought by speakers of London English not to "speak good English." In spite of their not being speakers of the standard English of their time, features of their language have paradoxically become part of what those coming after them know as standard. This fact underlines that point that, in English at least, standard languages *are* standard only for particular times and places. They do not have any universal validity or even a consistent history.

Of course, the history of English is not wholly inconsistent or random. We have seen how the shift of stress to the first syllable in Proto-Germanic created the conditions of pronunciation in which most inflectional endings would be pronounced indistinctly and then lost. There is also much continuity in the forms of commonly used nouns and pronouns and in basic sentence structure, particularly once word order became relatively fixed after the Old English period. On the other hand, we have seen many other changes—Grimm's Law, the Great Vowel Shift, the influx of French vocabulary, the adoption of pronouns ultimately derived from Old Norse—that depend on outside circumstances or that, while internal, could not be predicted by tendencies within the language itself. In particular, we've seen that features that in one period are non-standard can become standard in another.

None of this should be taken to imply that teaching our current standard language is unimportant, or that the history of English provides a reason *not* to teach it. Within any period, one variety of the language is the one used for communicating most broadly, and lacking command of that language can affect people's life chances negatively. We don't want such a circumstance to limit any of our students. On the other hand, we should help them acquire as much command of the standard language as they want to with appropriate humility about just how arbitrary and historically specific that standard is.

THEORY AND IMPLICATIONS

1. What kinds of language change have occurred during the history of English? Give an example or two from the reading to illustrate each kind of change.

2. What kinds of language change do you still see going on in English today? Think about the number of different groups that speak English and the ways they can influence each other; describe how changes are occurring either within groups or through the influences of one group on another.

3. More and more new immigrants to the United States are coming from countries that speak Spanish or Asian languages. What influence do you think their languages will have on the future development of American English? Why?

4. Choose a substantial paragraph from something you are reading and use the etymologies in your dictionary to find the ultimate origins of the words in it. Do your findings support this essay's statement about the importance of words of French or Latin origin? Are there languages represented in your sample that surprise you?

5. Do you think that a change of English pronunciation as basic as the Great Vowel Shift is still possible in the modern world? Why or why not? As you think about this question, you should take into account the many places English is spoken today and the broad reach of television and other telecommunications.

PROFESSIONAL CONCERNS

1. Suppose you worked for a principal who made sarcastic comments about the English spoken by some students in your school and bewailed the loss of the language of Shakespeare and Dr. Johnson. How could you use material from this reading or from elsewhere in this book to try to change his/her point of view?

2. Black English is a variety of English that has long existed side by side with more standard varieties. How has BE influenced language use in the United States? How would you anticipate it will continue to do so? How does this influence confirm or question what this reading says about language change in English? Write a speculative paper for a teacher in-service.

The King Case: Implications for Educators*

JERRIE COBB SCOTT

"The King Case: Implications for Educators" focuses on the stigma attached to a nonstandard dialect, not on the students' inability to understand. In this legal case, parents did not necessarily want teachers to change the language

---

* Scott, J. C., "The King Case: Implications for Educators," from *Tapping Potential English and Language Arts for the Black Learner,* edited by Charlotte K. Brooks. Copyright 1985 by the National Council of Teachers of English. Reprinted with permission.

of instruction; they had no objection to the teaching of SE. Rather, they objected to the negative attitudes toward BE, attitudes they claimed affected their children's learning. The results of this case reveal the legal thinking on issues of nonstandard dialects and provide teachers with a legal context for their own instruction and classroom responses.

Scott recommends that teachers learn about the complexities of BE and understand that divergent forms are not "errors." Such knowledge is the basis for a change in attitude. She does not, however, view changes in attitude as automatic with this knowledge, so she outlines a program of self-monitoring that must accompany it. Thus Scott's view also encompasses teachers' actual behavior. And like Labov's essay, which follows, it argues against "deficit models" of education for BE speakers.

In 1978, the parents of eleven black children charged school officials with denying their children equal educational opportunities by failing to help the children overcome a language barrier. The court found it appropriate to: require the defendant Board to take steps to help its teachers to recognize the home language of the students and to use that knowledge in their attempts to teach reading skills in standard English (Court Memorandum and Opinion 1978: 41). This case, *Martin Luther King Junior Elementary School Children v. Ann Arbor School District Board,* has attracted the attention of people from virtually the whole spectrum of American society. Naturally, the responses to the decision varied, but by and large, the case brought to the attention of educators two important points about black English. First, the decision recognizes the existence of a language system that elicits negative attitudes when used in the school environment. Negative attitudes are transformed into low expectations; low expectations are transmitted to and fulfilled by students. This cycle, described as either the Pygmalion effect or the pattern of self-fulfilling prophecies, has been shown to be a major factor in the academic failure of black students, though other factors contribute as well. Second, the decision legitimizes the use of information about the language of Afro-Americans for planning educational programs, especially reading programs.

Before discussing the two major points of this paper, it is useful to review some of the key points about the case. First, note the statute under which this case was tried:

> No state shall deny equal educational opportunity to an individual on account of his or her race, color, sex, or national origin, by . . . the failure by an educational agency to take appropriate action to overcome language barriers that impede equal participation by its students in its instructional programs. (U.S.C. 1703)

Contrary to popular opinion, the case was not directed toward settling the language vs. dialect controversy which had been debated in academic settings over the last decade; rather, it was directed toward determining whether or not the language system used by the eleven black children constituted a barrier in the educational process and whether or not the schools might have taken more appropriate action to help youngsters overcome these barriers. The language barrier, it was argued by the plaintiffs, was not based on students' inability to understand English. The language is a barrier in the educational process because of the stigma attached to it, the lack of respect given to it, and the lack of knowledge about it. All of the above factors have been shown to lead to damaged self-concepts of students, low expectations regarding the educability of students, ineffective instructional methods, and sometimes to inappropriate placement of students, e.g. classes for the learning disabled, the mentally handicapped, and the speech impaired.

A variety of views on the implications of the decision for educators can be found. At one extreme, there are those who interpret the decision as an explicit mandate not to teach standard English but to teach black English only. At the other extreme is the view that large scale language programs will be implemented for the purpose of teaching standard English to speakers of black English. There is also the interpretation that the ruling implies that no changes need take place at all in that some school programs have been acting in accordance with the ruling all along. The interpretation of the Ann Arbor School District Board was that the mandate required the Board to provide inservice training that would give school personnel wider exposure to the language and language learning patterns of black students. Finally, the response that best reflects the view of the lawyers and the expert witnesses in this case is that *King* implies the need for educators to reexamine the academic progress of blacks and other speakers of low prestige dialects in desegregated or language diverse educational settings. Educators might ask, then, what it means to recognize the existence of a language system other than the idealized standard English language system and what it means to legitimize the use of information about a variety of linguistic systems in planning educational programs.

THE RECOGNITION OF A LANGUAGE SYSTEM

To recognize that a language system exists is to admit that black children engage in highly complex language learning processes, as do children from any other ethnic group. Many of the readiness experiences thought to be important in developing communication skills are provided within the Afro-American speech community. For example, at a very early age black children learn to construct rhyming patterns; they are given numerous opportunities to use contextual cues for making distinctions between words that sound alike but have different meanings—homophones. Black students are quite apt at expressing a single idea in a variety of ways—paraphrasing. And they enjoy, even at kindergarten age, rearranging words to create new ideas or novel expressions, e.g. Ronald MacDonald to MacDonald Ronald. One could go on with numerous other features of language that are learned by children prior to entering school, features that might also be associated with readiness for school related language tasks. However, the point here is that the recognition of a language system would suggest the need for different attitudes about what black children learn, i.e., systematic rule-governed language patterns, and about how they acquire these language patterns, i.e., through natural yet complex language learning processes.

Attitudes are important. In his discussion of impediments to learning, Judge Joiner refers specifically to nonacceptance attitudes in the Court Memorandum of *King:*

> The research evidence supports the theory that the learning of reading can be hurt by teachers who reject students because of the "mistakes" or "errors" made in oral speech by black English speaking children who are learning standard English. This comes about because "black English" is commonly thought of as an inferior method of speech and those who use this system may be thought of as "dumb" or "inferior." (1978:18)

By implication, attitudes toward the language and the users of the language can influence the teaching-learning process. However simple it might sound, the task of changing attitudes is deceptively complex. Research findings reported by such people as Williams (1970), Williams, Whitehead, and Miller (1971), Taylor (1975), and Seligman, Tucker, and Lambert (1972) have shown that negative associations between speech patterns and other characteristics of a speaker, including educability of students, are made in seemingly unjustifiable ways. But more important, the negative associations seem to shape some of the expectations that teachers have about the language, personality traits, motivational levels, and academic potential of students who either speak a low-prestige dialect or who happen to be members of an ethnic group whose language patterns are stigmatized (Williams, Whitehead, and Miller 1971). Another important point about these research findings is that they suggest that attitudes about language are often formed unconsciously. Certainly it is difficult to change feelings that we are unconscious of. It is also difficult to change behaviors that communicate unconsciously formed attitudes, as is indicated by research on teacher behaviors that communicate low expectations.

That negative attitudes lead to negative results is not by any means new information, but we have just begun to investigate how negative attitudes are communicated in the classroom. Research by Dworkin and Dworkin (1979) has led to the identification of teacher behaviors that communicate low expectations to students, perhaps unintentionally. Some examples are limited opportunities for responses, emphasis on weaknesses rather than on strengths, absence of challenging questions, and the failure to ask probing questions when a response seems to be partially correct (Kernan 1979). So, in addition to the already complex problem of changing attitudes which are formed unconsciously, we have another complex problem—changing behaviors that communicate low expectations to students.

CHANGING ATTITUDES

When we speak of changing attitudes toward language, we are forced to deal with the fact that we are talking about changing feelings that people may not be consciously aware of and changing behaviors that people may not consciously control. These two factors suggest that attitudinal changes must be approached in a systematic way. Following is a brief description of three important steps in approaching attitudinal changes in a systematic way.

The First Step

First in the sequence is the recognition of the need for attitudinal changes. Information such as that presented in workshops and in the growing body of literature on the topic of language variation and related educational problems offer convincing evidence that many of the negative attitudes toward both low-prestige dialects and their speakers interfere with important educational goals. After being exposed to more objective descriptions of language and to empirically based findings on the negative influence of negative attitudes toward language and learning, educators tend to agree that attitudes should be changed. For example, workshop consultants have indicated that participants are more tolerant of language differences after they have received more information about different varieties of English. Acceptance on this level does not guarantee that the more positive attitudes will be communicated to students in the classroom. Thus, a second step is needed.

The Second Step

The next step involves the careful monitoring of behaviors that communicate low expectations. In addition to those teacher behaviors identified by researchers, we might add still another—insensitive patterns of correction. (For a fuller discussion of student anxieties which are created through insensitive patterns of correcting students, see Scott's discussion of cross-cultural communication conflicts in the classroom, 1978.) Each of these behaviors, i.e. providing response opportunities, positive feedback, challenging questions, sensitive corrections, can be observed, evaluated and controlled; they lend themselves well to monitoring.

It seems that the implementation of monitoring plans works best when conducted with other colleagues. That is, small groups or teams might meet periodically to discuss their observations, evaluations, and progress with monitoring behaviors that communicate low expectations. Interesting discoveries can be made. For example, one teacher reported that he discovered that he engaged in nonacceptance behaviors, not because of his negative attitudes toward students or their language, but because he was quite sensitive to the embarrassment caused by asking students challenging and probing questions when he knew full well that they could not answer the questions. When a team member asked, "What can the students do well? What are their strengths?," he admitted that he wasn't quite sure. This kind of response points to the need for a third step in our systematic approach to attitudinal changes: observing for positive attributes of students.

The Third Step

The third step involves careful observation of students' language learning behaviors and communication patterns and monitoring of evaluative statements about students, particularly students who have been unsuccessful in performing school-related tasks. In the same way that we accumulate data on students' weaknesses, we can accumulate data on their strengths. In other words, we can design a "balanced data bank" on students' performance. I am suggesting that a list of positive evaluations to match the list of negative evaluations of students' performance and behaviors would provide a more accurate profile of a student. From my experience with teacher workshops on this topic, I have found that school personnel tend to respond to this last suggestion enthusiastically, noting that the balanced data bank technique is practical and easy to implement. Some teachers have used the technique with students and with parents. Unsuccessful students have a difficult time finding enough positive attributes of themselves to balance the negative attributes. Their responses are quite similar to that of the teacher mentioned above—they're not quite sure what the strengths are. Armed with the information provided from the balanced data bank technique, the teacher can avoid the problem mentioned in step two, i.e., changing one set of behaviors only to take on another set that might be no more effective than the first. And ideally, the three steps mentioned here would complement each other, thereby fulfilling my criteria for a systematic approach to attitudinal changes.

Admittedly though, I have not been successful with selling the entire approach to any single group, though many have shown strong preferences for the balanced data bank technique. What seems more important than the total acceptance of my model is the acceptance of the basic principle of the model: attitudinal changes are dependent upon systematic approaches. The approach offered here involves the dissemination of information, observation and self-monitoring of teacher behaviors, observation and evaluation of students' strengths and weaknesses.

This discussion of attitudes has more to do with the learning environment than with the instructional materials. The focus on attitudes and learning environment is, however, in keeping with the ruling in *King*. A careful reading of the court order will reveal that the language barrier is often referred to in connection with nonsupportive learning environments that are created from negative attitudes toward the home language of some students. If the language is no longer perceived as illogical, unprincipled bundles of mistakes, then those attitudes shown to interfere with the educational process can no longer be supported.

THE USE OF THE LANGUAGE SYSTEM FOR PLANNING INSTRUCTION

To legitimize the use of the black English language system for planning instructional programs is to admit that information is available that can and should be used to better accommodate the learning needs of black English speakers. Usually when we think of accommodating the needs of minority students, we think of remedial programs. It should be noted that the plaintiffs in *King* did not request special programs for the eleven children. Parents were already concerned about the amount of time their children spent out of the regular classroom, most often in remedial programs. One objection to remedial programs is that they are generally based on deficit models. With language this means that language differences are, in effect, treated as language deficiencies. In addition, when dialect variation is addressed in regular programs, language differences are seldom given respectable treatment. Considering the notion that we are dealing with a language system, and that information about the system can be incorporated into instructional programs, the implications are that special programs need not be remedial and that regular programs need not always present information about dialect variation in a negative way. The problem of changing instructional materials is, in many ways, similar to that of changing attitudes. People tend to be willing to acknowledge the existence of different linguistic systems or sub-systems but unwilling to behave as though the differences are anything but deficiencies. Resistances to change are found in both special and regular instructional programs.

To illustrate my point, I will consider one of the proposals offered for accommodating students in language diverse classrooms. The basic design features for a special instructional program are offered by Anastasiow and Hanes in their book *Language Patterns of Poverty Children.* The authors maintain that "poverty children" (rural whites, blacks, and Puerto Ricans) speak a "structured and rule-governed language, . . . are equal to their middle class peers in language development, . . . and are capable of achieving in school" (1976, 101). But they also note that "until poverty children have ample experience in matching their own language with that of the school, formal reading instructions should be replaced with an intensive oral language program" (1976, 104). As late as 1976 we find the advocacy of pedagogy that was rendered as unacceptable nearly a decade before. That is, most investigations of dialect and reading problems agreed that it was impractical and unnecessary to delay teaching reading until after students have learned to speak standard English. It is equally important that such a proposal comes after the acknowledgement that linguistic differences do not reflect linguistic deficiencies. From the perspective of language pedagogy, the notion advanced by these authors is that instead of remediating deficits, we should be remediating differences. Put more dramatically, students must give up, "the right to be" for "the right to read." The language that students bring to school, different though it may be, is an intimate part of their being.

In legitimizing the use of information about the black English language system for educational planning, one would expect for goals of special instructional programs to be targeted towards expanding language competencies rather than towards remediating language differences.

Seldom do we find references to changes in regular classroom material with regard to accommodating diverse language and cultural background of ethnic minorities. In regular instructional programs, language samples associated with dialect variation usually serve as examples of incorrect, unacceptable, uneducated, or inappropriate language patterns. It is possible, however, to include information about the language and cultural patterns of ethnic minorities in a more positive light.

For example, spelling textbooks often contain sections on word-etymologies. African and Afro-American derived words could be included in such sections. In literature textbooks, analyses of literary forms could include samples of metaphors, alliteration, etc., from speech samples representing the Afro-American speech community. In reading textbooks, exercises for developing inferential skills might contain samples of proverbs frequently used in Afro-American speech communities. Excellent examples of each are provided by Smitherman (1977) in her book *Talkin and Testifyin.*

Whether one takes *King* or the current literature as a point of reference, the recognition of black English as a language system implies the need for attitudinal changes, and the legitimacy given to using information about the black English language system suggests that we must find more positive ways to treat dialect variation in the classroom. Indeed one might take as a point of reference the observations of the well-known author Toni Morrison. In response to the questions "What do you think is distinctive about your fiction? What makes it good?" She replied:

> The language, only the language. It is the thing that black people love so much—the saying of the words, holding them on the tongue, experimenting with them, playing with them. It's a love, a passion. . . . The worst of all possible things that could happen would be to lose that language. There are certain things I cannot say without recourse to my language. It's terrible to think that a child with five different present tenses comes to school to be faced with those books that are less than his own language, which is him, that are sometimes permanently damaging. He may never know the etymology of Africanisms in his language, not even know that "hip" is a real word or that "the dozens" meant something. This is a really cruel fallout of racism. I know the standard English. I want to use it to help restore the other language, the lingua franca. (1981, 27)

REFERENCES

Anastasiow, N., and M. Hanes. *Language Patterns of Poverty Children.* Springfield, Ill.: Charles C. Thomas, 1976.

Dworkin, N., and Y. Dworkin. "The Legacy of Pygmalion in the Classroom." *Phi Delta Kappan* 60 (June 1979).

Kernan, S. "Teacher Expectations and Student Achievement." *Phi Delta Kappan* (June 1979): 716–18.

Morrison, T. "An Interview with Toni Morrison." *New Republic* (March 1981).

Scott, J. "Black Modes of Communication and Conflicts in the Schools." In *Cross-Cultural Communications in the Schools,* edited by C. Moody and K. Lind. Ann Arbor, Mich.: Program for Educational Opportunity, University of Michigan, 1978.

Seligman, D., G. Tucker, and W. Lambert. "The Effects of Speech, Style and Other Attributes on Teachers' Attitudes toward Pupils." *Language in Society* (April 1972).

Smitherman, Geneva. *Talkin and Testifyin: The Language of Black America.* Boston: Houghton Mifflin, 1977.

Taylor, O. "Black Language and What to Do about It: Some Black Community Perspectives." In *Ebonics: The True Language of Black Folks,* edited by R. Williams. St. Louis: Institute of Black Studies, 1975.

Williams, F. "Psychological Correlates of Speech Characteristics." *Journal of Speech and Hearing* 13 (1970).

Williams, F., J. Whitehead, and L. Miller. "Attitudinal Correlates of Children's Speech Characteristics." Project #0-0336, U.S. Department of Health, Education and Welfare, Washington, D.C.: Office of Education, 1971.

THEORY AND IMPLICATIONS

1. The case this essay describes highlights the issue of language attitude barriers—the problem of self-fulfilling prophecies. Why do you think this is a crucial problem yet one that is not often directly addressed? Can you think of other examples of language barriers that have remained unexamined? Explain.
2. How are the language problems faced by nonstandard dialect speakers like or unlike those faced by second language learners? Explain.
3. The parents did not want special programs. Do you feel that they were right not to want them? Why?
4. Why do you think that the ruling on this case did not have any immediate practical effect on specific pedagogy? What practices do you feel the case mandates?
5. Do you feel that a change in attitude will automatically follow from a change in knowledge about BE? Why?
6. Do you feel that the self-monitoring program would work? Why or why not? What modifications would you make?

PROFESSIONAL CONCERNS

1. Devise methods other than those suggested here for incorporating into regular classrooms "the diverse language and cultural background of ethnic minorities."
2. What do you think the legal implications of this case might be for specific classroom pedagogies? Present a case to a principal or other educator, explaining what steps you think the school must take to comply with the laws. Offer evidence.

The Logic of Nonstandard English*

WILLIAM LABOV

"The Logic of Nonstandard English" is an eloquent critique of the "deficit model" view of BE. This model presumes that BE speakers come to the classroom without a fully developed, logical language, capable of abstraction; that their home life is impoverished in language use; and that BE speakers need a drill-based, remedial program to improve their language skills.

---

* Labov, W., "The Logic of Nonstandard English," 1979, in Alatis, James E., Editor, *Report of the Twentieth Annual Round Table Meeting on Linguistics and Language Studies* (Monograph Series on Languages and Linguistics, No. 22).

Labov's criticism of sociologists with little linguistic knowledge, who make inductions from contrived interviews about BE speakers' logic, abstract thought, and verbality in the home, has become a classic on misinterpretation and bias. To support his view, Labov contrasts the pithy, aphoristic, quick-witted verbal style of one BE speaker with the repetitive, vague, and bombastic style of a middle-class speaker. He helps us to see how our own biases allow us to read content into middle-class style, even where no content exists. Like Scott, Labov asks us to monitor ourselves—to watch our own biases at play. Furthermore he offers a useful overview of the key characteristics of BE.

In the past decade, a great deal of federally sponsored research has been devoted to the educational problems of children in ghetto schools.[1] In order to account for the poor performance of children in these schools, educational psychologists have attempted to discover what kind of disadvantage or defect they are suffering from. The viewpoint that has been widely accepted and used as the basis for large-scale intervention programs is that the children show a cultural deficit as a result of an impoverished environment in their early years. Considerable attention has been given to language. In this area the deficit theory appears as the concept of verbal deprivation. Black children from the ghetto area are said to receive little verbal stimulation, to hear very little well-formed language, and as a result are impoverished in their means of verbal expression. They cannot speak complete sentences, do not know the names of common objects, cannot form concepts or convey logical thoughts.

Unfortunately, these notions are based upon the work of educational psychologists who know very little about language and even less about black children. The concept of verbal deprivation has no basis in social reality. In fact, black children in the urban ghettos receive a great deal of verbal stimulation, hear more well-formed sentences than middle-class children, and participate fully in a highly verbal culture. They have the same basic vocabulary, possess the same capacity for conceptual learning, and use the same logic as anyone else who learns to speak and understand English.

The notion of verbal deprivation is a part of the modern mythology of educational psychology, typical of the unfounded notions which tend to expand rapidly in our educational system. In past decades linguists have been as guilty as others in promoting such intellectual fashions at the expense of both teachers and children. But the myth of verbal deprivation is particularly dangerous, because it diverts attention from real defects of our educational system to imaginary defects of the child. As we shall see, it leads its sponsors inevitably to the hypothesis of the genetic inferiority of black children that it was originally designed to avoid.

The most useful service which linguists can perform today is to clear away the illusion of verbal deprivation and to provide a more adequate notion of the relations between standard and nonstandard dialects. In the writings of many prominent educational psychologists, we find very poor understanding of the

---

[1] This chapter first appeared in *Georgetown Monographs in Languages and Linguistics No. 22* (1969).

nature of language. Children are treated as if they have no language of their own in the preschool programs put forward by Bereiter and Engelmann (1966). The linguistic behavior of ghetto children in test situations is the principal evidence of genetic inferiority in the view of Jensen (1968). In this paper, we will examine critically both of these approaches to the language and intelligence of the populations labeled "verbally deprived" and "culturally deprived,"[2] and attempt to explain how the myth of verbal deprivation has arisen, bringing to bear the methodological findings of sociolinguistic work and some substantive facts about language which are known to all linguists. Of particular concern is the relation between concept formation on the one hand, and dialect differences on the other, since it is in this area that the most dangerous misunderstandings are to be found.

VERBALITY

The general setting in which the deficit theory arises consists of a number of facts which are known to all of us. One is that black children in the central urban ghettos do badly in all school subjects, including arithmetic and reading. In reading, they average more than two years behind the national norm (see *New York Times,* December 3, 1968). Furthermore, this lag is cumulative, so that they do worse comparatively in the fifth grade than in the first grade. Reports in the literature show that this poor performance is correlated most closely with socioeconomic status. Segregated ethnic groups seem to do worse than others— in particular, Indian, Mexican-American, and black children. Our own work in New York City confirms that most black children read very poorly; however, studies in the speech community show that the situation is even worse than has been reported. If one separates the isolated and peripheral individuals from members of central peer groups, the peer-group members show even worse reading records and to all intents and purposes are not learning to read at all during the time they spend in school.

In speaking of children in the urban ghetto areas, the term *lower class* frequently is used, as opposed to *middle class.* In the several sociolinguistic studies we have carried out, and in many parallel studies, it has been useful to distinguish a lower-class group from a working-class one. Lower-class families are typically female-based, or matrifocal, with no father present to provide steady economic support, whereas for the working-class there is typically an intact nuclear family with the father holding a semiskilled or skilled job. The educational problems of ghetto areas run across this important class distinction. There is no evidence, for example, that the father's presence or absence is closely correlated with educational achievement (e.g., Coleman et al. 1966). The peer groups we have studied in south-central Harlem, representing the basic vernacular culture,

[2] I am indebted to Rosalind Weiner of the Early Childhood Education group of Operation Head Start in New York City and to Joan Baraiz of the Education Study Center, Washington, D.C., for pointing out to me the scope and seriousness of the educational issues involved here and the ways in which the cultural deprivation theory has affected federal intervention programs in recent years.

include members from both family types. The attack against cultural deprivation in the ghetto is overtly directed at family structures typical of lower-class families, but the educational failure we have been discussing is characteristic of both working-class and lower-class children.

This paper, therefore, will refer to children from urban ghetto areas rather than lower-class children. The population we are concerned with comprises those who participate fully in the vernacular culture of the street and who have been alienated from the school system.[3] We are obviously dealing with effects of the caste system of American society—essentially a color-marking system. Everyone recognizes this. The question is: By what mechanism does the color bar prevent children from learning to read? One answer is the notion of cultural deprivation put forward by Martin Deutsch and others (Deutsch and associates 1967; Deutsch, Katz, and Jensen 1968). Black children are said to lack the favorable factors in their home environment which enable middle-class children to do well in school (Deutsch and assoc. 1967; Deutsch, Katz, and Jensen 1968). These factors involve the development of various cognitive skills through verbal interaction with adults, including the ability to reason abstractly, speak fluently, and focus upon long-range goals. In their publications, these psychologists also recognize broader social factors.[4] However, the deficit theory does not focus upon the interaction of the black child with white society so much as on his failure to interact with his mother at home. In the literature we find very little direct observation of verbal interaction in the black home; most typically, the investigators ask the child if he has dinner with his parents, and if he engages in dinner-table conversation with them. He is also asked whether his family takes him on trips to museums and other cultural activities. This slender thread of evidence is used to explain and interpret the large body of tests carried out in the laboratory and in the school.

The most extreme view which proceeds from this orientation—and one that is now being widely accepted—is that lower-class black children have no language at all. The notion is first drawn from Basil Bernstein's writings that "much of lower-class language consists of a kind of incidental 'emotional' accompaniment to action here and now." (Jensen 1968:118). Bernstein's views are filtered through a strong bias against all forms of working-class behavior, so that middle-class language is seen as superior in every respect—as "more abstract, and necessarily somewhat more flexible, detailed and subtle." One can proceed through a range of such views until one comes to the practical program of Carl Bereiter, Siegfried Engelmann and their associates (Bereiter et al. 1966; Bereiter and Engelmann 1966). Bereiter's program for an academically oriented preschool is based upon their premise that black children must have a language with which they can learn, and their empirical finding that these children come to school without such a

---

[3] The concept of the black English vernacular (BEV) and the culture in which it is embedded is presented in detail in CRR 3288; section 1.2.3 and 4.1.

[4] For example, in Deutsch, Katz and Jensen 1968 there is a section on "Social and Psychological Perspectives" which includes a chapter by Proshansky and Newton on "The Nature and Meaning of Negro Self-Identity" and one by Rosenthal and Jacobson on "Self-Fulfilling Prophecies in the Classroom."

language. In his work with four-year-old black children from Urbana, Bereiter reports that their communication was by gestures, "single words," and "a series of badly connected words or phrases," such as *They mine* and *Me got juice*. He reports that black children could not ask questions, that "without exaggerating . . . these four-year-olds could make no statements of any kind." Furthermore, when these children were asked "Where is the book?", they did not know enough to look at the table where the book was lying in order to answer. Thus Bereiter concludes that the children's speech forms are nothing more than a series of emotional cries, and he decides to treat them "as if the children had no language at all." He identifies their speech with his interpretation of Bernstein's restricted code: "the language of culturally deprived children . . . is not merely an under-developed version of standard English, but is a basically nonlogical mode of expressive behavior" (Bereiter et al. 1966:112–113). The basic program of his preschool is to teach them a new language devised by Engelmann, which consists of a limited series of questions and answers such as *Where is the squirrel? The squirrel is in the tree.* The children will not be punished if they use their vernacular speech on the playground, but they will not be allowed to use it in the schoolroom. If they should answer the question *Where is the squirrel?* with the illogical vernacular form *In the tree* they will be reprehended by various means and made to say, *The squirrel is in the tree.*

Linguists and psycholinguists who have worked with black children are apt to dismiss this view of their language as utter nonsense. Yet there is no reason to reject Bereiter's observations as spurious. They were certainly not made up. On the contrary, they give us a very clear view of the behavior of student and teacher which can be duplicated in any classroom. In our own work outside of adult-dominated environments of school and home, we have not observed black children behaving like this. However, on many occasions we have been asked to help analyze the results of research into verbal deprivation conducted in such test situations.

Here, for example, is a complete interview with a black child, one of hundreds carried out in a New York City school. The boy enters a room where there is a large, friendly, white interviewer, who puts on the table in front of him a toy and says: "Tell me everything you can about this." (The interviewer's further remarks are in parentheses.)

    (12 seconds of silence)
(What would you say it looks like?)
    (8 seconds of silence)
A space ship.
(Hmmmm.)
    (13 seconds of silence)
Like a je-et.
    (12 seconds of silence)
Like a plane.
    (20 seconds of silence)
(What color is it?)
Orange. (2 seconds) An' whi-ite. (2 seconds) An' green.

   (6 seconds of silence)
(An' what could you use it for?)
   (8 seconds of silence)
A je-et.
   (6 seconds of silence)
(If you had two of them, what would you do with them?)
   (6 seconds of silence)
Give one to some-body.
(Hmmmm. Who do you think would like to have it?)
   (10 seconds of silence)
Cla-rence.
(Mm. Where do you think we could get another one of these?)
At the store.
(Oh ka-ay!)

We have here the same kind of defensive, monosyllabic behavior which is reported in Bereiter's work. What is the situation that produces it? The child is in an asymmetrical situation where anything he says can literally be held against him. He has learned a number of devices to avoid saying anything in this situation, and he works very hard to achieve this end. One may observe the intonation patterns of

$$^2a \ ^{3\prime}o^\prime \ ^2know$$

and

$$a \ ^2space \ ^2sh \ ^{3}ip$$

which black children often use when they are asked a question to which the answer is obvious. The answer may be read as: "Will this satisfy you?"

   If one takes this interview as a measure of the verbal capacity of the child, it must be as his capacity to defend himself in a hostile and threatening situation. But unfortunately, thousands of such interviews are used as evidence of the child's total verbal capacity, or more simply his verbality. It is argued that this lack of verbality explains his poor performance in school. Operation Head Start and other intervention programs have largely been based upon the deficit theory—the notions that such interviews give us a measure of the child's verbal capacity and that the verbal stimulation which he has been missing can be supplied in a preschool environment.

   The verbal behavior which is shown by the child in the situation quoted above is not the result of the ineptness of the interviewer. It is rather the result of regular sociolinguistic factors operating upon adult and child in this asymmetrical situation. In our work in urban ghetto areas, we have often encountered such behavior. Ordinarily we worked with boys 10 to 17 years old, and whenever we extended our approach downward to eight- or nine-year-olds, we began to see the need for different techniques to explore the verbal capacity of the child. At one point we began a series of interviews with younger brothers of the Thunderbirds. Clarence Robins interviewed eight-year-old Leon L., who showed the following minimal response to topics which arouse intense interest in other interviews with older boys.

CR: What if you saw somebody kickin' somebody else on the ground, or was using a stick, what would you do if you saw that?
LEON: Mmmm.
CR: If it was supposed to be a fair fight—
LEON: I don' know.
CR: You don' know? Would you do anything? . . . huh I can't hear you.
LEON: No.
CR: Did you ever see somebody got beat up real bad?
LEON: . . . Nope . . .
CR: Well—uh—did you ever get into a fight with a guy
LEON: Nope.
CR: That was bigger than you?
LEON: Nope . . .
CR: You never been in a fight?
LEON: Nope.
CR: Nobody ever pick on you?
LEON: Nope.
CR: Nobody ever hit you?
LEON: Nope.
CR: How come?
LEON: Ah 'o' know.
CR: Didn't you ever hit somebody?
LEON: Nope.
CR: [*incredulously*] You never hit nobody?
LEON: Mhm.
CR: Aww, ba-a-a-be, you ain't gonna tell me that!

It may be that Leon is here defending himself against accusations of wrong-doing, since Clarence knows that Leon has been in fights, that he has been taking pencils away from little boys, and so on. But if we turn to a more neutral subject, we find the same pattern:

CR: You watch—you like to watch television? . . . Hey, Leon . . . you like to watch television? [*Leon nods*] What's your favorite program?
LEON: Uhhmmmm . . . I look at cartoons.
CR: Well, what's your favorite one? What's your favorite program?
LEON: Superman . . .
CR: Yeah? Did you see Superman—ah—yesterday, or day before yesterday? When's the last time you saw Superman?

LEON: Sa-aturday . . .

CR: You rem—you saw it Saturday? What was the story all about? You remember the story?

LEON: M-m.

CR: You don't remember the story of what—that you saw of Superman?

LEON: Nope.

CR: You don't remember what happened, huh?

LEON: Hm-m.

CR: I see—ah—what other stories do you like to watch on TV?

LEON: Mmmm? . . . umm . . . [*glottalization*]

CR: Hmm? [*four seconds*]

LEON: Hh?

CR: What's th' other stories that you like to watch?

LEON: Mi-ighty Mouse . . .

CR: And what else?

LEON: Ummmm . . . ahm . . .

This nonverbal behavior occurs in a relatively favorable context for adult-child interaction. The adult is a black man raised in Harlem, who knows this particular neighborhood and these boys very well. He is a skilled interviewer who has obtained a very high level of verbal response with techniques developed for a different age level, and he has an extraordinary advantage over most teachers or experimenters in these respects. But even his skills and personality are ineffective in breaking down the social constraints that prevail here.

When we reviewed the record of this interview with Leon, we decided to use it as a test of our own knowledge of the sociolinguistic factors which control speech. In the next interview with Leon we made the following changes in the social situation:

1. Clarence brought along a supply of potato chips, changing the interview into something more in the nature of a party.
2. He brought along Leon's best friend, eight-year-old Gregory.
3. We reduced the height imbalance by having Clarence get down on the floor of Leon's room; he dropped from six feet, two inches to three feet, six inches.
4. Clarence introduced taboo words and taboo topics, and proved, to Leon's surprise, that one can say anything into our microphone without any fear of retaliation. The result of these changes is a striking difference in the volume and style of speech. (The tape is punctuated throughout by the sound of potato chips.)

CR: Is there anybody who says *your momma drink pee?*

{ LEON: [*rapidly and breathlessly*] Yee-ah!

{ GREG: Yup!

LEON: And *your father eat doo-doo for breakfast!*

CR: Ohhh!! [*laughs*]

LEON: And they say your father—*your father eat doo-doo for dinner!*

GREG: When they sound on me, I say C.B.S. C.B.M.

CR: What that mean?

LEON: Congo booger-snatch! [*laughs*]

GREG: Congo booger-snatcher! [*laughs*]

GREG: And sometimes I'll curse with B.B.

CR: What that?

GREG: Black boy! [*Leon crunching on potato chips*] Oh that's a M.B.B.

CR: M.B.B. What's that?

GREG: 'Merican Black Boy.

CR: Ohh . . .

GREG: Anyway, 'Mericans is same like white people, right?

LEON: And they talk about Allah.

CR: Oh yeah?

GREG: Yeah.

CR: What they say about Allah?

LEON: Allah—Allah is God.

GREG: Allah—

CR: And what else?

LEON: I don' know the res'.

GREG: Allah i—Allah is God, Allah is the only God, Allah . . .

LEON: Allah is the son of God.

GREG: But can he make magic?

LEON: Nope.

GREG: I know who can make magic.

CR: Who can?

LEON: The God, the *real* one.

CR: Who can make magic?

GREG: The son of po'—[CR: *Hm?*] I'm sayin' the po'k chop God![5] He only a po'k chop God! [*Leon chuckles*].

(The "nonverbal" Leon is now competing actively for the floor; Gregory and Leon talk to each other as much as they do to the interviewer.)

---

[5] The reference to the *pork chop God* condenses several concepts of black nationalism current in the Harlem community. A *pork chop* is a black who has not lost the traditional subservient ideology of the South, who has no knowledge of himself in Muslim terms, and the *pork chop God* would be the traditional God of Southern Baptists. He and His followers may be pork chops, but He still holds the power in Leon and Gregory's world.

We can make a more direct comparison of the two interviews by examining the section on fighting. Leon persists in denying that he fights, but he can no longer use monosyllabic answers, and Gregory cuts through his facade in a way that Clarence alone was unable to do.

> CR: Now, you said you had this fight now; but I wanted you to tell me about the fight that you had.
>
> LEON: I ain't had no fight.
>
> { GREG: Yes you did! He said Barry . . .
> { CR: You said you had one! you had a fight with Butchie.
>
> { GREG: An he say Garland! . . . an' Michael!
> { CR: an' Barry . . .
>
> { LEON: I di'n'; you said that, Gregory!
> { GREG: You did!
>
> { LEON: You know you said that!
> { GREG: You said Garland, remember that?
>
> { GREG: You said Garland! Yes you did!
> { CR: You said Garland, that's right.
>
> GREG: He said Mich—an' I say Michael.
>
> { CR: Did you have a fight with Garland?
> { LEON: Uh-Uh.
>
> CR: You had one, and he beat you up, too!
>
> GREG: Yes he did!
>
> LEON: No, I di—I never had a fight with Butch! . . .

The same pattern can be seen on other local topics, where the interviewer brings neighborhood gossip to bear on Leon, and Gregory acts as a witness.

> CR: . . . Hey Gregory! I heard that around here . . . and I'm 'on' tell you who said it, too . . .
>
> LEON: Who?
>
> CR: about you . . .
>
> { LEON: Who?
> { GREG: I'd say it!
>
> CR: They said that—they say that the only person you play with is David Gilbert.
>
> { LEON: Yee-ah! yee-ah! yee-ah! . . .
> { GREG: That's who you play with!
>
> { LEON: I 'on' play with him no more!
> { GREG: Yes you do!
>
> LEON: I 'on' play with him no more!
>
> GREG: But remember, about me and Robbie?
>
> LEON: So that's not—

GREG: and you went to Petey and Gilbert's house, 'member? *Ah haaah!!*

LEON: So that's—so—but I would—I had came back out, an' I ain't go to his house no more. . . .

The observer must now draw a very different conclusion about the verbal capacity of Leon. The monosyllabic speaker who had nothing to say about anything and cannot remember what he did yesterday has disappeared. Instead, we have two boys who have so much to say they keep interrupting each other and who seem to have no difficulty in using the English language to express themselves. In turn we obtain the volume of speech and the rich array of grammatical devices which we need for analyzing the structure of black English vernacular; for example: negative concord ("I 'on' play with him no more"), the pluperfect ("had came back out"), negative perfect ("I ain't had"), the negative preterite ("I ain't go"), and so on.

We can now transfer this demonstration of the sociolinguistic control of speech to other test situations, including IQ and reading tests in school. It should be immediately apparent that none of the standard tests will come anywhere near measuring Leon's verbal capacity. On these tests he will show up as very much the monosyllabic, inept, ignorant, bumbling child of our first interview. The teacher has far less ability than Clarence Robins to elicit speech from this child. Clarence knows the community, the things that Leon has been doing, and the things that Leon would like to talk about. But the power relationships in a one-to-one confrontation between adult and child are too asymmetrical. This does not mean that some black children will not talk a great deal when alone with an adult, or that an adult cannot get close to any child. It means that the social situation is the most powerful determinant of verbal behavior and that an adult must enter into the right social relation with a child if he wants to find out what a child can do. This is just what many teachers cannot do.

The view of the black speech community which we obtain from our work in the ghetto areas is precisely the opposite from that reported by Deutsch or by Bereiter and Engelmann. We see a child bathed in verbal stimulation from morning to night. We see many speech events which depend upon the competitive exhibition of verbal skills—sounding, singing, toasts, rifting, louding—a whole range of activities in which the individual gains status through his use of language. We see the younger child trying to acquire these skills from older children, hanging around on the outskirts of older peer groups, and imitating this behavior to the best of his ability. We see no connection between verbal skill in the speech events characteristic of the street culture and success in the schoolroom.

VERBOSITY

There are undoubtedly many verbal skills which children from ghetto areas must learn in order to do well in the school situation, and some of these are indeed characteristic of middle-class verbal behavior. Precision in spelling, practice in handling abstract symbols, the ability to state explicitly the meaning of words, and a richer knowledge of the Latinate vocabulary, may all be useful acquisitions. But is it true that all of the middle-class verbal habits are functional and desirable in the school situation? Before we impose middle-class verbal style upon children from other cultural groups, we should find out how much of this is useful for the main work of analyzing and generalizing, and how much is merely stylistic— or even dysfunctional. In high school and college, middle-class children spontaneously complicate their syntax to the point that instructors despair of getting them to make their language simpler and clearer. In every learned journal one can find examples of jargon and empty elaboration, as well as complaints about it. Is the elaborated code of Bernstein really so "flexible, detailed and subtle" as some psychologists believe (e.g., Jensen 1968:119)? Isn't it also turgid, redundant, bombastic, and empty? Is it not simply an elaborated style, rather than a superior code or a system?[6]

Our work in the speech community makes it painfully obvious that in many ways working-class speakers are more effective narrators, reasoners, and debaters than many middle-class speakers who temporize, qualify, and lose their argument in a mass of irrelevant detail. Many academic writers try to rid themselves of that part of middle-class style that is empty pretension and keep that part that is needed for precision. But the average middle-class speaker that we encounter makes no such effort; he is enmeshed in verbiage, the victim of sociolinguistic factors beyond his control.

I will not attempt to support this argument here with systematic quantitative evidence, although it is possible to develop measures which show how far middle-class speakers can wander from the point. I would like to contrast two speakers dealing with roughly the same topic—matters of belief. The first is Larry H., a fifteen-year-old core member of the Jets, being interviewed by John Lewis. Larry is one of the loudest and roughest members of the Jets, one who gives the least recognition to the conventional rules of politeness.[7] For most readers of this book, first contact with Larry would produce some fairly negative reactions on both sides. It is probable that you would not like him any more than his teachers do. Larry causes trouble in and out of school. He was put back from the eleventh grade to the ninth, and has been threatened with further action by the school authorities.

JL: What happens to you after you die? Do you know?

LARRY: Yeah, I know. (What?) After they put you in the ground, your body turns into—ah—bones, an' shit.

---

[6] The term *code* is central in Bernstein's (1966) description of the differences between working-class and middle-class styles of speech. The restrictions and elaborations of speech observed are labeled as codes to indicate the principles governing selection from the range of possible English sentences. No rules or detailed description of the operation of such codes are provided as yet, so that this central concept remains to be specified.

[7] A direct view of Larry's verbal style in a hostile encounter is given in CRR 3288 Vol 2:39–43. Gray's Oral Reading Test was being given to a group of Jets on the steps of a brownstone house in Harlem and the landlord tried unsuccessfully to make the Jets move. Larry's verbal style in this encounter matches the reports he gives of himself in a number of narratives cited in section 4.8 of the report.

JL: What happens to your spirit?

LARRY: Your spirit—soon as you die, your spirit leaves you. (And where does the spirit go?) Well, it all depends . . . (On what?) You know, like some people say if you're good an' shit, your spirit goin' t'heaven . . . 'n' if you bad, your spirit goin' to hell. Well, bullshit! Your spirit goin' to hell anyway, good or bad.

JL: Why?

LARRY: Why? I'll tell you why. 'Cause, you see, doesn' nobody really know that it's a God, y'know, 'cause I mean I have seen black gods, pink gods, white gods, all color gods, and don't nobody know it's really a God. An' when they be sayin' if you good, you goin' t'heaven, tha's bullshit, 'cause you ain't goin' to no heaven, 'cause it ain't no heaven for you to go to.

Larry is a paradigmatic speaker of black English vernacular as opposed to standard English. His grammar shows a high concentration of such characteristic BEV forms as negative inversion ("don't nobody know"), negative concord ("you ain't goin' to no heaven"), invariant *be* ("when they be sayin'"), dummy *it* for standard *there* ("it ain't no heaven"), optional copula deletion ("if you're good . . . if you bad") and full forms of auxiliaries ("I have seen"). The only standard English influence in this passage is the one case of "doesn't" instead of the invariant "don't" of BEV. Larry also provides a paradigmatic example of the rhetorical style of BEV: he can sum up a complex argument in a few words, and the full force of his opinions comes through without qualification or reservation. He is eminently quotable, and his interviews give us many concise statements of the BEV point of view. One can almost say that Larry speaks the BEV culture (see CRR 3288, vol. 2: 38, 71-73, 291-92).

It is the logical form of this passage which is of particular interest here. Larry presents a complex set of interdependent propositions which can be explicated by setting out the standard English equivalents in linear order. The basic argument is to deny the twin propositions:

(A) If you are good, (B) then your spirit will go to heaven.

(~A) If you are bad, (C) then your spirit will go to hell.

Larry denies B and asserts that if A or ~A, then C. His argument may be outlined as follows:

1. Everyone has a different idea of what God is like.
2. Therefore nobody really knows that God exists.
3. If there is a heaven, it was made by God.
4. If God doesn't exist, he couldn't have made heaven.
5. Therefore heaven does not exist.
6. You can't go somewhere that doesn't exist.
(~B) Therefore you can't go to heaven.
(C) Therefore you are going to hell.

The argument is presented in the order: *C* because 2 because 1, therefore 2, therefore ~*B* because 5 and 6. Part of the argument is implicit: the connection 2 therefore ~*B* leaves unstated the connecting links 3 and 4, and in this interval Larry strengthens the propositions from the form 2 "Nobody knows if there is . . ." to 5 "There is no. . . ." Otherwise, the case is presented explicitly as well as economically. The complex argument is summed up in Larry's last sentence, which shows formally the dependence of ~*B* on 5 and 6:

> An' when they be sayin' if you good, you goin' t'heaven, (The proposition if *A,* then *B*)
> tha's bullshit, (is absurd)
> 'cause you ain't goin' to no heaven (because *B*)
> 'cause it ain't no heaven for you to go to (because 5 and 6).

This hypothetical argument is not carried on at a high level of seriousness. It is a game played with ideas as counters, in which opponents use a wide variety of verbal devices to win. There is no personal commitment to any of these propositions, and no reluctance to strengthen one's argument by bending the rules of logic as in the 2-5 sequence. But if the opponent invokes the rules of logic, they hold. In John Lewis's interviews, he often makes this move, and the force of his argument is always acknowledged and countered within the rules of logic. In this case, he pointed out the fallacy that the argument 2-3-4-5-6 leads to ~*C* as well as ~*B*, so it cannot be used to support Larry's assertion *C*:

JL: Well, if there's no heaven, how could there be a hell?

LARRY: I mean—ye-eah. Well, let me tell you, it ain't no hell, 'cause this is hell right here, y'know! (This is hell?) Yeah, this is hell right here!

Larry's answer is quick, ingenious, and decisive. The application of the 3-4-5 argument to hell is denied, since hell is here, and therefore conclusion *C* stands. These are not ready-made or preconceived opinions, but new propositions devised to win the logical argument in the game being played. The reader will note the speed and precision of Larry's mental operations. He does not wander, or insert meaningless verbiage. The only repetition is 2, placed before and after 1 in his original statement. It is often said that the nonstandard vernacular is not suited for dealing with abstract or hypothetical questions, but in fact speakers from the BEV community take great delight in exercising their wit and logic on the most improbable and problematical matters. Despite the fact that Larry does not believe in God and has just denied all knowledge of him, John Lewis advances the following hypothetical question:

JL: . . . but, just say that there is a God, what color is he? White or black?

LARRY: Well, if it is a God . . . I wouldn' know what color, I couldn' say,—couldn' nobody say what color he is or really *would* be.

JL: But now, jus' suppose there was a God—

LARRY: Unless'n they say . . .

JL: No, I was jus' sayin' jus' suppose there is a God, would he be white or black?

LARRY: . . . He'd be white, man.

JL: Why?

LARRY: Why? I'll tell you why. 'Cause the average whitey out here got everything, you dig? And the nigger ain't got shit, y'know? Y'unnerstan'? So—um—for— in order for *that* to happen, you know it ain't no black God that's doin' that bullshit.

No one can hear Larry's answer to this question without being convinced that they are in the presence of a skilled speaker with great "verbal presence of mind," who can use the English language expertly for many purposes. Larry's answer to John Lewis is again a complex argument. The formulation is not standard English, but it is clear and effective even for those not familiar with the vernacular. The nearest standard English equivalent might be: "So you know that God isn't black, because if he were, he wouldn't have arranged things like that."

The reader will have noted that this analysis is being carried out in standard English, and the inevitable challenge is: why not write in BEV, then, or in your own nonstandard dialect? The fundamental reason is, of course, one of firmly fixed social conventions. All communities agree that standard English is the proper medium for formal writing and public communication. Furthermore, it seems likely that standard English has an advantage over BEV in explicit analysis of surface forms, which is what we are doing here. We will return to this opposition between explicitness and logical statement in subsequent sections on grammaticality and logic. First, however, it will be helpful to examine standard English in its primary natural setting, as the medium for informal spoken communication of middle-class speakers.

Let us now turn to the second speaker, an upper-middle-class, college-educated black adult (Charles M.) being interviewed by Clarence Robins in our survey of adults in central Harlem.

CR: Do you know of anything that someone can do, to have someone who has passed on visit him in a dream?

CHARLES: Well, I even heard my parents say that there is such a thing as something in dreams, some things like that, and sometimes dreams do come true. I have personally never had a dream come true. I've never dreamt that somebody was dying and they actually died, (Mhm) or that I was going to have ten dollars the next day and somehow I got ten dollars in my pocket. (Mhm). I don't particularly believe in that, I don't think it's true. I do feel, though, that there is such a thing as—ah—witchcraft. I do feel that in certain cultures there is such a thing as witchcraft, or some sort of *science* of witchcraft; I don't think that it's just a matter of believing hard enough that there is such a thing as witchcraft. I do believe that there is such a thing that a person can put himself in a state of *mind* (Mhm), or that—er—something could be given them to intoxicate them in a certain—to a certain frame of mind—that—that could actually be considered witchcraft.

Charles M. is obviously a good speaker who strikes the listener as well-educated, intelligent, and sincere. He is a likeable and attractive person, the kind of person that middle-class listeners rate very high on a scale of job suitability and equally high as a potential friend.[8] His language is more moderate and tempered than Larry's; he makes every effort to qualify his opinions and seems anxious to avoid any misstatements or overstatements. From these qualities emerge the primary characteristic of this passage—its verbosity. Words multiply, some modifying and qualifying, others repeating or padding the main argument. The first half of this extract is a response to the initial question on dreams, basically:

1. Some people say that dreams sometimes come true.
2. I have never had a dream come true.
3. Therefore I don't believe 1.

Some characteristic filler phrases appear here: *such a thing as, some things like that,* and *particularly.* Two examples of dreams given after 2 are afterthoughts that might have been given after 1. Proposition 3 is stated twice for no obvious reason. Nevertheless, this much of Charles M.'s response is well-directed to the point of the question. He then volunteers a statement of his beliefs about witchcraft which shows the difficulty of middle-class speakers who (a) want to express a belief in something but (b) want to show themselves as judicious, rational, and free from superstitions. The basic proposition can be stated simply in five words: *But I believe in witchcraft.* However, the idea is enlarged to exactly 100 words and it is difficult to see what else is being said. In the following quotations, padding which can be removed without change in meaning is shown in parentheses.

1. "I (do) feel, though, that there is (such a thing as) witchcraft." *Feel* seems to be a euphemism for 'believe.'
2. "(I do feel that) in certain cultures (there is such a thing as witchcraft)." This repetition seems designed only to introduce the word *culture,* which lets us know that the speaker knows about anthropology. Does *certain cultures* mean 'not in ours' or 'not in all'?
3. "(or some sort of *science* of witchcraft.)" This addition seems to have no clear meaning at all. What is a "science" of witchcraft as opposed to just plain witchcraft?[9] The main function is to introduce the word *science,* though it seems to have no connection to what follows.
4. "I don't think that it's just (a matter of) believing hard enough that (there is such a thing as) witchcraft." The speaker argues that witchcraft is not merely a belief; there is more to it.

---

[8] For a description of subjective reaction tests which utilize these evaluative dimensions see CRR 3288:4.6.

[9] Several middle-class readers of this passage have suggested that *science* here refers to some form of control as opposed to belief. The science of witchcraft would then be a kind of engineering of mental states. Other interpretations can of course be provided. The fact remains that no such difficulties of interpretation are needed to understand Larry's remarks.

5. "I (do) believe that (there is such a thing that) a person can put himself in a state of mind . . . that (could actually be considered) witchcraft." Is witchcraft as a state of mind different from the state of belief, denied in 4?

6. "or that something could be given them to intoxicate them (to a certain frame of mind) . . ." The third learned word, *intoxicate,* is introduced by this addition. The vacuity of this passage becomes more evident if we remove repetitions, fashionable words and stylistic decorations:

> But I believe in witchcraft.
> I don't think witchcraft is just a belief.

> A person can put himself or be put in a state of mind that is witchcraft.

Without the extra verbiage and the "OK" words like *science, culture,* and *intoxicate,* Charles M. appears as something less than a first-rate thinker. The initial impression of him as a good speaker is simply our long-conditioned reaction to middle-class verbosity. We know that people who use these stylistic devices are educated people, and we are inclined to credit them with saying something intelligent. Our reactions are accurate in one sense. Charles M. is more educated than Larry. But is he more rational, more logical, more intelligent? Is he any better at thinking out a problem to its solution? Does he deal more easily with abstractions? There is no reason to think so. Charles M. succeeds in letting us know that he is educated, but in the end we do not know what he is trying to say, and neither does he.

In the previous section I have attempted to explain the origin of the myth that lower-class black children are nonverbal. The examples just given may help to account for the corresponding myth that middle-class language is in itself better suited for dealing with abstract, logically complex, or hypothetical questions. These examples are intended to have a certain negative force. They are not controlled experiments. On the contrary, this and the preceding section are designed to convince the reader that the controlled experiments that have been offered in evidence are misleading. The only thing that is controlled is the superficial form of the stimulus. All children are asked "What do you think of capital punishment?" or "Tell me everything you can about this." But the speaker's interpretation of these requests and the action he believes is appropriate in response is completely uncontrolled. One can view these test stimuli as requests for information, commands for action, threats of punishment, or meaningless sequences of words. They are probably intended as something altogether different—as requests for display,[10] but in any case the experimenter is normally unaware of the problem of interpretation. The methods of educational psychologists used by Deutsch, Jensen, and Bereiter follow the pattern designed for animal experiments where

---

[10] The concept of a request for verbal display is here drawn from a treatment of the therapeutic interview given by Alan Blum.

motivation is controlled by simple methods as withholding food until a certain weight reduction is reached. With human subjects, it is absurd to believe that identical stimuli are obtained by asking everyone the same question.

Since the crucial intervening variables of interpretation and motivation are uncontrolled, most of the literature on verbal deprivation tells us nothing about the capacities of children. They are only the trappings of science, approaches that substitute the formal procedures of the scientific method for the activity itself. With our present limited grasp of these problems, the best we can do to understand the verbal capacities of children is to study them within the cultural context in which they were developed.

It is not only the black English vernacular which should be studied in this way, but also the language of middle-class children. The explicitness and precision which we hope to gain from copying middle-class forms are often the product of the test situation, and limited to it. For example, it was stated in the first part of this paper that working-class children hear more well-formed sentences than middle-class children. This statement may seem extraordinary in the light of the current belief of many linguists that most people do not speak in well-formed sentences, and that their actual speech production, or performance, is ungrammatical.[11] But those who have worked with any body of natural speech know that this is not the case. Our own studies (Labov 1966) of the grammaticality of everyday speech show that the great majority of utterances in all contexts are complete sentences, and most of the rest can be reduced to grammatical form by a small set of editing rules. The proportions of grammatical sentences vary with class backgrounds and styles. The highest percentage of well-formed sentences are found in casual speech, and working-class speakers use more well-formed sentences than middle-class speakers. The widespread myth that most speech is ungrammatical is no doubt based upon tapes made at learned conferences, where we obtain the maximum number of irreducibly ungrammatical sequences.

It is true that technical and scientific books are written in a style which is markedly middle-class. But unfortunately, we often fail to achieve the explicitness and precision which we look for in such writing, and the speech of many middle-class people departs maximally from this target. All too often, standard English is represented by a style that is simultaneously overparticular and vague. The accumulating flow of words buries rather than strikes the target. It is this verbosity which is most easily taught and most easily learned, so that words take the place of thoughts, and nothing can be found behind them.

---

[11] In several presentations, Chomsky has asserted that the great majority (95 percent) of the sentences which a child hears are ungrammatical. Chomsky (1965:58) presents this notion as one of the arguments in his general statement of the nativist position: "A consideration of the character of the grammar that is acquired, *the degenerate quality and narrowly limited extent of the available data* [my emphasis], the striking uniformity of the resulting grammars, and their independence of intelligence, motivation, and emotional state, over wide ranges of variation, leave little hope that much of the structure of the language can be learned . . ."

When Bernstein (e.g., 1966) describes his elaborated code in general terms, it emerges as a subtle and sophisticated mode of planning utterances, where the speaker is achieving structural variety, taking the other person's knowledge into account, and so on. But when it comes to describing the actual difference between middle-class and working-class speakers (Bernstein 1966), we are presented with a proliferation of *I think,* of the passive, of modals and auxiliaries, of the first-person pronoun, of uncommon words, and so on. But these are the bench marks of hemming and hawing, backing and filling, that are used by Charles M., the devices that so often obscure whatever positive contribution education can make to our use of language. When we have discovered how much of middle-class style is a matter of fashion and how much actually helps us express ideas clearly, we will have done ourselves a great service. We will then be in a position to say what standard grammatical rules must be taught to nonstandard speakers in the early grades.

GRAMMATICALITY

Let us now examine Bereiter's own data on the verbal behavior of the children he dealt with. The expressions *They mine* and *Me got juice* are cited as examples of a language which lacks the means for expressing logical relations, in this case characterized as "a series of badly connected words" (Bereiter, et al. 1966:113). In the case of *They mine,* it is apparent that Bereiter confuses the notions of logic and explicitness. We know that there are many languages of the world which do not have a present copula and which conjoin subject and predicate complement without a verb. Russian, Hungarian, and Arabic may be foreign, but they are not by the same token illogical. In the case of BEV we are not dealing with even this superficial grammatical difference, but rather with a low-level rule which carries contraction one step farther to delete single consonants representing the verbs *is, have,* or *will.* We have yet to find any children who do not sometimes use the full forms of *is* and *will,* even though they may frequently delete them. Our recent studies with black children four to seven years old indicate that they use the full form of the copula more often than preadolescents 10 to 12 years old or the adolescents 14 to 17 years old.[12]

Furthermore, the deletion of the *is* or *are* in BEV is not the result of erratic or illogical behavior; it follows the same regular rules as standard English contraction. The appropriate use of the deletion rule, like the contraction rule, requires a deep and intimate knowledge of English grammar and phonology. Such knowledge is not available for conscious inspection by native speakers. The rules worked out for standard contraction have never appeared in any grammar and are certainly not a part of the conscious knowledge of any standard English speakers. Nevertheless, the adult or child who uses these rules must have formed

---

[12] This is from work on the grammars and comprehension of black children, four to eight years old, carried out by Prof. Jane Torrey of Connecticut College 1972 in extension of the research cited above in Labov, et al. (1968).

at some level of psychological organization, clear concepts of tense marker, verb phrase, rule ordering, sentence embedding, pronoun, and many other grammatical categories which are essential parts of any logical system.

Bereiter's reaction to the sentence *Me got juice* is even more puzzling. If Bereiter believes that *Me got juice* is not a logical expression, it can only be that he interprets the use of the objective pronoun *me* as representing a difference in logical relationship to the verb—that the child is in fact saying 'the juice got him' rather than 'he got the juice'! If on the other hand, the child means 'I got juice' then this sentence shows only that he has not learned the formal rules for the use of the subjective form *I* and oblique form *me*. We have in fact encountered many children who do not have these formal rules in order at the ages of four, five, six, or even eight. It is extremely difficult to construct a minimal pair to show that the difference between *he* and *him* or *she* and *her* carries cognitive meaning. In almost every case, it is the context that tells us who is the agent and who is acted upon. We must then ask: What differences in cognitive, structural orientation are signalled by the fact that the child has not learned this formal rule? In the tests carried out by Jane Torrey it is evident that the children concerned do understand the difference in meaning between *she* and *her* when another person uses the forms; all that remains is that the children themselves do not use the two forms. Our knowledge of the cognitive correlates of grammatical differences is certainly in its infancy; for this is one of very many questions which we simply cannot answer. At the moment we do not know how to construct any kind of experiment which would lead to an answer; we do not even know what type of cognitive correlate we would be looking for.

Bereiter shows even more profound ignorance of the rules of discourse and of syntax when he rejects *In the tree* as an illogical or badly-formed answer to *Where is the squirrel?* Such elliptical answers are of course used by everyone; they show the appropriate deletion of subject and main verb, leaving the locative which is questioned by *WH + there*. The reply *In the tree* demonstrates that the listener has been attentive to and apprehended the syntax of the speaker.[13] Whatever formal structure we wish to write for expressions such as *Yes* or *Home* or *In the tree*, it is obvious that they cannot be interpreted without knowing the structure of the question which preceded them and that they presuppose an understanding of the syntax of the question. Thus if you ask me "Where is the squirrel?" it is necessary for me to understand the processes of *WH*-attachment, *WH*-attraction to the front of the sentence, and flip-flop of auxiliary and subject to produce this sentence from an underlying form which would otherwise have produced *The squirrel is there*. If the child had answered *The tree*, or *Squirrel the tree*, or *The in tree*, we would then assume that he did not understand the syntax of the full form, *The squirrel is in the tree*. Given the data that Bereiter presents, we cannot conclude that the child has no grammar, but only that the investigator does not understand the rules of grammar. It does not necessarily do any harm to use the full form *The squirrel is in the tree*, if

---

[13] The attention to the speaker's syntax required of the listener is analyzed in detail in a series of unpublished lectures by Prof. Harvey Sacks, Department of Sociology, University of California–Irvine.

one wants to make fully explicit the rules of grammar which the child has internalized. Much of logical analysis consists of making explicit just that kind of internalized rule. But it is hard to believe that any good can come from a program which begins with so many misconceptions about the input data. Bereiter and Engelmann believe that in teaching the child to say *The squirrel is in the tree* or *This is a box* and *This is not a box* they are teaching him an entirely new language, whereas in fact they are only teaching him to produce slightly different forms of the language he already has.

LOGIC

For many generations, American school teachers have devoted themselves to correcting a small number of nonstandard English rules to their standard equivalents, under the impression that they were teaching logic. This view has been reinforced and given theoretical justification by the claim that BEV lacks the means for the expression of logical thought.

Let us consider for a moment the possibility that black children do not operate with the same logic that middle-class adults display. This would inevitably mean that sentences of a certain grammatical form would have different truth values for the two types of speakers. One of the most obvious places to look for such a difference is in the handling of the negative, and here we encounter one of the nonstandard items which has been stigmatized as illogical by schoolteachers—the double negative, or as we term it, *negative concord*. A child who says *He don't know nothing* is often said to be making an illogical statement without knowing it. According to the teacher, the child wants to say 'He knows nothing' but puts in an extra negative without realizing it, and so conveys the opposite meaning. 'He does not know nothing', which reduces to 'He knows something.' I need not emphasize that this is an absurd interpretation. If a nonstandard speaker wishes to say 'He does not know *nothing*', he does so by simply placing contrastive stress on both negatives as I have done here (*He don't know nothing*) indicating that they are derived from two underlying negatives in the deep structure. But note that the middle-class speaker does exactly the same thing when he wants to signal the existence of two underlying negatives: *He doesn't know nothing.* In the standard form with one underlying negative (*He doesn't know anything*), the indefinite *anything* contains the same superficial reference to a preceding negative in the surface structure as the nonstandard *nothing* does. In the corresponding positive sentences, the indefinite *something* is used. The dialect difference, like most of the differences between the standard and nonstandard forms, is one of surface form, and has nothing to do with the underlying logic of the sentence.

We can summarize the ways in which the two dialects differ:

	SE	*BEV*
Positive:	He knows something.	He know something.
Negative:	He doesn't know anything.	He don't know nothing.
Double Negative:	He *doesn't* know *nothing.*	He *don't* know *nothing.*

This array makes it plain that the only difference between the two dialects is in superficial form. When a single negative is found in the deep structure, standard English converts *something* to the indefinite *anything*. BEV converts it to *nothing*. When speakers want to signal the presence of two negatives, they do it in the same way. No one would have any difficulty constructing the same table of truth values for both dialects. English is a rare language in its insistence that the negative particle be incorproated in the first indefinite only. The Anglo-Saxon authors of the Peterborough Chronicle were surely not illogical when they wrote *For ne wœren nan martyrs swa pined alse he wœron,* literally. 'For never weren't no martyrs so tortured as these were'. The "logical" forms of current standard English are simply the accepted conventions of our present-day formal style. Russian, Spanish, French, and Hungarian show the same negative concord as nonstandard English, and they are surely not illogical in this. What is termed "logical" in standard English is of course the conventions which are habitual. The distribution of negative concord in English dialects developed in the last chapter can be summarized as follows:

1. In all dialects of English, the negative is attracted to a lone indefinite before the verb: *Nobody knows anything,* not *Anybody doesn't know anything.*
2. In some nonstandard white dialects, the negative also combines optionally with all other indefinites: *Nobody knows nothing, He never took none of them.*
3. In other white nonstandard dialects, the negative may also appear in preverbal position in the same clause: *Nobody doesn't know nothing.*
4. In black English vernacular, negative concord is obligatory to all indefinites within the clause, and it may even be added to preverbal position in the following clauses: *Nobody didn't know he didn't* (meaning, 'Nobody knew he did').

Thus all dialects of English share a categorical rule which attracts the negative to an indefinite subject, and they merely differ in the extent to which the negative particle is also distributed to other indefinites in preverbal position. It would have been impossible for us to arrive at this analysis if we did not know that black speakers are using the same underlying logic as everyone else.

Negative concord is more firmly established in black English vernacular than in other nonstandard dialects. The white nonstandard speaker shows variation in this rule, saying one time *Nobody ever goes there* and the next *Nobody never goes there.* Core speakers of BEV consistently use the latter form. In repetition tests which we conducted with black adolescent boys (CRR 3288: section 3.9), standard forms were repeated with negative concord. Consider again three trials by two 13-year-olds, Boot and David, Thunderbirds:

Model by interviewer: Nobody ever sat at any of those desks, anyhow.
BOOT:
  1. Nobody never sa—No [whitey] never sat at any o' tho' dess, anyhow.
  2. Nobody never sat any any o' tho' dess, anyhow.
  3. Nobody as ever sat at no desses, anyhow.

DAVID:
1. Nobody ever sat in-in-in-in- none o'—say it again?
2. Nobody never sat in none o' tho' desses anyhow.
3. Nobody—aww! Nobody never ex—Dawg!

It can certainly be said that Boot and David fail the test; they have not repeated the sentence back correctly—that is, word for word. But have they failed because they could not grasp the meaning of the sentence? The situation is in fact just the opposite: they failed because they perceived only the meaning and not the superficial form. Boot and David are typical of many speakers who do not perceive the surface details of the utterance so much as the underlying semantic structure, which they unhesitatingly translate into the vernacular form. Thus they have the asymmetrical system we saw in responses to embedded questions.

MODEL: I asked Alvin if he knows how to play basketball.
BOOT: I ax Alvin do he know how to play basketball.
MONEY: I ax Alvin if—do he know how to play basketball.

Here the difference between the words used in the model sentence and in the repetition is striking. Again, there is a failure to pass the test. But it is also true that these boys understand the standard sentence, and translate it with extraordinary speed into the BEV form—which is here the regular southern colloquial form. This form retains the inverted order to signal the underlying meaning of the question, instead of the complementizer *if* or *whether* which standard English uses for this purpose. Thus Boot and Money perceive the deep structure of the model sentence in the diagram below.

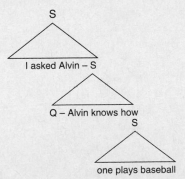

The complementizers *if* or *whether* are not required to express this underlying meaning: they are merely two of the formal options which one dialect selects to signal the embedded question. The colloquial southern form utilizes a different device—preserving the order of the direct question. To say that this dialect lacks the means for logical expression is to confuse logic with surface detail.

To pass the repetition test, Boot and the others have to learn to listen to surface detail. They do not need a new logic; they need practice in paying attention to the explicit form of an utterance rather than its meaning. Careful attention to surface features is a temporary skill needed for language learning—and neglected thereafter by competent speakers. Nothing more than this is involved in the language training in the Bereiter and Engelmann program, or in most methods of "teaching English." There is of course nothing wrong with learning to be explicit—as we have seen, that is one of the main advantages of standard English at its best—but it is important that we recognize what is actually taking place, and what teachers are in fact trying to do.

I doubt if we can teach people to be logical, though we can teach them to recognize the logic that they use. Piaget has shown us that in middle-class children logic develops much more slowly than grammar, and that we cannot expect four-year-olds to have mastered the conservation of quantity, let alone syllogistic reasoning. The problems working-class children may have in handling logical operations are not to be blamed on the structure of their language. There is nothing in the vernacular which will interfere with the development of logical thought, for the logic of standard English cannot be distinguished from the logic of any other dialect of English by any test that we can find.

WHAT'S WRONG WITH BEING WRONG?

If there is a failure of logic involved here, it is surely in the approach of the verbal deprivation theorists, rather than in the mental abilities of the children concerned. We can isolate six distinct steps in the reasoning which has led to positions such as those of Deutsch or Bereiter and Engelmann:

1. The lower-class child's verbal response to a formal and threatening situation is used to demonstrate his lack of verbal capacity, or verbal deficit.
2. This verbal deficit is declared to be a major cause of the lower-class child's poor performance in school.
3. Since middle-class children do better in school, middle-class speech habits are seen to be necessary for learning.
4. Class and ethnic differences in grammatical form are equated with differences in the capacity for logical analysis.
5. Teaching the child to mimic certain formal speech patterns used by middle-class teachers is seen as teaching him to think logically.
6. Children who learn these formal speech patterns are then said to be thinking logically and it is predicted that they will do much better in reading and arithmetic in the years to follow.

In the preceding sections of this paper I have tried to show that the above propositions are wrong, concentrating on 1, 4, and 5. Proposition 3 is the primary logical fallacy which illicitly identifies a form of speech as the cause of middle-class achievement in school. Proposition 6 is the one which is most easily shown to be wrong in fact, as we will note below.

However, it is not too naive to ask: What is wrong with being wrong? There is no competing educational theory which is being dismantled by this program, and there does not seem to be any great harm in having children repeat "This is not a box" for twenty minutes a day. We have already conceded that BEV children need help in analyzing language into its surface components and in being more explicit. But there are serious and damaging consequences of the verbal deprivation theory which may be considered under two headings: theoretical bias and consequences of failure.

Theoretical Bias

It is widely recognized that the teacher's attitude toward the child is an important factor in his success or failure. The work of Rosenthal and Jacobson (1968) on self-fulfilling prophecies shows that the progress of children in the early grades can be dramatically affected by a single random labeling of certain children as "intellectual bloomers." When the everyday language of black children is stigmatized as "not a language at all" and "not possessing the means for logical thought," the effect of such a labeling is repeated many times during each day of the school year. Every time that a child uses a form of BEV without the copula or with negative concord, he will be labeling himself for the teacher's benefit as "illogical," as a "nonconceptual thinker." Bereiter and Engelmann, Deutsch, and Jensen are giving teachers a ready-made, theoretical basis for the prejudice they already feel against the lower-class black child and his language (for example, see Williams 1970). When teachers hear him say *I don't want none* or *They mine,* they will be hearing through the bias provided by the verbal deprivation theory—not an English dialect different from theirs, but the "primitive mentality of the savage mind."

But what if the teacher succeeds in training the child to use the new language consistently? The verbal deprivation theory holds that this will lead to a whole chain of successes in school and that the child will be drawn away from the vernacular culture into the middle-class world. Undoubtedly this will happen with a few isolated individuals, just as it happens for a few children in every school system today. But we are concerned not with the few but the many, and for the majority of black children the distance between them and the school is bound to widen under this approach.

Proponents of the deficit theory have a strange view of social organization outside of the classroom. They see the attraction of the peer group as a substitute for success and gratification normally provided by the school. For example, Whiteman and Deutsch (1968:86–87) introduce their account of the deprivation hypothesis with an eyewitness account of a child who accidentally dropped his school notebook into a puddle of water and walked away without picking it up: "A policeman who had been standing nearby walked over to the puddle and stared at the notebook with some degree of disbelief." The child's alienation from school is explained as the result of his coming to school without the "verbal, conceptual, attentional, and learning skills requisite to school success." The authors see the child as "suffering from feelings of inferiority because he is failing; he withdraws or becomes hostile, finding gratification elsewhere, such as in his peer group."

To view the peer group as a mere substitute for school shows an extraordinary lack of knowledge of adolescent culture. In our studies in south-central

Harlem we have seen the reverse situation—the children who are rejected by the peer group are most likely to succeed in school. Although in middle-class suburban areas, many children do fail in school because of their personal deficiencies, in ghetto areas it is the healthy, vigorous, popular child with normal intelligence who cannot read and fails all along the line. It is not necessary to document here the influence of the peer group upon the behavior of youth in our society, but we may note that somewhere between the time that children first learn to talk and puberty, their language is restructured to fit the rules used by their peer group. From a linguistic viewpoint, the peer group is certainly a more powerful influence than the family (e.g., Gans 1962). Less directly, the pressures of peer-group activity are also felt within the school. Many children, particularly those who are not doing well in school, show a sudden sharp downward turn in the fourth and fifth grades, and children in the ghetto schools are no exception. It is at the same age, at nine or ten years old, that the influence of the vernacular peer group becomes predominant (see Wilmott 1966). Instead of dealing with isolated individuals, the school is then dealing with children who are integrated into groups of their own, with rewards and value systems which oppose those of the school. Those who know the sociolinguistic situation cannot doubt that reaction against the Bereiter-Engelmann approach in later years will be even more violent on the part of the students involved, and their rejection of the school system will be even more categorical.

The essential fallacy of the verbal deprivation theory lies in tracing the educational failure of the child to his personal deficiencies. At present, these deficiencies are said to be caused by his home environment. It is traditional to explain a child's failure in school by his inadequacy. But when failure reaches such massive proportions, it seems to us necessary to look at the social and cultural obstacles to learning and the inability of the school to adjust to the social situation. Operation Head Start is designed to repair the child, rather than the school; to the extent that it is based upon this inverted logic, it is bound to fail.

Consequences of Failure

The second area in which the verbal deprivation theory is doing serious harm to our educational system is in the consequences of this failure and the reaction to it. As failures are reported of Operation Head Start, the interpretations which we receive will be from the same educational psychologists who designed this program. The fault will be found not in the data, the theory, nor in the methods used, but rather in the children who have failed to respond to the opportunities offered to them. When black children fail to show the significant advance which the deprivation theory predicts, it will be taken as further proof of the profound gulf which separates their mental processes from those of "civilized," middle-class mankind.

A sense of the "failure" of Head Start is already in the air. Some prominent figures in the program have reacted to this situation by saying that intervention did not take place early enough. Caldwell (1967:16) notes that:

. . . the research literature of the last decade dealing with social-class differences has made abundantly clear that all parents are not qualified to provide even the basic essentials of physical and psychological care to their children.

The deficit theory now begins to focus on the "long-standing patterns of parental deficit" which fill the literature. "There is, perhaps unfortunately," writes Caldwell (1967:17), "no literacy test for motherhood." Failing such eugenic measures, she has proposed "educationally oriented day care for culturally deprived children between six months and three years of age." The children are returned home each evening to "maintain primary emotional relationships with their own families," but during the day they are removed to "hopefully prevent the deceleration in rate of development which seems to occur in many deprived children around the age of two to three years."

There are others who feel that even the best of the intervention programs, such as those of Bereiter and Engelmann, will not help the black child no matter when such programs are applied—that we are faced once again with the "inevitable hypothesis" of the genetic inferiority of the black people. Many readers of this chapter may be familiar with the paper of Arthur Jensen in the *Harvard Educational Review* (1969), which received immediate and widespread publicity. Jensen (p. 3) begins with the following quotation from the United States Commission on Civil Rights as evidence of the failure of compensatory education:

> The fact remains, however, that none of the programs appear to have raised significantly the achievement of participating pupils, as a group, within the period evaluated by the Commission. (U.S. Commission on Civil Rights 1967, p. 138)

Jensen believes that the verbal-deprivation theorists with whom he had been associated—Deutsch, Whiteman, Katz, Bereiter—have been given every opportunity to prove their case, and have failed. This opinion is part of the argument which leads him to the overall conclusion (p. 82) that "the preponderance of the evidence is . . . less consistent with a strictly environmental hypothesis than with the genetic hypothesis." In other words, racism—the belief in the genetic inferiority of blacks—is the most correct view in the light of the present evidence.

Jensen argues that the middle-class white population is differentiated from the working-class white and black population in the ability for "cognitive or conceptual learning," which Jensen calls Level II intelligence as against mere "associated learning" or Level I intelligence.

> . . . certain neural structures must also be available for Level II abilities to develop, and these are conceived of as being different from the neural structures underlying Level I. The genetic factors involved in each of these types of ability are presumed to have become differentially distributed in the population as a function of social class, since Level II has been most important for scholastic performance under the traditional methods of instruction. (Jensen 1968:114)

Jensen found, for example, that one group of middle-class children were helped by their concept-forming ability to recall 20 familiar objects that could be classified into four categories: animals, furniture, clothing, or foods. Lower-class black children did just as well as middle-class children with a miscellaneous set, but showed no improvement with objects that could be so categorized.

The research of the educational psychologists cited here is presented by them in formal and objective style and is widely received as impartial scientific evidence. Jensen's paper has been reported by Joseph Alsop and William F. Buckley, Jr. (*New York Post,* March 20, 1969) as "massive, apparently authoritative . . ." It is not my intention to examine these materials in detail, but it is important to realize that we are dealing with special pleading by those who have a strong personal commitment. Jensen is concerned with class differences in cognitive style and verbal learning. His earlier papers incorporated the cultural deprivation theory which he now rejects as a basic explanation.[14] Jensen (1968:167) classified the black children who fail in school as "slow learners" and "mentally retarded" and urged that we find out how much their retardation is due to environmental factors and how much is due to "more basic biological factors." His conviction that the problem must be located in the child leads him to accept and reprint some truly extraordinary data. To support the genetic hypothesis Jensen (1969:83) cites the following percentage estimates by Heber (1968) of the racial distribution of mental retardation (based upon IQs below 75) in the general population:[15]

Socioeconomic Status	*Percent of Whites*	*Percent of Blacks*
1 (highest)	0.5	3.1
2	0.8	14.5
3	2.1	22.8
4	3.1	37.8
5 (lowest)	7.8	42.9

These estimates, that almost half of lower-class black children are mentally retarded, could be accepted only by someone who has no knowledge of the children or the community. If he had wished to, Jensen could easily have checked

---

[14] In Deutsch et al. (1968), Jensen expounds the verbal deprivation theory in considerable detail, for example (p. 119): "During this 'labeling' period . . . some very important social-class differences may exert their effects on verbal learning. Lower-class parents engage in relatively little of this naming or 'labeling' play with their children . . . That words are discrete labels for things seems to be better known by the middle-class child entering first grade than by the lower-class child. Much of this knowledge is gained in the parent-child interaction, as when the parent looks at a picture book with the child . . . "

[15] Heber's (esp. 1968) studies of 88 black mothers in Milwaukee are cited frequently throughout Jensen's paper. The estimates in this table are not given in relation to a particular Milwaukee sample, but for the general United States population. Heber's study was specifically designed to cover an area of Milwaukee which was known to contain a large concentration of retarded children, black and white, and he has stated that his findings were "grossly misinterpreted" by Jensen (*Milwaukee Sentinel,* June 11, 1969).

this against the records of any school in any urban ghetto area. Taking IQ tests at their face value, there is no correspondence between these figures and the communities we know. For example, among 75 boys we worked with in central Harlem who would fall into status categories 4 or 5 above, there were only three with IQs below 75. One spoke very little English; one could barely see; the third was emotionally disturbed. When the second was retested, he scored 91, and the third retested at 87.[16] There are of course hundreds of realistic reports available to Jensen. He simply selected one which would strengthen his case for the genetic inferiority of black children.

The frequent use of tables and statistics by educational psychologists serves to give outside readers the impression that this field is a science and that the opinions of the authors should be given the same attention and respect that we give to the conclusions of physicists or chemists. But careful examination of the input data will often show that there is no direct relationship between the conclusions and the evidence (in Jensen's case between I.Q. Tests in a specially selected district of Milwaukee and intelligence of lower-class black children). Furthermore, the operations performed upon the data frequently carry us very far from the common-sense experience which is our only safeguard against conclusions heavily weighted by the author's theory. As another example, we may take some of the evidence presented by Whiteman and Deutsch for the cultural deprivation hypothesis. The core of Deutsch's environmental explanation of poor performance in school is the Deprivation Index, a numerical scale based on six dichotomized variables. One variable is "the educational aspirational level of the parent for the child." Most people would agree that a parent who did not care if a child finished high-school would be a disadvantageous factor in the child's educational career. In dichotomizing this variable Deutsch was faced with the fact that the educational aspiration of black parents is in fact very high, higher than for the white population, as he shows in other papers.[17] In order to fit this data into the Deprivation Index work, he therefore set the cutting point for the deprived group as "college or less" (see Whiteman and Deutsch 1968:100). Thus if a black child's father says that he wants his son to go all the way through college, the child will fall into the "deprived" class on this variable. In order to

---

[16] The IQ scores given here are from group rather than individual tests and must therefore not be weighed heavily; the scores are from the Pintner-Cunningham test, usually given the first grade in New York City schools in the 1950's.

[17] In Table 15.1 in Deutsch and associates (1967:312), section C shows that some degree of college training was desired by 96, 97, and 100 percent of black parents in class levels I, II, and III, respectively. The corresponding figures for whites were 79, 95, and 97 percent. In an earlier version of this chapter, this discussion could be interpreted as implying that Whiteman and Deutsch had used data in the same way as Jensen: to rate the black group as low as possible. As they point out (pers. comm.), the inclusion of this item in the Deprivation Index had the opposite effect, and it could easily have been omitted if that had been their intention. They also argue that they had sound statistical grounds for dichotomizing as they did. The criticism which I intended to make is that there is something drastically wrong with operations which produce definitions of deprivation such as the one cited here. It should of course be noted that Whiteman and Deutsch have strongly opposed Jensen's genetic hypothesis and vigorously criticized his logic and data.

receive the two points given to the "less deprived" on the index, it would be necessary for the child's parent to insist on graduate school or medical school! This decision is not discussed by the author; it simply stands as a *fait accompli* in the tables. Readers of this literature who are not committed to one point of view would be wise to look as carefully as possible at the original data which lies behind each statement and check the conclusions against their own knowledge of the people and community being described.

No one can doubt that the reported inadequacy of Operation Head Start and of the verbal deprivation hypothesis has now become a crucial issue in our society.[18] The controversy which arose over Jensen's article typically assumed that programs such as Bereiter and Engelmann's have tested and measured the verbal capacity of the ghetto child. The cultural sociolinguistic obstacles to this intervention program are not considered, and the argument proceeds upon the data provided by the large, friendly interviewers whom we have seen at work in the extracts given above.

THE LINGUISTIC VIEW

Linguists are in an excellent position to demonstrate the fallacies of the verbal deprivation theory. All linguists agree that nonstandard dialects are highly structured systems. They do not see these dialects as accumulations of errors caused by the failure of their speakers to master standard English. When linguists hear black children saying *He crazy* or *Her my friend,* they do not hear a primitive language. Nor do they believe that the speech of working-class people is merely a form of emotional expression, incapable of expressing logical thought.

All linguists who work with BEV recognize that it is a separate system, closely related to standard English but set apart from the surrounding white dialects by a number of persistent and systematic differences. Differences in analysis by various linguists in recent years are the inevitable products of differing theoretical approaches and perspectives as we explore these dialect patterns by different routes—differences which are rapidly diminishing as we exchange our findings. For example, Stewart (1970) differs with me on how deeply the invariant *be* of *She be always messin' around* is integrated into the semantics of the copula system with *am, is, are,* and so on. The position and meaning of *have. . . . ed* in BEV is very unclear, and there are a variety of positions on this point. But the grammatical features involved are not the fundamental predicators of the logical system. They are optional ways of contrasting, foregrounding, emphasizing, or

---

[18] The negative report of the Westinghouse Learning Corporation and Ohio University on Operation Head Start was published in the *New York Times* (April 13, 1969). The evidence of the failure of the program is accepted by many, and it seems likely that the report's discouraging conclusions will be used by conservative Congressmen as a weapon against any kind of expenditure for disadvantaged children, especially black children. The two hypotheses mentioned to account for this failure are that the impact of Head Start is lost through poor teaching later on, and more recently, that poor children have been so badly damaged in infancy by their lower-class environment

deleting elements of the underlying sentence. There are a few semantic features of BEV grammar which may be unique to this system. But the semantic features we are talking about here are items such as "habitual," "general," "intensive." These linguistic markers are essentially *points of view*—different ways of looking at the same events, and they do not determine the truth values of propositions upon which all speakers of English agree.

The great majority of the differences between BEV and standard English do not even represent such subtle semantic features as those, but rather extensions and restrictions of certain formal rules and different choices of redundant elements. For example, standard English uses two signals to express the progressive, *be* and *-ing,* while BEV often drops the former. Standard English signals the third person in the present by the subject noun phrase and by a third singular *-s;* BEV uses redundant negative elements in negative concord, in possessives like *mines,* uses *or either* where standard English uses a simple *or,* and so on.

When linguists say that BEV is a system, we mean that it differs from other dialects in regular and rule-governed ways, so that it has equivalent ways of expressing the same logical content. When we say that it is a separate subsystem, we mean that there are compensating sets of rules which combine in different ways to preserve the distinctions found in other dialects. Thus as noted above BEV does not use the *if* or *whether* complementizer in embedded questions, but the meaning is preserved by the formal device of reversing the order of subject and auxiliary. Linguists therefore speak with a single voice in condemning Bereiter's view that the vernacular can be disregarded. The exact nature and relative importance of the structural differences between BEV and standard English are not in question here. It is agreed that the teacher must approach the teaching of the standard through a knowledge of the child's own system. The methods used in teaching English as a foreign language are recommended, not to declare that BEV is a foreign language, but to underline the importance of studying the native dialect as a coherent system for communication. This is in fact the method that should be applied in any English class.

Linguists are also in an excellent position to assess Jensen's claim that the middle-class white population is superior to the working-class and black populations in the distribution of Level II, or conceptual, intelligence. The notion that large numbers of children have no capacity for conceptual thinking would inevitably mean that they speak a primitive language, for even the simplest linguistic rules we discussed above involve conceptual operations more complex than those used in the experiment Jensen cites. Let us consider what is involved in the use of the general English rule that incorporates the negative with the first indefinite. To learn and use the rule we worked out, one must first identify the class of indefinites involved—*any, one, ever,* which are formally quite diverse. How is this done? These indefinites share a number of common properties which can be expressed as the concepts 'indefinite,' 'hypothetical,' and 'nonpartitive.' One might argue that these indefinites are learned as a simple list, by association learning. But this is only one of the many syntactic rules involving indefinites—rules known to every speaker of English, which could not be learned except by an understanding of their common, abstract properties.

What are we then to make of Jensen's contention that Level I thinkers cannot make use of the concept "animal" to group together a miscellaneous set of toy animals? It is one thing to say that someone is not in the habit of using a certain skill. But to say that his failure to use it is genetically determined implies dramatic consequences for other forms of behavior, which are not found in experience. The knowledge of what people must do in order to learn language makes Jensen's theories seem more and more distant from the realities of human behavior. Like Bereiter and Engelmann, Jensen is handicapped by his ignorance of the most basic facts about human language and the people who speak it.

There is no reason to believe that any nonstandard vernacular is in itself an obstacle to learning. The chief problem is ignorance of language on the part of all concerned. Our job as linguists is to remedy this ignorance; but Bereiter and Engelmann want to reinforce it and justify it. Teachers are now being told to ignore the language of black children as unworthy of attention and useless for learning. They are being taught to hear every natural utterance of the child as evidence of his mental inferiority. As linguists we are unanimous in condemning this view as bad observation, bad theory, and bad practice.

That educational psychology should be strongly influenced by a theory so false to the facts of language is unfortunate; but that children should be the victims of this ignorance is intolerable. It may seem that the fallacies of the verbal deprivation theory are so obvious that they are hardly worth exposing. I have tried to show that such exposure is an important job for us to undertake. If linguists can contribute some of their available knowledge and energy toward this end, we will have done a great deal to justify the support that society has given to basic research in our field.

REFERENCES

Bereiter, Carl, et al. 1966. An academically oriented pre-school for culturally deprived children. In *Pre-school education today,* ed. Fred M. Hechinger. New York: Doubleday.

Bereiter, Carl, and Engelmann, Siegfried. 1966. *Teaching disadvantaged children in the pre-school.* Englewood Cliffs, N.J.: Prentice-Hall.

Bernstein, Basil. 1966. Elaborated and restricted codes: their social origins and some consequences. In *The ethnography of communication,* eds. J. Gumperz and D. Hymes. Special publication. *American Anthropologist* 66 (no. 6, part 2).

Caldwell, Bettye M. 1967. What is the optimal learning environment for the young child? *Am. J. of Orthopsychiatry* 37:8–21.

Chomsky, Noam. 1965. *Aspects of the theory of syntax.* Cambridge, Mass.: MIT Press.

Coleman, J. S., et al. 1966. *Equality of educational opportunity.* Washington, D.C.: U.S. Government Printing Office.

Deutsch, Martin, and associates. 1967. *The disadvantaged child.* New York: Basic Books.

Deutsch, Martin; Katz, Irwin; and Jensen, Arthur. 1968. eds. *Social class, race, and psychological development.* New York: Holt, Rinehart and Winston.

Gans, Herbert. 1962. *The urban villagers.* New York: The Free Press.

Heber, R.; Dever, R.; and Conry, J. 1968. The influence of environmental and genetic variables on intellectual development. In *Behavioral research in mental retardation,* eds. J. H. Prehm, L. A. Hamerlynck, and J. E. Crossom. Eugene, Oregon: University of Oregon Press.

Jensen, Arthur. 1968. How much can we boost IQ and scholastic achievement? *Harvard Educational Review:* no. 39.

Labov, William. 1966. The linguistic variable as a structural unit. *Washington Linguistics Review* 3:4–22.

Labov, William; Cohen, Paul; Robins, Clarence; and Lewis, John. 1968. *A study of the non-standard English of Negro and Puerto Rican speakers in New York City.* Report on Co-operative Research Project 3288. New York: Columbia University.

Rosenthal, R., and Jacobson, Lenore. 1968. *Pygmalion in the classroom.* New York: Holt, Rinehart and Winston.

Stewart, William. 1970. Toward a history of Negro dialect. In *Language and poverty,* ed. Frederick Williams. Chicago: Markham.

Whiteman, Martin, and Deutsch, Martin. 1968. Social disadvantage as related to intellective and language development. In *Social class, race, and psychological development,* eds. Deutsch, Katz, and Jensen. New York: Holt, Rinehart and Winston.

Williams, Frederick. 1970. Language, attitude, and social change. In *Language and poverty,* ed. F. Williams. Chicago: Markham.

Wilmott, Peter. 1966. *Adolescent boys of East London.* London: Routledge and Kegan Paul.

THEORY AND IMPLICATIONS

1. What other manifestations of the "deficit model" have you seen applied to nonstandard English speakers? Recount your own experiences.

2. How does this essay confirm the need for a strong linguistics background for all teachers?

3. What were your own initial reactions to Charles's responses? Did you find yourself approving certain features? Why?

4. What features of Leroy's language did you react to negatively? What attributions about him did you make? Why?

5. Does this article make "logic" seem culturally based? Explain.

6. If manifestations of logic are relative to different cultures, how do teachers ever suspend their ethnocentric views so they can appreciate the logic of other cultures?

7. What kinds of social conditions in the classroom put dialect speakers at a disadvantage? How might teachers address these conditions?

PROFESSIONAL CONCERNS

1. Analyze a student essay or tape-recorded verbal exchange from a BE student for its underlying logic. Explain how a teacher might mistakenly apply a "deficit model" to the student. Look for elements of both lower-class and middle-class style. What do you think is the most productive way to assess this student's verbality?

2. Analyze a student essay or tape-recorded verbal exchange from a middle-class student. Analyze its underlying logic. Determine what features make this style more "socially acceptable." What are its weaknesses?

3. Studies of cultural differences in logic, called studies in contrastive rhetoric, examine the different strategies of different cultures for developing ideas. Examine some of this research initiated by Robert Kaplan in 1966. What insights does it offer? Does it suffer from the same drawbacks as contrastive analysis, which looks only at differences in grammar to predict error?

"The Forms of Things Unknown": Black Modes of Discourse*

GENEVA SMITHERMAN

Smitherman's "The Forms of Things Unknown," from her book Talkin and Testifyin, *extends contrastive concerns to discourse. The four discourse modes explained and illustrated by Smitherman reveal the distinctive genres that African Americans draw on as part of their folklore tradition. The richness and versatility of these traditions confirm the verbality of African Americans and contradict the "deficit theory" of BE depicted in Labov's essay. Teachers aware of such traditions can further appreciate the forms of discourse familiar to their African-American students and allow them to draw on and extend that expertise.*

These discourse modes, expressed in Africanized English or BE, have been ignored largely because of the dialect in which they are uttered and the migratory status of the people uttering them. Despite this lack of attention, these modes reveal highly sophisticated verbal strategies and rhetorical devices, and a consistent worldview expressing the hopes and desires of a people for things unknown. Smitherman helps us to see how grammar, discourse, and culture intertwine, thereby giving us an appreciation for similar connections in other nonstandard dialect groups.

Dr. John Mason Brewer was one of the two men most responsible for recording the Black English folk expression of African-Americans. The other was Richard Wright, 1908–1960. While Brewer, the folklore scholar, collected and documented the "authentic Negro folklore tradition," Wright, the prolific, self-taught writer and father of all modern Black American literature, used this tradition as literary source material and incorporated it extensively in his novels and short stories.

> These two main streams of Negro expression [are] the Narcissistic level and the Forms of Things Unknown . . . This division in Negro life can be described in psychological as well as in class terms. It can be said there were Negroes who naively accepted what their lives were, lived more or less unthinkingly in their environment, mean as they found it,

---

and sought escape either in religion, migration, alcohol, or in what I've called a sensualization of their sufferings in the form of jazz and blues and folk and work songs.

Then there were those who hoped and felt that they would ultimately be accepted in their native land as free men, and they put forth their claims in a language that their nation had given them. These latter were more or less always middle class in their ideology. But it was among the migratory Negro workers that one found, rejected and ignorant though they were, strangely positive manifestations of expression, original contributions in terms of form and content . . .

. . . I feel personally identified with the migrant Negro, his folk songs, his ditties, his wild tales of bad men; . . . my own life was forged in the depths in which they live . . . Numerically, this formless folk utterance [the Forms of Things Unknown] accounts for the great majority of the Negro people in the United States . . .

Speaking thus before European audiences in the years 1950–1955, Richard Wright was attempting to account for the two broad divisions of Black American experience in these United States, the one being that experience of the small number of literate, well-educated blacks, the other being the folk-oral tradition of the black masses. The black experience of the former has typically been expressed in Americanized English, that of the latter group in Africanized English. We must thus look to the "original contributions" of the folk—their folklore, folk utterances, songs, and tales of folk expression—to complete our definition and understanding of Black English. Comprising the formulaic structure of these contributions are verbal strategies, rhetorical devices, and folk expressive rituals which derive from a mutually understood notion of modes of discourse, which in turn is part of the "rich inheritance" of the African background acclaimed by Brewer. Following Richard Wright, I have chosen to call these black discourse modes the "Forms of Things Unknown."

We may classify black modes of discourse into the following broad categories: call-response; signification (of which the Dozens is a strictly secular, "streetified" example); tonal semantics; narrative sequencing (of which the Toasts is a strictly secular, "streetified" example). Before we get into the nitty-gritty of analyzing each of these communicative modalities, two important points must be reaffirmed. First, recall the unity of the sacred and secular in the Black American oral tradition and in the traditional African world view. Each discourse mode is manifested in Black American culture on a sacred-secular continuum. Second, recall that the traditional African world view emphasizes the synthesis of dualities to achieve balance and harmony in the universe and in the community of men and women. Thus, while the rituals of black discourse have an overall formulaic structure, individuals are challenged to do what they can within the traditional mold. Centuries-old group norms are balanced by individualized, improvisational emphases. By virtue of unique contributions to the group-approved communicative structure, the individual can actualize his or her sense of self within the confines of the group.

§

The African-derived communication process of call-response may be briefly defined as follows: spontaneous verbal and nonverbal interaction between speaker and listener in which all of the speaker's statements ("calls") are punctuated by expressions ("responses") from the listener. In the traditional black church, call-response is often referred to as the congregation's way of "talking back" to the preacher, the most well-known example of which is "A-men." (However, traditional black church members also call and respond between themselves as well as the preacher, and church musicians frequently will get a Thang goin between themselves and their instruments.) Like most other Africanisms in Black American life, call-response has been most carefully preserved in the church. But it is a basic organizing principle of Black American culture generally, for it enables traditional black folk to achieve the unified state of balance or harmony which is fundamental to the traditional African world view. Since that world view does not dichotomize life into sacred and secular realms, you can find call-responses both in the church and on the street. . . .

Now, obviously, some calls and responses are more strictly limited to either church or street; similarly the subject matter of the discourse is different in sacred and secular contexts. But we are here talking about the *process* of communication, not the substance: the communication vehicle or channel is the same, and sometimes the underlying message is also, though the subject matter differs. Below is a summary list of various responses you might hear and observe in black discourse. (Asterisks indicate those which are strictly secular; the others are found in both sacred and secular contexts.)

Verbal

*Dig it!

*No shit! (also bullshit,
  ain't that some shit)

Amen!

Say so!

Tell it!

Speak on it!

Yeah! (also Naw! Aw!)

Yessuh!

*Rap on!

Well, all right!

Un-huh

*Who you humping!

*Oh, you mean nigger!
  (said with affinity and approval)

Really!

You on the case, now!

Go head!

Look out!

Lord, ha' mercy!

Do Jesus!

I hear you!

Well, Iah be . . .

Mercy!

*I swear!

*Get down man! (baby, girl)

*Get back!

Shonuff!

*Do it, baby! (man, girl)

Teach! Teach! (however, "Preach"
  is strictly sacred)

*Hip me!

*You lyin! (said only semiseriously)

Tell the truth!

Verbal comments made to people near you, hollering and whooping at the same time the speaker is talking, to affirm approval of what the speaker has said, are not regarded as discourteous behavior.

Nonverbal

*giving skin

waving hand in the air

stomping feet

hitting back of chair (wall, etc.)

*black power sign (raised, clenched fist)

rolling eyes

pursing lips

sucking teeth

laughing (simply to indicate a strong point has been made, not necessarily in response to joke or humorous statement)

looking from side to side

moving around (sometimes in a dance-like fashion, sometimes when seated, turning to person next to you or in back of you)

nodding head (also shaking head)

clapping hands

jumping up and down (out of your seat)

If you observe black speakers interacting, whether in casual conversation or in a "speech-giving" set, you can witness certain specific functions that these various responses serve. We can thus categorize the responses according to the purpose accomplished or the effect achieved:

CO-SIGNING [*affirming, agreeing with speaker*]: Amen; Well; Yes; Un-huh; I hear you; Dig that; Praise the Lord

ENCOURAGING [*urging speaker to continue in direction he has started*]: Take yo time; Come on up; You on the case; Watch yoself; Speak on it; What?!; Aw, naw! (meaning really Aw, yes!)

REPETITION [*using same words speaker has said*]: Speaker says: "Some folk ain't got no mother wit." Response is: "No mother wit! That's right, no mother wit!"

COMPLETER [*completing speaker's statement, sometimes in response to "request" from speaker, sometimes in spontaneous talking with speaker*]: Speaker says: "And, what did the Lord say about His time, what did He say, church?" Response: "Yassuh, he may not come when you want Him, but He's right on time." Preacher: "And Job said, of my appointed time, uhm gon wait [*congregation spontaneously joins in here*] till my change shall come."

ON T [*an extremely powerful co-signing response, acknowledging that something the speaker has just said is dead on time, that is, "psychological" time*]: Shonuff; Yassuh!; Ooooo-weeeee!; Gon wit yo bad self! (Also waving hand in air, giving five; jumping up; hollering; clapping hands.)

Some calls from the speaker might elicit a co-signing response from one person, an encouraging type of response from someone else, a completer response from still another listener. Whatever is being said at a particular moment will affect different listeners in different ways. The dynamics of black communication allow for individual variation within the structure. Thus all responses are "correct"; the only "incorrect" thing you can do is *not respond* at all.

To get a further understanding of call-response in Black English, we should look more closely at the relationship between this communication dynamic and the traditional African world view, as well as its relationship to black music. Now, y'all got to follow me cause it gon git deep right long in here, you dig?

Recall that the traditional African world view conceptualizes a cosmos which is an interacting, interdependent, balanced force field. The community of men and women, the organization of society itself, is thus based on this assumption. Consequently, communication takes on an interactive, interdependent nature. As Oliver Jackson succinctly states it:

> The moral sanctity of . . . life [in African society] derived from the idea that all is spiritual and that the Supreme Power embodies the totality of the cosmos in one spiritual unity . . . the African continuum is essentially harmonious. Men, in building their societies, endeavor to reproduce this 'divine or cosmic harmony.' This is the basis of all ethical and moral behavior in community life. This human microcosm must reaffirm the harmonious modality of the cosmic macrocosm.

Thus, call-response seeks to synthesize speakers and listeners in a unified movement. It permeates Black English communication and reaffirms the "modality of the cosmic macrocosm." . . .

§

Signification, our second mode of discourse, refers to the verbal art of insult in which a speaker humorously puts down, talks about, needles—that is, signifies on—the listener. Sometimes signifyin (also siggin) is done to make a point, sometimes it's just for fun. This type of folk expression in the oral tradition has the status of a customary ritual that's accepted at face value. That is to say, nobody who's signified on is supposed to take it to heart. It is a culturally approved method of talking about somebody—usually through verbal indirection. Since the signifier employs humor, it makes the put-down easier to swallow and gives the recipient a socially acceptable way out. That is, if they can't come back with no bad signification of they own, they can just laugh along with the group.

For example, the following dialogue took place in a group of six black adolescents:

SHERRY: I sho am hongy. Dog!
REGINALD: That's all you think bout, eating all the time.
JOHN [*Sherry's brother*]: Man, that's why she so big.
SHERRY: Aw, y'all shut up!
JOHN: Come on, Sherry, we got to go. We'll catch you later, man.

REGINALD [*to John*]: Goodnight
                      Sleep tight
                      Don't let Sherry
                      Eat you up tonight.
[*Everybody laughs—including Sherry—and gives skin.*]

In ending his little ditty the way he does, Reginald has cleverly substituted signification for the original lines of this folk rhyme, which goes: "Goodnight / Sleep tight / Don't let the bed bugs bite." Though not addressing Sherry directly, Reginald is obviously still on her case about her enormous appetite which, he suggests, is so huge that even her brother may be in danger! His farewell to Sherry and John, playful, exaggerated, and quick-witted, is approved by all as good signifyin. Thus excellence and skill in this verbal art helps build yo rep and standing among yo peers.

Some Black Semantic terms that are somewhat synonymous with signification are: dropping lugs; joanin; capping; sounding. All are characterized by exploitation of the unexpected and quick verbal surprises. The difference is that signification tends to be more subtle and circumlocutory than the other verbal activities. For example, one traditional black church preacher hurled the following linguistic social corrective at his congregation: "Seen some mens out drankin and gamblin last night—I know I ain gon get no A-men!" He didn't get too much response; it was a *lug*, pure and simple. By contrast "Reben Nap" did it this way: "Y'all know, the Lord sees and watches everything we do; whether we be in the church or out. And I just wanta let y'all know one thang: Everybody talkin bout Heaven ain goin there!" This effective siggin got both laughter and applause. . . .

. . . The Dozens is a form of signification, but as a discourse mode it has some rules and rituals of its own, thus it constitutes a kind of subcategory within the signification mode. A crucial difference, though, is that the Dozens is found only in secular contexts (not that church folk don't play them, they just don't play them in the church). What you do in playing the Dozens is sig on a person's kinfolk—usually the mother, the closest kin—instead of siggin on the person. The player can extend the put-down, by analogy, to include other immediate relatives, and even ancestral kinfolk. . . .

. . . The objective of the Dozens is to better your opponent with more caustic, humorous "insults." Played for fun or viciousness—and it can be either— the Dozens is a competitive oral test of linguistic ingenuity and verbal fluency. The winner, determined by the audience's responses, becomes a culture hero. . . .

In its indigenous folk style, the Dozens consists of set responses in versified form, usually rhymed couplets. Some refer to various sexual acts committed with "yo momma"—the mother of whoever is being addressed. The term "Dozens" probably comes from the fact that the original verses involved twelve sex acts, each stated in such a way as to rhyme with the numbers 1 to 12. Other folk verses refer to aspects of "yo momma's" sexuality rather than to direct sexual activities. As an example, Richard Wright's short story "Big Boy Leaves Home" opens with a group of young black Southern cats playing the Dozens on their way to the swimming hole.

Yo mama don wear no drawers . . .
Clearly, the voice rose out of the woods, and died away. Like an echo another voice caught it up:
Ah seena when she pulled em off . . .
Another, shrill, cracking, adolescent:
N she washed 'em in alcohol . . .
Then a quartet of voices blending in harmony, floated high above the tree tops:
N she hung 'em out in the hall . . .
Laughing easily, four black boys came out of the woods into cleared pasture. They walked lollingly in bare feet, beating tangled vines and bushes with long sticks.
"Ah wished Ah knowed some mo lines t tha song."
"Yeah, when yuh gits t where she hangs em out in the hall yuh has t stop."
"Shucks, whut goes wid *hall*?"
"*Call.*"
"*Fall.*"
"*Wall.*"
"*Quall.*"
They threw themselves on the grass, laughing.
"Big Boy?"
"Huh?"
"Yuh know one thing?"
"Whut?"
"Yuh sho is crazy!"
"Crazy?"
"Yeah, yuh crazys a bed-bug!"
"Crazy bout whut?"
"Man, whoever hearda *quall*?"
"Yuh said yuh wanted something to go wid *hall,* didn't yuh?"
"Yuh, but whuts a *quall?*"
"Nigger, a *qualls* a *quall.*"
They laughed easily, catching and pulling long green blades of grass with their toes.
"Waal, ef a *qualls* a *quall,* whut IS a *quall?*"
"Oh, Ah know."
"What?"
"Tha ol song goes something like this:
> *Yo mama don wear no drawers,*
> *Ah seena when she pulled em off,*
> *N she washed em in alcohol,*
> *N she hung em out in the hall,*
> *N then she put em back on her QUALL!*"

As blacks have become more urbane, the Dozens have become more sophisticated and today the game is played with fewer of its original programmatic responses. The player who reaches into his or her linguistic bag and comes up with something fresh and original is given heavy audience approval. The most recent popular addition to the game, though now somewhat dated, was: "I fucked yo momma for a solid hour / Baby came out hollin 'Black Power.'" . . .

§

Tonal semantics, the third category of discourse, refers to the use of voice rhythm and vocal inflection to convey meaning in black communication. In using the semantics of tone, the voice is employed like a musical instrument with improvisations, riffs, and all kinds of playing between the notes. This rhythmic pattern becomes a kind of acoustical phonetic alphabet and gives black speech its songified or musical quality. Black rappers use word sound to tap their listeners' souls and inner beings in the same way that the musician uses the symbolic language of music to strike inward responsive chords in his listeners' hearts. The speech rhythms and tonal inflections of Black English are, of course, impossible to capture in print. But you have heard these rhythms in the speech-music of James Brown and Aretha Franklin, in the preaching-lecturing of Martin Luther King, Jr., and Jesse Jackson, in the political raps of Stokely Carmichael and Malcolm X, in the comedy routines of Flip Wilson and Richard Pryor. The key to understanding black tonal semantics is to recognize that the sound of what is being said is just as important as "sense." Both sound and sense are used to deliver the Word. Reverend McKenzie of Memphis intoned: "I say Lo-rd, Lo-rd, Lo-rd, do you hear me, do you hear—ear-ear-ear—me-mee-mee." And Martin Luther King, Jr., once said, "Lord, we ain what we ought to be, and we ain what we want to be, we ain what we gon be, but thank God, we ain what we was." In tonal semantics then, strictly semantic meaning is combined and synthesized with lyrical balance, cadence, and melodious voice rhythm. The effect achieved is the conveyance of a psychocognitive message. These songified patterns of speech reach down to the "deep structure" of life, that common level of shared human experience which words alone cannot convey.

To both understand and "feel" tonal semantics requires the listener to be of a cultural tradition that finds value and meaning in word sound. In Black America, that tradition, like other aspects of Black English style, is located in the African background. From a strictly linguistic viewpoint, we may note that West African languages are *tone languages*. That is, speakers of these languages rely on the tone with which they pronounce syllables, sounds, and words to convey their meaning. The closest example of tone used to distinguish meaning in English is the difference in word pairs like: permit/permit (pronounced one way, you have the verb, pronounced another way, it's a noun); suspect/suspect (again, difference in pronunciation signals whether the verb or noun form is being used). Whereas English is quite limited in its use of the features of tone to signal meaning, African languages have a very complex, highly sophisticated system of tone. Caught between a tone language (i.e., their native African tongue) and a "toneless" language (i.e., the English they were forced to adopt), Africanized English speakers seem to have mediated this linguistic dilemma by retaining in their cultural consciousness the abstract African concept of tone while applying it to English in obviously different ways. . . .

. . . the retention of tone as a register of meaning in Black English was buttressed by two cultural forces. First, the emphasis on balance and the synthesis of opposites in the traditional African world view, hence emotion and intellect, word *sound* and word *meaning,* are combined in Afro-American communication dynamics. The second cultural force relates to the use of the drum in African culture. Not only does the drum function to convey cognitive messages, it has a sociopsychological purpose as well. In *Indaba My Children,* African scholar Credo Mutwa put it this way:

> The drumbeat can summon tears from the springs of our eyes and drive our souls deep into the caverns of sorrow, or it can raise us to the very peak of elation . . . Drums can be sounded in such a way that they have a soothing effect, and create a restful feeling. The beat of the drums can cure what no medicines can cure! It can heal the ills of the mind— it can heal the very soul. Where Americans and Europeans have their evil drugs and the couches of their psychiatrists, the Africans still have their drums.

Although Afro-Americans no longer have their drums, they have retained this African cultural concept in the use of word-sound combinations to achieve spiritual equilibrium and psychological balance.

Tonal semantics has many varied representations in black speech. These may be grouped according to the following types: talk-singing, repetition and alliterative word play, intonational contouring, rhyme. Given the limitations of print, it will be difficult to illustrate these properly. But we gon do our best!

§

Talk-singing in tonal semantics achieves its meaning from the listener's association of the tone with the feeling of being "happy" and gittin the Spirit. (That feeling, as we've noted, is behaviorally expressed in the black cultural ritual of "shouting.") By extension, then, talk-singing is associated with any state of feeling good (whether you "shout" or not). The black preacher's vocalization is the most widely known example of talk-singing. He combines straightforward talk with the cadence and rhythm of traditional black preaching style. This style is characterized by elongated articulation of single words, by heavy breathing, by lengthy pauses between words and phrases, and by constant interjections of the standard key expressions "ha," "aha," and "un-huh." . . .

The preacher himself uses talk-singing at times other than when he is giving his sermon. He may sprinkle his off-the-cuff general remarks with it (as the signification example shows). He may be discussing church business or finance and shift into talk-singing. He may also use it in exhorting the members to pay attention to upcoming church events. The point is that talk-singing is not restricted to Sunday morning sermons, nor is it limited to the preacher. From a practical viewpoint, perhaps it is widely used because it is an excellent attention-getting device. The listener recognizes the shift from straight talk to talk-singing and becomes extra alert and attentive to the speaker, since the tone derives meaning from its use as a signal that the ritual of intense emotion and spirit possession is about to come down. Whether it comes down or not, the fact is that the listener is moved to sit up and take notice. . . .

Another feature of tonal semantics is repetition and alliterative word-play. Key words and sounds are repeated in succession, both for emphasis and effect. Believing that meaningful sounds can move people, the black speaker capitalizes on effective uses of repetition: the disc jockey's "call, cop, and qualify"; Jesse Jackson's "pimp, punk, prostitute, preacher, Ph.D."; the preacher's "I am nobody talking to Somebody Who can help anybody"; the preacher's repetition of words and sounds of emotion, especially in the shift to talk-singing; the phrasal structured repetition of King's "we ain what we ought to be, and we ain what we want to be, we ain what we gon be, but thank God, we ain what we was." . . .

Intonational contouring is the specific use of stress and pitch in pronouncing words in the black style. For example, *yeah* and *un-huh,* when pronounced in a certain way characteristic of black speakers, take on special meaning. Namely, that of registering a notion of sarcastic disbelief or contradiction about what somebody has just said. Hence, depending on context, the speaker can mean the exact opposite of "yeah" and "un-huh." This use of voice inflection does not always operate on a strictly semantic level, but can be used to trip a familiar sociocultural type of semantic lever. That is, the special black pronunciation may not register a different meaning, but it locates the speaker dead into the Black Thang, thus giving greater psychological weight to his words. As one brother said, "it ain the police—it's the PO-lice." Whereupon another brother turned around and gave the word a truly semantically distinct pronunciation, contending: "Naw, it's the po-lice" [poor lice].)

Preachers employ intonational contouring in their deliberately halting, slow, exaggerated pronunciation of important words. Rather than saying simply "God," they will say "Godt," or, "There is a PURson here who is PO-sessed."

§

Modern free verse notwithstanding, rhyme remains a basic ingredient of poetry. Its widespread cultural use and approval in nonpoetic contexts is unique to Black English speakers. While both sacred and secular speech employ rhyme, it is more frequently used in secular discourse. When it is used in sacred contexts, it is usually found in the incorporation of Gospel and old standby hymn lyrics into a sermon, testifying, church speech, or welcome on a church program. A newly "saved" member joining the church said: "I thank God for being here today. And I want y'all to know today that it's a sweet sound cause I once was lost but now uhm found." (The reference is to the church song Amazing Grace": "Amazing Grace / how sweet the sound / I once was lost / but now am found.") . . .

Turning to the use of rhyme in secular style, where it is most prevalent, we should note that some of the rhyming sounds form semantically meaningful words, others constitute so-called nonsense rhymes. Yet all make sense on one level of meaning or another when located in the cultural tradition that applauds mood rappin rhymers . . .

. . . Modern-day examples of the black rapper's overwhelming preference for rhymes include the following: "See you later, alligator . . . After while, crocodile

. . . Split the scene, jelly bean." And: "You dead, skillet head . . . You ain nowhere, square." Or: "I would if I could, but I ain't cause I cain't."

The most effective signifyin and cappin have rhyme as a prime ingredient. For instance, Malcolm X's heavy sig on the non-violent revolution: "In a revolution, you swinging, not singing." (Referring to the common practice of singing "We Shall Overcome" in Civil Rights marches and protests of the sixties). And Muhammad Ali's cap on Sonny Liston: "Yes, the crowd did not dream when they laid down their money / that they would see a total eclipse of the Sonny." . . .

§

Narrative sequencing is the final mode of discourse to be considered. The story-telling tradition is strong in Black American culture and is most often associated with Toasts and other kinds of folklore, as well as the plantation tales of old. But alongside these more ritualized kinds of story-telling is narrative speech as a characteristic register of black communication generally. Black English speakers will render their general, abstract observations about life, love, people in the form of a concrete narrative—as the saying goes, "a nigguh always got a story." The relating of events (real or hypothetical) becomes a black rhetorical strategy to explain a point, to persuade holders of opposing views to one's own point of view, and in general to "win friends and influence people." This meandering away from the "point" takes the listener on episodic journeys and over tributary rhetorical routes, but like the flow of nature's rivers and streams, it all eventually leads back to the source. Though highly applauded by blacks, this narrative linguistic style is exasperating to whites who wish you'd be direct and hurry up and get to the point.

That the story-telling tradition harks back to an African past is fairly well-established by now. We spoke of the role of the griot in African tribal culture. This revered person, always an elder, was responsible for maintaining tribal history. Comprising this history was not merely the chronicles of who did what when, but composite word-pictures of the culture, belief, ethics, and values of the tribe. As part of their training for this sacred position, the story-tellers took oaths never to alter the history, customs, and truths of their people. Village story-tellers are like walking museums. The "old ones" tell their stories to "boys and girls seated with open mouths around the spark-wreathed fire in the center of the villages in the dark forests and on the aloe-scented plains of Africa." Thus, as the Akan saying goes, "the words of one's elders are greater than an amulet," for African elders constitute the "repository of communal wisdom." (In black American culture, this reverence for elders can be witnessed in the rearing of children, who are told that they "bet not be sassin dem ol folks—don't somethin bad happen to you." However, in the chaos and contemporary disintegration of black urban life, one does not hear this expression nor witness this practice as often.)

Every black neighborhood in every city in the United States comes equipped with its own story-tellers. Some can be found on street corners with fifths of whiskey in their hands. Bars, churches, hospitals, unemployment lines, welfare lines—all are possible places where one might find story-tellers. The ghetto porch is home base for some of these "walking historians." . . .

To testify is to tell the truth through "story." In the sacred context, the subject of testifying includes such matters as visions, prophetic experiences, the experience of being saved, and testimony to the power and goodness of God. In the secular context, the subject matter includes such matters as blues changes caused by yo man or yo woman, and conversely, the Dr. FEEL-GOOD power of yo man or yo woman; experiences attesting to the racist power of the white oppressor; testimonials to the power of a gifted musician or singer. The retelling of these occurrences in lifelike fashion recreates the spiritual reality for others who at that moment vicariously experience what the testifier has gone through. The content of testifying, then, is not plain and simple commentary but a dramatic narration and a communal reenactment of one's feelings and experiences. Thus one's humanity is reaffirmed by the group and his or her sense of isolation diminished. . . .

In the oral tradition, there are a number of different narrative forms that tell a kind of folk story revelatory of the culture and experiences of Black America. Some of these are ghost stories (such as "Uncle Henry and the Dog Ghost"); some are general human interest stories (such as "The Palacious Rancher and the Preacher"); some are stories explaining the origin of events and men (such as "Why the Negro is Black"). One well-known narrative form is the folk tale about underdog animals who outsmart their larger-sized enemies. An example of this type is the "Brer Rabbit" cycle of stories in which the rabbit always outfoxes the fox. Some black folklorists attribute an African origin to the Brer Rabbit tales. To be sure, many people question the authenticity of these stories made popular by the Southern white writer, Joel Chandler Harris, who distorts the context of the stories in a number of ways—for instance, by adding a black Uncle Remus figure as a "playmate" for the young whites. But Harris, in fact, did not invent these stories. All his life he had heard them from black people who had adapted their African folk tale to American slave conditions. Thus the cunning and deceit of the rabbit personifies the slave outwitting his more powerful master.

Another type of folk tale in this category is the trickster tale, with a black male, usually known as "Buck" or "John," as central figure. A well-known cycle of stories of this type are the "High John de Conquer" stories. Masters of duplicity and guile, capable or working hoo-doo, witchcraft, and conjuration, these characters do it to death to the white man. Using this kind of material as literary source, nineteenth-century black writer Charles Waddell Chesnutt developed his brilliant short story "the Goophered Grapevine." In the story, Uncle Julius, a "venerable-looking colored man," vainly tries to dissuade a white Northerner from buying the vineyard that has been Uncle Julius's hustle all these years. Julius's "story" deals with the way the vineyard has been "goophered—cunju'd, bewitch."

Another type of narrative folklore based on the values and techniques used by the trickster is the less formalized but no less significant tradition of lying. Meant to be taken semiseriously, the lie is a contrived story about some unusual event or outstanding feat that usually has an element of truth in it—somewhere. (Recall that Riley accuses Buster of working out of this tradition when he begins to narrate the story of Toussaint L'Ouverture.) Contemporary examples are found in the "game" used by hustlers, con men, and rappers in general, who will invent intricate and complex narratives designed to get what they want or to provide "rational" excuses for their behavior. "Shucking and jiving" is a variation on this theme.

All of these folk narrative forms have as their overriding theme the coping ability, strength, endurance, trickeration capacity, and power of black people. . . .

The narratives mentioned thus far are told in prose, conversational style. The Toast is a variation on the trickster, bad nigguh theme done in poetic form. While the High John and Brer Rabbit stories are rural and older in time, the Toast is a modern urban continuance of this tradition. In contrast to the lack of profanities and sexual allusions in the older folk stories, Toasts are replete with funk in practically every rhymed couplet. While the older stories reveal black power in subtle forms (such as blacks deceiving white folks), the Toasts let it all hang out. The hero is fearless, defiant, openly rebellious, and full of braggadocio about his masculinity, sexuality, fighting ability, and general badness. Narrated in first person, this epic folk style is a tribute—that is, a "toast"—to this superbad, omnipotent black hustler, pimp, player, killer who is mean to the max:

> I'm m - e - a - n . . .
> . . . mean/mean/mean . . .
> I been walking the streets
> trying to find
> Miss hard time,
> But all I seen
> Was the dust off her feet
> As she was running from me.

Toasts are usually kept alive in black culture by males, although some females, having heard Toasts from their male friends or relatives, will recite them occasionally (such as the present writer, who learned them from her male cousins, much to the dismay of her Baptist preacher father!). You used to hear Toasts quite regularly in the pool halls, barbershops, and on the street corners in the community; nowadays they are mostly heard among black prisoners who sit around for hours passing the time away reciting various Toasts learned in their adolescence. . . .

In recent years, folklorists and linguists have popularized the Toasts, much to the chagrin of some blacks who disdain this display of our "bad side." Yet viewed from another perspective, Toasts represent a form of black verbal art requiring memory and linguistic fluency from the narrators. Akin to grand epics in the Graeco-Roman style, the movement of the Toast is episodic, lengthy, and detailed. While exactness of wording is not demanded, creative use of language is. The Toast-teller must be adept at linguistic improvisation in order to capture the rhythmic structure and narrative sense of each line in his or her own words. Since the overall narrative structure is loose and episodic, there is both room and necessity for individual rhetorical embellishments and fresh imaginative imagery. Moreover, critics of this narrative form forget that the material is simply an extension of black folk narrative in the oral tradition. Thus contemporary black writers in the black consciousness movement have used this material since it reflects much of the fundamental essence of Afro-American values (such as belief in black male superiority over white males, stress on black verbal ability, coolness, and grace under pressure). Employing this material as an artistic framework for the conveyance of black ideology, contemporary writers capture the spirit, intent, and poetic power of the Toasts without "problem" words. As an example, Nikki Giovanni, in her "Ego Tripping" gives us an inno-vative and powerful poetic Toast to the archetypal black person, source of the creative principle:

> I was born in the congo
> I walked to the fertile crescent and built
>   the sphinx
> I designed a pyramid so tough that a star
>   that only glows every one hundred years falls
>   into the center giving divine perfect light
> I am bad
> . . . . . .
> I sowed diamonds in my back yard
> My bowels deliver uranium
>   the filings from my fingernails are
>   semi-precious jewels
> On a trip north
> I caught a cold and blew
> My nose giving oil to the arab world
> I am so hip even my errors are correct
> I sailed west to reach east and had to round off
>   the earth as I went
> The hair from my head thinned and gold was laid
>   across three continents
>
> I am so perfect so divine so ethereal so surreal
> I cannot be comprehended
>   except by my permission
>
> I mean . . . I . . . can fly
>   like a bird in the sky . . .

The story element is so strong in black communicative dynamics that it pervades general everyday conversation. An ordinary inquiry is likely to elicit an extended narrative response where the abstract point or general message will be couched in concrete story form. The reporting of events is never simply objec-tively reported, but dramatically acted out and narrated. The Black English speaker thus simultaneously conveys the facts and his or her personal sociopsychological perspective on the facts.

Now naturally, when you tellin a story, you include details, characterization, plot, and related digressions. Unaware of the black cultural matrix in which narrative sequencing is grounded, whites, as mentioned earlier, often become genuinely irritated at what they regard as "belabored verbosity" and narration in an "inappropriate" context—thus we have yet another case of cross-cultural communication interference. A fascinating look at this type of interference comes from the courtrooms in which young black males are tried for criminal offenses. In many urban areas, the overload of trial cases is overwhelming, and the judges anxiously try to move the cases as quickly and judiciously as possible. Naturally they don't reckon on the narrative style of the young bloods before them.

A twenty-year-old black male, charged as an accessory to armed robbery, appears before a white judge at the pretrial hearing. His court-appointed attorney had already entered a plea of guilty for him, and, as is customary in trial proceedings, the judge had a copy of the defendant's statement before him. From all indications, it's an open-and-shut case, and the judge need do nothing more than go through the legal motions, ordering the defendant to be bound over for trial. Yet, in the interests of humanitarian fairness, or perhaps due to judicial conscience, the judge makes the cultural "mistake" of soliciting information from the defendant himself. He inquires whether the defendant wishes to add anything in his behalf. The blood begins:

> Well, sir, like the lawyer said, I guess uhm guilty since I *was* there when everythang went down. But see, Your Honor, what happen was that Keif and Mac—Keif, he bout, I say bout this high, with a big natural and Mac, he drive a Deuce, but his car wasn't working. So I went to the job—they work at, Dodge Main and see, I work there too, but I work the midnight shift. So I went to pick 'em up—oh, yeah, Mac, he real tall with a fly [superfly hair do]. And so I pick 'em up from work and Keif, he say he wahn't feelin good so he want to go straight on home. Then Mac ask Keif what he mean, he wahn't feelin good, he look okay to him. And so Keif was the one had the gun, but I didn't know what was goin down, or what they had been rap—discussin—before I got there.

JUDGE: You say this Keifer had a gun?

DEFENDANT: Yes, sir.

JUDGE: Well, why didn't you leave then?

DEFENDANT: Well, see, like, I didn't know that, cause Keif—he had on his maxie leather, and the gun was inside. And so Mac, he had a knife, I think, I mean, I found out later, that's what the police said. So Mac said he was gon stop at the credit union and get his check. And I said, what check? And Keif start lookin funny, and I figure he was really sick like he said, and—

JUDGE [*interrupting, again, with a tone of surprise in his voice*]: Just a minute, who did you say had the gun—Keifer? Who is he? His name doesn't appear on the record here.

DEFENDANT: Yes, it was Keif, Your Honor.

JUDGE: Keif, or Keifer?

DEFENDANT: Keif, sir, K-E-I-T-H.

JUDGE [*with an I-give-up-attitude*]: Oh . . .

. . . At this point, thoroughly exasperated, and perhaps realizing that this "story" is going to go on and on to its detailed max, the judge asks the attorney and defendant to approach the bench, after which he orders the defendant bound over for trial and goes on to the next case, which is . . . yeah, you guessed it . . . another young black male on a similar charge.

NOTES

Wright's 1960 essay, reprinted in Wright (1964), is a concise, informative overview of Black American literature in the United States. The Jackson quote is found in the Preface to *Kuntu Drama,* Paul Harrison, ed. (New York: Grove, 1974), pp. ix-xiii. The brief quote on African communication is from Doob (1961). Thompson's work was cited earlier. Brewer (1972) contains the folk material cited here. For more on tone in African languages, see Turner (1949). The introduction to *Sundiata* in Pickett (1965), discusses the African story-telling tradition; also Mutwa (1966). The reference to Akan culture and African elders comes from Abrahams (1969), whose work should be added to those mentioned above in connection with African philosophical thought. In addition to Brewer, examples of folk stories and "tall" tales can be found in Hughes and Bontemps (1958) and Hurston (1935). Chesnutt's story appears in most standard anthologies of Black American literature, such as *Cavalcade,* Davis and Redding, eds. (Boston: Houghton Mifflin, 1971). The "Malitis" story is found in Botkin (1945), pp. 4–5. The excerpt from Henry Alsup's poem "mean" is in *Get It Up Set It Out* (Detroit: Ink & Soul, 1973), p. 27. Collections of Toasts are Abrahams (1964) and Jackson (1974). Labov (1972; 1973) gives a brilliant analysis of the aesthetic, versification, and metrical style of the Toasts as well as a critical evaluation and comparison of the verbal abilities of various Toast-tellers. "Ego Tripping" by Nikki Giovanni is reprinted from *The Women and the Men* (Copyright © 1970, 1974, 1975 by Nikki Giovanni) by permission of William Morrow & Company, Inc.

BIBLIOGRAPHY

Abrahams, Roger. *Deep Down in the Jungle.* Chicago: Aldine Publishing Co., 1970 (originally published in Hatboro, Pennsylvania, 1964).
Abrahams, W. E. *The African Mind.* Chicago: University of Chicago Press, 1969.
Alsup, Henry. *Get It Up Set It Out.* Detroit: Ink & Soul, 1973.
Botkin, B. A., ed. *Lay My Burden Down: A Folk History of Slavery.* Chicago: University of Chicago Press, 1945.
Brewer, J. Mason. *American Negro Folklore.* Chicago: Quadrangle Books, 1972.
Davis, Arthur P., and Redding, Saunders, eds. *Cavalcade.* Boston: Houghton Mifflin, 1971.
Doob, Leonard. *Communication in Africa.* New Haven: Yale University Press, 1961.
Harrison, Paul, ed. *Kuntu Drama.* New York: Grove Press, 1974.
Hughes, Langston, and Bontemps, Arna. *The Book of Negro Folklore.* New York: Dodd, Mead, 1958.
Hurston, Zora Neale. *Mules and Men.* Philadelphia: J. B. Lippincott, 1935.
Jackson, Oliver, in Preface to *Kuntu Drama,* Paul Harrison, ed. New York: Grove Press, 1974, pp. IX–XIII.

Labov, William. *Language in the Inner City*. Philadelphia: University of Pennsylvania Press, 1972.

———. "Toasts," in Alan Dundes, ed., *Mother Wit from the Laughing Barrel*. New Jersey: Prentice-Hall, 1973.

Mutwa, Vusamazulu Credo. *Indaba My Children*. London: Blue Crane Books, 1966.

Pickett, G. D., ed. and trans. *Sundiata: An epic of old Mali*. London: Longman Group Ltd. Edition, 1965.

Turner, Lorenzo D. *Africanisms in the Gullah Dialect*. Chicago: University of Chicago Press, 1949.

Wright, Richard. *Black Boy*. New York: Harper & Row, 1966.

———. *Lawd Today*. New York: Walker and Company, 1963.

———. "The Literature of the Negro in the United States," in *White Man, Listen!* New York: Anchor Books, 1964.

———. *The Long Dream*. Garden City, N.Y.: Doubleday, 1958.

———. *Uncle Tom's Children*. New York: Harper & Row, 1965.

THEORY AND IMPLICATIONS

1. What are some of the cultural reasons why the African-American discourse mode of call-response might create negative reactions in many white, middle-class teachers?

2. Why might Playing the Dozens be seen as scandalous? Why should teachers know something about it?

3. How might student behavior in the classroom, including responses to teachers' questions and imperatives, be affected by these modes?

4. How might teachers build lessons on a knowledge of these discourse modes?

5. How might these folklore traditions be presented in the classroom so that African Americans could benefit? What is the value of teaching these modes to all children?

6. What do the connections between these modes and the traditional African worldview reveal about the value of oral traditions?

PROFESSIONAL CONCERNS

1. Devise and defend a detailed lesson on one of the discourse modes. Assume that you are presenting your lesson plan to your master teacher. How would you explain it as an art form and encourage children to use its conventions?

2. Defend to an administrator the need for any teacher of African-American students to have an appreciation for these discourse modes. Assume an antagonistic or a skeptical audience.

chapter 5

Achieving Grammatical Competence

THE ISSUES

This chapter attempts to answer the questions, What do teachers need to know about grammar and how can that knowledge be translated into effective teaching methods? Recent research identifies different levels of grammar in an effort to distinguish grammarians' abstract knowledge of language systems from the simpler rules provided by textbooks and from the etiquette involved in appropriate usage. This chapter briefly describes and compares several abstract systems developed by grammarians, helping teachers to realize how relative grammatical descriptions are and how different descriptions lead to different sets of textbook rules and teaching methods. Also offered are practical applications of grammar to writing instruction within a writing process approach. A few notes about this chapter's limitations: Clearly, students' grammatical competence, in both writing and speech, involves more than grammatical rules or systems, and grammatical choice depends on larger choices of discourse frames. However, the focus here on sentence-level grammatical choices fits with the process approach to initial literacy addressed in chapter 6.

Some of the answers to the above question have been misleading. Although some studies show that grammar instruction in the form of definitions and drills, isolated from communicative contexts, does not improve writing, such studies should not be used to justify abandoning all grammar knowledge. Some teachers, recalling their own early frustrations with grammar, have concluded that grammar automatically leads to a focus on error, to students' fear of experimentation, and even to regressions due to hypercorrection.

Because of these views, many prospective teachers have not been taught grammatical approaches and lack even a minimal grammar terminology. But though terminology alone may not help reduce students' errors, an understanding of central grammatical relationships helps one teacher to analyze sentence problems and devise revising strategies. Without a working understanding of grammar, teachers lack the ability to perceive and later call students' attention to possible sentence expansions, variations, reformulations, or edits. Finally, the lack of a working grammar can lead to teachers' resistance to giving writing assignments; they may think, "I'm not a writing teacher; I don't know anything about grammar." What, then, do teachers need to know, and how can they put this knowledge to use?

PRINCIPLES OF GRAMMAR KNOWLEDGE AND INSTRUCTION

The principles of grammar instruction highlighted in this chapter are ways to address the confusions that dominate grammar instruction. The first, most important misconception is that there exists one monolithic, static, consistent grammar, and that all of us must learn it. Yet linguists have shown us that there are various approaches to grammar based on specific historical and philosophical concerns. Each approach describes the language differently, emphasizing different features for different purposes. Furthermore, because language itself changes, no grammar stays the same. Thus there is no one grammar that language specialists should use to measure correctness.

This difference among grammars can be demonstrated by an extended example that contrasts traditional and transformational-generative (TG) grammar. These two grammars begin their analysis focused on different units: Traditional English grammar begins with individual words involving nouns, verbs, adjectives, and prepositions; TG grammar begins with the sentence, for instance S = NP + VP, which is a formula for indicating that a sentence is a noun phrase plus a verb phrase. This difference in starting point reflects each grammar's different purpose and resulting problems. For example, the purpose of traditional English grammar is classification, as was that of the Latin grammar on which it is modeled. Indeed, traditional grammar attempts to answer the question, What kind of word (phrase, clause) is this? and goes on to classify all words into eight parts of speech, all phrases into six types of phrases, all clauses into two types of clauses, and all sentences into four types of sentences. Because elements do not fit neatly into such a scheme, this classification system sometimes seems vague, circular, or inconsistent. Consider the vagueness and circularity of such definitions as "A pronoun takes the place of a noun" or "A preposition is a word placed before a noun or pronoun to form a phrase modifying another word in the sentence." Such definitions assume that one has knowledge of the words to be defined and of such key grammatical concepts as "modification."

Transformational-generative grammar, to the contrary, attempts to explain how sentences are "generated" from certain rules, not simply how we might classify them once they have been produced. It posits certain base or "kernel" sentences that, through cognitive processes, undergo transformations to create more complex structures. Thus TG asks what unconscious rules we must apply in order to create, combine, or reposition structures, helping us to distinguish intuitively between a grammatical and an ungrammatical sentence as we produce sentences. Hence, whereas traditional grammar analyzes products to serve as models and to dictate usage, TG grammar attempts to explain our knowledge of grammaticality as we produce sentences, offering a cognitive model for the creation of increasingly complex structures. Applications of TG grammar also offer criteria for judging complexity based on the number of TG rules applied to the kernel sentences. TG grammar's problems lie in the fact that formal complexity in itself does not indicate maturity of thought, as was once proposed.

A second key misunderstanding about grammar concerns teaching methods. When grammar is taught as a body of information to be memorized and then applied in isolated drills and exercises, it has little effect on writing. When grammar is taught within the framework of revising writing for both content and form, however, it becomes more meaningful. Research shows that teachers need to find ways to help students evolve rule systems that fit their writing needs. Students need to tie such rules to the larger purposes of communicating, such as writing a story, persuading an adult to do something, or conveying information to classmates about an experiment. And teachers need to tap students' intuitive rule hypothesizing, helping them to evolve approximate rules that increase their fluency as well as their accuracy. Indeed, given the number of potential grammatical rules, teaching grammar in isolation and then expecting it to be applied in context seems impossible. As with first language errors, writers, like children, evolve rules to fit their needs and, like children making L1 errors, they can be stymied by corrections based on a model of absolute correctness.

A third key misconception about grammar follows from the first. When teachers assume there is a monolithic, static body of knowledge, they mistakenly believe that they need a linguist's knowledge of grammar even to approach student problems, and probably consider such full grammatical knowledge to be unobtainable. Indeed, teachers often view terminology like "predicate complement" and "dative" as obscure and intimidating; they believe such concepts are based on a cumulative knowledge that they somehow lack. Yet a need for extensive knowledge of grammatical rules is not supported by research. Teachers can begin responding to students' sentences with a basic terminology and use it to help students combine sentences, vary sentence structure, and use punctuation stylistically. The simple distinction between "bound" and "free" modifiers can help a teacher show students how they can move parts of sentences around, where punctuation is appropriate, and where additions can most easily be made. Other simple distinctions can be added when a teacher tries to increase students' stylistic options or when a teacher encounters consistent underlying errors. Thus, although conscious rules do not produce writing, they can help us to revise or extend it. Most important is that teachers should have knowledge of underlying assumptions of a particular grammatical approach so that they can make informed decisions about how to apply their knowledge.

A fourth key misunderstanding about grammar involves the confusion between grammar and usage. A grammar attempts to describe systematically a language's central elements. As indicated above, different descriptions have different starting points. Usage, however, comprises the forms of speaking or writing based on "acceptability." Usage features change with time, given social factors, and are usually taught prescriptively. Indeed, teachers often worry about "good grammar" when they are really concerned with "good usage." Although knowledge of grammar can help teachers with the production stages of their students' writing—helping students to generate sentences and use structures they have not used before—knowledge of usage helps with the editing stage. Understanding the distinction between grammar and usage relieves teachers of the burden of knowing all usage rules and helps them to explain such rules within a context of social acceptability rather than one of absolute correctness.

A fifth key misunderstanding lies in the notion that language does not and should not change—that rules serve to correct faulty usage and restore language to its pure forms. However, the history of changes in the English language challenges the notion that there ever *was* a pure language. Instead it shows that ungrammatical forms like the double negative ("He don't have no money") were once grammatical and that word order, on which modern English now relies, was once less important than word endings to indicate parts of speech. Furthermore the history of English shows changes in pronunciation and in word meanings. The learning of grammar should therefore be a descriptive, not a prescriptive, task.

PROFESSIONAL APPLICATIONS

A number of professional benefits follow from clearing up such misunderstandings and establishing principles of grammar knowledge. First, when teachers understand that different grammars serve different purposes, and that all systems are problematic in isolation from real writing contexts, they can use grammar more flexibly. Clearly they do not need to know or teach extensive abstract rules in isolation from a communicative purpose; students who are taught traditional grammar in this fashion learn and relearn the rules and seldom find a means of remembering this knowledge. Rather, teachers need a rough system of grammar derived from a knowledge of how different grammars can serve writing. A knowledge of the comparative features of different grammars will help teachers to flexibly adopt and extend a practical terminology in their classrooms. This terminology can help them to further such literacy goals as increasing the length, complexity, and variety of sentences and addressing the specific kinds of errors that follow from such advances. As teachers find an increasing need to develop their own terminology, they will increase their own knowledge and use of grammar and can help students extend their terminology in ways that tap students' intuitive knowledge about how language works.

A second professional application is that teachers who formerly resisted assigning writing in the classroom can begin to ask for and respond to writing without self-doubt. When teachers understand that explicit instruction in grammar rules has minimal effect on writing, they are encouraged to respond to errors in the editing stage with inductive methods that provoke students' own rule formation. Rather than looking to a circular, vague terminology as an end in itself, teachers can develop a simple set of terms appropriate to the writing needs and levels of their students.

A third benefit is that teachers can look at language change positively. Although changes occur slowly, our language is constantly changing. Semantic changes reflect our different values and needs, and syntactic changes indicate moves toward greater logic and economy. Out of this recognition comes the understanding that grammar describes rather than dictates language.

With these benefits in mind, this chapter first explains the underlying differences between traditional and transformational-generative grammar. These differences indicate areas where each system can help the teacher to encourage increasingly complex sentence structures, to predict and address errors, and to better understand the language processes accounting for the errors. The chapter then offers specific practical applications of grammar. Throughout this chapter underscores central assumptions in the study of grammar for use: (1) that different grammars reflect different purposes and concerns, (2) that teachers and students each have all the resources to develop their own grammars, and (3) that grammar must be integrated with the practice of speaking and writing.

OVERVIEW OF THE READINGS

The readings selected here provide a number of perspectives on grammar. The essays at the beginning of the chapter attempt to compare different theoretical approaches, the history of these approaches, and how different grammars describe different structures. The essays at the end of the chapter show explicitly how grammars can be used. Readers who come to see the historically contingent nature of any description of grammar can thus see the practical applications for grammatical concepts, which include not only addressing errors in the editing stages of writing but also inventing or developing ideas.

Erika Lindemann's "Approaches to Grammar" broadly contrasts traditional, structural, and transformational-generative grammars in terms of origin and purpose. Lindemann reveals the origins of traditional grammar in Latin grammar, itself based on the written form of Greek grammar. Most of the key elements from the classical tradition, now dysfunctional, remain with traditional grammar today, including its prescriptive emphasis on correctness and on dissecting sentences rather than producing them. Lindemann then contrasts traditional grammar with structural grammar, which derives from a more objective, anthropological approach seeking descriptions of actual language use. Finally she addresses transformational-generative grammar, with its key distinctions between competence and performance, surface and deep structure, and kernel and transformed sentences.

Doris T. Myers's "What Petey Forgot" points out specific differences between traditional and structural grammars in classifying parts of speech. Myers contrasts the often vague and confusing definitions of traditional grammar with the more objective, position-based definitions of structural grammar, showing that whereas traditional grammar defines categories inconsistently—sometimes using meaning, sometimes function—structural grammar is more consistent in using place, or "distribution," in the sentence. Despite this useful contrast, the essay leaves the reader with unresolved issues: One, neither system appears to be free from overlap or shifting criteria; and two, the focus here is limited to the classification of parts of speech, which is not the main goal of structural grammar. However, this essay serves the important purpose of showing that any system relies on intuitive knowledge of grammar in order for a definition to make sense. It confirms why we all learn and relearn grammar, yet still forget it.

Ellery Sedgwick's "Alternatives to Teaching Formal, Analytical Grammar" is a practical overview of the "grammar dilemma." Given that research demonstrates that direct grammar instruction does not eradicate errors in writing, much less improve syntax or style, Sedgwick offers needed alternatives to traditional instruction. He favors indirect over direct methods, with grammar instruction made part of larger projects and writing purposes. Students need not acquire a conscious knowledge of grammatical forms, but they can learn grammatical options through practice. His essay thus builds on L1 and L2 acquisition theories that favor unconscious over conscious learning, emphasize communication, and view error tolerantly. It also anticipates the next two essays in advocating sentence expansion and integrating grammar into the writing process.

Francis Christensen's "A Generative Rhetoric of the Sentence" offers a way in which grammar can be used for writing. He addresses the invention stage of writing, using grammatical distinctions to show how a sentence is "built." This approach offers a rough-hewn grammar—one that begins with a simple distinction between movable and nonmovable parts of the sentence—and then identifies three places for sentence expansion and three types of expansions. Using little more than these "productive" grammatical distinctions, Christensen demonstrates how sentences can be created (not simply revised) in ways that duplicate the natural flow from general idea to specific detail.

The last reading, "Grammar in Context: Why and How" by Jim Meyer, Jan Youga, and Janis Flint-Ferguson, offers a practical lesson in how grammar might be given a "natural context." Unlike the previous essays, it attempts, through a particular example, to show how teachers might integrate a grammatical feature into a whole language lesson. A specific grammatical feature, in this case the pronoun, is used to analyze literature, to write about literature, and to edit one's own writing. These authors thus show how grammar can become part of an entire reading and writing curriculum.

Approaches to Grammar*

ERIKA LINDEMANN

"Approaches to Grammar," from A Rhetoric for Writing Teachers, *is a helpful background to grammar instruction. It reveals the history of grammar texts and grammar instruction, showing how dependent traditional grammar is on*

---

* Lindemann, E., "Approaches to Grammar," from *A Rhetoric for Writing Teachers*, Second Edition, by Erika Lindemann. Copyright © 1987 by Oxford University Press, Inc. Reprinted by permission.

*the particular values and concerns of the seventeenth century, and thus
counters the view that grammar is based on certain absolute truths about the
language. Also informative are the contrasts it offers among the three main
approaches to grammar: traditional, structural, and transformational-generative.
This comparative overview underscores the relative nature of any systematic
approach to language description, as being dependent on the questions asked
and the purpose of the analysis. From this analysis we can see the origins of
the current practice of sentence combining, which evolved out of transformational-generative grammar.*

If teaching grammar per se doesn't improve writing ability, why include in this
chapter a section called "Approaches to Grammar"? Because *teachers* do need to
know grammar, the theories which explain how English functions systematically.
Beginning teachers, especially, should know that the study of grammar can be
approached from several perspectives. Each perspective offers ways of helping
students expand their powers of expression and increase their linguistic options,
especially in editing their work. Furthermore, when teachers understand grammatical theories, they can respond to concerns that parents, administrators, and
other teachers express about what should be basic in a writing curriculum.
Grammatical knowledge also helps teachers evaluate curricula, instructional
materials, and teaching practices.

Many contemporary methods of teaching English originate in past theories
about language which ought to be reexamined. The teaching of English as a school
subject began in the seventeenth century, when England was filled with foreigners
and members of the middle class who wanted to read and write English. Formerly
education had belonged to the nobility and the clergy, but in the Renaissance
teachers were forced quickly to adapt old methods of teaching Latin and Greek
to new students and a new subject, English.

Even though English is structurally quite different from Latin and Greek,
nevertheless English instruction was modeled on a classical tradition. As early as
100 B.C., Dionysius Thrax had compiled a grammar of Greek, based on the written,
not the spoken, language. He classified Greek into parts of speech. Latin grammar
books were based on the Greek classification system. They also included material
on metrics and established the practice of imitating literary "models." The tradition
of teaching parts of speech, of asking students to memorize verb, noun, and
pronoun paradigms, of defining "excellence" with reference to great works of
literature, remains virtually unchanged after centuries of employing the classical
tradition to teach English.

A second characteristic of English education, making judgments about
language, legislating "correctness," stems from classical precepts which were
reinforced during the Middle Ages, when the church fostered education. Christian
theology tended to view change negatively, as emblematic of the human condition
since the fall from grace in the Garden of Eden. Language was believed to be
devolving from Hebrew (erroneously thought to be the oldest language). Language
change was seen as further evidence that sin pervaded human existence. To
prevent further degeneration, scholars and teachers sought to "fix" language by
rigid rules, by establishing classical models and the formal writing of the Church

Fathers as standards for correctness. Language study became error-oriented. Students were expected to learn the rules and gain practice in recognizing "deviant" constructions.

The two traditions, a reliance on classical models and an orientation toward correctness, were reemphasized in the eighteenth century, when "scientific rationalism" exerted tremendous influence on the study of language. Scholars of this period sought to make language "logical," reasonable in a scientific, mathematical sense. Wherever possible, they reinforced their explanations of logical rules with examples from classical authors. In an effort to promote and codify the logic of English, eighteenth-century grammarians adopted the following aims:[1]

1. *To devise rules governing "correct" English usage.* Many rules resorted to mathematical principles. For example, writing two negatives in a sentence began to be "incorrect," given the logic of mathematics. Similarly, since the verb *to be* was viewed as a mathematical equals sign, the nominative, not the objective, case became the appropriate form to use after *to be:*

> It   is   I (not *me*).
> Nominative =   Nominative

2. *To refine the language, removing "deviant" constructions and introducing "improvements."* Supposedly inferior words of Anglo-Saxon origin were replaced with Latinate vocabulary. Dr. Samuel Johnson's *Dictionary of the English Language* (1755), the first true English dictionary and a remarkable achievement in its day, often resorts to Latin terms in defining English words. His definition of *network,* for example, reads: "Any thing reticulated or decussated, at equal distances, with interstices between the intersections." Many of the terms we encounter in studying grammar—*antecedent, accusative, intransitive, passive*—originate in this period and reflect a preference for Latin, the "superior" authority as a model.

3. *To fix the English language and prevent further deterioration.* Working from the mistaken notion that Greek and Latin hadn't changed, grammarians wanted to codify the new refinements and rules they had developed for English. In this way, they thought, writers (and speakers) could be guided by the collective wisdom of texts and other reference works. Samuel Johnson's *Dictionary* and the grammar books of Robert Lowth (1762) and Lindley Murray (1795) became important school texts, prototypes of instructional materials used for over 150 years to the present.

Traditional grammar reflects this legacy. It is rules-oriented, Latin-based, prescriptive and proscriptive. It legislates constructions which must be adhered to or avoided. It focuses on the written language. The principal method of teaching traditional grammar is called *parsing,* a rote process which analyzes a given sentence in four steps:

1. By identifying the largest structural components of the sentence (subject and predicate, dependent and independent clauses);

---

[1] For a detailed discussion of these aims, see Baugh and Cable.

2. By classifying each word as one of eight parts of speech (nouns, pronouns, verbs, adverbs, adjectives, prepositions, conjunctions, interjections);
3. By describing individual words in terms of their inflectional or derivational prefixes or suffixes;
4. By explaining the relationship of each word to other words in the sentence through a "sentence diagram."

Traditional grammarians developed terminology useful to discussing language and codified many conventions governing edited American English. Nevertheless, the traditional approach to grammar has many disadvantages. In the first place, traditional grammarians did not describe what spoken English was but rather legislated what written English ought to be. They failed to respect the role of change in language and refused to recognize that forms appropriate in some kinds of writing might not be appropriate for other audiences.

Second, they based their approach on Latin and Greek, assuming that what was logical for those languages was also logical for English. They failed to recognize English's unique logic and structure. Because English has lost most of its inflectional endings, it differs in many significant ways from its distant Latin and Greek cousins. For example, a paradigm may be useful for teaching the Latin verb *amo* ("I love") in the present tense indicative mood. All the endings are different. In English, however, most verbs show only one inflectional variant in the third person singular; modal verbs show no variants at all.

Latin		*English*			
amo	amamus	love	love	may	may
amas	amatis	love	love	may	may
amat	amant	loves	love	may	may

A paradigm, then, represents a time-consuming, inefficient means of teaching students where English demands final -*s* on present tense verbs.

Third, traditional grammar's preoccupation with parts of speech leaves little room to study other, equally important, areas of the English language. We've probably memorized the definitions so well that we don't recognize how vague some of them are: "A sentence expresses a *complete thought.*" (What, then, is an "incomplete" thought?) "A verb expresses action or *state of being.*" (How's a tenth grader supposed to understand "being-ness"?) Other definitions are circular: "An adverb modifies a verb, adjective, or *another adverb.*" Still other definitions seem inconsistent; some explain what the part of speech *means,* while others describe what the part of speech *does,* how it functions.

Finally, although traditional grammar claims to study the sentence, the approach focuses on taking language apart, not on putting it together. Students analyze and dissect sentences by diagramming them or labeling each word as a part of speech. Generally, they are someone else's sentences, not the student's. As a result, students may learn terminology and doubtless some principles of editing, but they haven't learned how to *create* discourse, only how to label, diagram, or analyze it. Since the traditional approach doesn't encourage students to apply grammatical principles to the composing process, teachers must. If grammar is taught at all, it should be tied to writing instruction. The student's own prose, not the chapter-by-chapter arrangement of a text, should determine which grammatical principles offer workable solutions to writing problems.

STRUCTURAL GRAMMAR

Although descriptive approaches to the study of language developed more slowly than the traditional prescriptive approach, they have found favor among the majority of modern linguists as well as a good many writing teachers. As long ago as the eighteenth century, Joseph Priestley (*Rudiments of English Grammar,* 1761) and George Campbell (*Philosophy of Rhetoric,* 1776) advanced the theory that contemporary usage, not classical authority, must determine what's appropriate or standard in English. For them, English speakers, not Latin models, were the best authority for describing the grammar of English. When Darwin's studies (1859) asserted that "progress" was beneficial, not harmful, changes in language also began to be viewed more objectively. Scholars began to be more interested in what changes had occurred than in determining whether those changes were right or wrong. In contrast to the prescriptivists, descriptive linguists are primarily interested in examining the language as it is, not advancing notions about what it should be.

In 1933 Leonard Bloomfield, widely regarded as the father of modern linguistics in America, published *Language,* a work which defines the methodology of the descriptive linguist. Working only with data that can be objectively verified, the descriptive linguist must describe, classify, and analyze samples of language before making generalizations about the evidence. Limiting himself only to that which is measurable, Bloomfield relegated the rest of language study, especially thought processes, to other disciplines.

The structural grammarian, one kind of descriptive linguist, sorts language data into three levels: the smallest units of language or individual sounds (phonology), groups of sounds that have meaning (morphology), and the arrangement of morphs which signal complex relationships in phrases, clauses, and sentences (syntax). A major difference between the traditional and structural grammarian can be seen in how they treat parts of speech. Unwilling to classify nouns, for example, on the basis of a word's meaning, structuralists use other evidence. *Gangsters* is a noun, not because it names persons, but because it shows an inflectional plural *-s* and because the derivational suffix *-ster* is a morph reserved exclusively for nouns in English. In addition to form-criteria, position-criteria (syntax) may also determine "nounness." In the sentence, "The gangsters robbed the bank," *gangsters* is a noun because it occupies one of many slots or positions nouns hold in English sentence patterns. Students find these criteria—what a word looks like and where it appears in the sentence—much more reliable and concrete than criteria which resort to a word's meaning.

The structuralists' descriptions of basic English sentence patterns also help students identify the order and arrangement of sentence elements. Without making abstract determinations about a clause's "dependence" or "independence," students can study how words behave in their writing by examining where they appear in sentences. A common technique structuralists advocate for teaching syntax asks students to analyze nonsense sentences like "The trasky gleebers were miffling holps wombly." Deprived of clues to the word's meaning, students must base their understanding of sentence construction on morphological and syntactic evidence.

These and other techniques derived from structural grammar help us teach students about words and sentences more objectively, concretely, and descriptively than the traditional approach permits.

GENERATIVE-TRANSFORMATIONAL GRAMMAR

Oddly enough, our ability to decode nonsense sentences points up a shortcoming in the approach and methodology of structural grammar. Dependent on samples of spoken language, the structuralist can't explain how speakers of a language constantly create sentences they've never heard before. Structuralists aren't able to analyze the infinite possibilities of a complex, living language because they limit themselves to investigating only measurable data. They exclude from their studies mental processes, what speakers know, and focus only on performance, the results of speakers' putting what they know to use.

This distinction between *competence* and *performance* is of special interest to generative-transformational grammarians. They attempt to explain how speakers and hearers of English create and understand unique sentences, based on the same code, yet permitting infinite variations. All human beings acquire the ability to use language without formal instruction. We master the code we share with other English speakers long before we know that language has rules, let alone what those rules are. It's this intuitive knowledge that the transformational grammarian seeks to describe.

Noam Chomsky's *Syntactic Structures* sets forth the principles of this recent approach to descriptive linguistics. Chomsky maintains that native speakers know the grammar of their language intuitively. By *grammar* he means not only the rules whereby we combine words into sentences (syntax), but also our knowledge of sounds (phonology) and units of meaning (morphology). A single body of intuitive linguistic knowledge, a grammar, governs all our uses of language, as speakers, hearers, writers, or readers. Whereas the structuralists begin their study with the smallest units of speech, individual sounds, and proceed to analyze ever larger units of language, the transformationalist describes the native speaker's intuitive grammar beginning with the sentence. Defining *sentence* is the heart of transformational grammar. An analogy to mathematics may help to explain the transformationalist's approach.[2]

---

[2] The analogy was suggested by Jeanne Herndon, *A Survey of Modern Grammars* (New York: Holt, Rinehart and Winston, 1970). The second edition (1976) offers an excellent overview of traditional, structural, and transformational approaches to the study of language. For a brief, readable discussion of transformational grammar alone, consult Suzette Haden Elgin, *A Primer of Transformational Grammar: For the Rank Beginner* (Urbana, Ill.: NCTE, 1975).

When we learn mathematics, we don't have to store in our memories the fact that $126 \times 157 = 19,782$. We simply learn a finite set of multiplication tables and then memorize a few simple rules—how to "carry" numbers, shift columns, add the columns—for reusing the basic tables. Given a finite set of multiplication tables and a finite set of rules for using them, we can perform an infinite number of math problems. Similarly, the transformationalist suggests that we learn, at a very early age, a finite set of phrase-structure rules and a second finite set of transformations which, used over and over or recursively, give us the linguistic capability of generating an infinite number of sentences.

The phrase-structure rules, corresponding to multiplication tables in math, describe the nature and order of the parts in a simple declarative sentence. Written in mathematical notation, the phrase-structure rule S→NP + VP reads, "The sentence may be rewritten or defined as 'noun phrase plus verb phase.'" That is, all declarative sentences *in English* must contain a noun phrase and a verb phrase. A second phrase-structure rule then defines NP:

$$NP \rightarrow \begin{Bmatrix} (\text{Determiner}) + \text{N} \\ \text{Pronoun} \end{Bmatrix}$$

As the braces indicate, all English noun phrases must contain *either* a pronoun *or* a noun. If a noun is present, a determiner or article *may* also be present. In English, then, we may generate three kinds of noun phrases:

1. N   Dogs
2. Determiner + N   The dogs   barked.
3. Pronoun   They

Notice, too, that the phrase-structure rules prescribe the order of the parts; determiners, if present, always precede the noun. Since the phrase-structure rules are also recursive, a noun phrase, regardless of where it appears in the sentence, will always have the same components.

Long before the sentence is spoken, the speaker selects items from the phrase-structure rules to generate mentally a simple declarative sentence, called a *kernel sentence.* Once the kernel sentence has been generated, a series of operations, called *transformations,* may be applied to the declarative sentence. Transformations are analogous to the multiplication rules for carrying numbers, shifting columns, and adding them up. Each transformation modifies the kernel sentence in a specific way. Some transformations are obligatory; others remain optional; all of them add to, delete from, or reorder the elements of the kernel sentence. The negative transformation, for example, adds *not* to the kernel sentence in a specific place depending on the nature of the verb phrase. Transformations performed on a single kernel sentence are known as *single-base transformations.* Transformations which embed one kernel sentence within a second kernel sentence are called *double-base* (or *multiple-base*) *transformations.* The following sentences, then, are said to be transformationally related to the simple declarative sentence, "Michael painted the picture":

Single-Base Transformations
Michael did not paint the picture. (Negative transformation)

Did Michael paint the picture? (Yes-No question transformation)

The picture was painted by Michael. (Passive transformation)

What was Michael painting? (Wh-question transformation)

Double-Base Transformations (Embedding or sentence combining)
Michael, who painted the picture, won first prize. (Relative clause transformation)

The picture that Michael painted was beautiful. (Relative clause transformation)

Michael's painting the picture took time. (Gerund transformation)

For Michael to paint the picture took time. (Infinitive transformation)

That Michael painted the picture was obvious. (Noun clause transformation)

Michael painted the picture and cleaned the brushes. (Conjunctive transformation)

Michael painted the beautiful picture. (Adjective transformation)

Both generating a kernel sentence and transforming it are mental operations which yield ordered slots for vocabulary items. The sentence to this point is said to have a *deep structure,* as contrasted with a *surface structure,* the appearance it has when it's spoken or written. The sentences "Michael painted the picture" and "The picture was painted by Michael" show a difference in surface structure only; underlying both is the same kernel sentence, the same deep structure, the same meanings, and the same relationships between parts. Their surface structures differ because in the second example the kernel sentence underwent a passive transformation which wasn't applied to the first sentence.

A sentence receives a surface structure when the ordered slots of a transformed kernel sentence are filled with appropriate selections from the English *lexicon,* a kind of internalized, mental dictionary in which we store the countless vocabulary items we learn throughout life. When we learn new words, we remember not only their pronunciations and meanings, but also other information about their use. Generative-transformationalists characterize this information by marking the features of words with a plus or minus. Feature analysis assumes importance in the final stages of creating sentences, when transformed kernel sentences are filled with lexical items sharing compatible features. Although "The building is eating a steak" certainly sounds English and conforms to English sentence structure, it doesn't make sense, except perhaps in the context of a children's story. The "sense" is disturbed because *building* carries the features –animate and –human, whereas the verb *eat* shows +animate and +human features. Substituting a +animate and a +human noun for *building* rids the sentence of semantic distortions: "The boy is eating a steak."

Generative-transformationalists focus their attention on the creative aspect of language, on the ability of human beings regularly to produce and understand new utterances, on a language system which holds an infinite number of possible sentences. Furthermore, the approach assumes that native speakers intuitively "know" how English works, that students have a competence for language many teachers have ignored. Sentence-combining represents one way of tapping this intuitive resource. Through sentence-combining, students practice transforming simple declarative sentences and constructing increasingly complex sentences, enlarging their repertoire of syntactic options, improving their ability to "perform" sentences. As Frank O'Hare and John Mellon have demonstrated,[3] sentence-combining may increase "syntactic fluency" without formal grammar instruction or elaborate terminology.

If grammatical competence is intuitive, why do students have sentence problems? Fragments, run-on sentences, and confused syntax reflect not deficient competence, but difficulties in performance. They represent problems in "code-switching," transferring spoken English into writing. When students understand that both codes are systematic but that the systems don't always overlap, they can bring to their writing a greater conscious awareness of their linguistic options.

Studying grammar in the context of (not in lieu of) writing practice, then, may foster linguistic flexibility and improve students' abilities to edit their work. Whether it does or not depends on how we approach the study of language in a writing class. Students don't need to "know" grammar in the same way their teachers do. If we teach our students grammar as a subject matter, it remains isolated from and irrelevant to writing. If, on the other hand, we apply what we know about grammar to our teaching, we can help students become more effective writers. When we understand grammatical principles and methods, we can examine intelligently how people use language and then design courses which effectively increase our students' awareness of the choices both the spoken and written language allow.

LIST OF WORKS CONSULTED

Baugh, Albert C., and Thomas Cable. *A History of the English Language.* 3rd ed. Englewood Cliffs, N.J.: Prentice-Hall, 1978.

Beale, Walter, Karen Meyers, and Laurie White. *Stylistic Options: The Sentence and the Paragraph.* Glenview, Ill.: Scott, Foresman, 1982.

Campbell, George. *The Philosophy of Rhetoric.* Ed. Lloyd F. Bitzer. Carbondale, Ill.: Southern Illinois University Press, 1963.

Daiker, Donald, Andrew Kerek, and Max Morenberg, eds. *Sentence Combining and the Teaching of Writing.* Conway, Ark.: L & S Books, 1979.

---

[3] John C. Mellon, *Transformational Sentence-Combining: A Method for Enhancing the Development of Syntactic Fluency in English Composition* (NCTE Research Report No. 10; Champaign, Ill.: NCTE, 1967) and Frank O'Hare, *Sentence Combining* (1973) describe the effects of this technique on groups of students participating in research studies. Two good sentence-combining textbooks for college students are Donald Daiker, Andrew Kerek, and Max Morenberg, *The Writer's Options: Combining to Composing,* 3rd ed. (New York: Harper & Row, 1986) and Walter Beale, Karen Meyers, and Laurie White, *Stylistic Options: The Sentence and the Paragraph* (Glenview, Ill.: Scott, Foresman, 1982). The best resource for sentence-combining practice, of course, remains the students' own papers.

Elgin, Suzette Haden. *A Primer of Transformational Grammar: For the Rank Beginner.* Urbana, Ill.: NCTE, 1975.

Herndon, Jeanne. *A Survey of Modern Grammars.* New York: Holt, Rinehart and Winston, 1970.

Robert Lowth, 1762. "A Short Introduction to English Grammar." Menston (Yorks). In Scolar, P., 1967. *English Linguistics 1500–1800: A Collection of Facsimilie Reprints* #18.

Mellon, John C. *Transformational Sentence-Combining: A Method for Enhancing the Development of Syntactic Fluency in English Composition.* NCTE Research Report No. 10. Champaign, Ill.: NCTE, 1967.

Lindley Murray, 1795. "English Grammar." Menston (Yorks). In Scolar, P., 1968. *English Linguistics 1500–1800: A Collection of Facsimilie Reprints* #106.

O'Hare, Frank. *Sentence Combining: Improving Student Writing without Formal Grammar Instruction.* NCTE Research Report No. 15. Urbana, Ill.: NCTE, 1973.

THEORY AND IMPLICATIONS

1. What elements of traditional grammar carried over from the seventeenth and eighteenth centuries seem most dysfunctional today?

2. Why do you think that the distinction between "dependent" and "independent" clauses is dropped out in structural grammar? Do you think the distinction is problematic? Why?

3. What is useful and/or problematic about such distinctions as "performance" and "competence"; deep structure and surface structure; and "kernel sentence" and its "transformations"?

4. Traditional grammar and TG grammar both seem to begin with the sentence; the formula S→NP+VP seems to translate: "A sentence has a subject and a predicate." How, then, are these systems different?

5. The concepts of kernel sentences and their transformations offer a different perspective from traditional grammar and structural grammar. What is this difference? Why is it important?

6. What is important about distinguishing between single-based and double-based transformations? What are the underlying propositions in each of the double-based transformations listed?

7. What questions do you think that the structuralists and transformational-generativists had to answer if the structuralists were focused on performance while the transformational-generativists were focused on competence?

8. How do first and second language acquisition studies build on this important distinction between competence and performance?

PROFESSIONAL CONCERNS

1. How might the three different grammars be applied in the classroom? Could each of them offer students a new understanding of language? How?

2. How might you offer an explicit contrast among different grammars? Would such an exercise be useful? Why?

3. How might you use your knowledge of grammar to encourage students' intuitive grammar knowledge? As a principal, write a report to your faculty on the use of grammar in the classroom.

What Petey Forgot*

DORIS T. MYERS

"What Petey Forgot," from Understanding Language, *offers an explicit contrast between traditional and structural (here called "syntactical") descriptions of parts of speech. In a way, such an endeavor favors traditional grammar because traditional grammar emphasizes parts of speech, whereas structural grammar emphasizes larger constituent elements. The contrast provided here, however, underscores the differences between a prescriptive and a descriptive grammar; between a grammar using traditional explanations based on Latin and Greek texts and one using scientific descriptions of language heard; and between explanations that rely on abstract knowledge and deduction and those that rely on intuitive understanding. This essay supports the view that structural grammar is much more empirical and descriptive than traditional grammar. It also, however, raises questions about the need for such a terminology at all.*

Along with the breakfast food commercials on Saturday morning there is, or was, a commercial break called "Grammar Rock." With smooth lyrics and humorous cartoons, it tries to indoctrinate the Bugs Bunny set with the slogan, "A noun is the name of a person, place, or thing." What the young viewers are supposed to do with this information is never made clear, but apparently it's important. I knew a sixth grade teacher who used to spend quite some time in conversations like this:

TEACHER: Petey, a noun is the name of a person, place or thing.
[*Petey remains silent.*]
TEACHER [*encouragingly*]: Petey, what's a noun?
PETEY [*after a long pause*]: I done forgot.

This definition of a noun and seven other such definitions make up a body of wisdom called "the parts of speech." It's a traditional part of childhood, like spelling and orthodontia. Most people resist learning them, though perhaps not as stubbornly as Petey did.

Petey's resistance, however, was perfectly justified: the whole complex mechanism of language works best when we're unaware of what we're doing. We resist analyzing the parts of speech because doing so makes the easy matter of talking seem strange and difficult. The person who wrote "Please engage brain

---

before putting mouth in motion" just didn't understand how important it is for language to be automatic.

We also resist studying the parts of speech because there seems to be no security in them. The "right answer" changes mysteriously. The following sentences, for example, show that the word *down* can be used as five different parts of speech:

NOUN: Life has its little ups and *downs.*

VERB: He can *down* more beer than any other man in his club.

ADJECTIVE: She was depressed when she received her *down* notices, because she hadn't realized that her grades were *down.*

ADVERB: Jump *down,* now.

PREPOSITION: Little Red Riding Hood ran *down* the path.

[*It's no wonder that Petey "done forgot."*]

Nevertheless, being able to name parts of speech does have value, as we find when we begin to acquire a second language. In English we say "tomato sauce," but French reverses the order: "sauce tomate." If we know such terminology as "adjective," "noun," and "attributive" we can formulate this difference very simply and learn it once and for all. (At least some of the traditional part-of-speech names are used for every language of the world.) In fact, it's easier to learn the parts of speech for a foreign language than it is for English because we lack the automatic, "natural" ability to use the foreign language. This is the reason you sometimes hear people say, "I never understood English grammar until I took French (or German, or Arabic, or Japanese)."

If a person doesn't plan to learn a foreign language, then, why bother with the parts of speech? Why not just leave well enough alone?

First, one goal of linguistic study is to understand language competence—what people know about their language. Apparently one thing we all know intuitively is a rough classification of our lexicon into parts of speech. Second, English is a world language with a complex history and a sophisticated literature. It consists of much more than the routine phrases and sentences with which we conduct our daily affairs. In attaining this broader understanding, a knowledge of terminology is helpful, if not absolutely essential. In this chapter we'll discuss how English words are classified into parts of speech and the way these parts are combined into phrases.

If part-of-speech classifications are to be useful in describing sentence structures, the words must be classified on the basis of *syntax* (arrangement) rather than *semantics* (meaning). In classifying anything into categories, you get different groups if you use different criteria. If you classify the members of your class on the basis of sex, you'll get one grouping; if you classify them on the basis of whether they live on-campus or off-campus or whether they pay in-state or out-of-state tuition, you'll get entirely different groupings. The same thing is true of linguistic classifications. If we classify *no, not, un-,* and *-less* on the basis of semantics, they all belong in the same category because they all have a negative meaning; but if we classify them on the basis of syntax, they all belong in different categories because they fit in different arrangements. *No* goes with nouns, as in "No solicitors"; *not* goes in groups like "not at home" and "could not see"; *un-* is a prefix, *-less* a suffix.

Much of the difficulty in learning part-of-speech categories comes because textbooks do not always emphasize sufficiently the distinction between syntax and semantics. There is some correlation between meaning and syntactic class, but the relationship is unreliable. Petey once said that *run* is a verb in the sentence "Robin hit a home run" because he had learned the definition, "A verb is an action word." Semantically, *run* is certainly an action, but in that sentence the syntactic pattern makes it a noun. Likewise, two words can belong to the same syntactic category but not the same semantic category. Consider these sentences:

1. The child *hits* the new kid on the block.
2. The child *knows* the new kid on the block.

Syntactically both "hits" and "knows" are verbs, but "hits" is an action word while "knows" is not, except in a very figurative sense.

Besides the difficulties caused by the confusion between syntax and semantics, there are difficulties caused by the unnecessary assumptions that there are eight and only eight parts of speech. The ancient Romans first classified their words into three categories: (1) those which change form to show number and case; (2) those which change form to show person and tense; and (3) those which do not change form. Class 1 included what we today would call nouns, pronouns, adjectives, and participles; Class 2 included verbs; and Class 3 included prepositions, adverbs, conjunctions, and interjections. During the Middle Ages the number of parts of speech for Latin—no other languages were being analyzed—varied between seven and ten. Finally, one medieval grammarian asserted that eight was the proper number because there were eight kind of clergy in the Church.[1] (This reason is just as sensible as many of the rules Petey failed to learn.)

To have eight parts of speech works pretty well for Latin and languages like Latin, but when linguists began to work on American Indian, African, and Oriental languages, new parts of speech had to be defined and named. For example, in Thai an important unit of syntax is the classifier, a word which comes before a noun and tells what kind of noun it is. English has something like classifiers in phrases like "a *pair* of pants," "a *game* of tennis," and "twenty *head* of cattle," but we analyze them as nouns rather than classifiers because of the way they fit into our noun phrase pattern.

How many parts of speech are necessary for English? More than eight, certainly. The traditional class of adverbs needs to be broken up because it contains such a wide variety of words: descriptive words like "slowly," the negator

---

[1] Karl W. Dykema, "Where Our Grammar Came From," *College English* 22 (1961), 455–65. In *Language: Introductory Readings,* ed. Virginia P. Clark, Paul A. Eschholz and Alfred F. Rosa, 2nd ed. (New York: St Martin's Press, 1977), p. 281.

"not," intensifiers like "really," "hardly," and "almost," and transition words like "however," "thus," and "therefore." The traditional class of pronouns also contains a wide variety of words: personal pronouns like "I" and "we," pointers like "this" and "that," and question words like "who" and "which."

In an ideal situation, all the words of one class would fill the same slot and have the same inflectional and derivational forms. But human languages are never ideal, and English is especially hard to classify. Because we have so few inflections, we're able to use a noun as a verb or an adjective (or any other combination of those three categories). It becomes the new part of speech just by the place it occupies in the sentence. Because the language has changed so much over the centuries, even members of the same category do not behave alike. Thus "we" is used for subjects and objects. And some words—"that" for example—have so many functions that they have to be classified several ways.

Although it's confusing to have too many different types of words in one class, it's equally confusing to make unnecessary distinctions. For example, in describing English it's not necessary to have separate parts of speech for abstract and concrete nouns because the two types of words occur in the same patterns. We say, "I admire her *determination*" (abstract noun) or "I admire her *garden*" (concrete noun).

One of the most successful efforts to get away from the traditional eight parts of speech was made by linguist C. C. Fries (rhymes with *freeze*) in the 1930s. Fries ended up with nineteen classifications, but he called only four of them "parts of speech." The other fifteen were structure words, words that communicate how the sentence units are related. To emphasize the freshness of his analysis and get away from traditional associations, Fries numbered his parts of speech as Classes 1 through 4 and lettered his structure words as Groups A through O. Theoretically it doesn't matter what a class of words is called as long as the definition is clear, but in practice we find grammar easier to tolerate when the names are familiar. So we'll use Fries's definition of the "Class 1 Word," but call such words "nouns."

The four parts of speech which Fries defined coincide pretty well with what we might call nouns, main verbs, adjectives, and descriptive adverbs. These are the content words of our language. They're also called the *open* classes because the new words we add to our vocabulary always belong to one of these classes. The noun class is the most open one. We're constantly inventing or discovering new things, and of course they have to have names. The verb class is less open than the noun class, but we make new verbs freely by adding verb suffixes such as -*ify* or -*ize*. Adjectives and adverbs are somewhat less open than the verb class, but occasionally we find a new adjective like *humongous*, and almost any noun can become an adverb by the addition of the suffix -*wise*.

The open classes are also called *form classes*, because all of them have inflectional forms. The nouns change form by adding *s* to show plural and possessive. The verbs change form to show tense, as in start-starts-started-starting. Some adjectives and adverbs change form by adding -*er* and -*est*, as in sweet-sweeter-sweetest, although many of them use "more" or "most" instead. Many members of the form classes can also be recognized by their derivational affixes, such as -*tion* for nouns, -*ify* for verbs, -*ous* for adjectives, and -*ly* for adverbs.

TABLE 1 Comparison of part-of-speech categories

Traditionally Defined	Syntactically Defined
NOUN—the name of a person, place, or thing.	NOUN—recognized by plural inflection, derivational affixes, determiners.
VERB—a word that shows action or state of being.	VERB—recognized by tense inflection, derivational affixes, auxiliaries.
ADJECTIVE—a word that modifies a noun.	ADJECTIVE—recognized by comparison inflection, derivational affixes, ability to fit this slot: It was very _____.
ADVERB—a word that modifies a verb, adjective, or another adverb.	ADVERB—same comparison inflections as adjective, different derivational affixes. Fits slot in verb phrase; never modifies adjective or adverb.
PRONOUN—a word that takes the place of a noun.	
Personal—I, mine, me, etc.	PERSONAL PRONOUN—Occupies a noun phrase slot.
Demonstrative—this, that, these, those.	DEMONSTRATIVE—Same list. Also classed with determiners.
Indefinite—one, someone, nothing, none, etc.	INDEFINITE—inflected for possessive like nouns; otherwise patterns like personal pronouns.
Relative: who, whose, whom, which what, that.	RELATIVE—Same.
Interrogatives—who, whose, whom, what, which.	QUESTION WORD—introduces questions and noun clauses. Same list plus where, when, why, how.
PREPOSITION—a word that shows the relationship between a noun and the rest of the sentence.	PREPOSITION—defined by slot, distribution.
CONJUNCTION—a word that joins two parts of a sentence. Types:	
Coordinating—and, but, etc.	COORDINATOR—Same list.
Subordinating—words like if, because, after; also relative and interrogative pronouns.	SUBORDINATOR—words like if, because, after; relatives, question words not always included.
INTERJECTION—a word that shows strong feeling.	Not listed, since the word has no syntactic relationship to the rest of the sentence.
Classified with adjectives or pronouns.	DETERMINER—defined by position in noun phrase.

(continued)

TABLE 1 continued

Traditionally Defined	Syntactically Defined
Classified with adverbs.	INTENSIFIER—precedes adjectives, adverbs; may occur within verb phrase; not inflected like adverbs.
Classified with verbs.	AUXILIARY—occurs in VP's according to a definite formula.
Classified with adverbs; sometimes called "conjunctive adverbs."	TRANSITION WORD—occurs at beginning or parenthetically within clause; discourse-level connectives; examples: thus, therefore, then, furthermore, consequently, however.

Thus the four biggest classes of words—nouns, verbs, adjectives, and adverbs—may be referred to as the content words, the open classes, or the form classes.

Fries defined fifteen classes of structure words. Some of these, such as "well," the sentence opener, seemed of marginal usefulness to later analysts, so that Table 1 shows only twelve structure classes.

Another good name for the structure words is syntactic markers, because they signal what syntactic category the content words belong to. For example, it's impossible to know whether "run" is a noun or verb in isolation. But if it's preceded by "the" in "the run," we know it's a noun. If it's preceded by "will" in "will run," we know it's a verb. Structure words also signal the relationships of larger units of syntax, as in the sentence, "*While* I am gone, don't run *after* other women." "While" and "after" introduce important groups of content words. The structure words do not have inflections or derivational affixes. Thus, the only syntactic basis for classifying them is *distribution*—what slot they fit into. As Table 2 shows, many of them can fit into a number of slots, so that all classifications of them are somewhat confusing.

The classes of structure words are all *closed* classes, because we seldom add any new ones to the language. Although some advocates of women's liberation have tried to create a new non-gendered pronoun to replace *he* and *she*, the various suggestions have been slow in catching on. Instead, people who wish to avoid specifying sex use a pronoun we already have, *they*, to mean "he or she." "They" was a new addition to the language in the Middle English period, borrowed from Scandinavian. And lately I've noticed people using "plus" as a conjunction instead of "and." So it is possible to add to the closed classes.

Thus, various names for these small classes of words are structure words, the closed classes, and syntactic markers. They are also called *function words* in some texts because they are classified according to function—i.e., the slot they fill.

Some of the structure words have traditionally been put into one of the large open classes. For example, noun markers like *a* and *the* were classified with the adjectives, or described as "a special kind of adjective, the article." To make a strict separation of the open classes from the closed classes clarifies the way English syntactic structure actually works.

TABLE 2 Distribution of relatives and question words

Words	Determiner	Pronoun (NP Slot)	Relative (in Adj. Cl.)	Introducing Noun Cl.	Subordinator (Adv. Cl.)	Question
who, whom		✓	✓	unusual		✓
whose	✓		✓	unusual		✓
which	✓	✓	✓	unusual		✓
what	✓	✓		✓		✓
that	✓	✓	✓	✓	in phrase "so that"	
when			✓	✓	✓	✓
where			✓	✓		✓
why			✓	✓		✓
how				✓		✓

COMPARING THE CLASSIFICATIONS

Noun

Traditional: A noun is the name of a person, place, or thing.
Syntactic: A noun can be recognized by these characteristics:

1. inflection for *plural* and *possessive*
2. derivational affixes: -ness, -ment, -hood, -ation, -ship, -ity, -ism, -ist, -er, -ee, -ance
3. the headword of a noun phrase
4. may be preceded by a determiner

Since the traditional definition of a noun is based on meaning, it's necessary to know the meaning of a word in order to classify it as a noun. With the syntactic approach, one can be sure the "toves" in Lewis Carroll's "the slithy toves" is a noun by the determiner and the plural inflection, without having the slightest idea what a tove is. The traditional definition also fails to identify as nouns such words as "poor" in "The poor you always have with you" and "run" in "He scored a home run." "Poor" is, according to the definition, an adjective rather than a person, and "run" is an action (verb).

The syntactic classification also has its problems. Words like "scissors" and "tennis" have no plural inflections, and apparently no inflection for possessive. Should they still be called nouns? Most of us would vote yes, since either one can be a headword in a noun phrase, but at least one textbook votes no.

Verb

Traditional: A verb is a word that expresses action or state of being.
Syntactic: A verb can be recognized by these characteristics:

1. inflection for *tense*
2. derivational prefixes and suffixes such as be-, for-, fore-, em-, in-, re-, -ify, -ize, en, -ate, etc.
3. the headword, or main verb, in a verb phrase
4. may be preceded by one of more auxiliaries as structure words

Again, the traditional definition of the verb is based on meaning, while the syntactic definition allows one to recognize a verb without knowing what it means. The only problem with this category has to do with the auxiliaries, words such as "will," "can," "am," and "do." The traditional approach merely distinguishes them as "helping verbs." The syntactic approach puts them in a category of their own, but this isn't entirely satisfactory. Occasionally a sentence comes up in which one of them is the main verb: for example, Popeye's "I am what I am and that's all I am" and "She cans peaches every year." With "can," the meaning is so different that the main verb "can" and the auxiliary "can" probably ought to be considered homonyms, but there's no such clear difference between Popeye's use of "am" as a main verb and its use as an auxiliary.

Adjective

Traditional: An adjective is a word that modifies a noun.
Syntactic: An adjective can be recognized by these characteristics:

1. inflection for *comparison* by the use of -er and -est, or *more* and *most*
2. derivational affixes such as -ful, -less, -ly, -y, -like, -ish, -esque, -able, -some, -ic, -ical, -al, -ive, -ous, etc.
3. fits between determiner and noun in a noun phrase
4. can be a predicate adjective in a sentence like this:
   The thing was very_____.

Although the traditional definitions classify nouns and verbs by meaning, with adjectives the basis of classification switches to *function*—what the adjective does. Also, the traditional approach cannot differentiate between descriptive adjectives and determiners. Articles, for example, are often mentioned as "a special kind of adjective." The syntactic approach has a minor problem with adjectives that cannot be compared, such as "pregnant." (It makes no sense to say "more pregnant" or "most pregnant.") However, the syntactic pattern is so dominant in people's minds that many "uncomparable" adjectives are compared. The preamble to the U.S. Constitution calls for "a more perfect union" and we hear people say that a tourist attraction is "one of the most unique," even though "unique" means "one of a kind" and therefore logically can have no comparison. Despite these problems, there's no major difference in results between the traditional and the syntactic approaches.

Adverb

Traditional: An adverb is a word that modifies a verb, adjective, or another adverb.

Syntactic: An adverb can be recognized by these characteristics:

1. inflection for *comparison* by the use of -er and -est or *more* and *most*
2. derivational affixes such as -ly, -ward, -wise, -fashion, -style, a-, etc.
3. movability: the adverb can be placed in or near the verb phrase, at the beginning of the sentence, or at the end.

It's in dealing with the adverb that the traditional and the syntactic approaches are most at odds. The syntactic approach identifies as adverbs only those words that modify the verb phrase. The words that modify "verbs, adjectives, and other adverbs" are, according to the newer system, *intensifiers* (sometimes called *qualifiers*). The intensifier changes the intensity with which a statement is made, as in "The hand of the artist is particularly adept." The syntactic approach puts intensifiers in a separate class because they lack the movability of the open-class adverbs. On the other hand, the traditional approach has something in its favor: some words can be used both as intensifiers and as open-class adverbs. "Particularly," for example, can mean "in a fussy manner," as in "He examined the tomatoes *particularly,* turning each one over and over."

The characteristics of the open classes are summarized in Table 3.

Pronoun

Traditional: A pronoun is a word that takes the place of a noun.

Syntactic: The *personal* pronouns are a small class of words inflected for person, gender, number, and case that can occupy a noun phrase slot. Other types of words traditionally called pronouns should be put in other categories.

To say that the personal pronouns are inflected does not mean that they add endings, as nouns and verbs do. Instead, they change form completely. Also, they have changed over the centuries, so that the inventory of inflections is not complete. The differentiations of *person* have to do with viewpoint. First person is the speaker (I, we), second person the person spoken to (you), and third person the person(s) spoken about (he, she, it, they). Some languages have additional distinctions in person, such as first person inclusive (speaker and hearers) and the first person exclusive (speaker only). In all its history English has never had inclusive/exclusive distinctions in pronouns. The differentiation of *gender* is, in English, a matter of sex, and it's made only in the third person (he, she, it). In Arabic, there are gender distinctions in first and second persons also. *Number* is the distinction between singular and plural. It's made in all the personal pronouns except the second person. *Case* is the distinction between subjects, possessives, and objects, such as I, my, me, and he, his, him.

TABLE 3 The open classes

Inflectional Forms	Derivational Affixes	Positions	Structure Words
NOUNS Plural: -s Possession: -'s, -'	-ness, -ment, -y, -hood, -ation, -ship, -ity, -ism, -ist, -er, -ance, -ee, -dom, -ure	Head word in Noun Phr.	Determiners

VERBS
Pres: walk, walks
      see, sees
Past: walked
     saw
-ing Participle:
  walking, seeing
Past Participle:
  walked, seen
	be-, for-, fore-, em-, in-, re-, -ify, -ize, -en, -ate	Head word in Verb Phr.	Auxiliaries

ADJECTIVES Positive: ø Comparative: -er Superlative: -est	-ful, -less, -ly, -y, -al, -like, -ish, -esque, -ic, -able, -some, -ical, -ive, -ous	1. Between det., noun in noun phrase 2. After Be-verb as predicate adjective 3. As post-modifier (rare)	Intensifiers
ADVERBS Same as adjectives	-ly, -ward(s), -wise, -fashion, -style	1. Within verb phrase 2. Beginning or end of clause	Intensifiers

The words other than personal pronouns which are traditionally called pronouns are put into categories of their own when a syntactic basis of classification is used. No classification is entirely satisfactory.

For example, the *indefinites* (words like "one," "someone," "somebody," "anything," etc.) are like pronouns in that they sometimes "take the place" of a noun phrase. But they form possessives like nouns: somebody, somebody's. They can also appear in a typical noun phrase with a determiner and adjective, as in "the lonely one." (See the discussion of noun phrase structure further along in the chapter.) Thus the traditional approach of calling them pronouns has some validity, but they act a lot like nouns.

The *demonstratives* (this, that, these, those) are traditionally called pronouns, and they "take the place" of a noun phrase in such sentences as "*This* is my kind of place." But they also fill the same slot as words like *a* and *the*, which is a justification for putting them in a class of their own.

The *relatives* (who, which, what, that) are so called because they relate one part of a sentence to another, as in "I saw the child *who* stole the magazine." This group overlaps with a category of *question words*. All of the relatives except *that* can be used to introduce a question. In addition, there are some question words that cannot fill a noun phrase slot as the relatives do. Table 2 shows the various functions these words can have. In "*Who* stole the magazine?" "who" is a pronoun because it fills the noun phrase slot, but it's a question word because it introduces a question. How did our language get into such a mess?

Preposition

Traditional: A preposition is a word that shows the relationship between a noun and the rest of the sentence.
Syntactic: Prepositions are words like *of, in,* and *to* which are usually followed by a noun phrase called the object of the preposition.

The two approaches to classification here result in exactly the same list of words. The traditional approach defines the preposition (as it does the adjective and adverb) by *function*. The syntactic approach defines it by *distribution*. All the words that fit into the same slot in a particular sentence make up a distribution class. For example, in the sentence, "The clue to the murderer's identity was _____ the desk," the list of words that can fill the blank include "in," "on," "inside," "within," "outside," "under," etc. They're all prepositions. They're also related semantically, since all express some kind of physical position, although the early attempts to classify parts of speech syntactically tried to ignore semantics. This was a practical policy, since a word like "with" would not fit the slot only because of the noun's meaning. Change it to "The clue to the murderer's identity was _____ the other papers," and additional words like "with," "between," and "among" are revealed as prepositions.

The big problem of classification—one that nobody can make easy—is that many words belong to three distribution classes. They not only appear in the preposition slot before a noun phrase, but also as conjunctions to introduce a clause or as adverbs modifying a verb. Consider the word "after." In "The baby bear scampered *after* its mother," the word fills the same slot as other prepositions such as *before, with, to.* In "*After* the bears had left, we began to assess the damage to our camp," it fills the same slot as other conjunctions such as *when, although,* and *since.* In "The mother bear left, and the baby followed *after,*" it fills the same slot as other adverbs such as *quickly, clumsily,* and *immediately.* If the three lists of words coincided completely, we would have only one classification, but they don't. Thus, the categories cannot be neat and logical, for the structure of the language isn't.

Also, classifications may change as the language changes. In addition to introducing the prepositional phrase, certain prepositions are used more and more to complete or intensify the meanings of verbs. For example, we say that someone will "head up" a committee, "finish up" a task, "do in" an enemy, or "pig out" at the pizza parlor. Not all prepositions are used in this way. "In," "out," "up," and "down" are the most common. Perhaps in the future, linguists analyzing the English language will feel that these words should be put in a class of their own, since their distribution into syntactic patterns is so different from that of other prepositions.

Conjunction

Traditional: a word that joins words or groups of words.
Syntactic: Since classification is made on the basis of distribution, the traditional conjunction becomes two separate categories: *coordinators*—that is, joiners of syntactically equal elements—and *subordinators,* joiners of unequal elements. The distinction is somewhat confusing because a number of coordinators and subordinators are almost identical in meaning. *But,* for example, is a coordinator and *although* is a subordinator. They have about the same meaning (and even the same position) in the following sentences:

1. They gave a concert in Reno last year, *but* I didn't attend.
2. They gave a concert in Reno last year, *although* I didn't attend.

The distribution is different, however, in that *although* can introduce the first clause in the sentence while *but* can't:

1. **But* I didn't attend, they gave a concert in Reno last year.
2. *Although* I didn't attend, they gave a concert in Reno last year.

(The asterisk shows that the first sentence is ungrammatical.) Another difference in distribution is that *but* can be used to introduce a single clause and relate it to the rest of the paragraph. *Although* can't be used in this way:

1. *But* I didn't attend. (compete sentence)
2. **Although* I didn't attend. (sentence fragment)

In the first example, *but* is apparently being used as a sentence adverb (see explanation below) rather than as a conjunction. Since *although* can't be used this way, the two words differ in distribution. Why? As the bureaucrat said to the citizen, "There's no reason for it—it's just our policy." See Table 4 for a list of joining words most often used as coordinators, subordinators, and sentence adverbs.

TABLE 4   Joining words

Coordinators	Subordinators (can begin sentence)	Transition Words
And	Time: after, before, since, when, until, as soon as	Time: then
but		
or	Concessive: although, even though, while	Concessive: however, still, nevertheless
for		
so	Cause or reason: since because, as, so that	Cause or reason: thus, therefore, consequently as a result
	Purpose: in order that, so that, that, that . . . not	
	Comparison: as, as if, as though, as . . . as, so . . . that	Comparison: instead
	Universal conditions: whether, whatever, wherever, etc.	
		Additive: furthermore, moreover

Interjection

Traditional: a word that shows strong feeling.
Syntactic: If language is being analyzed syntactically, the interjection is ignored, since it stands by itself, never combining with other words to make phrases. It doesn't really fill a slot, so analysts have no interest in it.

Determiner

Traditional: no definition; all these words are classed with adjectives or pronouns.
Syntactic: Determiners are words that can be substituted for *the,* or that fill the same slot as *the.*

The determiner is an important structure word in English, because it enables us to turn any word into a noun. For this reason it's sometimes called a *noun indicator,* but in some ways that's an unsatisfactory classification. Only the articles, *a, an,* and *the,* invariably fill the determiner slot. Other determiners simultaneously belong to other classifications, such as demonstratives (*that* book, *That* is silly), question words (*What* amount would you accept?), and possessive nouns (*Jerry's* bike is broken) or pronouns (*My* phone bill is too high). Despite the remaining classification problems, it has been an improvement to take them out of the adjective class.

Intensifier

These are the words which, in the traditional definition, modify "verbs, adjectives, or other adverbs." The open-class adverb modifies only verbs, or perhaps the sentence as a whole. The words that can modify adjectives or other adverbs are the intensifiers, and their syntactic function is quite different from that of open-class adverbs. The most common intensifiers are *more, most, very, pretty, rather, really, fairly, somewhat, too, quite, less, least, hardly, scarcely.* See the previous discussion of adverbs for additional comments on intensifiers.

Auxiliary

In traditional grammar, these are classified with the verbs, but their function in the verb phrase is quite different from that of the open-class verbs. Open-class verbs are always the headword, or main verb, of the verb phrase; auxiliaries are the "helping verbs." See the heading "The Verb Phrase" below for a fuller discussion of the auxiliaries.

Transition Word

Another name for these is *conjunctive adverbs.* They appear within a sentence but they don't modify the verb or whole sentence as an adverb does, and they don't join one part of the sentence to another as a conjunction does. Instead, they join sentences to other sentences or even paragraphs. Some examples of transition words are *thus, therefore, nevertheless, furthermore, consequently, however, still, moreover, as a result, then,* and *instead.*

As this comparison of traditional and syntactic classifications has shown, there's nothing sacred about any particular analysis of language. Traditional classification is useful because it provides a rough-and-ready tool for the native speaker to use in handling many language problems. Most dictionaries use the traditional terminology as set forth here, although the *Oxford English Dictionary* follows an even older tradition by recognizing one class, the noun, and then further dividing it into *substantives* and *adjectives,* so that you may see references to "noun substantives" and "noun adjectives." Syntactic classification is useful because it helps us focus on the grammatical machinery of English—features like the determiner, the auxiliary, and the transition word—which we might otherwise ignore. For a closer look at that language machinery we'll now examine the structure of phrases.

THE NOUN PHRASE

The easiest way to recognize the noun phrase is to look for three slots: determiner, adjective, and noun: *the sneaky snake.* Each of the words is the filler of a different slot, and each filler has the same distribution (pattern of occurrence) as the other words which can fill that slot. We can think of the slot as a point of choice and the different fillers as the list of choices for that slot. In the adjective slot, we can choose "slimy," "scaly," "green," or "little." In the noun slot we can choose "grasshopper," "ocelot," or "professor," or any number of words. (Remember that both adjective and noun are open classes.) The determiner class includes *a, this, no, which, my, John's,* and *each.* Any one of these can substitute for *the* in the typical noun phrase.

The syntactic pattern for the noun phrase may be stated, for convenience, in an algebra-like formula. Since the noun phrase pattern consists of determiner, adjective, and noun, the formula is as follows:

$$NP = Det + Adj + N$$

The formula says that there are three slots in the noun phrase and specifies the part-of-speech category for the fillers of each slot. The formula is a first effort to understand the patterns of the English language. If we're unable to apply this pattern to a sample of the language, it doesn't mean that the writer or speaker is using language wrongly. Instead, it means that the formula is somehow wrong or incomplete. We can test the formula by applying it to a passage of ordinary English prose:

> The recent evolution of man certainly begins with the advancing development of the hand, and the selection for a brain which is particularly adept at manipulating the hand. We feel the pleasure of that in our actions, so that for the artist the hand remains a major symbol: the hand of Buddha, for instance, giving man the gift of humanity in a gesture of calm, the gift of fearlessness.[2]

The recent evolution, the advancing development, and *a major symbol* fit the formula precisely. But we also want to call *selection* and *fearlessness* nouns, since they have typical noun suffixes, *-tion* and *-ness.* Since the formula is intended to state what English-speaking people do when they produce a noun phrase, rather than what they "should" do, we revise it to show that the adjective is not always present, as in *the selection,* and that the determiner also is not always present, as in *fearlessness.* We can use parentheses to mean "optional slot." "The formula becomes: NP = (Det) (Adj) N. Now we're able to identify as noun phrases *man, the hand, the selection, a brain, the pleasure, our actions, the artist, Buddha, the gift, humanity, a gesture, calm,* and *fearlessness.* Since the noun slot is the only one in the NP which must be filled, the noun is called "the *headword* of the noun phrase."

There's another type of noun phrase in the passage which the formula doesn't cover. *We* in the second sentence and *which* in the first sentence are both called noun phrases because they fill a noun phrase slot in a higher level of syntax, the clause. Both these words belong to the class traditionally called the *pronoun.* We can correct the formula to include the pronoun as follows:

$$NP = (Det) (Adj) N$$
or
$$Pro$$

---

[2] Jacob Bronowski, *The Ascent of Man* (Boston: Little, Brown, 1973).

As it stands, the formula still fails to deal with compound structures like "the quiet, well-mannered girls and boys" and noun phrases containing different kinds of determiners like "all the many annoyances." We could set up a formula to cover these structures also, but it's more practical to use an oversimplified formula while remaining aware of its limitations. After all, the oversimplified formula does apply to the majority of noun phrases.

Much of Petey's discouragement with English syntax came from trying to analyze sentences with oversimplified formulas and categories, and then assuming that he was a failure because the analysis failed. We can avoid such discouragement by constantly remembering that we are using an inadequate formula.

THE PREPOSITIONAL PHRASE

Now that we have the noun phrase pattern, the formula for the second basic pattern, the prepositional phrase, is easy:

$$PrepPh = Prep + NP$$

The preposition slot is filled by a small group of words that all have original meanings of space relationships. Some examples of prepositions and their space relationships are as follows:

1. The runner walked *to* the starting line.
2. The cake is *in* the oven.
3. The book is *by* the vase.

Since we think of time as a sort of pseudo-space, it's natural to use prepositions to express time relationships:

1. The class meets from eleven *to* twelve.
2. The secretary can type five pages *in* an hour.
3. I expect the boss to arrive *by* four o'clock.

By extending the meaning of the prepositions still further, we can use them to express many other relationships, some of them quite surprising:

1. I gave the plant *to* Mary. (*To* shows that Mary is the receiver.)
2. Alphonse is *in* business for himself. (*In* introduces Alphonse's activity.)
3. The best ad presentation was created *by* Rhoda. (*By* shows that Rhoda is the doer, or agent.)

If you ever find yourself with some thumb-twiddling time, you might look up one of the prepositions in the dictionary. The great range of meanings will astonish you, and you can derive a certain sly satisfaction out of seeing what a hard time the dictionary-makers have in writing definitions for such a "simple" word. You will also see the futility of trying to define the preposition as a part of speech on the basis of semantics.

Here's the same prose passage with the prepositions italicized:

> The recent evolution *of* man certainly begins *with* the advancing development *of* the hand, and the selection *for* a brain which is particularly adept *at* manipulating the hand. We feel the pleasure *of* that *in* our actions, so that *for* the artist the hand remains a major symbol: the hand *of* Buddha, *for* instance, giving man the gift *of* humanity *in* a gesture *of* calm, the gift *of* fearlessness.

The passage contains five prepositions; and some of them are repeated, so that there are actually 14 prepositions in all. Each preposition is followed by a noun phrase. (The construction, "at manipulating the hand," which seems to be an exception, will be discussed later.) Notice that the prepositional phrases tend to be attached to the word that comes immediately before them in two ways:

1. Semantically: they complete, specify, or add to the meaning of the preceding word. For example, *of man* specifies what creature is evolving with respect to the noun *evolution.*
2. Phonologically: they are attached to the preceding word by the melody and rhythm of your voice when you read the sentence naturally.

Thus *the recent evolution of man* hangs together as a semantic and phonological unit. Furthermore, we can replace these five words with *it* and say "*It* certainly begins . . ." Since *the recent evolution of man* is a unit of some sort, and since it contains a phrase *(of man)* not mentioned in the formula, we must either find a new name for it or revise the noun phrase formula. When we study clause-level units, we find that either *the recent evolution* or *the recent evolution of man* can appear in the same clause-level slot, indicating that these two word groups belong to the same unit category. Therefore, it will make sense to revise the noun phrase formula to account for both. The following seems logical: NP = (Det) (Adj.) N (PrepPh). However, the language unit after the noun is not always a prepositional phrase. Sometimes it's a unit like this: *which we have studied,* as in *the recent evolution which we have studied.* Therefore, we need a more general term for the unit after the noun. One common name is *post-modifier.* The revised noun phrase formula, then, is this:

$$NP = (Det) (Adj.) N (Post-Mod.)$$

The noun of any prepositional phrase may have its own post-modifier, and the headword in that post-modifier may have its own post-modifier. This is normal. Language has wheels within wheels within wheels. It's like the old bit of doggerel:

And so we see that all the fleas
Have smaller fleas to bite 'em

And so it goes, and so it goes,
Ad infinitum.

THE VERB PHRASE

The verb phrase is the most difficult word cluster to recognize because it comes in such a great variety of patterns. Also, it's easily confused with the *verbal phrase,* which we'll attack later. Traditional terminology adds to the difficulty, as you see in the confusing similarity between the names *verb phrase* and *verbal phrase*. A further difficulty is the subtle and complex relationship between syntactic and semantic categories which apply to verb phrases. Finally, our English-speaking ancestors made a hopeless mess of the morphology. But with reasonable attentiveness and good cheer we can learn to recognize some important regularities within the verb phrase pattern. To do so, we'll use separate formulas for different parts of the total range of verb phrase possibilities.

The verb phrase must have at least one word called the *main verb*. It may also contain one or more *auxiliaries,* which Petey's teacher called *helping words* or *helping verbs*. Open-class adverbs, a few of the intensifiers, and the negator *not* may also be tucked into the verb phrase. These may or may not be considered part of the verb phrase, depending on the purpose or whims of the grammarian. In the sentence "The tour guide was not speaking comprehensibly," it's correct to say that the verb phrase is "was not speaking comprehensibly"; but since our purpose is to understand the way main verbs and auxiliaries work together, we'll leave out the "not" and the open-class adverb and say that the verb phrase is "was speaking."

The simplest verb phrase consists of two slots—a main verb such as "speak" and another slot called *tense*. The two slots are often combined in a single word. "Walked," for example, consists of only one word, but it contains the main verb *walk* and the tense marker *-ed*. The verb phrase "walks" also has two slots, *walk* and *-s,* a present tense marker. "Walk," as in "The companions *walk* as far as Moria together," also has a tense slot. The absence of any other tense marker shows that the verb is in the present tense. (As anyone waiting for the phone call that never comes could tell you, the absence of a signal communicates just as emphatically as the presence of one.) We can state this simplest verb phrase in a formula as follows:

Basic formula: VP = Tns + MV
Example: Jughead *laughed*.

For historical reasons, English has many verbs which use something other than *-ed* as the past tense marker—a vowel change, as in *speak-spoke,* or a change of the whole word form, as in *think-thought* or *go-went*.

As in other processes of syntactic analysis, we must distinguish carefully between syntax and semantics. When we speak of the tense slot or tense markers, we're speaking of syntactic forms rather than meaning. *Tense* is not the same thing as *time*. Tense is a syntactic category while time is semantic. In the sentence

"I *speak* whenever and wherever I am invited," *speak* has the syntactic form of present tense, but the meaning refers to a recurrent action. It's a peculiarity of English verb morphology that there are only two syntactic tenses, *present* and *past*.

Besides the two obligatory slots of main verb and tense, the verb phrase may have the following optional slots: modal, perfective, progressive, and passive. The presence of each of these slots is signaled by a combination of morphemes.

Modal: The term *modal* (pronounced / mow dəl/) is related to the word mood, and the modal auxiliaries, generally speaking, express moods—things like politeness, determination, hope, regret. The list of modal auxiliaries includes *can, will, may, shall,* and *must* in the present tense and *could, would, might,* and *should* in the past tense. Since *must* has no past tense, we use *had to* as a past tense form of it. To say that *could* is the past tense of *can* etc. is a convenience of syntactic analysis. It has nothing to do with time. For example, "You can go now" and "You could go now" both refer to the present time, but they convey subtle differences in mental attitude. The justification for listing the modals into present and past categories is this: every verb phrase must have a tense slot. When there's a modal in the verb phrase, the tense marker can not appear anywhere else in the phrase. It seems easier to put the tense slot in every verb phrase and call the modals present and past than to make a rule that every verb phrase has a tense marker unless it begins with a modal. Since the kind of rule we make doesn't change the way people speak, we might as well construct rules which have as few exceptions as possible. When the modal option is chosen, the formula looks like this:

> *Modal formula:* VP = Tns + Modal + MV
> Example: Jughead *will pay* for all of us.
> (Is the mood hope—or determination?)

Perfective: The presence of the perfective slot in the verb phrase brings into focus the whole scope of an action. It's so named because the original meaning of the word "perfect" is "complete." To say "I *had sung* in the choir for two years," focuses on the fact that the whole action took place in the past. "I *have sung* in the choir for two years" emphasizes that the whole action extends up to the present time. To say "I sing" or "I sang" avoids emphasis on the wholeness of the action. Two morphemes are required to express perfective: the *have* auxiliary (*have* and *has* in the present, *had* in the past) and an inflectional ending called past participle. For most verbs, the past participle is the same as the past tense marker: *-ed.* Other verbs have other past participle forms, often the *-en* or *-n* endings.

> *Perfective formula:* VP = Tns + Have + Past Part. + MV
> Examples: Jughead *had shown* talent in goofing off, his chosen field.
> He *has received* honorable mention.

Notice that the *Past Part.* morpheme is listed *before* the MV, even though in the actual verb phrase it appears on the end of the MV. When several of the optional elements are chosen, Past Part. combines with the following word, whatever it may be.

Progressive: In addition to the perfective option, which focuses on the wholeness of an action, English has the progressive, which focuses on the continuousness of an action. It shows that the action is or was a process, something extended in time. If we say "The child was squeezing the toothpaste out of the tube," we are focusing on the fascinating process of producing a long worm. To say "The child squeezed the toothpaste out of the tube" leaves undetermined whether it came out slowly or in a big squirt. The progressive option is expressed by some form of the *be* auxiliary (is, am, are, was, were, etc.) plus the present participle *(-ing)*.

> *Progressive Formula:* VP = Tns + Be + -ing + MV
>
> Example: Jughead *is learning* English grammar. (If you believe
> that, maybe you would like to buy the Brooklyn Bridge.)

Notice that the form of be is combined with the tense, and the *-ing* attaches to the MV.

Both progressive and perfective are technically called *aspects,* because they express a focus, a way of looking at the action. Textbooks often list such things as "present perfect" or "present progressive" as tenses in a tabular presentation of verb forms, but technically speaking, these "complex tenses" are a combination of tense and aspect.

Passive: The passive option shows that the subject of the verb phrase, instead of doing, had something done to it. The passive option is expressed by some form of the *be* auxiliary (is, am, are, was, were, etc.) plus the past participle (-ed, -en, -n, etc.) Both progressive and passive use the *be* auxiliary, but they use different participle forms. "The scouts were seeing" is progressive, while "The scouts were seen" is passive.

> *Passive Formula:* VP = Tns + Be + Past Part. + MV
>
> Examples: Jughead *was seen* by teachers as a disruptive influence.
> The meeting *was chaired* efficiently.

All four of the options—modal, perfective, progressive, and passive—can appear in the same verb phrase. Consider the sentence "The client *could have been being seen* for the past six weeks if the referral system had been working properly." *Could* fills the optional slot of modal and the obligatory slot of tense. *Have* is the sign of the perfective. There are two *be* verbs, one for progressive and one for passive. And *seen* is the main verb. Very few verb phrases use all the options at once. Although such long phrases are within our language *competence,* in actual *performance* we avoid verb phrases of more than three words.

Now that we've examined the verb phrase structure, let's look again at the passage from Bronowski. In the previous analyses of the passage we identified all the noun phrases and prepositional phrases. What we have left are the following:

certainly begins   and
is particularly adept   so that
feel
remains

The word groups in the left-hand column all contain one word which is inflected for tense: *begins, is, feel* (with the ø inflection), and *remains. And* and *so that* in the right-hand column do not and could not have a tense inflection. By morphology we can recognize *certainly* and *particularly* as *-ly* adverbs, and the appearance of adverbs is a good indicator of verb phrases. It's safe, then, to call the left-hand word groups verb phrases.

The word *adept* presents a problem. Morphologically, it's an adjective, since it can take the *-er* and *-est* inflections: "more adept," "most adept." In syntax it often fills the adjective slot in a noun phrase: "the adept mechanic." Yet we feel that "to be adept" is an action. But whether a thing is an *action* is a matter of semantics; whether it's a *verb* is a matter of syntax. Since we're studying syntax at the moment, we delete "adept" from the verb phrase. The second verb phrase is not "is particularly adept," but merely "is."

Before leaving the verb phrase, let's look at some additional syntactic patterns not covered by the formulas we've discussed, such as the use of the auxiliary *do* and its inflections, *does* and *did.* When a verb phrase needs to have two words and has no other auxiliaries, one of the forms of *do* fills the slot. When does a verb phrase need two words? One instance is the negative. The structure of English doesn't allow us to say, "I not studied." The negative must be associated with an auxiliary, as in "I could not study" or "I have not studied." When there's no other auxiliary, *do* must be supplied: "I did not study." If there's more than one auxiliary, the negative normally comes after the first: "I could not have done it." Placing the negative after the second, as in "I could have not done it," creates a subtle difference in meaning. This, incidentally, is the kind of rule that native speakers of English automatically obey. To foreigners, it seems awkward and arbitrary, and they must practice to get it right.

There's a further complication: the auxiliaries *have, has,* and *had; do, does, did,* and *done;* and *be, being, been, am, is, are, was,* and *were* are sometimes not auxiliaries at all, but main verbs. When used as a main verb the various forms of *have* mean "to possess" or "to be associated with" as in "I *have* a new car" (possession) and "I *have* a cold" (association). Sometimes a word can appear in both auxiliary and main verb slots at the same time, producing correct but awkward-sounding sentences such as, "The stereo was stolen before he *had had* it even a week." Such a sentence may make the speaker feel, "Wait a minute! That can't be right." But it is. The forms of *do* are used when a generalized verb is needed, as in "He *does* interior decorating and landscape design." This sentence is smoother and clearer than saying "He interior decorates and landscape designs." The forms of *be,* when used as lexical verbs, mean "to exist" or "to equal" or "to have the quality of." The slogan, "Love is," means "Love exists." "Mary is the boss," expresses equality: Mary and the boss are the same person. "War is hell" means that war has the quality of hell.

A third complication in analyzing verb phrases involves a special use of prepositions. Consider the sentence, "The revolutionaries blew up the street." The action is "to blow up," not "to blow." "Blow up" is an idiom, because the two words combine into a new meaning which is quite different from the meaning they have separately. Contrast the first sentence with this one: "The wind blew up the street." We can see that semantically the two actions are not the same. Must we analyze them the same way syntactically? The answer is "No," because the first sentence can be restated "The revolutionaries blew the street up." The second cannot be restated this way. We have found a syntactic difference. We solve the problem by creating a new part of speech. When a preposition combines with a verb in this way we call it a *particle*. If a preposition can be moved to the end of the sentence, it's not a preposition but a particle. Some writers eliminate the extra term by calling the particle an adverb, but it's not an adverb like "noisily" as in "The toddler blew noisily into his cereal bowl." Another test of the particle is that the idiomatic combination of verb plus particle can often be replaced by a single word. "Exploded," for example, can replace "blew up."

VERBAL PHRASES

The final complication is that verb phrases are often difficult to separate from verbal phrases. Consider this sentence: "The young women planned to go skiing." When asked to state the verb phrase, Petey's first impulse was to say "planned to go skiing," because the whole thing makes up a single action; but according to syntactic rather than semantic analysis, only "planned" is the verb phrase. "To go skiing" fills a noun phrase slot. It's a verbal phrase, not a verb phrase.

A verbal phrase is a word cluster containing a verb form which fills a noun phrase, post-modifier, or adjunct slot in a clause. There are three kinds of verbal phrases: the infinitive, the *ing*-participle, and the past participle. Let's look at the infinitive first.

The infinitive is easy to recognize because it has a clear structure word, *to*. (It would be logical to give *to* its own part-of-speech category, but no grammarian ever does.) The verb part of the infinitive phrase can be a single word, as in "to go," or it can include perfective, progressive, or passive options as in "to have gone," "to be going," and "to be seen." The modal option is expressed by a double infinitive phrase such as "to be able to go" for "can go" and "to have to go" for "must go." When a noun phrase or a prepositional phrase completes the thought of an infinitive (or of any other verbal phrase), then it's considered part of the phrase, as in "His purpose was *to see the world by himself.*" The infinitive phrase can have adverb modifiers just as verb phrases do: "to be easily seen." (Incidentally, this phrase is wrong according to Petey's teacher, who told Petey to say "to be seen easily" because one should "never split an infinitive." This is the one rule Petey learned thoroughly. It's also the one rule he didn't need. The best writers and speakers of English have always split infinitives when it pleased them to do so. The writers of "Star Trek" were entirely correct, and stylistically sensitive, in choosing to say "To boldly go where no man has gone before" rather than "To go boldly.")

The *ing*-participle contains a main verb ending with *-ing,* and it usually has a noun phrase or prepositional phrase to complete the thought. If the *ing*-participle fills an adjective or post-modifier slot, it's traditionally called a *present participle,* as in the following sentences:

Adjective: the *skiing* criminal was chased by helicopters.

Post-modifier: The criminal *skiing along the ridges* contributed some dramatic photography to an otherwise dull film.

The present participle can also appear before or after the main clause of the sentence, loosely connected with the thought:

Finding himself in a tight spot, the criminal surrendered.

When the *ing* participle fills a noun phrase slot, it's traditionally called a *gerund.* Here the gerund phrase is the subject of the sentence, and the whole thing could be replaced by *it:*

Skiing in well-run competitions is not particularly dangerous.

The Bronowski passage contains two *-ing* verbals—"advancing" and "manipulating." Can you tell the present participle from the gerund without a score card?[3]

The past participle contains a main verb ending with *-ed* or a special past participle form such as *seen* or *written.* Like the other verbal phrases, it may have a noun or prepositional phrase to complete the thought. It can appear in the same slots as the present participle, but it cannot be a gerund. Unless there is a special past-participle form like *seen,* telling the difference between it and a simple past-tense verb can be tricky. Consider this sentence: "The money, advanced under a low-interest loan plan, simply disappeared." "Advanced" is the past participle, and the whole past participle phrase is set off by commas. (Not all past participles are set off in this way.) "Disappeared" is the verb phrase. The key to identifying them is to ask which one needs a passive auxiliary. The money did disappear; no extra auxiliary is needed. But the money did not advance; it *was* advanced by someone, presumably the banker. Thus "advanced" is the past participle.

There are more problems with part-of-speech categories and their combination into phrases than the ones we have discussed. If, however, we pay attention to inflectional endings and the formulas for phrase types, we can classify most of the words in a particular sentence and pick out most of the phrases. When we can't classify a word or group of words, the unit may belong to a different level of syntactic structure—clause, sentence, or paragraph—or it may represent a dialect or speech style not covered by the analysis. A person ought to be content to leave these unclassifiables as unknowns instead of confusing the issue by making a wild guess. In many cases, two or three classifications might be equally

---

[3] "Advancing" is a participle and "manipulating" a gerund.

valid, and it could be fun to discuss the reasons for choosing one rather than another. Perhaps one reason Petey decided to forget the whole thing was that he had too many teachers who insisted that there was one and only one way of looking at a problem in analysis. Let's hope that someday he'll meet a teacher who agrees with linguist Edward Sapir that "All grammars leak," and who will accept "I don't know" as a valid answer.

THEORY AND IMPLICATIONS

1. Clearly, Myers favors structural (called "syntactical") over traditional explanations. What are some of the problems with traditional explanations of parts of speech? Do you agree that the structural explanations are much more helpful? Why or why not?

2. What confusions between semantics and syntax do you recall from your own grammar instruction?

3. How does Fries's grammar reinforce linguists' distinctions between content and function words for first language acquisition? Do you agree with Fries that this central distinction between class (content) and structure (function) words should lie at the heart of a grammar? Why?

4. Classes 1–4 can also be called the "form classes" because these classes of words have inflectional forms—they take word endings that change their meaning. Why should this feature be so important to mark in a grammar?

5. Structure (function) words in the revisions of Fries's grammar have 12 classes (see Table 1). Does this expansion of four in traditional grammar seem helpful? Why or why not?

6. Intensifiers are placed in a separate class (they are no longer simply adverbs) because of their lack of movability. Why do you think movability is so important a criterion?

7. What is problematic about such traditional grammar terminology as "modification"?

8. The formula N = (det) (adj) N provides an example of an objective description based on our intuitive knowledge of arrangement, one that avoids the unreliability of an appeal to semantics. However, the formula seems circular—a noun, ultimately, is a noun. What are the advantages and disadvantages of such a notational system?

9. A key lesson in this reading is the relativity of all classification systems. Why is this such an important lesson to learn when it comes to language descriptions?

10. Does the emphasis on parts of speech in "What Petey Forgot" seem contrary to the purposes of structural and transformational grammar? Why? How might you resolve this contradiction?

PROFESSIONAL CONCERNS

1. If questions have been raised about the usefulness of identifying parts of speech as a way of improving writing, does the syntactic system offer significant advantages over the traditional one? Do you agree with the author that to produce more than routine phrases we need to understand this grammar?

2. Devise a lesson that enables students, using their own notations, to determine the syntactic characteristics of parts of speech. Present your views in a journal article or letter to a principal.
3. Do you think that syntactical definitions, presented here as superior to traditional ones, might prove equally troublesome for students to learn? As a teacher informing other teachers, write a response explaining why or why not.

Alternatives to Teaching Formal, Analytical Grammar*

ELLERY SEDGWICK

This reading is an overview of practical solutions to the "grammar dilemma." As summarized at the beginning of the essay, teachers do not wish to ignore the plethora of errors in student writing, yet research confirms that direct analytical instruction in grammar neither improves writing overall nor eliminates error. So what should teachers do?

Sedgwick offers no definitive solutions, but does help clarify the issues. First, the research on grammar does not suggest that all *grammar instruction is ineffective. Rather, ineffective instruction usually involves analytical methods that emphasize labeling (e.g., parts of speech and types of phrases and clauses), diagramming sentences, and filling in blanks in workbooks. Second, the research suggests that "indirect" methods* are *effective, although they are often not consistently applied. Third, the research indicates that an entirely new curriculum, one that is integrated into the writing process, is needed for teaching syntax and usage. Old methods based on memorized rules and applications of such rules in isolated exercises, as well as teachers' correction of all errors, clearly do not work.*

Sedgwick makes an important distinction between direct and indirect methods, one that corresponds to what we know about language acquisition. Children do not learn language through direct teaching, correction, and sequenced skills; they learn it indirectly while they are doing something functional such as conveying a message. Thus children can learn syntax and usage so long as they are integrated into larger writing purposes. Other readings about developing literacy in this book confirm this need for integration. Editing for errors becomes one stage in the writing process.

Sedgwick's overview of indirect grammar methods is an introduction to more detailed discussions in other readings in this chapter. These methods include sentence combining and sentence expansions, discussed at length by Francis Christensen. Although the methods are not without problems, this overview offers teachers possible avenues for addressing a central problem in language instruction.

---

* Sedgwick, E., "Alternatives to Teaching Formal, Analytical Grammar," from *Journal of Developmental Education, 12* (3), 8-10, 12, 14. Published by Appalachian State University, Boone, NC 28608.

Many English teachers currently face a frustrating dilemma in teaching syntax and usage. Most of us believe strongly that our students need to be able to write syntactically fluent standard English; that college teachers, employers, and others who will make judgments affecting our students' lives still consider correctness very important; and that, like it or not, we are responsible for teaching it. We may also feel pressure from parents and administrators to teach standard English as one of the educational "basics."

On the other hand, we are aware that 80 years of research, much of it flawed but some of it impressively designed and in composite overwhelming, concludes that the study of formal grammar taught by traditional methods has very little or no effect on students' use of language. Braddock, Lloyd, and Schoer (1963), reviewing studies from 1945 to 1962, stated that "in view of the widespread agreement of research studies based upon many types of students and teachers, the conclusion can be stated in strong and unqualified terms: the teaching of formal grammar has a negligible or, because it usually displaces some instruction and practice in actual composition, even a harmful effect on the improvement of writing" (pp. 37–38). Sherwin (1969), reviewing more than 20 studies between 1906 and 1968, concluded that "after a tally of procedural and other limitations, the research still overwhelmingly supports the contention that instruction in grammar is an ineffective and inefficient way to help students achieve proficiency in writing" (p. 168). More recently, Hillocks (1986), reviewing a large number of studies over the past 20 years, reached essentially the same conclusion: "None of the studies reviewed for the present report provide any support for teaching grammar as a means of improving composition skills" (p. 138).

Caught between our conviction that our students need to be able to use the patterns and conventions of written English and our awareness of the research, we have four basic options. The first two are essentially evasions of the problem. But the second two together constitute at least part of a real solution.

First, we can reject the research and continue to teach formal grammar by traditional methods. Unfortunately some interpreters of the research have made disbelief easier by simplistically claiming that the research proves that all grammar instruction is not only a waste of time, but punitive. Some further imply that any concern with usage or syntax is antipathetic to teaching the process. In fact, we should be very skeptical of these simplistic summaries and look carefully at exactly what the major studies do indicate. If we do so, we find that they demonstrate that teaching formal grammatical systems by methods emphasizing analysis—defining and labeling parts, learning rules about how the parts function, diagramming sentences, filling in blanks—does not significantly affect the overall quality, or even the correctness, of student writing. The research is, then, an indictment of traditional methods for teaching formal grammar, not of the possibility or aim of teaching usage and syntax. Although we must examine the evidence carefully, to rationalize or dismiss the mass of empirical research data as flawed or irrelevant to our practice is an act of cynicism, a rejection of reason and evidence in favor of habit, prejudice, or political expediency.

A second response is to acknowledge the weight of the evidence but to continue teaching formal grammar by traditional methods despite serious doubts about its usefulness. Sharon Taylor (1986), in "Grammar Curriculum: Back to

Square One," indicates that many of the teachers she worked with to try to develop a new grammar curriculum decided on this course because they lacked materials and training in alternative methods of grammar instruction and because of pressures from parents and administrators. The problem with this course, aside from its pedagogical ineffectiveness, is that if we continue to teach what we don't believe in, we will do it half-heartedly and develop a defeating sense of frustration and futility.

The third response is to give up all systematic teaching of syntax and usage in favor of "naturalistic" instruction focusing on the writing process, including some work on editing and proofreading. This response has considerable merit, particularly when it shifts the focus of instruction from a heavy emphasis on analyzing grammatical systems to an emphasis on writing and editing. Over the past 10 years methods have been developed to teach editing and proofreading systematically and effectively, and these are undoubtedly a major part of a solution to the "grammar dilemma." Many of these methods are summarized in an excellent *English Journal* article by Lois Rosen (1987); these and others will be mentioned later in this article.

Some teachers cite three potential problems with this approach. First, instruction in editing and proofreading tends to focus on error correction rather than development of new syntactic patterns. Second, instruction in items of usage and sentence structure is often haphazard; it gives students no usable generalizations about how language works, and the specific items discussed are not likely to be practiced enough to become part of the student's usable repertoire. Third, in the pursuit of process, both teacher and students may relegate editing to such a low priority that it is seldom addressed. If overemphasis on sentence structure and standard usage ignores the purpose of writing and inhibits student writers, ignoring issues of correctness and syntactic development is also a disservice, albeit a somewhat lesser one.

While acknowledging the value of the editing approach, many teachers still feel that more systematic ways of developing students' ability to use syntactic patterns and the conventions of punctuation and usage are discoverable and necessary. For these teachers, a fourth response to the grammar dilemma is to develop an entirely new curriculum for teaching syntax and usage based on what has been learned from the research and integrated with constant practice of the writing process. Sharon Taylor's (1986) group of teachers felt that this was the best solution. But they also knew that it would require materials and training, and they felt that they lacked the resources, expertise, time, and administrative support to accomplish it.

Developing and implementing a new curriculum for teaching standard usage and punctuation and for developing syntactic fluency will require considerable time for teacher preparation, effective coordination among teachers, and substantial support from administrators. But individual teachers who are convinced that formal instruction in traditional grammar is ineffective can take a great number of steps in the meantime that will immediately improve instruction and speed large-scale change. The remainder of this article will suggest some practical strategies in three main areas: developing syntactical patterns, teaching editing and proofreading, and selecting and adapting textbooks. Little of this information is new; it is simply a partial list of ideas and methods that teachers over the past 20 years or so have developed for dealing with the grammar dilemma. In many cases, I have included references to materials or fuller discussions of the strategies reviewed. My inclination was to be inclusive on the assumption that readers would be selective for themselves.

DEVELOPING SYNTACTICAL PATTERNS

The following methods offer systematic instruction in sentence structure, punctuation, and usage that emphasize language use rather than analysis. Their purpose is to develop a student's syntactic range and to make standard sentence patterns habitual. But to transfer effectively to the student's writing, they should be integrated with and applied to composing, revising, and editing whole pieces of writing in some of the ways suggested at the end of this section.

Research over the past 15 years offers considerable evidence that methods involving sentence combining and sentence construction do increase students' command of English syntax (Hillocks, 1986, pp. 141–147). Hillocks summarizes a large number of studies by confirming an earlier finding that "extensive reviews of the research are unanimous in concluding that sentence combining, 'has been proven again and again to be an effective means of fostering growth in syntactic maturity.'" Research on sentence construction methods showed similar gains in ability to manipulate syntax. Further, several studies indicate that sentence combining and sentence construction not only improve students' syntax, but improve the overall quality of their writing as well (Hillocks, 1986, pp. 143, 147).

1. *Sentence combining* is the most widely accepted alternative to traditional grammar. It draws on students' intuitive knowledge of the syntax of their native language, and teaches through practice of correct patterns rather than by calling attention to error. While sentence combining cannot directly teach usage, it does give students practice in writing standard English while developing their abilities to manipulate an increasing variety of grammatical constructions such as coordination, subordination, relative clauses, infinitives, participles, prepositional phrases, appositives, and absolutes. It can also be used to teach sentence boundaries and many marks of punctuation. Recently, materials have been developed to teach sentence combining in a rhetorical context so that students learn to choose among alternative sentence structures to express appropriate tone, emphasis, and coherence.

Several widely used composition texts now use sentence combining exercises. The most popular has been *The Writer's Options* by Daiker, Kerek, and Morenberg (1986) which presents sentence combining in a rhetorical context. This text asks students not only to combine simple sentences to form more complex sentence structures, but also to combine sentences into effective paragraph and essay structures. It uses sentence combining to teach organization, emphasis, coherence, and tone as well as syntax, and punctuation. Other texts include *Easy Writer II* by Campbell and Meier (1987) and William Strong's *Sentence Combining: A Composing Book* (1983). Strong's short book *Creative*

Approaches to Sentence Combining (1986) is a very useful summary of research on sentence combining and is filled with practical suggestions on teaching it.

2. *Sentence expansion* derives mainly from the work of Francis Christensen and differs from sentence combining partly in that students generate their own content. The instructor may ask students to observe something and generate a basic subject and verb (or give them the kernel); then expand the basic sentence by adding various syntactic structures. Students may be asked to focus on adding certain kinds of modifiers ("who clauses," participial phrases, etc.) and using certain position slots (e.g., introductory position, between s and v). Instructors may add as much or as little naming and discussion of constructions as they wish. If they fear sentence expansion may encourage a bloated style, they can give practice in deconstructing sentences by eliminating modifiers.

Sentence construction requires no formal instructional materials. It is also very easy to integrate into the revision stage simply by asking students to add specific kinds of elements to sentences in drafts in progress. Killgallon's *Sentence Composing* (1984) has some good expansion exercises that focus on adding to certain slots or positions.

3. *Sentence modeling or imitation* was well known to every British school-boy of Winston Churchill's generation (and way before), but most teachers now don't feel obliged to use sentences from Latin for imitation. Imitation can be used to teach not only sentence structure but also punctuation. For a brief discussion of the method, see Constance Weaver, *Grammar for Teachers* (1979, p. 90). If the teacher selects model sentences from literary works that students are reading, sentence imitation can provide students with real insights into the style of particular authors and stimulate discussion of stylistic choices or effects.

Sentence modeling does not require elaborate instructional materials. The teacher may simply write a pattern on the board (say, two independent clauses joined by a semicolon) and ask the students to write five sentences of their own using the same pattern. If students need more direction, the teacher can provide a sequence of model sentences leaving certain slots blank; students rewrite the whole sentence completing the blanks. Patterns should be introduced system-atically in a planned progression which could be borrowed from whatever grammar text is available. Again, Killgallon's *Sentence Composing* (1984) contains a good sequence of imitation exercises.

Sentence combining, sentence construction, and modeling all encourage students to play with syntactic structures using their intuitive knowledge of the language. If not overdone, they lend themselves well to being treated as or turned into competitive or noncompetitive games.

4. *Transformation exercises* can help develop control over certain elements of standard usage such as agreement and tense. This is a technique borrowed from foreign language teaching and may be most appropriate for students with dialect interference problems. Students practice correct usage by rewriting passages transforming, for instance, present tense verbs to past tense, positive statements to negative, first person pronouns to third person, or passive constructions to active. The best materials for transforming practice are the student's own writings.

5. *Inductive grammar instruction* may be an alternative for teachers who are convinced of the ineffectiveness of traditional rule-governed teaching of grammar, yet still believe that if students consciously understand how language works they will use it better. In inductive instruction, students observe how a particular aspect of English functions. Then, drawing on their observations and their intuitive knowledge, they derive principles of grammar themselves in their own language rather than by memorizing the "rules." As a culmination of inductive instruction, older students might be asked to write their own class handbook on certain points of punctuation or grammar, stating and illustrating their own strategies for writing standard English.

Unfortunately, working out lesson plans and materials for inductive instruction is, like many good teaching practices, time consuming. Sources offering guidelines and samples of exercises are: Robert DeBeaugrande (1984), "Forward to the Basics: Getting Down to Grammar;" Robert Pooley, *Teaching English Grammar* (1957), and *The Teaching of English Usage* (1974); and Mina Shaughnessy, *Errors and Expectations,* chapter 4 (1977).

Instruction in syntactic development and standard usage using the aforementioned methods should be applied to the student's own writing at every opportunity. Since students should be free to develop ideas without worrying too much about form in the early stages of the process, most practice in sentence structure and usage is best integrated into the editing stage. The most effective time for a formal exercise in usage of sentence structure is while students are revising and editing, when it can be applied immediately to their own writing. Half the period can be given to discussion and systematic practice of an item and the other half to revising their writing to incorporate what they have learned.

Writing assignments can also be constructed to encourage the transfer of instruction to the student's own writing in the following ways:

1. Specify or encourage students to specify an exact audience and purpose for their writing and discuss the appropriate level of usage. Be sure that students understand that usage is not a matter of morality or logic but of effectiveness with a particular audience.
2. Designate writing topics, in some cases, that require students to use certain grammatical constructions. For example, to practice the past perfect tense, students could write an account of a past experience in which they were influenced by a memory of something that had happened before.
3. Ask students, either in composing (sparingly) or in revising, to use constructions they have studied. For example, assignment directions could ask students to use at least three parallel constructions or introductory participial phrases, or revise to combine at least three pairs of sentences by either coordination or subordination. These constructions could be marked or labelled in the margin. Research indicates that the easiest type of revision is adding information which can improve narrative or descriptive writing by adding modifiers or specific nouns that make the writing more concrete.

TEACHING EDITING AND PROOFREADING

The most direct, most easily implemented, and perhaps the most effective methods for developing correct usage involve teaching students to edit and proofread their own writing. This approach has the advantages of individualizing instruction, focusing only on usage errors a student actually makes, and not requiring elaborate materials. A good deal of research attests to the effectiveness of "process methods" such as peer editing and teacher/student conferences in improving the overall quality of student writing. Less research has been done on the effect of these methods on correctness, but studies by Calkins (1980) and by DiStefano and Killion (1984) have shown strong gains in spelling, usage, sentence structure, and ability to punctuate.

1. *Peer editing* not only provides more audience feedback for student writers than the teacher alone can, but, perhaps more importantly, gives the peer readers practice in editing which will transfer to their own writing. Peer editors should respond to larger issues of voice, content, and organization as well as issues of correctness and style. Most practitioners recommend that the teacher tie peer editing to recent instruction, provide teacher- or student-made evaluation sheets to focus peer response, and model with the class by applying the evaluation sheets to sample drafts that are mimeographed or projected with an overhead projector. Some teachers have found guideline questions calling for descriptive response (e.g., "State the main idea.") more effective than those calling for judgment (e.g., "Is the introduction interesting?"). For a more complete discussion of methods and results of peer editing see Stephen and Susan Judy, *An Introduction to the Teaching of Writing* (1981, pp. 96–103), and Thom Hawkins's "Group Inquiry Techniques for Teaching Writing" (1976).

One variation on peer editing is to divide the class into groups of four to eight on the day the paper is due and hold a round table at which each student in a group is to proofread other students' papers, looking for one or two particular types of problems of usage, syntax, or style. Students should mark the general area of a problem, but not correct it. At the end of the session marked papers are returned to each writer to complete the actual editing.

2. *Teacher/student conferences* can be an effective way to teach and give guided practice in editing. After students have dealt with larger issues and while they are in the editing stage, teachers can conduct one- to three-minute conferences either at their desks or moving around the room. The teacher might focus on one or two major problems, mark one or more examples, ask the student to explain and resolve the problem, supply a brief explanation if the student can't, and ask the student to edit the rest of the paper looking particularly for that problem. Having students read their writing aloud to you, checking what they read against their text, also helps them to spot syntax and usage errors.

3. *Proofreading instruction:* Shaughnessy (1977) suggests that part of the reason why traditional grammar instruction is ineffective is that it teaches students to spot errors only in highly controlled exercises, not in the context of their papers. Teachers need to show students how to proofread and apply "grammar" to their own editing. Students may be most highly motivated to apply grammatical knowledge to proofreading when they are asked to work on their own papers

or each other's just before handing them in for grading or, even better, for "publication." The following are some suggestions:

a. Focus on a limited number of types of errors (1 to 3). The teacher might give instruction in one or more of these just before students are asked to proofread their papers for it. Students could be asked to underline or label various features of their text that might cause problems (e.g., draw a line from each pronoun to its referent) and to focus proofreading attention on these features.

b. Have students review a checklist of errors they have made on previous papers before proofreading. They should keep this checklist, which can cite handbook page references for each type of error, as a regular part of their writing folder.

c. Have students read the paper aloud *slowly,* emphasizing punctuation. Students could work in teams: one reading the paper aloud slowly, the other noting any oral corrections of written errors.

d. Ask students to practice proofreading by reading one sentence at a time, beginning at the end and reading backwards sentence by sentence, or using a piece of paper to cover all but the line being read. This slows reading and encourages focusing on form rather than meaning.

4. *Editing syntax* for clarity and conciseness, rather than simply for correctness, can be especially profitable for more advanced students. Richard Lanham's "Paramedic Kit to Fix Sick Sentences" outlined in *Revising Prose* (1979) provides a good system for editing to clarify meaning. After modeling the system extensively with the class, the teacher can mark (or ask peer editors to mark) sentences in students' drafts and require students to rewrite them using the system. The basic points of Lanham's method are to state as clearly as possible "who is doing what here" by using concrete subjects and action verbs, minimizing "to be" verbs and passive forms, reducing phrases and clauses to single words, and eliminating hedges and redundancies.

5. *Writing for real audiences* and publishing student writing should be encouraged whenever possible. Students will expend more effort on editing and proofreading if they know their writing will be "public" rather than read only by the teacher. Modes of publication include classroom displays, class or school magazines, letters, writing for students in other classes or schools, oral readings local newspapers or radio broadcasts, and contests sponsored by civic clubs, etc.

6. *Selective marking of errors* should focus on major items in which you have given instruction. Then require your students to respond to any marking of grammar or usage errors by revising to correct the problem. Most students learn nothing from the time and energy you spend marking their papers unless they are required to make the effort to understand and correct the errors themselves. Selective revision makes students focus on particular usage problems and tells them that they, not you, are responsible for editing their writing. It also shows the teacher whether the student has understood written comments and can correct the problem. (Teachers who for years have assumed that students understand their editing marks and comments may be surprised to find that they don't.)

I prefer to make marks or comments for editing on a draft in progress but, even in the final paper, I mark sentences containing major errors "R" for rewrite and require students to rewrite each sentence or passage marked in full on a separate sheet. The best time for students to rewrite is in class immediately after the teacher returns the draft or paper because the student has the chance to ask questions and the teacher is available to explain comments or give instruction. (Some instructors who believe in "applied grammar" ask students not only to revise to correct the error, but to explain in their own words why it is an error.)

Viera (1986) suggests that older students not only rewrite but could also a) cite a text reference for errors, b) write out an explanation of major errors in their own words, c) write several sentences using the pattern or usage item correctly, and d) give lessons (including a quiz) on a major error they make to the class or a subgroup of the class.

7. *Evaluation and error:* Many writers on the relation of usage errors to evaluation of writing seem to reason by false dilemma. Which has more merit, they ask, the paper that is compelling but grammatically flawed or the vacuous but correct paper? This misses the point, which is that if teachers have not only assigned and graded the paper, but taught strategies for and devoted time to all stages of the process including editing, they should be able to expect a higher level of performance in all areas, including *both* substance and correctness.

Obviously, in evaluating papers teachers should make holistic judgments rather than an error count and should comment on content as well as form. A considerable body of research indicates that intensive marking of most or all errors is at least inefficient and quite possibly counterproductive (Sherwin, 1969, p. 167; Hillocks, 1986, pp. 160–166). Shaughnessy (1977, pp. 90–160) and other advocates of error analysis suggest focusing on specific types of errors, analyzing patterns and causes of these errors, and developing instruction strategies specifically to deal with these patterns. In marking or commenting on error, teachers should keep in mind the research, limits on their own time, usefulness of the comment, need to respond to substance rather than merely critique form, and the fact that some errors reflect syntactic growth. They should not forget that a lot of evidence indicates that parents and employers take standard usage seriously and a consensus remains that English teachers are responsible for teaching it.

SELECTING AND ADAPTING TEXTBOOKS

The methods reviewed thus far for teaching syntactic development and standard usage are alternatives to teaching formal grammar by traditional methods which the research has repeatedly shown to be ineffective. The selection and adaptation of the text used to teach grammar offers another set of options.

1. *Use the text selectively* no matter what textbook is chosen. One important option the teacher has is to shift the focus of instruction from covering the grammar book to constant practice in composing and editing. Many textbooks intentionally include material on every conceivable point so that every potential buyer will find comfortable material in them. Publishers also fill texts with drills and exercises so that they will have something that looks substantial to sell. This

doesn't mean that teachers need to drag students through the whole book. A good teacher can teach most of the important points about writing with simply pen and paper.

2. *List a few major problems* of grammar and usage on which you want to focus rather than trying to cover everything in the book again, and teach these major items to the point of application to the student's own writing. Selecting and focusing grammar instruction will also free up more time for actual writing. State curriculum guidelines are useful in focusing grammar instruction appropriate for each grade level. Robert Pooley, in *The Teaching of English Usage* (1974, pp. 183, 188–190, 206–107), compiles helpful lists of major usage items appropriate for elementary, junior high, and high school instruction. Don't waste time on minor or archaic points of usage such as "never end a sentence with a preposition, never split an infinitive, never start a sentence with 'and' or 'but.'"

3. *Revise the order and emphasis* of the text if you are stuck with a textbook that emphasizes formal analytical grammar. Begin with the sections that develop fluency and give strategies for the writing process, rather than with definitions of the parts of speech and analyses of sentence and paragraph forms. Integrate chapters on particular usage problems into the editing stage of writing assignments.

Rewrite the directions to exercises requiring diagramming, filling in blanks, or labelling so that they require students to use the constructions studied to generate their own sentences or longer units. This often works best if the teacher suggests subjects. For instance, if a textbook exercise asks students to underline adjectives and draw an arrow to the nouns they modify, give students a list of 10 items of clothing and ask them to make up sentences using adjectives to describe the color, condition, or style of these items or write a description of a person wearing them. If you feel it useful, students could underline adjectives and draw arrows to nouns in their own writing.

4. *Write your own grammar exercises* and instructional plans. Textbook publishers like to convince teachers that they need a lot of printed instructional materials. But teaching techniques such as sentence expansion and imitation require very little in the way of written materials. Students, not publishers or teachers, need to do most of the writing if they are to learn how to write. If you are interested in creating your own sentence combining exercises, Charles Cooper's article "An Outline for Writing Sentence Combining Problems" (1973) shows how.

5. *Create a bibliography* and a file of instructional materials, including sentence combining and expanding exercises, that can be reproduced and shared with other teachers. A thermofax machine, which makes a ditto master from a photocopy, is invaluable and well worth including in your equipment budget.

6. *Take an active part on committees* selecting composition or language arts textbooks. This is one important step teachers can take to bring about wide-scale changes in the way standard English is taught. Obviously, the textbook has an enormous effect on what gets taught, and there are very major differences in the way current texts treat grammar and usage. Some texts separate grammar from writing and emphasize analysis. These often begin with long sections on grammar, diction, and sentence structure before asking students actually to write anything longer than a sentence. Other texts, reflecting current research, begin with the

writing process, integrate grammar with editing, and emphasize application. As members of text selection committees, we can summarize for colleagues the research on grammar instruction in support of texts that a) give appropriate emphasis from the beginning to actual writing, not rules and drills, b) integrate instruction on sentence structure and usage with editing, not treating it as an end in itself, and c) contain sentence combining and other exercises requiring use of grammatical structures, not just labelling and filling in the blanks. One good summary of the research on grammar and its implications for instruction is the SLATE starter sheet "Back to Basics: Composition" (August, 1976) available from NCTE (National Council of Teachers of English). (NCTE encourages reproduction of these materials for distribution to any interested party.)

7. *Evaluate carefully any computer-aided instruction software* that the school is considering and do not confuse technical innovation with pedagogical progress. Much current CAI on grammar/usage is reminiscent of the worst aspects of traditional workbook grammar drills: A rule is given and students are asked to identify forms, fill in blanks, or punctuate according to the rule. The programs very seldom require students to write even sentences, much less longer pieces of discourse. Some programs have been developed to analyze the student's text itself (WANDAH, HB Writer, Epistle, etc.) but many of these yield information of dubious value (readability ratings, word counts, etc.) and few seem appropriate to beginning writers. CAI reviews can be found in journals such as *Classroom Computer News, The Computing Teacher, Creative Computing,* and *Electronic Learning.* The NCTE also has a set of guidelines for evaluating instructional software.

CONCLUSION

The "grammar dilemma" is soluble. Teachers aware of the extensive research demonstrating that formal analytical grammar is ineffective in improving either the quality or correctness of student writing do not have to give up teaching standard usage and the varieties of sentence structure. Alternatives to traditional instruction in formal grammar do exist. Some have been practiced for long enough to have been demonstrated effective and incorporated into texts. Others are still being developed, refined, and researched by innovative teachers who believe that teaching syntactic development and standard usage is important, possible, and compatible with teaching the writing process.

REFERENCES

Braddock, R., Lloyd Jones, R., & Schoer, L. (1963). *Research in writing composition.* Champaign, IL: NCTE.

Calkins, L. (1980, May). When children want to punctuate: Basic skills belong in context. *Language Arts, 57,* 567–573.

Campbell, D., & Meier, T. (1987). *Easy writer II.* New York: Harper and Row.

Cooper, C. (1973, January). An outline for writing sentence combining problems. *English Journal, 62,* 98–108.

Daiker, D., Kerek, A., & Morenberg, M. (1986). *The writer's options* (3rd ed.) New York: Harper.

DeBeaugrande, R. (1984, October). Forward to the basics: Getting down to grammar. *College Composition and Communication, 35,* 358-367.

DiStephano, P., & Killion, J. (1984, December). Assessing writing skills through a process approach. *English Education, 16,* 203-207.

Hawkins, T. (1976, March). Group inquiry techniques for teaching writing. *College English, 37,* 637-646.

Hillocks, G. (1986). *Research on written composition.* Urbana, IL: NCRE/ERIC.

Judy, S., & Judy, S. (1981). *An introduction to the teaching of writing.* New York: Wiley.

Killgallon, D. (1984). *Sentence composing.* Upper Montclair, NJ: Boynton/Cook.

Lanham, R. (1979). *Revising prose.* New York: Scribner's.

Pooley, R. (1957). *Teaching English grammar.* Urbana, IL: NCTE.

Pooley, R. (1974). *The teaching of English usage.* Urbana, IL: NCTE.

Rosen, L. (1987, March). Developing correctness in student writing. *English Journal, 76,* 62-69.

Shaughnessy, M. (1977). *Errors and expectations.* New York: Oxford.

Sherwin, J. S. (1969). *Four problems in teaching English.* Urbana, IL: NCTE.

SLATE Steering Committee. (1976, August). *Back to the basics: Composition,* (4). Urbana, IL: NCTE.

Strong, W. (1986). *Creative approaches to sentence combining.* Urbana, IL: ERIC.

Strong, W. (1983). *Sentence combining: A composing book* (2nd ed.) New York: Random House.

Taylor, S. (1986, January). Grammar curriculum: Back to square one. *English Journal, 75,* 94-98.

Viera, C. (1986, February). Helping students to help themselves: An approach to grammar. *College Composition and Communication, 37,* 94-96.

Weaver, C. (1979). *Grammar for teachers.* Urbana, IL: NCTE.

THEORY AND IMPLICATIONS

1. What might be the problems with sentence-combining exercises, given that the author emphasizes that increasing students "syntactic range" needs to be "integrated with and applied to composing, revising, and editing whole pieces of writing"?

2. What are the benefits and problems with sentence expansion?

3. What are the potential advantages and disadvantages of sentence modeling? What language principles does it support or contradict?

4. What potential advantages and disadvantages do you see in transformation exercises?

5. What benefits do you see in using inductive grammar? What questions does its use raise?

6. When teachers selectively respond to grammar errors, how should they determine which errors to mark?

7. What if students neither understand error nor have the grammar vocabulary to understand a teacher's explanation? To what extent do teachers necessarily rely on a grammar vocabulary they assume to be in place? What problems does this create?

8. How does the teaching of an inductive grammar support or contradict language acquisition principles?

PROFESSIONAL CONCERNS

1. Describe to another teacher or to a principal how you might create an inductive grammar.
2. Write a critique of this essay explaining what was helpful and not helpful about its approach to the "grammar dilemma." What do teachers gain from it? What questions are they still left with? Does it offer them a point of departure? Explain.

A Generative Rhetoric of the Sentence*

FRANCIS CHRISTENSEN

"A Generative Rhetoric of the Sentence" is an application of modern grammars that encourages the productive use of grammatical structures. Christensen is concerned not only with sentence complexity—a complexity resulting from the "combining" of structures already created—but also with a means of "generating" or creating new structures, a method that duplicates thought processes. Thus his grammar-based "rhetoric" addresses such issues as the writer's shifting levels of generality and direction of movement in the sentence. Such concerns mean that Christensen's grammar serves the prewriting or discovery stage, rather than simply the editing stage, of writing.

Christensen posits four key principles that relate the linear structures of writing to thought processes, offering a method for producing, not merely analyzing, those structures: the principle of addition, the principle of direction of modification or direction of movement, the principle of levels of generality, and the principle of texture. Addition involves the notion of writing sentences as adding modifiers—especially free modifiers, which modify the sentence as a whole and can be moved around. Direction of movement involves the placement of modifiers to shape the mind's movement forward or backward as it "ponders" an idea. Level of generality involves the meaning in these structures, which tends to be more abstract in the base clause and to move to particulars in the modifying structures. Texture is the number of levels in any sentence, which reveals the depth of modification.

Because Christensen seeks to relate grammar to thought, his grammar begins with a distinction not typically emphasized in traditional, structural, or transformational-generative grammars: the distinction between free and bound modifiers. (Interestingly, this distinction also plays a role in the classifications offered by structural grammar for parts of speech, whereas class and structure words differ on this same basis.) Christensen's interest lies in creating free modifiers because they are "sentence" modifiers—they qualify the

---

entire idea of the main clause and duplicate the movement of the mind as it rethinks, qualifies, and ponders a broad idea through example, detail, or explanation. Therefore, instead of seeing the writer as adding on discrete bits of information (as in "The bright red balloon sailed treacherously out over the jagged, high rocks . . ."), Christensen views the writer as adding modifying phrases and clauses to the whole "base" idea. This analysis offers teachers methods for helping students to analyze and produce complex sentences.

We do not have time in our classes to teach everything about the rhetoric of the sentence. I believe in "island hopping," concentrating on topics where we can produce results and leaving the rest, including the "comma splice" and the "run-on sentence," to die on the vine. The balanced sentence deserves some attention in discursive writing, and the enormous range of coordinate structures deserves a bit more. The rhythm of good modern prose comes about equally from the multiple-tracking of coordinate constructions and the downshifting and backtracking of free modifiers. But the first comes naturally; the other needs coaxing along.

This coaxing is the clue to the meaning of *generative* in my title. (It is not derived from generative grammar; I used it before I ever heard of Chomsky.) The teacher can use the idea of levels of structure to urge the student to add further levels to what he has already produced, so that the structure itself becomes an aid to discovery.

This system of analysis by levels is essentially an application of immediate constituent analysis. IC analysis reveals what goes with what. In such analysis the free modifiers are cut off first. The order in which initial, medial, and final elements are cut off is immaterial, but one might as well start at the beginning. Thus, in sentence 2 below, the first cut would take off the whole set of initial modifiers. Then the members of a coordinate set are separated and, if the dissection is to be carried out to the ultimate constituents, analyzed one by one in order. In sentence 1, the first cut would come at the end of the base clause, taking off levels 2, 3, and 4 together since they are dependent on one another. Another cut would come at the end of level 2, taking off levels 3 and 4 together since 4 is a modifier of 3. Medial modifiers have to be cut *out* rather than *off.*

If the new grammar is to be brought to bear on composition, it must be brought to bear on the rhetoric of the sentence. We have a workable and teachable, if not a definitive, modern grammar; but we do not have, despite several titles, a modern rhetoric.

In composition courses we do not really teach our captive charges to write better—we merely *expect* them to. And we do not teach them how to write better because we do not know how to teach them to write better. And so we merely go through the motions. Our courses with their tear-out workbooks and four-pound anthologies are elaborate evasions of the real problem. They permit us to put in our time and do almost anything else we'd rather be doing instead of buckling down to the hard work of making a difference in the student's under-standing and manipulation of language.

With hundreds of handbooks and rhetorics to draw from, I have never been able to work out a program for teaching the sentence as I find it in the work of contemporary writers. The chapters on the sentence all adduce the traditional rhetorical classification of sentences as loose, balanced, and periodic. But the term *loose* seems to be taken as a pejorative (it sounds immoral); our students, no Bacons or Johnsons, have little occasion for balanced sentences; and some of our worst perversions of style come from the attempt to teach them to write periodic sentences. The traditional grammatical classification of sentences is equally barren. Its use in teaching composition rests on a semantic confusion, equating complexity of structure with complexity of thought and vice versa. But very simple thoughts may call for very complex grammatical constructions. Any moron can say "I don't know who done it." And some of us might be puzzled to work out the grammar of "All I want is all there is," although any chit can think it and say it and act on it.

The chapters on the sentence all appear to assume that we think naturally in primer sentences, progress naturally to compound sentences, and must be taught to combine the primer sentences into complex sentences—and that complex sentences are the mark of maturity. We need a rhetoric of the sentence that will do more than combine the ideas of primer sentences. We need one that will *generate* ideas.

For the foundation of such a generative or productive rhetoric I take the statement from John Erskine, the originator of the Great Books courses, himself a novelist. In the essay "The Craft of Writing" (*Twentieth Century English*, Philosophical Library, 1946) he discusses a principle of the writer's craft which, though known he says to all practitioners, he has never seen discussed in print. The principle is this: "When you write, you make a point, not by subtracting as though you sharpened a pencil, but by adding." We have all been told that the formula for good writing is the concrete noun and the active verb. Yet Erskine says, "What you say is found not in the noun but in what you add to qualify the noun. . . . The noun, the verb, and the main clause serve merely as the base on which meaning will rise. . . . The modifier is the essential part of any sentence." The foundation, then, for a generative or productive rhetoric of the sentence is that composition is essentially a process of *addition*.

But speech is linear, moving in time, and writing moves in linear space, which is analogous to time. When you add a modifier, whether to the noun, the verb, or the main clause, you must add it either before the head or after it. If you add it before the head, the direction of modification can be indicated by an arrow pointing forward; if you add it after, by an arrow pointing backward. Thus we have the second principle of a generative rhetoric—the principle of *direction of modification* or *direction of movement*.

Within the clause there is not much scope for operating with this principle. The positions of the various sorts of close, or restrictive, modifiers are generally fixed and the modifiers are often obligatory—"The man who came to dinner remained till midnight." Often the only choice is whether to add modifiers. What I have seen of attempts to bring structural grammar to bear on composition usually boils down to the injunction to "load the patterns." Thus "pattern practice" sets students to accreting sentences like this: "The small boy on the red bicycle who lives with his happy parents on our shady street often coasts down the steep street until he comes to the city park." This will never do. It has no rhythm and hence no life; it is tone-deaf. It is the need that will burgeon into gobbledegook. One of the hardest things in writing is to keep the noun clusters and verb clusters short.

It is with modifiers added to the clause—that is, with sentence modifiers—that the principle comes into full play. The typical sentence of modern English, the kind we can best spend our efforts trying to teach, is what we may call the *cumulative sentence*. The main clause, which may or may not have a sentence modifier before it, advances the discussion; but the additions move backward, as in this clause, to modify the statement of the main clause or more often to explicate or exemplify it, so that the sentence has a flowing and ebbing move-ment, advancing to a new position and then pausing to consolidate it, leaping and lingering as the popular ballad does. The first part of the preceding compound sentence has one addition, placed within it; the second part has 4 words in the main clause and 49 in the five additions placed after it.

The cumulative sentence is the opposite of the periodic sentence. It does not represent the idea as conceived, pondered over, reshaped, packaged, and delivered cold. It is dynamic rather than static, representing the mind thinking. The main clause ("the additions move backward" above) exhausts the mere fact of the idea; logically, there is nothing more to say. The additions stay with the same idea, probing its bearings and implications, exemplifying it or seeking an analogy or metaphor for it, or reducing it to details. Thus the mere form of the sentence generates ideas. It serves the needs of both the writer and the reader, the writer by compelling him to examine his thought, the reader by letting him into the writer's thought.

Addition and direction of movement are structural principles. They involve the grammatical character of the sentence. Before going on to other principles, I must say a word about the best grammar as the foundation for rhetoric. I cannot conceive any useful transactions between teacher and students unless they have in common a language for talking about sentences. The best grammar for the present purpose is the grammar that best displays the layers of structure of the English sentence. The best I have found in a textbook is the combination of immediate constituent and transformation grammar in Paul Roberts's *English Sentences*. Traditional grammar, whether oversimple as in the school tradition or overcomplex as in the scholarly tradition, does not reveal the language as it operates; it leaves everything, to borrow a phrase from Wordsworth, "in discon-nection dead and spiritless." *English Sentences* is oversimplified and it has gaps, but it displays admirably the structures that rhetoric must work with—primarily sentence modifiers, including nonrestrictive relative and subordinate clauses, but, far more important, the array of noun, verb, and adjective clusters. It is para-doxical that Professor Roberts, who has done so much to make the teaching of composition possible, should himself be one of those who think that it cannot be taught. Unlike Ulysses, he does not see any work for Telemachus to work.

Layers of structure, as I have said, is a grammatical concept. To bring in the dimension of meaning, we need a third principle—that of *levels of generality* or *levels of abstraction.* The main or base clause is likely to be stated in general or abstract or plural terms. With the main clause stated, the forward movement of the sentence stops, the writer shifts down to a lower level of generality or abstraction or to singular terms, and goes back over the same ground at this lower level.[1] There is no theoretical limit to the number of structural layers or levels, each[2] at a lower level of generality, any or all of them compounded, that a speaker or writer may use. For a speaker, listen to Lowell Thomas; for a writer, study William Faulkner. To a single independent clause, he may append a page of additions, but usually all clear, all grammatical, once we have learned how to read him. Or, if you prefer, study Hemingway, the master of the simple sentence: "George was coming down in the telemark position, kneeling, one leg forward and bent, the other trailing, his sticks hanging like some insect's thin legs, kicking up puffs of snow, and finally the whole kneeling, trailing figure coming around in a beautiful right curve, crouching, the legs shot forward and back, the body leaning out against the swing, the sticks accenting the curve like points of light, all in a wild cloud of snow." Only from the standpoint of school grammar is this a simple sentence.

This brings me to the fourth, and last, principle, that of texture. *Texture* provides a descriptive or evaluative term. If a writer adds to few of his nouns or verbs or main clauses and adds little, the texture may be said to be thin. The style will be plain and bare. The writing of most of our students is thin—even threadbare. But if he adds frequently or much or both, then the texture may be said to be dense or rich. One of the marks of an effective style, especially in narrative, is variety in the texture, the texture varying with the change in pace, the variation in texture producing the change in pace. It is not true, as I have seen it asserted, that fast action calls for short sentences; the action is fast in the sentence by Hemingway above. In our classes, we have to work for greater density and variety in texture and greater concreteness and particularity in what is added.

I have been operating at a fairly high level of generality. Now I must downshift and go over the same points with examples. The most graphic way to exhibit the layers of structure is to indent the word groups of a sentence and to number the levels. The first three sentences illustrate the various positions of the added sentence modifiers—initial, medial, and final. The symbols mark the grammatical character of the additions: SC, subordinate clause; RC, relative clause; NC, noun cluster; VC, verb cluster; AC, adjective cluster; A + A, adjective series; Abs, absolute (i.e., a VC with a subject of its own); PP, prepositional phrase. The elements set

---

[1] Cf. Leo Rockas "Abstract and Concrete Sentences," *CCC,* May 1963. Rockas describes sentences as abstract or concrete, the abstract implying the concrete and vice versa. Readers and writers, he says, must have the knack of apprehending the concrete in the abstract and the abstract in the concrete. This is true and valuable. I am saying that within a single sentence the writer may present more than one level of generality, translating the abstract into the more concrete in added levels.

[2] This statement is not quite tenable. Each helps to make the idea of the base clause more concrete or specific, but each is not more concrete or specific, than the one immediately above it.

off as on a lower level are marked as sentence modifiers by junctures or punctuation. The examples have been chosen to illustrate the range of constructions used in the lower levels; after the first few they are arranged by the number of levels. The examples could have been drawn from poetry as well as from prose. Those not attributed are by students.

1

1 He dipped his hands in the bichloride solution and shook them,
    2 a quick shake, (NC)
        3 fingers down, (Abs)
            4 like the fingers of a pianist above the keys. (PP)

Sinclair Lewis

2

    2 Calico-coated, (AC)
    2 small-bodied, (AC)
        3 with delicate legs and pink faces in which their mismatched eyes rolled
           wild and subdued, (PP)
1 they huddled,
    2 gaudy motionless and alert, (A + A)
    2 wild as deer, (AC)
    2 deadly as rattlesnakes, (AC)
    2 quiet as doves. (AC)

William Faulkner

3

1 The bird's eye, / , remained fixed upon him;
    2 / bright and silly as a sequin (AC)
1 its little bones, / , seemed swooning in his hand.
    2 / wrapped . . . in a warm padding of feathers (VC)

Stella Benson

4

1 The jockeys sat bowed and relaxed,
    2 moving a little at the waist with the movement of their horses. (VC)

Katherine Anne Porter

5

1 The flame sidled up the match,
    2 driving a film of moisture and a thin strip of darker grey before it. (VC)

6

1 She came among them behind the man,
    2 gaunt in the gray shapeless garment and the sunbonnet, (AC)
    2 wearing stained canvas gymnasium shoes. (VC)

Faulkner

7

1 The Texan turned to the nearest gatepost and climbed to the top of it,
   2 his alternate thighs thick and bulging in the tight trousers, (Abs)
   2 the butt of the pistol catching and losing the sun in pearly gleams. (Abs)

Faulkner

8

1 He could sail for hours,
   2 searching the blanched grasses below him with his telescopic eyes, (VC)
   2 gaining height against the wind, (VC)
   2 descending in mile-long, gently declining swoops when he curved and
      rode back, (VC)
   2 never beating a wing. (VC)

Walter Van Tilburg Clark

9

1 They regarded me silently,
   2 Brother Jack with a smile that went no deeper than his lips, (Abs)
      3 his head cocked to one side, (Abs)
      3 studying me with his penetrating eyes; (VC)
   2 the other blank-faced, (Abs)
      3 looking out of eyes that were meant to reveal nothing and to stir
         profound uncertainty. (VC)

Ralph Ellison

10

1 He stood at the top of the stairs and watched me,
   2 I waiting for him to call me up, (Abs)
   2 he hesitating to come down, (Abs)
      3 his lips nervous with the suggestion of a smile, (Abs)
      3 mine asking whether the smile meant come, or go away. (Abs)

11

1 Joad's lips stretched tight over his long teeth for a moment, and
1 he licked his lips,
   2 like a dog, (PP)
      3 two licks, (NC)
         4 one in each direction from the middle. (NC)

Steinbeck

12

1 We all live in two realities:
   2 one of seeming fixity, (NC)
      3 with institutions, dogmas, rules of punctuation, and routines, (PP)
         4 the calendared and clockwise world of all but futile round on round;
         (NC) and

2 one of whirling and flying electrons, dreams, and possibilities, (NC)
3 behind the clock. (PP)

Sidney Cox

13

1 It was as though someone, somewhere, had touched a lever and shifted gears, and
1 the hospital was set for night running,
  2 smooth and silent, (A + A)
  2 its normal clatter and hum muffled, (Abs)
  2 the only sounds heard in the whitewalled room distant and unreal: (Abs)
    3 a low hum of voices from the nurses' desk, (NC)
      4 quickly stifled, (VC)
    3 the soft squish or rubber-soled shoes on the tiled corridor, (NC)
    3 starched white cloth rustling against itself, (NC) and, outside,
    3 the lonesome whine of wind in the country night (NC) and
    3 the Kansas dust beating against the windows. (NC)

14

1 The beach sounds are jazzy,
  2 percussion fixing and the mode— (Abs)
    3 the surf cracking and booming in the distance, (Abs)
    3 a little nearer dropped bar-bells clanking, (Abs)
    3 steel gym rings, / , ringing, (Abs)
      4 / flung together, (VC)
    3 palm fronds rustling above me, (Abs)
      4 like steel brushes washing over a snare drum, (PP)
    3 troupes of sandals splatting and shuffling on the sandy cement, (Abs)
      4 their beat varying, (Abs)
        5 syncopation emerging and disappearing with changing paces. (Abs)

15

1 A small Negro girl develops from the sheet of glare-frosted walk,
  2 walking barefooted, (VC)
    3 her bare legs striking and coiling from the hot cement, (Abs)
      4 her feet curling in, (Abs)
        5 only the outer edges touching. (Abs)

16

1 The swells moved rhythmically toward us,
  2 irregularly faceted, (VC)
  2 sparkling, (VC)
  2 growing taller and more powerful until the shining crest bursts, (VC)
    3 a transparent sheet of pale green water spilling over the top, (Abs)
      4 breaking into blue-white foam as it cascades down the front of the wave, (VC)

    4 piling up in a frothy mound that the diminishing wave pushes up
       against the pilings, (VC)
      5 with a swishmash, (PP)
    4 the foam drifting back, (Abs)
      5 like a lace fan opened over the shimmering water as the spent
       wave returns whispering to the sea. (PP)

The best starting point for a composition unit based on these four principles is with two-level narrative sentences, first with one second-level addition (sentences 4, 5), then with two or more parallel ones (6, 7, 8). Anyone sitting in his room with his eyes closed could write the main clause of most of the examples; the discipline comes with the additions, provided they are based at first on immediate observation, requiring the student to phrase an exact observation in exact language. This can hardly fail to be exciting to a class: it is life, with the variety and complexity of life; the workbook exercise is death. The situation is ideal also for teaching diction—abstract-concrete, general-specific, literal-metaphorical, denotative-connotative. When the sentences begin to come out right, it is time to examine the additions for their grammatical character. From then on, the grammar comes to the aid of the writing, and the writing reinforces the grammar. One can soon go on to multilevel narrative sentences (1, 9–11, 15, 16) and then to brief narratives of three to six or seven sentences on actions with a beginning, a middle, and an end that can be observed over and over again—beating eggs, making a cut with a power saw, or following a record changer's cycle or a wave's flow and ebb. (Bring the record changer to class.) Description, by contrast, is static, picturing appearance rather than behavior. The constructions to master are the noun and adjective clusters and the absolute (13, 14). Then the descriptive noun cluster must be taught to ride piggyback on the narrative sentence, so that description and narration are interleaved: "In the morning we went out into a new world, a glistening crystal and white world, each skeleton tree, each leafless bush, even the heavy, drooping power lines sheathed in icy crystal." The next step is to develop the sense for variety in texture and change in pace that all good narrative demands.

In the next unit, the same four principles can be applied to the expository paragraph. But this is a subject for another paper.

I want to anticipate two possible objections. One is that the sentences are long. By freshman English standards they are long, but I could have produced far longer ones from works freshmen are expected to read. Of the sentences by students, most were written as finger exercises in the first few weeks of the course. I try in narrative sentences to push to level after level, not just two or three, but four, five, or six, even more, as far as the students' powers of observation will take them. I want them to become sentence acrobats, to dazzle by their syntactic dexterity. I'd rather have to deal with hyperemia than anemia. I want to add my voice to that of James Coleman (*CCC,* December 1962) deploring our concentration on the plain style.

The other objection is that my examples are mainly descriptive and narrative—and today in freshman English we teach only exposition. I deplore this limitation as much as I deplore our limitation to the plain style. Both are a sign that we have sold our proper heritage for a pot of message. In permitting them, the English department undercuts its own discipline. Even if our goal is only utilitarian prose, we can teach diction and sentence structure far more effectively through a few controlled exercises in description and narration than we can by starting right off with exposition (Theme One, 500 words, precipitates *all* the problems of writing). There is no problem of invention; the student has something to communicate—his immediate sense impressions, which can stand a bit of exercising. The material is not already verbalized—he has to match language to sense impressions. His acuteness in observation and in choice of words can be judged by fairly objective standards—is the sound of a bottle of milk being set down on a concrete step suggested better by *clink* or *clank* or *clunk?* In the examples, study the diction for its accuracy, rising at times to the truly imaginative. Study the use of metaphor, of comparison. This verbal virtuosity and syntactical ingenuity can be made to carry over into expository writing.

But this is still utilitarian. What I am proposing carries over of itself into the study of literature. It makes the student a better reader of literature. It helps him thread the syntactical mazes of much mature writing, and it gives him insight into that elusive thing we call style. Last year a student told of rereading a book by her favorite author, Willa Cather, and of realizing for the first time *why* she liked reading her: she could understand and appreciate the style. For some students, moreover, such writing makes life more interesting as well as giving them a way to share their interest with others. When they learn how to put concrete details into a sentence, they begin to look at life with more alertness. If it is liberal education we are concerned with, it is just possible that these things are more important than anything we can achieve when we set our sights on the plain style in expository prose.

I want to conclude with a historical note. My thesis in this paragraph is that modern prose like modern poetry has more in common with the seventeenth than with the eighteenth century and that we fail largely because we are operating from an eighteenth-century base. The shift from the complex to the cumulative sentence is more profound than it seems. It goes deep in grammar, requiring a shift from the subordinate clause (the staple of our trade) to the cluster and the absolute (so little understood as to go almost unnoticed in our textbooks). And I have only lately come to see that this shift has historical implications. The cumulative sentence is the modern form of the loose sentence that characterized the anti-Ciceronian movement in the seventeenth century. This movement, according to Morris W. Croll,[3] began with Montaigne and Bacon and continued with such men as Donne, Browne, Taylor, Pascal. To Montaigne, its art was the

---

[3] "The Baroque Style in Prose," *Studies in English Philology: A Miscellany in Honor of Frederick Klaeber* (1929), reprinted in *Style, Rhetoric, and Rhythm: Essays by Morris W. Croll* (1966) and A. M. Witherspoon and F. J. Warnke, *Seventeenth-Century Prose and Poetry,* 2nd ed. (1963). I have borrowed from Croll in my description of the cumulative sentence.

art of being natural; to Pascal its eloquence was the eloquence that mocks formal eloquence; to Bacon, it presented knowledge so that it could be examined, not so that it must be accepted.

But the Senecan amble was banished from England when "the direct sensuous apprehension of thought" (T. S. Eliot's words) gave way to Cartesian reason or intellect. The consequences of this shift in sensibility are well summarized by Croll:

> To this mode of thought we are to trace almost all the features of modern literary education and criticism, or at least of what we should have called modern a generation ago: the study of the precise meaning of words; the reference to dictionaries as literary authorities; the study of the sentence as a logical unit alone; the careful circumscription of its limits and the gradual reduction of its length; . . .[4] the attempt to reduce grammar to an exact science; the idea that forms of speech are always either correct or incorrect; the complete subjection of the laws of motion and expression in style to the laws of logic and standardization—in short, the triumph, during two centuries, of grammatical over rhetorical ideas. (*Style, Rhetoric and Rhythm,* p. 232)

Here is a seven-point scale any teacher of composition can use to take stock. He can find whether he is based in the eighteenth century or in the twentieth and whether he is consistent—completely either an ancient or modern—or is just a crazy mixed-up kid.

POSTSCRIPT

I have asserted that "syntactical ingenuity" can best be developed in narrative-descriptive writing and that it can be made to carry over into discursive writing. The count made for the article on sentence openers included all sentence modifiers—or free modifiers, as I prefer to call them. In the total number of free modifiers, the 2000 word samples were almost identical—1545 in the fiction and 1519 in the nonfiction, roughly one in three sentences out of four. But they differ in position:

Nonfiction	initial	575	medial	492	final	452
Fiction	initial	404	medial	329	final	812

And they differ in some of the grammatical kinds used in the final position:

Nonfiction	NC	123	VC	63	Abs	9
Fiction	NC	131	VC	218	Abs	108

---

[4] The omitted item concerns punctuation and is not relevant here. In using this scale, note the phrase "what we should have called modern a generation ago" and remember that Croll was writing in 1929.

Thus the differences are not in the structures used, only in the position and in the frequency of the various kinds of structures. It will be well to look at a few more sentences of discursive prose.

17

1 His [Hemingway's] characters, / , wander through the ruins of Babel,
   2 / expatriates for the most part, (NC)
   2 smattering many tongues (VC) and
   2 speaking a demotic version of their own. (VC)

Harry Levin

18

1 From literal to figurative is one range that a word may take:
   2 from *foot* of a person to *foot* of a mountain, (PP)
     3 a substituted or metaphoric use. (NC)
1 From concrete to abstract is another range:
   2 from *foot to extremity,* (PP)
     3 stressing one of the abstract characteristics of foot, (VC)
       4 a contrast for which the terms *image* and *symbol* as distinguished
         from *concept* are also used. (NC)

Josephine Miles

19

   2 Going back to his [Hemingway's] work in 1944, (VC)
1 you perceive his kinship with a wholly different group of novelists,
   2 let us say with Poe and Hawthorne and Melville: (PP)
     3 the haunted and nocturnal writers, (NC)
     3 the men who dealt in images that were symbols of an inner world. (NC)

Malcolm Cowley

20

1 Even her style in it is transitional and momentous,
   2 a matter of echoing and reminiscing effects, and of little clarion notes
     of surprise and prophecy here and there; (NC)
     3 befitting that time of life which has been called the old age of youth
       and the youth of old age, (AC or VC)
       4 a time fraught with heartache and youthful tension. (NC)

Glenway Wescott, of Colette's Break of Day

21

   2 Aglow with splendor and consequence, (AC)
1 he [Sterne] rejoined his wife and daughter,
   2 whom he presently transferred to his new parsonage at Coxwold, (RC)
     3 an old and rambling house, (NC)
       4 full of irregular, comfortable rooms, (AC)
       4 situated on the edge of the moors, (VC)

    5 in a neighborhood much healthier than the marshy lands of
       Sutton. (PP)

Peter Quennell

22

1 It is with the coming of man that a vast hole seems to open in nature,
  2 a vast black whirlpool spinning faster and faster, (NC)
    3 consuming flesh, stones, soil, minerals, (VC)
    3 sucking down the lightning, (VC)
    3 wrenching power from the atom, (VC)
      4 until the ancient sounds of nature are drowned out in the cacophony
        of something which is no longer nature, (SC)
      5 something instead which is loose and knocking at the world's
        heart, (NC)
      5 something demonic and no longer planned— (NC)
        6 escaped, it may be— (VC)
        6 spewed out of nature, (VC)
        6 contending in a final giant's game against its master. (VC)

Loren Eiseley

    The structures used in prose are necessarily the structures used in poetry,
necessarily because prose and poetry use the same language. Poets may take more
liberties with the grammar than prose writers are likely to do; but their departures
from the norm must all be understood by reference to the norm. Since poets,
like the writers of narrative, work more by association than by logical connection,
their sentences are likely to have similar structures. They seem to know the values
of the cumulative sentence.

    The first example here consists of the first two stanzas of "The Meadow
Mouse"; the slashes mark the line ends. The other example constitutes the last
four of the five stanzas of "The Motive for Metaphor." It shows well how structural
analysis of the sentence reveals the tactics of a difficult poem.

23

1 In a shoebox stuffed in an old nylon stocking / Sleeps the baby mouse I
   found in the meadow, /
  2 Where he trembled and shook beneath a stick / Till I caught him up by
    the tail and brought him in, / (RC)
    3 Cradled in my hand, / (VC)
    3 a little quaker, (NC)
      4 the whole body of him trembling, / (Abs)
    3 His absurd whiskers sticking out like a cartoon mouse, / (Abs)
    3 His feet like small leaves, /(Abs)
      4 Little lizard-feet, / (NC)
      4 Whitish and spread wide when he tried to struggle away, / (AC)
        5 Wriggling like a minuscule puppy. (VC)

1 Now he's eaten his three kinds of cheese and drunk from his bottlecap
    watering trough— /
  2 So much he just lies in one corner, / (AC)
    3 His tail curled under him, (Abs)
    3 his belly big / As his head, (Abs)
    3 His bat-like ears / Twitching, (Abs)
      4 tilting toward the least sound. (VC)

Theodore Roethke

24

  2 In the same way, (PP)
1 you were happy in spring,
  2 with the half colors of quarter-things, (PP)
    3 The slightly brighter sky, (NC)
    3 the melting clouds, (NC)
    3 the single bird, (NC)
    3 the obscure moon— (NC)
      4 The obscure moon lighting an obscure world of things that would
        never be quite expressed, (NC)
        5 where you yourself were never quite yourself and did not want
          nor have to be, (RC)
      6 desiring the exhilirations of changes: (VC)
        7 the motive for metaphor, (NC)
      6 shrinking from the weight of primary noon, (VC)
        7 the ABC of being, (NC)
        7 the ruddy temper, (NC)
        7 the hammer of red and blue, (NC)
        7 the hard sound— (NC)
          8 steel against intimation— (NC)
        7 the sharp flash, (NC)
        7 the vital, arrogant, fatal, dominant X. (NC)

Wallace Stevens

THEORY AND IMPLICATIONS

1. The principle of the writer's craft that Christensen quotes is, "When you write, you make a point, not by subtracting as though you sharpened a pencil, but by adding." What assumptions about the writing process are implicit here?

2. Christensen distinguishes modification within the clause from modification of the clause as a whole. What is his rationale for valuing the latter and downplaying the former? Can you think of other justifications? Do you think that all linguists, rhetoricians, or professional writers would agree with such views? Why or why not?

3. Why do you think that the concept of "levels of generality" could be considered a needed combination of grammar and content?

4. What kind of critique of traditional notions of "complexity" does this grammar of the sentence offer? Keep in mind traditional grammar's classification of sentence types into simple, compound, complex, and compound/complex?

5. How is the concept of texture, like the concept of levels of generality, connected to thought or content?

6. Christensen deplores current style books that favor the plain style. What advice do you think he refers to here? Is he right to disparage it?

7. Do you agree that writing courses should include descriptive and narrative writing? Should they feature them over expository writing?

8. Identify the levels, kinds of phrases, and position (initial, medial, or final) in the following cumulative sentence:

   Without thought, his arms and legs working beautifully together, he headed right for the safety man, stiff-armed him, feeling blood spurt instantaneously from the man's nose onto his hand, seeing his face go awry, head turned, mouth pulled to one side.

9. Levels of generality allow one to see how structures are coordinate or subordinate; coordination is signaled by elements on a par with one another (as in a list), by elements that are in similar structures, or by elements that have the same function. Identify the clues for coordinate structure in the following sentence after rewriting the sentence to show levels of generality:

   We caught two bass, hauling them in as though they were mackerel, pulling them over the side of the boat, stunning them with a quick blow.

10. Punctuation helps clarify relationships—parts that are subordinate and parts that are coordinate. Place the following sentence in levels and punctuate it, defending your choices with the clues listed in sentence 12:

    We walked through the flaring streets jostled by drunken men and bargaining women amid the curses of laborers the shrill litanies of shop-boys who stood on guard by the barrels of pigs' cheeks the nasal chanting of street-singers who sang a come-all-you about O'Donovan Rossa or a ballad about the troubles of our native land.

PROFESSIONAL CONCERNS

1. Christensen offers suggestions for a course using his four principles. Devise a writing sequence using his four principles for any grade level. Explain and defend your practical application, anticipating possible objections.

2. Compare and contrast two prose documents of similar genre from the eighteenth and nineteenth centuries. Describe the shift that Christensen notes from the "complex sentence" to the "cumulative sentence." What implications do you see in this shift in style?

Grammar in Context: Why and How*

JIM MEYER, JAN YOUGA, AND JANIS FLINT-FERGUSON

This essay offers a practical application of grammar, illustrating how a grammatical feature can be integrated into a literature and composition class. When teachers connect pronouns with a literary point of view, they offer students an analytic tool and demonstrate the usefulness of understanding grammatical features. This essay serves as a model for other lessons that attempt to integrate grammar into wider reading and writing lessons.

These authors underscore Corder's point concerning L2 acquisition that what is taught is not what is learned. Children can be taught grammar in various grade levels and still not remember it. If teachers provide context, however, grammar can be learned, if not as a formal system then as a tool of analysis for other language activities. The context offered should be an integrated language arts lesson in which reading, writing, literature, and grammar come together. The lesson described here provides such a context and presents an example of grammar in use.

If we were to summarize the state of grammar in most American schools today in one sentence, it would be this: Grammar is very often taught but very seldom learned. This fact seems odd since grammar, unlike many other aspects of the middle-school curriculum, receives continuous support from teachers, parents, and administrators. Yet, despite efforts made on various fronts, the grammar of their own language remains a mystery to most students. Rather than making them more comfortable with their mother tongue, a few lessons in the difference between *lie* and *lay* or restrictive and nonrestrictive clauses seem to produce a greater uncertainty bordering on panic. Many people, even some very well-educated people, simply learn ways to avoid rules they never really understood or learn to make excuses for their mistakes by apologizing lamely, "I never was any good at diagramming sentences."

Although students do not appear to be learning grammar the way it is presently taught, most grammar curricula do not reflect new ways of teaching but simply rely on the same old techniques despite their ineffectiveness. In many schools, the same grammar objectives—"students will be able to identify verbs in sentences," for example—show up for several different grades, sometimes even being listed as an objective for grades as different as second and ninth. That fact alone should indicate to us that something is seriously wrong. Why should it be necessary to repeat the same instruction year after year? Why should students be taught, over and over again, the same definition for parts of speech, with only the examples changing? A calculus class does not spend the first week identifying numbers and reviewing addition and subtraction, and yet after many years of study

---

and even more years of use, students at all grade levels are given grammar lessons that start at square one over and over again.

The reasons for this state of affairs are many, but there is one that seems particularly important to us: Traditional grammar instruction is bound to fail because it is given without any realistic *context*. In Ed Vavra's words, "Students are never asked to do anything with [grammatical knowledge]" (1987, 42). People who feel comfortable and confident with the grammar of our language developed that confidence by becoming "natural language users" of standard English (Smith et al. 1982, 35). They spoke it and heard it spoken, they read it, and they wrote it. Grammar lessons showed them the patterns for what they already knew and in that sense were irrelevant. Now, however, we want the grammar lessons to do what life used to accomplish, and the old drills will not work. The classroom must now become the place where students become natural language users and learn grammar as part of the life of reading, writing, and speaking.

Yet when language is taught in the middle grades, context is often ignored. Students are made to learn definitions—of parts of speech, kinds of sentences— and then are given worksheets on which each sentence contains an example of the feature in question. Language is often divorced from reading, literature, vocabulary, and spelling: although traditionally grammar has been connected to writing, this link is often poorly conceived. Writing a paragraph using as many adjectives as possible is as artificial as a contrived worksheet. And so grammar is "taught" in a separate unit, six or nine weeks spent solely on diagramming sentences and doing exercises from a book, with no reference to language in use.

Instead of considering ways to provide a meaningful context for grammar, many teachers focus on making traditional kinds of grammar exercises interesting or cute. Magazines and publishers provide eye-catching charts, based on song lyrics or movie titles, that are meant to stimulate interest in grammar. (For an example of this approach, see Elgin 1982.) Computerized versions of exercises with special effects are now readily available. These can perhaps sustain student interest for a little while, but unless this grammar instruction means something to the students, it, too, will fail to achieve lasting results.

The notion of context has always been important in theoretical work and research on natural uses of language, from reading (see, for example, Smith et al.) to children's acquisition of their mother tongue (Moskowitz 1978). If the classroom now must replicate the condition of natural language use, we must see the context of language instruction as crucial.

We believe that grammar instruction can be made more effective by putting it in a realistic context in these two ways:

1. Grammar should be part of an integrated curriculum which includes reading, literature, vocabulary, spelling, and writing and should not be taught as an isolated unit in a language-arts class.
2. Grammar instruction should be concentrated on the proofreading stage of writing assignments. In the writing workshop approach championed by Nancie Atwell (1987), teachers base mini-lessons on the students' own writing, aiming "to be as relevant as possible to the

whole group and what it needs," not letting these mini-lessons "become occasions for preaching abstract formulas and rules" (148).

The middle-school years provide the perfect opportunity to begin this integration of context and grammar. Developmentally, adolescents do not grow simply quantitatively, but qualitatively as well. "An adolescent not only knows more but also thinks differently about what is known" (Forisha 1983, 22). Students have already spent five or six years learning what parts of speech are; they are now ready to begin thinking about that knowledge and why it is important. It seems natural to use that interest to lead students into a more analytic approach to how they use grammar and how grammar is used in the literature they read. This approach also moves students into critical-thinking skills which are much more important than rote-memory skills.

AN INTEGRATED CURRICULUM

In order to provide a natural context for grammar instruction, we believe it must be part of an integrated curriculum. In other words, we believe that each "unit" should cover objectives in all the areas of the language arts. Spelling and vocabulary, for example, should not be separated from reading since it is through reading that vocabulary is learned most naturally. Reading instruction should also not be separated from literature, as one cannot appreciate literature unless one can read it. And the true test of students' understanding of vocabulary, spelling, and reading is their ability to use these skills in their own writing.

To illustrate how we integrate the various components of a language-arts curriculum into a unit, we will briefly describe a unit we have developed for Edgar Allan Poe's short story, "The Tell-Tale Heart."

Reading Instruction

The unit begins with reading instruction by illustrating effective prereading techniques. Students are asked to explain or guess what "tell-tale" means and to predict how a heart might be "tell-tale." They are also asked to explain what they know (to tap their prior knowledge) about the term "evil eye." Finally, to help them identify with the perspective of the narrator, students write for a few minutes about a habit someone has that drives them crazy. As students read the story, during-reading questions focus their attention on the significant details of the story, such as the narrator's preparation for the murder or the narrator's emotions during the story.

Vocabulary

Vocabulary instruction occurs as a natural part of the reading process. Some words which might hinder students' reading and prevent them from getting through the story are discussed ahead of time. During reading, students' attention is drawn to certain valuable vocabulary words that can easily be defined by noting the context in which they are used ("First of all I *dismembered* the corpse. I cut off the head and the arms and the legs") or by thinking of related words (sagacity/sage, gesticulation/gesture). Students' vocabulary and spelling lists are drawn from words in the story. Learning words within their natural contexts raises ample and spontaneous opportunities for lessons in roots, prefixes, suffixes, etymologies, and dictionary use. However, we distinguish between words that students are likely to need to know as part of their expanding vocabulary and words that many students will never meet again. Only words of the first kind become part of their vocabulary lists; students do not need to memorize words from Poe's archaic, nineteenth-century vocabulary.

Literature

Literary terms and techniques are then discussed as postreading activities and within an appropriate context as well. For example, a lesson on point of view grows naturally out of "The Tell-Tale Heart" since the entire story is told from the perspective of the insane narrator.

One natural element of this discussion is the use of pronouns. Pronouns are a stylistic element used by authors to create point of view. Discussed within this context, pronouns are discovered to be more than just lists of words for fill-in-the-blank exercises; they are an integral part of literary style.

Writing

Finally, students are asked to write something that grows out of the selection they have just read. This writing can be either fiction or nonfiction and should serve as one of the ways in which the students' reading of the story is evaluated. (See Flint-Ferguson and Youga [1987] for further discussion of this.) To reinforce the lesson on point of view, we have asked students to retell the story from the point of view of one of the policemen or to tell a story from their own lives from two different points of view. The paper goes through drafts, and in the final draft this piece of writing becomes the basis for the grammar lesson.

Grammar and Proofreading

Once students have become familiar with the story of "The Tell-Tale Heart," both through reading it and through a writing assignment based on it, they have a realistic context for a language lesson. It is important that the grammar instruction relate naturally both to the reading selection and to the students' own writing. (See, for example, the discussion of "knowing grammar" and "teaching of formal grammar" in Neuleib and Brosnahan [1987].) Students should not be asked to use a grammatical construction just because it comes next on a list of items to cover; we want students to write as naturally as possible. Our job is to structure the writing assignment so it will naturally elicit writing that contains a particular grammatical feature.

In other words, the grammar lesson must build naturally from the previous instruction. In this unit, students do a prewriting which asks them to put themselves in the place of the narrator; during reading they look for the emotions that reveal the narrator's perspective; they then explore the significance of the narrator's point of view in the literature lesson; and finally, they rewrite the story from a different point of view. The language lesson, then, must focus on a grammatical feature that is important in revealing perspective and determining point of view and that will have occurred naturally as students choose a point of view for their stories.

The appropriate grammar lesson obviously focuses on pronouns, a lesson for which they have been prepared by the literature discussion. Students are asked first to find examples of all the first-person singular pronouns in Poe's story ("*I* heard many things in hell"; "the idea . . . haunted *me* day and night"; "the disease had sharpened *my* senses"; "a watch's minute hand moves more quickly than did *mine*"). From these sentences we elicit all the pronoun forms and their uses in sentences. Students make charts that will help them keep track of these uses. Although such charts are found in every grammar text, the crucial difference here is that the students are not merely passive receptacles for information from teacher or text; instead, students are generating this information themselves through their active involvement with the story.

Students then turn to their own writing and are asked to circle all the pronouns they have used. This exercise helps them to see if they are keeping a consistent point of view and also reinforces pronoun identification.

Now, with the final draft of the students' papers, we incorporate a lesson on correct pronoun usage. It is important that in the early drafts students are working on vivid details, on organization, on a clear focus, and on developing a consistent tone. Only when they are ready to proofread do we focus their attention on correct grammar. We do not want students to feel that this writing assignment is rigged or is a camouflaged attempt to evaluate grammar. Neither should students feel that they must use as many pronouns as possible nor that they should avoid pronouns in order to avoid errors. Their grammar lessons are to be based on language in natural use, and determining correct usage is a natural part of the proofreading process.

It is at this point that we can begin to deal with some of the most common problems of pronoun usage—as they occur, not as they are envisioned by a textbook author. One usage lesson that arises, for example, deals with the correct form of a pronoun next to a conjunction. Having found their own pronouns, students can look for any pronoun that is discussed, and students are guided to determine if they have used the correct forms. For those students who have persistent problems with pronoun usage, an entry on their "editing list" will serve as a reminder to check this on future writing assignments as well. (For an example of an editing list, see Atwell 109.)

LANGUAGE IN USE

The focus for grammar instruction in this unit has been on language in use. The grammar lesson occurred in a natural context. Students first interacted with the reading selection as a story, not as an example of pronoun use; the writing assignment was a purposeful task on its own, not simply writing to be evaluated for pronoun usage. The primary message we hope to communicate to students is that they are already skilled users of language, that they know quite a bit about language (in this case, pronouns), and that they demonstrate that knowledge whenever they read and write. The grammar lesson is designed to correspond to the abilities of students in the middle grades, students who are ready to go beyond learning parts of speech but not ready for grammar as a formal, abstract system, as Sanborn (1986) points out. Through this lesson, students are made more aware of the way they and others use language, and thus they learn more control over it.

Language instruction in an integrated unit will be more effective than six or nine weeks spent on isolated grammar lessons because it has a context and a purpose. Pronouns are part of both literary style and everyday vocabulary; they are part of language in a natural use. Students are not treated as if they know nothing about the language they use every day; their ability to read and write is recognized and serves as the basis for the lesson. If students find errors in pronoun usage in their own writing, they are helped to correct them; if not, they are not made to spend classroom time on a problem they do not have.

These writing/grammar assignments can be repeated with different pieces of literature. Instead of spending two weeks on nouns and then "moving on" to adjectives, we need to see grammar instruction as ongoing. After all, grammar does not build one part of speech on top of another. All parts of speech exist simultaneously within our language.

Because the lessons are based on the students' own writing, they will become more complex as the students' writing becomes more sophisticated. By increasing exposure to grammatical features at different times rather than confining them to their own isolated unit, we provide for constant review and reinforcement. It is thus part of a spiral curriculum, to use Jerome Bruner's term (1979). We build into our lesson plans the recognition that some students may not be ready to learn that lesson the first time but will be ready later. And we give students the chance to become more proficient at language use, to recognize the usefulness of grammar, and to develop a more positive attitude towards language. Through this method, grammar is not only taught; it is also learned.

WORKS CITED

Atwell, Nancie. 1987. *In the Middle: Writing, Reading, and Learning with Adolescents.* Portsmouth, NH: Boynton/Cook.

Bruner, Jerome. 1979. *On Knowing: Essays for the Left Hand.* Expanded ed. Cambridge, MA: Belknap.

Elgin, Suzette Haden. 1982. "The Top Forty Mistakes in English Usage: A Bulletin." *College English* 44: 529–31.

Flint-Ferguson, Janis, and Jan Youga. 1987. "Making Evaluation a Part of the Learning Process." *Journal of Reading* 31: 140–45.

Forisha, Barbara. 1983. *The Experience of Adolescence: Development in Context.* Glenview, IL: Scott.

Moskowitz, Breyne Arlene. 1978. "The Acquisition of Language." *Scientific American* 18: 92–94.

Neuleib, Janice, and Irene Brosnahan. 1987. "Teaching Grammar to Writers." *Journal of Basic Writing* 6: 28–35.

Sanborn, Jean. 1986. "Grammar: Good Wine before Its Time." *English Journal* 75.3: 72–80.

Smith, Sharon L., et al. 1982. "The Contexts of Reading." *Secondary School Reading: What Research Reveals for Classroom Practice.* Ed. Allen Berger and H. Alan Robinson. Urbana: NCRE/ERIC, 21–37.

Vavra, Ed. 1987. "Grammar and Syntax: The Students' Perspective." *English Journal* 76.6: 42–48.

THEORY AND IMPLICATIONS

1. What is problematic about the way teachers try to make traditional grammar exercises "interesting"?

2. Does grammar necessarily have to be relegated to the editing stages of writing instruction? How can grammar help in the prewriting or invention stage?

3. The authors refer to Smith and Moskowitz, two authors included in this text. What additional insights from Moskowitz seem most applicable here?

4. Read the essay by Frank Smith in chapter 6. How do these authors build on Smith's insights?

5. What other ways can context be made important in the learning of grammar?

6. How does this reading reflect various L1 and L2 researchers' ideas?

7. Use a grammatical feature from BE to analyze a passage from a book using BE forms such as those in Alice Walker's novel, *The Color Purple*. What insights about the characters and themes does this analysis provide?

PROFESSIONAL CONCERNS

1. Devise a similar grammar lesson offering an integrated curriculum. Explain it as these authors have explained their lesson.

2. Devise a lesson using Christensen's distinction between bound and free modifiers. What literature might you use? How would you draw students' attention to grammatical features?

chapter 6

Developing Literacy

THE ISSUES

Children's literacy—their ability not only to decode and encode print but to construct meaning with it—affects their mastery of all subjects. Most subjects, including social studies, mathematics, and science, depend on children's increasing ability to identify key ideas from reading, to understand the contexts of what they read, and to write effectively about those ideas. It is important for teachers of all levels to understand the multitude of influences on early literacy and how children initially master the written code. This knowledge will help teachers to address later issues of literacy, including the application of learning strategies to various subjects; it will also help them to judge whether teaching methods support or interfere with children's developing ability to create meaning.

Such an understanding depends on teachers' grappling with key questions: Do the methods for teaching literacy draw on children's innate language abilities? Do children come to school as blank slates, with no literacy training but only oral competency? Do children need a formal, step-by-step introduction to subskills— one that begins, for instance, with knowledge of the alphabet, moves to letter blends, and finally reaches word identification? If such a skills-based program ignores children's previous knowledge of print, how can teachers build on children's home-based knowledge, supporting and developing it rather than departing from it? In addition, what are the special needs of children who are learning standard English as a second language or second dialect? How should error be addressed?

An understanding of first and second language acquisition, as well as of dialect and grammar issues, can help teachers to answer such questions. In sum, children have innate capacities to decipher and produce print, and through social interaction they gain extensive knowledge about the meaning of print. They

404

actively participate in literacy events such as memorizing books, "reading" environmental print, and "writing" scribble messages to parents and friends. These "natural" learning processes can be interrupted by lockstep, formal, school-based methods that emphasize correctness and the achievement of subskills. Indeed, damaging myths about the need to correct errors in oral language can become even more damaging myths about the need to correct reading and writing errors. Just as children's oral mistakes reflect their developing competencies, so their reading and writing errors reflect a certain stage of competency.

Research shows that children first learn to read and write by making increasingly accurate hypotheses about the nature, meaning, and sequence of print. Global hypotheses give way to more refined views. For instance, at the word level the hypothesis that each cluster of letters represents one syllable shifts to the hypothesis that a cluster represents an entire word. Similarly, the guess that the number of letters corresponds to the size of the object represented ("bear" must have more letters than "mouse") precedes a grasp of the arbitrary relationship between symbol and object. Furthermore hypotheses that rely solely on one clue system, say context (a child guesses "shoes" instead of "footwear" for a department store sign), are replaced by more accurate hypotheses combining more than one clue system. Studies that examine children's natural growth in literacy reveal that reading "miscues," as well as errors in spelling and punctuation, are necessary to the learning process. Extensive error correction is especially inappropriate for nonstandard dialect speakers and ESL students, who can rely less on oral language as a clue system than can native standard speakers.

Indeed children learn to read and write in much the same way that they learn to speak: by focusing on content and identifying rudimentary patterns that globally communicate their intent. Just as children begin oral language with the holophrastic or one-word stage, yet use these single words to stand in place of a complete syntax, so they begin to write by drawing a global "picture" of their idea. They may then move to using scribbles or balls and lines, resembling cursive or print, or they may move to using single letters to represent words. Similarly, children begin to read by using previous knowledge of context to read books they have memorized or books whose repetitive patterns help them to anticipate words. They may guess words that neither look nor sound like the written word but convey its meaning. If teachers concentrate on decoding skills, however (the use of sound-letter correspondences or phonics), they can undermine children's active hypothesizing. Given the abstract, irregular nature of sound-letter correspondences, children necessarily make mistakes using phonics and come to doubt their ability to guess.

A concentration on error correction and a lockstep syllabus are particularly harmful to the literacy development of nonstandard English and ESL speakers, who are often thought to need extensive oral practice in the standard dialect before they can be taught to read and write. Yet it is a misconception that nonstandard spoken forms necessarily impede reading comprehension or produce spelling errors. This view is based on the oversimplified idea that writing is nothing but sounds written down, and that children need only "decode" through phonics the sounds encoded in the letters. In addition, this view ignores the irregularities in the sound-letter system as well as the reader's need to use context clues and sight patterns to determine word meaning. An emphasis on pronunciation has led to the problematic assumption that standard pronunciation is a prerequisite for reading and writing, a view that has denied whole groups of children equal access to the literacy training necessary for mastery of subject matter.

For all students—standard and nonstandard English and ESL students alike— the teaching of literacy as a programmed group of subskills may produce good decoders and spellers but does not teach comprehension or expression. Nor does it enhance in children the love for reading and writing that remains fundamental to education. Whole language approaches to literacy—the attempt to keep texts and purposes "whole"—began as a reaction to such programming and social dimensions. Separating reading and writing instruction from speaking and listening can lead to formal, workbook methods of teaching literacy that are based on repetition and drill. This division of language modalities can drive a wedge between home and school learning. Formal language learning in the school setting that is based on competency levels and sequenced materials can contradict the naturalistic, intuitive learning strategies encouraged in the home. These instruction methods can thus exaggerate differences between learning environments, learning strategies, and language speakers, further segmenting an already divided society.

The emphasis on similar approaches for students with different language backgrounds needs an important qualification. Significantly, the initial literacy methods suggested in this chapter have different implications for ESL children in U.S. schools, who represent very different L1 literacy skill levels and home language approaches to literacy. Some students with high literacy in their L1 can carry over knowledge to literacy experiences in the L2. Students with literacy training that differs significantly from U.S. literacy training may have more trouble. For example, Arabic-speaking students face a special literacy challenge: Arabic requires students to read from right to left and to write *through* lines, not *between* them; furthermore, these students are taught to strive for balanced, coordinated syntax rather than a hierarchical, subordinated one. Another example is Japanese students, who rely more on memorization than do U.S. children. It is not just the system, but also the way it is learned, that affects the learning strategies of already literate ESL students. This chapter focuses on the tie between general language processes and initial literacy; it only suggests the implications of such variables and the need for teachers to account for them in the classroom. In addition, it only suggests the importance of later reading skills, such as inferring and in-depth paraphrasing, skills that will also be informed by a whole language rather than a skills-based approach.

PRINCIPLES OF TEACHING LITERACY

The relationship between spoken and written forms of language is too complex to be fully treated here. However, research on reading and writing instruction clearly draws on key cognitive and social principles from first and second oral language acquisition. Research from the cognitive perspective indicates that children begin with global approximations of print, based on a search for meaning, and then gradually refine their understanding of the code to more nearly approximate the adult model. Thus they actively hypothesize or guess about print, as they do in first and second oral language acquisition, and necessarily make errors along the way. Furthermore children bring to the task extensive knowledge of print that they have learned intuitively through close interactions with adults in contexts that help clarify meanings; they do not learn through imitation and behavioristic drill.

Extending the implications of context, research from the social perspective emphasizes interactive literacy environments and children's understanding of the social purposes of print and the need for social interaction, collaboration, and cultural knowledge to motivate literacy. It also emphasizes individual differences in the development of literacy, based on such social factors as home attitude toward literacy, story listening, and opportunities to read and write for meaning.

Reading

Research on literacy has important implications with respect to reading. Young children begin to read by bringing background information and social purposes to the text, and they decipher words by "guessing" from a limited clue system in the code. For example, when children first try to guess the crayon color represented by letter clusters on a color-labeled drawing, they often use their limited knowledge of consonant sound-letter correspondences to determine the first letter of a word; then they guess at the word's meaning from that single clue and from the knowledge that the word must be a color. As a result, they often mistake "blue" and "brown," which both begin with the sound /b/. At a later stage, they might make the correct choice, based on more particularized knowledge of both first and last letters, when they continue to try to recognize color names to make a drawing. Outside of such a specific purpose and context, children might have more difficulty decoding the word *blue*. The *ue* vowel combination would provide few clues, given that consonants are learned long before vowels and vowels have varying pronunciations. From this example, we see that children are not simply decoding—translating the letters into sounds that are meaningful words—but are also using social purpose, context, and a gradually increasing knowledge of the code to narrow down possibilities.

This reading guessing-game characterizes nonstandard and ESL as well as standard English speakers. All these groups must rely on a variety of clue systems and must learn to recognize code patterns that do not translate into predictable sound patterns. To delay reading for nonstandard and ESL speakers until they pronounce standard English is not justified by what is known about the reading processes of standard English speakers. Both standard and nonstandard English speakers and ESL students have to use a variety of clue systems to narrow down possibilities, and both face baffling inconsistencies in sound-letter correspondences. Because writing is another code—not simply speech written down—all groups of speakers must hypothesize rules, identify patterns, and go through stages of more closely approximating the target code.

Writing

Research on literacy also has important implications for writing. In their developing writing, children also begin by approximating the adult model. From the cognitive perspective, they start globally, perhaps using wavy lines to represent cursive or balls and lines to represent print. As they start to narrow down their approximations, attempting to encode individual words, children use their knowledge of context and sound-letter correspondences to guess which letters belong in particular words. They necessarily make errors that reflect their developing competence. From the social perspective, they use knowledge of writing's social purposes and enact social roles to help them produce the content of the text.

This mastery takes place through tacit learning. Indeed much of what children know about writing they bring from home—from experiences with the social purposes for producing and deciphering print and from attempts at realizing those purposes. Children see adults writing letters, making lists, filling out forms, and taking down messages. They then exhibit these same global purposes in their own expressions, seldom practicing a single skill isolated from such a purpose.

As with reading, children necessarily make writing errors, often progressing through somewhat predictable stages of spelling approximations (called "invented spellings"), which represent logical guesses built on knowledge of sound-letter correspondences and spelling patterns. Similarly, nonstandard English and ESL speakers actively hypothesize the rules of the writing system, using a variety of clue systems to approximate the adult model. Their errors are not necessarily caused by dialect or L1 interference, and thus they do not need to have mastered standard pronunciation before they learn to write. Like standard English speakers, they need to address global writing tasks with identifiable purposes.

Listening to Stories

Initial reading and writing skills are of paramount importance to teachers, but according to some researchers, they may not predict long-range literacy.

Although the everyday purposes of print—to convey information, make lists, write recipes, and compose letters—are very obvious to young children and offer important social functions, some research suggests that listening to stories offers the kind of tacit learning most closely tied to long-range literacy success. This research also suggests that listening to stories or narratives lies at the heart of meaning-making, not only by helping children experience the gradual meaning-building of all extended text, but also by embodying children's thought processes, itself a form of *storying*. As children listen to stories, their own inner storying or meaning-building is validated. They tacitly learn how word structures build contexts—meanings removed from the here and now of speech. Most important, the narrative structures of stories teach the interpretive, ultimately narrative structures on which history, science, and even chemistry are built. In addition, through stories children's own skills in narrating, describing, and following directions are enhanced. Therefore, because stories unconsciously teach the active construction of meaning and correspond to children's own thought processes, they have long-range effects on children's literacy that extend far beyond the skills of learning to read and write.

OVERVIEW OF THE READINGS

This chapter does not attempt to provide the full spectrum of theory on reading and writing. Rather, it offers readings that reveal how theory and practice in these areas build on first and second language acquisition theory as well as on grammar and dialect concerns. These studies suggest common principles, offer cognitive and social perspectives, and address, through another avenue, this book's central concern with approaches to error. Although they are theoretical, these readings also offer extensions of theory into the immediate practice of teaching reading and writing. These methods should be grounded on a knowledge of research in other language areas, especially language acquisition.

The selection from Gordon Wells's *The Meaning Makers,* "The Sense of Story," provides an overview of issues involved in acquiring literacy and suggests concerns far beyond the achievement of reading and writing skills per se. These issues include identifying factors that predict literacy success, describing the relationship between and motives for reading and writing, determining how initial literacy extends into the content areas, and identifying methods most appropriate for enhancing literacy. With a spotlight on listening to stories, Wells offers a broad view of children's unconscious, tacit acquisition of literacy in an intimate setting that fosters interpretation. He claims that exposure to stories leads to children's assimilation and later re-creation of extended text. Wells here presumes children's active interpretation and offers a theory based not on skills but rather on children's meaning-building itself. His essay thus offers a philosophical grounding not only for a meaning-based, whole language pedagogy but also for language use itself.

Frank Smith's essays, "Learning to Read by Reading" and "Making Sense of Reading—And of Reading Instruction," from his book *Essays into Literacy,* are classic observations and explanations of children's early reading abilities. He corroborates Wells's view of children's tacit, meaning-building approach to literacy and offers support for whole language pedagogies that stress using full texts and avoiding subskills. Groundbreaking, readable, and often cited, Smith's essays capture the essence of much recent theory on initial reading: that children learn to read through unconscious, informal means; that they are active learners who seek out meaning in text; that children's reading begins much earlier than formal schooling; that children bring knowledge and meaning to text rather than simply decode it; and that phonics is but one clue system among many that help students to construct meaning. His studies thus reveal that the acquisition of literacy, like language acquisition generally, is meaning-based, with children concentrating on communication. By using context to narrow down alternatives, children show how much knowledge they bring to the reading task. An early advocate of observing children's abilities, Smith reveals the astonishing capacities and tenacities of a three-and-one-half-year-old, a boy not yet able to "decode" print.

Along similar lines, Glenda L. Bissex's "Watching Young Writers" focuses on the parallels between learning to write and learning to speak. Children learn both skills by informal means, in an environment that offers reasons for language use and a close, tutorial relationship with others. As active learners, children hypothesize rules for writing even before they learn that in our society writing is alphabetic. When they begin to spell, they hypothesize rules as they did to develop speech: They pass through predictable stages of increasing spelling accuracy. Bissex shows that in writing as in speech, children move from generalized global strategies to refined, analyzed ones—a view that L. S. Vygotsky posits for all language learning and that Moskowitz confirms for first language acquisition. Bissex thus underscores the analogy between L1 acquisition and other forms of language acquisition. She implies that teachers of writing should duplicate in the classroom the rich interactions of the home environment, and like Smith, she encourages teachers to pay attention to what children already can do, by observing their abilities instead of their errors. She suggests that a standardized, preset syllabus would make certain children appear to learn more than others, when in fact they may have learned equal amounts, with some beginning at different stages.

Lucy McCormick Calkins's "Learning to Think through Writing" describes the kind of writing workshop that embodies much of current writing theory for children, which emphasizes self-expression and voice. The workshop embodies a rich literacy environment: Students write as authors to express their own meanings. Teachers who believe in the natural acquisition of skills work with students on a tutorial basis to help them develop their writing skills. Assuming the role of facilitator rather than of transmitter of knowledge, they attend to what children can do and encourage them to do more. There is no preset syllabus: The students' writing is the focus of the class, and interaction among students both motivates and enhances their writing. With this focus on meaning, error is de-emphasized and relegated to the editing stage. Significantly, the writing that Calkins's children perform is typically narrative, confirming Wells's emphasis on the closeness of this form to children's thought process itself. And the self-motivation of Calkins's young authors further supports Wells's claim that the essence of meaning-making is narrative. Calkins's students write to discover meanings—to interpret their own experience. Because they alone have access to that experience, they write as experts and retain ownership of their work. The workshop she describes fits the new paradigm for teaching composition, involving a shift from product to process. Product instruction concentrates on isolated skills, models, formal patterns, and error; process instruction concentrates on writing strategies such as invention, drafting, revision, and editing. This shift supports the general principles of language acquisition stressed throughout this text: The adults—the teachers—must follow the lead of the child; learning follows predictable stages but is achieved by individual children at different times; and the best learning environment encourages learning through children's active construction of meaning and rejects lockstep, sequenced syllabi focused on subskills.

Sarah Hudelson's "Kan Yu Ret an Rayt en Ingles: Children Become Literate in English as a Second Language" reveals that though research on ESL literacy has changed oral language development methods, it has not affected methods of teaching ESL literacy. Although her essay was written in 1984, the situation has not changed today. Reading and writing instruction in second language classrooms relies heavily on workbooks, drill, isolated skills, and lockstep, sequenced syllabi designed to eliminate errors; grammar drills foreground instruction. Hudelson suggests that ESL children, like native speakers, can read environmental print and can write using invented spelling, even before they have mastered the language orally. The children reveal the same use of context, background knowledge, and active learning strategies described by Smith and Bissex. Hudelson describes a variety of methods that can be used in ESL classrooms, including Sylvia Ashton-Warner's key words, language experience stories, journal writing, practical writing, and writing in the content areas.

The Sense of Story*

GORDON WELLS

Wells's book, The Meaning Makers, *from which this selection is taken, forms the surprising conclusion that children's listening to stories is more closely associated with literacy acquisition than with either drawing and coloring or looking at picture books and talking about them. His longitudinal study of preliterate through fifth-grade children reveals that listening to stories lies at the heart of understanding the nature of print. Stories teach children the "sustained meaning-building organization of written language and its characteristic rhythms and structures" (p. 151). Wells means that through listening to stories, children see* context *built up through structures of words, not, as in oral language, simply through references to immediate surroundings; all the clues from which the child constructs meaning lie in the words. Such meaning-building prepares them for the less contextualized language that teachers use and is associated with children's later ability to "narrate an event, describe a scene, and follow instructions" (p. 157). More important, it is tied to children's own inner "storying," which they use to create meaning.*

In this selection, Wells shows that even beyond the early acquisition of literacy, stories are associated with the interpretive meaning-building we perform in all the disciplines and that they underlie the abstract "knowledge" we think of as fact. Quoting a letter to Harold Rosen, Wells asks, "What is geology but a vast story that geologists have been composing and revising through the existence of their subject?" And, like Rosen, he thinks that "every chemical reaction is a story compressed into the straitjacket of an equation." The succession of contributions to disciplines are themselves stories—Einstein added to Newton who added to Galileo. Wells argues that even along the road toward more abstract thinking, stories provide fundamental ways of "grappling with new knowledge."

Significantly, Wells's theories support much of language acquisition theory generally and current reading and writing theory specifically. Literacy is an

* Wells, G., "The Sense of Story," from *The Meaning Makers,* 1986. Heinemann, a Division of Reed Publishing (USA) Inc., Portsmouth, NH. Reprinted by permission of Gordon Wells.

active, meaning-making process, with reading and writing being integrated activities. These theories lend credence to the kind of writing workshop atmosphere, based on ownership and collaboration, described by Calkins. Furthermore they provide an umbrella of theory for the expressivist, narrative emphasis in early writing theory. Wells claims that although children willingly perform real-world writing tasks such as list-making, they gravitate toward stories because stories express and validate their own experience. Writing stories provides a way of directing one's own thought processes—finding out what one feels, thinks, or imagines. Children who express their experiences in stories not only learn to be authors—to create authentic texts, as Calkins would explain it—but also learn to discover what their experiences mean.

In Wells's scheme, however, story writing depends on a wealth of early experience in listening to stories. Children deprived of such early experience lack knowledge of story structure and do not develop the writing abilities of other, more fortunate children. Wells thus suggests different roots of literacy from those posited in other essays in this chapter. Whereas Smith, Bissex, and Calkins emphasize that literacy is achieved through children's active, self-initiated reading and writing of texts, Wells sees literacy's roots in earlier experiences—unconscious text-building achieved through listening to stories. Furthermore he views narrative as extending beyond the acquisition of initial literacy and as underlying our knowledge of all the disciplines, remaining part of our thought even as that thought becomes more and more abstract.

As children progress through the primary years, the content of the curriculum comes increasingly to be presented symbolically through uses of language that are more characteristic of writing than of conversation. Without the ability to cope with this literate form of language, therefore—that is to say, with the linguistic representation of ideas that are disembedded from a context of specific personal experience—children become progressively less able to meet the demands of an academic curriculum and, whether justly or not, are judged to be intellectually limited.

This is not a new discovery, of course, but what has become increasingly clear from our longitudinal study is just how early these crucial differences between children begin to be established. By the time they came to school, the rank order of the children in our study was already fairly firmly established. This is not to say that school made no difference. Indeed, all the children made considerable progress during the five years of school through which we followed them. But, because the schools provided rather similar learning environments, individual children did not change their relative position in the rank order very much. Several gained or lost a few places, it is true, and there is good reason to believe that this was partly due to the quality of the teaching they received.[1] However, there is little doubt that, in accounting for the *differences* between children, the major influence was that of the home, particularly during the preschool years and the first year or two at school.

There are many ways in which parents foster their children's development in these years, not least through the quality of their conversation with them. But what this study clearly demonstrates is that it is growing up in a literate family environment, in which reading and writing are naturally occurring, daily activities, that gives children a particular advantage when they start their formal education. And of all the activities that were characteristics of such homes, it was the sharing of stories that we found to be most important.

On the surface, this may not appear remarkable. We have always known that reading stories to children is a worthwhile activity. However, as I thought about our results, I began to wonder whether there was not more to stories than was suggested by the simple relationship between reading stories and learning to read. At the same time, I began to read some of the work that had been carried out on stories from other perspectives. Gradually, the various findings from our study began to fit together for me, forming a pattern around the concept of storying. This chapter is a first attempt to sketch out that pattern.

What I want to suggest is that stories have a role in education that goes far beyond their contribution to the acquisition of literacy. Constructing stories in the mind—or *storying*, as it has been called—is one of the most fundamental means of making meaning; as such, it is an activity that pervades all aspects of learning. When storying becomes overt and is given expression in words, the resulting stories are one of the most effective ways of making one's own interpretation of events and ideas available to others. Through the exchange of stories, therefore, teachers and students can share their understandings of a topic and bring their mental models of the world into closer alignment. In this sense, stories and storying are relevant in all areas of the curriculum.

MAKING SENSE THROUGH STORIES

There has probably never been a human society in which people did not tell stories. Many of them went unrecorded, of course; but, as is still the case in non-literate societies, the most important were preserved in oral form and handed down from one generation to the next. These formed the culture's heritage of myths and legends: stories that attempted to explain and give coherence to the otherwise inexplicable. This continued to be, at least in part, the function of literature in literate societies, in which a sizable proportion of the population has both the ability and the time to read. There are, of course, important differences between the essentially social conditions under which stories are created and recreated in an oral culture and the much more solitary conditions under which most written literature is created and interpreted. But the underlying purpose is the same: to provide a cultural interpretation to those aspects of human experience that are of fundamental and abiding concern.

Such public stories, however, are only the most highly developed and polished instances of a form of human behavior that is both universal and ubiquitous. Whenever people come together socially, they begin to exchange stories—personal narratives, anecdotes, or just snippets of gossip. James Britton refers to such stories as language used "in the spectator role," and he contrasts this with the use that is made of language when we are involved as "participants" in getting things done. Freed from the demands that are made on us when we are actually engaged in practical events, we are able as spectators to adopt a more reflective attitude—to look for their inner consistency and structure and to express it in the stories of everyday conversation and later, perhaps, in writing.[2]

Such stories do not offer a personal interpretation of experience, however. Because they occur in the context of social interaction and are produced in conversation, they, like all other conversational meanings, are jointly constructed and require collaboration and negotiation for their achievement. In this way, members of a culture create a shared interpretation of experience, each confirming, modifying, and elaborating on the story of the other. Whether at home or at work, in the playground or in the club, it is very largely through such impromptu exchanging of stories that each one of us is inducted into our culture and comes to take on its beliefs and values as our own.

Even this, however, does not take us to the heart of the pervasive significance of stories. For what is done socially and verbally in conversation has its roots in the perceptual and cognitive processes through which, as individuals, we make sense of all of our experience. Each act of recognition, whether it be of objects in the external world perceived through our senses or of a conceptual relationship "seen" through an act of the mind, involves a sort of inner storying. This is how we make sense of it.

Rarely, if ever, do we have all the necessary visual or other sensory information to decide unambiguously what it is we are seeing, hearing, or touching. Instead we draw on our mental model of the world to construct a story that would be plausible in the context and use that to check the data or sense the predictions that the story makes possible.[3]

Waking in the middle of the night, for example, I creep downstairs without switching on the light to get a cool drink from the refrigerator. But as I pass the table in the dining room, I decide to have an apple instead and reach out my hand to the fruit bowl, which I know is in the middle of the table. To my surprise, however, the object that I touch, although spherical and apple-sized, is furry and slightly springy. It does not match my expectations at all. At this point, processes that had been going on unattended now become the focus of my attention. I search for a story that will enable me to make sense of my sensations and finally I recall an episode earlier in the afternoon when my son had found a tennis ball in the garden and asked what he should do with it. I had suggested putting it in the fruit bowl so that we would remember to give it back to our neighbors. So now, with this story, I am able to interpret my sensation: what I am grasping is not an apple but a misplaced tennis ball.

This example concerns an occasion unusual enough for the task of finding an interpretative story to require conscious attention. However, it illustrates rather clearly the processes whereby, in every act of perception, the world "out there" is interpreted in relation to the inner mental model in terms of which that world is represented. Making sense of an experience is thus to a very great extent being able to construct a plausible story about it.

Stories in this sense surround the infant from the moment of birth. Even before they can talk, infants begin to construct a mental model of their world, based on the regularities in their experience, and in due course this model plays a major part in helping them to make sense of their linguistic experience and so to learn the language of their community. By reference to it they construct mental stories about the shared context—Mummy preparing dinner, the birds eating berries—and use them to predict the meanings of the utterances that are addressed to them. At the same time, stories provide the framework within which their own behaviors are interpreted; and, as children begin to speak and understand the speech of others, their view of the world is strongly influenced by the stories that other people offer them, as they interpret their experience for them and recount the stories of other people's experiences. In this way, stories are woven into the tapestry of a child's inner representations, producing the patterns that give it significance.

Thus, although storying may have its roots in the biologically given human predisposition to construct mental stories in order to make sense of perceptual information, it very quickly becomes the means whereby we enter into a shared world, which is continually broadened and enriched by the exchange of stories with others. In this sense, the reality each one of us inhabits is to a very great extent a distillation of the stories that we have shared: not only the narratives that we have heard and told, read, or seen enacted in drama or news on television, but also the anecdotes, explanations, and conjectures that are drawn upon in everyday conversation, in our perpetual attempts to understand the world in which we live and our experiences in it. . . .

THROUGH STORIES INTO READING AND WRITING

. . . I think we can now see more clearly why the early experience of listening to stories is such a good preparation for learning to read and write. In conversation, children discover the forms of oral language that correspond to their inner storying. But in listening to stories read aloud they not only extend the range of experience they are able to understand but also begin to assimilate the more powerful and more abstract mode of representing experience that is made available by written language. Then, having already discovered one of the chief functions of reading and writing—that of conveying stories—they are prepared for the task of mastering this new medium and the conventions and skills that this involves.

What is needed at this stage, I am convinced, is opportunities to discover how meaning and graphic representation are related, through activities involving reading and writing that have purpose and significance in their own right. As in learning to talk, children have to construct their own understanding of written language and how to use it, and the best way of helping them to do so is by enabling them to approach the tasks of reading and writing as means of communicating meaning. Guidance will certainly be necessary but, as in conversation, it will be most helpful if it is responsive to the connections that children are making between their own meaning intentions and expectations and the written language forms of the texts that they are creating or interpreting.

What this implies is that reading and writing should be treated as complementary activities, work on one informing and enhancing the other. In some schools, the practice is to concentrate first on reading and to introduce writing only when a sight vocabulary of a certain size has been acquired. Not only is this artifical—it would be odd to suggest that children should only learn to talk when they had reached a fair degree of competence in comprehending the speech of others—but it is also counterproductive. Children who already know enough about the functions of written language to be able to embark on learning to read also know enough to be able to begin to write. This has been amply demonstrated recently by a variety of experimental and observational studies of children's spontaneous learning about literacy.

What all these studies show is that, by the time they enter school, almost all children are able to write—at least in a rudimentary way—and that they gain a geat deal of satisfaction from doing so and from having what they have written read by other people. In the early stages it may well be necessary to provide a transcription service—typing what the child has composed so that it can be read by other children and by the child him- or herself on a later occasion. The important thing, however, is that children make the discovery that they have experiences to share, stories to tell that others find interesting; that they belong to the fraternity of writers.

At the same time, in order to write, they must necessarily also learn to read, so that they can later interpret what they have written. For, if what a child has experienced is sufficiently significant to write about, it is likely to prove equally meaningful as material to read. An additional advantage of giving equal attention to writing in the early stages, moreover, is that writing requires a focus on the graphic display with an attention to detail that is more concentrated than in reading. An emphasis on writing as composing can thus also be a powerful spur to the development of reading.[4]

The range of situations in which children may find it meaningful to read and write is extremely wide, ranging from organizing routines around the classroom (such as feeding the hamsters or recording the stages in the development of tadpoles) to corresponding with parents and other people outside the classroom. But it is likely that for the majority of children it will be stories that assume the greatest importance.

. . . Similar arguments apply to stories as the form in which most children will find it easiest and most meaningful to learn to write. As will be clear by now, this does not only mean imaginary stories—though some children find their greatest satisfaction in creating stories about exciting worlds of princesses and dragons, monsters and space ships. Stories arise equally appropriately out of personal experience, at home or in the classroom, or from reading, watching television, or visiting places outside the school. One of David's earliest achievements as a writer, for example, was a book about insects, some of which he had encountered personally while others he had only met in picture reference books or through watching television. Whether based in reality or in fantasy, what is important is that what children write should be their own stories, not ones that are written to someone else's design. "Ownership" is vital if the child is to make a real commitment of time and effort to the task of learning the craft of writing.[5]

But perhaps the most important reason for advocating a strong emphasis on writing right from the beginning is its potential as a tool for learning. Once some proficiency in composing in this new medium has been acquired, writing provides a means of recording what has been observed or discovered through talking, listening, and reading and through reflection on those observations and discoveries. And because what has been written remains, it can form the basis for further discovery as the text that has been created is reread in order to launch off anew or engage in the process of revision. If, as Margaret Donaldson suggests, one of the prime aims of schooling is to become able to direct one's thought processes in a thoughtful manner, this is most effectively learned through writing. Writing is, par excellence, the activity in which we consciously wrestle with thoughts and words in order to discover what we mean. "The process itself unfolds the truths which the mind then learns. Writing informs the mind, it is not the other way round."[6]

These suggestions for facilitating children's entry into literacy are based on the assumption that they have already had a wealth of experience of creating and responding to stories in a variety of interpersonal situations. Where such is the case, the transition to the more private activity of making meaning in writing, with all the new processes that this involves, is likely to be made without undue difficulty. But, as we have seen, there is a substantial proportion of children who come to school without this advantage. It is not that they lack stories to tell or write, it is rather that they lack familiarity with the way in which stories are constructed and given expression in writing.

For these children it is even more important that the emphasis should not be placed on the conventions and associated skills *in dissociation* from the purpose of reading and writing. Learning the sounds and names of the letters of the alphabet is clearly essential if they are to take possession of this new and exciting medium, but without an equal emphasis on the purpose and meaning of reading and writing *for them,* the mechanical skills may eventually be acquired, but the children will have no personal commitment to using them. On the other hand, what better way could there be to help these children achieve this commitment than through experiences that involve the creation, interpretation, and discussion of stories, first in speech and then also in writing?

For *all* children, then, stories continue to provide one of the most enriching contexts for the development of language, both spoken and written. As has been emphasized, facility in using language is a means to achieving communicative purposes, not an end in itself. For the most part, it is best achieved by attending to the purposes for which language is used, rather than to the linguistic form itself. Stories provide a real purpose for extending control over language, all the more effective because they also tap one of the child's most powerful ways of understanding, enlarging, and working on experience. In listening to, telling, reading, and writing stories, children simultaneously enrich and reorganize that experience and extend their linguistic resources the better to allow them to do so.

STORIES ARE FOR UNDERSTANDING

Having gained this enhanced understanding of the significance of stories and storying as a fundamental way of making meaning, I began to look at their place in education more generally. What I found was that, beyond the early years, they received little official recognition, except in the literature lesson and in "creative writing" sessions. School, it appears, is for learning about the "real" world and, for most teachers, a concern with stories seems frivolous and pupils' personal anecdotes an annoying and irrelevant interruption of the official matter of the curriculum. Stories are all very well for preschoolers and for learning to read and write. But, once the skills of literacy have been acquired, the emphasis should shift to facts—to real-world knowledge and the subject disciplines in terms of which that knowledge is organized. However, in the light of what we now understand about the fundamental significance of storying, I believe that such a view is inappropriate and the assumptions upon which it is based are mistaken.

The first mistake is in assuming that the imaginative and affective response to experience is of less value than the practical and analytic—or, indeed, in thinking that they are in competition. The education of the whole person, which is the declared aim of probably every school system, can only be achieved if there are opportunities to explore feelings and values in specific real or imagined situations as well as lessons devoted to the consideration of general principles. Indeed, as pupils get older, it is probably more rather than less important to help them to recognize that the knowledge that they encounter in the various subjects of the curriculum is arrived at as the result of the activities of specific individuals and that it has implications for the lives and actions of other individuals in the future. Inevitably, therefore, knowledge has moral and aesthetic dimensions as well as practical and conceptual ones, and a fully mature response is one that achieves a balance between them.

Such issues are raised, for example, when studying history, by the consequences of European conquest and settlement for the indigenous populations of all the other continents; in geography, by the exploitation of the earth's resources; in biology, by the possibilities of birth control or genetic engineering. But the same need for a balanced response to knowledge applies equally in other subject areas; and, in all areas, stories have a major role to play in achieving this, in the form of biographies, historical novels, newspaper and magazine feature articles and, of course, the stories the students bring in speech or writing from their own experience.

The second mistaken assumption concerns the simple opposition that is often made between fact and fiction: facts are true while stories, if not false, are certainly less accurate or reliable. Quite apart from the difficulty involved in deciding what is a fact, such a simple dichotomy fails to do justice to the interpenetration of fact and fiction in all branches of human knowledge.

All fiction—novels, plays, even fairy tales and science fiction—is firmly based in fact, in the sense that it is about recognizable people acting in recognizable ways, but in a "possible world" that differs in certain ways from any that has actually existed. To read or write fiction is not to abandon the search for truth, therefore, but to search for the truth within the world created by the imagination rather than the truth provided by documentary evidence, measurement, and so on.

However, if fiction is rooted in fact, so are facts embedded in something very similar to fiction. Isolated facts—items of information—only take on significance when they are related to other facts, and connections of various kinds made between them. Such coherent assemblages of related facts may then appear to correspond in a direct way to the reality that forms the background to our existence. Knowledge just is: given and unquestionable. Certainly, this is the impression that is created by many textbooks and works of reference. However, such a view is seriously misleading. As Richard Gregory showed in the article referred to above, the facts in any academic discipline are only facts within the framework of some theory, and theories share many of the imaginative "as if" characteristics of fiction. Moreover, as theories change through radical reconceptions of the subject matter with which they deal, so do the facts they underpin.

This point is put in a somewhat more humorous vein by Harold Rosen, when he writes:

> A few days ago my son passed on to me a paper of his. It was sufficiently opaque for the title itself to be, for me, completely opaque. If I have understood the drift of one part of his argument, it is that if you aspire to becoming an invertebrate paleontologist you must be someone given to storytelling. What is geology but a vast story which geologists have been composing and revising throughout the existence of their subject? Indeed what has the recent brouhaha about evolution been but two stories competing for the right to be the authorized version, the authentic story, a macro-narrative? There are stories wherever we turn. How do we understand foetal development except as a fundamental story in which sperm and ovum triumph at the denouement of parturition? Every chemical reaction is a story compressed into the straitjacket of an equation. Every car speeds down the road by virtue of that well-known engineer's yarn called the Otto cycle.[7]

If theories are "macro-narratives," similar in many respects to the stories we class as fictions, what about the way in which theories are constructed and knowledge built up? Does that not too form a story, in the succession of contributions of different thinkers to a particular discipline (for example, the progression in physics from Galileo to Newton to Einstein)? Equally, if we were to study the way in which intellectual and scientific advances are made by any one of these individual thinkers, would we not find that at a rather abstract level, it involved a form of storying, as alternative hypothetical worlds were considered in order to decide which made the best sense of the available evidence?

On closer inspection, then, thinking—even advanced thinking—involves imagination as well as logical reasoning. To use Gregory's words:

> By neither being tied to fact nor quite separate, fiction is a tool, necessary for thought and intelligence, and for considering and planning possibilities. Fiction is vitally important—indeed we may live more by fiction than fact.[8]

This is equally true for the developing thinker as well. Very young children, it is readily accepted, find it easier to assimilate new ideas when they are presented within the framework of a story. Only gradually do they learn to move from the particularized example to the general principle and from a narrative mode of expression to an expository or argumentative one. However, even older students find that illustrative anecdotes make general principles easier to grasp and, given the opportunity, will frequently look for such anecdotal examples in their own experience, as they work at new ideas in speech or writing in the attempt to assimilate the new material to what they already know. As students of all ages encounter new ideas, therefore, it is helpful to illustrate these ideas with stories—with particular contextualized examples—and to support their inner storying by encouraging them to work through the story mode themselves on the way to the expression of a more abstract formulation.

In the end, of course, it is important that students should be able to deal with abstractions and generalizations and to express them in the appropriate modes of discourse. But if, as has been suggested, storying is the most fundamental way of grappling with new experience, the best path to this achievement is likely, both developmentally and in the tackling of each new problem, to take them through the domain of stories, their own and other people's. Stories provide a major route to understanding.

STORIES ACROSS THE CURRICULUM

If these arguments are correct, we should expect to see stories continuing to occur in all subjects of the curriculum, in both speech and writing. Of course, the major function of stories will vary from one subject to another. In English or Language Arts, for example, there will be a concern with stories, along with plays and poems, for their own sake as works of verbal art. In science or humanities subjects, on the other hand, stories may have a much more incidental role—as a way of considering particular instances on the way to a more abstract understanding of a general principle or as illustration once that principle has been formulated. But, underpinning this diversity, we should expect to find a recognition that, in both speech and writing, a story drawn from experience can be an essential step on the route to more differentiated modes of knowing and of working on what is known.

Unfortunately, observations in classrooms suggest that this is rarely the case. In secondary schools, except in the English lesson, there is little opportunity for stories of any kind, particularly in the written mode.[9] When a student does proffer a story from personal experience, it is often cut short as an irrelevant departure from the point of the lessons. Even in many elementary classrooms, the importance of stories is only recognized within the narrow confines of creative writing; and, if stories are read by the teacher or by individual pupils, it is often only as a way of filling odd moments when the "serious" work has been completed.

There are classrooms, however, at both elementary and secondary levels, where the curriculum is not fragmented in this way—where activities in one area are planned to lead into activities in another and where each is enriched by connections made with the others. In such classrooms, too, pupils are encouraged to collaborate on the tasks they undertake and, as a result, they learn from each other and discover the value of their own knowledge by having it accepted and validated by their peers. Not surprisingly, perhaps, when pupils are given the freedom and the responsibility to work in this way, there is ample evidence that it is indeed their natural impulse to tell and write stories as a means of achieving understanding and of making connections between what they are learning and what they already know.

Since this more integrated approach to learning is still not particularly common, I should like to describe in some detail one particular class of 10-year-olds who were working in this way. All the activities to be described took place in the course of a single day in a longer period during which this class was being recorded.[10]

The school, which was in southwest London, was celebrating its centenary, and this occasion provided the starting point for the greater part of the curriculum for most of a term. Within the theme of "Life a Hundred Years Ago," small groups of children, twos or threes, undertook individual projects in which they explored, through reading, writing, drama, painting, practical work, and discussion, some aspect of late-nineteenth-century life.

. . . the teacher called on two of the girls, Syena and Niki. They had been finding out about schools a hundred years ago and had chosen to present the results of their research in the form of two related stories about a particular school. The following is a transcription of the dramatic presentation of Syena's version.

SYENA: It's a story, um, about a Dame School and I'm the dame and Niki's the child. But I'm going to read my story. [*Reads*] The morning started when the children came in. When I thought everybody was here, I got one piece of paper—it was the only piece of paper that I had. On it was all the names in the class.
"Susan?" "Yes, Miss Dame."
"Abigail?" "Yes, Miss Dame."
"Nicolette?"
"Nicolette? Nicolette?"
Then I looked up and saw Nicolette sleeping and said, "Susan, go and get the cane." So Susan got the cane and brought it to me. I walked slowly to the place where Nicolette was sleeping and I tapped the back of her neck. She suddenly woke up. I said, "Why were you sleeping in class? Stand up!" She got up and bent down. She knew what was going to happen. I got off the shelf a metal top which fitted onto the cane. Then I took Nicky—that is what we called her for short—by the ear and I took the cane and hit her two times on her bottom. In a way I felt a little sorry for her. Then I asked her why—then I asked her why she was sleeping in class. She said:

NIKI: "Miss Dame, I am very sorry but, er—but my mother and father had to work in the shop and because it was very busy I had to work too. So I went to bed very late. And I had to get up very early and clean the shop."

SYENA: In the afternoon, I did some—we did some sums and Nicky got hers wrong. I hit her on the hand with the cane and put a dunce cap on her. The next day we did our chanting out. I found that Nicky could not sit down on her bottom for a long time. She did not look at me for a long time.

TEACHER: Start that bit again.

SYENA: So I said, "Nicky, tell me your letters, A to Z, and don't get them wrong or else!"

NIKI: "A, B, C, D, E, F, G, H, I, M, N—"

SYENA: "Stop! Stop!" I cried. "You've done it wrong. Why don't you learn them at home? Oh, I've forgotten, you have to work at your mother's and father's shop. I will come to your shop and see your mother and father and talk to them about your sums and letters." So after school I went with Nicky to her house and talked to her mother and father. In the morning, Nicky came to school on time. I asked her, "Tell me your five times table."

NIKI: "One five is five. Two fives are . . .

SYENA: [*whispering*]: Ten.

NIKI: "Ten. Three fives are . . fif—er, sixteen."

NIKI: "Sixteen is not in the five table. I thought I told your mother and father you had to learn your letters and sums."

The other children were clearly appreciative of the story. But they also saw it, and its authors, as a source of information. Several questions followed about the school and its organization, with one of the other girls showing a particular interest in the dunce cap.

The teacher indicated that these questions should be addressed to the authors, the experts on this subject. And indeed their story does give a very accurate picture of a dame school, with its emphasis on rote learning and the use of corporal punishment for minor misdemeanors. It also captures another aspect of Victorian life—the exploitation of child labor. But what is equally impressive is the quality of the writing: the dramatic conception, the characterization, and such features as the aside, "that is what we called her for short," and the dame's moment of empathy, "In a way I felt a little sorry for her." Given the chance to choose a dramatic narrative form, these two girls have been able to convey what they have learned in a way that their classmates are obviously able to understand and appreciate. . . .

. . . This classroom thus illustrates, probably as well as any could, the way in which meaning is negotiated and the collaborative quality of teacher-pupil interaction that enables pupils to make knowledge their own. What is particularly striking is the central place of stories: stories read to the class by the teacher; stories read by pupils individually and in small groups; and, most obviously, stories told and written by pupils.

It also provides a fitting end to my story of the development of the making of meaning. Let me end, then, with another quotation from Harold Rosen, for it is from him and from the other writers quoted in this chapter that I have learned the value of stories for my own work as a researcher and as a reporter of that research to others:

We are in error if we believe narrative . . . stands in complete contrast to other kinds of discourse. In fact it is an explicit resource in all intellectual activity.[11]

NOTES

1. In the first follow-up study, a significant relationship was found between the amount of progress children made in their first two years at school and the subjectively assessed quality of the teaching that we observed them to receive. This suggests that,

with better teaching, many more children could make better progress at school, though this would not necessarily lead to a significant change in the rank order, since this is largely determined by factors outside the school's control. (Gordon Wells and Bridie Raban, *Children Learning to Read*, Final Report to the Social Science Research Council [U.K.], 1978.)

2. James Britton, "Writing and the story world," in B. M. Kroll and C. G. Wells (eds.), Explorations in the Development of Writing (Chichester, Sussex: Wiley, 1983). As Britton acknowledges, this distinction was first made by D. W. Harding in "The role of the onlooker," *Scrutiny* 6 (1937): 247-58.

3. Richard Gregory, in an article entitled "Psychology: towards a science of fiction" (New Society, 23 May 1974), refers to such stories as "brain fictions." He goes on to argue that essentially the same processes are involved when, in more formal contexts, we make sense of the evidence obtained through scientific observations or through other forms of research.

4. This point is made more fully by Marie Clay in "Getting a theory of writing," in B. M. Kroll and C. G. Wells (eds.), *Explorations in the Development of Writing* (Chichester: Wiley, 1983).

5. This is one of a number of very important points about learning to write that is made by Donald Graves in *Writing: Teachers and Children at Work* (Portsmouth, NH: Heinemann Educational Books, 1982). Another very helpful suggestion that Graves makes concerns the importance of individual "conferencing" at various stages in the process of writing. As I understand this proposal, it is a particularly clear instance of the contingent responsiveness that I have suggested should characterize the guidance that the teacher gives to help children develop their mastery of this or any other craft or area of knowledge.

6. I have been unable to trace the source of this quotation, but I would not wish to claim the credit for phrasing this insight so aptly.

7. Harold Rosen, "The nurture of narrative," *Stories and Meanings* (National Association for the Teaching of English, 1984), p. 16.

8. Richard Gregory, "Psychology: towards a science fiction," *New Society,* 23 May 1974, pp. 439-41.

9. See, for example, the results of the studies of writing by the "Writing across the Curriculum" group (N. Martin, P. D'Arcy, B. Newton, and R. Parker, *Writing and Learning across the Curriculum* [London: Ward Lock Educational, 1976], 11-16), reading by the Schools Council Project (E. Lunzer and K. Gardner, *The Effective Use of Reading* [London: Heinemann Educational Books, 1979]) and of the ORACLE study of the primary school (M. Galton, B. Simon, and P. Croll, *Inside the Primary Classroom* [London: Routledge and Kegan Paul, 1980]).

10. This material comes from the video program *Extending Literacy.* For descriptions of similar secondary school classrooms, see Mike Torbe and Peter Medway, *The Climate of Learning* (Montclair, NI: Boynton/Cook, 1981).

11. Rosen, "The nurture of narrative," p. 15. My emphasis.

THEORY AND IMPLICATIONS

1. What questions does Wells leave you with about the relationship between reading and writing and "inner storying"? Does he answer them? Do you have answers for them? Explain.

2. What do you think Wells means when he says that internal storying is "validated" through listening to external stories? What relation does he posit between thought and experience?

3. How does Wells's theory offer a combination of cognitive and social perspectives? How does he combine these perspectives? Does he also offer a larger cultural perspective? Explain.

4. Wells claims that making up stories is involved in all interpretation. Do you agree? Can you think of examples where stories do not underlie interpretation? Explain.

5. Wells provides an uncommon view of stories. Many educators view stories as simply a beginning point for early literacy but inconsequential to later knowledge. Wells calls into question such conventional distinctions as fact and fiction. Can you think of how even the simplest stories might be fact? Give an example and discuss it.

6. Explain how your own inner storying helps you make sense of experience.

7. Why does Wells's theory that stories are a way of making sense of our world help to justify his view that reading and writing should be taught as complementary activities?

8. In terms of your own experience, how does writing extend inner storying rather than simply duplicate it? Does writing help you control the thought process itself? How?

9. How has Wells presented his insights as a story? Has this method helped you to better understand? Why?

PROFESSIONAL CONCERNS

1. How does storying underlie your own major field of study? In what ways do writers in that discipline rely on stories to convey knowledge in the field?

2. Write a story about your own writing and how you might better integrate stories into your writing within your field of study. Address this story to an instructor in your major field.

Learning to Read by Reading*
and Making Sense of Reading—
And of Reading Instruction†

FRANK SMITH

The work of Frank Smith is cited in most recent reading theory. His essays, classic because of their clarity and observation, have supported whole language approaches to reading and writing. Whole language theory suggests that children learn to read and write not by going from part to whole but from whole to part. For example, children gradually differentiate letters, particular

---

word meanings, and punctuation devices; they do not learn each separately, gradually amassing whole meanings. In whole language classrooms, children work with complete texts in an environment where language is functional; they do not learn pieces of language devoid of context and function. The part to whole approach wrongly assumes that subskills, taught in a preset sequence, "accumulate" or build up into larger skills. In reality, such an approach eliminates the context clues that young readers need to predict larger meaning and thus impedes reading.

Smith's depiction of children's early reading shows that they learn to read much as they learn to talk—simply by doing it. Rather than divide the task into subskills they attempt it whole. The key to this is the construction of meaning from the text: Whereas children cannot derive meaning from books designed to teach isolated skills—books with repetitive syntax, nonsensical stories, and limited vocabulary—they can derive meaning from books that tell coherent, involving stories, even if the children mistake individual words. Having the subskills involved in reading is no guarantee that children will read, however. In fact having good "decoding" skills—the ability to translate the written symbols into sounds—does not guarantee comprehension. Smith depicts the essence of reading more as active hypothesizing: Children recognize that print has meaning, use general language skills gradually to construct that meaning, and experience the pleasure books offer so that they are motivated to continue developing their language skills.

Clearly, Smith argues against the use of basals—books that are created with a hidden agenda to teach skills. These books are often boring, repetitious, and illogical, designed by curriculum specialists interested only in developing a particular skill in a particular sequence. Smith's humorous "case study" reveals that children learn to read on their own. Indeed they determine their own agendas, find regularities in the print, use context to narrow down possibilities, and make guesses based on diverse cue systems. Given its concentration on children's abilities, Smith's work supports a child-centered classroom in which children's learning dictates the instruction. The case study engagingly portrayed here supports the view that children are in charge of their own learning.

At what point in their literate development can children be said to begin to read? Can the roots of reading be detected before children begin to read in any formal sense?

I have argued elsewhere (Smith, 1971, 1973) that children learn to read by reading, and that a teacher's prime concern must be to do as much reading as is necessary for children until they can make further progress on their own. An occasional objection to this view is that children cannot begin reading until they have mastered some of the mechanics of the task, which usually means some familiarity with phonics. It is also sometimes objected that any "meaningful" approach to reading must surely wait until children can put enough words together to read a meaningful sentence. And a few teachers and theorists have feared that children who have beginning reading made too easy for them might become intellectually lazy and content with minimal progress.

Some insights into all these issues became available recently when I was involved in part of a television film on the topic of reading instruction.[1] As is the nature of both educational research and the filming of young children, the most illuminating incidents occurred when the subject was doing something quite unexpected and even irrelevant to the task at hand. Some events of particular interest also occurred when the camera was not running, so an informal written report may be in order. Since the study involved an N of only one and an observation period of not more than 3 hours, it would be reckless to claim too much generality. Nevertheless, results were obtained which suggest research of a more formal nature and which meanwhile, I think, warrant some thoughtful consideration.

THE CASE STUDY

The objectives were clearly defined. I was to take a young child "on the threshold of learning to read" to a supermarket and a department store and demonstrate (1) that the world of children can be full of meaningful print, and (2) that children not only know how to learn, but will always turn to find something to learn if they have exhausted all the learning possibilities of the situation they are in.

The subject was Matthew, aged 3½. He happens to be the older of two children in a middle-class family in suburban Toronto, but there is no reason to suspect that his natural curiosity and learning ability differ markedly from those of other children of about the same age, whatever their sex and family circumstances. Matthew's parents both work, and if anything, he probably watches more television than many children. He is not a precocious reader; his interest in books is limited to looking at their illustrations and having them read to him.

To demonstrate the richness of printed language in Matthew's environment, we first let him wander through the supermarket, following with the camera at eye level. From this perspective it is obvious that Matthew was surrounded by print, reaching literally (but not metaphorically) over his head. There were words all around him, and they were all meaningful, even though most of them were not yet recognizable. He knew that all the words meant something and could certainly distinguish one brand of ketchup from another by the names on the labels. Where did Matthew learn this? Probably from television commercials, which are a rich source of information about reading for children (Torrey, 1970), since commercials frequently present words several times in both their written and spoken form as well as in meaningful contexts.

The amount of written language confronting a child can come as a surprise to an adult who normally pays only passing attention to it. But adult readers have learned to ignore this plethora of print, while to an inquiring, learning child it must be a stimulating situation. It suggests that a child's world may sometimes be as rich in meaningful written language as it is in meaningful spoken language

---

[1] *How do you read?* A BBC "Horizon" television film, 1975. Produced by Stephen Rose.

in the home, and it is generally acknowledged that such immersion is essential for learning speech.

There were a few words that Matthew could read on sight and a number that he got wrong, such as "corn flakes" when the package he was looking at gave a brand name. But he knew a good deal about what the print ought to say on a package label, which indicates how well he understood the function of print, and he could apply a probable meaning to a word long before he could recognize the word on sight.

Incidentally, Matthew obviously did not recognize the few words that were familiar to him on the basis of phonics. When asked how he had been able to identify a stop sign correctly, he said it was because it was spelt "*p-o-t-s.*"

Does Matthew have a reversal problem? When asked what a street name sign said, he gave the name of his own street, which was nothing like the word he was looking at. Does this mean that Matthew knows nothing about reading, or does it suggest that he will not be long in picking up the additional clues about how to distinguish one word from another, especially since he clearly has a good idea about the alternatives that particular words might be?

In the department store, Matthew was taken to buy a greeting card. Asked if he could identify the sign over the section, he correctly responded "cards." Was he cheating or demonstrating an aspect of reading even though he would not have been able to identify the word out of context? He showed a similar 100-percent ability to predict the sign over the toy department. And he enjoyed this game, although he was not interested in telling us letters. He knew those, so they were boring.

At the luggage department there was a revealing miscue (Goodman, 1969). Matthew took one glance around him and said that the sign said "cases." Would he have done better if he had tried to decode the word by phonics? An answer to that question was suggested when he was tested in the department labeled "footwear." This time the camera was running. Aware, perhaps, that the situation was somehow critical, Matthew now tried to use both a letter-by-letter and a meaning approach. He looked carefully at the sign and its context and said "It either says eff-off or shoes."

To summarize so far, Matthew had made both the points we wanted him to make. A young child can be immersed in printed language, and our sample of one certainly knew how to make sense of it. He also knew how to learn; no one had told him how to use context cues to identify words. Incidentally, it is worth reflecting upon how much a child of Matthew's age can have learned about department stores, not to mention the rest of the world. He was familiar with the layout, knew where he could walk and where not to walk, how items were organized in departments, that they should be paid for, where to pay, how to pay, and to be sure to wait for change. He knew as much as an adult. Who had been giving him all this instruction?

There were still two lessons to be learned by the adults who were following Matthew. Both involved situations in which Matthew might have been said to be acting perversely. He was not doing what we wanted, but his behavior was instructive.

The first occasion was after Matthew had thrown aside in disinterest a book that he had examined with some concentration a few minutes earlier. We thought this action demonstrated that children will not dwell too long in a situation where there is nothing to learn; he had quickly realized that there was nothing further to be gained by studying that book. But when we tried to set up the situation again for filming, Matthew steadfastly refused to reject the book once more. While the camera ground on and on and on, Matthew lay awkwardly immobile on the floor, engrossed in the book, oblivious to any distraction. He had discovered something new, the fact that some pages had a hole in the middle and could be turned by the new method of hooking a finger in them. He was checking to see if every page was the same. He was now demonstrating not that a child will refuse to attend if there is nothing for him to learn, but the complementary point that a child can scarcely be prevented from attending if there is something he wants to learn.

Finally, Matthew picked up a book that he was familiar with, a "scratching book" with pictures with fruit and other objects that gave off an appropriate aroma if their printed surface was scratched with a fingernail. The camera was running and I wanted to turn Matthew's attention elsewhere because I did not want any viewer to conclude from his interest that we might be advocating a smelly-book theory of reading instruction. But Matthew thought I was doubting that the pictures actually smelled so, while the filming continued, he forced me to lower my nose to floor level and sniff at every picture in the book. What did he demonstrate, apart from the well-known propensity of children to embarrass grown-ups in public? He showed that learning for children is an exciting experience which everyone should enjoy. He did not want me to miss the satisfaction of learning something.

CONCLUSIONS

At the beginning of this report I stated five issues on which I think my brief case study has had something to say. The first is that children probably begin to read from the moment they become aware of print in any meaningful way, and the second is that the roots of reading are discernible whenever children strive to make sense of print, before they are able to recognize many of the actual words.

Third, not only are the formal mechanics of reading unnecessary in these initial stages, but they may well be a hindrance. It is the ability of children to make sense of the printed word that will enable them to make use of the mechanics we offer. Fourth, words do not need to be in sentences to be meaningful; they just have to be in a meaningful context. It is the reader who brings sense to words. And finally, there is no cause to fear that a child's learning ability will be smothered by too much adult assistance. If children have nothing to learn because they understand the lesson already, they will be bored and will want to move on to something else. But they will also be bored and distractible when there is nothing to learn because they cannot make sense of a task. Therefore, we must be careful to distinguish the two possible causes of inattentiveness.

To sum up, my brief case study tells me that children learn a great deal about reading without adult assistance ·or even adult awareness. But adults who hope to learn more about learning to read should certainly use the assistance of children.

REFERENCES

Goodman, Kenneth S., "Analysis of oral reading miscues: Applied psycholinguistics." *Reading Research Quarterly,* 1969, *5,* 1, 9-30.

Smith, Frank, *Understanding Reading.* Holt, 1971.

Smith, Frank, *Psycholinguistics and Reading.* Holt, 1973.

Smith, Frank, "The Role of Prediction in Reading." *Elementary English,* 1975, *52,* 3, 305-311.

Torrey, Jane W., "Illiteracy in the Ghetto." *Harvard Educational Review,* 1970, *40,* 2, 253-259.

Making Sense of Reading—
And of Reading Instruction

Children must have two fundamental insights before they can learn to read. These two insights are rarely discussed in the research literature on reading and are generally ignored in reading instruction, which may even suppress the insights in children who have already managed to acquire them. Without these insights reading instruction will remain incomprehensible to children and have the adverse effect of making nonsense of reading.

The two fundamental insights are (1) that print is meaningful and (2) that written language is different from speech. I shall discuss each of the two insights in turn, considering first why the insight is essential for learning to read, then how it is normally acquired, and finally how it may be overlooked or even impeded in reading instruction.

INSIGHT I: PRINT IS MEANINGFUL

Children are often immersed in spoken language—at home, at play, and even while watching television. But they would make little progress in learning to produce and understand speech unless they could bring meaning to it,[1] and this would be impossible without the fundamental insight that the sounds of speech are not unrelated to other events but in fact make things happen in the world. Children learn language by making sense of the differences that language makes.

---

[1] John Macnamara, "Cognitive Basis of Language Learning in Infants," *Psychological Review,* 79 (1972), 1-13.

By "making sense" I mean that children are able to relate the sounds of the language they hear to understandings they already have. Language makes sense—it is meaningful—when meaning can be brought to it. In fact, I would define "meaning" as the relevance that can be imposed on an utterance.[2]

It is not clear how or when infants acquire the insight that different sequences of language sounds are related to different meanings, that one sequence of sounds cannot be substituted arbitrarily for another sequence. This insight is unlikely to be explicit; I do not see how adults can explain the meaningfulness of language to children, nor how children might formulate the insight in words for themselves. Rather, I regard the insight as an implicit decision that certain events warrant attention because they are related to situations and intentions that the child can make sense of and is interested in. I suspect that the key lies in Halliday's observation that children do not learn language independently of its functions.[3] Language to a child always has a use, and the various uses could provide the child a clue to the purposes underlying differences among utterances. A child soon ignores sounds that do not seem to make a difference. There is, in fact, a powerful mechanism in all children preventing them from wasting time on sounds that they can not make sense of, that do not appear to have a purpose; that mechanism is boredom. Even if the strangeness of the sounds initially stimulates their interest, children will not continue to pay attention to sounds that do not make meaningful differences. That is why they grow up speaking language and not imitating the noise of the air conditioner.

A similar insight—that differences on a printed page have a function, that they are meaningful—must also be the basis for learning written language. As long as children see print as purposeless or nonsensical, they will find attention to print aversive and will be bored. Children will not learn by trying to relate letter to sounds, partly because the task does not make sense to them and partly because written language does not work that way. In my view reading is not a matter of decoding letters to sound but of bringing meaning to print.[4] Orthography only indirectly relates print to spoken language.[5] Phonic generalizations are both cumbersome and unreliable; over two hundred rules with hundreds of exceptions apply to the most common words in our language. Relatively few words can be "blended" from the sounds of their spelling. To overcome this problem, instruction usually tries to limit alternatives by placing severe restrictions on the words a child will meet. In normal reading, unlikely alternatives are more efficiently eliminated through the sense of the context. Phonics will never enable a child to decode the words *horse, mule,* or *donkey* in isolation. There are at least ten different ways of pronouncing *ho* at the beginning of a word, and /horse/ contains one of the uncommon ones; but if context indicates that a word is either

---

[2] Frank Smith, *Comprehension and Learning* (New York: Holt, Rinehart & Winston, 1975).

[3] Michael A. K. Halliday, *Explorations in the Functions of Language* (London: Edward Arnold, 1973).

[4] Frank Smith, *Understanding Reading* (New York: Holt, Rinehart & Winston, 1971); *Psycholinguistics and Reading* (New York: Holt, Rinehart & Winston, 1973).

[5] Noam Chomsky and Morris Halle, *The Sound Pattern of English* (New York: Harper & Row, 1968); Carol Chomsky, "Reading, Writing and Phonology," *Harvard Educational Review,* 40 (1970), 287–309.

horse, mule, or *donkey* then phonics will indeed work. My view on this controversial issue is that teachers often give phonics too much credit because of the limited objectives to which phonics are usually directed, and children contribute to the myth because the best readers are always good at phonics. It is, however, the sense of the text, if the text has any sense, that enables readers to use spelling-to-sound correspondences effectively.

Prediction through meaningfulness is the basis of language comprehension.[6] By prediction I do not mean reckless guessing but rather the elimination of unlikely alternatives on the basis of prior knowledge. The child predicts that a limited range of relationships is likely to occur between language and its setting or within the language itself. Meaning then is the relationships the child finds. If there is no meaning to be found, there can be no prediction, no comprehension, and no learning. But, to repeat, before meaning can assist a child in learning to read, there must be the insight that print is meaningful.

Acquiring the Insight

Research to date has little to offer in the way of relevant data, but it seems a reasonable hypothesis that the majority of children are as much immersed in written language as in speech. I refer to the wealth of print to be found on every product in the bathroom, on every jar and package in the kitchen, in the television guide and television commercials, in comics, catalogs, advertising fliers, street signs, store fronts, billboards, supermarkets, and department stores. All of this print is meaningful; it makes a difference. We do not expect corn flakes in a package labeled *detergent.*

The question is whether children who cannot yet read pay very much attention to all this print.[7] I have reported on a three-and-a-half-year-old boy who obviously could not read the words *luggage* and *footwear* on signs in a department store but who nevertheless asserted that the first sign said "cases" and the second said "shoes."[8] Here was one child who could bring meaning to print long before he could read the actual words—who had acquired the insight that differences in print are meaningful.

I can think of only one way in which such an insight might be achieved, and that is when a child is being read to or observes print being responded to. At this point I am not referring to the reading of books or stories but to the occasions when a child hears "That sign says 'Stop,'" "That word is 'Boy,'" or "There's the bus for downtown." Television commercials may do the same for a child. They not only announce the product's name, desirability, and uniqueness in spoken and written language, but they even demonstrate the product at work. The point in all of these cases is that no substitution could be made; the print

---

6 Frank Smith, "The Role of Prediction in Reading," *Elementary English,* 52 (1975), 305–11.
7 The only researchers I know who are working in this area are Yetta Goodman at the University of Arizona, Martha Evans at the University of Maryland, and Ingrid Ylisto at Eastern Michigan University.
8 Frank Smith, "Learning to Read by Reading: A Brief Case Study," *Language Arts,* 53 (1976), 297–99, 322.

is directly related to the setting in which it occurs, just as is the spoken language of the home. Once the fundamental insight about the meaningfulness of written language is attained, I see no reason why children should not go on spontaneously elaborating upon it as they do with speech. Children can test hypotheses about the meaning of the word *toys* not because anyone reads it to them but because it indicates the location of the toy department.

The Relevance of Instruction

I must reiterate that to make sense of any aspect of language a child must perceive a purpose for it. In school, I believe, this need implies that children must understand not only the content of the instruction—the materials they are expected to read—but also the purpose of the instruction. However, this often does not occur, and in the next few paragraphs I describe what I consider to be some aspects of reading instruction which are fundamentally incomprehensible.

One such aspect is the decomposition of spoken words to sounds. The spoken word "cat" makes sense in some contexts, but the sounds /kuh/, /a/, /tuh/ do not. It should not be surprising that children find it difficult to detect these units in speech (until and unless they catch on to the highly conventionalized game that is being taught) because such units do not in fact exist in spoken language, where individual sounds and even words are slurred together. Speech is certainly not understood through an analysis and subsequent synthesis of its parts.[9] Auditory acuity is not essential for reading, although it may be a prerequisite for reading instruction.

Another incomprehensible exercise is the decomposition of written words to letters. The printed word *cat* can make sense in some contexts, since it refers to an object in the real world with which children can meaningfully interact. But the letters, *c, a,* and *t* do not have that status. They refer to specialized visual symbols that have nothing to do with anything else in the child's life. Until children have had substantial experience reading, they must find it profoundly unsettling to be confronted with the information that *cat* begins with /see/ or that *bat* and *ball* both start with the same letter. Children who know the alphabet tend to be good readers, but teaching letter names will not turn a poor reader into a good one.[10] Rather, it would seem, fluency with the alphabet comes with being a competent reader.

A third problematic aspect of instruction is the relating of letters to sounds. For a child who has no conception of reading to be told that some peculiar shapes called letters (which have no apparent relevance in the real world) are related in any way to some improbable sounds (that have no existence in the real world) must be the purest Jabberwocky. Of course, with a certain amount of good will and diligence a child might succeed in learning to recite a few of

---

[9] Alvin M. Liberman, "The Grammar of Speech and Language," *Cognitive Psychology,* 1 (1970), 301–23.

[10] S. Jay Samuels, "The Effects of Letter-Name Knowledge on Learning to Read," *American Educational Research Journal,* 9 (1972), 65–74.

these correspondences. At best, however, such correspondences will not make sense until the child is able to read; at worst, they may persuade the child that reading is a matter of trying to produce meaningless sounds at an impossibly high speed.

The use of metalinguistic terms poses yet other problems. Many of the words that children are expected to understand in order to benefit from reading instruction, in fact, make sense only when one is able to read. The word *letter* is a case in point and so is the word *word*. The status of a word in spoken language is extremely dubious; words cannot be segregated by any mechanical or electronic device from the continuous flow of normal speech[11] and linguists prefer not to use the term at all. The usual definitions of a word—letters surrounded by white space or a separate item in a dictionary—obviously apply only to written language. It should not be surprising that many novice readers cannot make sense of this and other metalinguistic terms, such as *sentence, paragraph, capital letter,* or even *space*, since only more skilled readers have experienced them meaningfully. Teaching children the definitions of such terms will not make them readers[12] because until they can read, the terms will remain entirely senseless to them.

Finally, many drills and exercises are meaningless. It does not matter how much a teacher might believe or hope that certain exercises have a point; anything that is opaque to a child can contribute nothing positive to reading. Children frequently learn to achieve high scores on boring, repetitive, and nonsensical tasks (especially, once more, those children who happen to be competent readers), but such a specialized skill will not make children into readers. Low scores, on the other hand, can certainly interfere with reading development and not simply because children risk being stigmatized as potential poor readers, but because they may begin to regard rote, meaningless, and difficult activities as a model for what reading is all about.

The content of the material which children are expected to begin reading may also be incomprehensible. As a general rule, isolated words—which are the basis of much initial reading instruction—make no more sense than isolated letters. However, words in a meaningful context—if a child is encouraged to use context—promote prediction, comprehension, and learning. But some elaboration is required. Words that appear by themselves are not necessarily meaningless. In the world outside school, individual words—for example, *gas, exit, burgers*—make a lot of sense. But these single words are not in fact devoid of context; they are given meaning and function by the settings in which they are found. This is not the case when individual words are isolated from any apparent function and are printed alone in lists, on chalkboards, in exercise books, and even under some pictures. Many of the words that are likely to appear in isolation in school have a multiplicity of meanings and grammatical functions. Words like *shoe, house,* and *chalk* can be nouns

---

[11] Colin Cherry, *On Human Communication: A Review, a Survey and a Criticism,* 2nd ed. (Cambridge, Mass.: M.I.T. Press, 1966).

[12] John Downing and Peter Oliver, "The Child's Conception of 'A Word,'" *Reading Research Quarterly,* 4 (1974), 568-82.

or verbs, and *open* and *empty* can be adjectives or verbs. To ask children to identify such words is simply to ask them to put a name to them, not a meaning. Conversely, the fact that a word is embedded in a grammatical sentence does not make it meaningful. Sentences can be just as devoid of purpose and meaning as isolated words—*Sam the fat cat sat on the flat mat*—and so can whole paragraphs and "stories" made up of such sentences.

A consequence of all this potential meaninglessness in reading instruction may be to confound children who are striving to learn through making sense of what they are doing. More seriously, the ultimate danger is that children who have not got the insight that written language should make sense will never achieve it, while children who have got it may be persuaded that they are wrong. Unfortunately, a good deal of reading instruction seems to be based on the premise that sense should be the last, not the first, concern of readers.

Such instruction may not be ineffectual. Many students identified as having reading problems in high school struggle to get every word right, drawing on all their resources of phonics, and in this way they may succeed. But they show no apparent concern for meaning and no evident expectation that sense has any bearing on what they are trying to do. As a cure for their obvious disability, they may often be removed entirely from any possibility of reading meaningful text and returned to a meaningless form of beginning reading. Such meaningless materials and activities are occasionally supposed to exemplify "getting back to basics."

INSIGHT II: PRINT IS DIFFERENT FROM SPEECH

Obviously, spoken language and written language are not the same. It is not difficult to detect when a speaker is reading from a prepared text, especially one written for publication, or when a speaker is reading the unedited transcript of a spontaneous talk. Speech and print are not different languages; they share a common vocabulary and the same grammatical forms. But they are likely to contain different distributions of each. It is not surprising that differences exist between spoken and written language, since each is frequently used for quite different purposes and audiences. Spoken language itself varies radically depending on the purpose for which it is used and the relationships among the people using it. Although it is difficult to specify exactly how or why written and spoken language differ, I believe this difference has a simple and distinct basis; spoken language has adapted itself to being heard while written language is more appropriately read.

To understand how such specialized adaptation might have come about, it is necessary to examine the different demands that the two language forms make upon their recipients. For, consider the obvious fact that spoken language is ephemeral. The word dies the moment it is uttered and can be recaptured only if it is held in one's fallible memory or if one asks the speaker to go to the trouble of recapitulating. In contrast to the facile way in which we can move back and forth through written text, even tape recording does little to mitigate the essential transience of speech. Writing, unlike speech, is largely independent of the constraints of time. Put in another way—and this is still an untested hypothesis—

spoken language often makes a considerable short-term demand on memory while written language does not. The reader can not only attend to several words at a time but can also select what those words will be, the order in which they will be dealt with, and the amount of time that will be spent on them.

There is, however, another demand that written language places upon the reader, related not to memory but to the far more fundamental question of how we make sense of language in the first place. The question concerns how language is verified—how we confirm that the information we are receiving is true, that it makes sense, or, indeed, that we understand the message correctly. For everyday spoken language, the matter of verification is simple: look around. An utterance is usually related to the situation in which it occurs. But, if we do not understand or believe what we read, the ultimate recourse can only be back to the text itself. With written language, difficult and possibly unique skills are required in order to verify, disambiguate, and avoid error. Specifically, the skills involve following an argument, looking for internal consistencies, and thinking abstractly.

These requirements of written language have so impressed some theorists that they have argued that writing has introduced a whole new mode to our repertoire of intellectual skills.[13] It might be objected that spoken language is often as abstract, argumentative, and unrelated to the circumstances in which it is comprehended as a scientific paper. But Olson claims that our ability to produce and understand such spoken language is simply a by-product of our being literate.[14] Only because of our experience in reading can we make sense of abstract speech, which in its form is more like writing than everyday spoken language.

The Need for the Insight

Children who expect to read in the way they make sense of spoken language are likely to have difficulty in comprehending print and thus in learning to read. Their predictions will be all wrong. It does not matter that we cannot define exactly the differences between spoken and written language. We cannot say what the rules of spoken language are; yet children learn to make sense of speech. Nor is there convincing evidence that children need to have the conventions of written language explained to them, provided they can make sense of print. The general requirements of immersion in the problem, of making sense, and of getting feedback to test hypotheses would seem to be just as easily met with written language as with speech. In fact, since a number of alternative tests can be conducted on the same material, written language might seem to have advantages as far as hypothesis testing is concerned. By virtue of its internal consistency, the text itself can provide feedback about the correctness of hypotheses, just as the surrounding situation may provide feedback that is relevant to

---

[13] Eric Havelock, *Origins of Western Civilization* (Toronto: Ontario Institute for Studies in Education, 1976); Jack Goody and Ian Watt, "The Consequences of Literacy." In *Literacy in Traditional Societies,* ed. Jack Goody (Cambridge, Eng.: Cambridge Univ. Press, 1968); and David R. Olson, "Utterance to Text: The Bias of Language," *Harvard Educational Review,* 47 (1977), pp. 257–81.

[14] Olson.

speech. When reading something you comprehend, you can usually tell if you make a mistake that makes a difference—for the very reason that it *makes* a difference—and you can probably go back to find out why. However, none of this will be of any value to children learning to read if the language from which they are expected to learn is not in fact written language or if they do not have the fundamental insight that written language and speech are not the same.

Acquiring the Insight

How might children acquire and develop the insight that speech and written language are not the same? There can be only one answer: by hearing written language read aloud. When a child's predictions about written language fail because they are based on prior knowledge of spoken language, then an occasion exists for gaining the insight that spoken and written language are different. As written language is heard and comprehended, hypothesis testing will also help children develop an implicit understanding of the particular characteristics of written language. And children can considerably augment this understanding as they become able to do more and more of their own reading.

I suspect it is the higher probability of hearing written language that accounts for the finding that children tend to become proficient readers if they come from homes where a good deal of reading occurs. (Sartre has related his experience of learning to read in this way.[15]) Children are unlikely to learn to read by osmosis (by the mere fact that books are around them), from direct parental instruction, or because they see the value of reading by watching adults perform what initially must seem a pretty meaningless, silent activity. Rather, I would be inclined to credit the simple possibility that such children are merely more likely than other children to hear written language being read.

Actual stories are the kind of reading that I think most familiarizes children with written language. These can range from the contemporary material found in newspapers and magazines, elaborating perhaps upon something already experienced, to the traditional content of fairy tales and adventure stories, to history and myth. These traditional stories fascinate children—possibly fulfilling some of their deepest needs[16]—without pandering to an alleged inability to handle complex language or ideas. All of these story types are truly written language, produced for a purpose in a conventional medium. There is no evidence that children find it harder to understand such complex texts (when they are read to them) than it is for them to understand complex adult speech. In both cases it usually does not matter if large parts of the language are incomprehensible, provided the general theme and interest carry the reader or listener along. Indeed, it is through exposure to such meaningful complexity that children are able to develop and test their hypotheses about the nature of spoken or written language.

---

[15] Jean-Paul Satre, *The Words* (New York: Braziller, 1964).

[16] Bruno Bettelheim, *The Uses of Enchantment: The Meaning and Importance of Fairy Tales* (New York: Knopf, 1976).

Most of the material which interests children at school—and from which they would be likely to learn—tends to be too difficult for them to read by themselves. This poses a problem for teachers. One solution would be to help children read or listen to such material. But the alternative often selected is to seek or produce less complex material—pseudo forms—in the expectation that children will find them simpler. And if this specially tailored material also confounds beginners, the assumption may be made that the fault lies with the children or with their language development.

Indeed, the language of school texts is probably unfamiliar to most children. But this situation need not have its roots in the particular kind of spoken language with which a child is familiar nor even in the child's possibly limited experience with print. The source is more likely to be the artificial language of school books, whether of the truncated "cat on the mat" variety or the more florid "down the hill hand in hand skipped Susie and her friend." This language is so different from any other spoken or written form that is probably most appropriate to put it into an exclusive category, "school language."

Of course, such language tends to be quite unpredictable for many children, who may then have enormous difficulty understanding and learning to read from it. Ironically, it is often concluded that written language is intrinsically difficult for children who would be better off learning from "spoken language written down." The source for such a hybrid is either someone's intuition of what constitutes spoken language or, worse still, a dialect of that language or even "children's language," the description of any of which confounds professional linguists. The result may be something that is quite unlike written language yet has none of the advantages of everyday speech, since it has to be comprehended out of its setting. Children may learn to recite such print, but I have seen no evidence that it makes them readers. Any insight they might have in advance about the nature of written language is likely to be undermined. Worse, children may be persuaded that the print they first experience in school is a model for all the written language that will confront them throughout their lives—a conviction that would be as discouraging as it is misleading.

CONCLUSIONS

I have argued that children need two basic insights to begin to learn to read. Also, I have implied that with these insights children can solve all the other problems associated with print by themselves provided that no extraneous confusion or hindrance is put in their way. They must be able to predict and make sense of language in the first place, and they can do this only by bringing meaning to it. This is certainly the way that all children learn spoken language and is probably the reason that many of them succeed in learning to read despite the instructional method used.

As I have argued elsewhere, the implications for instruction are that a child learns to read by reading and that the teacher's role is to make reading easy. I do not mean that reading is made easy by the use of simple material, which can indeed be difficult because of its probable irrelevance and unpredictability. Rather,

I suggest helping children to understand any written material that interests them—whether the help is provided by the teacher, an aide, another child, or a tape recording—or simply by permitting children to make errors and omissions without penalty and without the disruption of unwanted correction. Children seek help when they need it and ignore it when they do not.

There are, of course, many factors that can contribute to failure in reading, including lack of motivation, low expectations, fear of failure, and hostility to the school or to the teacher. But failure also implies that a child sees no sense in what is involved in learning to read. A child's commitment to learn reflects an economic decision made on the basis of perceived cost and return. The problem for the teacher is not just to make reading comprehensible (which may be hard enough) but also to make sure that the instruction makes sense and is relevant to all of the child's concerns. Children who can make sense of instruction should learn to read; children confronted by nonsense are bound to fail. The issue is as simple—and as complicated—as that.

THEORY AND IMPLICATIONS

1. Written context is as important as the referenced world in helping children read. How does a text create context to help children read? Do words have to be in whole sentences to have a context? Explain.

2. The study illustrates how children bring background information to help them construct meaning. What kinds of background information did Matthew bring to bear on his reading tasks? How might such knowledge be less available to children who have recently come from other cultures?

3. What problems do teachers face in determining the kinds of background information their children might lack?

4. Some researchers advocating the teaching of phonics stress that it offers an unbiased system, one that does not depend on variable cultural knowledge. Thus all children would be given the same tools for unlocking the code. How would you respond to such an argument?

5. How have educators sometimes wrongly interpreted inattentiveness? What underlying false assumptions are such interpretations based on?

6. What implications for language learning generally do you see in the fact that adults cannot explain the meaningfulness of language? If language growth is based on the assumption of meaning, yet neither adults nor language researchers can explain meaningfulness, how, then, do children learn?

7. Smith stresses that meaning must be related to purpose and that children find much reading instruction fundamentally without meaning. Can you imagine a way in which some phonics instruction could be made meaningful? Explain.

8. How does Smith's theory support the view of literacy developed by Wells? How does it differ?

9. Does Smith emphasize primarily a cognitive or a social view of reading? What implications does this theory have for older readers?

PROFESSIONAL CONCERNS

1. Phonics instructions, and subskills generally, have been disparaged in much research on reading. Argue why you would not like to see all phonics instruction removed from the curriculum. How might phonics be taught within a whole language framework? How could it be taught to children so that they see "meaning" in it?

2. Smith seems to argue that written language is more logical and abstract than spoken language, a view that is shared by certain literacy researchers who claim that literacy offers a "great divide" in abstract reasoning between cultures that have remained oral and those that have become literate. Such an argument may unfairly disparage the analytical thought of many cultures that remained oral yet were capable of abstract and analytical thought. Write an essay in which you argue for similarities as well as differences between speech and writing. You may make this a formal paper for your class or choose an audience and shape your response to anticipated audience concerns.

Watching Young Writers*

GLENDA L. BISSEX

Glenda L. Bissex's study traces the increasing literacy of two children whose written products at the end of first grade might lead teachers to think that they learned different amounts. By tracing their development, Bissex shows that children begin at different stages, pass through similar kinds of competencies, and end at stages that are different but significantly more advanced than where they began. Both children learned; they hypothesized spelling rules and used increasingly appropriate writing systems to convey ideas. As with learning to speak, they did not need correction or drills to advance.

Bissex thus draws similarities between learning to write and learning to speak. Children progress through similar stages but at different times. She shows that all children devise spelling systems that are systematic, rule-governed, and uniform across children. Most important, she stresses that children bring to school extensive knowledge about print and years of experience with its functions; many bring some knowledge of letters and phonics. It is therefore the teacher's job to find out what children already know and to encourage their growth from that point.

This study's major import for teachers lies in the methods it suggests for finding out what children already know and for encouraging tacit learning— the rule hypothesizing that will increase their learning. Bissex recommends a writing atmosphere in which teachers observe children composing: The teacher

* Bissex, Glenda, "Watching Young Writers," in *Observing the Language Learner,* Angela Jaggar and M. Trika Smith-Burke (Eds.), 1985. Reprinted with permission of the International Reading Association.

observes what children use to select letters, asks them what they know about words, and listens to them sounding out letters. As with first and second language acquisition, the teacher avoids direct instruction of the whole class.

Bissex's study suggests the validity of several views posited by Wells. The roots of literacy lie in the home and not in formal schooling; given their different backgrounds, children will not begin at the same place, but this does not mean that they should be instructed differently. Teachers need to replicate the rich environment of the home, not turn to subskills—a point especially true for students lacking a literate home environment. Specifically teachers need to encourage the kind of story writing that allows children to control their writing and learning.

When a child who is just beginning to talk refers to water as "wa-wa," parents are thrilled that the child has successfully identified the name with the thing and come close enough to adult pronunciation to be understood. When a child who is beginning to write puts down DRAKTHENS for "directions," adults see an error and may worry that the child will form a wrong habit if it is not corrected. The focus is on what the child does not yet know (the conventional spelling) rather than on the knowledge the child has demonstrated of the alphabetic principle of our writing system, of specific sound-letter relationships, and of letter forms and sequencing.

Adults seem to have faith that children will develop accuracy in speech without constant corrections—how many ten year olds do you know who still say "wa-wa"?—but we respond differently to beginning writers (and readers). Because an error is in writing, it may appear permanent and thus in need of immediate erasure and correction lest it become established. Yet the child who wrote DRAKTHENS did not regard that spelling as permanent, for a month later the child wrote DRAKSHINS, two years after that DIRECKSHONS, and in another year spelled the word conventionally. Although the child had correctly copied several *-tion* words two years before mastering "directions," the correct spelling had not made sense in terms of what the child understood about sound-spelling relationships and so he had not learned from this instruction.

Is learning to write such a different process from learning to speak that we must take a different approach to it, that we can have faith children will learn to speak correctly yet believe they need constant instruction and correction in order to learn to write? How much of the difference lies in the different conditions under which speaking and writing have generally been learned, that is, the home and school environments? At home, children hear speech, are spoken to and practice speaking frequently; they have adult models, functional as well as emotional motivation to learn, and a tutorial relationship with at least one accomplished speaker of the language. If we enlarge the notion of "instruction" to include not only explicit teaching but also the availability of information in the children's environment and the presence of reasons for them to engage with it, then we see that children are indeed "taught" to speak at home. We see also that children may learn to write in school through means other than formal instruction; by writing every day and for reasons that are real to the child, by being written to, by seeing writing and writers, by asking questions and receiving wanted information about print.

Studies of child language development show us that children do not learn merely by imitation since they use constructions and forms of words that are not spoken around them. For example, after children become aware of plural and past tense endings, they tend to regularize all plurals and past tenses: "mouses," "goed" or even "wented." Children certainly have not been taught to do this, but have over generalized rules learned from their observations of the speech around them and through their own reasoning. Children do not regard these learnings as permanent. Continuing to listen critically to the language around them, they find they have to revise such "rules," and these forms drop out of their speech. Like little scientists, they are constantly making and testing hypotheses about language, among other things.

LEARNING ABOUT WRITING

Children in a literate society start learning about written language long before they enter school. They learn from television, they learn from cereal boxes and tooth-paste tubes, they learn from road signs—they learn from the print in their environment and from the adults they see using print. Before they can write conventionally, they write in their own ways but with the knowledge that writing communicates meanings and words, as these early recollections from young adults suggest:

> I remember, before school years, doing a lot of scribbling. Although this scribbling meant nothing to my family, I can recall being able to read the whole thing. As the family giggled and thought how "cute" it was, I would sit in my chair and read my scribbles.

> Since I can remember, I wrote. I remember taking crayons and writing on the walls and my mother would yell at me because it was scribbling. But wouldn't it be funny if I wrote a word—she probably wouldn't have yelled at me then. I really remember wanting to express with my pencil, pen, or whatever, but I couldn't; no one understood.

From looking closely at scribbles, Harste, Burke, and Woodward (1981) concluded that:

> Children as young as three, regardless of race or socioeconomic status, differentiated writing from drawing. . . . Generally the children's art was characterized as being global, centralized and connected. Children, prior to the product being particularly representational to the adult eye, usually drew a large figure in the center of the page having a unity or cohesive-ness of lines converging about this point. Their writing, on the other hand, was typically linear, spaced, and located off center. (pp. 127–128)

When children first write, Ferreiro's studies (1982) of three to six year olds show us, they will represent an object by a single letter-like shape. Then, moving closer to our writing system, they will use a combination of several varied shapes to represent a name. For some time, the number of letter-like forms required for a word corresponds to the size or quantity of the object named: more letters for "horse" than "chicken" and more for "carrots" than "carrot." Only after trying out this theory do children discover the correspondence between writing and speech, first reasoning that letters represent syllables and, finally, sounds. Children puzzle over the relationship between print and meaning or speech before schooling compels them to do so, and their understanding evolves through a series of hypotheses about that relationship. Many of the theories they try out and the conventions they invent (such as syllabic writing, dots to separate words, and writing from left to right) are or were used in other written language systems (Bissex, 1980; Harste, Burke & Woodward, 1981). Children do not leap from illiteracy to an understanding that our writing system is alphabetic when they receive their first phonics lesson.

> Children go a long and complicated way before discovering that writing surrounding them is alphabetic in nature. They explore other hypotheses, some of them not being adequate for the alphabetical system, although they would be appropriate for other systems of writing.
>
> The writing that precedes the alphabetical period is far from unstructured: It provides evidence of children's efforts in the search for an understanding of the laws of the system. (Ferreiro, 1982, p. 36)

Once children have grasped the alphabetic principle (that our writing system is based on letters representing speech sounds) and know the names of at least some letters, they invent their own systematic spellings—a further stage in their active search for the laws of our writing system. Read (1971) has shown us how these young spellers reason. Consider how the spelling FEGR (finger) might have been invented. Without benefit of phonics lessons, this young writer could have abstracted the sounds *f* and *r* from the letter names *"F"* and *"R"*: FEGR. The *G* whose sound cannot be derived from its letter name, was probably supplied by an adult in response to the child's question about it. The nasal *(n)* before a consonant is typically not represented by inventive spellers because the nasal sound cannot be heard or felt in the mouth as a separate segment. The jaw and tongue remain in one position for *-ng*. Since the *e* in "finger" cannot be heard or felt as separate from the *r*, it is not represented by children who are spelling by ear and by mouth, using everything they know about the spoken language they have already mastered in order to figure out written language. Many very young spellers, Read found, represent short *i* with the letter *E* as in FEGR. Why? Either because the place of articulation in the mouth for "ih" and "ee" are closely related, or because the letter name *"E,"* when pronounced slowly ("ih-ee"), starts with short *i*. As well as abstracting sounds from letter names, inventive spellers use letters to stand for letter names, as in DA (day) and AGRE (angry).

In sum, children use their knowledge of speech sounds and of the alphabet, combined with some information requested from adults, to devise a spelling system. Read stresses the systematic nature of invented spellings; children's judgments about how to represent sounds are consistent and rule-governed and, as subsequent research has confirmed, amazingly uniform across the different groups of children studied. Yet this immature system is not fixed but is in a constant state of reevaluation and change, moving increasingly toward more complete and conventional spellings.

Knowing that writing has meaning and functions, understanding the alphabetic principle of our writing system, and establishing rules for representing speech sounds are not all a child must have accomplished in order to write. Clay (1975) reveals the many graphic and spatial principles children master as they move into writing. They learn that writing is linear and that in our system it goes from left to right and top to bottom of a page. Before children represent speech sounds in their writing, they learn not only about directionality and the use of space but about patterns, for example, the "generating principle"—that letters recur in variable patterns—so that with knowledge of only a few letter shapes a child can produce strings of print that resemble conventional writing.

OBSERVING WHAT CHILDREN
HAVE LEARNED ABOUT WRITING

Children spend several years learning about print *before they enter first grade*. Since the start of schooling marks only the beginning of formal instruction in writing, not the beginning of children's learning about written language, what does this mean for first grade teachers? It means that teachers need to find out right away what children *already know* about written language in order to tell where effective instruction can start. By the end of the year, if writing folders are kept for each child with pieces accurately dated, his or her progress will be clearly visible.

This is how one first grade teacher, Mary Ellen Giacobbe (1981), found out what her children could do as writers. Each day during the first week of school she introduced five or six children to journals (books containing 40 pages of unlined 9" × 12" paper for them to write in). These children worked at the writing table while the others were assigned elsewhere in the classroom.

> I circulated around the classroom observing and talking with the children. "Tell me about your building." . . . "Why do you think the sand goes through this strainer faster than through that strainer?" . . . "How many cubes do you think it will take to fit across the top of the desk?"
>
> Someone tugged at my sleeve and I turned to see Mark standing by my side with his journal. "Tell me about your drawing, Mark," I said.
>
> He pointed to each part of the drawing and said, "This is the ocean and this is a sailboat and this is the anchor. These are clouds."
>
> He had written BD for boat and KLD for cloud. (p. 99)

If Giacobbe had not asked Mark about his drawing, she might not have understood his writing. She watched Ellen write: THE TRCE WAS TACAN A WEC (The turkey was taking a walk).

She read it to herself, crossed out the *T* in *Tacan*, changed it to a *w* and on top of a *wec*, she wrote *D the hall*. Her message now read: THE TRCE WAS WACAN D THE HALL. (The turkey was walking down the hill). Already Ellen knew that she could change her message so that it said exactly what she wanted it to say. She was rereading and revising.

My attention was drawn to the tap, tap, tapping of the black marker on David's page as he was creating a snowstorm. He wrote: I SO SO (I saw snow). David said, "This is a big snowstorm. A real blizzard." As he touched each word, he read, "I saw snow."

I asked David, "What do you notice about the words *saw* and *snow?*" He replied, "They both begin with the same sound." (p. 100)

Giacobbe found out that David understood what a written word was and already knew some phonics.

As the blank pages in their journals came alive with drawings and words telling of their experiences, I could see these children had entered school ready to engage in the active process of writing. They were writing their own workbooks. They were showing me what they knew as well as what they needed to know. There were no errors to be red penciled. Just information showing me what the next step of instruction should be. (pp. 100–101)

Other teachers ask the whole class to write at the same time, using single sheets of paper, while the teachers circulate around the room to observe how the children are writing: Are they sounding out spellings? Which children are not yet using letters to represent sounds but rather are showing a more visual knowledge of print by writing strings of letters or other symbols? Are children writing from left to right and from top to bottom of the paper? Are children asking or giving one another information about spellings or letter formations? Are some children able to read back what they have written? (In the early phase of invented spelling it is not unusual for children to have difficulty reading their writing.) Do some writers make self-corrections and revisions as they work? Have children already memorized the spellings of some words? Did someone at home teach those spellings, the teacher might inquire, or were the spellings picked up from reading? The teachers need not instruct at the beginning; they are essentially finding out information about their children's learning by observation, listening, and questions.

Teachers will learn much about their students' concerns and interests as they draw and write if children generally choose their own topics rather than respond to assigned topics. First graders usually have no trouble taking this initiative, especially if they start out by drawing. As they share their writings, in small groups or as a class, they gather more ideas. From observing children writing and from talking with them about what they write, teachers will come to know their student's lives as well as their skills. Teachers will find that ground, between their own knowledge and their student's knowledge, between their own lives and their student's lives, where they can meet those children and thus truly teach.

When teachers ask children to show what they know, teachers are faced with more diverse responses than are revealed through filling in worksheets or following assignments. Having evidence of how children are not the same at the beginning of school, teachers will not expect them to be at the same, standardized place in their writing development by the end of the year. They will expect children to grow and learn, and will see their essential role as being responsible for that *learning* rather than for *teaching*, in the sense of covering a curriculum and correcting errors.

OBSERVING DEVELOPMENT IN WRITING

In another first grade room, near the end of the year, we could see these two examples of writing.

We might conclude that Scott (Figure 1) and Kenny (Figure 2) had learned a very different amount, especially since this is only one of six pages Kenny wrote while Scott did his sentence. Leafing through their writing folders, however, we see what different places they started from and the different paths their learning took—information that standardized tests could not give us.

The first few weeks of school, Scott's writing was largely in the form of drawing. When his teacher asked him to tell her about his picture, he told elaborated, action-filled stories that sounded vivid and exciting but appeared somewhat incoherent when written down, such as this one from the second day

FIGURE 1 Scott

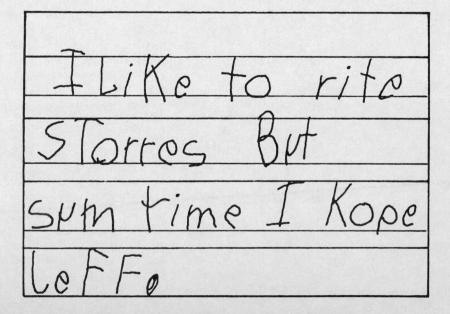

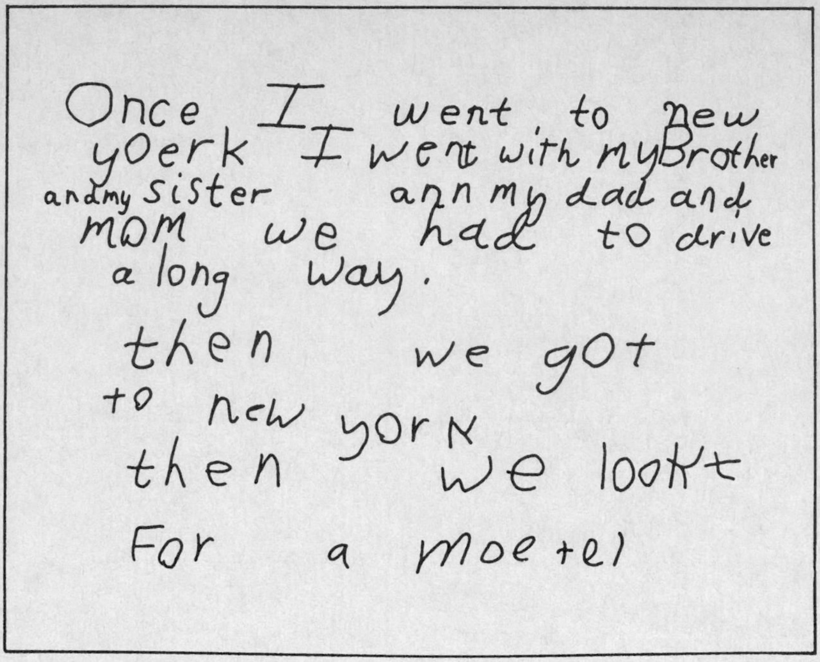

Once I went to new
yOerk I went with myBrother
andmy sister   ann my dad and
mOM   we   had   to drive
a long   way.
then   we got
to new yorN
then   we lookt
For   a moe+el

FIGURE 2 Kenny

of school: "The rocket was starting to take off and the people got in. They saw treasure on the ground. The people jumped out. The rocket was starting to blow up." The only writing on his drawing of the rocket (see Figure 3) was his name, copied from a placard on his desk, and the date, copied from the blackboard.

The first week of school, Kenny drew a detailed picture of three pigs standing in front of three houses and the big bad wolf approaching. He wrote (not copied) his name and APBBW (*a pig, a big bad wolf*). "A pig made a house out of straw and then a big bad wolf came" was what he said about his writing.

The influence of children's literature on both the content and form of Kenny's writing was clear from the start. Many of his pieces the first weeks of school began "Once upon a time."

Scott, two weeks after his rocket drawing, made a house with a door and a window and a face in the window—a sort of revised rocket (see Figure 4). Starting with the bottom line and working upward when he ran out of space, he wrote two strings of letters, many of them reversed. When asked about his piece, Scott told this story:

It was getting sunny and he was thinking about his old friend named Puff the Magic Dragon. He wished he was here. He was watching if he would come. He writed a letter to him. He wanted to sail away with him. Finally he got there. Puff the Magic Dragon says go home because

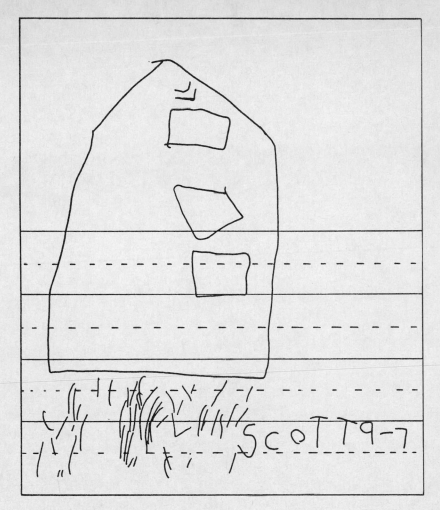

FIGURE 3

he had the sneezes. It was so sad that he comed back that boy because the big man poured some soup to make the sneezes go away.

Although Scott's teacher worked with him on identifying and writing letters to represent a few of the sounds in his dictated stories, he did not move readily into invented spelling but rather seemed to need more practice with letter forms first. Two months later, he wrote a solid page of letter strings (Figure 5) and "read" what he had written: "This is Sheldon. He is a big dog and he jumps on the man. He goes to bed and he sleeps for one hour and a half and I got a pony with him. My dog hunts for rabbits." While his letters did not seem to correspond to sounds, the amount he had written was much more in proportion to the amount he told.

FIGURE 4

    Ten days later, he invented his own phonetic spellings as for "rocket" in Figure 6, although he was still writing strings of letters that did not represent sounds.

    Thus, after nearly three months of school, Scott approached the point of writing development Kenny had reached before any first grade instruction: writing labels for drawings, using accurate representations of consonant sounds. Figure 6 is one page from a seven-page booklet Scott wrote that day. When he read the booklet to his teacher, he expanded the labels he had written into complete sentences: "This is my rocket," "This is my donkey," etc. Two months later he wrote out the full statement behind the labels, as in Figure 7: "This is my little house."

    What had happened to Scott's imaginative tales and vivid language? Scott, like some other storytellers in his classroom, had limited his language to what he could write. When they started spelling inventively, and even shortly before— as if in anticipation of the limits of their own ability to represent language in print,—they reduced their stories to simple, repetitive sentence patterns, such as "This is . . ." and "I see. . . ." These formulas could be kept easily in mind while the children labored to sound out spellings and recall correct letter shapes. Scott's early action narratives tumbled out so fast even an adult writer could barely keep up transcribing them. Just as children start reading at a level far below the level

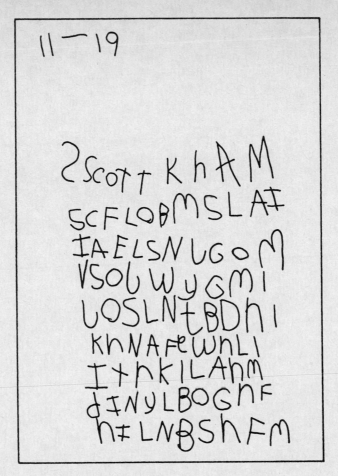

FIGURE 5

of oral language they comprehend, children start writing at a level far below the language of their own speech. Transcriptions by the teacher preserve the vitality and zany charm of children's oral stories, and may help to develop basic reading concepts and skills, but keep the power of writing in the hands of the teacher. Scott's written language was less interesting than his oral language—but he had done it all himself!

In February Scott wrote four solid pages of print—no drawings at all. Looking at one page of this unusually long story about his dog (Figure 8), we can see what, in retrospect, he was rehearsing with his letter strings almost three months earlier (see Figure 5). This page reads: "My dog was very smart. He knows how to roll over."

Scott's last first grade writings (see Figure 1) and one of his earliest (see Figure 3) show the full course of writing development. It no longer appears that he has learned little about writing during first grade.

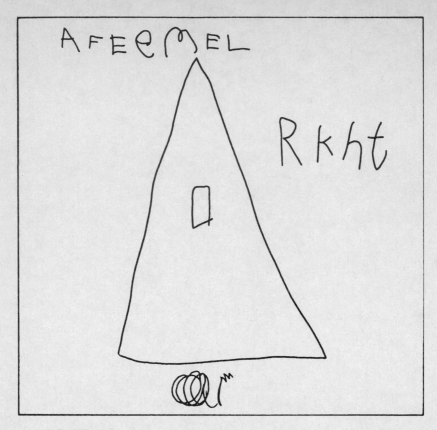

FIGURE 6

Scott was not pushed to copy writing beyond what he could produce, nor was he removed from his writing classroom to do directionality and readiness exercises. His teacher gave him time and faith and encouragement to continue to learn from his own writing. And he did. "Children have shown to us that they need to reconstruct the written system in order to make it their own. Let us allow them the time and the opportunities for such a tremendous task" (Ferreiro, 1982, p. 56).

CONCLUSION

When we appreciate the depth of children's understanding—how they start from the most fundamental and difficult questions about literacy, when we understand how much they need to know and do manage to learn beyond what is in our textbooks and worksheets and lesson plans, we become more aware of the many ways in which children learn about writing. We are then led to appreciate the many ways in which we teach: For instance, by allowing children space to ask their own questions to guide their own learning and to inform us of what they need to be taught. We teach by surrounding children with a richly literate environment which evokes their questions about print and draws them toward

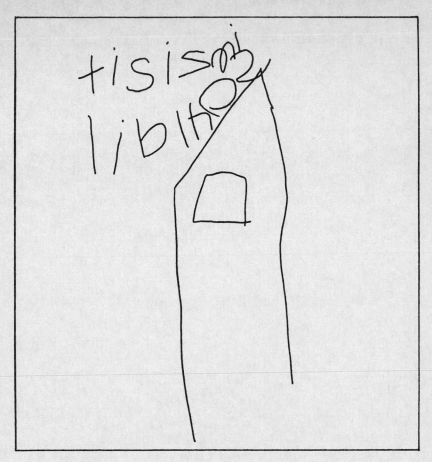

FIGURE 7

using print. We teach by confirming what children know—the knowledge they can grow on—as well as by supplying new information.

Children come to see themselves as they are seen by others. Do we see our students as learners or as mistake-makers? Do we see ourselves as nurturers of growth or as collectors of errors—as gardeners or as animated red pencils? We teach by what we see as well as by what we say.

REFERENCES

Bissex, G. *Gnys at Wrk: A Child Learns to Write and Read.* Cambridge, Massachusetts: Harvard University Press, 1980.

Clay, M. *What Did I Write?* Auckland, New Zealand: Heinemann Educational Books, 1975.

Ferreiro, E. "The Relationship between Oral and Written Language: The Children's Viewpoints," in Y. Goodman, M. Haussler, & D. Strickland (Eds.), *Oral and Written Language Development Research: Impact on the Schools.* Urbana, Illinois: National Council of Teachers of English, 1982.

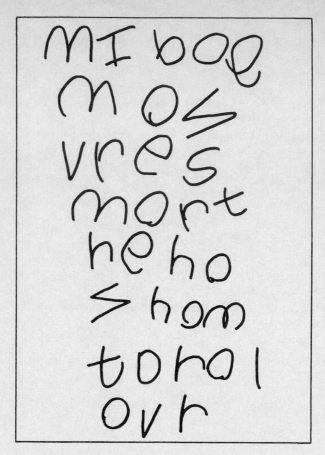

FIGURE 8

Giacobbe, M. E. "Who Says That Children Can't Write the First Week?" in R. D. Walshe (Ed.), *Donald Graves in Australia: "Children Want to Write. . . ."* Rozelle, Australia: Primary English Teaching Association, 1981. (Distributed by Heinemann Educational Books, Exeter, New Hampshire.)

Harste, J., Burke, C., & Woodward, V. *Children, Their Language and World: Initial Encounters with Print,* NIE Final Report. Bloomington, Indiana: Indiana University School of Education, 1981.

Read, C. "Preschool Children's Knowledge of English Phonology," *Harvard Educational Review, 41* (February 1971), 1-34.

THEORY AND IMPLICATIONS

1. Bissex indicates that "many of the theories that [children] try out and the conventions they invent are or were used in other written language systems." She refers here to such conventions as syllabic writing, writing from right to left, and dots to separate words. What do these spontaneous inventions matching other writing systems suggest?

2. These parallels among conventions may reflect the parallels Bickerton draws between the spontaneous creole forms children produce and the kinds of errors children typically make when learning a first language. What similarities do you see?

3. What might dots between words suggest concerning a child's early hypotheses about writing? How are these hypotheses similar to the ones Matthew makes in Smith's study?

4. In the spelling of *finger*, why must the child progress beyond phonics? Choose a different word and show the limitations of phonics in producing correct spelling.

5. Choose a word that is not spelled phonetically and anticipate how a child of five or six might guess at the spelling. Explain the clues the child might use.

6. Bissex suggests that first-grade teachers are essentially learners, finding out what children already know and how they use what they know. What difficulties do you expect teachers to have in finding out what children know? Why might it be very difficult? What strategies beyond those suggested by Bissex might you use?

7. Scott appears to "regress" to a writing level far below his speech level (e.g., to simple repetitive patterns). What are the implications of such "regression" for teachers?

8. Bissex is skeptical about the use of dictation to help children write, whereas Wells applauds it as a way to enable children to construct meaning. What underlies their possible disagreement? Which position do you agree with more? Why?

9. Why do you think that drawing is necessary to writing? Why do you suppose that children do not confuse the two?

PROFESSIONAL CONCERNS

1. How does this article reflect the ideas of Moskowitz, Krashen, and Corder that seem to support a naturalistic development of language skills? Write a position paper using these theories and apply them to classroom situations.

2. Take samples from young writers who use invented spelling and analyze the "hypotheses" you think they are using. Explain to skeptical parents or a principal what is logical and consistent about such hypotheses. Explain also what you assume will be the next stage of hypotheses these writers might use.

Learning to Think through Writing*

Lucy McCormick Calkins

Lucy McCormick Calkins describes a type of writing workshop that incorporates the insights of Smith and Bissex. Perhaps more important, she describes the kind of collaborative, supportive, and meaning-making environment that Wells values, and she encourages the use of narrative in ways that Wells would judge to support literacy.

---

* Calkins, L. M., "Learning to Think Through Writing," in *Observing the Language Learner*, Angela Jaggar and M. Trika Smith-Burke (Eds.), 1985. Reprinted with permission of the International Reading Association.

Calkins advocates a student-centered and whole language writing environ-ment in which the teacher as well as other students learn from the young writer. The workshop setting she describes encourages students to create and revise for meaning. Students read their works to the teacher or to other students and obtain feedback on the clarity of their ideas, but the "authority" remains with the writer. A student of writing teacher Donald Graves, from whom she takes many of her ideas, Calkins emphasizes the need for students to "author" their own texts—to become authorities who write for their own purposes and communicate ideas on self-chosen topics. Such choice creates "authentic" as opposed to school generated, artificial writing and helps to develop "voice"—the particular combi-nation of words and syntax that distin-guishes one writer from another.

Calkins's work lies in the "expressionist" tradition that builds on the theories of such writing teachers as Peter Elbow, Donald Murray, and Donald Graves. Chil-dren write to express themselves—to convey their unique perceptions, responses, and experiences. Calkins stresses that they need to know they have worthwhile stories to tell, for most children consider their own experiences too trivial or common to write about. Once aware that others learn from and sympathize with the uniqueness of their experiences, children happily see themselves controlling the content and purpose of their writing, for only they have the knowledge to expand and clarify that writing. These views are supported and extended by Wells's work, for Wells sees narrative as the essence of thought itself.

Although researchers generally accept expressive writing as appropriate for young children, they often criticize its use with older children, viewing it as self-absorbed—an avoidance of social realities. They prefer to look at writing as "social construction," analyzing social demands on writing such as genre, reader expectations, stylistic conventions, and specified bodies of knowledge and skills. Social construction theory sometimes stresses the acquisition of culture-specific forms through imitation yet sometimes encourages a critical revolt against such disempowering social forms through social action. This theory would put limits on the usefulness for the upper grades of a writing workshop like the one described by Calkins.

Recently, however, Stanley Fishman and Lucille Parkinson McCarthy (College English, Vol. 54, #6, Oct 1992) have argued that expressive writing enhances social cohesion and generates social action. Rather than encouraging isolated, individualistic writing, expressionism leads to the discovery of common sympathies among individuals. As writers clarify personal experience through writing, they discover sympathies larger than the contractual, narrowly professional social agreements that characterize existing social forms. For classrooms of students from diverse cultural backgrounds, expressionism offers a way of validating personal experience and of building new social connections.

But perhaps the opposition of these perspectives is unnecessary. Wells presents a different but equally cogent argument favoring expressive writing, but not at the expense of writing for social purposes. He argues that narrative does not oppose other modes but is integral to all intellectual activity and views narrative as underlying more abstract formulations such as summary and argument. These reconsiderations of expressionism and narrative further support the kind of early writing strategies suggested here. Although Calkins's description of a writing workshop might leave one wondering about the limits of expressionism and narrative, other researchers have demonstrated its connection to later literacy and to social forms of discourse.

"You can conference with yourself," nine year old Diane said to me one morning. "You just read the writing over to yourself and it's like there is another person there. You think thoughts to yourself. . . . You say things others might ask you." The brown eyed youngster paused, her glance shifting to my clipboard. "I talk it over with myself. I ask myself questions."

In his recent article, "Teaching the Other Self: The Writer's First Reader," Donald M. Murray (1982) describes writing as a conversation between two workers muttering to each other at the bench. "The self speaks, the other self listens and considers. The self proposes, the other self considers. The self makes, the other self evaluates. The two selves collaborate" (p. 140). Diane is in fourth grade and already she has developed an articulate other self.

Greg is seven and he, too, dialogues with his emerging text. I watched him scowl as he reread his homemade book. "This story should go in the trash can." he muttered. "See, it is a disaster. The kids will have so many questions."

I SAW MY FATHER'S COLLECTIONS. THEN WE LEFT.

"I go through it wicked fast. The kids will say, "What are the collections? What'd ya see?" " Greg's voice trailed off as he began to squeeze words into the margin of his page. He read the insert to me.

WE SAW BUTTONS, COINS, STAMPS AND OTHER STUFF.

"The kids will have questions still," Greg said, "but at least I got rid of some of them."

Heather, a second grader, reread each page of her book. "I'm having an individual writing conference with myself," she said in a prim, matter-of-fact voice. "On each page I ask myself the questions the other kids would ask me." Then Heather opened her book, "Here I wrote, 'I HAVE A HORSE.' The kids would ask me if I ride it, so I'm going to add 'I RIDE MY HORSE EVERYDAY UNLESS IT'S RAINING.' "

Nine year old Birger paused midway through "The Bottle Story." "In my first story last year, I wrote two stories in one," he said, "and so now I'm always thinking, 'Is this one story?' 'Is this two stories?' "After rereading his story twice, Birger crossed out the title. He explains, "I was going to write about getting 20 cents worth of bottles adding up to a dollar, but on the way my bike was crashed into the wheat field and so I'm going to drop the bottle story." Beside the crossed-out title, Birger wrote "The Wheat Field."

Like most writers, Birger, Heather, and Greg pull in to write, then pull back to reconsider. Closeness and distance, pushing forward and pushing back, creation and criticism; it is this combination of forces which makes writing such a powerful tool for learning. Whereas spoken words fade away, with print we can fasten our thoughts onto paper. We can hold our ideas in our hands; we can carry them in our pockets. We can think about our thinking. Through writing, we can re-see, reshape and refine our thoughts. Smith (1982) explains, "Writing separates our ideas from ourselves in a way that is easiest for us to examine, explore, and develop" (p. 15).

I have always believed that revision is essential to the writing process; that writing becomes a wedge that develops our thinking precisely because it enables us to revisit our first thoughts. But recently I've begun to realize that our alterations and drafts are not the cutting edge—the growing edge—of writing, but the traces of it. Instead, the cutting edge of writing is the interaction between writer and emerging text. The writer asks, "What am I trying to say?" "How does this sound?" "Where's this leading me?" When children learn to ask these questions of their emerging texts, they gain a tool for developing not only their information but also their skills as writers. When Heather has an individual writing conference with herself, when Birger asks himself, "Is this one story?" these youngsters develop not only their texts, but also their thinking and writing skills.

MY CHANGING CONCEPT OF HOW CHILDREN LEARN REVISION

Several years ago, the National Institute of Education funded Donald Graves (1982), Susan Sowers, and me to spend two years documenting the day-to-day changes in children's writing behaviors. In order to do this, we became live-in researchers in a public school in Atkinson, New Hampshire. . . . and it was there that I met Birger, Greg, Heather, and the others (Calkins, 1983). When I began collecting field notes on the children's activities during writing, I recorded voicing behaviors, eye movements, occasional pauses. But that was all. If the children revised, it was only to correct their spelling. Rarely did they even reread their texts. Writing, for these children, was certainly not an interaction with their emerging texts—instead it was an ongoing process of adding on.

Within a few months, however, I was startled to see our case study subjects were drafting and revising. "I've got mounds of drafts!" one youngster announced to his teacher. "Look at how many crossouts I did," another would chime in. I thought Eureka had been reached.

Then I began noticing curious things. Sometimes children's drafts were sequels rather than variations of each other. Often their drafts were copies of each other, with just a line added or a detail changed. One boy learned revision involved cutting and pasting and so he "revised" by carefully scissoring out each word of his story and then pasting them together again,—with the only addition being glue and tape. Although most of the children were happily revising, were they rereading, reconsidering, and reexploring their first thoughts? Were they using writing as a tool for thinking? I decided children could learn to sustain work on a piece of writing and to view drafts as tentative, but they probably were too young to interact with their emerging texts.

Kids. No sooner do you begin to understand them than they begin to change. No sooner had I built a tentative description of children's writing than some youngsters began defying the description.

Diane, Greg, Heather, and the others began having those individual writing conferences with themselves. Some children—but not all—began rereading their work and then interacting with their texts. "Is this one story?" "What else should

I say?" "Is this really true?" "How else could I write this?" Rather than being age-related, the development of this Other Self seemed classroom-related. It wasn't necessarily the older kids who were having those individual conferences with themselves. Instead, in some classrooms at all levels (K-5), children interacted with their emerging texts, while in other classrooms, children waited for teachers to ask questions, spot problems, or suggest solutions.

I do not have "hard data" about why some teachers succeeded in recruiting children's other selves. But I do have informed hunches. I believe, and our data suggest, that children learn to interact with their emerging texts when classroom environments and teacher-child conferences are structured in ways which help writers assume responsibility and ownership of their craft.

CLASSROOM ROUTINES

When methods for teaching writing and classroom routines and schedules are always changing, children are not apt to monitor their own writing processes, steering their way through a piece. Instead they wait for their teacher's changing agenda. I once assumed "creative" writing required "creative" classroom structures. Each week, my writing class would host new rules, agendas, and approaches. Now I suspect kaleidoscope classrooms keep children dependent on our changing plans. Only when schedules and routines are kept predictable can the unpredictable happen.

In some Atkinson classrooms, children knew they would write each day at the same time. In these rooms, I saw children planning for writing, and writing as if there was a tomorrow. "You need to know you've got all the time you want for a piece of writing," eight year old Susie explains. "Otherwise you're afraid to look back, afraid to see it's not all you could do."

There was not only a regular schedule in these classrooms for when children would write, there was also a predictable flow to each session. Birger, Diane, and their classmates knew each writing class would begin with a brief mini-lesson, followed by a workshop for writing, and conferences, followed by a meeting to share their writing. Some might ask, "Didn't the sameness bore children?" On the contrary, it allowed children to invest themselves in the workshop, making plans, developing their own strategies for writing. Susie began each day by rereading her pieces. Birger often met with several friends to share plans for their writing. Others mapped upcoming sections of their pieces. The simplicity of the schedule gave children a framework within which they could ask, "What am I going to do next?" Like artists in a studio, they discovered that the juxtaposition of a changing craft with a simple predictable environment can free us to make choices throughout the process of our craft.

TEACHER-CHILD CONFERENCES

Now, as I look back I also realize that children learned to interact with their texts in the classrooms where teacher-child conferences became models for child-child conferences. Children internalized the process and began asking themselves the questions which had been asked of them. In these classrooms teachers sensed the impact their conferences could have on young writers. They interacted with children in conferences in such a way that children learned to interact with their emerging texts. They were teaching the writer, not the writing.

Other teachers believed their job was to improve the texts. In conferences, they'd rush in and offer evaluations and solutions, not realizing the lasting effect of such conferences was to perpetuate children's dependence on their evaluations, solutions, and strategies.

I do not blame those teachers. It is so easy for us to take over a child's text, often without realizing what we've done. How easy it is for us to begin a writing conference by taking up the text and thinking, "What would I do if this were mine?" Sometimes I take a draft out of the writer's hands and hold it in my own—what a message! Then, too, sometimes, I take control by eagerly imposing my agendas on a conference, perhaps asking specific questions meant to coax writers to expand on my favorite section, perhaps rushing in with my compliments and criticisms. "Your story is perfect," I say, as if I could know when a piece matches the writer's intentions. How hard it is for us to approach a conference asking questions which return authorship to the writer: "How's it coming?" "How can I help?" "What do you think of it?" "What will you do next?" Our job in a writing conference is to interact with children in such a way that they learn to interact with their emerging text. Our job in a writing conference is to put ourselves out of a job.

The data from our study suggest that when teacher-child conferences are predictable, children are more likely to internalize the temporary structure of a conference. In classrooms where teachers' responses are ever-changing and kaleidoscopic, children do not anticipate their teacher's responses, but instead wait for their changing agendas.

CONTENT CONFERENCES

Several teachers at Atkinson intuitively developed several predictable "kinds" of conferences. Most frequently, teachers focused on the child's emerging subject (I call these content conferences). "Children need to know they are being heard," Currier said, explaining her purpose in a content conference. The pattern in most content conferences was that the teachers listened to the child's evolving subject and then repeated the child's story, as if to say, "I heard you . . . your meaning is coming through." Sometimes this active listening involved questions which would clear away little snags and tangles which prevented the teacher from hearing what the child was saying, but the focus was on the child's content, not on trumped-up questions asked by teachers who wanted to tug out more information. Ironically, this kind of real listening seems to recruit additional information better than a barrage of questions. The force of listening helps writers see the value of their message and so content conferences often lead youngsters to further develop their subjects—and their confidence.

Because the pattern of these conferences was a predictable one, in their peer conferences first graders and fourth graders alike were soon telling what they'd heard in a draft and asking questions that could clear away the snags and gaps which clouded the meaning. These peer conferences were later internalized. And so seven year old Greg reread his piece and said, "This story should go in the trash can. The kids will have so many questions. The kids will say, 'What were the collections?' 'What'd ya see?' "

In her fourth grade classroom, Susie reread her lead:

> I was at a beach in Florida. I pressed my toes in the hot sand. I saw my sister jumping out in the waves with my Aunt. She was jumping around as the waves hit her, she was out deep—I wanted to go and play in the waves but I was too nervous.

Susie reread her lead and then said to herself, "How did it feel? What was it like?" Then she muttered, "I'm realizing my whole first draft is like that—blah." Susie wrote a second draft, adding details:

> I pressed my toes in the hot sand. I wiggled them around. The gritty sand felt good on my sunburnt toes. I looked out over the ocean. My sister was out deep, jumping over the waves with my Aunt. Sometimes the waves got too big and they would knock her over, then my Aunt would pull her up and she'd be dripping wet and they'd start laughing.

Sometimes the teachers' content conferences were directed not only towards learning about the child's subject but, more specifically, towards helping children focus their topic. Whether the writer is a first grader whose stories are a list, a fifth grader who writes without highlighting a specific theme, or a professional writer, searching for the thread of his book, a crucial question we can ask is "What are you trying to say?" This question can be rephrased. "Why did you select this topic; what's the important thing about it?" "What do you want to leave your reader with?" "What's the heart of your piece?" Soon Birger and the others were asking these same questions of their own emerging drafts.

Sometimes the teacher's content conference had a different purpose and a different pattern. If the piece was a skeleton, lacking in details, or if a child had just focused his or her topic and needed to embellish it with more details, teachers geared their content conference toward helping children expand their information. When Eric narrowed his topic from "All about My Trip" to "The Bunk Beds," he worried that his piece would be awful short. Eric's teacher helped him realize how much he had to say. She did this not with specific questions meant to eke out more details, but instead with general, open-ended questions meant to tap into Eric's energy. "What exactly happened, Eric?" "How did you feel?" "It's hard for me to imagine what it was like. Will you help me picture it?" The significant thing about these questions is that they leave control in the writer's hands. They don't pull the writer this way and that, distracting him from what he wanted to say. But also, the questions give writers tools which can be used another day, on another piece of writing. They are universal questions, they could be asked of almost any piece of writing. And so it was not long before children were asking these same questions of each other and of themselves.

Sometimes the teachers mostly listened to a child's subject, repeating what they heard to the child. Sometimes they asked questions which helped children select a focus for their pieces. Sometimes they asked questions which drew more detail and more energy from the child. In any case, teachers mostly paid attention to the subject of the child's paper, and so I called these "content conferences." Because the teachers' content conferences were predictable, because their questions were often universal ones, children soon began asking these same questions of each other and of themselves.

PROCESS CONFERENCES

But then something surprising happened. A new kind of conference entered the classroom, and it seemed to come from nowhere. In their conferences with themselves, children began to center on their process of writing rather than on their evolving subjects. Many of the children's questions to themselves were not about the subject at all, but about writing strategies.

> What should I do next? Let's see, I could see if my story goes into parts and then work on each part.
>
> I've got heaps of drafts, I don't know why. . . . This piece was the hardest for me because I wanted to tell exactly what it's like to snuggle with my father, and the words kept being wrong.
>
> I've got five drafts! Now, how are they different?

Along with these surprising new questions, it became clear that the children had an astonishing ability to articulate their process of writing, to select and critically review their strategies, and to consciously guide and control their thinking (Calkins, 1983).

> BIRGER: Now I'm going to reread my story, trying to make parts longer, like Susie did in her piece. I'm going to add on at this part when I come out of the garage to the accident. I'll tell about when I was walking across the driveway, how I heard sounds, like the vet with the siren, and I smelled the air. It wasn't bad air and I remember thinking, it was hard to believe a part of me had just died, the air smelled so nice and clean. I'm going to put all that in, spreading it out with more details.
>
> AMY: When I write, it's like I have a movie in my mind and the words just come off of me. I'm like a typewriter, clicking them off.
>
> SUSIE: Usually I put down a sentence that I don't even like. It isn't even going to be in the piece. I just put it down and keep going right through it.

It was not magic which had led these children to such an awareness and control of their strategies for writing. The children's process conferences had not emerged from nowhere. The children were again asking themselves the questions which had been asked of them—this time, not by their teachers, but by the researchers who were observing in the school. How could I have overlooked the impact our presence would have on the children? Day by day for two years, these children had been asked process questions. "How'd you go about writing this draft?" "What new problems did you run into?" "What are you planning to do next?"

All of my efforts not to teach the children had been to no avail. My presence at the child's side, my interest in the process of their craft, and my predictable questions had been a powerful teaching force. Because I continually asked children to put their thinking into words, the children had become exceptionally aware of their intentions and strategies. The children had seen my fascination with their thinking and they, too, began looking at it, asking, "So what am I doing now?" "What kinds of things could I do next?"

Because children were reflecting on their strategies for writing, they were also learning to steer their thinking. Donaldson (1978) writes:

> The point to grasp is how closely the growth of consciousness is related to the growth of the intellect. . . . If the intellectual powers are to develop, the child must gain a measure of control over his own thinking and he cannot control it while he remains unaware of it.

It is not by accident that we learn dance in a room full of mirrors.

I'd meant to observe children's growth, and in doing so, I'd participated in it. I'd meant to study learning, and in doing so, I learned teaching.

REFERENCES

Calkins, L. M. *Lessons from a Child.* Exeter, New Hampshire: Heinemann Educational Books, 1983.

Donaldson, M. *Children's Minds.* New York: Norton, 1978.

Graves, D. H. *A Case Study Observing the Development of Primary Children's Composing, Spelling, and Motor Behaviors During the Writing Process.* Final Report, Project No. 8-3419-0963. Washington, D.C.: National Institute of Education, 1982.

Murray, D. M. "Teaching the Other Self: The Writer's First Reader," *College Composition and Communication, 33* (May 1982), 140-147.

Smith, F. *Writing and the Writer.* New York: Holt, Rinehart & Winston, 1982.

THEORY AND IMPLICATIONS

1. How does the collaborative nature of Calkins's classroom correspond to the collaborative story making Wells sees as part of children's essential meaning-making?

2. How are language events kept "whole" in this environment?

3. How does the revision process correspond to Wells's description of writing as a way of directing thought? How does it extend oral storytelling in ways that prepare children to make meaning in other disciplines?

4. Interaction with an emerging text, Calkins claims, is more classroom-related than age-related. Does this contradict Wells's view that home environments, particularly listening to stories, best predict achievement of literacy? Why? How do you think that teachers can promote such interactions with texts?

5. When children internalize the questions that teachers ask in conferences, do they simply learn to add on? Do you think that children can learn to become good writers only from responding to such questions or that children also require extensive previous experiences in listening to stories, as Wells might argue? Why?

6. How did the conferences illustrate general cognitive and social principles of language acquisition?

7. Do process conferences differ substantially from content conferences in demonstrating how children learn? Explain.

PROFESSIONAL CONCERNS

1. Justify to a parent, teacher, principal, or other interested person the use of a writing workshop. Anticipate objections: that some children will write nothing; that children teach each other skills; that many children will talk or draw rather than write (given that writing is hard); that children need more structure; and that some children will do better than others in this environment, thus biasing the instruction.

2. Explain to other educators why Calkins describes a writing environment without "prompts," topics, or teacher-created leads of any sort. Why do you think that children must choose their own topics? What potential problems does this choice involve?

Kan Yu Ret an Rayt en Ingles: Children Become Literate in English as a Second Language*

SARAH HUDELSON

Although studies in second language development have shaped the teaching of L2 oral language, they have not significantly changed L2 literacy instruction. Second language literacy instruction has been mostly concerned with eradicating error, ensuring reading comprehension before teaching writing, and teaching both reading and writing as a series of subskills such as pronunciation, sound-letter correspondences, and spelling lists. Hudelson's research contradicts such views. She shows that eradicating error is not the point. Indeed children with few oral skills can read environmental print, and can read print in class if it is kept "whole" and functional.

---

* Hudelson, S., "Kan Yu Ret an Rayt En Ingles: Children Become Literate in a Second Language," *TESOL Quarterly, Vol. 18/No. 2.* Copyright 1984. Reprinted by permission.

*Hudelson draws on L2 theories that emphasize natural language develop-
ment, with children progressing through predictable stages and benefiting from
interaction. She also seems to draw on L1 literacy theories that similarly view
reading and writing as interactions within social contexts, involving predictions
and approximations. She agrees with Smith that students bring background
knowledge and a cultural framework to build meaning out of texts, and
believes that they do so with minimal oral ability in the L2. They need literacy
materials to be kept "whole" and functional so that they can use context to
guess at meanings. As Wells, Bissex, and Calkins suggest, the four modes of
speaking, listening, reading, and writing should not be separated into subskills
but instead integrated into a whole language framework.*

*The implications of Hudelson's work are that ESL children learn to read
and write the way native speakers learn: by reading and writing. Although
ESL children bring knowledge to the text, their cultural knowledge differs from
the knowledge of native speakers, so they can, indeed, misread a text. Many
miscues are surface level though, and do not affect underlying meaning.
Teachers should not presume that ESL students need attention to subskills
simply because they make more errors; a more likely implication is that they
need more cultural knowledge.*

INTRODUCTION

During the last ten to fifteen years, significant studies in second language
development have provided researchers and practitioners with important information about how children learn a second language. Often this information has been
applied to ESL teaching practices and curriculum development. Unfortunately,
many of the innovations in teaching children have been limited to or have focused
upon oral language (Gonzalez-Mena 1975, Urzua 1981, Ventriglia 1982), with less
consideration given to innovation in literacy (reading and writing) practices. In
spite of recent research that presents findings with implications for practice,
children's ESL literacy is dominated by materials and procedures that have been
created with the following perspective in mind: that ESL reading and writing
should be strictly controlled so that errors do not occur; that children should
be asked to read and write only what they have practiced orally in formal lessons;
that early experiences with English reading should consist of "linguistic" materials
that emphasize phonetically and orthographically regular words; that there should
be a time gap between the presentation of oral and written forms of English;
that writing, especially at the initial stages, should consist of copying, filling in
blanks, and taking dictation rather than creating one's own messages; that reading
and writing should always follow listening and speaking instruction, with writing
always following reading. Reading materials such as *The Miami Linguistics
Readers* (Robinett, Bell, and Rojas 1970), the *Crane Reading System—English*
(Crane 1977), and the reading/writing components of programs such as *Steps to
English* (Kernan 1983), *English Around The World* (Marquardt, Miller, and
Housman 1976), and *YES English for Children* (Mellgren and Walker 1977)
exemplify this perspective. Aspects of this position have been articulated in

methods textbooks such as those written by Ching (1976), Donoghue and Kunkle (1979) , and Finocchiaro (1974), among others. Elley (1981) has suggested that the dominance of these kinds of materials and approaches may be traced to the influence of the audio lingual school of language teaching, whose methods and principles Elley sees in practice in elementary second language classrooms and curricula around the world.

Until recently, the perspective delineated above reflected our understanding of second language literacy development in children. However, in recent years researchers have made exciting discoveries about the growth of reading and writing abilities in children learning a second language. Many of these findings, in addition to coming from descriptive and classroom-based research, have direct implications for and applications to classroom practice. Without intending to reject outright all previous notions or efforts of the past, this article offers some alternative views of second language literacy development in children. This article, then, has two purposes: 1) to provide an overview of some findings of recent research in second language literacy (reading and writing), and 2) to provide some examples of how these findings speak to classroom practice.

RECENT RESEARCH FINDINGS

Finding/Generalization 1

Even children who speak no or very little English are reading some of the print in their environment and are using that reading to increase their English. In the United States, non- or limited English-speaking children find themselves surrounded by English outside of school. These learners acquire a lot of English and often begin reading English from living and coping with English in their daily lives (K. Goodman, Y. Goodman, and Flores 1979).

A few years ago, in several settings, Y. Goodman investigated the print awareness of preschool, supposedly preliterate children, both native English speakers and non- or limited English-speaking children from such native language backgrounds as Arabic, Navajo, and Spanish. She found that even children who were virtually non-speakers of English in such isolated areas as the Navajo Nation in Northern Arizona could read items such as *Crest, Coca Cola, McDonalds, Cheerios, Wonder Woman, Dracula,* and *Spider Man* (Y. Goodman 1980, Y. Goodman and Altwerger 1981, K. Goodman, Y. Goodman, and Flores 1979). They were able to do this because these items from the media and from real life were salient for them. Older non-English-speaking children, too, have demonstrated an ability to read such environmental print items, even though they have resided in the United States for only a month or two (Hudelson 1981). An example comes from a case study of a third grader who, when asked by the researcher about English print in his neighborhood, could tell her that a sign that said *BEWARE OF THE DOG* meant "que no se acerque al perro" ('don't get close to the dog') and that *TV's FIXED HERE* meant "que se compongan televisiones aquí" ('televisions fixed here').

What does this mean for classroom instruction? For teachers who say that children are reading only because they see the entire label and therefore are not really reading, it means little. But for ESL teachers who take this as evidence that children are interacting with and learning from their environment, a host of instructional possibilities appear. Some examples appear below.

A first-grade teacher took her ESL children on a walking field trip around the school. The children had received no formal English reading instruction at the time of this activity. The children's job was to point out, read, and write down all of the English words they could find. If the children were unable to read the print they discovered, the teacher read the word for them. Considerable English vocabulary teaching occurred as the children developed their lists. The teacher read several words to the class (for example, *fire extinguisher*). Others she pronounced with standard English phonology and explained their meaning in English (*custodian* and *caution*). In some cases one child would read for the others. Back in the classroom, the lists were reread and the items were then used in categorizing activities.

In two first and second-grade classrooms, as a substitute for structured ESL time, teachers set up a class grocery store, requesting that students bring in items for the store (in the form of empty boxes, cartons, tin cans, and so on), identify the items, arrange them on shelves as a grocer would, and roleplay grocer and customers. These children also had not received any formal English reading instruction. All transactions had to be conducted in English, and the customers had to write out shopping lists before they went to the store in order to be able to buy their groceries. On the lists that the children wrote and read were such items as *Coors Lite beer, pizza, soup, milk,* and *gum*.

In a combination third-fourth grade, the teacher assigned students to bring in product labels, identify the products, and then describe them orally and in writing. One young writer, who read her paper to the class, described Trix cereal as soft (*sofet*), crunchy (*cranchi*), and lemon and orange flavored (*flavert limen and oreng*).

In a junior high school class, some advanced ESL students working in small groups invented their own products and created commercial messages. Actual television commercials were used for listening/speaking and reading activities before the students came up with their own inventions. One of the commercial messages is reproduced as Figure 1.

These are a few examples of ways in which ESL teachers have made use of their students' interaction with English environmental print. These teachers have taken advantage of what students already know (and are interested in) in their second language; they have validated this knowledge by bringing it into school and have used it as part of literacy instruction. This instruction has raised children's awareness of themselves as English readers while simultaneously developing and revealing their English vocabularies.

Finding/Generalization 2

ESL learners are able to read English before they have complete oral control of the language. As in a first language, reading in a second language is a psycho-sociolinguistic process, an experience in which readers build meaning by interaction

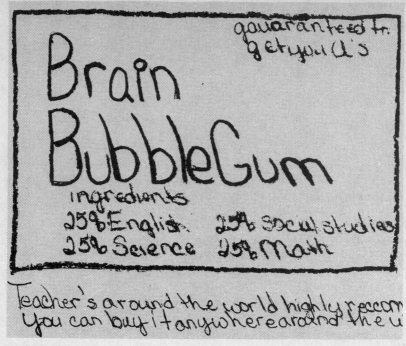

FIGURE 1

with print and by utilizing in these interactions their own background of experiences and personal information as well as their developing knowledge of the language (Grove 1981). Using their language and experiential background, readers predict their way through a text. As ESL readers build meaning, their own levels of language development and their own background influence what is created.

A clear view of the second language reader as a predictor presents itself when *miscue analysis*, a reading research technique originally developed to examine the oral reading of native speakers of English (K. Goodman and Burke 1973), is utilized. Miscue analysis requires that a person read a story orally and then retell the contents. Both the retelling and the reader's miscues (deviations from the printed text) are examined. In recent years, several researchers have used miscue analysis with ESL readers (Barrera 1978, Clarke 1981, Devine 1981, K. Goodman and Y. Goodman 1978, Mott 1981, Rigg 1977). Their research has yielded the following generalizations: 1) like native speakers, ESL readers make miscues when they read English; 2) some of these miscues change the meaning of what is being read, while others do not; 3) those miscues that change the meaning of what is being read are more likely to be self-corrected than those that do not; 4) some of the miscues that ESL readers make reflect the reader's English language development; 5) the ESL reader may be able to demonstrate more understanding of material that has been read if retelling is done in the native language rather than in English; 6) ESL readers do not need to pronounce the surface phonology of what they are reading as a native speaker would in order to understand what they are reading; and 7) ESL readers demonstrate greater comprehension of material that is culturally close to their own experiences.

These findings suggest several applications. First, ESL teachers do not need to wait until children are highly fluent in English before offering reading materials. Care must be taken in selecting the kinds of materials to be offered, but reading can and should begin fairly soon after children begin studying English. Second, teachers should avoid judging children's ESL reading ability on the basis of the number of oral reading errors the children make and/or on the basis of heavily accented reading. Informal reading inventories, widely used in elementary school classrooms (see Harris and Sipay 1979), suggest that teachers total the number of oral reading errors in order to determine whether a child is able to read certain material. Applying this practice to ESL readers can be especially misleading since ESL children make many surface errors that do not affect understanding. Rather, the teacher should consider the child's ability to talk about what has been read. Third, teachers should avoid interrupting ESL children while they are reading in order to correct them. Allowing children to make pronunciation errors does not reinforce incorrect English, and the practice of interrupting and correcting may actually disrupt rather than facilitate the readers' construction of meaning from a text. Fourth, in working with ESL children reading English, it is crucial to focus on comprehension of text material. An appropriate beginning is to encourage children to retell as much as possible of what they have read. Specific questions may also be asked, but it is important that the children do as much of the talking as possible in response to a general request to "tell me everything you can about what you just read." Children's retellings often reveal what they *do not* understand as well as what they do. This information is valuable to the teacher in returning the children to the story to re-examine parts of the text. And fifth, when possible (either through the teacher or through peers), ESL children should be allowed to discuss texts in the native language as well as in English. In this way the teacher may get a more accurate picture of what children understand.

Finding/Generalization 3

Reading comprehension in a second language, as in a first, is influenced by the background knowledge and the cultural framework that the reader brings to the text (Grove 1981). Even quite proficient ESL readers recall more from a text based on their own culture than they do from a text based on a foreign culture (Steffensen, Joag-dev, and Anderson 1979, Steffensen and Joag-dev 1981). In two studies of ESL readers, Johnson (1981, 1982) found that simplification of vocabulary and syntax were less important factors in ESL readers' comprehension of a text than the cultural contents of the passage being read. She also found that real cultural experiences prior to reading (as contrasted to formal study of vocabulary items) had a positive effect on ESL students' reading comprehension of a passage linked to the cultural experience.

The classroom applications of these findings are several. First, whenever possible the teacher should select reading materials that reflect the children's cultural and experiential background. Children's comprehension also may be enhanced if the teacher utilizes the children's experiences as background preparation for reading. Making the children aware of what they already know about a topic contributes positively to subsequent reading comprehension. Second, as often as possible, if children are reading culturally unfamiliar material, teachers need to build a background of knowledge prior to reading. Ideally this will take the form of a real experience (as in Johnson's example of the Halloween carnival). Knowledge (and language) may also be built through television, films or filmstrips, demonstrations, and materials shared with children. Third, instructional strategies that do not depend upon prepared texts but which utilize the readers' cultural and experiential backgrounds are also appropriate. Two such strategies are the use of key words and language experience stories.

Developed by Ashton-Warner (1963) as a way of teaching non-English-speaking Maori children to read English, *key words* are words that individual children decide they want to learn to read because the words are personally important to them. On a daily basis, the teacher elicits a key word from each child. The teacher writes down each child's word on a card, which the child then retains in order to read the words over, copy them, make a picture of them, read them to others, write sentences with them, and so on. Since Ashton-Warner first proposed the use of key words, the practice has been used effectively in the United States as a beginning reading strategy for both native speakers of English and ESL children (Veatch 1979).

Language experience stories also utilize the students' knowledge and cultural background as well as their developing language (Murphy 1980, Feeley 1979, 1983). Research has shown that the language experience approach is an effective method for teaching reading both to native and non-native speakers of English (Colvert 1973, Hall 1979, Mallett 1977). Basically, the students have an experience which they discuss, after which they dictate to the teacher (scribe) what they want written about the experience. The teacher listens and transcribes the story exactly as the children dictate it. Because both the contents of the stories and the language used come from the students, these stories are especially comprehensible, an important factor in working with ESL students.

Rigg (1981) has utilized language experiences with ESL learners of all ages. Using wordless picture books as the stimulus (experience), she has found that students are willing and able to use their background knowledge to create stories. To address the concern that accepting children's stories as dictated reinforces their incorrect language patterns, Rigg has demonstrated that first draft stories may be used as the basis for oral language activities (diagnosing which structures to practice from their dictations) as well as for revising and editing by the students. In the example below, a Russian-speaking student dictated two stories using picture stimuli. Each of the stories was subsequently corrected by the student without being prompted to do so.

First Effort	*Self-Revision*
Two ladies playing in tennis.	Two ladies are playing in tennis.
In the hand they holding the rackets.	In the hand they are holding the
One from they is coming to the	rackets. One from they is running
ball.	to the ball.

The boy live in the ranch. He help
for his parents. He give the food
for the cocks . . . The cows eat the
grass and he watch for them.

The boy lives on the ranch. He
helps his parents. He gives the food
for the cocks . . . The cows eat the
grass and he watches them.

(Rigg 1981:85)

The second drafts suggest that many ESL learners are able to reflect on the form
of what they have said and have seen written down and that they are able to
make revisions as they learn more English. The drafts also are useful to the ESL
teacher as a way of documenting student learning.

Students learning English as a second language, then, show teachers both
that they are able to read and understand some material in English that they do
not yet control orally and that they are able to read English when the material
comes from within themselves, that is, when the approach used is an organic
one that relies on what the students know rather than on what they do not know.

Finding/Generalization 4

As in a first language, writing in a second language interacts with reading. The
two processes are closely related and complement each other (Edelsky 1982,
Staton 1981). Bissex (1980), Chomsky (1971), and Read (1975) have demonstrated
that for some young native speakers of English, writing—the composing of one's
own message—precedes formal reading. The messages generally are characterized
by a variety of unconventional aspects (for example, spelling and segmentation)
which signify that the young composers use their existing knowledge to solve
their writing problems. These researchers have also shown that these young
writers read their own creations, often before they read conventional English
texts. Bissex discovered that Paul, the child in her longitudinal case study, used
his writing as his personal reading material for several months.

What has been found for native speakers is also being shown to be true for
child second language learners. For some ESL children, written expression in
English may precede formal reading instruction (Edelsky 1982). For some, their
English writing forms their first reading (Rigg 1981). For others, writing may help
other school work (Searfoss, Smith, and Bean 1981, Staton 1981).

The classroom application is this: we should encourage ESL learners to write,
to express themselves in writing as well as orally, and to use written expression
as one means of developing English. The previous examples have shown that ESL
speakers can write shopping lists and product descriptions based on environmental print. Other kinds of writing also have been encouraged by teachers who
consider writing an integral part of second language development.

Figure 2 is a journal entry from a first-grade child enrolled in a bilingual
program where initial literacy, including a great deal of writing, was in Spanish
(see Edelsky 1981, 1982, 1983). With no formal literacy instruction in English,
one day late in the spring the child produced this journal entry in English when
the teacher asked the class if they could write in their journals in English rather
than in Spanish.

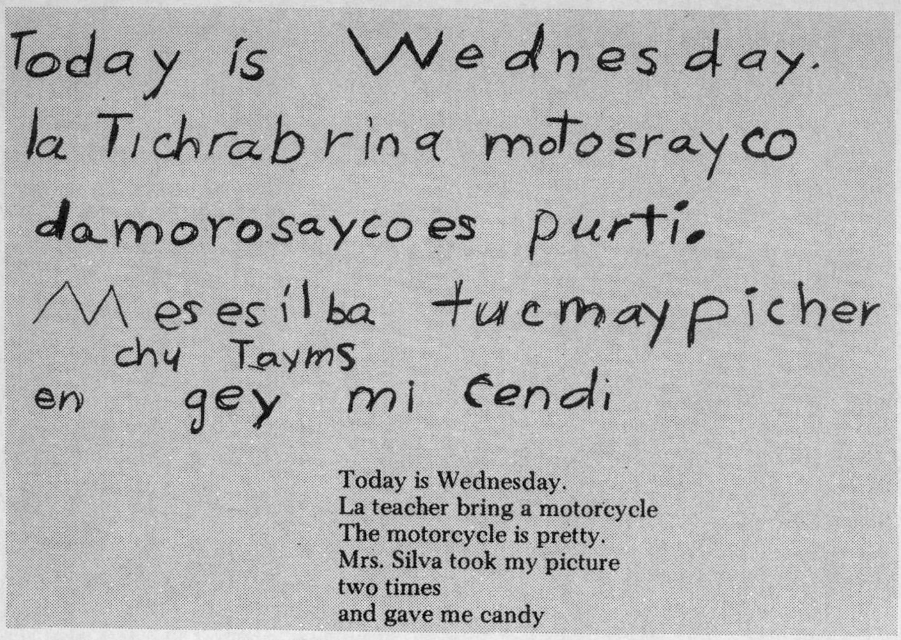

Today is Wednesday.
la Tichrabrina motosrayco
damorosaycoes purti.
Mesesilba tucmaypicher
chy Tayms
en   gey mi Cendi

Today is Wednesday.
La teacher bring a motorcycle
The motorcycle is pretty.
Mrs. Silva took my picture
two times
and gave me candy

FIGURE 2

In reading the entry, the influence of Spanish on English is obvious. But looking beyond the invented spelling, one is struck both by the ability of this child to express himself in English and to reveal what he already knows about English, without having received training in that language. This child was not afraid to try to write in English, and he read what he wrote.

Other ESL students may express themselves more easily in writing than orally. The following journal entry was written by a fourth grader described by her teacher as extremely shy in class. At the time of the writing, this child had been in the United States less than two years. In her writing this child expressed several personal feelings that perhaps she was unwilling or unable to say out loud. Her incomplete mastery of English did not prevent her from using her journal to express some things that were on her mind.

Some girl act beautiful cause shake their but and has feather back hear and act big. And they act smart ibe day I was playing woth Pola and somebody called me to the teetotter and told me not to play with pola because she would make me black. I feel that are are bad becuase they dress in tight pants tight shirt because they act that they could beet up everibody.[1]

---

[1] (Spelling, punctuation, and word choice have not been changed.)

In middle school settings, interactive journal writing has been used to promote student expression (Staton, Shuy, and Kreeft 1982). In this practice, students use daily journals to write to their teacher about whatever they choose to discuss. The teacher writes back to them responding to content, not form, and creates a written conversation. The use of interactive journals has been studied using both native and non-native speakers of English (Staton 1981, 1983). The findings suggest that ESL students are able to make progress toward understanding and producing more formal discourse by using the less formal, more "oral" style of a journal. The research has also documented that, for ESL students, the journals become a vehicle for obtaining information about school subjects and about English (1981).

ESL writing may also play a role in content area construction. In second-grade social studies, for example, a class of limited English speakers studied several Native American tribes. During class time set aside for ESL, the teacher told the class about each tribe, and the class then participated in such activities as creating sand paintings, constructing totem poles, and making dioramas. The teacher shared some books about Indians, but no formal reading was required. At the end of the unit, the teacher asked the students to write about something they had learned. One child wrote what appears in Figure 3, using writing to reflect upon what he had studied.

FIGURE 3

totem poles protect you. they have faces of
animals   my totem pole has a lion on
it   totem poles are big and they
have wings and they are too
big and they are too big
and they are too big and
they are from the Navajos

For ESL students working with content area textbooks, the use of the "guided writing procedure" may contribute both to ESL students' understanding of text material and to their ability to express that understanding in writing (Searfoss, Smith, and Bean 1981). The guided writing procedure involves children in brainstorming what they know about the topic they will read about, putting their knowledge in writing, reading, and discussing the text, and writing again. Writing serves both to set expectations for reading and to provide a mechanism for rethinking the contents of the text.

Finding/Generalization 5[2]

ESL learners can (and should) write English before they have complete control over the oral and written systems of the language. Second language acquirers' written products reflect their language development at a given point in time. As learners gain more control over the language, their writing will reflect this development (Hudelson 1983). Consider these examples (see Figure 4) from a second grader from Puerto Rico who was enrolled in a public school in Florida. They were gathered by an ESL tutor who encouraged the child's early and continued written expression but did not correct the writing efforts.

In October this child hypothesized that English was spelled like Spanish, and while she was unable to write sentences, she did come up with a phrase she knew. By December the overwhelming influence on her writing was the material *(The Miami Linguistic Readers)* she was reading in her classroom. She was willing to write only what she thought she could spell correctly, what she had copied in class. In February and March she began to use some of the words she had learned to read in her classroom, but she was also willing to predict the spelling of words that were in her oral vocabulary even though they were not in her spelling repertoire. As the school year continued, she used a combination of reading words, words from spelling, and words for which she invented the spelling. She also became more willing to venture beyond the safe topic of her house. Over time, both the quantity and quality of her writing improved. Although in May she still did not demonstrate complete control over the oral or written systems of English, she did exhibit growth in her ability to express herself in English. Additionally, her writing over time helps the teacher document her progress in English.

This child's writing was nurtured by a situation in which the adult working with her believed that she was capable of writing in English while still acquiring and refining the language. This ESL tutor encouraged the child's writing with the awareness that it would develop over time and believed that the mistakes this child made were an integral part of her growth as an English user.

---

[2] Although this generalization relates closely to the one just discussed, it merits separate comment because many elementary-level ESL teachers fear that if they allow children to write "incorrectly" they will contribute to the children's continued use of those forms.

October

myja us Muymodcrayamuyeeder

myjaus may model ayamayppder

my house my mother and my father

December

Do cat

siduringking

sDobstifasitting

Do cat
si durinking
sDobsitifasitting

The cat is drinking
Dog sit Tiff is sitting

March

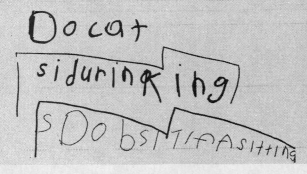

myHaus is Red aRd dlue and Iigat faurr aRd three and I gat aporl dad is Haus my ~~GarRflo~~ Grandmother

My Haus is Red and dlue and Iigat faurr and three and I gat aporl dad is Haus my grandmother

My house is red and blue and I got
flowers and trees and I got apples
That is house my Grandmother

May

The Boe is fisehing
He going to fodaun
He fodaun
Hear toaring to gereout
the Wetre
the therin gad hasfishhut

The Boe is fisehing
He goin to fo daun
He fo daun
He toaring to gereout
the wetre
the therin gad has fish

The boy is fishing
He going to fall down
He fall down
He trying to get out the water
The turtle got his fish

Other Samples from May

The dog going fighting
with the turtle
the turtle going
bite the dog
the boy going to
take the dog and the turtle
going bite the dog

The boy take the dog
He take the dog
He put he tail in the water
He fall down
He going jump to take
the dog to the water

The turtle dies
He going to XXXX out
The boy take the
turtle in his
hand and the frog and the
dog going walking
the boy digging the hole

FIGURE 4 (*continued*)

Finding/Generalization 6

As many examples in this article illustrate, the processes of writing, reading, speaking, and listening in a second language are interrelated and interdependent. It is both useless and, ultimately, impossible to separate out the language processes in our teaching (i.e., to attempt to teach only listening or speaking or only reading or writing, although some elementary ESL curricula still try to do so), or try to present ESL material in a linear sequence of listening, speaking, reading, and writing. The examples presented here refute both that separation and that notion of sequencing. Second language learners demonstrate that they are dealing with and making sense of language as a totality rather than dealing with the language processes as separate entities.

CONCLUSION

Research on second language literacy in children has the following applications. Teachers should: 1) give children credit for interacting with and acting upon their environment; 2) use the students' lives and living environments for literacy experiences (that take advantage of what students know); 3) ask children both to respond to and to create meaningful language in meaningful contexts (that is, listening to or reading whole texts and writing for real purposes, as compared with filling in ditto sheets and labeling parts of speech); 4) realize that mistakes are a necessary part of second language development and, that they are critical to language growth; and 5) respond to student products, whether oral or written, more as work in progress (Graves 1982) than as final product by reacting primarily to what students are trying to express and only secondarily to form. These kinds of activities will help English as a second language learners in elementary schools to become the proficient users of English that all teachers want them to be.

REFERENCES

Ashton-Warner, Sylvia. 1963. *Teacher.* New York: Bantam Books.

Barrera, Rosalinda. 1978. Analysis and comparison of the first language and second language oral reading behavior of native Spanish speaking Mexican American children. Ph.D. dissertation, University of Texas at Austin.

Bissex, Glenda. 1980. *GYNS AT WK.* Cambridge, Massachusetts: Harvard University Press.

Ching, Dorothy. 1976. *Reading and the bilingual child.* Newark, Delaware: International Reading Association.

Chomsky, Carol. 1971. Invented spelling in the open classroom. *Word* 27: 1–3.

Clarke, Mark. 1981. Reading in Spanish and English: evidence from adult ESL students. In *Learning to read in different languages,* Sarah Hudelson (Ed.), 69–92. Washington, D.C.: Center for Applied Linguistics.

Colvert, John D. 1973. An exploratory study to adapt the language experience approach to remedial 7th and 10th grade Mexican American pupils. Ph.D. dissertation, Arizona State University.

Connor, Ulla. 1981. The application of reading miscue analysis to diagnosis of English as a second language learners' reading skills. In *Reading English as a second language: moving from theory,* C. W. Twyford, William Diehl, and Karen Feathers (Eds.), 47–55. *Monographs in Teaching and Learning* 4. Bloomington, Indiana: Indiana University.

Crane, Barbara. 1977. *Crane reading system—English.* Trenton, New Jersey: Crane Publishing Company.

Devine, Joanne. 1981. Development patterns in native and nonnative reading acquisition. In *Learning to read in different languages,* Sarah Hudelson (Ed.), 103–114. Washington, D.C.: Center for Applied Linguistics.

Donoghue, Mildred R., and John F. Kunkle. 1979. *Second languages in primary education.* Rowley, Massachusetts: Newbury House.

Edelsky, Carole. 1981. From "JIMOSALSCO" to "7 naranjas se calleron e el arbol -est -triste en lagrymas": writing development in a bilingual program. In *The writing needs of linguistically different students,* Bruce Cronnel (Ed.), 63–98. Los Alamitos, California: SWRL Educational Research and Development.

Edelsky, Carole. 1982. Writing in a bilingual program: the relation of L1 and L2 texts. *TESOL Quarterly* 16 (2): 211–228.

Edelsky, Carole. 1983. Segmentation and punctuation: developmental data from young writers in a bilingual program. *Research in the Teaching of English* 17 (2): 135–156.

Elley, Warwick. 1981. The role of reading in bilingual contexts. In *Comprehension and teaching: research reviews.* John T. Guthrie (Ed.). 227–254. Newark, Delaware: International Reading Association.

Feeley, Joan. 1979. A workshop tried and true: language experience for bilinguals. *The Reading Teacher* 33 (1): 25–27.

Feeley, Joan. 1983. Help for the reading teacher: dealing with the limited English proficient (lep) child in the elementary classroom. *The Reading Teacher* 36 (7): 650–655.

Finocchiaro, Mary. 1974. *English as a second language: from theory to practice.* New York: Regents Publishing Company.

Gonzalez-Mena, Janet. 1975. *English experiences.* Silver Spring, Maryland: Institute of Modern Languages.

Goodman, Kenneth, and Carolyn Burke. 1973. *Theoretically based studies of patterns of miscues in oral reading performance.* Detroit, Michigan: Wayne State University (ERIC Document Reproduction Service ED 079 708).

Goodman, Kenneth and Yetta Goodman. 1978. *Reading of American children whose language is a stable rural dialect of English or a language other than English.* Washington, D.C.: NIE Final Report, C-00-3-0087.

Goodman, Kenneth, Yetta Goodman, and Barbara Flores. 1979. *Reading in the bilingual classroom:literacy and biliteracy.* Rossyln, Virginia: National Clearinghouse for Bilingual Education.

Goodman, Yetta. 1980. The roots of literacy. Keynote address to the Claremont Reading Conference, March, 1980.

Goodman, Yetta, and Bess Altwerger. 1981. *Print awareness in preschool children: a study of the development of literacy in preschool children. Occasional Paper* 4. Tucson, Arizona: Program in Language and Literacy, Arizona Center for Research and Development.

Graves, Donald. 1982. *Writing: teachers and children at work.* Exeter, New Hampshire: Heinemann Educational Books.

Grove, Michael. 1981. Psycholinguistic theories and ESL reading. In *Reading English as a second language: moving from theory,* C. W. Twyford, William Diehl, and Karen Feathers (Eds.), 3–20. *Monographs in Teaching and Learning* 4. Bloomington, Indiana: Indiana University.

Hall, Maryanne. 1979. *The language experience approach for teaching reading: a research perspective.* Second Edition. Newark, Delaware: International Reading Association.

Harris, Albert J., and Edward Sipay. 1979. *How to teach reading.* New York: Longman.

Hudelson, Sarah, 1981. Beginning reading and writing in a second language. In *Reading: a foundation for success.* Fourth Yearbook of the Arizona State University Reading Conference. Tempe, Arizona: Arizona State University.

Johnson, Patricia. 1981. Effects on reading comprehension of language complexity and cultural background of a text. *TESOL Quarterly* 15 (2): 169–181.

Johnson, Patricia. 1982. Effects on reading comprehension of building background knowledge. *TESOL Quarterly* 16 (4): 503–516.

Kernan, Doris. 1983. *Steps to English.* Second Edition. New York: McGraw-Hill.

Mallett, Graham. 1977. Using language experience with junior high native Indian students. *Journal of Reading* 21 (1); 25–28.

Marquardt, William, Jean Miller, and Eleanor Houseman. 1976. *English around the world.* Glenview, Illinois: Scott Foresman.

Mellgren, Lars, and Michale Walker. 1977. *YES English for children.* Reading, Massachusetts: Addison-Wesley Publishing Company.

Mott, Barbara. 1981. A miscue analysis of German speakers reading in German and English. In *Learning to read in different languages.* Sarah Hudelson (Ed.), 54–68. Washington, D.C.: center for Applied Linguistics.

Murphy, Barbara. 1980. Second language reading and testing in bilingual education. *TESOL Quarterly* 14 (2): 189–198.

Read, C. 1975. *Children's categorization of speech sounds.* Urbana, Illinois: National Council of Teachers of English.

Rigg, Pat. 1977. The miscue ESL project. In *On TESOL '77,* H. Douglas Brown, Carlos Yorio, and Ruth Crymes (Eds.), 109–118. Washington, D.C.: TESOL.

Rigg, Pat. 1981. Beginning to read in English the LEA way. In *Reading English as a second language: moving from theory.* C. W. Twyford, William Diehl, and Karen Feathers (Eds.), 81–90. *Monographs in Teaching and Learning* 4. Bloomington, Indiana: Indiana University.

Robinett, Ralph, Paul Bell, and Pauline Rojas. 1970. *The Miami linguistic readers.* Lexington, Massachusetts: D. C. Heath Company.

Searfoss, Lyndon, Christine Smith, and Thomas Bean. 1981. An integrated language strategy for second language learners. *TESOL Quarterly* 15 (4): 383-392.

Staton, Jana. 1981. Literacy as an interactive process. *The Linguistic Reporter* 24 (2): 1-5.

Staton, Jana. 1983. Dialogue journals: a new tool for teaching communication. *ERIC/CLL News Bulletin* 6 (2): 1-6.

Staton, Jana, Roger Shuy, and Joy Kreeft. 1982. *Analysis of dialogue journal writing as a communicative event.* Volumes I and II. Washington, D.C.: Center for Applied Linguistics.

Steffensen, Margaret, Chitra Joag-dev, and Richard Anderson. 1979. A cross cultural perspective on reading comprehension. *Reading Research Quarterly* 15 (10): 10-29.

Steffensen, Margaret, and Chitra Joag-dev. 1981. Cultural knowledge and reading: interference or facilitation. In *Reading English as a second language: moving from theory,* C. W. Twyford, William Diehl, and Karen Feathers (Eds.), 29-46. *Monographs in Teaching and Learning* 4. Bloomington, Indiana: Indiana University.

Urzua, Carole. 1981. *Using language purposefully.* Silver Spring, Maryland: Institute of Modern Languages.

Veatch, Jeanette. 1979. *Key words to reading: the language experience approach begins.* Columbus, Ohio: Merrill Publishing.

Ventriglia, Linda. 1982. *Conversation of Miguel and Maria: how children learn a second language.* Rowley, Massachusetts: Addison-Wesley.

THEORY AND IMPLICATIONS

1. Why do you think that L2 language deveopment theory has not been applied to issues of literacy? Why would errors in L2 writing seem to teachers more problematic than errors in L2 oral language?

2. Why do you think that outdated methods—subskills—prove even more ineffective for L2 writers than for L1 writers?

3. What key principles from Moskowitz's essay seem to apply to L2 writing? How?

4. Would you characterize the writing environment Hudelson recommends as whole language? Why?

5. How would Wells characterize the kinds of predicaments ESL writers face in becoming literate? Would his characterizations be similar to those Smith might offer? Explain.

6. If ESL students have minimal oral English skills and if they write using these minimal skills, falling back on L1 vocabulary to complete ideas, will these students learn bad habits? Why?

7. How would Calkins respond to ESL students in her writing workshop? Would she change her procedures? Explain why.

PROFESSIONAL CONCERNS

1. Write a letter to parents of L1 students explaining why the ESL students in the class, who can barely speak English, should not be placed in a separate class to practice their oral skills.

2. Write a formal paper showing how research from various language areas, including L1 and L2 acquisition and the study of dialects and grammar, support a whole language approach to literacy for ESL as well as native speakers.

3. Using the essay and other research in this book, argue for literacy instruction for dialect speakers that is similar to that recommended for ESL speakers.

Index